Sex and Marriage in the Catholic Tradition

Sex and Marriage in the Catholic Tradition

An Historical Overview

Edited by Douglas R. Letson

Foreword by Michael W. Higgins

NOVALIS

© 2001 Novalis, Saint Paul University, Ottawa, Canada

Cover: Miriam Bloom

Layout: Robert Vienneau, Suzanne Latourelle, Caroline Gagnon

Business Office:
Novalis
49 Front Street East, 2nd Floor
Toronto, Ontario, Canada
M5E 1B3
Phone: 1-800-387-7164 or (416) 363-3303
Fax: 1-800-204-4140 or (416) 363-9409
E-mail: novalis@interlog.com

Canadian Cataloguing in Publication Data

National Library of Canada Cataloguing in Publication Data

Main entry under title:

　　Sex and marriage in the Catholic tradition : an historical overview

Includes bibliographical references.

ISBN 2-89507-175-6

　　1. Marriage—Religious aspects—Catholic Church.　2. Sex—Religious aspects—Catholic Church.　3. Family—Religious aspects—Catholic Church.　I. Letson, Douglas Richard, 1939–

BX1795.S48S494 2001　　　　　261.8'35　　　　　C2001-901535-6

Printed in Canada.

We acknowledge the financial support of the Government of Canada through the Book Publishing Industry Development Program (BPIDP) for our publishing activities.

Dedicated to the Congregation of the Resurrection,
who introduced me to Thomas Aquinas,
the medieval tradition, and the intellectual life.
DRL

Contents

Foreword

Papal Politics and Sexual Politics

We are all sexual beings; sexuality is at the heart of our human self-definition; we live in and through our bodies. This is orthodox Catholic teaching. And this very teaching is at its core liberating, organic, suffused with a special beauty. But it is also a teaching controverted, misunderstood, and divisive.

The selected writings in this volume are designed to acquaint or re-acquaint the reader with the history of the Roman Catholic Church's teaching on sexuality, a history that reflects both continuity of teaching and respectful diversity. You will find in this collection writings ancient and modern, biblical passages and excerpts from the Fathers of the Church, commentaries on the evolution of the tradition, literary specimens from diverse periods, official documents both papal and episcopal, synod interventions, investigative articles, sections from professional studies, and several selections drawn from contemporary journalists. In short, you will find that this anthology contains representative works that cross the spectrum of Catholic thinking on sexual morality, works that contribute to the shaping of the tradition and works that call the continued relevance of that very tradition into question.

Discussion and debate over the Church's teaching on sexual morality, however, must always take into consideration the contemporary context; that context, in our own time, is greatly determined and directed by the teaching of Pope John Paul II. To better appreciate the current context, then, I think it best to provide you with a general overview of John Paul's foundational thinking on the matter of morality, life issues, sexuality and sexual behaviour. To that end I will single out for specific treatment two of his most important encyclicals.

What kind of work is an encyclical? One should say it quickly to avoid the pain, like the mercifully swift extraction of a tooth by a master dentist. It hurts less that way. Non-Catholics are mystified by papal nomenclature and Catholics are either generally embarrassed or uninterested. Parish priests, in my experience, seldom preach on the matter of a new encyclical, partly because they divine minimum interest in their congregants, and partly because they have not perse-vered in their own slow savouring of the text.

Admittedly, papal prose is not the most arresting feature of an encyclical, and unlike the ever popular whodunit, there's no mystery about the conclusion. Charac-terization and plot don't figure, the personal voice is all but obliterated, the oracular tone can be off-putting for the educated reader, general truths and abstractions abound with little in the nature of specifics and particulars, and the contemporary taste for lengthy exhortations being at a premium, it is easy to see why the art of encyclical writing, or indeed encyclical reading, has yet to become the newest rage.

Still, they are important documents; they can be genuinely inspirational; they provide a valuable tool whereby to gauge the direction and substance of a pontifi-cate. Popes have been using encyclicals – technically circular letters of a pastoral nature – since Benedict XIV's *Ubi primum* in 1740. But frequent or standardized use of the encyclical actually began during the reign of Pius IX, or Pio Nono. The encyclical does not enjoy the authority attached to a pronouncement or declaration made by the extraordinary infallible magisterium, and is often a collaborative work, if not in genesis or execution, then certainly with the fine tuning. Some of the major modern encyclicals include: *Rerum novarum* (1891); *Pacem in terris* (1963); *Populorum progressio* (1967); and *Humanae vitae* (1968).

John Paul II is the most prolific encyclical writer of them all. Bernard Lonergan once quipped of Andrew Greeley that he never had an unpublished thought; a latter-day wag, Richard McBrien, I think, when reflecting on Greeley's growing literary oeuvre, opined that Greeley never had an unpublished fantasy. Could it be said of Karol Wojtyla that he never had an unpublished encyclical? Certainly, those whose business it is to track and catalogue papal writings must find themselves gainfully employed during this pontificate. No fear of downsizing in this industry. There is something to be said for papal prolixity after all.

Papal encyclicals may enjoy a bad press, but they are not inconsequential things. Quite simply, they matter.

John Paul's first encyclical, *Redemptor hominis,* provided us with a clue to his christological thinking, and subsequent encyclicals have dealt with suffering, with Mary the Mother of the Redeemer and, very importantly, with social justice and integral humanism. The trilogy of his social encyclicals – *Laborem exercens* (1981); *Sollicitudo rei socialis* (1987); *Centesimus annus* (1991) – is a hallmark of papal social teaching, the most sophisticated and substantive treatment of social issues by any modern pope. They are taken very seriously in the corridors of power – by the lords temporal and the lords spiritual.

On August 6, 1993, the Feast of the Transfiguration of the Lord, John Paul issued *Veritatis splendor,* an encyclical addressed pointedly to all the bishops of the Roman Catholic Church "regarding certain fundamental questions of the Church's moral teaching."

Very clearly the alarum bells are sounded in the Introduction wherein the pontiff writes:

a new situation has come about *within the Christian community itself,* which has experienced the spread of numerous doubts and objections of a human and psychological, social and cultural, religious and even properly theological nature, with regard to the Church's moral teachings. It is no longer a matter of limited and occasional dissent, but of an overall and systematic calling into question of traditional moral doctrine, on the basis of certain anthropological and ethical presuppositions. At the root of these presuppositions is the more or less obvious influence of currents of thought which end by detaching human freedom from its essential and constitutive relationship to truth. Thus the traditional doctrine regarding the natural law, and the universality and the permanent validity of its precepts, is rejected; certain of the Church's moral teachings are found simply unacceptable; and the Magisterium itself is considered capable of intervening in matters of morality only in order to "exhort consciences" and to "propose values", in the light of which each individual will independently make his or her decisions and life choices.

The remaining 170-odd pages addresses this "crisis." The language is philosophical and abstract. It speaks of first principles and categories of thought, modes of discourse and inquiry, which are largely foreign to contemporary readers unfamiliar with Neo-Scholastic and Thomistic thinking.

The first of the three sections which comprise the encyclical consists of a biblical meditation, one of John Paul II's favourites: Jesus' dialogue with the rich young man in the Gospel of St. Matthew. The young man asks Jesus: "Teacher, what good must I do to have eternal life?" The pope examines Jesus' answer to this question, the question itself, and its spiritual significance for all followers of Jesus with rudimentary exegetical tools that yield a rich harvest:

Jesus' way of acting and his word, his deeds and his precepts constitute the moral rule of Christian life. Indeed, his actions, and in particular his Passion and Death on the Cross, are the living revelation of his love for the Father and for others.

The pope then moves on to section two of the encyclical. In this section the pope examines various tendencies in present-day moral theology, reaffirms the validity of universal moral absolutes, deplores the dangerous post-Enlightenment drift into subjectivism, reminds Christians of the true nature of freedom and of the relationship of morality to faith, restates the classic teaching of God's eternal law and of the natural law as the human expression of this eternal law, denounces the liberality of interpretation regarding the role and judgments of conscience, repudiates the arguments of proportionalists, consequentialists, and ethicists who espouse a "fundamental option" approach rather than a traditional acts-directed ethical methodology, and restates with vigorous clarity the existence of intrinsically evil acts.

In the third and final section John Paul explores the pastoral dimensions of his argument and reminds the bishops that "before the demands of morality we are all absolutely equal." He especially laments the dechristianization process that has succeeded in severing the inextricably woven relationship of faith with morality:

> Today's widespread tendencies towards subjectivism, utilitarianism and relativism appear as not merely pragmatic attitudes or patterns of behaviour, but rather as approaches having a basis in theory and claiming full cultural and social legitimacy.

He then proceeds to speak of the role and value of the magisterium and lobs the following ecclesiological grenade: "Dissent, in the form of carefully orchestrated protests and polemics carried on in the media, is opposed to ecclesial communion and to a correct understanding of the hierarchical constitution of the People of God."

He concludes with a meditation on Mary.

Not surprisingly, the reception of the encyclical varied. *The Globe & Mail, Le Monde, The New York Times,* among a legion of others, applauded its publication and the courage of its author. The universal episcopate responded with deference of mind and spirit. Conservative Catholics exploded with pleasure; moderates felt cowed; progressives regrouped; radicals went ballistic.

But it was only the first step.

There was more to come.

On March 25, 1995, the Solemnity of the Annunciation of the Lord, *Evangelium vitae* appeared. This encyclical letter – on the value and inviolability of human life – was addressed to bishops, priests, deacons, men and women religious, lay faithful, and all people of good will. The Roman Church is nothing if not hierarchical.

Evangelium vitae stands on the foundations of *Veritatis splendor.*

In Chapter One of *Evangelium vitae* John Paul makes clear his case: euthanasia, abortion, contraception, sterilization, doctor-assisted suicide, in vitro fertilization, surrogacy, and the death penalty are all manifestations – symptoms – of a world held captive by an ideology and ethic deeply hostile to the Christian world view:

> While the climate of widespread moral uncertainty can in some way be explained by the multiplicity and gravity of today's social problems, and these can sometimes mitigate the subjective responsibility of individuals, it is no less true that we are confronted by an even larger reality, which can be described as a veritable structure of sin. This reality is characterized by the emergence of a culture which denies solidarity and in many cases takes the form of a veritable "culture of death." This culture is actively fostered by powerful cultural, economic and political currents which encourage an idea of society excessively concerned with efficiency. Looking at the situation from

this point of view, it is possible to speak in a certain sense of a war of the powerful against the weak: a life which would require greater acceptance, love and care is considered useless, or held to be an intolerable burden, and is therefore rejected in one way or another. A person who, because of illness, handicap or, more simply, just by existing, compromises the well-being or life-style of those who are more favoured, tends to be looked upon as an enemy to be resisted or eliminated. In this way a kind of "conspiracy against life" is unleashed. This conspiracy involves not only individuals in their personal, family or group relationships, but goes far beyond, to the point of damaging and distorting, at the international level, relations between peoples and States.

The pope proceeds – this time lacing his argument with an extended meditation of the Cain and Abel story to be found in the Book of Genesis – to outline the consequences of a notion of freedom that is uni-dimensional, defined in terms of individual rights only, disengaged from truth, and grounded on "the shifting sands of complete relativism" – a notion of freedom that has no place for the Transcendent.

Freedom for the pontiff is inherently relational. It is tied to the Other. It draws its meaning from the dialectic "between the experience of the uncertainty of human life and the affirmation of its value" that so completely marks the life of Jesus:

He is certainly accepted by the righteous, who echo Mary's immediate and joyful "yes". But there is also from the start, rejection on the part of the world which grows hostile and looks for the child in order "to destroy him". ... In this contrast between threats and insecurity on the one hand and the power of God's gift on the other, there shines forth all the more clearly the glory which radiates from the house at Nazareth and from the manger at Bethlehem: this life which is born is salvation for all humanity.

The only adequate antidote to the poison of the culture of death is the culture of life embodied in the gospel of life – a life distinguished by its self-donation, self-emptying, *kenosis*. "Jesus proclaims that life finds its centre, its meaning and its fulfillment when it is given up."

But the pope does not restrict himself to theology. He reviews the Roman Catholic position on many highly controverted areas of sexual morality and restates the Church's uncompromising opposition to any technological undertaking that further sunders the integral relationship of the procreative with the unitive in every single act of sexual intercourse. His forays into biology and history earn him correction from such distinguished thinkers as the Catholic scientist John-Erik Stig Hansen, Head of Research at the Hvidore Hospital in Denmark, and the late Jesuit Richard McCormick, professor of Christian Ethics at Notre Dame University. Both make the point that inaccuracies or misunderstandings seriously weaken the credibility of an encyclical they largely and soundly applaud.

The pope doesn't hesitate to scold nations that enact legislation that diminishes human life in all its forms. He wrestles with the complex issue of civil and moral law and has little time for a morality governed by poll, personal whim, social licence, or majority opinion.

He also makes it clear, as if it weren't already apparent in *Veritatis splendor,* that he has little patience for dissent in these critical matters, especially dissent in those quarters where adherence to the organic teaching of the Church is vital.

We must use appropriate means to defend the faithful from all teaching which is contrary to it. We need to make sure that in theological faculties, seminaries and Catholic institutions sound doctrine is taught, explained and more fully investigated.

The bottom line, if you like, of the encyclical's argument – an argument less abstruse and more user-friendly than *Veritatis splendor* – is simply this: the essential connection between life and freedom and between freedom and truth is at the heart of an authentic culture of life.

He concludes, predictably, with a meditation on Mary.

Encyclicals are not known for their nuance. They do not deal with particularities. They mention neither dates nor names. They take the long view. They advance a position, exhort, and warn. We shouldn't demand that they be other than what they are. But it is incumbent upon us to know the nature of the beast. To rightly do that we need to appreciate the historical context; the time of its planning and release; the politics of composition; the advisors, consultants, and editors; its place in the chronology of the pontiff's oeuvre; the personal signature, with the present case its length, dabbling in biblical exegesis, its Marian note; and its reception by both the Catholic and the non-Catholic world.

In between *Veritatis splendor* and *Evangelium vitae* we had the Cairo International Conference on Population and Development, and following very shortly after the publication of *Evangelium vitae* we had the Beijing Conference. Both of these conferences involved significant input from the Holy See. In the case of Cairo we had considerable controversy over the Vatican's opposition to issues of reproductive freedom, sex education, and planned parenthood. The Holy See responded to the aggressively driven platform by playing the "integrity of life" argument from conception and by underscoring the critical role of the parents in matters of sex education and family planning. The Vatican delegation was composed of men – nearly all clerics – and they found themselves pitted against a formidable consortium of women's groups, NGOs, and left-leaning governments. They often found themselves linked by the media with Latino governments enmeshed in the sinister world of machismo with its dread of liberal values, or forming unholy alliances with Islamic fundamentalists hell-bent on preserving the pernicious enslavement of women. This is the stuff of dangerous stereotyping. It was a sorry mess. But the Vatican survived and managed to score major points on the abortion issue in the final Cairo document. And the Vatican survived, despite calls for the formal revocation of its international status as a member state of the UN and despite a universal uproar in liberal Catholic circles over Vatican politicking. And the

Vatican survived the scores of editorials that eulogized its hitherto distinguished, if not occasionally arcane, record of achievement.

The Vatican, in fact, won more than a pyrrhic victory.

It returned in September 1995, not a pariah as had been prophesied, but humbled by its previous experience, with a delegation where women were in the majority. The delegation was headed by the respected U.S. jurist Mary Ann Glendon, Professor of Law at Harvard University. It again negotiated significant changes and enjoyed the confidence of Gertrude Mongella, Secretary-General of the UN Conference, and even merited muted approval from one of the hard-line Vatican critics, Baroness Chalker, the British Minister for Overseas Development.

The positions stipulated and the strategies employed at these conferences are public and practical instances of the Vatican's efforts to implement the thinking that undergirds *Veritatis splendor* and *Evangelium vitae.*

John Paul's millenarian concerns – outlined specifically in his justice, suffering and life-issue encyclicals – reveal his preoccupation with sustaining and indeed nurturing a culture of life in the darkest of centuries. All else takes a back seat. At the Cairo and Beijing Conferences, in his various publications and addresses – *Mulieris dignitatem,* his 1995 "Letter to Women," his Marian documents and apostolic letters – John Paul celebrates the equality and full dignity of women. But it is often of women as *type* rather than of women as persons that he speaks and writes. It's what he knows. It is reminiscent of the argumentation and discourse of the concluding Address to Women delivered at the Final Session of the Second Vatican Council: quaint, civil, rhapsodic, and disturbingly unreal.

You hear it again in *Evangelium vitae*:

Women first learn and then teach others that human relations are authentic if they are open to accepting the other person: a person who is recognized and loved because of the dignity which comes from being a person and not from other considerations, such as usefulness, strength, intelligence, beauty or health. This is the fundamental contribution which the Church and humanity expect from women. And it is the indispensable prerequisite for an authentic cultural change.

There are many who disagree. Perhaps the substance of that disagreement is most persuasively encapsulated in a *Tablet* piece by Catholic journalist Melanie McDonagh, who reminds us of the limits of papal and sexual politics:

It is simply inconceivable that the UN could be organizing a conference about Men. It is impossible to imagine the Pope talking about the genius of Men, thanking them for their special role in the world.... just take the way the Pope addressed women: "Thank you, women who are mothers.... You become God's own smile upon the newborn child.... Thank you, women who are wives....Thank you, women who are daughters and women who are sisters.... Thank you, women who work." If he were to address his own sex in this way men would not know what to make of it.... But we are [just as] unlikely to patronise men by holding UN conferences about them.... It is bad enough to have minority status if, by race, religion or whatever, you are actually in a minority. But to pretend to minority status when you are the tougher, healthier part of the population, the part that reads more, goes to prison less and to church more.... that is bizarre. (*The Tablet,* 26 August 1995, p. 1070)

A reasonable, if not bracing, corrective for a world of conflicting anthropologies, lacerating rhetoric, and polarizing postures.

We need to attend to the writings of John Paul with a critical eye and a nod of sympathy. His is the voice of a reasoned and firm conservatism.

For some it is a voice that is simply the final word. And for others, an invitation to reflect critically on a vital faith and an integrated sexual morality.

Michael W. Higgins
Waterloo, Ontario

Part I

Historical Background

INTRODUCTION

In Geoffey Chaucer's late-fourteenth-century *Canterbury Tales*, the Wife of Bath poses a key question, one which has quite often become an empathetic reference point for today's theology of liberation in its many forms. "Who painted the lion?" the Wife challenges, referring to one of Aesop's fables. It was Aesop's, Chaucer's, and the Wife of Bath's way of pointing out that the perspective assumed in the painting of any picture is inevitably influenced by the dispositions of the painter: the king of the jungle would obviously image the world wholly differently from the hunter who sees the lion as the object of his sport. In the same way, proponents of a female theology of liberation contend that history has been written by the (male) victors, whereas Latin American theologians often view traditional Catholic theology as Euro-centered and intellectually imperialistic. Similarly, the fact that the lion's share of the theological thinking that has shaped the Christian tradition was shaped by male celibates has surely had an influence on the predispositions within that tradition. Moreover, insofar as Vatican documents and Vatican spokesmen – popes, cardinals, and bishops – are accustomed to speak of the "constant tradition," anyone who wishes to understand the doctrine being articulated by modern churchmen needs also to understand the tradition they are referring to as ratification for their doctrinal determinations. So, if the past colours the present, as indeed it does, one ought to have at least an introductory grasp of the early authorities, of their attitudes and the influences that affected their own thinking; one ought also to be somewhat familiar with what has been incorporated from their work into the constant tradition and what has been quietly laid aside.

St. Thomas Aquinas, the great thirteenth-century philosopher and theologian who introduced the Greek philosopher Aristotle to the Christian world, was a Dominican scholar with an encyclopedic grasp of the Christian and pagan past as well as a master of the medieval passion for order. Saint since 1323, Angelic Doctor since 1567, and patron saint of Catholic schools since 1879, Aquinas was, nonetheless, a product both of his time and of his circumstances. Given the nature of thirteenth-century biology and scientific insight, and given the hierarchical world view that Aquinas inherited uncritically from his philosophical predecessors, his unflattering translation of Aristotle's teaching with respect to women and sexuality into the Christian Middle Ages is thoroughly consistent with the predispositions of the scholarly clerical celibate at work within his monastic cell in the high Middle Ages. As a result, Aquinas incorporates into his world view the time-honoured wisdom contained in the three Genesis stories as they had been interpreted through the spectrum of the Hellenistic insights of St. Paul; together, St. Paul and Aquinas helped to lay the foundation for the Christian churches' anthropological perception of what it is to be male and female: both as a representative member of one's sex and as a complementary component of the human household. Aristotle's description of woman as mutilated male and as material cause in the generative process places her by nature in a position inferior to man; it is a concept that coincides conveniently with the divinely imposed anthropological order as it appears in the second Genesis story, and as it is presented in the first letter of St. Paul to the Corinthians, chapter 11: "I would have you know that the head of every man is Christ; and the head of the woman is the man; and the head of Christ is God.... A man indeed ought not to cover his head [while praying and prophesying], because he is the image of God. But woman is the glory of man. For man is not from woman, but woman from man. For man was not created for woman, but woman for man." St. Paul's explication of Genesis 2 becomes a cornerstone for the constant tradition on marriage and domestic relationships: not only for the fathers of the church but for the pope of Rome well into the twentieth century. The starkness of the hierarchical relationship may now be somewhat muted, but its echoes are still to be heard not only in Vatican documents but in those emanating from other Christian churches as well.

St. Augustine of Hippo is another of the fathers of the church who has had a dramatic impact on contemporary attitudes towards sexuality, marriage, and gender differences. Pius XI, for example, quotes Augustine as justification for positions he takes in his encyclical *Casti connubii,* and the authors of *Humanae vitae* do the same; even John Paul II refers to Augustine as one of those who helped to shape the perduring tradition, as indeed he was, especially with respect to the indissolubility of the marriage bond, the innate superiority of the virgin state, a deeply seated suspicion of the pleasure of conjugal intimacy, and an insistence on the procreative purpose of sexual intercourse. Although he did see a value in sexual intimacy beyond the procreative, Augustine viewed sex that was without the intention of procreation as a venial sin and wondered if procreation could have taken place without it had Adam and Eve remained blameless. For his part, Augustine was not merely a trained rhetorician and insightful exegete; he was also a flesh-and-blood human being whose 33-year quest as a pagan in search of meaning and whose fathering of a child out of wedlock undoubtedly had their own influence on his attitudes concerning women, sexuality and the married state. These attitudes Augustine honed while doing verbal battle with several of the heretical thinkers of his day and has passed on to us in his tracts on marriage and virginity as well as in his *Confessions* and *City of God.*

The poet is the voice for the popular imagination, as our opening reference to the Wife of Bath is intended to make clear. The fact that the poets turned to the thinking of the early fathers of the church – characterized here in the writings of Augustine, Bede and Aquinas – as a source for their poetic inspiration affirms that patristic teachings were hardly the arcane preserve of the monk in his cloister. In fact, the elements of effective preaching outlined in Augustine's *De doctrina christiana* were specifically adapted by poets like Chaucer, Dante, and Boccaccio as the philosophical underpinning for an art whose purpose was specifically designed to teach, to please and to move an audience to better behaviour. As a result, poets like Geoffrey Chaucer extend the influence of these churchmen by popularizing their opinions and incorporating them into the aristocratic poetry that formed the chief means of entertainment throughout the Middle Ages. Attitudes towards the hierarchical relationship of body and soul, marriage and celibacy, for example, are not only captured in the medieval penitential – the confessor's handbook – but are imbedded within the poetic image. The image of the soul incarcerated within the human body, the higher component of the rational animal imprisoned by the lower, therefore, expresses the sense of the *contemptus mundi* inherent in medieval Christian attitudes expressed not just towards the body but towards all things material. That Body and Soul poems should appear in representative literature from the eleventh century, the Renaissance and the Victorian period is one sure sign that this hierarchical relationship is intellectually well-entrenched and is indeed a ubiquitous part of the archetypal reflex. It is also a clear example of the constant tradition that will echo throughout the writings contained within this book.

1.

FROM ARISTOTLE'S *POLITICS*
(fourth century B.C.)

Book I

Every state is a community of some kind, and every community is established with a view to some good; for mankind always act in order to obtain that which they think good. But, if all communities aim at some good, the state or political community, which is the highest of all, and which embraces all the rest, aims at good in a greater degree than any other, and at the highest good.

Some people think that the qualifications of a statesman, king, householder, and master are the same, and that they differ, not in kind, but only in the number of their subjects. For example, the ruler over a few is called a master; over more, the manager of a household; over a still larger number, a statesman or king, as if there were no difference between a great household and a small state. The distinction which is made between the king and the statesman is as follows: When the government is personal, the ruler is a king; when, according to the rules of the political science, the citizens rule and are ruled in turn, then he is called a statesman.

But all this is a mistake; for governments differ in kind, as will be evident to any one who considers the matter according to the method which has hitherto guided us. As in other departments of science, so in politics, the compound should always be resolved into the simple elements or least parts of the whole. We must therefore look at the elements of which the state is composed, in order that we may see in what the different kinds of rule differ from one another, and whether any scientific result can be attained about each one of them.

He who thus considers things in their first growth and origin, whether a state or anything else, will obtain the clearest view of them. In the first place there must be a union of those who cannot exist without each other; namely, of male and female, that the race may continue (and this is a union which is formed, not of deliberate purpose, but because, in common with other animals and with plants, mankind have a natural desire to leave behind them an image of themselves), and of natural ruler and subject, that both may be preserved. For that which can foresee by the exercise of mind is by nature intended to be lord and master, and that which can with its body give effect to such foresight is a subject, and by nature a slave; hence master and slave have the same interest. Now nature has distinguished between the female and the slave. For she is not niggardly, like the smith who fashions the Delphian knife for many uses; she makes each thing for a single use, and every instrument is best made when intended for one and not for many uses. But among barbarians no distinction is made between women and slaves, because there is no natural ruler among them: they are a community of slaves, male and female. Wherefore the poets say,—

It is meet that Hellenes should rule over barbarians;[1]

as if they thought that the barbarian and the slave were by nature one.

Out of these two relationships between man and woman, master and slave, the first thing to arise is the family, and Hesiod is right when he says,—

First house and wife and an ox for the plough.[2]

FROM ARISTOTLE'S *ON THE GENERATION OF ANIMALS*

From Book II, chapter 3

Let us return to the material of the semen, in and with which comes away from the male the spiritus conveying the principle of soul. Of this principle there are two kinds; the one is not connected with matter, and belongs to those animals in which is included something divine (to wit, what is called the reason), while the other is inseparable from matter. This material of the semen dissolves and evaporates because it has a liquid and watery nature. Therefore we ought not to expect it always to come out again from the female or to form any part of the embryo that has taken shape from it; the case resembles that of the fig-juice which curdles milk, for this too changes without becoming any part of the curdling masses.

It has been settled then, in what sense the embryo and the semen have soul, and in what sense they have not; they have it potentially but not actually.

Now semen is a secretion and is moved with the same movement as that in virtue of which the body increases (this increase being due to subdivision of the nutriment in its last stage). When it has entered the uterus it puts into form the corresponding secretion of the female and moves it with the same movement wherewith it is moved itself. For the female's contribution also is a secretion, and has all the parts in it potentially though none of them actually; it has in it potentially even those parts which differentiate the female from the male, for just as the young of mutilated parents are sometimes born mutilated and sometimes not, so also the young born of a female are sometimes female and sometimes male instead. For the female is, as it were, a mutilated male, and the catamenia are semen, only not pure; for there is only one thing they have not in them, the principle of soul. For this reason, whenever a wind-egg is produced by any animal, the egg so forming has in it the parts of both sexes potentially, but has not the principle in question, so that it does not develop into a living creature, for this is introduced by the semen of the male. When such a principle has been imparted to the secretion of the female it becomes an embryo.

From Book I, chapters 20-21

That, then, the female does not contribute semen to generation, but does contribute something, and that this is the matter of the catamenia, or that which is analogous to it in bloodless animals, is clear from what has been said, and also from a general and abstract survey of the question. For there must needs be that which generates and that from which it generates; even if these be one, still they must be distinct in form and their essence must be different; and in those animals that have these powers separate in two sexes the body and nature of the active and the passive sex must also differ. If, then, the male stands for the effective and active, and the female, considered as female, for the passive, it follows that what the female would contribute to the semen of the male would not be semen but material for the semen to work upon. This is just what we find to be the case, for the catamenia have in their nature an affinity to the primitive matter.

So much for the discussion of this question. At the same time the answer to the next question we have to investigate is clear from these considerations, I mean how it is that the male contributes to generation and how it is that the semen from the male is the cause of the offspring.

From Book II, chapter 1

This is why there is always a class of men and animals and plants. But since the male and female essences are the first principles of these, they will exist in the existing individuals for the sake of generation. Again, as the first efficient or moving cause, to which belong the definition and the form, is better and more divine in its nature than the material on which it works, it is better that the superior principle should be separated from the inferior. Therefore, wherever it is possible and so far as it is possible, the male is separated from the female. For the first principle of the movement, or efficient cause, whereby that which comes into being is male, is better and more divine than the material whereby it is female. The male, however, comes together and mingles with the female for the work of generation, because this is common to both.

From Book II, chapter 4

Now the reason why it is not all males that have a generative secretion, while all females do, is that the animal is a body with soul or life; the female always provides the material, the male that which fashions it, for this is the power that we say they each possess, and this is what is meant by calling them male and female.

Thus while it is necessary for the female to provide a body and a material mass, it is not necessary for the male, because it is not within the work of art or the embryo that the tools or the maker must exist. While the body is from the female, it is the soul that is from the male, for the soul is the reality of a particular body.

---

[1] Euripides, *Iphegenia in Aulis,* 1400.

[2] *Works and Days,* 405.

2.

FROM THOMAS AQUINAS' *SUMMA THEOLOGICA*
(late thirteenth century)

FIRST PART

QUESTION XCII

The Production of the Woman
(In Four Articles)

We must next consider the production of the woman. Under this head there are four points of inquiry: (1) Whether the woman should have been made in that first production of things? (2) Whether the woman should have been made from man? (3) Whether of man's rib? (4) Whether the woman was made immediately by God?

Article 1. *Whether the Woman Should Have Been Made in the First Production of Things?*

We proceed thus to the First Article: It would seem that the woman should not have been made in the first production of things.

Objection 1. For the Philosopher says[1] that "the female is a misbegotten male." But nothing misbegotten or defective should have been in the first production of things. Therefore woman should not have been made at that first production.

Obj. 2. Further, subjection and lessening were a result of sin, for to the woman was it said after sin (Gen. 3:16): *Thou shalt be under the man's power;* and Gregory says that, "Where there is no sin, there is no inequality."[2] But woman is naturally of less strength and dignity than man, for the agent is always more honourable than the patient, as Augustine says *(Gen. ad lit.* xii, 16).[3] Therefore woman should not have been made in the first production of things before sin.

Obj. 3. Further, occasions of sin should be cut off. But God foresaw that the woman would be an occasion of sin to man. Therefore He should not have made woman.

On the contrary, It is written (Gen. 2:18): *It is not good for man to be alone; let us make him a helper like to himself.*

I answer that, It was necessary for woman to be made, as the Scripture says, as a helper to man; not, indeed, as a helpmate in other works, as some say,[4] since man can be more efficiently helped by another man in other works, but as a helper in the work of generation. This can be made clear if we observe the mode of generation carried out in various living things. Some living things do not possess in themselves the power of generation, but are generated by an agent of another species, such as some plants and animals by the influence of the heavenly bodies, from some fitting matter and not from seed. Others possess the active and passive generative power together, as we see in plants which are generated from seed. For the noblest vital function in plants is generation, and so we observe that in these the active power of generation invariably accompanies the passive power. Among perfect animals the active power of generation belongs to the male sex, and the passive power to the female. And as among animals there is a vital operation nobler than generation, to which their life is principally directed, therefore the male sex is not found in continual union with the female in perfect animals, but only at the time of coition; so that we may consider that by coition the male and female become one, just as in plants they are always united, although in some cases one of them preponderates, and in some the other. But man is yet further ordered to a still nobler vital action, and that is to understand. Therefore there was greater reason for the distinction of these two forces in man, so that the female should be produced separately from the male, although they are carnally united for generation. Therefore directly after the formation of woman, it was said: *And they shall be two in one flesh* (Gen. 2:24).

Reply Obj. 1. As regards the particular nature, woman is defective and misbegotten, for the active force in the male seed tends to the production of a perfect likeness in the masculine sex, while the production of woman comes from defect in the active force or from some material indisposition, or even from some external change, such as that of a south wind, which is moist, as the Philosopher observes.[5] On the other hand, in relation to the universal nature, woman is not misbegotten, but is included in nature's intention as ordered to the work of generation. Now the universal intention of nature depends on God, Who is the universal Author of nature. Therefore, in producing nature, God formed not only the male but also the female.

Reply Obj. 2. Subjection is twofold. One is servile, by virtue of which a superior makes use of a subject for his own benefit, and this kind of subjection began after sin. There is another kind of subjection, which is called economic or civil, whereby the superior makes use of his subjects for their own benefit and good; and this kind of subjection existed even before sin. For good order would have been wanting in the human family if some were not governed by others wiser than themselves. So by such a kind of subjection woman is naturally subject to man, because in man the discretion of reason predominates. Nor is inequality among men excluded by the state of innocence, as we shall prove (Q. XCVI, A. 3).

Reply Obj. 3. If God had deprived the world of all those things which proved an occasion of sin, the universe would have been imperfect. Nor was it fitting for the common good to be destroyed in order that individual evil might be avoided, especially as God is so powerful that He can direct any evil to a good end.

Article 2. *Whether Woman Should Have Been Made from Man?*

We proceed thus to the Second Article: It would seem that woman should not have been made from man.

Objection 1. For sex belongs both to man and animals. But in the other animals the female was not made from the male. Therefore neither should it have been so with man.

Obj. 2. Further, things of the same species are of the same matter. But male and female are of the same species. Therefore, as man was made of the slime of the earth, so woman should have been made of the same, and not from man.

Obj. 3. Further, woman was made to be a helpmate to man in the work of generation. But close relationship makes a person unfit for that office; hence near relations are debarred from intermarriage, as is written (Lev. 18:6). Therefore woman should not have been made from man.

On the contrary, It is written (Ecclus. 17:5): *He created of him,* that is, out of man, *a helpmate like to himself,* that is, woman.

I answer that, When all things were first formed, it was more suitable for the woman to be made from the man than (for the female to be from the male) in other animals. First, in order thus to give the first man a certain dignity, so that just as God is the principle of the whole universe, so the first man, in likeness to God, was the principle of the whole human race. And so Paul says that *God made the whole human race from one* (Acts 17:26). Secondly, that man might love woman all the more, and cleave to her more closely, knowing her to be fashioned from himself. Hence it is written (Gen. 2:23, 24): *She was taken out of man, wherefore a man shall leave father and mother, and shall cleave to his wife.* This was most necessary as regards the human race, in which the male and female live together for life, which is not the case with other animals. Thirdly, because, as the Philosopher says,[6] "the human male and female are united not only for generation, as with other animals, but also for the purpose of domestic life, in which each has his or her particular duty, and in which the man is the head of the woman." Therefore it was suitable for the woman to be made out of man, as out of her principle. Fourthly, there is a sacramental reason for this. For by this is signified that the Church takes her origin from Christ. Therefore the Apostle says (Eph. 5:32): *This is a great sacrament; but I speak in Christ and in the Church.*

Reply Obj. 1. is clear from the foregoing.

Reply Obj. 2. Matter is that from which something is made. Now created nature has a determinate principle; and since it is determined to one thing, it has also a determinate mode of proceeding. Therefore from determinate matter it produces something in a determinate species. On the other hand, the Divine Power, being infinite, can produce things of the same species out of any matter, such as a man from the slime of the earth, and a woman from a man.

Reply Obj. 3. A certain affinity arises from natural generation, and this is an impediment to matrimony. Woman, however, was not produced from man by natural generation, but by the Divine Power alone. Hence Eve is not called the daughter of Adam; and so this argument does not prove.

Article 3. *Whether the Woman Was Fittingly Made from the Rib of Man?*

We proceed thus to the Third Article: It would seem that the woman should not have been formed from the rib of man.

Objection 1. For the rib was much smaller than the woman's body. Now from a smaller thing a larger thing can only be made either by addition (and then the woman ought to have been described as made out of that which was added, rather than out of the rib itself), or by rarefaction, because, as Augustine says *(Gen. ad lit.* X):[7] "A body cannot increase in bulk except by rarefaction." But the woman's body is not more rarefied than man's—at least, not in the proportion of a rib to Eve's body. Therefore Eve was not formed from a rib of Adam.

Obj. 2. Further, in those things which were first created there was nothing superfluous. Therefore a rib of Adam belonged to the integrity of his body. So, if a rib was removed, his body remained imperfect, which is unreasonable to suppose.

Obj. 3. Further, a rib cannot be removed from man without pain. But there was no pain before sin. Therefore it was not right for a rib to be taken from the man, that Eve might be made from it.

On the contrary, It is written (Gen. 2:22): *God built the rib, which He took from Adam, into a woman.*

I answer that, It was right for the woman to be made from a rib of man. First, to signify the social union of man and woman, for the woman should neither use authority over man, and so she was not made from his head; nor was it right for her to be subject to man's contempt as his slave, and so she was not made from his feet. Secondly, for the sacramental signification; for from the side of Christ sleeping on the Cross the Sacraments flowed—namely, blood and water—on which the Church was established.

Reply Obj. 1. Some say that the woman's body was formed by a material increase, without anything being added, in the same way as our Lord multiplied the five loaves.[8] But this is quite impossible. For such an increase of matter would either be by a change of the very substance of matter itself, or by a change of its dimensions. Not by change of the substance of the matter, both because matter, considered in itself, is altogether unchangeable, since it has a potential existence, and has nothing but the character of being a subject, and because multiplication and size are extraneous to the essence of matter itself. Therefore multiplication of matter is quite unintelligible, as long as the matter itself remains the same without anything added to it, unless it receives greater dimensions. This implies rarefaction, which is for the same matter to receive greater dimensions, as the Philosopher says.[9] To say, therefore, that matter is multiplied, without being rarefied, is to combine contradictories—namely, the definition with the absence of the thing defined.

Therefore, as no rarefaction is apparent in such multiplication of matter, we must admit an addition of matter, either by creation or, which is more probable, by conversion. Hence Augustine says (*Tract.* XXIV, *in Joan.*)[10] that "Christ filled five thousand men with five loaves in the same way as from a few seeds He produces the harvest of corn"—that is, by conversion of the nourishment. Nevertheless, we say that the crowds were fed with five loaves, or that woman was made from the rib, because an addition was made to the already existing matter of the loaves and of the rib.

Reply Obj. 2. The rib belonged to the integral perfection of Adam, not as an individual, but as the principle of the human race; just as the semen belongs to the perfection of the begetter, and is released by a natural and pleasurable operation. Much more, therefore, was it possible that by the Divine power the body of the woman should be produced from the man's rib without pain.

From this it is clear how to answer the *third objection.*

Article 4. *Whether the Woman Was Formed Immediately by God?*

We proceed thus to the Fourth Article: It would seem that the woman was not formed immediately by God.

Objection 1. For no individual is produced immediately by God from another individual alike in species. But the woman was made from a man who is of the same species. Therefore she was not made immediately by God.

Obj. 2. Further, Augustine (*De Trin.* iii, 4)[11] says that corporeal things are governed by God through the angels. But the woman's body was formed from corporeal matter. Therefore it was made through the ministry of the angels, and not immediately by God.

Obj. 3. Further, those things which pre-exist in creatures as to their causal principles are produced by the power of some creature, and not immediately by God. But the woman's body was produced in its causal principles among the first created works, as Augustine says (*Gen. ad lit.* ix, 15).[12] Therefore it was not produced immediately by God.

On the contrary, Augustine says, in the same work:[13] "God alone, to Whom all nature owes its existence, could form or build up the woman from the man's rib."

I answer that, As was said above (A. 2, Ans. 2), the natural generation of every species is from some determinate matter. Now the matter from which man is naturally begotten is the human semen of man or woman. Therefore from any other matter an individual of the human species cannot naturally be generated. Now God alone, the Author of nature, can produce a thing in being outside the ordinary course of nature. Therefore God alone could produce either a man from the slime of the earth, or a woman from the rib of man.

Reply Obj. 1. This argument is verified when an individual is begotten, by natural generation from that which is like it in the same species.

Reply Obj. 2. As Augustine says (*Gen. ad lit.* ix, 15),[14] we do not know whether the angels were employed by God in the formation of the woman; but it is certain that, as the body of man was not formed by the angels from the slime of the earth, so neither was the body of the woman formed by them from the man's rib.

Reply Obj. 3. As Augustine says (*ibid.* 18):[15] "The first creation of things did not demand that woman should be made thus; it made it possible for her to be thus made." Therefore the body of the woman did indeed pre-exist in these causal principles, in the things first created; not as regards active potency, but as regards a potency ordered to the active potency of the Creator.

QUESTION XCIII

The End or Term of the Production of Man
(In Nine Articles)

We now treat of the end or term of man's production, according as he is said to be made to the image and likeness of God. There are under this head nine points of inquiry: (1) Whether the image of God is in man? (2) Whether the image of God is in irrational creatures? (3) Whether the image of God is in the angels more than in man? (4) Whether the image of God is in every man? (5) Whether the image of God is in man by comparison with the Essence, or with all the Divine Persons, or with one of them? (6) Whether the image of God is in man, as to his mind only? (7) Whether the image of God is in man's power or in his habits and acts? (8) Whether the image of God is in man by comparison with every object? (9) Of the difference between image and likeness.

• • •

Article 4. *Whether the Image of God Is Found in Every Man?*

We proceed thus to the Fourth Article: It would seem that the image of God is not found in every man.

Objection 1. For the Apostle says that *man is the image of God, but woman is the image* (Vulg., *glory) of man (I Cor. 11. 7).* Therefore, as woman is an individual of the human species, it is clear that every individual is not an image of God.

Obj. 2. Further, the Apostle says (Rom. 8. 29): *Whom God foreknew, He also predestinated to be made conformable to the image of His Son.* But all men are not predestined. Therefore all men have not the conformity of image.

Obj. 3. Further, likeness belongs to the notion of image, as above explained (A. 1). But by sin man becomes unlike God. Therefore he loses the image of God.

On the contrary, it is written (Ps. 38:7): *Surely man passeth as an image.*

I answer that, Since man is said to be the image of God by reason of his intellectual nature, he is the most perfectly like God according to that in which he can best imitate God in his intellectual nature. Now the intellectual nature imitates God chiefly in this, that God understands and loves Himself. And so we see that the image of God is in man in three ways. First, because man possesses a natural aptitude for understanding and loving God; and this aptitude consists in the very nature of the mind, which is common to all men. Secondly, because man actually or habitually knows and loves God, though imperfectly; and this image consists in the conformity of grace. Thirdly, because man knows and loves God perfectly; and this image consists in the likeness of glory. Therefore on the words, *The light of Thy countenance, O Lord, is signed upon us* (Ps. 4:7), the gloss distinguishes a threefold image, of creation, of re-creation, and of likeness.[16] The first is found in all men, the second only in the just, the third only in the blessed.

Reply Obj. 1. The image of God, in its principal signification, namely the intellectual nature, is found both in man and in women. Hence after the words, *To the image of God He created him,* it is added, *Male and female He created them* (Gen. 1:27). Moreover it is said "them," in the plural, as Augustine (*Gen. ad lit.* iii, 22)[17] remarks, lest it should be thought that both sexes were united in one individual. But in a secondary sense the image of God is found in man, and not in woman, for man is the beginning and end of woman, just as God is the beginning and end of every creature. So when the Apostle had said that *man is the image and glory of God, but woman is the glory of man,* he adds his reason for saying this: *For man is not of woman, but woman of man; and man was not created for woman, but woman for man.*

Reply Objs. 2 and 3. These reasons refer to the image which consists in the conformity of grace and glory.

QUESTION XCVIII

Of the Preservation of the Species
(In Two Articles)

We next consider what belongs to the preservation of the species; and, first, of generation; secondly, of the state of the offspring (Q. XCIX). Under the first head there are two points of inquiry: (1) Whether in the state of innocence there would have been generation? (2) Whether generation would have been through coition?

Article 1. *Whether in the State of Innocence Generation Existed?*

We proceed thus to the First Article: It would seem there would have been no generation in the state of innocence.

Objection 1. For, as stated in the *Physics,*[18] "corruption is contrary to generation." But contraries affect the same subject. And there would have been no corruption in the state of innocence. Therefore neither would there have been generation.

Obj. 2. Further, the object of generation is the preservation in the species of that which cannot be preserved through the individual. Therefore there is no generation in those individual things which last for ever. But in the state of innocence man would have lived for ever. Therefore in the state of innocence there would have been no generation.

Obj. 3. Further, by generation man is multiplied. But the multiplication of masters requires the division of property, to avoid confusion of mastership. Therefore, since man was made master of the animals, it would have been necessary to make a division of overlordship when the human race increased by generation. This is against the natural law, according to which all things are in common, as Isidore says (*Etym.* V, 4).[19] Therefore there would have been no generation in the state of innocence.

On the contrary, It is written (Gen. 1:28): *Increase and multiply, and fill the earth.* But this increase could not come about save by generation, since the original number of mankind was two only. Therefore there would have been generation in the state of innocence.

I answer that, In the state of innocence there would have been generation of offspring for the multiplication of the human race; otherwise man's sin would have been very necessary, in order that such a great blessing be its result. We must, therefore, observe that man, by his nature, is established as it were midway between corruptible and incorruptible creatures, his soul being naturally incorruptible, while his body is naturally corruptible. We must also observe that nature's purpose appears to be different as regards corruptible and incorruptible things. For that seems to be the direct purpose of nature, which is invariable and perpetual, while what is only for a time is seemingly not the chief purpose of nature, but, as it were, subordinate to something else; otherwise, when it ceased to exist, nature's purpose would become void.

Therefore, since in things corruptible none is everlasting and permanent except the species, it follows that the chief purpose of nature is the good of the species, for the preservation of which natural generation is ordained. On the other hand, incorruptible substances survive not only in the species, but also in the individual; and so even the individuals are included in the chief purpose of nature.

Hence it pertains to man to beget offspring, on the part of the naturally corruptible body. But on the part of the soul, which is incorruptible, it is fitting that the multiple of individuals should be the direct purpose of nature, or rather of the Author of nature, Who alone is the Creator of the human soul. Therefore, to provide for the multiplication of the human race, He established the begetting of offspring even in the state of innocence.

Reply Obj. 1. In the state of innocence the human body was in itself corruptible, but it could be preserved from corruption by the soul. Therefore, since generation belongs to things corruptible, man was not to be deprived of it.

Reply Obj. 2. Although generation in the state of innocence might not have been required for the preservation of the species, yet it would have been required for the multiplication of the individual.

Reply Obj. 3. In our present state a division of possessions is necessary on account of the multiplicity of masters, since community of possession is a source of strife, as the Philosopher says.[20] In the state of innocence, however, the will of men would have been so ordered that without any danger of strife they would have used in common, according to each one's need, those things of which they were masters—a state of things to be observed even now among many good men.

Article 2. *Whether in the State of Innocence There Would Have Been Generation by Coition?*

We proceed thus to the Second Article: It would seem that generation by coition would not have existed in the state of innocence.

Objection 1. For, as Damascene says (*De Fid. Orth.* ii, 11),[21] the first man in the terrestrial Paradise was "like an angel." But in the future state of the resurrection, when men will be like to the angels, *they shall neither marry nor be married,* as it is written Matt. 22:30. Therefore neither in Paradise would there have been generation by coition.

Obj. 2. Further, our first parents were created at the age of perfect development. Therefore, if generation by coition had existed before sin, they would have had intercourse while still in Paradise, which was not the case according to Scripture (Gen. 4:1).

Obj. 3. Further, in carnal intercourse, more than at any other time, man becomes like the beasts, on account of the vehement delight which he takes therein; and so continency, by which man refrains from such pleasures, is praiseworthy. But man is compared to beasts by reason of sin, according to Psalm 48:13: *Man, when he was in honour, did not understand; he is compared to senseless beasts, and is become like to them.* Therefore, before sin, there would have been no such intercourse of man and woman.

Obj. 4. Further, in the state of innocence there would have been no corruption. But virginal integrity is corrupted by intercourse. Therefore there would have been no such thing in the state of innocence.

On the contrary, God made man and woman before sin (Gen. 1:2). But nothing is void in God's works. Therefore, even if man had not sinned, there would have been such intercourse, to which the distinction of sex is ordained.

Moreover, we are told that woman was made to be a help to man (Gen. 2:18, 20). But she was not fitted to help man except in generation, because another man would have proved a more effective help in anything else. Therefore there would have been such generation also in the state of innocence.

I answer that, Some of the earlier doctors,[22] considering the nature of concupiscence as regards generation in our present state, concluded that in the state of innocence generation would not have been effected in the same way. Thus Gregory of Nyssa says (*De Hom. Opif.* xvii)[23] that in Paradise the human race would have been multiplied by some other means, just as the angels were multiplied without coition by the operation of the Divine Power. He adds that God made man male and female before sin because He foreknew the mode of generation which would take place after sin, which He foresaw.

But this is unreasonable. For what is natural to man was neither acquired nor forfeited by sin. Now it is clear that generation by coition is natural to man by reason of his animal life, which he possessed even before sin, as above explained (Q. XCVII, A. 3), just as it is natural to other perfect animals, as the corporeal members make it clear. So we cannot allow that these members would not have had a natural use, as other members had, before sin.

Thus, as regards generation by coition, there are, in the present state of life, two things to be considered. One, which comes from nature, is the union of man and woman; for in every act of generation there is an active and a passive principle. Therefore, since wherever there is distinction of sex, the active principle is male and the passive is female, the order of nature demands that for the purpose of generation there should be concurrence of male and female. The second thing to be observed is a certain deformity of excessive concupiscence, which in the state of innocence would not have existed, when the lower powers were entirely subject to reason. Therefore Augustine says,[24] "We must be far from supposing that offspring could not be begotten without concupiscence. All the bodily members would have been equally moved by the will, without ardent or wanton incentive, with calmness of soul and body."

Reply Obj. 1. In Paradise man would have been like an angel in his spirituality of mind, yet with an animal life in his body. After the resurrection man will be like an angel, spiritualized in soul and body. And so there is no parallel.

Reply Obj. 2. As Augustine says (*Gen. ad lit*. ix, 4),[25] our first parents did not come together in Paradise, because on account of sin they were ejected from Paradise shortly after the creation of the woman; or because, having received the general Divine command relative to generation, they awaited the special command relative to the time.

Reply Obj. 3. Beasts are without reason. In this way man becomes, as it were, like them in coition, because he cannot moderate concupiscence. In the state of innocence nothing of this kind would have happened that was not regulated by reason, not because delight of sense was less, as some say[26] (rather indeed would sensible delight have been the greater in proportion to the greater purity of nature and the greater sensibility of the body), but because the force of concupiscence would not have so inordinately thrown itself into such pleasure, being curbed by reason, whose place it is not to lessen sensual pleasure, but to prevent the force of concupiscence from cleaving to it immoderately. By "immoderately" I mean going beyond the bounds of reason, just as a sober person does not take less pleasure in food taken in moderation than the glutton, but his concupiscence lingers less in such pleasures. This is what Augustine means by the words quoted, which do not exclude intensity of pleasure from the state of innocence, but the ardour of desire and restlessness of the soul. Therefore continence would not have been praiseworthy in the state of innocence, whereas it is praiseworthy in our present state, not because it removes fecundity, but because it excludes disordered desire. In that state fecundity would have been without lust.

Reply Obj. 4. As Augustine says,[27] In that state *intercourse would have been without prejudice to virginal integrity; thus would have remained intact, as it does in the menses. And just as in giving birth the mother was then relieved not by groans of pain, but by the instigations of maturity, so in conceiving, the union was one not of lustful desire, but of deliberate action.*

QUESTION 152

Of Virginity

(In Five Articles)

WE must now consider virginity: and under this head there are five points of inquiry: (1) In what does virginity consist? (2) Whether it is lawful? (3) Whether it is a virtue? (4) Of its excellence in comparison with marriage. (5) Of its excellence in comparison with the other virtues.

Article 1. *Whether Virginity Consists in Integrity of the Flesh?*

We proceed thus to the First Article:

Objection 1. It would seem that virginity does not consist in integrity of the flesh. For Augustine says *(De Nup. et Concup.)* [28] that *virginity is the continual meditation on incorruption in a corruptible flesh.* But meditation does not concern the flesh. Therefore virginity is not situated in the flesh.

Obj. 2. Further, virginity denotes a kind of purity. Now Augustine says *(De Civ. Dei* i. 18) that *purity dwells in the soul.* Therefore virginity is not incorruption of the flesh.

Obj. 3. Further, the integrity of the flesh would seem to consist in the seal of virginal purity. Yet sometimes the seal is broken without loss of virginity. For Augustine says *(De Civ. Dei, ibid.)* that *those organs may be injured through being wounded by mischance. Physicians, too, sometimes do for the sake of health that which makes one shudder to see: and a midwife has been known to destroy by touch the proof of virginity that she sought.* And he adds: *Nobody, I think, would be so foolish as to deem this maiden to have forfeited even bodily sanctity, though she lost the integrity of that organ.* Therefore virginity does not consist in incorruption of the flesh.

Obj. 4. Further, corruption of the flesh consists chiefly in resolution of the semen: and this may take place without copulation, whether one be asleep or awake. Yet seemingly virginity is not lost without copulation: for Augustine says *(De Virgin.* xiii) that *virginal integrity and holy continency that refrains from all sexual intercourse is the portion of angels.* Therefore virginity does not consist in incorruption of the flesh.

On the contrary, Augustine says *(ibid.* viii) that *virginity is continence whereby integrity of the flesh is vowed, consecrated and observed in honor of the Creator of both soul and flesh.*

I answer that, Virginity takes its name apparently from *viror* (freshness), and just as a thing is described as fresh and retaining its freshness, so long as it is not parched by excessive heat, so too, virginity denotes that the person possessed thereof is unseared by the heat of concupiscence which is experienced in achieving the greatest bodily pleasure which is that of sexual intercourse. Hence, Ambrose says *(De Virgin.* i. 5) that *virginal chastity is integrity free of pollution.*

Now venereal pleasures offer three points for consideration. The first is on the part of the body, viz. the violation of the seal of virginity. The second is the link between that which concerns the soul and that which concerns the body, and this is the resolution of the semen, causing sensible pleasure. The third is entirely on the part of the soul, namely the purpose of attaining this pleasure. Of these three the first is accidental to the moral act, which as such must be considered in reference to the soul. The second stands in the relation of matter to the moral act, since the sensible passions are the matters of moral acts. But the third stands in the position of form and complement, because the essence of morality is perfected in that which concerns the reason. Since then virginity consists in freedom from the aforesaid corruption, it follows that the integrity of the bodily organ is accidental to virginity; while freedom from pleasure in resolution of the semen is related thereto materially; and the purpose of perpetually abstaining from this pleasure is the formal and completive element in virginity.

Reply Obj. 1. This definition of Augustine's expresses directly that which is formal in virginity. For *meditation* denotes reason's purpose; and the addition *perpetual* does not imply that a virgin must always retain this meditation actually, but that she should bear in mind the purpose of always persevering therein. The material element is expressed indirectly by the words *on incorruption in a corruptible body.* This is added to show the difficulty of virginity: for if the flesh were incorruptible, it would not be difficult to maintain a perpetual meditation on incorruption.

Reply Obj. 2. It is true that purity, as to its essence, is in the soul; but as to its matter, it is in the body: and it is the same with virginity. Wherefore Augustine says *(De Virgin.* viii) that *although virginity resides in the flesh,* and for this reason is a bodily quality, *yet it is a spiritual thing, which a holy continency fosters and preserves.*

Reply Obj. 3. As stated above, the integrity of a bodily organ is accidental to virginity, in so far as a person, through purposely abstaining from venereal pleasure, retains the integrity of a bodily organ. Hence if the organ lose its integrity by chance in some other way, this is no more prejudicial to virginity than being deprived of a hand or foot.

Reply Obj. 4. Pleasure resulting from resolution of semen may arise in two ways. If this be the result of the mind's purpose, it destroys virginity, whether copulation takes place or not. Augustine, however, mentions copulation, because such like resolution is the ordinary and natural result thereof. In another way this may happen beside the purpose of the mind, either during sleep, or through violence and without the mind's consent, although the flesh derives pleasure from it, or again through weakness of nature, as in the case of those who are subject to a flow of semen. In such cases virginity is not forfeit, because such like pollution is not the result of impurity which excludes virginity.

Article 4. *Whether Virginity Is More Excellent than Marriage?*

We proceed thus to the Fourth Article:

Objection 1. It would seem that virginity is not more excellent than marriage. For Augustine says (*De Bono Conjug.* xxi): *Continence was equally meritorious in John who remained unmarried and Abraham who begot children.* Now a greater virtue has greater merit. Therefore virginity is not a greater virtue than conjugal chastity.

Obj. 2. Further, the praise accorded a virtuous man depends on his virtue. If, then, virginity were preferable to conjugal continence, it would seem to follow that every virgin is to be praised more than any married woman. But this is untrue. Therefore virginity is not preferable to marriage.

Obj. 3. Further, the common good takes precedence of the private good, according to the Philosopher (Ethic. i. 2). Now marriage is directed to the common good: for Augustine says *(De Bono Conjug.* xvi): *What food is to a man's well-being, such is sexual intercourse to the welfare of the human race.* On the other hand, virginity is ordered to the individual good, namely in order to avoid what the Apostle calls the *tribulation of the flesh,* to which married people are subject (I Cor. vii. 28). Therefore virginity is not greater than conjugal continence.

On the contrary, Augustine says: *(De Virgin.* xix): *Both solid reason and the authority of Holy Writ show that neither is marriage sinful, nor is it to be equaled to the good of virginal continence or even to that of widowhood.*

I answer that, According to Jerome (*Contra Jovin.* i) the error of Jovinian consisted in holding virginity not to be preferable to marriage. This error is refuted above all by the example of Christ Who both chose a virgin for His mother, and remained Himself a virgin, and by the teaching of the Apostle who (1 Cor. vii) counsels virginity as the greater good. It is also refuted by reason, both because a Divine good takes precedence of a human good, and because the good of the soul is preferable to the good of the body, and again because the good of the contemplative life is better than that of the active life. Now virginity is directed to the good of the soul in respect of the contemplative life, which consists in thinking *on the things of God* (Vulg.,—*the Lord*), whereas marriage is directed to the good of the body, namely the bodily increase of the human race, and belongs to the active life, since the man and woman who embrace the married life have to think *on the things of the world,* as the Apostle says (1 Cor. vii. 34). Without doubt therefore virginity is preferable to conjugal continence.

Reply Obj. 1. Merit is measured not only by the kind of action, but still more by the mind of the agent. Now Abraham had a mind so disposed, that he was prepared to observe virginity, if it were in keeping with the times for him to do so. Wherefore in him conjugal continence was equally meritorious with the virginal continence of John, as regards the essential reward, but not as regards the accidental reward. Hence Augustine says *(De Bono Conjug.* xxi) that both *the celibacy of John and the marriage of Abraham fought Christ's battle in keeping with the difference of the times: but John was continent even in deed, whereas Abraham was continent only in habit.*

Reply Obj. 2. Though virginity is better than conjugal continence, a married person may be better than a virgin for two reasons. First, on the part of chastity itself; if to wit, the married person is more prepared in mind to observe virginity, if it should be expedient, than the one who is actually a virgin. Hence Augustine *(De Bono Conjug.* xxii) charges the virgin to say: *I am no better than Abraham, although the chastity of celibacy is better than the chastity of marriage.* Further on he gives the reason for this: *For what I do now, he would have done better, if it were fitting for him to do it then; and what they did I would even do now if it behooved me now to do it.* Secondly, because perhaps the person who is not a virgin has some more excellent virtue. Wherefore Augustine says *(De Virgin.* xliv): *Whence does a virgin know the things that belong to the Lord, however solicitous she be about them, if perchance on account of some mental fault she be not yet ripe for martyrdom, whereas this woman to whom she delighted in preferring herself is already able to drink the chalice of the Lord?*

Reply Obj. 3. The common good takes precedence of the private good, if it be of the same genus: but it may be that the private good is better generically. It is thus that the virginity that is consecrated to God is preferable to carnal fruitfulness. Hence Augustine says *(De Virgin.* ix): *It must be confessed that the fruitfulness of the flesh, even of those women who in these times seek naught else from marriage but children in order to make them servants of Christ, cannot compensate for lost virginity.*

Article 5. *Whether Virginity Is the Greatest of Virtues?*

We proceed thus to the Fifth Article:

Objection 1. It would seem that virginity is the greatest of virtues. For Cyprian says *(De Virgin.)*[29]: *We address ourselves now to the virgins. Sublime is their glory, but no less exalted is their vocation. They are a flower of the Church's sowing, the pride and ornament of spiritual grace, the most honored portion of Christ's flock.*

Obj. 2. Further, a greater reward is due to the greater virtue. Now the greatest reward is due to virginity, namely the hundredfold fruit, according to a gloss on Matth. xiii, 23. Therefore virginity is the greatest of the virtues.

Obj. 3. Further, the more a virtue conforms us to Christ, the greater it is. Now virginity above all conforms us to Christ; for it is declared in the Apocalypse (xiv. 4) that virgins *follow the Lamb whithersoever He goeth,* and *(verse* 3) that they sing *a new canticle,* which *no* other *man could say.* Therefore virginity is the greatest of the virtues.

On the contrary, Augustine says *(De Virgin.* xlvi): *No one, methinks, would dare prefer virginity to martyrdom,* and *(ibid.* xlv): *The authority of the Church informs the faithful in no uncertain manner, so that they know in what place the martyrs and the holy virgins who have departed this life are commemorated in the Sacrament of the Altar.* By this we are given to understand that martyrdom, and also the monastic state, are preferable to virginity.

I answer that, A thing may excel all others in two ways. First, in some particular genus: and thus virginity is most excellent, namely in the genus of chastity, since it surpasses the chastity both of widowhood and of marriage. And because comeliness is ascribed to chastity antonomastically, it follows that surpassing beauty is ascribed to chastity. Wherefore Ambrose says *(De Virgin.* i. 7): *Can anyone esteem any beauty greater than a virgin's, since she is beloved of her King, approved by her Judge, dedicated to her Lord, consecrated to her God?* Secondly, a thing may be most excellent simply, and in this way virginity is not the most excellent of the virtues. Because the end always excels that which is directed to the end; and the more effectively a thing is directed to the end, the better it is. Now the end which renders virginity praiseworthy is that one may have leisure for Divine things, as stated above (A. 4). Wherefore the theological virtues as well as the virtue of religion, the acts of which consist in being occupied about Divine things, are preferable to virginity. Moreover, martyrs work more mightily in order to cleave to God,—since for this end they hold their own life in contempt;—and those who dwell in monasteries,—since for this end they give up their own will and all that they may possess,—than virgins who renounce venereal pleasure for that same purpose. Therefore virginity is not simply the greatest of virtues.

Reply Obj. 1. Virgins are *the more honored portion of Christ's flock,* and *their glory more sublime* in comparison with widows and married women.

Reply Obj. 2. The hundredfold fruit is ascribed to virginity, according to Jerome,[30] on account of its superiority to widowhood, to which the sixtyfold fruit is ascribed, and to marriage, to which is ascribed the thirtyfold fruit. But according to Augustine *(De QQ. Evang.* i. 9), *the hundredfold fruit is given to martyrs, the sixtyfold to virgins, and the thirtyfold to married persons.* Wherefore it does not follow that virginity is simply the greatest of virtues, but only in comparison with other degrees of chastity.

Reply Obj. 3. Virgins *follow the Lamb whithersoever He goeth,* because they imitate Christ, by integrity not only of the mind but also of the flesh, as Augustine says *(De Virgin.* xxvii). Wherefore they follow the Lamb in more ways, but this does not imply that they follow more closely, because other virtues make us cleave to God more closely by imitation of the mind. The *new hymn* which virgins alone sing, is their joy at having preserved integrity of the flesh.

QUESTION 39 (Supplement to the Summa Theologica)

Of the Impediments to This Sacrament [Holy Orders]

We must next consider the impediments to this sacrament. Under this head there are six points of inquiry: (1) Whether the female sex is an impediment to receiving this sacrament? (2) Whether lack of the use of reason is? (3) Whether the state of slavery is? (4) Whether homicide is ? (5) Whether illegitimate birth is? (6) Whether lack of members is?

Article 1. *Whether the Female Sex Is an Impediment to Receiving Orders?*

We proceed thus to the First Article:

Objection 1. It would seem that the female sex is no impediment to receiving Orders. For the office of prophet is greater than the office of priest, since a prophet stands midway between God and priests, just as the priest does between God and people. Now the office of prophet was sometimes granted to women, as may be gathered from 4 Kings xxii. 14. Therefore the office of priest also may be competent to them.

Obj. 2. Further, just as Order pertains to a kind of pre-eminence, so does a position of authority as well as martyrdom and the religious state. Now authority is entrusted to women in the New Testament, as in the case of abbesses, and in the Old Testament, as in the case of Debbora, who judged Israel (Judges ii). Moreover martyrdom and the religious life are also befitting to them. Therefore the Orders of the Church are also competent to them.

Obj. 3. Further, the power of Orders is founded in the soul. But sex is not in the soul. Therefore difference in sex makes no difference to the reception of Orders.

On the contrary, It is said (1 Tim. ii. 12): *I suffer not a woman to teach (in the Church),*[31] *nor to use authority over the man.*

Further, the crown is required previous to receiving Orders, albeit not for the validity of the sacrament. But the crown or tonsure is not befitting to women according to 1 Cor. xi. Neither therefore is the receiving of Orders.

I answer that, Certain things are required in the recipient of a sacrament as being requisite for the validity of the sacrament, and if such things be lacking, one can receive neither the sacrament nor the reality of the sacrament. Other things, however, are required, not for the validity of the sacrament, but for its lawfulness, as being congruous to the sacrament; and without these one receives the sacrament, but not the reality of the sacrament. Accordingly we must say that the male sex is required for receiving Orders not only in the second, but also in the first way. Wherefore even though a woman were made the object of all that is done in conferring Orders, she would not receive Orders, for since a sacrament is a sign, not only the thing, but the signification of the thing, is required in all sacramental actions, thus it was stated above (Q. 32, A. 2) that in Extreme Unction it is necessary to have a sick man, in order to signify the need of healing. Accordingly, since it is not possible in the female sex to signify eminence of degree, for a woman is in the state of subjection, it follows that she cannot receive the sacrament of Order. Some, however, have asserted that the male sex is necessary for the lawfulness and not for the validity of the sacrament, because even in the Decretals (cap. *Mulieres,* dist. 32; cap. *Diaconissam,* 27, qu. i) mention is made of deaconesses and priestesses. But *deaconess* there denotes a woman who shares in some act of a deacon, namely who reads the homilies in the Church, and *priestess* (*presbytera*) means a widow, for the word *presbyter* means elder.

Reply Obj. 1. Prophecy is not a sacrament but a gift of God. Wherefore there it is not the signification, but only the thing which is necessary. And since in matters pertaining to the soul woman does not differ from man as to the thing (for sometimes a woman is found to be better than many men as regards the soul), it follows that she can receive the gift of prophecy and the like, but not the sacrament of Orders.

And thereby appears the *Reply* to the *Second* and *Third Objections.* However, as to abbesses, it is said that they have not ordinary authority, but delegated as it were, on account of the danger of men and women living together. But Debbora exercised authority in temporal, not in priestly matters, even as now woman may have temporal power.

Article 2. *Whether Boys and Those Who Lack the Use of Reason Can Receive Orders?*

We proceed thus to the Second Article:

Objection 1. It would seem that boys and those who lack the use of reason cannot receive Orders. For, as stated in the text (iv. *Sent.* D. 25), the sacred canons have appointed a certain fixed age in those who receive Orders. But this would not be if boys could receive the sacrament of Orders. Therefore, etc.

Obj. 2. Further, the sacrament of Orders ranks above the sacrament of matrimony. Now children and those who lack the use of reason cannot contract matrimony. Neither therefore can they receive Orders.

Obj. 3. Further, act and power are in the same subject, according to the Philosopher (*De Somn. et Vigil.* i). Now the act of Orders requires the use of reason. Therefore the power of Orders does also.

On the contrary, One who is raised to Orders before the age of discretion is sometimes allowed to exercise them without being reordained, as appears from Extra., *De Cler. per salt. prom.* But this would not be the case if he had not received Orders. Therefore a boy can receive Orders.

Further, boys can receive other sacraments in which a character is imprinted, namely Baptism and Confirmation. Therefore in like manner they can receive Orders.

I answer that, Boyhood and other defects which remove the use of reason occasion an impediment to act. Wherefore the like are unfit to receive all those sacraments which require an act on the part of the recipient of the sacrament, such as Penance, Matrimony, and so forth. But since infused powers like natural powers precede acts—although acquired powers follow acts—and the removal of that which comes after does not entail the removal of what comes first, it follows that children and those who lack the use of reason can receive all the sacraments in which an act on the part of the recipient is not required for the validity of the sacrament. but some spiritual power is conferred from above: with this difference, however, that in the minor Orders the age of discretion is required out of respect for the dignity of the sacrament, but not for its lawfulness, nor for its validity. Hence some can without sin be raised to the minor Orders before the years of discretion, if there be an urgent reason for it and hope of their proficiency, and they are validly ordained: for although at the time they are not qualified for the offices entrusted to them, they will become qualified by being habituated thereto. For the higher Orders, however, the use of reason is required both out of respect for, and for the lawfulness of the sacrament, not only on account of the vow of continency annexed thereto, but also because the handling of the sacraments is entrusted to them.[32] But for the episcopate whereby a man receives power also over the mystical body, the act of accepting the pastoral care of souls is required; wherefore the use of reason is necessary for the validity of episcopal consecration. Some, however, maintain that the use of reason is necessary for the validity of the sacrament in all the Orders; but this statement is not confirmed either by authority or by reason.

Reply Obj. 1. As stated in the Article, not all that is necessary for the lawfulness of a sacrament is required for its validity.

Reply Obj. 2. The cause of matrimony is consent, which cannot be without the use of reason. Whereas in the reception of Orders no act is required on the part of the recipients, since no act on their part is expressed in their consecration. Hence there is no comparison.

Reply Obj. 3. Act and power are in the same subject; yet sometimes a power, such as the free-will, precedes its act; and thus it is in the case in point.

QUESTION 41

Matrimony and Nature

Article 3. *Whether the Marriage Act Is Always Sinful?*

We proceed thus to the Third Article:

Objection 1. It would seem that the marriage act is always sinful. For it is written (1 Cor. vii. 29): *That they . . . who have wives, be as if they had none.* But those who are not married do not perform the marriage act. Therefore even those who are married sin in that act.

Obj. 2. Further, *Your iniquities have divided between you and your God.* Now the marriage act divides man from God, wherefore the people who were to see God (Exod. xix. 11) were commanded not to go near their wives (*ibid.* 20); and Jerome says (*Ep. ad Ageruch.: Contra Jovin.* i. 18) that in the marriage act *the Holy Ghost touches not the hearts of the prophets.* Therefore it is sinful.

Obj. 3. Further, that which is shameful in itself can by no means be well done. Now the marriage act is always connected with concupiscence, which is always shameful. Therefore it is always sinful.

Obj. 4. Further, nothing is the object of excuse save sin. Now the marriage act needs to be excused by the marriage blessings, as the Master says (iv. *Sent.* D. 26). Therefore it is a sin.

Obj. 5. Further, things alike in species are judged alike. But marriage intercourse is of the same species as the act of adultery, since its end is the same, namely the human species. Therefore since the act of adultery is a sin, the marriage act is likewise.

Obj. 6. Further excess in the passions corrupts virtue. Now there is always excess of pleasure in the marriage act, so much so that it absorbs the reason which is man's principal good, wherefore the Philosopher says (*Ethic.* vii. 11) that *in that act it is impossible to understand anything.* Therefore the marriage act is always a sin.

On the contrary, It is written (1 Cor. vii. 28): *If a virgin marry she hath not sinned,* and (1 Tim. v. 14): *I will . . . that the younger should marry, and bear children.* But there can be no bearing of children without carnal union. Therefore the marriage act is not a sin; else the Apostle would not have approved of it.

Further, no sin is a matter of precept. But the marriage act is a matter of precept (1 Cor. vii. 3): *Let the husband render the debt to his wife.* Therefore it is not a sin.

I answer that, If we suppose the corporeal nature to be created by the good God, we cannot hold that those things which pertain to the preservation of the corporeal nature and to which nature inclines, are altogether evil; wherefore, since the inclination to beget an offspring whereby the specific nature is preserved is from nature, it is impossible to maintain that the act of begetting children is altogether unlawful, so that it be impossible to find the mean of virtue therein; unless we suppose, as some are mad enough to assert, that corruptible things were created by an evil god, whence perhaps the opinion mentioned in the text is derived (iv. *Sent.* D. 26); wherefore this is a most wicked heresy.

Reply Obj. 1. By these words the Apostle did not forbid the marriage act, as neither did he forbid the possession of things when he said (*loc. cit., verse* 31): *They that use this world* (let them be) *as if they used it not.* In each case he forbade enjoyment;[33] which is clear from the way in which he expresses himself; for he did not say *let them not use it,* or *let them not have them,* but *let them be as if they used it not and as if they had none.*

Reply Obj. 2. We are united to God by the habit of grace and by the act of contemplation and love. Therefore whatever severs the former of these unions is always a sin, but not always that which severs the latter, since a lawful occupation about lower things distracts the mind so that it is not fit for actual union with God; and this is especially the case in carnal intercourse wherein the mind is withheld by the intensity of pleasure. For this reason those who have to contemplate Divine things or handle sacred things are enjoined not to have to do with their wives for that particular time; and it is in this sense that the Holy Ghost, as regards the actual revelation of hidden things, did not touch the hearts of the prophets at the time of the marriage act.

Reply Obj. 3. The shamefulness of concupiscence that always accompanies the marriage act is a shamefulness not of guilt, but of punishment inflicted for the first sin, inasmuch as the lower powers and the members do not obey reason. Hence the argument does not prove.

Reply Obj. 4. Properly speaking, a thing is said to be excused when it has some appearance of evil, and yet is not evil, or not as evil as it seems, because some things excuse wholly, others in part. And since the marriage act, by reason of the corruption of concupiscence, has the appearance of an inordinate act, it is wholly excused by the marriage blessing, so as not to be a sin.

Reply Obj. 5. Although they are the same as to their natural species, they differ as to their moral species, which differs in respect of one circumstance, namely intercourse with one's wife and with another than one's wife; just as to kill a man by assault or by justice differentiates the moral species, although the natural species is the same; and yet the one is lawful and the other unlawful.

Reply Obj. 6. The excess of passions that corrupts virtue not only hinders the act of reason, but also destroys the order of reason. The intensity of pleasure in the marriage act does not do this, since, although for the moment man is not being directed, he was previously directed by his reason.

Article 4. *Whether the Marriage Act Is Meritorious?*

We proceed thus to the Fourth Article:

Objection 1. It would seem that the marriage act is not meritorious. For Chrysostom[34] says in his commentary on Matthew: *Although marriage brings no punishment to those who use it, it affords them no meed.* Now merit bears a relation to meed. Therefore the marriage act is not meritorious.

Obj. 2. Further, to refrain from what is meritorious deserves not praise. Yet virginity whereby one refrains from marriage is praiseworthy. Therefore the marriage act is not meritorious.

Obj. 3. Further, he who avails himself of an indulgence granted him, avails himself of a favor received. But a man does not merit by receiving a favor. Therefore the marriage act is not meritorious.

Obj. 4. Further, merit like virtue, consists in difficulty. But the marriage act affords not difficulty but pleasure. Therefore it is not meritorious.

Obj. 5. Further, that which cannot be done without venial sin is never meritorious, for a man cannot both merit and demerit at the same time. Now there is always a venial sin in the marriage act, since even the first movement in such like pleasures is a venial sin. Therefore the aforesaid act cannot be meritorious.

On the contrary, Every act whereby a precept is fulfilled is meritorious if it be done from charity. Now such is the marriage act, for it is said (1 Cor. vii. 3): *Let the husband render the debt to his wife.* Therefore, etc.

Further, every act of virtue is meritorious. Now the aforesaid act is an act of justice, for it is called the rendering of a debt. Therefore it is meritorious.

I answer that, Since no act proceeding from a deliberate will is indifferent, as stated in the Second Book (ii. *Sent.* D. 40, Q. 1, A. 3; I-II, Q. 18, A. 9), the marriage act is always either sinful or meritorious in one who is in a state of grace. For if the motive for the marriage act be a virtue, whether of justice that they may render the debt, or of religion, that they may beget children for the worship of God, it is meritorious. But if the motive be lust, yet not excluding the marriage blessings, namely that he would by no means be willing to go to another woman, it is a venial sin; while if he exclude the marriage blessings, so as to be disposed to act in like manner with any woman, it is a mortal sin. And nature cannot move without being either directed by reason, and thus it will be an act of virtue, or not so directed, and then it will be an act of lust.

Reply Obj. 1. The root of merit, as regards the essential reward, is charity itself; but as regards an accidental reward, the reason for merit consists in the difficulty of an act; and thus the marriage act is not meritorious except in the first way.

Reply Obj. 2. The difficulty required for merit of the accidental reward is a difficulty of labor, but the difficulty required for the essential reward is the difficulty of observing the mean, and this is the difficulty in the marriage act.

Reply Obj. 3. First movements in so far as they are venial sins are movements of the appetite to some inordinate object of pleasure. This is not the case in the marriage act, and consequently the argument does not prove.

---

[1] *Generation of Animals,* II, 3 (737a27).

[2] *Moral.,*XXI, 15 (PL 76, 203).

[3] PL 34, 467.

[4] Cf. Augustine, *Gen. ad lit.,* IX, 3 (PL 34, 395); *City of God,* XIV, 21 (PL 41, 429).

[5] *Generation of Animals,* IV, 2 (766b33).

[6] *Ethics,* VIII, 12 (1162a19).

[7] Chap. 26 (PL 34, 428).

[8] Hugh of St. Victor, *De Sacram.,* I, VI, 36 (PL 176, 284); Peter Lombard, *Sent.,* II, d. 18, chap. 4 (QR 1, 389).

[9] *Physics,* IV, 9 (217a25).

[10] PL 35, 1593.

[11] PL 42, 873.

[12] PL 34, 404.

[13] PL 34, 403.

[14] PL 34, 404.

[15] PL 34, 407.

[16] *Glossa ordin.* (III, 92A); *Gloss* of Peter Lombard (PL 113, 88).

[17] PL 34, 294.

[18] Aristotle, V, 5 (229b12).

[19] PL 82, 199.

[20] *Politics,* 11, 5 (1263a21).

[21] PG 94, 916.

[22] John Chrysostom, *In Genesim,* XVI (PG 53, 126); XVIII (PG 53, 153); John Damascene, *De Fide Ortho.,* 11, 30 (PG 94, 976), IV, 24 (PG 94, 1208).

[23] PG 44, 189.

[24] *City of God*, XIV, 26 (PL 41, 434).

[25] PL 34, 395.

[26] Bonaventure, *In Sent.,* II, d. 20, A. 1, Q. 3 (QR II, 481); cf. also Alexander of Hales, *Summa Theol.*, 1-11, n. 496 (QR II, 703).

[27] *City of God*, XIV, 26 (PL 41, 434).

[28] The quotation is from *De Sancta Virgin*, xiii.

[29] *De Habitu Virg.*

[30] *Ep.* cxxiii, *ad Ageruch.*

[31] The words in parenthesis are from 1 Cor. xiv. 34, *Let women keep silence in the churches.*

[32] See Acts of the Council of Trent (*De Reform.,* Sess. xxiii, cap. 4, 11, 12).

[33] *Fruitionem,* i.e. enjoyment of a thing sought as one's last end.

[34] *Hom.* i, in the opus *Imperfectum,* falsely ascribed to St. John Chrysostom.

3.

THE BIBLE

The Book of Genesis

1 [1] In the beginning when God created the heavens and the earth, [2] the earth was a formless void and darkness covered the face of the deep, while a wind from God swept over the face of the waters. [3] Then God said, "Let there be light"; and there was light. [4] And God saw that the light was good; and God separated the light from the darkness. [5] God called the light Day, and the darkness he called Night. And there was evening and there was morning, the first day. [6] And God said, "Let there be a dome in the midst of the waters, and let it separate the waters from the waters." [7] So God made the dome and separated the waters that were under the dome from the waters that were above the dome. And it was so. [8] God called the dome Sky. And there was evening and there was morning, the second day. [9] And God said, "Let the waters under the sky be gathered together into one place, and let the dry land appear." And it was so. [10] God called the dry land Earth, and the waters that were gathered together he called Seas. And God saw that it was good. [11] Then God said, "Let the earth put forth vegetation: plants yielding seed, and fruit trees of every kind on earth that bear fruit with the seed in it." And it was so. [12] The earth brought forth vegetation: plants yielding seed of every kind, and trees of every kind bearing fruit with the seed in it. And God saw that it was good. [13] And there was evening and there was morning, the third day. [14] And God said, "Let there be lights in the dome of the sky to separate the day from the night; and let them be for signs and for seasons and for days and years, [15] and let them be lights in the dome of the sky to give light upon the earth." And it was so. [16] God made the two great lights – the greater light to rule the day and the lesser light to rule the night – and the stars. [17] God set them in the dome of the sky to give light upon the earth, [18] to rule over the day and over the night, and to separate the light from the darkness. And God saw that it was good. [19] And there was evening and there was morning, the fourth day. [20] And God said, "Let the waters bring forth swarms of living creatures, and let birds fly above the earth across the dome of the sky." [21] So God created the great sea monsters and every living creature that moves, of every kind, with which the waters swarm, and every winged bird of every kind. And God saw that it was good. [22] God blessed them, saying, "Be fruitful and multiply and fill the waters in the seas, and let birds multiply on the earth." [23] And there was evening and there was morning, the fifth day. [24] And God said, "Let the earth bring forth living creatures of every kind: cattle and creeping things and wild animals of the earth of every

kind." And it was so. ^{25} God made the wild animals of the earth of every kind, and the cattle of every kind, and everything that creeps upon the ground of every kind. And God saw that it was good. ^{26} Then God said, "Let us make humankind in our image, according to our likeness; and let them have dominion over the fish of the sea, and over the birds of the air, and over the cattle, and over all the wild animals of the earth, and over every creeping thing that creeps upon the earth." ^{27} So God created humankind in his image, in the image of God he created them; male and female he created them. ^{28} God blessed them, and God said to them, "Be fruitful and multiply, and fill the earth and subdue it; and have dominion over the fish of the sea and over the birds of the air and over every living thing that moves upon the earth." ^{29} God said, "See, I have given you every plant yielding seed that is upon the face of all the earth, and every tree with seed in its fruit; you shall have them for food. ^{30} And to every beast of the earth, and to every bird of the air, and to everything that creeps on the earth, everything that has the breath of life, I have given every green plant for food." And it was so. ^{31} God saw everything that he had made, and indeed, it was very good. And there was evening and there was morning, the sixth day.

2 ^{1} Thus the heavens and the earth were finished, and all their multitude. ^{2} And on the seventh day God finished the work that he had done, and he rested on the seventh day from all the work that he had done. ^{3} So God blessed the seventh day and hallowed it, because on it God rested from all the work that he had done in creation. ^{4} These are the generations of the heavens and the earth when they were created. In the day that the LORD God made the earth and the heavens, ^{5} when no plant of the field was yet in the earth and no herb of the field had yet sprung up – for the LORD God had not caused it to rain upon the earth, and there was no one to till the ground; ^{6} but a stream would rise from the earth, and water the whole face of the ground – ^{7} then the LORD God formed man from the dust of the ground, and breathed into his nostrils the breath of life; and the man became a living being. ^{8} And the LORD God planted a garden in Eden, in the east; and there he put the man whom he had formed. ^{9} Out of the ground the LORD God made to grow every tree that is pleasant to the sight and good for food, the tree of life also in the midst of the garden, and the tree of the knowledge of good and evil. ^{10} A river flows out of Eden to water the garden, and from there it divides and becomes four branches. ^{11} The name of the first is Pishon; it is the one that flows around the whole land of Havilah, where there is gold; ^{12} and the gold of that land is good; bdellium and onyx stone are there. ^{13} The name of the second river is Gihon; it is the one that flows around the whole land of Cush. ^{14} The name of the third river is Tigris, which flows east of Assyria. And the fourth river is the Euphrates. ^{15} The LORD God took the man and put him in the garden of Eden to till it and keep it. ^{16} And the LORD God commanded the man, "You may freely eat of every tree of the garden; ^{17} but of the tree of the knowledge of good and evil you shall not eat, for in the day that you eat of it you shall die." ^{18} Then the LORD God said, "It is not good that the man should be alone; I will make him a helper as his partner." ^{19} So out of the ground the LORD God formed every animal of the field and every bird of the air, and brought them to

the man to see what he would call them; and whatever the man called every living creature, that was its name. [20] The man gave names to all cattle, and to the birds of the air, and to every animal of the field; but for the man there was not found a helper as his partner. [21] So the LORD God caused a deep sleep to fall upon the man, and he slept; then he took one of his ribs and closed up its place with flesh. [22] And the rib that the LORD God had taken from the man he made into a woman and brought her to the man. [23] Then the man said, "This at last is bone of my bones and flesh of my flesh; this one shall be called Woman, for out of Man this one was taken." [24] Therefore a man leaves his father and his mother and clings to his wife, and they become one flesh. [25] And the man and his wife were both naked, and were not ashamed.

3 [1] Now the serpent was more crafty than any other wild animal that the LORD God had made. He said to the woman, "Did God say, 'You shall not eat from any tree in the garden'?" [2] The woman said to the serpent, "We may eat of the fruit of the trees in the garden; [3] but God said, 'You shall not eat of the fruit of the tree that is in the middle of the garden, nor shall you touch it, or you shall die.'"[4] But the serpent said to the woman, "You will not die; [5] for God knows that when you eat of it your eyes will be opened, and you will be like God, knowing good and evil." [6] So when the woman saw that the tree was good for food, and that it was a delight to the eyes, and that the tree was to be desired to make one wise, she took of its fruit and ate; and she also gave some to her husband, who was with her, and he ate. [7] Then the eyes of both were opened, and they knew that they were naked; and they sewed fig leaves together and made loincloths for themselves. [8] They heard the sound of the LORD God walking in the garden at the time of the evening breeze, and the man and his wife hid themselves from the presence of the LORD God among the trees of the garden. [9] But the LORD God called to the man, and said to him, "Where are you?" [10] He said, "I heard the sound of you in the garden, and I was afraid, because I was naked; and I hid myself." [11] He said, "Who told you that you were naked? Have you eaten from the tree of which I commanded you not to eat?" [12] The man said, "The woman whom you gave to be with me, she gave me fruit from the tree, and I ate." [13] Then the LORD God said to the woman, "What is this that you have done?" The woman said, "The serpent tricked me, and I ate." [14] The LORD God said to the serpent, "Because you have done this, cursed are you among all animals and among all wild creatures; upon your belly you shall go, and dust you shall eat all the days of your life. [15] I will put enmity between you and the woman, and between your offspring and hers; he will strike your head, and you will strike his heel." [16] To the woman he said, "I will greatly increase your pangs in childbearing; in pain you shall bring forth children, yet your desire shall be for your husband, and he shall rule over you." [17] And to the man he said, "Because you have listened to the voice of your wife, and have eaten of the tree about which I commanded you, 'You shall not eat of it,' cursed is the ground because of you; in toil you shall eat of it all the days of your life; [18] thorns and thistles it shall bring forth for you; and you shall eat the plants of the field. [19] By the sweat of your face you shall eat bread until you return to the ground, for out of it you were taken; you are dust, and to dust you shall

return." [20] The man named his wife Eve, because she was the mother of all living. [21] And the LORD God made garments of skins for the man and for his wife, and clothed them. [22] Then the LORD God said, "See, the man has become like one of us, knowing good and evil; and now, he might reach out his hand and take also from the tree of life, and eat, and live forever" – [23] therefore the LORD God sent him forth from the garden of Eden, to till the ground from which he was taken. [24] He drove out the man; and at the east of the garden of Eden he placed the cherubim, and a sword flaming and turning to guard the way to the tree of life.

Song of Songs

1 [1] The Song of Songs, which is Solomon's. [2] Let him kiss me with the kisses of his mouth! For your love is better than wine, [3] your anointing oils are fragrant, your name is perfume poured out; therefore the maidens love you. [4] Draw me after you, let us make haste. The king has brought me into his chambers. We will exult and rejoice in you; we will extol your love more than wine; rightly do they love you. [5] I am black and beautiful, O daughters of Jerusalem, like the tents of Kedar, like the curtains of Solomon. [6] Do not gaze at me because I am dark, because the sun has gazed on me. My mother's sons were angry with me; they made me keeper of the vineyards, but my own vineyard I have not kept! [7] Tell me, you whom my soul loves, where you pasture your flock, where you make it lie down at noon; for why should I be like one who is veiled beside the flocks of your companions? [8] If you do not know, O fairest among women, follow the tracks of the flock, and pasture your kids beside the shepherds' tents. [9] I compare you, my love, to a mare among Pharaoh's chariots. [10] Your cheeks are comely with ornaments, your neck with strings of jewels. [11] We will make you ornaments of gold, studded with silver. [12] While the king was on his couch, my nard gave forth its fragrance. [13] My beloved is to me a bag of myrrh that lies between my breasts. [14] My beloved is to me a cluster of henna blossoms in the vineyards of En-gedi. [15] Ah, you are beautiful, my love; ah, you are beautiful; your eyes are doves. [16] Ah, you are beautiful, my beloved, truly lovely. Our couch is green; [17] the beams of our house are cedar, our rafters are pine.

2 [1] I am a rose of Sharon, a lily of the valleys. [2] As a lily among brambles, so is my love among maidens. [3] As an apple tree among the trees of the wood, so is my beloved among young men. With great delight I sat in his shadow, and his fruit was sweet to my taste. [4] He brought me to the banqueting house, and his intention toward me was love. [5] Sustain me with raisins, refresh me with apples; for I am faint with love. [6] O that his left hand were under my head, and that his right hand embraced me! [7] I adjure you, O daughters of Jerusalem, by the gazelles or the wild does: do not stir up or awaken love until it is ready! [8] The voice of my beloved! Look, he comes, leaping upon the mountains, bounding over the hills. [9] My beloved is like a gazelle or a young stag. Look, there he stands behind our wall, gazing in at the windows, looking through the lattice. [10] My beloved speaks and says to me: "Arise, my love, my fair one, and come away; [11] for now the winter is

past, the rain is over and gone. ^{12} The flowers appear on the earth; the time of singing has come, and the voice of the turtledove is heard in our land. ^{13} The fig tree puts forth its figs, and the vines are in blossom; they give forth fragrance. Arise, my love, my fair one, and come away. ^{14} O my dove, in the clefts of the rock, in the covert of the cliff, let me see your face, let me hear your voice; for your voice is sweet, and your face is lovely. ^{15} Catch us the foxes, the little foxes, that ruin the vineyards – for our vineyards are in blossom." ^{16} My beloved is mine and I am his; he pastures his flock among the lilies. ^{17} Until the day breathes and the shadows flee, turn, my beloved, be like a gazelle or a young stag on the cleft mountains.

3 ^{1} Upon my bed at night I sought him whom my soul loves; I sought him, but found him not; I called him, but he gave no answer. ^{2} "I will rise now and go about the city, in the streets and in the squares; I will seek him whom my soul loves." I sought him, but found him not. ^{3} The sentinels found me, as they went about in the city. "Have you seen him whom my soul loves?" ^{4} Scarcely had I passed them, when I found him whom my soul loves. I held him, and would not let him go until I brought him into my mother's house, and into the chamber of her that conceived me. ^{5} I adjure you, O daughters of Jerusalem, by the gazelles or the wild does: do not stir up or awaken love until it is ready! ^{6} What is that coming up from the wilderness, like a column of smoke, perfumed with myrrh and frankincense, with all the fragrant powders of the merchant? ^{7} Look, it is the litter of Solomon! Around it are sixty mighty men of the mighty men of Israel, ^{8} all equipped with swords and expert in war, each with his sword at his thigh because of alarms by night. ^{9} King Solomon made himself a palanquin from the wood of Lebanon. ^{10} He made its posts of silver, its back of gold, its seat of purple; its interior was inlaid with love. Daughters of Jerusalem, ^{11} come out. Look, O daughters of Zion, at King Solomon, at the crown with which his mother crowned him on the day of his wedding, on the day of the gladness of his heart.

4 ^{1} How beautiful you are, my love, how very beautiful! Your eyes are doves behind your veil. Your hair is like a flock of goats, moving down the slopes of Gilead. ^{2} Your teeth are like a flock of shorn ewes that have come up from the washing, all of which bear twins, and not one among them is bereaved. ^{3} Your lips are like a crimson thread, and your mouth is lovely. Your cheeks are like halves of a pomegranate behind your veil. ^{4} Your neck is like the tower of David, built in courses; on it hang a thousand bucklers, all of them shields of warriors. ^{5} Your two breasts are like two fawns, twins of a gazelle, that feed among the lilies. ^{6} Until the day breathes and the shadows flee, I will hasten to the mountain of myrrh and the hill of frankincense. ^{7} You are altogether beautiful, my love; there is no flaw in you. ^{8} Come with me from Lebanon, my bride; come with me from Lebanon. Depart from the peak of Amana, from the peak of Senir and Hermon, from the dens of lions, from the mountains of leopards. ^{9} You have ravished my heart, my sister, my bride, you have ravished my heart with a glance of your eyes, with one jewel of your necklace. ^{10} How sweet is your love, my sister, my bride! how much better is your love than wine, and the fragrance of your oils than any spice! ^{11} Your lips

distill nectar, my bride; honey and milk are under your tongue; the scent of your garments is like the scent of Lebanon. ^{12} A garden locked is my sister, my bride, a garden locked, a fountain sealed. ^{13} Your channel is an orchard of pomegranates with all choicest fruits, henna with nard, ^{14} nard and saffron, calamus and cinnamon, with all trees of frankincense, myrrh and aloes, with all chief spices – ^{15} a garden fountain, a well of living water, and flowing streams from Lebanon. ^{16} Awake, O north wind, and come, O south wind! Blow upon my garden that its fragrance may be wafted abroad. Let my beloved come to his garden, and eat its choicest fruits.

5 ^{1} I come to my garden, my sister, my bride; I gather my myrrh with my spice, I eat my honeycomb with my honey, I drink my wine with my milk. Eat, friends, drink, and be drunk with love. ^{2} I slept, but my heart was awake. Listen! my beloved is knocking. "Open to me, my sister, my love, my dove, my perfect one; for my head is wet with dew, my locks with the drops of the night." ^{3} I had put off my garment; how could I put it on again? I had bathed my feet; how could I soil them? ^{4} My beloved thrust his hand into the opening, and my inmost being yearned for him. ^{5} I arose to open to my beloved, and my hands dripped with myrrh, my fingers with liquid myrrh, upon the handles of the bolt. ^{6} I opened to my beloved, but my beloved had turned and was gone. My soul failed me when he spoke. I sought him, but did not find him; I called him, but he gave no answer. ^{7} Making their rounds in the city the sentinels found me; they beat me, they wounded me, they took away my mantle, those sentinels of the walls. ^{8} I adjure you, O daughters of Jerusalem, if you find my beloved, tell him this: I am faint with love. ^{9} What is your beloved more than another beloved, O fairest among women? What is your beloved more than another beloved, that you thus adjure us? ^{10} My beloved is all radiant and ruddy, distinguished among ten thousand. ^{11} His head is the finest gold; his locks are wavy, black as a raven. ^{12} His eyes are like doves beside springs of water, bathed in milk, fitly set. ^{13} His cheeks are like beds of spices, yielding fragrance. His lips are lilies, distilling liquid myrrh. ^{14} His arms are rounded gold, set with jewels. His body is ivory work, encrusted with sapphires. ^{15} His legs are alabaster columns, set upon bases of gold. His appearance is like Lebanon, choice as the cedars. ^{16} His speech is most sweet, and he is altogether desirable. This is my beloved and this is my friend, O daughters of Jerusalem.

6 ^{1} Where has your beloved gone, O fairest among women? Which way has your beloved turned, that we may seek him with you? ^{2} My beloved has gone down to his garden, to the beds of spices, to pasture his flock in the gardens, and to gather lilies. ^{3} I am my beloved's and my beloved is mine; he pastures his flock among the lilies. ^{4} You are beautiful as Tirzah, my love, comely as Jerusalem, terrible as an army with banners. ^{5} Turn away your eyes from me, for they overwhelm me! Your hair is like a flock of goats, moving down the slopes of Gilead. ^{6} Your teeth are like a flock of ewes, that have come up from the washing; all of them bear twins, and not one among them is bereaved. ^{7} Your cheeks are like halves of a pomegranate behind your veil. ^{8} There are sixty queens and eighty concubines, and maidens

without number. ^{9} My dove, my perfect one, is the only one, the darling of her mother, flawless to her that bore her. The maidens saw her and called her happy; the queens and concubines also, and they praised her. ^{10} "Who is this that looks forth like the dawn, fair as the moon, bright as the sun, terrible as an army with banners?" ^{11} I went down to the nut orchard, to look at the blossoms of the valley, to see whether the vines had budded, whether the pomegranates were in bloom. ^{12} Before I was aware, my fancy set me in a chariot beside my prince. ^{13} Return, return, O Shulammite! Return, return, that we may look upon you. Why should you look upon the Shulammite, as upon a dance before two armies?

7 ^{1} How graceful are your feet in sandals, O queenly maiden! Your rounded thighs are like jewels, the work of a master hand. ^{2} Your navel is a rounded bowl that never lacks mixed wine. Your belly is a heap of wheat, encircled with lilies. ^{3} Your two breasts are like two fawns, twins of a gazelle. ^{4} Your neck is like an ivory tower. Your eyes are pools in Heshbon, by the gate of Bath-rabbim. Your nose is like a tower of Lebanon, overlooking Damascus. ^{5} Your head crowns you like Carmel, and your flowing locks are like purple; a king is held captive in the tresses. ^{6} How fair and pleasant you are, O loved one, delectable maiden! ^{7} You are stately as a palm tree, and your breasts are like its clusters. ^{8} I say I will climb the palm tree and lay hold of its branches. Oh, may your breasts be like clusters of the vine, and the scent of your breath like apples, ^{9} and your kisses like the best wine that goes down smoothly, gliding over lips and teeth. ^{10} I am my beloved's, and his desire is for me. ^{11} Come, my beloved, let us go forth into the fields, and lodge in the villages; ^{12} let us go out early to the vineyards, and see whether the vines have budded, whether the grape blossoms have opened and the pomegranates are in bloom. There I will give you my love. ^{13} The mandrakes give forth fragrance, and over our doors are all choice fruits, new as well as old, which I have laid up for you, O my beloved.

8 ^{1} O that you were like a brother to me, who nursed at my mother's breast! If I met you outside, I would kiss you, and no one would despise me. ^{2} I would lead you and bring you into the house of my mother, and into the chamber of the one who bore me. I would give you spiced wine to drink, the juice of my pomegranates. ^{3} O that his left hand were under my head, and that his right hand embraced me! ^{4} I adjure you, O daughters of Jerusalem, do not stir up or awaken love until it is ready! ^{5} Who is that coming up from the wilderness, leaning upon her beloved? Under the apple tree I awakened you. There your mother was in labor with you; there she who bore you was in labor. ^{6} Set me as a seal upon your heart, as a seal upon your arm; for love is strong as death, passion fierce as the grave. Its flashes are flashes of fire, a raging flame. ^{7} Many waters cannot quench love, neither can floods drown it. If one offered for love all the wealth of his house, it would be utterly scorned. ^{8} We have a little sister, and she has no breasts. What shall we do for our sister, on the day when she is spoken for? ^{9} If she is a wall, we will build upon her a battlement of silver; but if she is a door, we will enclose her with boards of cedar. ^{10} I was a wall, and my breasts were like towers; then I was in his eyes as

one who brings peace. [11] Solomon had a vineyard at Baal-hamon; he entrusted the vineyard to keepers; each one was to bring for its fruit a thousand pieces of silver. [12] My vineyard, my very own, is for myself; you, O Solomon, may have the thousand, and the keepers of the fruit two hundred! [13] O you who dwell in the gardens, my companions are listening for your voice; let me hear it. [14] Make haste, my beloved, and be like a gazelle or a young stag upon the mountains of spices!

4.

THE CITY OF GOD
St. Augustine
(Written 413–426 A.D.)

The Fourteenth Book of *The City of God*

CHAPTER XXII

That God first instituted and blessed the bond of marriage

BUT we doubt not at all that his increase, multiplying, and filling of the earth was by God's goodness bestowed upon the marriage which He ordained in the beginning, ere man sinned, when He made them male and female, sexes evident in the flesh. This work was no sooner done, but it was blessed: for the scripture having said: 'He created them male and female,' adds at once: 'And God blessed them, saying, Increase and multiply,' etc. All which though they may not unfitly be applied spiritually, yet male and female can in no wise be appropriate even in a figure of speech to two things in one man, as though there were one thing in him which rules and another which is ruled: but as it is evident in the real distinction of sex, they were made male and female, to bring forth fruit by generation, to multiply and fill the earth. This plain truth none but fools will oppose. It cannot be meant of the spirit ruling, and the flesh obeying; of the reason governing and the emotion working; of the contemplative part excelling, and the active serving; nor of the mind's understanding and the body's sense; but directly, of the bond of marriage, combining both the sexes in one. Christ being asked whether one might put away his wife for any cause, because Moses by reason of the hardness of their hearts suffered them to give her a bill of divorce, answered saying: 'Have ye not read, that He which made them at the beginning, made them male and female?' and said: 'For this cause shall a man leave his father and mother and cleave unto his wife, and they twain shall be one flesh. So that now they are no more two but one. Let no man therefore sunder what God has coupled together.'[1] Sure it is therefore that male and female were ordained at the beginning in the same form and difference that mankind is now in. And they are called one, either because of their conjunction, or the woman's origin, who came out of the side of man: for the apostle warns all married men by this example to love their wives.

CHAPTER XXIII

Whether if man had not sinned, he would have begotten children in paradise, and whether there should there have been any contention between chastity and lust

BUT he that says that there should have been neither copulation nor propagation but for sin, what does he else but make sin the origin of the holy number of saints? For if they two should have lived alone, not sinning, seeing sin (as these say) was their only means of generation, then verily was sin necessary to make the number of saints more than two. But if it be absurd to hold this, it is fit to hold that the number of God's citizens should have been as great then, if no man had sinned, as now shall be gathered by God's grace out of the multitude of sinners, as long as this worldly multiplication of the sons of the world shall endure; and therefore that marriage, that was held fit to be made in paradise, should have had increase, but no lust, had not sin been. How this might be, here is no fit place to discuss: but it need not seem incredible that one member might serve the will without lust then, so many serving it now. Do we now move our hands and feet so easily when we will unto their offices without resistance, as we see in ourselves and others, chiefly handicraftsmen, where industry has made dull nature nimble; and may we not believe that those members might have served our first father unto procreation, without their having been seized with lust, the reward of his disobedience, as well as all his others served him to other acts? Does not Tully, disputing of the difference of governments (in his treatise *Of the Commonwealth*[2]), and drawing a simile from man's nature, say, that we command our bodily members as sons, they are so obedient, and that we must keep a harder form of rule over our mind's vicious parts, as our slaves? In order of nature the soul is above the body, yet is it harder to rule than the body. But this lust whereof we speak is the more shameful in this, that the soul does neither rule itself therein, so that it may not lust, nor the body either, so that the will rather than lust might move these parts, which, if it were so, would be nothing to be ashamed of. But now the soul is ashamed that the body its inferior should resist it. It feels less shame in other rebellious emotions, because the resistance in this case comes from itself; and when it is conquered of itself, it conquers itself (although it be inordinately and viciously); for although these parts be reasonless that conquer it, yet are they parts of itself, and so, as I say, it is conquered of itself. For when it conquers itself in an orderly manner, and brings all the parts under reason, this is a laudable and virtuous conquest, if the soul be God's subject. But it is less ashamed when it is resisted by the vicious parts of itself, than when the body disobeys it, because the body is under it, depends on it, and cannot live without it. But so long as the other members are all under the will, without which members nothing can be performed against the will by those members which are incited by lust so to do, the chastity is kept unviolated, and the delight in sin is not permitted. This contention, fight, and altercation of lust and will, this need of lust to the sufficiency of the will, had not been laid upon wedlock in paradise, unless disobedience had become the punishment for the sin of disobedience. Otherwise these members had obeyed their wills as well as the rest. The seed of generation should have been sown in the vessel, as corn is now in the field. What I would say more in this kind, modesty bids me forbear a little, and first ask pardon of chaste ears. I need not do it, but might proceed in any discourse pertinent to this theme freely, and without any fear to be obscene, or imputation of impurity to the words, being as honestly spoken of these as others are of any other bodily members. Therefore he that reads this with unchaste suggestions, let him accuse his own guilt, not the nature of the question: and let him brand the effect of turpitude in himself, not the words necessity compels us to use, which the chaste and religious reader will easily allow us to use in confuting our experienced (not our credulous) adversary, who draws his arguments from proof not from belief. For he that abhors not the apostle's reprehension of the horrible beastliness of women, 'who perverted natural use and acted against nature,'[3] will read this without offence, especially seeing we neither rehearse nor reprehend that damnable bestiality that he condemns, but are investigating the emotions of human generation, yet with avoidance of obscene terms, as much as he avoids them.

CHAPTER XXIV

That our first parents, had they lived without sin, should have had their members of generation as subject unto their wills as any of the rest

MAN therefore would have sown the seed, and woman have received it, as need required, without any lust, and as their wills desired. For as we now are, not only do our articulate members obey our will—our hands, or feet, or fingers—but even those also that we move only by small sinews and tendons we contract and turn as we list; as you see in the voluntary motions of the mouth and face. And the lungs, the softest of all the organs except the brain, and therefore placed in the hollow of the breast for more safety in taking in and giving out the breath, and in modulating the voice, do serve a man's will entirely, like a pair of smith's or organist's bellows, to breathe, to speak, to cry, or to sing. I omit that it is natural in some creatures if they feel anything bite them, to move the skin there where it bites, and nowhere else; shaking off not only flies, but even darts or shafts by this motion of the skin. Man cannot do this. What then? Could not God give it unto what creatures He listed? Even so might man have had the obedience of his lower parts, which his own disobedience debarred. For God could easily have made him with all his members subjected to his will, even that which now is not moved but by lust: for we see some men's natures far different from others; acting those things strangely in their bodies, which others can neither do nor hardly will believe. There are those who can move their ears, one or both, as they please: there are those that can move all their hair towards their forehead, and back again, and never move their heads. There are those that can swallow twenty things whole, and pressing their stomach lightly, give you every thing up as whole as if they had but put into a bag. There are those that can mimic the voices of birds and other men so cunningly, that unless you see them, you cannot distinguish them at all. There are those that can break wind backward so artificially, that you would think they sung. I have seen one sweat whenever he pleased, and it is sure that some can weep when they list, and shed tears plentifully. But even more wonderful was the case lately seen by some of the brethren in a priest called Restitutus, of the village of Calama, who when he pleased (and they requested him to show them this rare experiment), at the imitation of funeral waiting drew himself into such an ecstasy, that he lay as if dead, senseless of all pinching, pricking, nay even of burning, but that he felt it sore after his awaking. And this rapture was found to be true, and not counterfeit in him, in that he lay still without any breathing: yet he said afterward, that if one spake aloud, he thought he heard him, as if he were afar off. Seeing therefore that in this frail state of ours, the body serves the will in such extraordinary emotions; why should we not believe that before his disobedience the first man might have had his means and members of generation without lust? But he taking delight in himself was left by God unto himself, and therefore could not obey himself, because he would not obey God. And this proves his misery the plainer, in that he cannot live as he would. For if he would do so, he might think himself happy; yet living, in obscenity, he would not be so indeed.

CHAPTER XXVI

That our first parents in paradise might have produced mankind without any shameful appetite

THEREFORE man lived in paradise as he desired, whilst he only desired what God commanded. He enjoyed God, from whence was his good. He lived without need, and had life eternal in his power. He had meat for hunger, drink for thirst, the tree of life to keep off age. He was free from all bodily corruption and feeling of molestation. He feared neither disease within nor violence without. Height of health was in his flesh, and fullness of peace in his soul; and as paradise was neither fiery nor frosty, no more was the inhabitants' good will offended either with desire, or fear. There was no true sorrow, nor vain joy. Their joy continued by God's mercy, whom they loved with a pure good conscience and an unfeigned faith. Their wedlock love was holy and honest; their vigilance and custody of the precept without any toil or trouble. They were neither weary of leisure, nor unwillingly sleepy. And can we not suppose that in all this happiness they might beget their children without lust, and move those members without concupiscential desire, the man being laid in his wife's lap without corruption of integrity? Lack of experience need not drive us from believing that their generative parts might be moved by will only, without exorbitance of hotter desire; and that the sperm of man might be conveyed into the place of conception without corruption of the instrument receiving, just as now it doth give forth the menstruous flux without breach of virginity. The one might be cast in as the other is cast forth. For as their childbirth would not have been forerun by pain but by maturity, which should open a way for the child without torment; so would their copulation have been performed without lustful appetite, only by voluntary use. This theme is immodest, and therefore let us conjecture as we can, how the first parents of man were, ere they were ashamed. Needs must our discourse hereupon rather yield to shamefacedness than trust to eloquence. The one restrains us much, and the other helps us little. For seeing they that might have tried, did not try this that I have said, desiring by sin to be expelled from paradise, before they had used their means of propagating man, how can man now conceive it should be done, except by the means of that headlong lust, not by any quiet will? This is that which stops my mouth, though I behold the reason in mine heart. But however, Almighty God, the Creator of all nature, the helper and rewarder of all good wills, the just condemner of the bad, and the ordainer of both, lacked no prescience how to fulfil the number of those whom He had destined to be of His city, even out of the condemned progeny of man, distinguishing them not by their merits (for the whole fruit was condemned in the corrupted stock) but by His own grace, freeing them both from themselves and the slavish world, and showing them what He bestowed on them; for each one now acknowledges that it is not his own deserts, but God's goodness that has freed him from evil, and from their society with whom he would have shared a just condemnation. Why then might not God create such as He knew would sin, thereby to show in them and their progeny both what sin deserved, and what His mercy bestowed; and that the perverse inordinate offence of them, under Him, could not pervert the right order which He had resolved?

THE GOOD OF MARRIAGE
(Written 401 A.D.)

Chapter 1

SINCE EVERY MAN is a part of the human race, and human nature is something social and possesses the capacity for friendship as a great and natural good, for this reason God wished to create all men from one, so that they might be held together in their society, not only by the similarity of race, but also by the bond of blood relationship. And so it is that the first natural tie of human society is man and wife. Even these God did not create separately and join them as if strangers, but He made the one from the other, indicating also the power of union in the side from where she was drawn and formed.[4] They are joined to each other side by side who walk together and observe together where they are walking. A consequence is the union of society in the children who are the only worthy fruit, not of the joining of male and female, but of sexual intercourse. For there could have been in both sexes, even without such intercourse, a kind of friendly and genuine union of the one ruling and the other obeying.

Chapter 2

(2) There is no need now for us to examine and put forth a final opinion on this question—how the progeny of the first parents might have come into being, whom God had blessed, saying, 'Be fruitful and multiply; fill the earth,'[5] if they had not sinned, since their bodies deserved the condition of death by sinning, and there could not be intercourse except of mortal bodies. Many different opinions have existed on this subject, and, if we must examine which of them agrees most with the truth of divine Scriptures, there is matter for an extended discussion:[6] Whether, for example, if our first parents had not sinned, they would have had children in some

other way, without physical coition, out of the munificence of the almighty Creator, who was able to create them without parents, and who was able to form the body of Christ in a virgin's womb, and who, to speak now to the unbelievers themselves, was able to grant progeny to bees without intercourse; whether, in that passage, much was spoken in a mystical and figurative sense and the written words are to be understood differently: 'Fill the earth and subdue it,' that is, that it should come to pass by the fullness and the perfection of life and power that the increasing and multiplying, where it is said: 'Be fruitful and multiply,' might be understood to be by the advancement of the mind and by the fullness of virtue, as it is expressed in the psalm: 'Thou shalt multiply me in my soul unto virtue,'[7] and that succession of offspring was not granted to man except that later, because of sin, there was to be a departure in death; whether, at first, the body of those men had been made spiritual but animal, so that afterwards by the merit of obedience it might become spiritual to grasp immortality, not after death, which came into the world through the envy of the Devil[8] and became the punishment for sin, but through that change which the Apostle indicates where he says: 'Then we who live, who survive, shall be caught up together with them in clouds to meet the Lord in the air,'[9] so that we may understand that the bodies of the first marriage were both mortal at the first formation and yet would not have died, if they had not sinned, as God had threatened,[10] just as if He threatened a wound, because the body was vulnerable, which, however, would not have happened, unless that was done which He had forbidden.

Thus, then, even through sexual intercourse generations of such bodies could have come into existence, which would have had increase up to a certain point and yet would not have inclined to old age, or they would have inclined as far as old age and yet not to death, until the earth should be filled with that multiplication of the blessing. For, if God granted to the garments of the Israelites[11] their proper state without any damage for forty years, how much more would He have granted a very happy temperament of certain state to the bodies of those who obeyed His command, until they would be turned into something better, not by the death of man, by which the body is deserted by the soul, but by a blessed change from mortality to immortality, from an animal to a spiritual quality.

Chapter 3

It would be tedious to inquire and to discuss which of these opinions is true, or whether another or other opinions can still be extracted from these words.

(3) This is what we now say, that according to the present condition of birth and death, which we know and in which we were created, the marriage of male and female is something good. This union divine Scripture so commands that it is not permitted a woman who has been dismissed by her husband to marry again, as long as her husband lives, nor is it permitted a man who has been dismissed by his wife to marry again, unless she who left has died. Therefore, regarding the good of marriage, which even the Lord confirmed in the Gospel,[12] not only because He

forbade the dismissal of a wife except for fornication, but also because He came to the marriage when invited,[13] there is merit in inquiring why it is a good.

This does not seem to me to be a good solely because of the procreation of children, but also because of the natural companionship between the two sexes. Otherwise, we could not speak of marriage in the case of old people, especially if they had either lost their children or had begotten none at all. But, in a good marriage, although one of many years, even if the ardor of youths has cooled between man and woman, the order of charity still flourishes between husband and wife. They are better in proportion as they begin the earlier to refrain by mutual consent from sexual intercourse, not that it would afterwards happen of necessity that they would not be able to do what they wished, but that it would be a matter of praise that they had refused beforehand what they were able to do. If, then, there is observed that promise of respect and of services due to each other by either sex, even though both members weaken in health and become almost corpse-like, the chastity of souls rightly joined together continues the purer, the more it has been proved, and the more secure, the more it has been calmed.

Marriage has also this good, that carnal or youthful incontinence, even if it is bad, is turned to the honorable task of begetting children, so that marital intercourse makes something good out of the evil of lust. Finally, the concupiscence of the flesh, which parental affection tempers, is repressed and becomes inflamed more modestly. For a kind of dignity prevails when, as husband and wife they unite in the marriage act, they think of themselves as mother and father.

Chapter 4

(4) There is the added fact that, in the very debt which married persons owe each other, even if they demand its payment somewhat intemperately and incontinently, they owe fidelity equally to each other. And to this fidelity the Apostle has attributed so much right that he called it power, when he said: 'The wife has not authority over her body, but the husband; the husband likewise has not authority over his body, but the wife.'[14] But the violation of this fidelity is called adultery, when, either by the instigation of one's own lust or by consent to the lust of another, there is intercourse with another contrary to the marriage compact. And so the fidelity is broken which even in material and base things is a great good of the soul; and so it is certain that it ought to be preferred even to the health of the body wherein his life is contained. For, although a small amount of straw as compared to much gold is as nothing, fidelity, when it is kept pure in a matter of straw, as in a matter of gold, is not of less importance on this account because it is kept in a matter of less value.

But, when fidelity is employed to commit sin, we wonder whether it ought to be called fidelity. However, whatever its nature may be, if even against this something is done, it has an added malice; except when this is abandoned with the view that there might be a return to the true and lawful fidelity, that is, that the sin might be amended by correcting the depravity of the will.

For example, if anyone, when he is unable to rob a man by himself, finds an accomplice for his crime and makes an agreement with him to perform the act together and share the loot, and, after the crime has been committed, he runs off with everything, the other naturally grieves and complains that fidelity had not been observed in his regard. In his very complaint he ought to consider that he should have observed his fidelity to human society by means of a good life, so that he would not rob a man unjustly, if he feels how wickedly fidelity was not kept with him in an association of sin. His partner, faithless on both counts, is certainly to be judged the more wicked. But, if he had been displeased with the wickedness which they had committed and so had refused to divide the spoils with his partner in crime on this account, that he could return them to the man from whom they were taken, not even the faithless man would call him faithless.

So, in the case of a woman who has broken her marriage fidelity but remains faithful to her adulterer, she is surely wicked, but, if she is not faithful even to her adulterer, she is worse. On the contrary, if she repents of her gross sin and returns to conjugal chastity and breaks off all adulterous unions and purposes, I cannot conceive of even the adulterer himself thinking of her as a violator of fidelity.

Chapter 5

(5) The question is also usually asked whether this case ought to be called a marriage: when a man and a woman (he not being the husband nor she the wife of another) because of incontinence have intercourse not for the purpose of procreating children but only for the sake of intercourse itself, with this pledge between them, that he will not perform this act with another woman, nor she with another man. Yet perhaps not without reason this can be called wedlock, if this has been agreed upon between them even until the death of one of them and if, although they do not have intercourse for the purpose of having children, they do not avoid it, so that they do not refuse to have children nor act in any evil way so that they will not be born. But, if both or either one of these conditions is lacking, I do not see how we can call this a marriage.

For, if a man lives with a woman for a time, until he finds another worthy either of his high station in life or his wealth, whom he can marry as his equal, in his very soul he is an adulterer, and not with the one whom he desires to find but with her with whom he now lives in such a way as not to be married to her. The same is true for the woman, who, knowing the situation and willing it, still has relations unchastely with him, with whom she has no compact as a wife. On the other hand, if she remains faithful to him and, after he has taken a wife, does not plan to marry and is prepared to refrain absolutely from such an act, surely I could not easily bring myself to call her an adulteress; yet who would say that she did not sin, when he knows that she had relations with a man though she was not his wife.

If from the union, as far as she is concerned, she wishes for nothing except children and whatever she endures beyond the cause of procreation she endures unwillingly, surely this woman is to be placed above many matrons, who, although they are not adulteresses, force their husbands, who often desire to be continent, to pay the debt of the flesh, not with any hope of progeny, but through an intemperate use of their right under the ardor of concupiscence, still, in the marriage of these women there is this good, that they are married. They are married for this purpose, that concupiscence may be brought under a lawful bond and may not waver disgracefully and loosely, having of itself a weakness of the flesh that cannot be curbed, but in marriage an association of fidelity that cannot be dissolved; of itself an increase of immoderate intercourse, in marriage a means of begetting chastely. For, although it is disgraceful to make use of a husband for purposes of lust, it is honorable to refuse to have intercourse except with a husband and not to give birth except from a husband.

Chapter 6

There also are men incontinent to such a degree that they do not spare their wives even when pregnant. Whatever immodest, shameful, and sordid acts the married commit with each other are the sins of the married persons themselves, not the fault of marriage.

(6) Furthermore, in the more immoderate demand of the carnal debt, which the Apostle enjoined on them not as a command but conceded as a favor, to have sexual intercourse even without the purpose of procreation, although evil habits impel them to such intercourse, marriage protects them from adultery and fornication. For this is not permitted because of the marriage, but because of the marriage it is pardoned. Therefore, married people owe each other not only the fidelity of sexual intercourse for the purpose of procreating children—and this is the first association of the human race in this mortal life—but also the mutual service, in a certain measure, of sustaining each other's weakness, for the avoidance of illicit intercourse, so that, even if perpetual continence is pleasing to one of them, he may not follow this urge except with the consent of the other. In this case, 'The wife has not authority over her body, but the husband; the husband likewise has not authority over his body, but the wife.' So, let them not deny either to each other, what the man seeks from matrimony and the woman from her husband, not for the sake of having children but because of weakness and incontinence, lest in this way they fall into damnable seductions through the temptations of Satan because of the incontinence of both or of one of them.

In marriage, intercourse for the purpose of generation has no fault attached to it, but for the purpose of satisfying concupiscence, provided with a spouse, because of the marriage fidelity, it is a venial sin; adultery or fornication, however, is a mortal sin. And so, continence from all intercourse is certainly better than marital intercourse itself which takes place for the sake of begetting children.

Chapter 7

While continence is of greater merit, it is no sin to render the conjugal debt, but to exact it beyond the need for generation is a venial sin; furthermore, to commit fornication or adultery is a crime that must be punished. Conjugal charity should be on its guard lest, while it seeks for itself the means of being honored more, it creates for the spouse the means of damnation. 'Everyone who puts away his wife, save on account of immorality, causes her to commit adultery.'[15] To such a degree is that nuptial pact which has been entered upon a kind of sacrament that it is not nullified by separation, since, as long as the husband, by whom she has been abandoned, is alive, she commits adultery if she marries another, and he who abandoned her is the cause of the evil.

(7) I wonder if, as it is permitted to put away an adulterous wife, it is accordingly permitted, after she has been put away, to marry another. Holy Scripture creates a difficult problem in this matter, since the Apostle says[16] that according to the command of the Lord a wife is not to depart from her husband, but, if she departs, she ought to remain unmarried or be reconciled to her husband. She surely ought not to withdraw and remain unmarried except in the case of an adulterous husband, lest, by withdrawing from him who is not an adulterer, she causes him to commit adultery. But, perhaps she can justly be reconciled with her husband either by tolerating him, if she on her own part cannot contain herself, or after he has been corrected. But I do not see how a man can have freedom to marry another if he leaves an adulteress, since a woman does not have freedom to marry another if she leaves an adulterer.

If this is so, that bond of fellowship between married couples is so strong that, although it is tied for the purpose of procreation, it is not loosed for the purpose of procreation. For, a man might be able to dismiss a wife who is barren and marry someone by whom he might have children, yet in our times and according to Roman law it is not permissible to marry a second wife as long as he has another wife living. Surely, when an adulteress or adulterer is abandoned, more human beings could be born if either the woman were wed to another or the man married another. But, if this is not permitted, as divine Law seems to prescribe, who will not be eager to learn what the meaning of such a strong conjugal bond is? I do not think that this bond could by any means have been so strong, unless a symbol, as it were, of something greater than that which could arise from our weak mortality were applied, something that would remain unshaken for the punishment of men when they abandon and attempt to dissolve this bond, inasmuch as, when divorce intervenes, that nuptial contract is not destroyed, so that the parties of the compact are wedded persons even though separated. Moreover, they commit adultery with those with whom they have intercourse even after their repudiation, whether she with a man, or he with a woman. Yet, except 'in the city of our God, His holy mountain,'[17] such is not the case with a woman.

Chapter 8

But who does not know that the laws of the pagans are otherwise. Among them, when repudiation intervenes, both she marries whomever she wishes and he whomever he wishes, without any offense that requires human punishment. Moses, because of the Israelites' hardness of heart,[18] seems to have permitted something similar to this practice regarding a written notice of dismissal.[19] In this matter there appears to be a rebuke rather than an approval of divorce.

(8) 'Let marriage be held in honor with all, and let the marriage bed be undefiled.'[20] We do not call marriage a good in this sense, that in comparison with fornication it is a good; otherwise, there will be two evils, one of which is worse. Or even fornication will be a good because adultery is worse—since violation of another's marriage is worse than associating with a prostitute. Or adultery will be a good because incest is worse—since intercourse with one's mother is worse than lying with another's wife—and so on, until we come to those things about which, as the Apostle says: 'It is shameful even to speak.'[21] All will be good in comparison with that which is worse. But who would doubt that this is false? Therefore, marriage and fornication are not two evils, the second of which is worse; but marriage and continence are two goods, the second of which is better. Just so, your temporal health and sickness are not two evils, the second of which is worse; but your health and immortality are two goods, the second of which is better.

Likewise, knowledge and vanity are not two evils, vanity being the worse of the two; but knowledge and charity are two goods, charity being the better of the two. For, 'knowledge will be destroyed,' says the Apostle, yet it is necessary for this life, but 'charity will never fall.'[22] So also, this mortal generation, which is the purpose of marriage, will be destroyed, but freedom from all sexual intercourse is both an angelic ideal here, and remains forever. But, as the meals of the just are better than the fastings of the sacrilegious, so the marriage of the faithful is placed above the virginity of the unbeliever. Nevertheless, neither is a meal preferable to fasting in the one case, but justice to sacrilege; nor in the second case is marriage preferred to virginity, but faith to unbelief. For, the just, when there is need, will dine for this purpose, that as good masters they may furnish for their slaves, their bodies, what is right and fitting; but the sacrilegious fast for this purpose, that they may serve devils. So, faithful women marry for this purpose, that they may join chastely with their husbands; but the unfaithful are virgins for this purpose, that they may commit fornication against the true God.

Therefore, just as that was good which Martha did when occupied with the ministering to holy souls, yet that was better which Mary her sister did, who 'seated herself at the Lord's feet, and listened to his words';[23] so we praise the good of Susanna[24] in married chastity, yet we place above it the good of the widow Anna[25] and much more so that of the Virgin Mary.[26] That was good which they were doing who out of their substance were supplying the necessaries to Christ and His disciples, but they did better who gave away all their substance that they might follow the same Lord more readily. In both these goods, whether what the latter did or what Martha and Mary did, the better could not be done without passing over and abandoning the other.

We must understand that marriage is not to be considered an evil for this reason, that widowed chastity or virginal purity cannot be possessed unless there is abstinence from marriage. Nor was that which Martha did an evil for this reason, that, unless her sister abstained from it, she would not be doing what was better; nor is it an evil to take a just man or a prophet into one's house, because he who wishes to follow Christ unto perfection, in order that he might do what is better, ought not to own any house at all.

Chapter 9

(9) Surely we must see that God gives us some goods which are to be sought for their own sake, such as wisdom, health, friendship; others, which are necessary for something else, such as learning, food, drink, sleep, marriage, sexual intercourse. Certain of these are necessary for the sake of wisdom, such as learning; others for the sake of health, such as food and drink and sleep; others for the sake of friendship, such as marriage or intercourse, for from this comes the propagation of the human race in which friendly association is a great good. So, whoever does not use these goods, which are necessary for something else, for the purpose for which they are given does well. As for him for whom they are not necessary, if he does not use them, he does better. In like manner, we wish for these goods rightly when we have need, but we are better off not wishing for them than wishing for them, since we possess them in a better way when we possess them as not necessary.

For this reason it is a good to marry, since it is a good to beget children, to be the mother of a family; but it is better not to marry, since it is better for human society itself not to have need of marriage. For, such is the present state of the human race that not only some who do not check themselves are taken up with marriage, but many are wanton and given over to illicit intercourse. Since the good Creator draws good out of their evils, there is no lack of numerous progeny and an abundance of generation whence holy friendships might be sought out.

In this regard it is gathered that in the earliest times of the human race, especially to propagate the people of God, through whom the Prince and Saviour of all peoples might both be prophesied and be born, the saints were obliged to make use of this good of marriage, to be sought not for its own sake but as necessary for something else. But now, since the opportunity for spiritual relationship abounds on all sides and for all peoples for entering into a holy and pure association, even they who wish to contract marriage only to have children are to be admonished that they practice the greater good of continence.

Chapter 10

(10) But I know what they murmur. 'What if,' they say, 'all men should be willing to restrain themselves from all intercourse, how would the human race survive?' Would that all men had this wish, if only in 'charity, from a pure heart and a good conscience and faith unfeigned.'[27] Much more quickly would the City of God be filled and the end of time be hastened. What else does it appear that the Apostle is encouraging when he says, in speaking of this: 'For I would that you all were as I am myself'?[28] Or, in another place: 'But this I say, brethren, the time is short; it remains that those who have wives be as if they had none; and those who weep, as though not weeping; and those who rejoice, as though not rejoicing; and

those who buy, as though not buying; and those who use this world, as though not using it, for this world as we see it is passing away. I would have you free from care.' Then he adds: 'He who is unmarried thinks about the things of the Lord, how he may please the Lord. Whereas he who is married thinks about the things of the world, how he may please his wife, and he is divided. And the unmarried woman and the virgin, who is unmarried, is concerned about the things of the Lord, that she may be holy in body and in spirit. Whereas she who is married is concerned about the things of the world, how she may please her husband.'[29]

And so it seems to me that at this time only those who do not restrain themselves ought to be married in accord with this saying of the same Apostle: 'But if they do not have self-control, let them marry, for it is better to marry than to burn.'[30]

(11) Such marriage is not a sin. If it were chosen in preference to fornication, it would be a lesser sin than fornication, but still a sin. But now what are we to say in answer to that very clear statement of the Apostle when he says: 'Let him do what he will; he does not sin if she should marry'[31] and 'But if thou takest a wife, thou hast not sinned. And if a virgin marries, she does not sin.'[32] Certainly from this it is not right to doubt that marriage is not a sin. And so it is not the marriage that the Apostle grants as a pardon—for who would doubt that it is most absurd to say that they have not sinned to whom a pardon is granted—but it is that sexual intercourse that comes about through incontinence, not for the sake of procreation and at the time with no thought of procreation, that he grants as a pardon. Marriage does not force this type of intercourse to come about, but asks that it be pardoned, provided it is not so great as to encroach on the times that ought to be set aside for prayer, and does not degenerate into that practice that is against nature, which the Apostle was not able to pass over in silence when he spoke of the extreme depravities of impure and impious men.[33]

The intercourse necessary for generation is without fault and it alone belongs to marriage. The intercourse that goes beyond this necessity no longer obeys reason but passion. Still, not to demand this intercourse but to render it to a spouse, lest he sin mortally by fornication, concerns the married person. But, if both are subject to such concupiscence, they do something that manifestly does not belong to marriage. However, if in their union they love what is proper rather than what is improper, that is, what belongs to marriage rather than that which does not, this is granted to them with the Apostle as an authority. They do not have a marriage that encourages this crime, but one that intercedes for them, if they do not turn away from themselves the mercy of God, either by not abstaining on certain days so as to be free for prayers, and by this abstinence as by their fasts they put their prayers in a favorable light, or by changing the natural use into that use which is contrary to nature, which is all the more damnable in a spouse.

Chapter 11

(12) For, although the natural use, when it goes beyond the marriage rights, that is, beyond the need for procreation, is pardonable in a wife but damnable in a

prostitute, that use which is against nature is abominable in a prostitute but more abominable in a wife. For, the decree of the Creator and the right order of the creature are of such force that, even though there is an excess in the things that have been granted to be used, this is much more tolerable than a single or rare deviation in those things which have not been granted. Therefore, the immoderation of a spouse in a matter that is permitted is to be tolerated lest lust may break forth into something that has not been granted. So it is that, however demanding one is as regards his wife, he sins much less than one who commits fornication even most rarely.

But, when the husband wishes to use the member of his wife which has not been given for this purpose, the wife is more shameful if she permits this to take place with herself rather than with another woman. The crown of marriage, then, is the chastity of procreation and faithfulness in rendering the carnal debt. This is the province of marriage, this is what the Apostle defended from all blame by saying: 'But if thou takest a wife, thou hast not sinned. And if a virgin marries, she does not sin'[34] and 'Let him do what he will; he does not sin, if she should marry.'[35] The somewhat immoderate departure in demanding the debt from the one or the other sex is given as a concession because of those things which he mentioned before.

(13) Therefore, what he says: 'The unmarried woman thinks about the things of the Lord, that she may be holy in body and spirit,'[36] is not to be understood in such a way that we think a chaste Christian wife is not holy in body. To all the faithful, indeed, it is said: 'Do you not know that your bodies are the temple of the Holy Spirit, who is in you, whom you have from God?'[37] Also holy, therefore, are the bodies of married people who remain faithful to themselves and to the Lord.

That an unbelieving spouse does not hinder this sanctity of either of the couple, but, rather, the sanctity of the wife profits the unbelieving husband or the sanctity of the husband profits the unbelieving wife, the same Apostle is a witness when he says: 'For the unbelieving husband is sanctified in the wife, and the unbelieving wife is sanctified in the believing husband.'[38]

Moreover, this was said in regard to the greater sanctity of the unmarried woman than of the married woman, and a more ample reward is due to this sanctity because it is better than the other good, because she thinks only of this, how she might please the Lord. For it is not that a faithful woman, observing conjugal chastity, does not think how she might please the Lord, but she does so less because she is thinking also of things of the world, how she might please her husband. This is what he wished to say about them, what they can expect, as it were, from the demands of marriage, namely, that they must think of the things of the world, how they might please their husbands.

Chapter 12

(14) Not without reason is it doubted whether he said this of all married women or of such women of this type who are so numerous that almost all women can be considered the same. Nor does this, which he says of the unmarried: 'The

unmarried woman thinks about the things of the Lord, that she may be holy in body and spirit,'[39] hold good for all unmarried women, since there are some widows who are dead in that they are living in sinful pleasures.[40] However, in regard to this certain distinction and *quasi* characteristic of unmarried and married, just as she is the most detestable who while refraining from marriage, that is, from a thing that has been granted, does not refrain from the sins whether of lust or pride or idle curiosity and gossip, so, too, rare is the married woman who in conjugal conduct thinks only how she might please God, by adorning herself 'not with braided hair or gold and pearls and expensive clothing, but by good behavior such as become women professing godliness.'[41]

The Apostle Peter also describes marriages of this type when he charges: 'In like manner also let wives be subject to their husbands; so that even if any do not believe the word, they may without word be won through the behavior of their wife, observing your reverence and chaste behavior. Let them not be such as are adorned with the curling of hair or clothed with gold or a fine robe; but let it be the inner life of your heart, in the imperishableness of a quiet and gentle spirit, which is of great price in the sight of the Lord. For after this manner certain holy women who hoped in the Lord, adorned themselves, while being subject to their husbands. So Sara obeyed Abraham, calling him lord. You have become daughters of hers when you do what is right and fear no vain disturbance. Husbands, in like manner dwell in peace and in chastity with your wives, pay honor to the weaker and subjected vessel, as if coheir of grace, and see that your prayers be not hindered.'[42]

Is it true that such spouses do not think about the things of the Lord, how they might please the Lord? They are very rare. Who denies this? And in the very rareness almost all the married people who are of this type were not joined to be this way, but, after they were united, then they became such.

Chapter 13

(15) What Christian men of our times, free from the bond of marriage, able to restrain themselves from all intercourse, when they see it is 'a time,' as it is written, 'not to embrace, but a time to abstain from embraces,'[43] would not choose to observe virginal continence or that of a widower rather than to undergo the tribulation of the flesh, without which marriage cannot exist—to pass over in silence other things which the Apostle spares us[44]—since now no duty of human society presses. But, when they have been joined under the rule of concupiscence, if they afterwards overcome it, since it is not permissible to dissolve the marriage, as it was permissible not to join together, they become such as the form of marriage professes, so that either by mutual consent they ascend to a higher grade of sanctity or, if both are not of this mind, he who is such will not be the one who demands the carnal debt but renders it, observing in all things a chaste and religious harmony.

In those times, when the mystery of our salvation was still veiled in prophetic signs, even those who were of this nature before marriage were accustomed to marry because of the obligation of procreation, not overcome by passion, but motivated by piety. If they had been given the free choice such as was given in the revelation of the New Testament when our Lord said: 'Let him accept it who can,'[45] that person does not doubt that they would have taken it upon themselves with joy who attentively and diligently reads how they used their spouses, when it was permissible for one man to have many wives, whom he had more chastely than any one of these in whose regard we see what the Apostle grants, by way of concession, now has his one wife. The patriarchs possessed their wives for the work of procreation, not 'in the passion of lust like the Gentiles who do not know God.'[46] This is so great that many today would contain themselves more easily for their whole life from all intercourse than to hold to the norm of not uniting except for offspring, if they were to be joined by marriage.

Indeed, we do have many continent brothers and associates of both sexes in the heavenly heritage, whether they have entered the marriage state or whether free from all such intercourse; in fact, they are numberless. Yet, whom have we heard in friendly talks, whether of those who are married or who have been married, saying to us that he never had intercourse with his wife except when hoping for conception? Therefore, what the Apostles prescribe for married people belongs to marriage; what they grant by way of a concession, or what interferes with prayer, marriage does not force but endures.

Chapter 14

(16) Still, if by chance—I do not know whether it can happen, and I rather think that it cannot—at any rate, if by chance a concubine taken for a time should seek only children from this same union, not for this reason is such a union to be preferred to the marriage of those women who take advantage of that which is pardonable. For, what belongs to marriage must be considered, not what is the action of those marrying and using marriage intemperately.

Neither does anyone, if he should use fields that have been wickedly and wrongly invaded so as to make large sums from their produce, therefore justify rapine; if another one, an avaricious man, takes over the incumbency of his father's farm or one rightly acquired, the civil statute of law whereby he became the rightful owner is not therefore to be found fault with. Neither will the wickedness of a tyrannical faction be praiseworthy if the tyrant treats his subjects with regal clemency; nor is the system of kingly power deserving of blame if a king conducts himself with tyrannical cruelty. It is one thing to wish to use an unjust power justly, and another to use a just power unjustly. So, concubines taken for a time, if they have intercourse for the sake of children, do not justify their concubinage; nor do the married wives, if they are wanton with their husbands, put a stain on the marriage state.

(17) It is clear that by a subsequent honorable agreement there can be a marriage for those who had not been rightly united.

Chapter 15

Once, however, marriage is entered upon in the City [that is, Church] of our God, where also from the first union of the two human beings marriage bears a kind of sacred bond, it can be dissolved in no way except by the death of one of the parties. The bond of marriage remains, even if offspring, for which the marriage was entered upon, should not follow because of a clear case of sterility, so that it is not lawful for married people who know they will not have any children to separate and to unite with others even for the sake of having children. If they do unite, they commit adultery with the ones with whom they join themselves, for they remain married people.

It was indeed permissible among the ancients to have another woman with the consent of the wife, from whom common children might be born by the union and seed of the husband, by the privilege and authorization of the wife. Whether this is permissible now, as well, I would not care to say. There is not the need for procreation which there was then, when it was permissible for husbands who could have children to take other women for the sake of a more copious posterity, which certainly is not lawful now. The mysterious difference of times brings so great an opportunity of doing or of not doing something justly that, now, he does better who does not marry even one wife, unless he cannot control himself; then, however, they had without fault several wives, even they who could restrain themselves much more easily, except that piety in that time demanded something else. For, as the wise and just man, who for a long time was desiring to be dissolved and to be with Christ[47] and was delighted rather by this greatest good, not the desire of living here but the duty of caring for others, took food that he might remain in the flesh, which was necessary for the sake of others, so, too, for the men of those times it was not lust but duty to be joined with women by the law of marriage.

Chapter 16

(18) For, what food is to the health of man, intercourse is to the health of the race, and both are not without carnal pleasure, which, however, when modified and put to its natural use with a controlling temperance, cannot be a passion.[48] However, what unlawful food is in the sustaining of life, this is the intercourse of fornication or adultery in seeking a child; and what unlawful food is in the excessive indulgence of the stomach and palate, this is unlawful intercourse in a passion seeking no offspring; and what is immoderate appetite for some as regards lawful food, this is that pardonable intercourse in spouses. Therefore, just as it is better to die of hunger than to eat food sacrificed to idols, so it is better to die childless than to seek progeny from an unlawful union.

However, from whatever source men are born, if they do not follow the vices of their parents and if they worship God rightly, they will be honest and safe. The seed of man, from any kind of man, is a creature of God and will prove bad for those who use it wrongly; of itself, it will not at any time be an evil. Yet, just as the good children of adulterers are no defense for adultery, so the bad children of married people do not constitute an accusation against marriage. Accordingly, just as the fathers of New Testament times, taking food because of the duty of caring for others, though they ate it with a natural delectation of the flesh—by no means, however, was their pleasure to be compared with the pleasure of those who were eating food sacrificed to idols or of those who, though they were consuming lawful foods, were doing so immoderately—so the fathers of Old Testament times had intercourse because of the duty of caring for others. That natural delight they derived was by no means given rein up to the point of unreasoning and wicked lust, nor is it to be compared to the debaucheries of lust or the intemperance of the married. Indeed, for the same fountainhead of charity, then carnally, now spiritually, were children to be propagated because of that great Mother Jerusalem; only the difference in times made the works of the fathers diverse. So, it was necessary that noncarnal Prophets copulate carnally, as it was necessary that noncarnal Apostles also eat carnally.

Chapter 17

(19) Therefore, as many women as there are now, to whom it is said: 'If they do not have self-control, let them marry,'[49] are not to be compared even to the holy women who married then. Marriage itself among all races is for the one purpose of procreating children, whatever will be their station and character afterwards; marriage was instituted for this purpose, so that children might be born properly and decently.

But the men who do not have self-control step up, as it were, into marriage by a step of honesty; those, however, who without a doubt would have practiced self-control, if the conditions of that time would have allowed this, step down, in a certain sense, into marriage by a step of piety. Therefore, the marriage of both, inasmuch as they are marriages because they exist for the sake of procreation, are equally good; yet, married men of our times are not to be compared to married men of those days. The former have something that is granted to them as a concession because of the dignity of marriage, although it does not pertain to marriage, that is, that departure which goes beyond the need for procreating, which the other men in question did not have. But neither can these, if any by chance are now to be found who do not seek or desire in marriage anything except that for which marriage was instituted, be put on the same footing with those men. For, in these the very desire for children is carnal; in those, however, it was spiritual, because it was in accord with the mystery of the time. In our day, it is true, no one perfect in piety seeks to have children except spiritually; in their day, however, the work of piety itself was to propagate children even carnally, because the generation of that people was a harbinger of future events and pertains to the prophetic dispensation.

(20) Therefore, while it was permitted for one husband to have several wives, it was not permitted for one woman to have several husbands, not even for the sake of offspring, if, perhaps, she was able to bear while her husband was not able to beget. For, by a hidden law of nature things that rule love singularity; things that are ruled, indeed, are subjected not only each one to an individual master, but also, if natural or social conditions allow, many of them are not unfittingly subjected to one master. Neither does one servant have many masters, as many servants have one master. And so we read where no one of the holy women served two or more living husbands; we do read, however, that one man had several wives when the

customs of that people permitted it and the nature of the time encouraged it, for it is not against the nature of marriage. Many women can conceive children by one man, but one woman cannot do so by many men—this is the nature of principals— just as many souls are properly subjected to the one God. Therefore, there is only the one true God of souls; one soul through many false gods can commit fornication, but not be made fruitful.

Chapter 18

(21) Since from many souls there is to be one City of those having one soul and one heart in regard to God,[50] this perfection of our unity is to be after this peregrination, when the thoughts of all will not be hidden from one another nor in any way opposed to one other; for this reason, the sacrament of marriage in our time has been reduced and confined to one man and one woman, so that it is not lawful to ordain a minister of the Church unless he is the husband of one wife.[51] This was more keenly understood by those who believed that the person should not be ordained who as a catechumen or as a pagan had had a second wife. It is a question of the sacrament, not of sin. In baptism all sins are remitted. But he who said: 'If thou takest a wife, thou hast not sinned. And if a virgin marries, she does not sin,'[52] and 'Let him do what he will, he does not sin if she should marry,'[53] has sufficiently declared that marriage is no sin.

However, because of the sanctity of the sacrament, just as a woman, even if she has had intercourse while still a catechumen, is not able after baptism to be consecrated among the virgins of God, just so it did not seem harsh that he who has had more than one wife did not commit any sin, but lost a certain standard, as it were, to the sacrament, necessary not for the reward of a good life, but for the seal of ecclesiastical ordination.

And on this account, just as the many wives of the ancient fathers signified our future churches of all races subject to one man-Christ, so our bishop, a man of one wife, signifies the unity of all nations subject to one man-Christ. This unity will be perfected at that time when He will reveal 'the things hidden in darkness' and make manifest 'the hidden things of the heart; and then everyone will have his praise from God.'[54] Now, however, there are open, there are hidden, dissensions, even though charity is preserved among those who are to be one and in One; these dissensions then, indeed, will be no more.

Therefore, just as the multiple marriages of that time symbolically signified the future multitude subject to God in all peoples of the earth, so the single marriages of our time symbolically signify the unity of all of us subject to God which is to be in one heavenly City. And so, just as serving two or more masters, so, too, passing from one husband while alive to the marriage of another was not lawful then, nor is it lawful now, nor will it ever be. Indeed, to apostatize from the one God and to go into the adulterous superstition of another is always wicked. Neither for the sake of a more numerous progeny did our holy father do what Cato the Roman is said to have done, that while he was still living he handed over his wife to fill the house of another with children. Indeed, in the marriage of our women the sanctity of the sacrament is of more importance than the fecundity of the womb.

(22) Therefore, even these who are joined for the sake of generation alone, for which marriage was instituted, are not to be compared with the ancients, who sought children in a much different way than they; since intrepid and devout Abraham, when he was ordered to sacrifice his son, whom he had received after great despair, would not have spared his sole child, but only he lowered his hand on being checked by Him at whose command he had raised it.

Chapter 19

It remains for us to see whether at least our continent men are to be compared with the married patriarchs; unless, perhaps, these continent men are to be preferred to the patriarchs, in respect to whom we have not yet found any to be compared. For there was a greater good in their marriage than the good proper to marriage, to which, without a doubt, the good of continence is to be preferred, because the ancients were not seeking children from their marriage out of an obligation such as the others are led by—a certain instinct of mortal nature requiring a replacement for a loss. Whoever denies that this is a good is ignorant of the fact that God is the creator of all good things from the heavenly even to the earthly, from the immortal even to the mortal. Yet, this instinct of generation not even the animals lack deep within, and especially the birds whose care for building a nest is obvious and to a certain extent comparable with married people as regards the procreation and nourishment of offspring.

But, the men of old, with much more holy minds, were surpassing this tendency of mortal nature whose own chastity in its kind, when the worship of God is added, is reckoned as producing fruit thirtyfold, as some have understood. They were seeking from their marriage children for the sake of Christ, to distinguish His descent according to the flesh from all others; as it pleased God to arrange it that this people before the rest should be able to prophesy Him because it was foretold from what family and from what people He was to come in the flesh.[55] Very much, then, was that a greater good that the chaste marriage of our faithful which father Abraham had known in his thigh, on which he ordered the servant to place his hand, that he might take an oath concerning the wife who was to be married by his son.[56] For, putting the hand under the thigh of a man and swearing by the God of heaven, what else did that signify except that in that flesh, which took its origin from that thigh, the God of heaven would come?

Marriage, therefore, is a good in which the married are better in proportion as they fear God more chastely and more faithfully, especially if they also nourish spiritually the children whom they desire carnally.

Chapter 20

(23) The fact that the Law orders a man to be purified even after marital intercourse does not mean that it is a sin; if it is not that intercourse which is granted as a concession, which, also, being intemperate, impedes prayers. But, just as the

Law placed many things in mysteries and in the shadows of things to come, a certain material shapelessness, as it were, in the seed, which when it is formed will produce the body of a man, is placed as a sign of a life shapeless and uninstructed; so, since it is fitting that men be cleansed from this shapelessness by the form and learning of doctrine, as a sign of this, purification after the loss of seed has been ordered.

Nor is loss of seed in sleep a result of sin; yet in this case, also, purification is prescribed. Or, if anyone considers this a sin, thinking that it does not happen except from some desire of this sort—which, without a doubt, is false—are, then, the cycle menstruations of women sins? However, the same Old Law ordered that the women be purified from them only because of the material shapelessness which, when conception takes place, is added, as it were, for the purpose of developing the body. And on this account, since there is a formless flow, the Law wished that by this the mind without the force of discipline, unseemly fluid and dissipated, be understood; it shows that the mind must be formed, when it orders such a flow of the body to be purified. Finally, is it a sin to die, or is not the burial of the dead also a good work of kindness? Still, purification was ordered after this, also,[57] because a dead body when life has left it is no sin, but it signifies the sin of a soul abandoned by justice.

(24) Marriage, I say, is a good and can be defended by right reason against all charges. However, with regard to the marriage of the holy patriarchs, I am asking not what marriage but what continence is comparable. Moreover, I am not comparing marriage with marriage—for a gift equal in all things has been given to the mortal nature of man—but men who make use of marriage. Since I do not find any to compare with those men of old who used marriages far differently, it must be asked what continent men can be compared to them—unless, perhaps, Abraham could not restrain himself from marriage because of the kingdom of heaven, who because of the kingdom of heaven could fearlessly immolate his single beloved son on whose account marriage was dear to him.

Chapter 21

(25) Continence, indeed, not of the body but of the soul is virtue. Virtues of the soul, however, sometimes are manifested in work, sometimes they lie dormant in habit and character, just as the virtue of martyrdom stood out and was manifested by bearing sufferings. But how many there are in that same virtuous condition of soul for whom the temptation is lacking by which that which within is in the sight of God might also come forth into the sight of men, and at the time not begin to exist but then begin to be known!

As an example, Job had possessed patience for a long time.[58] God knew this and He bore witness to it, but it became known to men by the trial of a temptation, and what was hidden within was not born, but was manifested, by the assaults made from without. Likewise, Timothy had the virtue of refraining from wine,[59] which Paul did not take from him by admonishing that he use a little wine for the stomach's sake and his frequent infirmities—otherwise, he would have taught perniciously that for the health of the body there should be a loss of virtue in the soul—but because it was possible to do what he ordered and safeguard virtue at the same time, so the advantage of drinking was relaxed as regards the body in such a way that the habit of temperance remained in the soul.

For habit is that by which something is done when the need arises, yet, when it is not being practiced, it can be, but there is no need. They do not have this habit in respect to the continence that is from intercourse, since it is said to them: 'But if they do not have self-control, let them marry.'[60] On the other hand, they do have the habit to whom the words are addressed: 'Let him accept it who can.'[61] Through this habit of continence perfect souls have so used worldly goods that are necessary for another purpose that by means of this habit they were not bound by these goods and were able not to use them when there was no need. Nor does anyone use them properly unless he is able also not to use them. Many, indeed, more easily abstain from them so as not to use them at all, rather than control themselves so as to use them well. Yet, no one can use them wisely except him who through continence is able not to use them. In consequence, Paul could say of this habit: 'I know how to have abundance and to suffer want.'[62] In any event, to suffer want is the lot of certain men, but to know how to suffer want belongs to great souls. So, who is not able also to have abundance? However, to know how to abound belongs only to those whom abundance does not corrupt.

(26) That it might be more clearly understood how virtue can be in habit, even if not in practice, I speak of an example regarding which there can be no doubt among Catholic Christians. That our Lord Jesus Christ in His true flesh was hungry and thirsty, ate and drank, no one doubts who is faithful in accordance with His Gospel. Therefore, was there not in Him the virtue of continence from food and drink such as was in John the Baptist? 'For John came neither eating nor drinking, and they said, "He has a devil!" The Son of Man came eating and drinking, and they said, "Behold a glutton and a wine-drinker, a friend of publicans and sinners!" '[63] Are not such things said of the members of His family, our fathers, of their use of earthly goods of another kind, such as pertain to intercourse; behold the lustful and unclean, the lovers of women and licentiousness? And just as in His case this was not true, although it was true that He did not abstain from eating and drinking as John did, for He Himself says very openly and truly: 'John came neither eating nor drinking. The Son of Man came eating and drinking,' so neither is this true as regards the patriarchs, although the Apostle of Christ came in our time neither married nor having children, yet the pagans say: he was a magician; at that time the Prophet of Christ came marrying and begetting children, and yet the Manichaeans say: he was fond of women. 'And wisdom is justified by her children.'[64] This is what our Lord added at that point when He said these things about John and Himself. 'Wisdom,' He said, 'is justified by her children.' They see that the virtue of continence ought always to be in the disposition of the souls, to be shown, however, in practice in accord with the opportunity of the time and circumstances. So the virtue of patience of the holy martyrs appeared, indeed, in act, although equally in habit it was in the rest of the saints. Therefore, just as there was not an

unequal reward for patience in Peter who suffered and in John who did not suffer, so there was not an unequal reward for continence in John who had no experience with marriage and in Abraham who begot sons. Both the celibacy of the one and the marriage of the other did service for Christ in accord with the needs of the time, but John possessed continence in practice; Abraham indeed possessed it, but only in habit.

Chapter 22

(27) Accordingly, when even the Law following the time of the patriarchs then called him accursed who did not rear children in Israel, even he who could did not show forth this continence, yet he possessed it. Afterwards, the fullness of time came,[65] so that it was said: 'Let him accept it who can';[66] from that time up till now and henceforward to the end, he who possesses this continence puts it into practice; he who is unwilling to practice it, let him not say untruthfully that he has it. Therefore, it is with a subtlety that is empty and of no use that they who corrupt good morals by evil conversation[67] say to the Christian man, continent and refusing marriage: 'You, then, are better than Abraham?' When he hears this, let him not be troubled or dare to say: 'Yes, better,' or to fall from his resolution—because the former he does not say truthfully, the latter he does not do rightly—but let him say: 'I am indeed not better than Abraham, but the chastity of the unmarried is better than the chastity of marriage. Abraham had one of them in practice, both in habit. He lived chastely in the married state, yet he could have been chaste without marriage, but then it was impossible. I, indeed, more easily do not make use of marriage, which Abraham made use of, than I could make use of marriage as Abraham used it. Therefore, I am better than those who through incontinence of mind cannot do what I am doing. I am not better than those who because of the difference of times did not do what I am doing. What I now do they would have done better, if it was to be done at that time. But what they did I would not be doing as they did, if it had to be done now.'

Or, if he feels and knows that he is of such a character that, if he would descend to the use of marriage because of some religious obligation, the virtue of continence remaining safe and secure in the habit of his mind, he would be the type of husband and the type of father that Abraham was, let him openly dare to respond to that captious questioner and to say: 'I am not even better than Abraham in at least this type of continence which he did not lack, though it was not apparent; but I am not such a one who has one thing but does another.' Let him say these things openly, because, even if he does wish to boast, he will not be foolish, for he speaks the truth. But, if he forbears, lest any man thinks that he is above what he sees in him or hears from him,[68] let him remove from his own person the knot of the question, and let him respond not about the man but about the thing itself, and say: 'Who can do so much, he is such a one as Abraham was.' Yet, it can happen that the virtue of continence is less in the soul of him who does not make use of marriage which Abraham made use of; still, it is greater than that in the soul of him who on this account observed the chastity of marriage because he could not observe the greater.

The same is the case of the unmarried woman who thinks about the things of the Lord, how she might be holy in body and in spirit.[69] When she hears that impudent inquirer saying: 'You are, then, better than Sara?' Let her answer: 'I am better, but better than those who lack the virtue of this continence, and I do not believe this in respect to Sara. Therefore, she possessed that virtue and did what was suited to that time. I am free from this duty so that in my body, also, there can appear what she had in her soul.'

Chapter 23

(28) Therefore, if we compare the things themselves, in no way can it be doubted that the chastity of continence is better than the chastity of marriage. Although both, indeed, are a good, when we compare the men, the one who has the greater good than the other is the better. Moreover, he who has the greater good of the same kind has also that which is less; however, he who has only what is less certainly does not have what is greater. For, thirty is contained in sixty, but not sixty in thirty. The failure to act in accordance with one's full capacity to act depends upon the distribution of duties, not upon the lack of virtue, because he does not lack the good of mercy who does not come upon the unfortunate ones whom he could help in his mercy.

(29) We must take this into account, too, that it is not right to compare men with men in some one good. For, it can happen that one does not have something that the other has, but he has something that is to be valued more highly. Greater, indeed, is the good of obedience than the good of continence. Marriage is nowhere condemned by the authority of our Scriptures; disobedience, however, is nowhere condoned.

If, then, we have to choose between one who remains a virgin who is at the same time disobedient and a married woman who could not remain a virgin but who is nevertheless obedient—which of the two shall we say is the better? Is it the one who is less laudable than she would be if she were a virgin, or the one worthy of reproach although she is a virgin? So, if you compare a drunken virgin with a chaste spouse, who would hesitate to pass the same judgment? Marriage and virginity are, it is true, two goods, the second of them is the greater. So with sobriety and drunkenness, obedience and disobedience—the former are goods; the latter, evils. However, it is better to have everything that is good in a lesser degree than to have a great good with a great evil, since even in the goods of the body it is better to have the stature of Zaccaeus[70] together with health than the height of Goliath[71] together with a fever.

(30) The right question is plainly not whether a virgin thoroughly disobedient should be compared with an obedient married woman, but a less obedient to a more obedient, for there is also nuptial chastity and it is indeed a good, but a lesser one

than virginal chastity. Therefore, if the woman who is inferior in the good of obedience in proportion as she is greater in the good of chastity is compared with the other, then he who sees, when he compares chastity itself and obedience, that obedience in a certain way is the mother of all virtues, judges which woman is to be placed first. On this account, then, there can be obedience without virginity, because virginity is of counsel, not of precept. I am speaking of that obedience whereby precepts are obeyed. There can be obedience to precepts without virginity, but there cannot be this obedience without chastity. For it is of the essence of chastity not to commit fornication, not to commit adultery, not to be stained with any illicit intercourse. Whoever do not observe these precepts act against the commands of God and on this account are banished from the virtue of obedience. Virginity can exist by itself without obedience, since a woman can, although accepting the counsel of virginity and guarding her virginity, neglect the precepts; just as we know many sacred virgins who are garrulous, inquisitive, addicted to drink, contentious, greedy, proud. All these vices are against the precepts and destroy them through their sin of disobedience, like Eve herself. Therefore, not only is the obedient person to be preferred to the disobedient one, but the more obedient wife is to be preferred to the less obedient virgin.

(31) In accord with this, that patriarch who was not without a wife was prepared to be without his only son and one to be slain by his own hand.[72] Indeed, I may speak of 'his only son' not unfittingly, concerning whom he had heard from the Lord: 'Through Isaac shall your descendants be called.'[73] Therefore, how much more readily would he have obeyed if it were ordered that he was not to have a wife.

So it is that not in vain do we often wonder at some of both sexes, who, containing themselves from all intercourse, carelessly obey the commands, though they have so ardently embraced the idea of not using things that have been granted. Seeing this, who doubts that the men and women of our times, free from all intercourse but inferior in the virtue of obedience, are not rightly compared to the excellence of those holy patriarchs and mothers begetting children, even if the patriarchs had lacked the habit of mind that is manifest in the actions of the men of our day?

Therefore, let the young men singing a new canticle follow the Lamb, as it is written in the Apocalypse: 'Who have not defiled themselves with women,'[74] on no other account than that they remained virgins. Let them not think, then, that they are better than the early patriarchs, who used their marriage, if I may put it this way, nuptially. The use, indeed, of marriage is such that there is a defilement if anything is done in marriage through the union of the flesh that exceeds the need for generation, though this is pardonable. For, what does pardon expiate, if that departure does not defile entirely. It would be remarkable if the children following the Lamb would be free from this defilement unless they remained virgins.

Chapter 24

(32) The good, therefore, of marriage among all nations and all men is in the cause of generation and in the fidelity of chastity; in the case of the people of God, however, the good is also in the sanctity of the sacrament. Because of this sanctity it is wrong for a woman, leaving with a divorce, to marry another man while her husband still lives, even if she does this for the sake of having children. Although that is the sole reason why marriage takes place, even if this for which marriage takes place does not follow, the marriage bond is not loosed except by the death of a spouse. Just as if an ordination of the clergy is performed to gather the people, even if the congregation does not follow, there yet remains in those ordained the sacrament of orders. And if, because of any fault, anyone is removed from clerical office, he retains the sacrament of the Lord once it has been imposed, although it remains for judgment.

The Apostle is a witness to the fact that marriage exists for the sake of generation in this way: 'I desire,' he says, 'that the younger widows marry.'[75] And—as if it were said to him: for what reason?—he added immediately: 'to bear children, to rule their households.' But this pertains to the faithfulness of chastity: 'The wife has not authority over her body, but the husband; the husband likewise has not authority over his body, but the wife.'[76] As to the sanctity of the sacrament, this is pertinent: 'A wife is not to depart from her husband, and if she departs, that she is to remain unmarried or be reconciled to her husband,' and 'Let not a husband put away his wife.'[77] These are all goods on account of which marriage is a good: offspring, fidelity, sacrament. Yet, not to seek carnal offspring now at this time, and on this account to retain a certain perpetual freedom from all such practice and to be spiritually subject to one man, Christ, is better and indeed holier; especially if men use this freedom so acquired in such a way as it is written, to think about the things of the Lord, how they may please God,[78] that is, that continence unceasingly consider lest obedience fall short in any way. The holy patriarchs practiced this virtue as basic and, as it is customarily called, a source and clearly a universal one; but continence they possessed in the disposition of the soul. Even if they had been ordered to abstain from all intercourse, they certainly would have done so by means of the obedience by which they were just and holy and prepared for every good work. For, how much more easily were they able not to have intercourse at the command or bidding of God who could by being obedient immolate the offspring whose propagation alone they were making possible by having intercourse.

Chapter 25

(33) Since these things are so, I have answered enough and more than enough to the heretics, whether Manichaeans or whoever else calumniate the patriarchs for their many wives, alleging that this is an argument by which they prove their incontinence, if, however, they understand that what is not done contrary to nature is not a sin, since they made use of their wives not for the sake of being wanton, but for procreation; nor against the customs, because at the time those things were

being done; nor contrary to the precept, because they were not prohibited by any law. Those, indeed, who illicitly made use of women, either that divine dictum in the Scriptures convicts, or the text puts them before us as ones who are to be judged and avoided, not to be approved or imitated.

Chapter 26

(34) However, as much as we can, we advise our people who have spouses not to dare to judge those patriarchs according to their weakness, comparing, as the Apostle says, themselves with themselves,[79] and therefore not understanding what great powers the soul that serves justice has against the passions, so that it does not acquiesce in carnal impulses of this kind and does not allow them to fall into or to proceed to intercourse beyond the need for generation, that is, beyond what the order of nature, beyond what customs, beyond what laws permit.

Men indeed have this suspicion concerning these patriarchs because they themselves either have chosen marriage because of incontinence or they make use of their wives immoderately. But let continent people, either men whose wives have died, or women whose husbands have died, or both, who with equal consent have pledged their continence to God, know that a greater reward is due them than conjugal chastity demands. But, as to the marriage of the holy patriarchs, who were joined in a prophetic way, who neither in intercourse sought anything but progeny, nor anything in the progeny itself except what would profit Christ who was to come in the flesh, let them not only not despise it in comparison with their own resolution, but also in accordance with their own resolution; let them prefer it with hesitation.

(35) Most especially do we warn the young men and the virgins dedicating their virginity to God, so that they may know that they ought to guard the life they are living in the meantime upon earth with the greatest humility, since the greater life which they have vowed is of heaven. For it is written: 'The greater thou art, the more humble thyself in all things.'[80] Therefore, it is for us to say something of their greatness; it is theirs to think of great humility. Thus, with the exception of certain of the married patriarchs and married women of the Old Testament—for these, though they are not married, are not better than they, because if they were married they would not be equal—let them not doubt that all the other married people of this time, even the ones who are continent after experiencing marriage, are surpassed by them, not as much as Susanna is surpassed by Anna, but as much as both are surpassed by Mary. I am speaking of what pertains to the holy integrity of the flesh, for who is ignorant of the other merits that Mary had?

Therefore, let them add a fitting conduct to such a high resolve, so that they may have a certain security in respect to obtaining such a splendid reward, knowing, indeed, that to themselves and to all the faithful beloved and chosen members of Christ coming from the East and the West, though shining with a light different in each case, because of their merits, this great reward is given in common, to recline with Abraham and Isaac and Jacob in the kingdom of God,[81] who, not for the sake of this world but for the sake of Christ, were spouses, for the sake of Christ were parents.

---

[1] Matt. xix. 4-6.

[2] *De Re Publ.* iii. 25.

[3] Rom. i. 26.

[4] Cf. Gen. 2.21.

[5] Gen. 1.28.

[6] Cf. *De civ. Dei* 1.14.

[7] Cf. Ps. 137.3.

[8] Cf. Wisd. 2.24.

[9] 1 Thess. 4.17.

[10] Cf. Gen. 2.17.

[11] Cf. Deut. 29.5.

[12] Cf. Matt. 19.9.

[13] Cf. John 2.

[14] 1 Cor. 7.4.

[15] Matt. 5.32.

[16] Cf. 1 Cor. 7.10,11.

[17] Ps. 47.2.

[18] Cf. Matt. 19.8.

[19] Cf. Deut. 24.1.

[20] Heb. 13.4.

[21] Eph. 5.12.

[22] 1 Cor. 13.8.

[23] Cf. Luke 10.39.

[24] Dan. 13.

[25] Cf. Luke 2.36.

[26] Cf. Luke 1.28.

[27] 1 Tim. 1.5.

[28] 1 Cor. 7.7.

[29] 1 Cor. 7.29-34.

[30] 1 Cor. 7.9.

[31] 1 Cor. 7.36.

[32] 1 Cor. 7.28.

[33] Cf. Rom. 1.26.

[34] 1 Cor. 7.28.

[35] 1 Cor. 7.36.

[36] 1 Cor. 7.34.

[37] 1 Cor. 6.19.

[38] 1 Cor. 7.14.

[39] 1 Cor. 7.34.

[40] Cf. 1 Tim. 5.6.

[41] 1 Tim. 2.9,10.

[42] 1 Peter 3.1-7.

[43] Eccle. 3.5.

[44] Cf. 1 Cor. 7-28.

[45] Matt. 19.12.

[46] Cf. 1 Thess. 4.5.

[47] Cf. Phil. 1.23.

[48] Cf. *Retractationes* 2.22: 'This was said since the good and proper use of passion is not a passion. Just as it is wicked to use good things wrongly, it is good to use wicked things rightly. I argued more carefully about this matter on another occasion, especially against the new Pelagian heretics.'

[49] 1 Cor. 7.9.

[50] Cf. Acts 4.32.

[51] Cf. 1 Tim. 3.2; Titus 1.6.

[52] 1 Cor. 7.28.

[53] 1 Cor. 7.36.

[54] Cf. 1 Cor. 4.5.

[55] Cf. Mich. 5.2.

[56] Cf. Gen. 24.2.

[57] Cf. Num. 19.11.

[58] Cf. Job 1.

[59] Cf. 1 Tim. 5.23.

[60] Cf. 1 Cor. 7.9.

[61] Matt. 19.12.

[62] Phil. 4.10.

[63] Matt. 11.18,19.

[64] Matt. 11.19.

[65] Cf. Gal. 4.4.

[66] Matt. 19.12.

[67] Cf. 1 Cor. 15.33.

[68] Cf. 2 Cor. 12.6.

[69] Cf. 1 Cor. 7.34.

[70] Cf. Luke 19.3.

[71] Cf. 1 Kings 17.4.

[72] Cf. *Retractiones* 2.22: 'What I said concerning Abraham . . . I do not entirely approve. It ought to be thought that he believed that his son, if he had been killed, must soon be returned to him by a resurrection from the dead, as it is read in the Epistle to the Hebrews' [11.19].

[73] Gen. 21.12.

[74] Apoc. 14.4.

[75] 1 Tim. 5.14.

[76] 1 Cor. 7.4.

[77] 1 Cor. 7.10.

[78] Cf. 1 Cor. 7.32.

[79] Cf. 2 Cor. 10.12.

[80] Eccli. 3.20.

[81] Cf. Matt. 8.11.

5.

BEDE'S ECCLESIASTICAL HISTORY OF THE ENGLISH NATION
(early eighth century)

Book I Chapter XXVII

St. Augustine, being made Bishop, sends to acquaint Pope Gregory with what had been done, and receives his answer to the doubts he had proposed to him. [A.D. 579.]

In the meantime, Augustine, the man of God, repaired to Arles, and, pursuant to the orders received from the holy Father Gregory, was ordained archbishop of the English nation, by Ætherius, archbishop of that city. Then returning into Britain, he sent Laurentius the priest, and Peter the monk, to Rome, to acquaint Pope Gregory, that the nation of the English had received the faith of Christ, and that he was himself made their bishop. At the same time, he desired his solution of some doubts that occurred to him. He soon received proper answers to his questions, which we have also thought fit to insert in this our history—

• • •

Augustine's Eighth Question. — Whether a woman with child ought to be baptized? Or how long after she has brought forth, may she come into the church? As also, after how many days the infant born may be baptized, lest he be prevented by death? Or how long after her husband may have carnal knowledge of her? Or whether it is lawful for her to come into the church when she has her courses? Or to receive the holy sacrament of communion? Or whether a man, under certain circumstances, may come into the church before he has washed with water? Or approach to receive the mystery of the holy communion? All which things are requisite to be known by the rude nation of the English.

Gregory answers. — I do not doubt but that these questions have been put to you, my brother, and I think I have already answered you therein. But I believe you would wish the opinion which you yourself might give to be confirmed by mine also. Why should not a woman with child be baptized, since the fruitfulness of the flesh is no offence in the eyes of Almighty God? For when our first parents sinned in Paradise, they forfeited the immortality which they had received, by the just judgment of God. Because, therefore, Almighty God would not for their fault wholly destroy the human race, He both deprived man of immortality for his sin, and, at the same time, of his great goodness, reserved to him the power of propagating his race after him. On what account then can that which is preserved to the human race, by the free gift of Almighty God, be excluded from the privilege of baptism? For it is very foolish to imagine that the gift of grace opposes that mystery in which all sin is blotted out. When a woman is delivered, after how many days she may come into the church, you have been informed by reading the Old Testament, viz. that she is to abstain for a male child thirty-three days, and sixty-six for a female. Now you must know that this is to be taken in a mystery; for if she enters the church the very hour that she is delivered, to return thanks, she is not guilty of any sin; because the pleasure of the flesh is in fault, and not the pain; but the pleasure is in the copulation of the flesh, whereas there is pain in bringing forth the child. Wherefore it is said to the first mother of all, "In sorrow shalt thou bring forth children." If, therefore, we forbid a woman that has brought forth, to enter the church, we make a crime of her very punishment. To baptize either a woman who has brought forth, if there be danger of death, even the very hour that she brings forth, or that which she has brought forth the very hour it is born, is no way prohibited, because, as the grace of the holy mystery is to be with much discretion provided for the living and understanding, so is it to be without any delay offered to the dying; lest, while a further time is sought to confer the mystery of redemption, a small delay intervening, the person that is to be redeemed is dead and gone.

Her husband is not to approach her, till the infant born be weaned. A bad custom is sprung up in the behaviour of married people, that is, that women disdain to suckle the children which they bring forth, and give them to other women to suckle; which seems to have been invented on no other account but incontinency; because, as they will not be continent, they will not suckle the children which they bear. Those women, therefore, who, from bad custom, give their children to others to bring up, must not approach their husbands till the time of purification is past. For even when there has been no child-birth, women are forbidden to do so, whilst they have their monthly courses, insomuch that the Law condemns to death any man that shall approach unto a woman during her uncleanness. Yet the woman, nevertheless, must not be forbidden to come into the church whilst she has her monthly courses; because the superfluity of nature cannot be imputed to her as a crime; and it is not just that she should be refused admittance into the church, for that which she suffers against her will. For we know, that the woman who had the issue of blood, humbly approaching behind our Lord's back, touched the hem of his garment, and her distemper immediately departed from her. If, therefore, she that had an issue of blood might commendably touch the garment of our Lord, why may not she, who has the monthly courses, lawfully enter into the church of God? But you may say, Her distemper compelled her, whereas these we speak of are bound by custom. Consider, then, most dear brother, that all we suffer, is ordained by the just judgment of God after the fall; for to hunger, to thirst, to be hot, to be cold, to be weary, is from the infirmity of our nature; and what else is it to seek food against hunger, drink against thirst, air against heat, clothes against cold, rest against weariness, than to procure a remedy against distempers? Thus to a woman her monthly courses are a distemper. If, therefore, it was a commendable boldness in her, who in her disease touched our Lord's garment, why may not that which is allowed to one infirm person, be granted to all women, who, through the fault of their nature, are distempered?

She must not, therefore, be forbidden to receive the mystery of the holy communion during those days. But if any one out of profound respect does not presume to do it, she is to be commended; yet if she receives it, she is not to be judged. For it is the part of noble minds in some manner to acknowledge their faults, even where there is no offence; because very often that is done without a fault, which, nevertheless, proceeded from a fault. Therefore, when we are hungry, it is no crime to eat; yet our being hungry proceeds from the sin of the first man. The monthly courses are no crime in women, because they naturally happen; however, because our nature itself is so depraved, that it appears to be so without the concurrence of the will, the fault proceeds from sin, and thereby human nature may herself know what she is become by judgment. And let man, who wilfully committed the offence, bear the guilt of that offence. And, therefore, let women consider with themselves, and if they do not presume, during their monthly courses, to approach the sacrament of the body and blood of our Lord, they are to be commended for their praiseworthy consideration; but when they are carried away with love of the same mystery to receive it out of the usual custom of religious life, they are not to be restrained, as we said before. For as in the Old Testament the outward works are observed, so in the New Testament, that which is outwardly done, is not so diligently regarded as that which is inwardly thought, in order to punish it by a discerning judgment. For whereas the Law forbids the eating of many things as unclean, yet our Lord says in the Gospel, "Not that which goeth into the mouth defileth a man; but that which cometh out of the mouth, this defileth a man." And presently after He added, expounding the same, "Out of the heart proceed evil thoughts." Where it is sufficiently shown, that that is declared by Almighty God to be polluted in fact, which proceeds from the root of a polluted thought. Whence also Paul the Apostle says, "Unto the pure all things are pure, but unto them that are defiled and unbelieving, nothing is pure." And presently after, declaring the cause of that defilement, he adds, "For even their mind and conscience is defiled." If, therefore, meat is not unclean to him who has a clean mind, why shall that which a clean woman suffers according to nature, be imputed to her as uncleanness?

A man who has approached his own wife is not to enter the church unless washed with water, nor is he to enter immediately although washed. The Law prescribed to the ancient people, that a man in such cases should be washed with water, and not enter into the church before the setting of the sun. Which, nevertheless, may be understood spiritually, because a man acts so when the mind is led by the imagination to unlawful concupiscence; for unless the fire of concupiscence be first driven from his mind, he is not to think himself worthy of the congregation of the brethren, whilst he thus indulges an unlawful passion. For though several nations have different opinions concerning this affair, and seem to observe different rules, it was always the custom of the Romans, from ancient times, for such an one to be cleansed by washing, and for some time respectfully to forbear entering the church. Nor do we, in so saying, assign matrimony to be a fault; but forasmuch as lawful intercourse cannot be had without the pleasure of the flesh, it is proper to forbear entering the holy place, because the pleasure itself cannot be without a fault. For he was not born of adultery or fornication, but of lawful marriage, who said, "Behold I was conceived in iniquity, and in sin my mother brought me forth." For he who knew himself to have been conceived in iniquity, lamented that he was born from sin, because the tree in its bough bears the moisture it drew from the root. In which words, however, he does not call the union of the married couple iniquity, but the pleasure of the copulation. For there are many things which are proved to be lawful, and yet we are somewhat defiled in doing them. As very often by being angry we correct faults, and at the same time disturb our own peace of mind; and though that which we do is right, yet it is not to be approved that our mind should be discomposed. For he who said, "My eye was disturbed with anger," had been angry at the vices of those who had offended. Now, in regard that only a sedate mind can apply itself to contemplation, he grieved that his eye was disturbed with anger; because, whilst he was correcting evil actions below, he was obliged to be withdrawn and disturbed from the contemplation of things above. Anger against vice is, therefore, commendable, and yet painful to a man, because he thinks that by his mind being agitated, he has incurred some guilt. Lawful commerce, therefore, must be for the sake of children, not of pleasure; and must be to procure offspring, not to satisfy vices. But if any man is led not by the desire of pleasure, but only for the sake of getting children, such a man is certainly to be left to his own judgment, either as to entering the church, or as to receiving the mystery of the body and blood of our Lord, which he, who being placed in the fire cannot burn, is not to be forbidden by us to receive. But when, not the love of getting children, but of pleasure prevails, the pair have cause to lament their deed. For this the holy preaching allows them, and yet fills the mind with dread of the very allowance. For when Paul the Apostle said, "Let him that cannot contain, have his wife;" he presently took care to subjoin, "But this I say by way of indulgence, not by way of command." For this is not granted by way of indulgence which is lawful, because it is just; and, therefore, that which he said he indulged, he showed to be an offence.

It is seriously to be considered, that when God was to speak to the people on Mount Sinai, He first commanded them to abstain from women. And if so much cleanness of body was there required, where God spoke to the people by the means of a subject creature, that those who were to hear the words of God should not do so; how much more ought women, who receive the body of Almighty God, to preserve themselves in cleanness of flesh, lest they be burdened with the very *greatness* of that unutterable mystery? For this reason, it was said to David, concerning his men, by the priest, that if they were clean in this particular, they should receive the shew-bread, which they would not have received at all, had not David first declared them to be clean. Then the man, who, afterwards, has been washed with water, is also capable of receiving the mystery of the holy communion, when it is lawful for him, according to what has been before declared, to enter the church.

Augustine's Ninth Question. — Whether after an illusion, such as happens in a dream, any man may receive the body of our Lord, or if he be a priest, celebrate the Divine mysteries?

Gregory answers. — The Testament of the Old Law, as has been said already in the article above, calls such a man polluted, and allows him not to enter into the church till the evening after being washed with water. Which, nevertheless, spiritual people, taking in another sense, will understand in the same manner as above; because he is imposed upon as it were in a dream, who, being tempted with filthiness, is defiled by real representations in thought, and he is to be washed with water, that he may cleanse away the sins of thought with tears; and unless the fire of temptation depart before, may know himself to be guilty as it were until the evening. But discretion is very necessary in that illusion, that one may seriously consider what causes it to happen in the mind of the person sleeping; for sometimes it proceeds from excess of eating or drinking; sometimes from the superfluity or infirmity of nature, and sometimes from the thoughts. And when it happens, either through superfluity or infirmity of nature, such an illusion is not to be feared, because it is rather to be lamented, that the mind of the person, who knew nothing of it, suffers the same, than that he occasioned it. But when the appetite of gluttony commits excess in food, and thereupon the receptacles of the humours are oppressed, the mind from thence contracts some guilt; yet not so much as to obstruct the receiving of the holy mystery, or celebrating mass, when a holy day requires it, or necessity obliges the sacrament to be administered, because there is no other priest in the place; for if there be others who can perform the ministry, the illusion proceeding from overeating is not to exclude a man from receiving the sacred mystery; but I am of opinion he ought humbly to abstain from offering the sacrifice of the mystery; but not from receiving it, unless the mind of the person sleeping has been filled with some foul imagination. For there are some, who for the most part so suffer the illusion, that their mind, even during the sleep of the body, is not defiled with filthy thoughts. In which case, one thing is evident, that the mind is guilty even in its own judgment; for though it does not remember to have seen any thing whilst the body was sleeping, yet it calls to mind that when waking it fell into bodily gluttony. But if the sleeping illusion proceeds from evil thoughts when waking, then the guilt is manifest to the mind; for the man perceives from whence that filth sprung, because what he had knowingly thought of, that he afterwards unwittingly revealed. But it is to be considered, whether that thought was no more than a suggestion, or proceeded to enjoyment, or, which is still more criminal, consented to sin. For all sin is fulfilled in three ways, viz., by suggestion, by delight, and by consent. Suggestion is occasioned by the Devil, delight is from the flesh, and consent from the mind. For the serpent suggested the first offence, and Eve, as flesh, was delighted with it, but Adam consented, as the spirit, or mind. And much discretion is requisite for the mind to sit as judge between suggestion and delight, and between delight and consent. For if the evil spirit suggest a sin to the mind, if there ensue no delight in the sin, the sin is in no way committed; but when the flesh begins to be delighted, then sin begins to grow. But if it deliberately consents, then the sin is known to be perfected. The beginning, therefore, of sin is in the suggestion, the nourishing of it in delight, but in the consent is its perfection. And it often happens that what the evil spirit sows in the thought, the flesh draws to delight, and yet the soul does not consent to that delight. And whereas the flesh cannot be delighted without the mind, yet the mind struggling against the pleasures of the flesh is somewhat unwillingly tied down by the carnal delight, so that through reason it contradicts, and does not consent, yet being influenced by delight, it grieviously laments its being so bound. Wherefore that principal soldier of our Lord's host, sighing, said, "I see another law in my members warring against the law of my mind, and bringing me into captivity to the law of sin, which is in my members." Now if he was a captive, he did not fight; but if he did fight, how was he a captive? he therefore fought against the law of the mind, which the law that is in the members opposed; if he fought so, he was no captive. Thus, then, man is, as I may say, a captive and yet free. Free on account of justice, which he loves, a captive by the delight which he unwillingly bears within him.

6.

MEDIEVAL PENITENTIALS

From: The Penitential of Columban
(Irish—ca. 600)

27. If anyone sitting in the bath, bathes himself completely, he shall do penance with a special fast. If one does this washing as permitted, standing in the presence of his brethren, if without necessity of an extensive removal of mud he shall be corrected with twenty-four stripes.

28. If anyone, indeed, in sitting in the bath, exposes his knees or arms without necessity of washing off mud, he shall not wash for six days, that is, until the second Sunday that disgraceful bather shall not wash his feet. A monk alone may wash his feet while standing in private; a senior, indeed, in public; but in the case of the latter when he washes his feet, he may be washed standing.

From: The Penitential of Theodore
(English—ca. 668–690)

A. *Of Matters Relating to Marriage*

1. Those who are married shall abstain from intercourse for three nights before they communicate.

2. A man shall abstain from his wife for forty days before Easter, until the week of Easter. On this account the Apostle says: "That ye may give yourselves to prayer."

3. When she has conceived a woman ought to obstain from her husband for three months before the birth, and afterward in the time of purgation, that is, for forty days and nights, whether she has borne a male or a female child.

4. It is also fully permitted to a woman to communicate before she is to bear a child.

5. If the wife of anyone commits fornication, he may put her away and take another; that is, if a man puts away his wife on account of fornication, if she was his first, he is permitted to take another; but if she wishes to do penance for her sins, she may take another husband after five years.

6. A woman may not put away her husband, even if he is a fornicator, unless, perchance, for [the purpose of his entering] a monastery.

B.   Of Excess and Drunkenness

16. A wife who tastes her husband's blood as a remedy shall fast for forty days, more or less.

17. Moreover, women shall not in the time of impurity enter into a church, or communicate—neither nuns nor laywomen; if they presume [to do this] they shall fast for three weeks.

18. In the same way shall they do penance who enter a church before purification after childbirth, that is, forty days.

19. But he who has intercourse at these seasons shall do penance for twenty days.

20. He who has intercourse on the Lord's day shall seek pardon from God and do penance for one or two or three days.

21. In case of unnatural intercourse with his wife, he shall do penance for forty days the first time.

22. For a graver offense of this kind he ought to do penance as one who offends with animals.

23. For intercourse at the improper season he shall fast for forty days.

24. Women who commit abortion before [the foetus] has life, shall do penance for one year or for the three forty-day periods or for forty days, according to the nature of the offense; and if later, that is, more than forty days after conception, they shall do penance as murderesses, that is for three years on Wednesdays and Fridays and in the three forty-day periods. This according to the canons is judged [punishable by] ten years.

25. If a mother slays her child, if she commits homicide, she shall do penance for fifteen years, and never change except on Sunday.

26. If a poor woman slays her child, she shall do penance for seven years. In the canon it is said that if it is a case of homicide, she shall do penance for ten years.

27. A woman who conceives and slays her child in the womb within forty days shall do penance for one year; but if later than forty days, she shall do penance as a murderess.

C.   Of Fornication

5. A male who commits fornication with a male shall do penance for ten years.

6. Sodomites shall do penance for seven years, and the effeminate man as an adulteress.

7. Likewise he who commits this sexual offense once shall do penance for four years. If he has been in the habit of it, as Basil says, fifteen years; but if not, one year less [?] as a woman. If he is a boy, two years for the first offense; if he repeats it, four years.

8. If he does this "in femoribus," one year, or the three forty-day periods.

9. If he defiles himself, forty days.

10. He who desires to commit fornication, but is not able, shall do penance for forty or twenty days.

11. As for boys who mutually engage in vice, he judged that they should be whipped.

12. If a woman practices vice with a woman, she shall do penance for three years.

13. If she practices solitary vice, she shall do penance for the same period.

14. The penance of a widow and of a girl is the same. She who has a husband deserves a greater penalty if she commits fornication.

15. "Qui semen in os miserit" shall do penance for seven years: this is the worst of evils. Elsewhere it was his judgment that both [participants in this offense] shall do penance to the end of his life; or twelve years; or as above seven.

From: The Penitential of Pseudo-Ecgbert
(late tenth century)

The original is from Josef Raith, *Die Altenglische Version des Halitgar'schen Bussbuches* (Darmstadt: Wissenschaftliche Buchgesellschaft, 1964), pp. 28-29.

The manner in which married couples ought to conduct their married life before God: a) Holy Books teach what each of the faithful is to do when he brings home his bride; that is, according to the teachings of the books, the newlyweds must first maintain their innocence for three days and three nights, and then on the third day they must attend mass, but without taking the eucharist, and afterwards they may consummate their marriage before God and the world as their need may be; b) and each must conduct his marriage so as to remain chaste during the forty days and forty nights of the holy Easter season and all of Easter week and every Sunday, Wednesday, and Friday; c) and every righteous woman must maintain her chastity three months before childbirth, and after childbirth she must hold herself chaste for forty days and forty nights, whether it be a male or a female child.

Translated by Douglas R. Letson

7.

SELECTIONS FROM "THE PARSON'S TALE," THE CANTERBURY TALES

Geoffrey Chaucer
(late fourteenth century)

The second part of penitence is confession, which is the sign of contrition. Now shall you understand what confession is, and whether it ought to be used or not, and which things are necessary to true confession.

First, you shall understand that confession is the true discovery of sins to the priest: I say "true," for a man must confess all the circumstances and conditions of his sin, in so far as he can. All must be told, and nothing excused or hidden, or covered up, and he must not vaunt his good deeds. And furthermore, it is necessary to understand whence his sins come, and how they increase, and what they are.

Of the birth of sins, Saint Paul says thus: "as by one man sin entered into the world, and death by sin; . . . so death passed upon all men, for that all have sinned." And this man was Adam, by whom sin entered into the world when he broke the commandment of God. And therefore, he that at first was so mighty that he should never have died became such a one as must needs die, whether he would or no; and all his progeny in this world, since they, in that man, sinned. Behold, in the state of innocence, when Adam and Eve were naked in Paradise, and had no shame for their nakedness, how that the serpent, which was the wiliest of all the beasts that God had made, said to the woman: "Yea, hath God said, ye shall not eat of every tree of the garden?" And the woman said unto the serpent: "We may eat of the fruit of the trees of the garden: but of the fruit of the tree which is in the midst of the garden, God hath said, 'Ye shall not eat of it, neither shall ye touch it, lest ye die.' " And the serpent said unto the woman: "Ye shalt not surely die: for God doth know, that in the day ye eat thereof, then your eyes shall be opened; and ye shall be as gods, knowing good and evil." And when the woman saw that the tree was good for food, and that it was pleasant to the eyes, and delectable in the sight, she took of the fruit thereof and did eat; and gave also unto her husband, and he did eat. And the eyes of them both were opened. And when they knew that they were naked, they sewed fig-leaves together into a kind of breeches to hide their members. There may you see that mortal sin had first suggestion from the Fiend, who is here figured by the serpent; and afterward the delight of the flesh, as shown here by Eve; and after that the acquiescence of reason, as is shown by Adam. For trust this well, though it were that the Fiend tempted Eve, that is to say, the flesh, and the flesh delighted in the beauty of the forbidden fruit, certainly until reason, that is, Adam, consented to the eating of the fruit, yet stood he in the state of innocence. From that same Adam caught we all that original sin; for we are all descended from him in the flesh, engendered of vile and corrupt matter. And when the soul is put into a body, immediately is contracted original sin; and that which was at first merely the penalty of concupiscence becomes afterwards both penalty and sin. And therefore are we all born the sons of wrath and of everlasting damnation, were it not for the baptism we receive, which washes away the culpability; but, forsooth, the penalty remains within us, as temptation, and that penalty is called concupiscence. When it is wrongly disposed or established in man, it makes him desire, by the lust of the flesh, fleshly sin; desire, by the sight of his eyes, earthly things; and desire high place, what of the pride of his heart.

Now, to speak of the first desire, that is, concupiscence, according to the law for our sexual parts, which were lawfully made and by rightful word of God; I say, for as much as man is not obedient to God, Who is his Lord, therefore is the flesh disobedient to Him, through concupiscence, which is also called the nourishing of and the reason for sin. Therefore all the while that a man has within himself the penalty of concupiscence, it is impossible but that he will be sometimes tempted and moved in his flesh to do sin. And this shall not fail so long as he lives; it may well grow feeble and remote by virtue of baptism and by the grace of God through penitence; but it shall never be fully quenched so that he shall never be moved within himself, unless he be cooled by sickness or by maleficence of sorcery or by opiates. For behold what Saint Paul says: "The flesh lusteth against the spirit, and the spirit against the flesh: and these are contrary, the one to the other; so that ye cannot do the things that ye would." The same Saint Paul, after his great penance on water and on land (on water by night and by day, in great peril and in great pain; on land in famine, in thirst, in cold, and naked, and once stoned almost unto death), yet said he: "O wretched man that I am! Who shall deliver me from the body of this death?" And Saint Jerome, when he had long lived in the desert, where he had no company but that of wild beasts, where he had no food but herbs, with only water to drink, and no bed but the naked earth, for which his flesh was black as an Ethiopian's with heat and well-nigh destroyed with cold, yet said he that the heat of lechery boiled through all his body. Wherefore I know well and surely that they are deceived who say that they are never tempted in the flesh. Witness Saint James the apostle, who says that everyone is tempted in his own concupiscence. That is to say, each of us has cause and occasion to be tempted by sin that is nourished in the body. And thereupon says Saint John the Evangelist: "If we say that we have no sin, we deceive ourselves, and the truth is not in us."

Now shall you understand in what manner sin waxes or increases in man. The first thing to be considered is this same nurturing of sin, whereof I spoke before, this same fleshly concupiscence. And after that comes the subjection to the Devil, that is to say, the Devil's bellows, wherewith he blows into man the fire of concupiscence. And after that a man bethinks himself whether he will do, or not, the thing to which he is tempted. And then, if a man withstand and put aside the first enticement of his flesh and the Fiend, then it is no sin; and if it be that he do not, he feels anon a flame of delight. And then it is well to be wary, and to guard himself, else he will fall anon into acquiescence to sin; and then he will do it, if he have time and place. And of this matter Moses says that the Devil says thus: "I will pursue, I will overtake, I will divide the spoil; my lust shall be satisfied upon them; I wilt draw my sword, my hand shall destroy them." For certainly, just as a sword may part a thing in two pieces, just so acquiescence separates God from man. "And then will I slay him in his sinful deed." Thus says the Fiend. For truly then is a man dead in soul. And thus is sin accomplished by temptation and by acquiescence; and then is the sin called actual.

Forsooth, sin is of two kinds; it is either venial or mortal sin. Verily, when man loves any creature more than he loves Jesus Christ our Creator, then is it mortal sin. And venial sin it is if a man love Jesus Christ less than he ought. Forsooth the effect of this venial sin is very dangerous; for it diminishes more and more the love that man should have for God. And therefore, if a man charge himself with many such venial sins, then certainly, unless he discharge them occasionally by shriving, they may easily lessen in him all the love that he has for Jesus Christ; and in this wise venial sin passes over into mortal sin. Therefore let us not be negligent in ridding ourselves of venial sins. For the proverb has it: "Mony a mickle mak's a muckle." And hear this example. A huge wave of the sea comes sometimes with so great violence that it sinks a ship. And the same harm is caused sometimes by the small drops of water that enter through the little opening in the seam into the bilge of the ship, if men be so negligent that they do not discharge it in time. And therefore, though there be a difference between these two ways of sinking, nevertheless the ship is sunk. Just so it is sometimes with mortal sin, and with vexatious venial sins when they multiply in a man so greatly that the worldly things he loves, for which he venially sins, have grown as great in his heart as the love for God, or greater. And therefore, the love for everything that is not fixed or rooted in God, or done principally for God's sake, though a man love it less than he love God, yet it is venial sin; and it is mortal sin when the love for anything weighs in the heart of man as much as the love for God, or more. "Mortal sin," as Saint Augustine says, "is when a man turns his heart from God, Who is the truly sovereign goodness and may not change, and gives his heart unto things that may change and pass away." And true it is that if a man give his love, the which he owes all to God, with all his heart, unto a creature, then certainly so much of his love as he gives unto the said creature he takes away from God; and thereby does he sin. For he, who is debtor to God, yields not unto God all of his debt, which is to say, all the love of his heart.

Now since man understands generally what venial sin is, it is fitting to tell especially of sins which many a man perhaps holds not to be sins at all, and for which he shrives not himself; yet, nevertheless, they are sins. Truly, as clerics write, every time a man eats or drinks more than suffices for the sustenance of his body, it is certain that he thereby sins. And, too, when he speaks more than it is necessary it is sin. Also, when he hears not benignly the complaint of the poor. Also, when he is in health of body and will not fast when other folk fast, and that without a reasonable excuse. Also, when he sleeps more than he needs, or when he comes, for that reason, too late to church, or to other places where works of charity are done. Also, when he enjoys his wife without a sovereign desire to procreate children to the honour of God, or when he does it without intention to yield to his wife the duty of his body. Also, when he will not visit the sick and the imprisoned, if he may do so. Also, if he love wife or child or any other worldly thing more than reason requires. Also, if he flatter or blandish more than, of necessity, he ought. Also, if he diminish or withdraw his alms to the poor. Also, if he prepare his food more delicately than is needful, or eat it too hastily or too greedily. Also, if he talk about vain and trifling matters in a church or at God's service, or if he be a user of idle words of folly or of obscenity; for he shall yield up an accounting of it at the day of doom. Also, when he promises or assures one that he will do what he cannot perform. Also, when he, through thoughtlessness or folly, slanders or scorns his neighbour. Also, when he suspects a thing to be evil when he has no certain knowledge of it. These things, and more without number, are sins, as Saint Augustine says.

Now shall men understand that while no earthly man may avoid all venial sins, yet may he keep them down by the burning love that he has to Our Lord Jesus Christ, and by prayer and confession, and by other good deeds. For, as Saint Augustine says: "If a man love God in such manner that all that he ever does is done in the love of God, and truly for the love of God, because he burns with the love of God: behold, then, how much a drop of water falling in a furnace harms or proves troublesome; and just so much vexes the venial sin a man who is perfect in the love of Christ." Men may also keep down venial sins by receiving deservingly the precious body of Jesus Christ; also by receiving holy water; by almsgiving; by general confession of *confiteor* at mass and at compline; and by the blessings of bishops and of priests, and by other good works.

* * *

Here followeth Gluttony

After avarice comes gluttony, which also is entirely against the commandment of God. Gluttony is immoderate appetite to eat or to drink, or else to yield corrupted all this world, as is well shown by the sin of Adam and Eve. Read, also, what Saint Paul says of gluttony: "For many walk, of whom I have told you often, and now tell you even weeping, that they are the enemies of the cross of Christ: whose end is destruction, whose God is their belly, and whose glory is in their shame, who mind earthly things." He that is addicted to this sin of gluttony may withstand no other sin. He may even be in the service of all the vices, for it is in the Devil's treasure house that he hides himself and rests. This sin has many species. The first is drunkenness, which is the horrible sepulture of man's reason; and therefore, when a man is drunk he has lost his reason; and this is deadly sin. But truly, when a man is not used to strong drink, and perhaps knows not the strength of the drink, or is feeble-minded, or has toiled, for which reason he drinks too much, then, though he be suddenly caught by drink, it is not deadly sin, but venial. The second kind of gluttony is when the spirit of man grows turbid, for drunkenness has robbed him of the discretion of his wit. The third kind of gluttony is when a man devours his food and has no correct manner of eating. The fourth is when, through the great abundance of his food, the humours in his body become distempered. The fifth is, forgetfulness caused by too much drinking, whereby sometimes a man forgets before the morning what he did last evening, or the night before.

In another manner are distinguished the kinds of gluttony, according to Saint Gregory. The first is, eating before it is time to eat. The second is when a man gets himself too delicate food or drink. The third is when men eat too much, and beyond measure. The fourth is fastidiousness, with great attention paid to the preparation and dressing of food. The fifth is to eat too greedily. These are the five fingers of the Devil's hand wherewith he draws folk into sin.

The Remedy against the Sin of Gluttony

Against gluttony abstinence is the remedy, as Galen says; but I hold that to be not meritorious if he do it only for the health of his body. Saint Augustine will have it that abstinence should be practised for the sake of virtue and with patience. Abstinence, he says, is little worth unless a man have a good will thereto, and save it be practised in patience and charity and that men do it for God's sake and in hope of the bliss of Heaven.

The companions of abstinence are temperance, which follows the middle course in all things; and shame, which eschews all indecency; and sufficiency, which seeks after no rich foods and drinks and cares nothing for too extravagant dressing of meats. Measure, also, which restrains within reason the unrestrained appetite for eating; sobriety, also, which restrains the luxurious desire to sit long and softly at meat, and because of which some folk, of their own will, stand, in order to spend less time at eating.

Here followeth Lechery

After gluttony, then comes lechery; for these two sins are such close cousins that oftentimes they will not be separated. God knows, this sin is unpleasing to God; for He said Himself, "Do no lechery." And therefore He imposed great penalties against this sin in the old law. If a bondwoman were taken in this sin, she should be beaten to death with rods. And if she were a woman of quality, she should be slain with stones. And if she were a bishop's daughter, she should be burnt, by God's commandment. Furthermore, for the sin of lechery, God drowned all the world by the deluge. And after that He burned five cities with thunderbolts and sank them into Hell.

Let us speak, then, of that stinking sin of lechery that men call adultery of wedded folk, which is to say, if one of them be wedded, or both. Saint John says that adulterers shall be in Hell "in the lake which burneth with fire and brimstone"—in the fire for the lechery, in brimstone for the stink of their filthiness. Certainly, the breaking of this sacrament is a horrible thing; it was ordained by God Himself in Paradise, and confirmed by Jesus Christ, as witness Saint Matthew in the gospel: "For this cause shall a man leave father and mother, and shall cleave to his wife; and they twain shall be one flesh." This sacrament betokens the knitting together of Christ and of Holy Church. And not only did God forbid adultery in deed, but also He commanded that "thou shalt not covet thy neighbour's wife." This behest, says Saint Augustine, contains the forbidding of all desire to do lechery. Behold what Saint Matthew says in the gospel: "Whosoever looketh on a woman to lust after her, hath committed adultery with her already in his heart." Here you may see that not only the doing of this sin is forbidden, but also the desire to do that sin. This accursed sin grievously troubles those whom it haunts. And first, it does harm to the soul; for it constrains it to sin and to the pain of everlasting death. Unto the body it is a tribulation also, for it drains it, and wastes and ruins it, and makes of its blood a sacrifice to the Fiend of Hell, also it wastes wealth and substance. And certainly, if it be a foul thing for a man to waste his wealth on women, it is a yet fouler thing when, for such filthiness, women spend on men their wealth and their substance. This sin, as says the prophet, robs man and woman of good name and of all honour; and it gives great pleasure to the Devil, for thereby won he the greater part of the world. And just as a merchant delights most in that trading whereof he reaps the greater gain, just so the Fiend delights in this filth.

This is the Devil's other hand, with five fingers to catch the people into his slavery. The first finger is the foolish interchange of glances between the foolish woman and the foolish man, which slays just as the basilisk slays folk by the venom of its sight; for the lust of the eyes follows the lust of the heart. The second finger is vile touching in wicked manner; and thereupon Solomon says that he who touches and handles a woman fares like the man that handles the scorpion which stings and suddenly slays by its poisoning; even as, if any man touch warm pitch, it defiles his fingers. The third is vile words, which are like fire, which immediately burns the heart. The fourth finger is kissing; and truly he were a great fool who would kiss the mouth of a burning oven or of a furnace. And the more fools they are who kiss in vileness; for that mouth is the mouth of Hell; and I speak specifically of these old dotard whoremongers, who will yet kiss though they cannot do anything, and so taste them. Certainly they are like dogs, for a dog, when he passes a rosebush, or other bushes, though he cannot piss, yet will he heave up his leg and make an appearance of pissing. And as for the opinion of many that a man cannot sin for any lechery he does with his wife, certainly that opinion is wrong. God knows, a man may slay himself with his own knife, and make himself drunk out of his own tun. Certainly, be it wife, be it child, or any worldly thing that a man loves more than he loves God, it is his idol, and he is an idolater. Man should love his wife with discretion, calmly and moderately; and then she is as it were his sister. The fifth finger of the Devil's hand is the stinking act of lechery. Truly, the five fingers of gluttony the Fiend thrusts into the belly of a man, and with his five fingers of lechery he grips him by the loins in order to throw him into the furnace of Hell; wherein he shall have the fire and the everlasting worms, and weeping and wailing, sharp hunger and thirst, and horror of devils that shall trample all over him, without respite and without end. From lechery, as I said, spring divers branches; as fornication, which is between man and woman who are not married; and this is deadly sin and against nature. All that is an enemy to and destructive of nature is against nature. Faith, the reason of a man tells him well that it is mortal sin, since God forbade lechery. And Saint Paul gives him over to that kingdom which is the reward of no man save those who do mortal sin. Another sin of lechery is to bereave a maiden of her maidenhead; for he that so does, certainly, he casts a maiden out of the highest state in this present life and he bereaves her of that precious fruit that the Book calls "the hundred fruit." I can say it in no other way in English, but in Latin it is called *centesimus fructus*. Certainly, he that so acts is the cause of many injuries and villainies, more than any man can reckon; just as he sometimes is cause of all damage that beasts do in the field, who breaks down the hedge or the fence, just so does the seducer destroy that which cannot be restored. For truly, no more may a maidenhead be restored than an arm that has been smitten from the body may return thereto to grow again. She may have mercy, this I know well, if she does penance, but it shall never again be that she is uncorrupted. And though I have spoken somewhat of adultery, it is well to show forth more dangers that come of adultery, in order that men may eschew that foul sin. Adultery, in Latin, means to approach another man's bed, by reason of which those that once were one flesh abandon their bodies to other persons. Of this sin, as the wise man says, follow many evils. First, breaking of faith; and certainly, in faith lies the key to Christianity. And when faith is broken and lost truly, Christianity stands barren and without fruit. This sin is also a theft; for theft commonly is to deprive a person of his own thing against his will. Certainly this is the vilest thievery that can be when a woman steals her body from her husband and gives it to her lecher to defile her; and steals her soul from Christ and gives it to the Devil. This is a fouler theft than to break into a church and steal the chalice; for these adulterers break into the temple of God spiritually and steal the vessel of grace, that is, the body and the soul, for which Christ will destroy them, as Saint Paul says. Truly, of this theft Joseph was much afraid when his master's wife besought him to lie with her, and he said: "Behold, my master wotteth not what is with me in the house, and he hath committed all that he hath to my hand: there is none greater in this house than I; neither hath he kept any thing from me but thee, because thou art his wife: how then can I do this great wickedness and sin against God?" Alas! All too little is such truth encountered nowadays. The third evil is the filth whereby they break the commandment of God and defame the Author of matrimony, Who is Christ. For certainly, in so far as the sacrament of marriage is so noble and honourable, so much the more is it a sin to break it; for God established marriage in Paradise, in the state of innocence, in order to multiply mankind to the service of God. And therefore is the breaking thereof the more grievous. Of which breaking come oftentimes false heirs, that wrongfully inherit. And therefore will Christ put them out of the Kingdom of

Heaven, which is the heritage of good folk. From this breaking it happens oftentimes, also, that people wed or sin with their own kindred; and specially the loose-livers who haunt the brothels of prostitutes who may be likened to a common privy wherein men purge themselves of their ordure. What shall we say, also, of whoremasters who live by the horrible sin of prostitution, yea, sometimes by the prostitution of their own wives and children as do pimps and procurers? Certainly these are accursed sins. Understand also that adultery is fitly placed in the ten commandments between theft and homicide; for it is the greatest theft that can be, being theft of body and of soul. And it is like homicide, for it cuts in twain and breaks asunder those that were made one flesh, and therefore, by the old law of God, adulterers should be slain. But nevertheless, by the law of Jesus Christ, which is a law of pity, He said to the woman who was taken in adultery and should have been slain with stones, according to the will of the Jews, as was their law: "Go," said Jesus Christ, "and have no more will to sin," or "will no more to do sin." Truly, the punishment of adultery is given to the torment of Hell, unless it be that it is hindered by penitence. And there are yet more branches of this wicked sin; as when one of them is a religious, or else both; or folk who have entered orders, as a sub-deacon, or deacon priest, or hospitaller. And ever the higher that he is in orders, the greater is the sin. The thing that greatly aggravates their sin is the breaking of the vow of chastity, taken when they received the order. And furthermore, the truth is that the office of a holy order is chief of all the treasury of God, and His special sign and mark of chastity, to show that those have entered it are joined to chastity, which is the most precious kind of life there is. And these folk in orders are specially dedicated to God, and are of the special household of God; for which, when they do deadly sin, they are especially traitors to God and to His people; for they live on the people in order to pray for the people, and while they are such traitors their prayers avail the people nothing at all. Priests are angels, by reason of the dignity of their ministry; but forsooth, as Saint Paul says: "Satan himself is transformed into an angel of light." Truly the priest that resorts to mortal sin, he may be likened to the angel of darkness transformed into the angel of light; he seems an angel of light, but, forsooth, he is an angel of darkness. Such priests are the sons of Eli, as is shown in the Book of the Kings that they were the sons of Belial, that is, the Devil. Belial means, "without judge"; and so fare they; they think they are free and have no judge, any more than has a free bull that takes whatever cow pleases him on the farm. So act they with women. For just as a free bull is enough for all a farm, just so is a wicked priest corruption enough for all a parish, or for all a county. These priests, as the Book says, teach not the functions of priesthood to the people and they know not God; they held themselves but ill satisfied, as the Book says, with the flesh that was boiled and offered to them and took by force the flesh that was raw. Certainly, so these scoundrels hold themselves not pleased with roasted flesh and boiled flesh, with which the people feed them in great reverence, but they will have the raw flesh of laymen's wives and of their daughters. And certainly these women that give assent to their rascality do great wrong to Christ and to Holy Church and all saints and all souls; for they bereave all these of him that should worship Christ and Holy Church and pray for Christian souls. And therefore such priests and their lemans also, who give assent to their lechery, have the cursing of all the Christian court, until they mend their ways. The third kind of adultery is sometimes practised between a man and his wife; and that is when they have no regard to their union save only for their fleshly delight, as says Saint Jerome; and care for nothing but that they are come together; because they are married, it is all well enough, as they think. But over such folk the Devil has power, as said the Angel Raphael to Tobias; for in their union they put Jesus Christ out of mind and give themselves to all filthiness. The fourth kind is the coming together of those that are akin, or of those that are related by marriage, or else of those whose fathers or other kindred have had intercourse in the sin of lechery; this sin makes them like dogs that pay no heed to relationship. And certainly, kinship is of two kinds, either spiritual or carnal; spiritual, as when one lies with one's sponsor. For just as he that engenders a child is its fleshly father, just so is his godfather his spiritual father. For which reason a woman is in no less sin when she lies carnally with her godfather or her godson than she would be in if she coupled with her own fleshly brother. The fifth kind is that abominable sin whereof a man ought scarcely to speak or write, notwithstanding it is openly discussed in holy writ. This wickedness men and women do with divers intentions and in divers manners; but though holy writ speaks of such horrible sin, holy writ cannot be defiled, any more than can the sun that shines upon the dunghill. Another form of sin appertains to lechery, and that comes often to those who are virgin and also to those who are corrupt; and this sin men call pollution, which comes in four ways. Sometimes it is due to laxness of the body; because the humours are too rank and abundant in the body of man. Sometimes it is due to infirmity; because of the weakness of the retentive virtue, as is discussed in works on medicine. Sometimes it is due to a surfeit of food and drink. And sometimes it comes from base thoughts that were enclosed in man's mind when he fell asleep; which thing may not happen without sin. Because of this, men must govern themselves wisely, or else they may fall into grievous sin.

The Remedy against the Sin of Lechery

Now comes the remedy for lechery, and that is, generally, chastity and continence, which restrain all the inordinate stirrings that come of fleshly desires. And ever the greater merit shall he have who restrains the wicked enkindlings of the ordure of this sin. And this is of two kinds, that is to say, chastity in marriage and chastity in widowhood. Now you shall understand that matrimony is the permitted coming together of man and of woman, who receive, by virtue of the sacrament, the bond of union from which they may not be freed in all their life, that is to say, while they both live. This, says the Book, is a very great sacrament. God established it, as I have said, in Paradise, and had Himself born into wedlock. And to sanctify marriage, He attended a wedding, where He turned water into wine, which was the first miracle that He wrought on earth before His disciples. The true result of marriage is the cleansing of fornication and the replenishing of Holy

Church with believers of good lineage; for that is the end of marriage; and it changes deadly sin to venial sin between those who are wedded, and makes one the hearts of them, as well as the bodies. This is true marriage, which was established by God ere sin began, when natural law occupied its rightful position in Paradise; and it was ordained that one man should have but one woman, and one woman but one man, as Saint Augustine says, and that for many reasons.

First, because marriage figures the union between Christ and Holy Church. And another is, because the man is the head of the woman; at any rate it has been so ordained by ordinance. For if a woman had more men than one, then should she have more heads than one, and that were a horrible thing before God; and also, a woman could not please too many folk at once. And also, there should never be peace or rest among them; for each would demand his own thing. And furthermore, no man should know his own get, nor who should inherit his property; and the woman should be the less beloved from the time that she were joined with many men.

Now comes the question, How should a man conduct himself toward his wife? and specifically in two things, that is to say, in tolerance and reverence, as Christ showed when He first made woman. For He made her not of the head of Adam, because she should not claim to exercise great lordship. For wherever the woman has the mastery she causes too much disorder; there are needed no instances of this. The experience of every day ought to suffice. Also certainly, God did not make woman of the foot of Adam, because she should not be held in too great contempt; for she cannot patiently endure: but God made woman of the rib of Adam, because woman should be a companion to man. Man should conduct himself toward his wife in faith, in truth, and in love; as Saint Paul says: "Husbands, love your wives, even as Christ also loved the Church, and gave Himself for it." So should a man give himself for his wife, if there be need.

Now how a woman should be subject to her husband, that is told by Saint Peter. First, by obedience. And also, as says the law, a woman who is a wife, as long as she is a wife, has no authority to make oath or to bear witness without the consent of her husband, who is her lord; in any event he should be so, in reason. She should also serve him in all honour and be modest in her dress. I know well that they should resolve to please their husbands, but not by the finery of their array. Saint Jerome says that wives who go apparelled in silk and in precious purple cannot clothe themselves in Jesus Christ. Also, what says Saint John on this subject? Saint Gregory, also, says that a person seeks precious array only out of vainglory, to be honoured the more before the crowd. It is a great folly for a woman to have a fair outward appearance and inwardly to be foul. A wife should also be modest in glance and demeanour and in conversation, and discreet in all her words and deeds. And above all worldly things she should love her husband with her whole heart, and be true to him of her body; so, also, should a husband be to his wife. For since all the body is the husband's, so should her heart be, or else there is between them, in so far as that is concerned, no perfect marriage. Then shall men understand that for three things a man and his wife may have carnal coupling. The first is with intent to procreate children to the service of God, for certainly, that is the chief reason for matrimony. Another is, to pay, each of them to the other, the debt of their bodies, for neither of them has power over his own body. The third is, to avoid lechery and baseness. The fourth is, indeed, deadly sin. As for the first, it is meritorious; the second also, for, as the law says, she has the merit of chastity who pays to her husband the debt of her body, aye, though it be against her liking and the desire of her heart. The third is venial sin, and truly, hardly any of these unions may be without venial sin, because of the original sin and because of the pleasure. As to the fourth, be it understood that if they couple only for amorous love and for none of the aforesaid reasons, but merely to accomplish that burning pleasure, no matter how often, truly it is a mortal sin; and yet (with sorrow I say it) some folk are at pains to do it more and oftener than their appetite really demands.

The second kind of chastity is to be a clean widow and eschew the embraces of man and desire the embrace of Jesus Christ. These are those that have been wives and have lost their husbands, and also women that have fornicated and have been relieved by penitence. And truly, if a wife could keep herself always chaste with leave and license of her husband, so that she should thereby give him never an occasion to sin, it were a great merit in her. These women that observe chastity must be clean in heart as well as in body and in thought, and modest in dress and demeanour; and be abstinent in eating and drinking, in speech and in deed. They are the vessel or the box of the blessed Magdalen, which fills Holy Church with good odour. The third kind of chastity is virginity, and it behooves her to be holy in heart and clean of body; then is she the spouse of Christ and she is the beloved of the angels. She is the honour of this world, and she is the equal of martyrs; she has within her that which tongue may not tell nor the heart think. Virginity bore Our Lord Jesus Christ, and virgin was He Himself.

Another remedy for lechery is, specially to withhold oneself from such things as give rise to this baseness; as ease, and eating and drinking: for certainly, when the pot boils furiously, the best measure is to withdraw it from the fire. Sleeping long in great security from disturbance is also a nurse to lechery.

Another remedy for lechery is, that a man or woman eschew the company of those by whom he expects to be tempted; for though it be that the act itself is withstood, yet there is great temptation. Truly a white wall, though it burn not from the setting of a candle near it, yet shall the wall be made black by the flame. Often and often I counsel that no man trust in his own perfection, save he be stronger than Samson and holier than David and wiser than Solomon.

Now, since I have expounded to you, as best I could, the seven deadly sins, and some of their branches, and their remedies, truly, if I could, I would tell you of the ten commandments. But so high a doctrine I leave to the divines. Nevertheless, I hope to God that they have been touched upon in this treatise, each of them all.

8.

THREE BODY AND SOUL POEMS

Soul and Body II
(eleventh century)

Of this, certainly, every man has need: that he should give attention to the fate of his soul and how grave it will be when death comes and cleaves those kinsmen who were before joined together – the body and the soul.

5 It will be long afterwards that the spirit receives from God himself either torment or glory exactly as that earthy vessel previously prepared for it in the world before. This spirit, the soul, must come, strident in its griefs, to find the bodily covering which it once long wore, every seven days for three hundred years – unless the everlasting Lord, almighty God, brings about the end of the world beforehand.

15 At that time the spirit so full of anxiety will cry out with a cold voice and say grimly to that dust:

17 'Listen, dreary dessicated thing! Why have you, a foul thing of earth, afflicted me? You, a semblance of clay, will rot wholly away. Little did you consider to what the fate of your soul might come after it was led forth from the body. What did you have against me, you criminal? Lo, worms' meat! little indeed did you consider how long this will go on. And to you, by an angel from the skies above, the almighty ordaining Lord out of his power and glory sent a soul through his own hand, and then bought you with that holy blood: and you have bound me with harsh starvation and held me captive in hellish torments.

30 'I dwelt within you – I could not get out from you, being engrossed in flesh – and your wicked lusts oppressed me so that it very often seemed to me that it would be thirty thousand years to your death-day. See! I reluctantly waited for our severance: now the outcome is none too good. You were extravagant with food and glutted with wine; full of your glory you flaunted yourself and I was thirsty for the body of God and spiritual drink. If you had made up your mind then, during your lifetime here while I was constrained to occupy you in this world, that you would be strictly steered through carnality and through wicked lusts, and stabilized by me, and that I was the spirit in you sent from God, you would never have prepared for me such harsh hellish torments by the lust of your needs. But now you must suffer the shame of my humiliations in that great day when the Only-begotten will muster all mankind.

49 'Now you are no more desired as a companion by any man among the living, by mother or by father or by any of your kindred, than the black raven, ever since I journeyed out alone from you by the hand of that Being by whom I was first sent. Now no ruby jewels can get you out of here, not gold nor silver, none of your goods, but here your bones must abide, robbed and ripped from their sinews; and I your soul, against my will, must repeatedly seek you out to revile you with my words in accordance with what you have done to me. You are dumb and deaf and your pleasures are come to naught; yet I, afflicted by sins, must needs seek you out by night and go from you again immediately upon the cock-crow, when holy men perform a song of praise to the living God, to seek out those abodes and that dishonourable dwelling-place to which you previously doomed me. And you the many earthworms shall gnaw; they shall rip you from your sinews, black creatures, gluttonous and greedy. Those vanities of yours which you showed off to people here on earth are come to naught; therefore it would have been very much better for you than if all the riches of the world had been yours – unless you had handed them over to the Lord himself – had you become at your creation a bird or a fish in the sea, or a beast of the soil, a field-trudging ox without understanding, and tilled for food, or the fiercest of wild animals in the wilderness if God so willed, yes, even though you had been the worst kind of snake, than that you ever became a man on earth or should ever have received baptism, since you will have to answer for us both in that great day when to all mortals will be revealed the wounds which sinful mortals perpetrated in the world once long ago.

86 'At that time the Lord himself will want to hear by word of mouth from each of all those people their achievements, their payment in compensation for his wounding: but what will you say to the Lord there in the day of judgment since there is no member matured into a limb so small but that for each one of them separately you will duly have to pay compensation.

92 'At that time the Lord will be wrathful in judgment, but what shall we two do when he has regenerated us for a second time? We shall then have to enjoy together thereafter such miseries as you doomed us to before.'

97 Thus it will revile that fleshy mass; then it will have to journey on its way, to seek not the joys of heaven but the abyss of hell, anguished by those deeds. The dust will remain where it was. It cannot articulate any reply to it nor offer any shelter, help or comfort there to the grieving spirit. The head is cracked apart, the hands are disjointed, the jaws dropped open, the palate ripped apart, the sinews have been sucked away, the neck gnawed through. Rampant worms rob the ribs and grip the corpse in swarms, thirsty for blood. The tongue is torn into ten pieces for the hungry worms' pleasure and therefore it cannot readily exchange words with the damned spirit.

111 The worm is called Gluttony, whose jaws are sharper than a needle, that first of them all sets to within the earthy grave. He tears the tongue apart and crawls among the teeth and eats through the eyes down into the head and clears the way to a surfeit of food, to a banquet, for the other worms.

117 When the vile body, which one long decked with clothes before, has grown chill, then it will be worm's meat, its food, in the earth.

121 To every man among the wise this may serve as a reminder.

THE METAPHYSICAL POETS
Andrew Marvell

A Dialogue between the Soul and Body
(seventeenth century)

SOUL

O who shall, from this Dungeon, raise
O Soul inslav'd so many wayes?
With bolts of Bones, that fetter'd stands
In Feet; and manacled in Hands.
Here blinded with an Eye; and there
Deaf with the drumming of an Ear.
A Soul hung up, as 'twere, in Chains
Of Nerves, and Arteries, and Veins.
Tortur'd, besides each other part,
In a vain Head, and double Heart.

BODY

Oh who shall me deliver whole,
From bonds of this Tyrannic Soul?
Which, stretcht upright, impales me so,
That mine own Precipice I go;
And warms and moves this needless[1] Frame:
(A Fever could but do the same.)
And, wanting where its spight to try,
Has made me live to let me dye.
A Body that could never rest,
Since this ill Spirit it possest.

SOUL

What Magick could me thus confine
Within anothers Grief to pine?
Where whatsoever it complain,
I feel, that cannot feel, the pain.
And all my Care its self employes,
That to preserve, which me destroys:
Constrain'd not only to indure
Diseases, but, whats worse, the Cure:
And ready oft the Port to gain,
Am Shipwrackt into Health again.

BODY

But Physick yet could never reach
The Maladies Thou me dost teach;
Whom first the Cramp of Hope does Tear:
And then the Palsie Shakes of Fear.
The Pestilence of Love does heat:
Or Hatred's hidden Ulcer eat.
Joy's chearful Madness does perplex:
Or Sorrow's other Madness vex.
Which Knowledge forces me to know;
And Memory wilt not foregoe.
What but a Soul could have the wit
To build me up for Sin so fit?
So Architects do square and hew,
Green Trees that in the Forest grew.

GERARD MANLEY HOPKINS
(nineteenth century)

THE CAGED SKYLARK

As a dare-gale skylark scanted in a dull cage
      Man's mounting spirit in his bone-house, mean house, dwells –
      That bird beyond the remembering his free fells;
This in drudgery, day-labouring-out life's age.

Though aloft on turf or perch or poor low stage,
      Both sing sometímes the sweetest, sweetest spells,
      Yet both droop deadly sómetimes in their cells
Or wring their barriers in bursts of fear or rage.

Not that the sweet-fowl, song-fowl, needs no rest –
Why, hear him, hear him babble and drop down to his nest,
      But his own nest, wild nest, no prison.

Man's spirit will be flesh-bound when found at best,
But uncumbered: meadow-down is not distressed
      For a rainbow footing it nor he for his bónes rísen.

9.

DIVINELY ORDAINED?
Joan Chittister

Religion is simultaneously mystery and meaning. Religion asks the great questions of life and purports to know their answers: Why do we exist? Where did we come from? How did life begin? What is God like? What does God expect of us? These are issues to which the other institutions of society relate.

On the answers to these questions depend both the ethics of our interpersonal relationships and the nature of our institutions. Religion names God, but religion names us as well. It is my belief that religion's name for woman is negative and that this diminishment of half the human race legitimates multiple forms of violence.

In the creation myths of a people are the grist of the social-moral system. Creation myths define at least by implication who God is to people, what kind of people they are, and how they are to relate to one another. The interpretation of the creation myth is, therefore, crucial to the development of society. In this era, sexism depends on it.

In every major world religion, though the feminine is part of the creative principle, women are nevertheless defined as the blighted and inferior part of the human race. Religious writings by men have said so, and the structures they have built to the honor and glory of their gods reflect that proposition.

Consequently, whatever the arguments for and against goddess religion, the primeval equality of the sexes, or archaic respect for the birthing power of women, the fact remains that modern religion has theologized the subordination of women—and obliquely, therefore, the subordination of any peoples—both explicitly and implicitly. The linkage between sexism, militarism, and theology in contemporary religion is subtle but discernible.

In India, early Hinduism described a universe replete with goddesses to whom were attached boundless fertility. This powerful fertility of Mother Earth, however, was considered as much danger as blessing since it brought both energy and matter, both good things and bad, into the world. Clearly, it was reasoned, such dangerous elements needed to be controlled. The conclusion, therefore, was that female fertility was ineffective unless practiced in conjunction with Father Heaven, whose spirit would fertilize the earth and bring order to the undisciplined feminine principle.

With this explanation the dualism of matter and spirit was firmly in place in Indian society, and social restrictions on women became both inevitable and necessary. In early Hindu society, consequently, women had a certain amount of freedom and status that emanated from a respect for the female power to give life, but they were expected to be dependent, docile wives whose husbands, like Father Heaven, were ordained to control them and their errant activities.

By the time of the Buddha (500 B.C.) the marriage age had been lowered to as young as five years, and whatever education or freedom had been part of the lives of Indian women of an earlier period, when the life-giving powers of females had been a source of religious awe, were lost. Feminine energy was then completely under control.

Centuries of this theology had made it perfectly clear to the traditional Hindu that no woman of any caste could gain salvation unless and until she had first been reborn as a man, a state that could be merited only by having been a good wife and bearing male children. In fact, even after his death, a husband controlled his wife: she could not remarry; she was to do penance ever after for having caused his death by virtue of her own bad *karma;* she was even expected to throw herself on his funeral pyre if her love for him was total, since without him she was nothing anyway.

Woman was, in effect, the creator of evil in the world. Whatever her power, however great her energy, she was obviously responsible for what came into the world and the disorder, disturbance, and downfall of social order that came with it. Moreover, though birthing power was woman's, this was a material process. The deduction that followed was debilitating: if women were responsible for the things of matter, men must be responsible for the spiritual or higher dimensions of life. The social effects of this thinking are with us still.

Buddha's new teaching that *nirvana* was within reach of anyone—female or male—who was willing to live out the Four Noble Truths had implications for women. If women were capable of enlightenment, they were candidates for instruction and had a capacity for the spiritual. Even so, what theoretically could have been gains were soon eroded.

Though the Buddha taught that women and men should share authority, property, management, and faithfulness, the ideal bowed in later days to the older model of the creation myth. True, Buddhist religious life, the *Sangha,* offered an alternative beyond marriage and motherhood that Indian women had not enjoyed in the past. But the institutionalization of male celibacy as a manifestation of a desireless state, the continuing image of women's insatiable sexual needs, and the merger over time of Buddhism with Hinduism led to women's fettering in other ways.

As Buddhism came to mirror Hindu norms of the past and the two lifestyles merged over time, women soon needed the permission of men to enter the *Sangha* or communities, only monks could interpret the religious duty required of these women, and women were considered a temptation to male celibacy, obstacles to monkish perfection to be shunned. Buddhist nuns, whatever their age and experience, were trained to obey the youngest monk just as all women were to be subject to men, since the lifeforce in women needed to be neutralized by men.

With these refinements women constituted not only matter, with its dangers according to classical Hinduism, but in Buddhism spiritual entrapment as well. The stage was set for systems that claimed to be equal, looked equal, and professed equality but which clung to patterns that justified the suppression of women in the name of salvation.

Only in popular Indian devotions—Mahayana Buddhism and Hindu *bhakti* or *tantrism*—was dualism suspect, wisdom feminine, and all things said to be capable of triggering enlightenment. In these faiths androgyny became the major religious symbol. Some depictions of divinity, in fact, were half male and half female beings, in which the soft and the strong, the beautiful and the powerful dimensions of life were joined. Consequently, in these 10th-century sects, women were accepted as partners of men, monastic life and celibacy were given less emphasis, enlightenment was considered possible in marriage, and women could also become gurus and masters.

But these cultic diversions were short-lived and without much social influence in the face of ancient beliefs. To this day and despite civil legislation to the contrary, dowries are still paid in India, marriages are still arranged, a woman's salvation still depends on docile subservience to a husband, women may still be abandoned for the sake of the man's spiritual enlightenment, women still have inferior religious status, daughters are still bad *karma*, and the life of a woman still depends on the gratuitous kindness of a man.

In China and Japan, Confucianism, Taoism, and Buddhism combine to give East Asia its moral and spiritual base and to determine the place of women in society.

Confucianism was a set of principles and protocols based on ancient Buddhist-Hindu beliefs and intended to bring them to perfection. Confucius himself (551 B.C.) said, "I communicate and do not invent. I have faith in antiquity and consecrate all my affection to its cause." Confucius, in other words, never questioned the female fertility fear. On the contrary, he simply set out to codify it.

Confucius, therefore, sought to bring harmony to society by training rulers who would embody and impose on the culture a highly structured sense of ordered behavior, filial piety, goodness, and social propriety. As a studied reflection of the fertility beliefs that preceded it, Confucianism was totally misogynistic.

Women were by nature simply inferior beings, whose undisciplined and corrupt natures polluted attempts to contact the divine and would be punished after death, as tradition maintained, for having produced this pollution. They existed solely for procreation and the ongoing development of the family and its ancestor veneration.

A woman could be beaten at will for the sake of docility and subservience. In fact, the common term for "girl" translated "slave girl" as well. "Educating a daughter is like weeding someone else's field," the proverb said. Female infanticide was endemic.

Confucianism was the state religion of China from 57 B.C. to 1911. On the prescriptions and protocol of Confucianism rested the social patterns of the Far East for centuries. For Confucius, the Tao, or Way of God, was hierarchy, order, and ethics. In that hierarchy, women were subject to men and inheritors of social controls designed to assure their fidelity.

Taoism (604 B.C.) softened the situation somewhat. Human nature, the Master Lao Tzu said, was an admixture of *yin* and *yang* energies that could be balanced through meditation and nonviolence. Tao, the way of nature, was gentle, "worthy to be the Mother of all things." The cardinal virtues of Taoism were humility and resignation rather than Confucian action and achievement.

The power gained by practicing Tao was symbolized by water, valley, infant, and female. *Yin* was not subservient to *yang* as tradition had it, the Taoist claimed, but correlative and indispensable for the balance and wholeness of nature. But Taoism was overshadowed by both Confucianism and Buddhism and in its ascendancy gained only one cultural consequence of note: the legal eradication of female infanticide.

The social profile in China is clear. In the face of a warring society and social upheaval, authoritarianism prevailed and with it the creation myth of domination rather than equality. Concubinage, female infanticide, girl sales, and footbinding—the height of Confucian misogyny—lasted until the 20th century. Order, it seems, is the need to assure power to the powerful and to equate those with force with the force of God.

In Japan, Shintoism—a blend of indigenous religion with Buddhism and Confucianism—created a religious reality very similar to that in China. Great goddess veneration, animism, and fear of fertility color the religious and social norms, with one major distinction. Tradition held that the creation of the Japanese Islands and Amaterasu, the Sun Goddess, was the result of the intercourse of a divine primal couple. The land itself, the ancient myth reported, was directly descended from Amaterasu, the Sun Goddess.

The way was laid for the elevation of women. In fact, *shamanesses,* female religious figures, could become channels for the spirits, the *kami,* and so women gained a modicum of social and cultural importance for a limited amount of time. But the Japanese, in their respect for Chinese culture, eventually adopted Confucian ethics and, in turn, its depreciation of women.

By the 12th century, Japanese landholders and their *samurai* warriors had already embarked on the militaristic feudalism that marked Japanese culture for almost 700 years and which matched well the Confucian ideals of hierarchy, rank, and social order. By the 15th century, Japanese women had lost all civil rights, political power, and opportunity for education. A young girl was instructed in the practice of suicide in case her chastity was violated, her husband was in danger, or her relationship with her husband threatened his loyalty to his lord; in case, in other words, her existence in any way violated the honor of a man.

Bushido, this unwritten code of disciplined loyalty to the master, touched women's lives in every aspect. Wives were used for management and posterity; other women were used for pleasure. Both existed as second-class citizens in a world that purported to bring harmony to a universe where rational men were intended to dominate the demonic power of women.

In Western civilization two religious world views predominate, one the root of the other. Judaism and Christianity claim a common vision of human creation: God created all things and people "in God's own image" as male and female and for their eternal happiness. Their sin led to their banishment from paradise and to their punishment, he to earn bread by the sweat of his brow and she to bear children in pain.

In both religious traditions women are said to be honored, but the stage is small and the lines are totally biological. Long gone is the commitment to a creation made "in the image of God," an implicit admission of the feminine as well as the masculine element in the creative source. Rather, women came quickly to be described as the afterthought of human life and the source of its trouble—the one made for the other, second and therefore secondary, inferior instead of identical and equal to the other as "bone of my bone."

Adam, the first man, says in Genesis, "The woman you gave me, she caused me to sin." Her seduction, not his equally bad judgment or co-conspiracy, was defined by male exegetes as the cause of humankind's loss of primitive grace, and so responsibility came to fall harshest on the woman. The social structures of each society reflect the ideology of male rationality and female immorality and decrepitude to this day.

Judaism defines marriage as a prime symbol for God's relationship with the people of Israel, and the good wife as one who bore male children. Unfortunately, what made a woman valuable also made her unclean and therefore a spiritual threat to Jewish men on whom all major religious responsibility devolved. Women were segregated, dependent, and limited. They did not have the right to full religious participation, public intervention, or authority. Inferior by nature and a temptress, a woman lost the right to the autonomy of full personhood because of Eve's sin.

In Christianity, Jesus' acceptance of women, his balance of images, his teaching, and his evenhanded expectations were soon overlaid with rabbinic morality and a preference for Genesis 2, the creation story of a later date that curses Eve to subordination. With vowed celibacy in the third century came the dread of women and the need to control them. Augustine argued that woman was no full image of God unless joined to a man who was her head. By the 13th century, Thomas Aquinas, working from Aristotle and Augustine, had defined women as weaker in substance than men, defiled in intellect and in moral character, sexually promiscuous, and without spiritual strength. God was exclusively "Father," not YHWH. Now God was male, though pure spirit. In this cosmology, males are, of course, closer to God. Everything else follows logically; the dictum marks Western culture to this day.

On the basis of this world view, Western women have taken vows of obedience to men, been denied full spiritual participation by their churches, and been defined by their biology. Their abilities are limited, their purpose sexual, their function domestic.

In seventh-century Arabia, Islam brought to life the same creation myth and religious history that Jewish monotheism had already described. Mohammed did not preach a new religion; he simply preached a new prophecy of the religion that was endemic to the area. In his telling, as in Genesis 1 and in Jesus' teachings, women enjoyed a fundamental religious equality with men. Mohammed outlined, too, the social effects of that philosophy in ways uncommon to the area: women were allowed consent to marriage, polygamy was limited, divorce was regulated, women had property rights, and in Mohammed's time were even permitted to pray in the mosques.

But whatever gains accrued to women were quickly eroded by the last line of the Koran itself: "Men are in charge of women because Allah hath made one of them to excel the other, and because they spend their property (for women's support). . . . Good women are obedient." On the basis of this dictum, later ages enforced veiling and *purdah*—seclusion and harems for women—to avoid the sexual danger presented by women, whose entire body was considered sexual and unfit for either mosque or marketplace. The move rendered women socially marginal and incompetent.

The husband's control was absolute. A wife could be imprisoned, even killed, for disobedience and divorced both without cause and without cult. All the man had to say was "I divorce you," and the woman was condemned to poverty and disgrace.

The established practice of clitoridectomy remains to this day to assure against women's infidelity and to release women from what is said to be their insatiable bondage to sex. More than 74 million clitoridectomies have been performed in continental Africa alone.

It is clear that religion validates violence against women. Creation stories are used to prove that some humans are more human than others. Whether creation is explained as the result of Mother Earth, the intercourse of a primeval couple, or the creative act of an integrated male/female being, the fall of humanity is attributed to the disordered appetite or polluting chemistry of woman.

It is religion, in other words, which teaches that inequality was built into the human race, that some people are by nature closer to God than others, that some are innately more virtuous than others, that some people are made for other people's use, that some people have both the right and the duty to control other people, and that these people know who they are.

The corruption of the creation myths of each major world religion, including Christianity, has been used by men to assure the ascendancy of men. Men were entitled to women as part of their birthright. Whether the women in question agreed or not, men took as divine decree the right to buy them, collect them, trade them, and fight over them.

Religion, in other words, in its derogation of half the human race, has created a theology of domination that, despite all spiritual maxims to the contrary, makes generalized violence, aggression, and international militarism not just logical but necessary in order to control what must be administered by men who have been "given dominion."

The natural inequality of women has been institutionalized by the woman's marriage vow of obedience and used to justify both discrimination and abuse. Dependence of women on men was both assumed and assured by legislation that denied to women in the name of God's will goods essential to the maintenance of life—property, education, credit, and economic advancement. So ingrained became the doctrine of female inferiority as a function of natural law that by the 1860s, it was used to validate the "naturalness" of slavery as well. In fact, when black slavery was instituted in the United States, the laws governing the rights of women in society served as the model for slave laws.

In the 20th century, psychologists wove elaborate schemes designed to distinguish between female and male sex differences. Dependence, passivity, emotionalism, compassion, and conformity were female traits; aggression, power, strength, objectivity, and intelligence were male—all of which suited the male religious assumptions that women were by nature inferior. Given the power to define creation, male literature, research, and legislation created it.

Every human institution built inequality into its basic philosophy, operational procedures, and social structures. The fact is that human rights are debatable when the explanation of humanity has a touch of the less than human in it and violence becomes virtue. In military societies, for instance, training programs are geared to "take the woman out of the recruit," to violate the enemy sexually, to link sex and aggression. The U.S. Army marching jingle asserts: "This is my rifle [slapping weapon]; this is my gun [slapping crotch]. One is for killing; the other for fun."

The historical-economic associations between the domination of woman and the making of war are lengthy and obvious. More subtle, more insidious, and more damaging perhaps are the associations between religion, sexism, and war.

By implication, by omission, and by design, religions have provided a construct of life in which God is male, woman's subordination to man is divinely ordained, and woman is by nature either evil or pure. Religion has been used to assert male superiority and so, by indirection, a theology of domination. Obedience and dominion have been used to justify hierarchy as well as control by the fittest.

Ironically, religion may well lie at the base of both sexism and militarism, as violence done to women legitimates violence done to others. If we believe that inferiority is built into the human race by the creative principle itself, then we must also believe that some people have the right and duty to control others. Thus we are only a short step away from the lynching of black people, the extermination of red people, the napalming of yellow people, and the gassing of the next generation of Jews. And all in the name of God.

The creation myth has been interpreted to justify the present social order and to perpetuate it—by force, if necessary. But there is another way to tell the same story. Two human beings were created by the God whose name is "I am who I am." Since they were made from the very same substance—"bone of my bone, flesh of my flesh," someone just like me—they were absolutely equal to one another and destined for eternal happiness together.

But because neither Adam nor Eve kept the commandments of God, they were both condemned to labor, he by the sweat of his brow, she in the throes of birth. It was their sin, not their natures, which condemned them. Their struggle for salvation—and ours—lies in the obligation not to institutionalize unjust relationships but to transcend and redeem them. The violence done to right relationships must end before it ends us all.

10.

"THIS FAIR DEFECT OF NATURE":
AN INTRODUCTION TO THE LITERARY IMAGE OF WOMAN
Douglas R. Letson

Nowhere will one find a better summary of the problem women have encountered historically in Western society than in the questions posed by Geoffrey Chaucer's Wife of Bath (*The Canterbury Tales,* c. 1384-1400), John Milton's Adam (*Paradise Lost,* 1674), and Nathaniel Hawthorne's Hester Prynne (*The Scarlet Letter,* 1850). Reacting to her husband's learned and thoroughly misogynic disquisition, the Wife of Bath enquires "Who painted first the lion, tell me who?"; lamenting the loss of paradise, and blaming Eve for the evil which has fallen on *man*kind, Adam moans: "O why did God, / Creator wise, that peopl'd highest Heav'n / With Spirits Masculine, create at last / This novelty on Earth, this fair defect / Of Nature . . . ?"(*Paradise Lost,* X, 888-892); and Hester Prynne, impregnated in an extramarital act of love and consequently ostracized by an unfeeling and judgemental society, muses: "Indeed, the same dark question often rose into her mind, with reference to the whole race of womanhood. Was existence worth accepting, even to the happiest among them? As concerned her own individual existence, she had long ago decided in the negative, and dismissed the point as settled. A tendency to speculation, though it may keep woman quiet, as it does man, yet makes her sad. She discerns, it may be, such a hopeless task before her. As a first step, the whole system of society is to be torn down, and built up anew. Then, the very nature of the opposite sex, or its long hereditary habit, which has become like nature, is to be essentially modified, before woman can be allowed to assume what seems a fair and suitable position." (*The Scarlet Letter*, p. 120).

Chaucer's Wife notes that the philosophy of Western society and the literature which popularizes that philosophy are virtually the private purview of men. Just as Aesop's lion would hardly have painted a picture of a vanquisher of lions, so the male cleric is equally unlikely to record accurately (i.e., realistically) the nature of woman. The Wife's point is clearly an important one, one fully accepted by women's liberationists (be they historians, theologians, or writers of fiction) – just as it has taken the Barabara MacHaffies to provide "Her Story" (herstory), the Rosemary Ruethers to uncover "Sexism and Godtalk", and the Elisabeth Schussler Fiorenzas to reconstruct Christian theology "In Memory of Her", so has it taken

Canada's women writers (the Margaret Atwoods, Margaret Laurences, Susan Musgraves, Marian Engels) to reveal with imaginative verve the essence of the real woman.

Milton's Adam echoes the "heart" of the patristic tradition when he blames woman for the fall of man. Eve is the archetype of evil in the Christian tradition, requiring expiation in the Virgin – conceived immaculately and conceiving immaculately. Reflecting the early patristic ruminations on the nature of women, Western literature, especially in the Middle Ages, is dotted with gardens and peopled by Eves and Marys – seldom with real women, women who are neither whore nor virgin but living composites of good and evil, sense and intellect, body and soul. But Milton's Adam retreats much further into philosophical history than the musings of the church fathers, returning to Aristotle's definition of woman as defective *by nature*. It is a definition which originates with the ruminations of men in ancient Greece, men who idealized homosexual love; and it is an idea which was transformed into the Christian tradition by celibate men, men usually living monastic existences out of the corrupting clutches of the real world. It is an idea which lives still, mostly (but not exclusively) in the philosophizing of men. In imitation of this fact, Nathaniel Hawthorne pictures Hester Prynne's judge as a minister of God, "a great scholar, like most of his contemporaries in the profession, and withal a man of kind and genial spirit. This last attribute, however, had been less carefully developed than his intellectual gifts, and was, in truth, rather a matter of shame than self-congratulation with him. There he stood, with a border of grizzled locks beneath his skull-cap; while his gray eyes, accustomed to the shaded light of his study, were winking, like those of Hester's infant, in the unadulterated sunshine." (p. 50). Can one so divorced from nature, so dead to the colour and splendour of this world, really contemplate the natural? Little wonder that Hester Prynne comes quickly to the heart of the matter: Is woman inferior and sensual by nature or by custom?

The literary odyssey which follows traces, in a general way, the pre-Christian origins of the issue from its fourth-century beginnings in the Greek Academy at Athens to its contemporary revision by Canada's writers of prose fiction.

By combining his observations of the world of animals with his philosophical proclivities, Aristotle posits in his *On the Generation of Animals* the notion that women are defective, material, and passive by nature, whereas men are the perfection of nature, are spiritual and active. Anticipating Freud's concept of penis envy (i.e., of the male as the desired product of the procreative act), Aristotle reasons that in the proper act of generation a male is formed, "for just as the young of mutilated parents are sometimes born mutilated and sometimes not, so also the young born of a female are sometimes female and sometimes male instead. For the female is, as it were, a mutilated male, and the catamenia are semen, only not pure; for there is only one thing they have not in them, the principle of soul." In the act of generation, Aristotle concludes, the male provides active semen and the psychic principle; the male, he reasons, is therefore the efficient cause, the actor; the woman, on the other hand, provides the matter to be disposed – she is the material cause. "Again, as the first efficient or moving cause, to which belong the definition and the form, is better and more divine in its nature than the material on which it works, it is better that the superior principle should be separated from the inferior. Therefore, wherever it is possible and so far as it is possible, the male is separated from the female. For the first principle of the movement, or efficient cause, whereby that which comes into being is male, is better and more divine than the material whereby it is female. The male, however, comes together and mingles with the female for the work of generation, because this is common to both."

Inherent in Aristotle's argument is a hierarchy which places the spiritual over the material, the active over the passive, the male over the female; in addition, Aristotle equates the male with the divine and relegates the association of male and female merely to the act of procreation. Such is no large mental step for a student whose mentor, Plato, had depicted the body as the prison of the soul and who had, logically, devalued the sexual as a hindrance to the proper spiritual flight of the mind. The implications of this hierarchical structure from the perspective of women and the church are numerous. But, that these implications have become part of our cultural response to male/female, maleness/femaleness is undeniable – it took a genesis myth and the fathers of the church who explicated that myth for Christian thinkers to give shape and vitality to the sexual suggestions implicit in the classical hierarchy; it took the poet to popularize, explore, and, ultimately, to explode them. Plato, Aristotle, and the church fathers functioned primarily in the male enclaves of the academy or the monastery, while the poet reformulated philosophical perception mimetically in imitation of the real world.

Anthony Kosnik explains that when St. Paul warns the early Christians about the inclinations and works of the flesh, Paul's concept of flesh extends beyond specific reference to the merely sexual: in keeping with Old Testament perceptions, Paul's word "flesh" embodies all of the temporal order (*Human Sexuality,* p. 42). Early English literature soon assigned the same role to woman as she became for the poet a symbol of flesh, of those transitory objects the love of which frustrates man's quest for the spiritual life (for Eden).

In the early eighth century, the respected English scholar, the Venerable Bede, records a late sixth-century exchange of letters between Augustine of Canterbury while on his mission to Christianize the English and Pope St. Gregory who had ordered the reluctant monk to the pagan island. Responding to Augustine's inquiry as to whether a man who has had a loss of sperm during a dream might receive communion, or celebrate mass if he is a priest, Gregory co-opts classical precepts on man and woman when he reasons that "all sin is fulfilled in three ways, viz. by suggestion, by delight, and by consent. Suggestion is occasioned by the Devil, delight is from the flesh, and consent from the mind. For the serpent suggested the first offense, and Eve, as flesh, was delighted with it, but Adam consented, as the spirit, or mind." Similar sentiments are recorded by Chaucer's Parson when he explains the origin of sin, using as his exemplars Adam and Eve, and concluding:

"There may ye seen that deedly synne hath first suggestion of the feend, as sheweth heere by the nadder [snake]; and afterward, the delit of the flessh, as sheweth heere by Eve; and after that, the consentynge of resoun, as sheweth heere by Adam. / Fortiust wel, though so were that the feend tempted Eve, that is to seyn the flessh, and the flessh hadde delit in the beautee of the fruyt defended, yet certes [certainly], til that resoun, that is to seyn Adam, consented to the etynge [eating] of the fruyt, yet stood he in th'estaat of innocence." (*The Complete Poetry and Prose of Geoffrey Chaucer*, p. 359).

While the Parson in Chaucer's fourteenth-century *Canterbury Tales* reiterates the identification of women with flesh, men with reason, Chaucer's translation of the sixth-century Boethian *Consolation of Philosophy* repeats the more all-embracing association of women with all things material and passing. In the poetic segment which concludes the third book of *Boece*, Chaucer translates and interprets Boethius' rendering of the story of Orpheus and Eurydice, noting that when Orpheus leaves the underworld with Eurydice, his beloved wife whom he has reclaimed from Pluto, he looks back on her (contrary to his agreement with the god of Hades) and consequently loses her. How does Chaucer explicate Boethius' use of the fable? To look back upon Eurydice, he explains, is to set one's eye on temporal things, to turn away from the celestial, and, hence, to lose all. "For whoso that ever be so overcomen that he fychche his eyen into the putte [pit] of helle (*that is to seyn, whoso sette his thowhtes in erthley thinges*), al that evere he hath drawen of the noble good celestial, he leseth [loses] it whan he loketh the helles [into hell] (*that is to seyn, into lowe thinges of the erthe*) (p. 869).

Though Chaucer could hardly escape unscathed from the temper of his times, it would be overly hasty to accuse him of rectifying women or harbouring blatantly sexist attitudes. In the case of *Boece* he is repeating Boethian and neo-Platonic philosophical concepts which have worked their way into ecclesial Christian thought; in the case of the Parson, he is imagining the thoughts and expressions typical of the ideal medieval cleric. For his part, Chaucer wrote a series of tales (the Wife's, Clerk's, Merchant's, Squire's, and Franklin's), which argued for a more equitable understanding of the male-female relationship; in addition, in his *Book of the Duchess, Parliament of Fowls,* and "Knight's Tale", he depicted as exemplary human relationships which reject both extremes of the stereotypical depiction of woman, and insisted instead on a comingling of the physical and the spiritual. His Parson, therefore, is an ideal medieval cleric, presenting mainline medieval philosophy. One need only look at the medieval penitentials popular in the seventh century and beyond to get a sense of typically medieval clerical perceptions of women. The advice Columban's penitential offers to confessors in the early seventh century, for example, is both typical and telling. "If any layman begets a child of another's wife," he counsels, "that is, commits adultery, violating his neighbor's bed, he shall do penance for three years, abstaining from juicy foods and from his own wife, giving in addition to the husband the price of the violated honor of his wife, and so shall his guilt be wiped off by the priest."

Columban's advice not only objectifies the woman by assessing a form of spiritual wergild to the sexual embrace, but it associates her sensually with the juices of the vegetable world, and assumes that the woman is there to service the man – she is a kind of catalyst to the action, a source of temptation and sin, not a wholly independent spiritual being in need of reconciliation for her willing involvement in an adulterous relationship. It is attitudes of this sort which are reflected in Chaucer's habit of providing moral summaries from which the woman is excluded. In his "Miller's Tale", for example, Chaucer sketches a summary scene while assigning a crude retributive justice: a covetous old carpenter who hoards his attractive young wife like an object securely kept is cuckolded; a lecherous but proud priest is humiliated by unwittingly providing his lusty lover (the carpenter's wife) with a clandestine kiss to the anus; and a scheming clerk is scalded (appropriately) with a hot poker for contriving to seduce this same lascivious young creature with the weasel-soft body. But for her there is no penalty, no restitution. She is Eve. As the principal character of Chaucer's "Nun's Priest's Tale" croons, *"In principio, mulier est hominis confusio"*: that is, co-existent with the Johannine Word of creation, woman was fashioned as man's downfall. Woman is object, she is temptress, she is mankind's Delilah, she is the captivating siren whose enchanting song is inherently bedeviling – but she is herself inconsequential. She is less than fully human.

What is one to conclude, for example, from the late seventh-century penitential of Theodore which states that a man who persists in engaging in "unnatural intercourse" i.e., sex in other than the missionary position – is to do penance "as one who offends with animals"? (The carpenter's libidinous wife in Chaucer's "Miller's Tale" is depicted in animalistic terms: she has a weasel's body, sings like Venus' sparrow, she skips like a calf, and is as jolly as a colt.) If woman is lower than man on the Platonic/Aristotelian/Christian scale of being, if she is relegated to the sensual, to the level of the animal, she is, nonetheless, given the opportunity to rise above her natural state – to become the Virgin Mary. Woman's "special status" is clear, for example, in the implications of the penitential directive that male masturbation is to be punished with a forty day penance, whereas female masturbation requires three years of similar atonement.

Medieval literature is replete with songs to the Virgin and catalogues of unfaithful women. The courtly love tradition, with its Marian imagery and Christian trappings, evokes exactly these conflicting models of womanhood. In the thirteenth-century allegorical (and overtly misogynic) handbook outlining the give-and-take of courtly love, *The Romance of the Rose,* and the romantic literature inspired by it, the woman is the leech whose healing power is borrowed from Boethius' Lady Philosophy whose salvation (i.e., salving) is expressly proper to wisdom, to the priestly confessor, and to the Sacrificial Priest. In the duplicity of the courtly tradition, however, the lady becomes the lover's pathway to paradise: she is either a paragon of virtue curing him of the fevered pursuit of the entrapments of this life, or she becomes his earthly paradise itself, healing his amourous wounds in an illicit sexual embrace and offering explicitly unrepentant adultery. (The word "paradise" derives from the Greek *paradeisos*, "walled garden"; as a result, medieval literary gardens abound, usually stylized on *The Romance of the Rose,* and the woman is the bud at its centre, the "queen of the rosary", who promises an earthly paradise of pleasure and delight.) So, in Chaucer's "Merchant's Tale" a silly old squire celebrates the buxomness (obeisance) of womankind by recalling how Eve was shaped from Adam's rib to be his helpmate. Inspired by the supposed example of Eve, the squire shops about for a young woman whose devotion will save his soul. Ultimately, covetous of his wife's charms he builds a walled garden in which she is encaged and in which he unwittingly stoops so that she might step over him into the arms of her lover who is waiting impatiently in the boughs of a tree of sexual knowledge centred in the garden – the squire's paradise is lost.

Chaucer's *Canterbury Tales* tells many a story of the ideal virtuous woman and the lusty unfaithful wife. The former are allegories and the women more bloodless abstractions of the medieval ideal than real people. In such stories, sex is an evil to be endured for the propagation of the species – a Platonic-Aristotelian "coming together and comingling"; in the consummation of the wedding of Constance and King Alla in Chaucer's "Man of Law's Tale", for example, Chaucer notes that "They goon to bedde, as it was skile and right; / For thogh wyves be ful hooly thynges, / They moste take in pacience at nyght / Swiche [such] manere necessaries as been plesynges [pleasing] / To folk than han ywedded hem with ringes, / And leye a lite hir hoolynesse aside, / As for the tyme . . ." (*The Complete Poetry and Prose of Geoffrey Chaucer,* p. 94). Similarly, in Chaucer's "Second Nun's Tale" as the organs make their melody and Cecelia takes a husband, she prays quietly: "O Lord, my soul and eek [also] by body gye / Unwemmed [keep undefiled], lest that it confounded be." (p. 313). She and Valerian live as brother and sister, and Cecelia is counted among the saints. That lady's not for burning!

Flesh and blood women abound in Chaucer. But there is no better symbol of woman as temporalia, as all things temporal and passing, than the Wife of Bath. She is grotesquely overweight, ostentaciously dressed, irrepressibly garrulous, naggingly irrational, and she is clearly on the pilgrimage of life in quest of all the pleasures it has to offer. The Wife of Bath is imaged as the Whore of Babylon and the Samaritan woman at the well whose five marriages allegorize an overindulgence in the five senses. She is an absurd caricature of everyman in love with the things of this life; as the Wife herself reflects, "I have had my world in my tyme." (p. 114). Her carefully patterned counterpart, the Clerk of Oxenford, is the medieval ideal, appropriately imaged: he is male, he is master of reason (Aristotle's logic) and of sententious discourse, and he is otherworldly – being threadbare in habit and abstemious in behaviour. He is reason, she is sense; he is living according to God's will, she is living according to hers; he is man, she is woman.

The misogynic catalogues which characterize the Wife's tale are present elsewhere in Chaucer, in post-Chaucerian poets like John Lydgate (e.g., his "Examples Against Women"), and in the literary classics of the high Middle Ages like *Sir Gawain and the Green Knight*. By recalling in list form the evil women of classical and biblical antiquity, medieval authors willy-nilly enshrine a misogynic world view which denigrates women and elevates men. Is it any wonder that when Marlowe's Faustus is in search of his world of profit and delight, it is the courtesaned representation of Helen of Troy whom he beseeches ironically to make him "immortal with a kiss"? Is it surprising that gifted renaissance poets like John Donne should celebrate "woman's inconstancy" in a litany of satiric poems, or that Milton's Eve should lament "inferior who is free?" (*Paradise Lost,* IX, 825). Indeed, Milton's Adam encapsulates the traditionalist's attitude succinctly when he observes of his Helpmate that Nature "at least on her bestow'd / Too much of Ornament, in outward show / Elaborate, of inward less exact. / For well I understand in the prime end / of Nature her th' inferior, in the mind and inward Faculties." (VIII, 537-542).

In the wake of the seventeenth-century Renaissance and the late eighteenth-century Enlightenment, however, intellectuals and social activists began to re-evaluate the relationship between reason and observation, between authority and the individual, between spirit and body. For the poet, nature was not perceived to be the designing mind of an abstract God; rather, nature was the breathing presence of divinity itself. Poets wrote of the harmony between nature and the individual, so that, stylistically, natural imagery was contrasted with the artificial and "civilized". To be in touch with nature was to act naturally – in accord with the goodness deep down in all things.

Wordsworth, Keats, and the Shelleys captured the Romantic spirit in England, Thoreau and Whitman in the United States. Walt Whitman's "Song of Myself" (1871) celebrates these new-found liberating attitudes: "I have said that the soul is not more than the body. / And I have said that the body is not more than the soul, / And nothing, not God, is greater to one than one's self is." There is a natural and non-hierarchical goodness inherent in body, soul, and individual.

What, therefore, is one to make of the time-honoured truths concerning the nature of man and woman? Are they accurately expressed in everyday reality; that is, is the traditionally dualistic separation of body and soul as it applies to the sexes empirically valid? The classical and medieval Ptolemaic view of the universe had put the earth rather than the sun at the centre of our solar system – a nicely packaged and totally rational thesis whose only flaw was that natural observation demonstrated conclusively that it happens to be dead wrong. Writers of imaginative fiction began to express the unpopular view that the philosophical ruminations which placed the male by nature at the centre of the universe was equally well-ordered intellectually, but equally wrong-headed. Nathaniel Hawthorne's *The Scarlet Letter* (1850) and Henrik Ibsen's *A Doll's House* (1879) challenged the myth of natural female inferiority, of the sentient and mindless role foisted on women. By analyzing the nature of love, by exposing the role of society and custom in perpetuating the sins of the fathers, and by imaging female characters who are in fact more capable of doing "manly" deeds than their male counterparts, they demonstrated an observable fact of everyday life which stands in complete contradiction to the long-embraced thesis of natural male superiority. In Canada, a host of novelists began to explode the misogynic myth. Prairie novelist Sinclair Ross, for example, has examined sexual stereotypes in his *As For Me and My House* (1941), a novel in which the wife is aggressive and the husband (a fundamentalist cleric who has rejected the tradition) is passive; it is a novel in which society prevents people from acting naturally.

More recently, a number of women writers have examined mimetically the traditional perceptions of women and the implications of these perceptions for everyday life. Margaret Atwood's *Edible Woman* (1969) pictures woman as sentient being, as consumable object, and argues for her rightful role which extends beyond the cheesecake and to the fully human. Her *Surfacing* (1972) depicts men as libidinous brute animals objectifying women, using them for their sensual amusement, and reducing them to disembodied genitalia; Atwood preaches a realistic recognition of the nature of male and female, of the imperfections in both sexes as well as in human society, and of the possibility of a more compatible and fully human relationship between women and men in the real world rather than in the fictional fantasy of a cerebrally created universe.

The view of woman as sensual enticement or, conversely, as virgin has found expression in Marian Engel's *Bear* (1976), a novel written for International Woman's Year and one in which the animal and intellectual are in psychic and sexual conflict. So too in several of Margaret Laurence's novels her women struggle to come to grips with natural sexual yearnings which force them to regress into stone angels making artificial angelic impressions in snow-cold sheets (*Stone Angel,* 1964) or which send them into the liberating fantasies of dream when the mortifying super-ego is mercifully at rest (*A Jest of God,* 1966).

Perhaps one of the most depressing analyses of traditional attitudes towards the relationship between the sexes is Susan Musgrave's *Charcoal Burners* (1980). It is a novel which lays bare in nauseous fashion society's consumer attitudes towards women, a novel in which the main character's request for Atwood's *Edible Woman* is mistakenly translated into the delivery of a cook book; it is a novel in which this same heroine is brutalized by sexually inept "monks" who reduce her body to commercial ash, a novel which plays to its macabre conclusion the theme of the yin and the yang of female passivity and male activity. It is also a novel in which the heroine witnesses her husband rape a slaughtered deer in imitation of their conjugal embrace. *Charcoal Burners* is a graphic cry for human understanding and redefinition.

One might add other voices – Brian Moore's, Gabrielle Roy's, Roch Carrier's, Marie-Claire Blais' – but the conclusion is clear. The images presented by our novelists are not always pleasant or uplifting, but they are imaginative representations of real people trying to find their way in the real world, mimetic representations sketched by men and women alike helping to shape a basis for more fulfilling relationships between the sexes, relationships based on our contemporary understanding of what it means to be fully man and fully woman.

References

Fisher, John H., ed. *The Complete Poetry and Prose of Geoffrey Chaucer.* Toronto: Holt, Rinehart and Winston, 1977.

Hawthorne, Nathaniel. *The Scarlet Letter.* New York: W.W. Norton, 1961.

Hughes, Merritt, Y. *John Milton, Paradise Lost.* New York: Odyssey Press, 1962.

Kosnik, Anthony, et al. *Human Sexuality: New Directions in American Catholic Thought.* New York: Doubleday & Company, 1979.

McNeill, John T. and Helena M. Gamer, eds. *Medieval Handbooks of Penance.* New York: Octagon Books, 1965.

Walt Whitman's "Song of Myself" in *Major American Writers.* Jones, Howard H. et al., eds. rpt. New York: Harcourt, Brace & World, 1935, 1952.

11.

THE SOUL INCARCERATE:
An Historical Overview of Body as Jailer of the Spirit
in English Literature
Douglas R. Letson

In his *Confession of a Catholic* Michael Novak states flatly that "Christianity is not about the soul, or in any case not the soul alone. It does not regard this body as a prison, a cage, a corruption".[1] The concept of body as cage, he suggests, is a platonic fiction – and, as a fiction, a lie not a Christian fact. Although there is no shortage of theological explorations into the dichotomous roads travelled by soul and body in Christian thought, Novak's theological contentions and, more pointedly, his specific use of the image of the incarcerated soul are so foreign to my own literary experience that I feel compelled to respond if not in an exhaustive at least in an historically suggestive fashion.

Although the question is apparently a literary one – it involves the use of an image – the implications are much more far-reaching, involving as they do matters of sexual self-understanding: the relationship of body and spirit, the relationship of women and men. These implications are clearly comprehended by the Roman Catholic bishops of the United States whose recent first draft of a pastoral letter on the status of women notes: "Commingled with women's general concerns for the integrity of family life are specific concerns pertaining to the integration of human sexuality into the universal call to holiness. Such a spirituality must be freed from the false notion that Christian sanctity is a matter of progressive separation of the soul or spirit from the body. Besides encouraging married couples to rejoice in the unitive and life-giving gift of their sexuality, the church must continue to deal pastorally and compassionately with the problems confronting spouses in their sexual lives".[2]

Although there is a semantic and philosophical sense in which Novak's assertion is certainly correct, there is often an immense gap between contemplative formulation and mundane reality. Plato does theorize that the body is the prison from which the soul strives relentlessly to escape,[3] but far from remaining a curious pagan rumination Plato's thesis was thoroughly Christianized by the practitioners of the Word. Insofar as the merging of poet and preacher was natural and early in the history of English letters – due largely to Augustine's transformation of Cicero's *docere, delectare, movere* into Christian rhetoric – Plato's image of body as prison was a familiar and enduring one, one through which the Christian artist was able to express an attitude he saw as dominant in the Christian ethics his poetry sought to inculcate.[4]

The sense of mortification (a word derived from the Latin *mortificare,* "to kill") is tenacious in the life of the ascetic Christian and is effectively epitomized in James Joyce's early twentieth-century scene of retreat and repentance at the heart of *A Portrait of the Artist as a Young Man.* Joyce's retreat master captures almost two thousand years of homiletic rhetoric familiar at least to Roman Catholic congregations when he depicts the horrors of hell in terms of retributive punishment for sensual misdeeds, a graphic description which reaches its climax in the homilist's numbing summary:

> Every sense of the flesh is tortured and every faculty of the soul therewith: the eyes with impenetrable utter darkness, the nose with noisome odours, the ears with yells and howls and execrations, the taste with foul matter, leprous corruption, nameless suffocating filth, the touch with redhot goads and spikes, with cruel tongues of flame.[5]

Joyce's youthful protagonist reacts to the priest's admonitions as the serious Christian has long been instructed to: the rigors of mortification will correct a sinful past.

> Each of his senses was brought under a rigorous discipline. In order to mortify the sense of sight he made it his rule to walk in the street with downcast eyes, glancing neither to right nor to left and never behind him. ... To mortify his hearing he exerted no control over his voice which was then breaking, neither sang nor whistled. ... To mortify his smell was more difficult as he found in himself no instinctive repugnance to bad odours. ... To mortify the taste he practised strict habits at table, observed to the letter all the fasts of the church and sought by distraction to divert his mind from the savours of different foods. (pp. 150f)

This sense of evil associated with the body is very strong in English letters from their very beginnings.[6] In Anglo-Saxon England, life was arduous and death a constant companion, the gulf between the powerful and dispossessed was agonizingly obvious so that the poet and the preacher returned constantly to the themes of earthly transience, of the evils of things temporal, of the equalizing capacity of the grave. Graveside scenes are legion – there is even extant a graphically sardonic poem entitled "The Grave" – and, in fact, two poems remain wherein a disembodied soul returns to chastise its former bondsman. "The Soul's Address to the Body" captures the elegiac lesson of old English poetry and in doing so uses as part of its poetic inspiration the emerging image of body as jailer.

and thou hast bound me with cruel hunger and fettered me in the torments of hell. I dwelt within thee; encompassed by flesh, I could not go from thee, and thy evil desires thronged upon me. ... [7]

During the High Middle Ages there is no writer more concerned with the effective presentation of Christian doctrine than the English poet Geoffrey Chaucer. Still, even though in his translations of Boethius and *The Romance of the Rose* Chaucer faithfully transmits official church teachings on things physical and temporal, his personal attitudes towards love, marriage, and sexuality are implicitly critical of the unnatural condemnation his church placed on the exercising of one's sexuality. Sensitive treatments of the subject of love and marriage in *The Book of the Duchess* and "The Knight's Tale" clearly argue for a union of bodies and of minds (a chain of love rather than a disincarnating hierarchy) in a spirit which anticipates the best of Renaissance ethical tradition; as a result, in *The Parliament of Fowls* Chaucer reduces to the absurd the clerical argument for ideal marital union "Let them be celibate", and in his "The Second Nun's Tale" he satirically rejects the hagiographic ideal of virginity in marriage.

So it is that in her invocation to the Virgin, the Second Nun piously utters a prayer which instinctively adopts the canonized image of body as jailer:

And of thy light my soule in prison lighte,
That troubled is by the contagioun
Of my body. ... [8]
[My soul lies imprisoned from your light, and is troubled by the contagion of my body.]

As the organ makes the melody of the nuptial rites, therefore, Cecelia implores her God to keep her soul and her body undefiled:

O Lord, my soule and eek my body gye
Unwemmed, lest that it confounded be. (11. 1366-37)
[O Lord, keep my soul and my body unfouled lest my soul should be confounded.]

A strange prayer indeed for a bride in the making. As master craftsman and student of medieval Christian philosophy, Chaucer characteristically reduces to the absurd what the Middle Ages holds to be sacred. Anyone looking for an affirmation of the traditional denigration of the corporeal in Chaucer will uncover it only in satire; such a quest were as fruitless as Emily's prayers to Diana, prayers answered with the symbolic shedding of virginal blood in the Knight's tale.

Chaucer knows his theory, he knows his Bible, and he has mastered the poetic fusion of the two so common in the Middle Ages. Hence, he concludes his *Canterbury Tales* with a meditative homily which preserves in essence both the form and the content of medieval sermon theology. Significantly, as the Parson expounds upon the nature of Penitence he discusses in some detail the foul contagion of the flesh and in so doing repeats in a Pauline context the canonized image of soul as prison:

The same Seint Paul, after his grete penaunce in water and in lond (in water by night and by day in greet peril and in greet peyne, in lond in famyne, in thrust, in coold and cloothless, and ones stoned almoost to the deeth), / yet seyde he "Allas, I, caytyf man, who shal delivere me fro the prisoun of my caytyf body?" (p. 360 11. 343-44)

[The same Saint Paul, after his great penance in water and on the land (in water by night and by day in great peril and in great pain, on land in famine, in thirst, in cold, naked, and once stoned almost to death); yet, he said, "Alas, prisoner that I am, who shall deliver me from the prison of my captive body?]

One might enumerate other medieval instances in which the image appears – the concluding lines of *Pearl* come to mind with their plea for release from the foul dungeon of this world; as does the timeless meandering of the old man in search of the freedom found only in death, an old man who wanders this earth "lyk a restless kaitif [captive]" in Chaucer's "Pardoner's Tale"; or the recurrent image of "this foule prisoun of this lyf" which informs the "Knight's Tale." Unquestionably, medieval Christian poets do take as their working hypothesis the evil associated with the body and the image of the body as the soul's prison as an apt expression of the relationship between body and soul. They may not totally accept the theology, but they do understand the power and the pertinacity of its expression.

It is noteworthy that this tradition passes unaltered into the English Renaissance. Some of the most noted clerical poets of the early sixteenth century assimilate the image into their poetry. In his thoroughly Christian "The Anniversarie", for example, John Donne celebrates that eternal union of lovers possible "When bodies to their graves, soules from their graves remove."[9] Similarly in his Holy Sonnet #2 Donne mediates on the nature of a parting soul as being:

like a thiefe, which till deaths doome be read,
Wisheth himselfe delivered from prison. (p. 83)

It is, however, not John Donne the churchman but Andrew Marvell the man of court and singer of lyrical verse who records the most extensive and most well-known Renaissance adaptation of this thoroughly Christianized image.[10] His "A Dialogue between the Soul and Body" begins:

O who shall, from this Dungeon, raise
A Soul inslav'd so many wayes?
With bolts of Bones, that fetter'd stands
In Feet; and manacled in Hands.
Here blinded with an Eye; and there
Deaf with the drumming of an Ear.
A Soul hung up, as 'twere, in Chains
Of Nerves, and Arteries, and Veins. (pp. 245-46)

Perhaps the most imaginative and most esthetic use of the image of the "bone-house", however, is that captured by the late nineteenth-century Jesuit priest Gerard Manley Hopkins. His "Caged Skylark" uses as its central image an idea which is far from pagan; rather, it is a canonized part of his cultural heritage as Roman Catholic and as Christian preacher of poetic sermons. Indeed, Hopkins found much of his imagery and his art in early Christian writing; his theology he found in the tireless reiterations of medieval Roman Catholicism.

Hopkins' "Caged Skylark" (see page 110) is thoroughly informed by the image of the soul's imprisonment; in addition, in this poem Hopkins has clearly relegated the physical nature of humankind to the realm traditionally assigned to it by his Christian forefathers.

In Hopkins' poem the soul clamours to escape its bodily bonds, but the body ceases to be jailor only when its nature has been altered through death and resurrection, when the body has shed its temporal contagion and is finally garbed in the glorified flesh of the hereafter.

One might discover instances of the concept of body as temple of the Holy Spirit (the tradition Novak argues is the proper one), but such discoveries would be restricted mostly to those mystical writers content to contemplate an ideal rather than to express a present reality. All of the poets noted in this paper wrestle with social reality as they see it, all are critical of the constraints of this life as they understand them, and all are in quest of a better world.

It is noteworthy that many of Canada's current writers inveigh against the social repressiveness fostered by a religiously inspired view of humankind which has too frequently denigrated the sanctity of the body. Contemporary Canadian belletrists such as Graeme Gibson, Margaret Atwood, Roch Carrier, Sinclair Ross, Marian Engel, Eric McCormack, Susan Musgrave, and Margaret Laurence come readily to mind. In *A Stone Angel* Margaret Laurence argues that Christian ethical philosophy has attempted to deny humankind's physical nature, has caused the Christian adherent to sublimate natural feelings, and has tended to view the Christian stonily as being bodiless and angelic. Just as in his *The Scarlet Letter* Nathaniel Hawthorne turns the image of the prison to exemplify the oppressiveness of the traditionalist puritanical society of nineteenth-century United States, so in *A Bird in the House* and *A Jest of God* Margaret Laurence selects the image of the caged bird to depict the human spirit shackled by a repressive religious Canadian environment which views the body as an unfortunate and inferior constituent of the *animal rationale,* a constituent to be subdued, mortified, confined. In *A Jest of God,* for example, Calla's caged bird struggles to climb Jacob's toy ladder in a futile quest for liberation, a mirror image of Rachel Cameron's effort to scale the walls of her Manawaka prison which separates her from her golden city; and Hagar Shipley, the wing-clipped questor of *A Stone Angel* muses the lyrics of "If I had the wings of an angel, over these prison walls I would fly", as she plots her escape from a society which has turned her to stone, which has caused her to deny her bodily urges, and which has confined her to cold sheets where she morosely fashions bloodless angels of snow.

"Christianity is not about the soul, or in any case not the soul alone. It does not regard this body as a prison, a cage, a corruption". Undoubtedly a celebration of the ways things might have been, might even yet be, but no accurate reflection of centuries of theological expression, nor of the artistic soul-searching embodied in the imaged aspirations of generations of Christian poets who knew their theology, loved their craft, and looked for a better world – often, in fact, they were looking for Michael Novak's world.

---

[1] New York: Harper and Row, 1983, p. 145.

[2] "Partners in the Mystery of Redemption: A Pastoral Response to Women's Concerns for Church and Society", *Origins,* 17 (April 21, 1988), p. 771.

[3] See, for example, Plato's "Phaedo" 81e pp. 65: "They continue wandering until at last, through craving for the corporeal, which unceasingly pursues them, they are imprisoned once more in a body"; "Phaedrus" 250c p. 497: "pure was the light that shone around us, and pure were we, without the taint of that prison house which now we are encompassed withall"; and "Cratylus" 400c p. 437: "the body is an enclosure or prison in which the soul is incarcerated". Edith Hamilton and Huntington Cairns, eds., *The Collected Dialogues of Plato* (1961; rpt. Princeton University Press, 1980).

Walter Kaufmann, "The Inevitability of Alienation", in *Alienation,* Richard Schacht, ed. (New York: Doubleday, 1970, p. xxx) recalls that "Plato cites approvingly an ancient play on the words that was dear to the Orphic sect: the body *(soma)* is the soul's tomb *(sema).* This means that the soul is buried in the body, that life is one long exile, and that salvation is to be found only in death".

[4] For an analysis of the convergence of the poetic and predicatory traditions in Anglo-Saxon England, see my "The Poetic Content of the Revival Homily" in Paul E. Szarmach and Bernard F. Huppe, eds. *The Old English Homily and Its Backgrounds* (Albany, New York: State University Press of New York, 1978), pp. 135-56.

[5] 1916; rpt., Penguin, 1966, p. 122.

[6] Perhaps one of the most telling sequences respecting the early Christian's attitude toward the body is captured in Pope Saint Gregory's response to Augustine, the monk who brought Christianity to England, when Augustine wrote to inquire about the purification of women after childbirth and other matters of sexual import. See, for example, the correspondence between Pope Saint Gregory and Augustine of Canterbury recorded in the Venerable Bede's eighth-century *Ecclesiastical History of the English Nation,* Book I Chapter XXVII. For example:

> Now you must know that this is to be taken in a mystery; for if she enters the church the very hour she is delivered, to return thanks, she is not guilty of sin; because the pleasure of the flesh is in fault, and not the pain; but the pleasure is in the copulation of the flesh, whereas there is pain in bringing forth the child.

In Michael W. Higgins and Douglas R. Letson, eds. *Women and the Church: A Sourcebook* (Toronto: Griffin House, 1986), p. 26.

> Nor do we, in so saying, assign matrimony to be a fault; but forasmuch as lawful intercourse cannot be had without the pleasure of the flesh, it is proper to forebear entering the holy place, because the pleasure itself cannot be without a fault. For he was not born of adultery or fornication, but of lawful marriage, who said, "Behold I was conceived in iniquity, and in sin my mother brought me forth". (p.28)

[7] W.S. Mackie, ed. *The Exeter Book* (1934; rpt., Oxford University Press, 1958), pp. 75-7.

[8] John H. Fisher, ed. *The Complete Poetry and Prose of Geoffrey Chaucer* (Toronto: Holt, Rinehart and Winston, 1977), p. 312, 11.71-3.

[9] Helen Gardner, ed. *The Metaphysical Poets* (1957; rpt., Penguin Books, 1975), p. 65.

[10] For other examples, see Miriam K. Starkman, ed. *Seventeenth-Century Poetry* (New York: Alfred A. Knopf, 1967):

Thomas Traherne, "Hosanna", which begins

No more shall Walls, no more shall Walls
confine
That glorious soul which in my Flesh doth
shine.
(vol. 1 p. 219)

Richard Crashaw, "To the Infant Martyrs", which begins

Goe smiling soules, your new built Cages
breake.
(vol. 1 p. 226)

Richard Lovelace, *"The* Vintage *to the* Dungeon", which begins

Sing out pent Soules, sing cheerfully!
(vol. 2 p. 182)

As one might expect, the image is also to be found in the plays of William Shakespeare. Note, for example, the reference in *King John,* III, iv, 17-19:

Look, who comes here! a grave unto a soul;
Holding the eternal spirit against her will,
In the vile prison of afflicted breath.
Hardin Craig, ed. *The Complete Works of Shakespeare* (Chicago: Scott, Foresman and Company, 1951).

[11] W.H. Gardner, ed. *Gerard Manley Hopkins* (1953; rpt., Penguin, 1961), pp. 31-2.

Part II

Humanae vitae:
The Document and Its Context

INTRODUCTION

No papal statement in modern times has had the popular impact or received the critical attention accorded to *Humanae vitae*. Pope Paul VI, under whose authority the encyclical was promulgated on July 25, 1968, has been variously praised for taking a principled and courageous stand against the materialistic and even hedonistic values of an increasingly acquisitive society and, at the same time, condemned for ignoring the advice of his own commission of experts, turning his back on the scientific and intellectual advances of the modern world, and opting to put his name to an encyclical not so much because he was convinced of the argument that the authors had marshalled as because he feared that by not signing the document he would be severing the tie with a continuous tradition that reached back through the Council of Trent and into the inheritance of the fathers of the church. Whatever his thinking, and whatever the rightness of the cause, the reception of *Humanae vitae* by the faithful – lay and clerical alike – was the apparent cause of the pope's decision never to disseminate another encyclical letter; at the same time, in the eyes of most Roman Catholic academics, *Humanae vitae* has been the most significant single determinant for the loss of papal authority and the introduction of the "cafeteria Catholic": the individual's conviction that one can dissent as a matter of conscience from a particular teaching of the church and still remain a Catholic in good standing.

The magisterial authors of *Humanae vitae* make repeated references to the constant tradition on which the encyclical letter is based, references that tend to affirm the argument that a principal motive behind its composition was a desire to remain constant with the tradition. But these same references naturally invite a study of the document by comparing it to its antecedents to determine exactly how it continues the tradition and how it might vary from the tradition. Although all papal documents refer ultimately to their biblical and patristic sources as the justification for their teachings, the two most immediate influences on *Humanae vitae* are Pope Leo XIII's *Arcanum* of 1880 and Pius XI's *Casti connubii,* released in 1930. While breaking with the hierarchical rigidity concerning the Pauline and medieval notions of the equality of husband and wife, Leo's *Arcanum* does, nonetheless, assume that the male is the image of domestic authority; in addition, while viewing the biblical edict to "increase and multiply" as the primary goal of marriage, Leo points also to "mutual love" and the giving of one another in an "unfailing and unselfish help" as a significant, though secondary, marital obligation. It is a direction that had been suggested by Augustine in his "Good of Marriage," but Augustine's aggressively negative attitudes towards sexuality had obscured his reference to mutual help that was included in "The Good of Marriage." Leo, however, was clearly concerned about the destructive impact that Marxist communism was having on the family unit, and he was determined to present the nuclear family not simply as an expression of the divine plan but also as a stabilizing element essential to the well-ordered state. In issuing his *Casti connubii*, on the other hand, Pius XI was intent on reaffirming traditional Catholic teaching with respect to the primary end of marriage: the procreation of children. Pius was reacting to a decision taken by the Lambeth Conference that had just broken long-standing Christian tradition by affirming that spouses might, for good reason and in good conscience, turn to artificial means to regulate the propagation of their children. As a result, Pius proclaimed the constant tradition on a wide range of topics, condemning contemporary notions of sexual equality and the emancipation of women, reaffirming traditional hierarchical structures within the family unit, underlining Augustinian teachings on indissolubility, and stating quite bluntly that artificial contraception was "intrinsically against nature."

By the 1960s, however, much had changed. Not only had Pius XII apparently opened the door for the legitimate regulation of birth by sanctioning the rhythm method as a natural means of preventing conception, but tremendous strides had been taken in our understanding of human nature as a result of developments in the social sciences, particularly psychology and sociology. In addition, there had been scientific advances in our understanding of the mechanics of reproduction, including the development of a birth control pill that seemed to function in harmony with nature. Moreover, demographic studies had begun to develop serious cautionary scenarios with respect to the expansion of human population, world hunger and environmental sustainability. When Pope John XXIII convened the Second Vatican Council in 1962 and threw open the windows of the Vatican to let the airs of change waft through the Council halls, when the Council itself began to affirm John's conviction that the church had to read the signs of the times, and when the Council seemed to have embraced the concept of mutual affirmation as an end of marriage that was as important as procreation, it seemed that new directions for Vatican teaching on human sexuality were imminent. Pope John's special commission, established to study the church's teaching on the regulation of birth, had not yet reported when the pope died; so, when Paul VI augmented the commission by adding a broad representation of clerical and lay experts, change seemed inevitable. In 1965 the Council concluded. Still no report. Then in 1967 both *The Tablet* and *The National Catholic Reporter* published a leaked copy of the commission report. The commission was not unanimous in its advice on the use of artificial contraception, but the vast majority were clearly in favour. Paul procrastinated. He looked for alternative input. Then, finally, in 1968 he released his own document with an unyielding reaffirmation: "every marriage act must remain open to the transmission of life." The Catholic world was in a state of shock. Many of those Catholics who took the directive seriously sought out confessors who would counsel against rigid interpretation of the directive. Bishops' conferences tried to put the encyclical into context, many of them arguing that for a Catholic to differ with Vatican teaching as a matter of properly informed conscience did not constitute a break with the church.

The Tablet, ever in the responsible vanguard with respect to media analysis, has not only made available the primary documents, but has also continued to provide informed discussion concerning the origin of and reaction to *Humanae vitae*. One cannot make conscientious decisions unless one is properly informed. On the 25th anniversary of the encyclical's proclamation, therefore, *The Tablet* published a series of articles by prominent Catholic writers analyzing *Humanae vitae* from the perspective of a commission insider, a proponent of the document, and a prominent Catholic theologian who was dismayed by the ultramontane inclinations within John Paul's consistories. *The Tablet* also published a series of articles written by eminent British Roman Catholic sexologist Jack Dominian, who raised serious problems with *Humanae vitae* from his particular professional perspective.

So the debate continues. The debate continues as Catholics in huge numbers have grown skeptical about the Vatican's teaching on sexuality, skeptical about Roman authority, and even cynical about a church whose spokesmen too often have not lived in fact by the teachings they have proposed in word.

12.

ARCANUM

Encyclical of Pope Leo XIII on Christian Marriage
February 10, 1880

To the Patriarchs, Primates, Archbishops, and Bishops of the Catholic World in Grace and Communion with the Apostolic See.

The hidden design of the divine wisdom, which Jesus Christ the Saviour of men came to carry out on earth, had this end in view, that, by Himself and in Himself, He should divinely renew the world, which was sinking, as it were, with length of years into decline. The Apostle Paul summed this up in words of dignity and majesty when he wrote to the Ephesians, thus: "That He might make known unto us the mystery of His will . . . to re-establish all things in Christ that are in heaven and on earth."[1]

2. In truth, Christ our Lord, setting Himself to fulfill the commandment which His Father had given Him, straightway imparted a new form and fresh beauty to all things, taking away the effects of their time-worn age. For He healed the wounds which the sin of our first father had inflicted on the human race; He brought all men, by nature children of wrath, into favor with God; He led to the light of truth men wearied out by longstanding errors; He renewed to every virtue those who were weakened by lawlessness of every kind; and, giving them again an inheritance of never-ending bliss, He added a sure hope that their mortal and perishable bodies should one day be partakers of immortality and of the glory of heaven. In order that these unparalleled benefits might last as long as men should be found on earth, He entrusted to His Church the continuance of His work; and, looking to future times, He commanded her to set in order whatever might have become deranged in human society, and to restore whatever might have fallen into ruin.

3. Although the divine renewal we have spoken of chiefly and directly affected men as constituted in the supernatural order of grace, nevertheless some of its precious and salutary fruits were also bestowed abundantly in the order of nature. Hence, not only individual men, but also the whole mass of the human race, have in every respect received no small degree of worthiness. For, so soon as Christian order was once established in the world, it became possible for all men, one by one, to learn what God's fatherly providence is, and to dwell in it habitually, thereby

fostering that hope of heavenly help which never confoundeth. From all this outflowed fortitude, self-control, constancy, and the evenness of a peaceful mind, together with many high virtues and noble deeds.

4. Wondrous, indeed, was the extent of dignity, steadfastness, and goodness which thus accrued to the State as well as to the family. The authority of rulers became more just and revered; the obedience of the people more ready and unforced; the union of citizens closer; the rights of dominion more secure. In very truth, the Christian religion thought of and provided for all things which are held to be advantageous in a State; so much so, indeed, that, according to St. Augustine, one cannot see how it could have offered greater help in the matter of living well and happily, had it been instituted for the single object of procuring or increasing those things which contributed to the conveniences or advantages of this mortal life.

5. Still, the purpose We have set before Us is not to recount, in detail, benefits of this kind; Our wish is rather to speak about that family union of which marriage is the beginning and the foundation. The true origin of marriage, venerable brothers, is well known to all. Though revilers of the Christian faith refuse to acknowledge the never-interrupted doctrine of the Church on this subject, and have long striven to destroy the testimony of all nations and of all times, they have nevertheless failed not only to quench the powerful light of truth, but even to lessen it. We record what is to all known, and cannot be doubted by any, that God, on the sixth day of creation, having made man from the slime of the earth, and having breathed into his face the breath of life, gave him a companion, whom He miraculously took from the side of Adam when he was locked in sleep. God thus, in His most far-reaching foresight, decreed that this husband and wife should be the natural beginning of the human race, from whom it might be propagated and preserved by an unfailing fruitfulness throughout all futurity of time. And this union of man and woman, that it might answer more fittingly to the infinite wise counsels of God, even from the beginning manifested chiefly two most excellent properties – deeply sealed, as it were, and signed upon it – namely, unity and perpetuity. From the Gospel we see clearly that this doctrine was declared and openly confirmed by the divine authority of Jesus Christ. He bore witness to the Jews and to His Apostles that marriage, from its institution, should exist between two only, that is, between one man and one woman; that of two they are made, so to say, one flesh; and that the marriage bond is by the will of God so closely and strongly made fast that no man may dissolve it or render it asunder. "For this cause shall a man leave father and mother, and shall cleave to his wife, and they two shall be in one flesh. Therefore now they are not two, but one flesh. What, therefore, God hath joined together, let no man put asunder."[2]

6. This form of marriage, however, so excellent and so pre-eminent, began to be corrupted by degrees, and to disappear among the heathen; and became even among the Jewish race clouded in a measure and obscured. For in their midst a common custom was gradually introduced, by which it was accounted as lawful for

a man to have more than one wife; and eventually when "by reason of the hardness of their heart,"[3] Moses indulgently permitted them to put away their wives, the way was open to divorce.

7. But the corruption and change which fell on marriage among the Gentiles seem almost incredible, inasmuch as it was exposed in every land to floods of error and of the most shameful lusts. All nations seem, more or less, to have forgotten the true notion and origin of marriage; and thus everywhere laws were enacted with reference to marriage, prompted to all appearance by State reasons, but not such as nature required. Solemn rites, invented at will of the law-givers, brought about that women should, as might be, bear either the honorable name of wife or the disgraceful name of concubine; and things came to such a pitch that permission to marry, or the refusal of the permission, depended on the will of the heads of the State, whose laws were greatly against equity or even to the highest degree unjust. Moreover, plurality of wives and husbands, as well as divorce, caused the nuptial bond to be relaxed exceedingly. Hence, too, sprang up the greatest confusion as to the mutual rights and duties of husbands and wives, inasmuch as a man assumed right of dominion over his wife, ordering her to go about her business, often without any just cause; while he was himself at liberty "to run headlong with impunity into lust, unbridled and unrestrained, in houses of ill-fame and amongst his female slaves, as if the dignity of the persons sinned with, and not the will of the sinner, made the guilt."[4] When the licentiousness of a husband thus showed itself, nothing could be more piteous than the wife, sunk so low as to be all but reckoned as a means for the gratification of passion, or for the production of offspring. Without any feeling of shame, marriageable girls were bought and sold, like so much merchandise,[5] and power was sometimes given to the father and to the husband to inflict capital punishment on the wife. Of necessity, the offspring of such marriages as these were either reckoned among the stock in trade of the common-wealth or held to be the property of the father of the family;[6] and the law permitted him to make and unmake the marriages of his children at his mere will, and even to exercise against them the monstrous power of life and death.

8. So manifold being the vices and so great the ignominies with which marriage was defiled, an alleviation and a remedy were at length bestowed from on high. Jesus Christ, who restored our human dignity and who perfected the Mosaic law, applied early in His ministry no little solicitude to the question of marriage. He ennobled the marriage in Cana of Galilee by His presence, and made it memorable by the first of the miracles which he wrought;[7] and for this reason, even from that day forth, it seemed as if the beginning of new holiness had been conferred on human marriages. Later on He brought back matrimony to the nobility of its primeval origin by condemning the customs of the Jews in their abuse of the plurality of wives and of the power of giving bills of divorce; and still more by commanding most strictly that no one should dare to dissolve that union which God Himself had sanctioned by a bond perpetual. Hence, having set aside the difficulties which were adduced from the law of Moses, He, in character of supreme

Lawgiver, decreed as follows concerning husbands and wives, "I say to you, that whosoever shall put away his wife, except it be for fornication, and shall marry another, committeth adultery; and he that shall marry her that is put away committeth adultery."[8]

9. But what was decreed and constituted in respect to marriage by the authority of God has been more fully and more clearly handed down to us, by tradition and the written Word, through the Apostles, those heralds of the laws of God. To the Apostles, indeed, as our masters, are to be referred the doctrines which "our holy Fathers, the Councils, and the Tradition of the Universal Church have always taught,"[9] namely, that Christ our Lord raised marriage to the dignity of a sacrament; that to husband and wife, guarded and strengthened by the heavenly grace which His merits gained for them, He gave power to attain holiness in the married state; and that, in a wondrous way, making marriage an example of the mystical union between Himself and His Church, He not only perfected that love which is according to nature,[10] but also made the naturally indivisible union of one man with one woman far more perfect through the bond of heavenly love. Paul says to the Ephesians: "Husbands, love your wives, as Christ also loved the Church, and delivered Himself up for it, that He might sanctify it... So also ought men to love their wives as their own bodies. . . For no man ever hated his own flesh, but nourisheth and cherisheth it, as also Christ doth the Church; because we are members of His body, of His flesh, and of His bones. For this cause shall a man leave his father and mother, and shall cleave to his wife, and they shall be two in one flesh. This is a great sacrament; but I speak in Christ and in the Church."[11] In like manner from the teaching of the Apostles we learn that the unity of marriage and its perpetual indissolubility, the indispensable conditions of its very origin, must, according to the command of Christ, be holy and inviolable without exception. Paul says again: "To them that are married, not I, but the Lord commandeth that the wife depart not from her husband; and if she depart, that she remain unmarried or be reconciled to her husband."[12] And again: "A woman is bound by the law as long as her husband liveth; but if her husband die, she is at liberty."[13] It is for these reasons that marriage is "a great sacrament";[14] "honorable in all,"[15] holy, pure, and to be reverenced as a type and symbol of most high mysteries.

10. Futhermore, the Christian perfection and completeness of marriage are not comprised in those points only which have been mentioned. For, first, there has been vouchsafed to the marriage union a higher and nobler purpose than was ever previously given to it. By the command of Christ, it not only looks to the propagation of the human race, but to the bringing forth of children for the Church, "fellow citizens with the saints, and the domestics of God";[16] so that "a people might be born and brought up for the worship and religion of the true God and our Saviour Jesus Christ."[17]

11. Secondly, the mutual duties of husband and wife have been defined, and their several rights accurately established. They are bound, namely, to have such feelings for one another as to cherish always very great mutual love, to be ever

faithful to their marriage vow, and to give one another an unfailing and unselfish help. The husband is the chief of the family and the head of the wife. The woman, because she is flesh of his flesh, and bone of his bone, must be subject to her husband and obey him; not, indeed, as a servant, but as a companion, so that her obedience shall be wanting in neither honor nor dignity. Since the husband represents Christ, and since the wife represents the Church, let there always be, both in him who commands and in her who obeys, a heaven-born love guiding both in their respective duties. For "the husband is the head of the wife; as Christ is the head of the Church. . . Therefore, as the Church is subject to Christ, so also let wives be to their husbands in all things."[18]

12. As regards children, they ought to submit to the parents and obey them, and give them honor for conscience' sake; while, on the other hand, parents are bound to give all care and watchful thought to the education of their offspring and their virtuous bringing up: "Fathers, . . . bring them up" [that is, your children] "in the discipline and correction of the Lord."[19] From this we see clearly that the duties of husbands and wives are neither few nor light; although to married people who are good these burdens become not only bearable but agreeable, owing to the strength which they gain through the sacrament.

13. Christ, therefore, having renewed marriage to such and so great excellence, commended and entrusted all the discipline bearing upon these matters to His Church. The Church, always and everywhere, has so used her power with reference to the marriages of Christians that men have seen clearly how it belongs to her as of native right; not being made hers by any human grant, but given divinely to her by the will of her Founder. Her constant and watchful care in guarding marriage, by the preservation of its sanctity, is so well understood as to not need proof. That the judgment of the Council of Jerusalem reprobated licentious and free love,[20] we all know; as also that the incestuous Corinthian was condemned by the authority of blessed Paul.[21] Again, in the very beginning of the Christian Church were repulsed and defeated, with the like unremitting determination, the efforts of many who aimed at the destruction of Christian marriage, such as the Gnostics, Manichaeans, and Montanists; and in our own time Mormons, St. Simonians, phalansterians, and communists.[22]

14. In like manner, moreover, a law of marriage just to all, and the same for all, was enacted by the abolition of the old distinction between slaves and free-born men and women;[23] and thus the rights of husbands and wives were made equal: for, as St. Jerome says, "with us that which is unlawful for women is unlawful for men also, and the same restraint is imposed on equal conditions."[24] The self-same rights also were firmly established for reciprocal affection and for the interchange of duties; the dignity of the woman was asserted and assured; and it was forbidden to the man to inflict capital punishment for adultery,[25] or lustfully and shamelessly to violate his plighted faith.

15. It is also a great blessing that the Church has limited, so far as is needful, the power of fathers of families, so that sons and daughters, wishing to marry, are

not in any way deprived of their rightful freedom;[26] that, for the purpose of spreading more widely the supernatural love of husbands and wives, she has decreed marriages within certain degrees of consanguinity or affinity to be null and void;[27] that she has taken the greatest pains to safeguard marriage, as much as is possible, from error and violence and deceit;[28] that she has always wished to preserve the holy chasteness of the marriage bed, the security of persons,[29] the honor of husband and wife,[30] and the sanctity of religion.[31] Lastly, with such foresight of legislation has the Church guarded its divine institution that no one who thinks rightfully of these matters can fail to see how, with regard to marriage, she is the best guardian and defender of the human race; and how, withal, her wisdom has come forth victorious from the lapse of years, from the assaults of men, and from the countless changes of public events.

16. Yet, owing to the efforts of the arch-enemy of mankind, there are persons who, thanklessly casting away so many other blessings of redemption, despise also or utterly ignore the restoration of marriage to its original perfection. It is a reproach to some of the ancients that they showed themselves the enemies of marriage in many ways; but in our own age, much more pernicious is the sin of those who would fain pervert utterly the nature of marriage, perfect though it is, and complete in all its details and parts. The chief reason why they act in this way is because very many, imbued with the maxims of a false philosophy and corrupted in morals, judge nothing so unbearable as submission and obedience; and strive with all their might to bring about that not only individual men, but families, also – indeed, human society itself – may in haughty pride despise the sovereignty of God.

17. Now, since the family and human society at large spring from marriage, these men will on no account allow matrimony to be the subject of the jurisdiction of the Church. Nay, they endeavor to deprive it of all holiness, and so bring it within the contracted sphere of those rights which, having been instituted by man, are ruled and administered by the civil jurisprudence of the community. Wherefore it necessarily follows that they attribute all power over marriage to civil rulers, and allow none whatever to the Church; and, when the Church exercises any such power, they think that she acts either by favor of the civil authority or to its injury. Now is the time, they say, for the heads of the State to vindicate their rights unflinchingly, and to do their best to settle all that relates to marriage according as to them seems good.

18. Hence are owing *civil marriages,* commonly so called; hence laws are framed which impose impediments to marriage; hence arise judicial sentences affecting the marriage contract, as to whether or not it have been rightly made. Lastly, all power of prescribing and passing judgment in this class of cases is, as we see, of set purpose denied to the Catholic Church, so that no regard is paid either to her divine power or to her prudent laws. Yet, under these, for so many centuries, have the nations lived on whom the light of civilization shone bright with the wisdom of Christ Jesus.

19. Nevertheless, the naturalists,[32] as well as all who profess that they worship above all things the divinity of the State, and strive to disturb whole communities with such wicked doctrines, cannot escape the charge of delusion. Marriage has God for its Author, and was from the very beginning a kind of foreshadowing of the Incarnation of His Son; and therefore there abides in it a something holy and religious; not extraneous, but innate; not derived from men, but implanted by nature. Innocent III, therefore, and Honorius III, our predecessors, affirmed not falsely nor rashly that a sacrament of marriage existed ever amongst the faithful and unbelievers.[33] We call to witness the monuments of antiquity, as also the manners and customs of those people who, being the most civilized, had the greatest knowledge of law and equity. In the minds of all of them it was a fixed and foregone conclusion that, when marriage was thought of, it was thought of as conjoined with religion and holiness. Hence, among those, marriages were commonly celebrated with religious ceremonies, under the authority of pontiffs, and with the ministry of priests. So mighty, even in the souls ignorant of heavenly doctrine, was the force of nature, of the remembrance of their origin, and of the conscience of the human race. As, then, marriage is holy by its own power, in its own nature, and of itself, it ought not to be regulated and administered by the will of civil rulers, but by the divine authority of the Church which alone in sacred matters professes the office of teaching.

20. Next, the dignity of the sacrament must be considered, for through addition of the sacrament the marriages of Christians have become far the noblest of all matrimonial unions. But to decree and ordain concerning the sacrament is, by the will of Christ Himself, so much a part of the power and duty of the Church that it is plainly absurd to maintain that even the very smallest fraction of such power has been transferred to the civil ruler.

21. Lastly should be borne in mind the great weight and crucial test of history, by which it is plainly proved that the legislative and judicial authority of which We are speaking has been freely and constantly used by the Church, even in times when some foolishly suppose the head of the State either to have consented to it or connived at it. It would, for instance, be incredible and altogether absurd to assume that Christ our Lord condemned the long-standing practice of polygamy and divorce by authority delegated to Him by the procurator of the province, or the principal ruler of the Jews. And it would be equally extravagant to think that, when the Apostle Paul taught that divorces and incestuous marriages were not lawful, it was because Tiberius, Caligula, and Nero agreed with him or secretly commanded him so to teach. No man in his senses could ever be persuaded that the Church made so many laws about the holiness and indissolubility of marriage,[34] and the marriages of slaves with the free-born,[35] by power received from Roman emperors, most hostile to the Christian name, whose strongest desire was to destroy by violence and murder the rising Church of Christ. Still less could anyone believe this to be the case, when the law of the Church was sometimes so divergent from the civil law that Ignatius the Martyr,[36] Justin,[37] Athenagoras,[38] and Tertullian[39] pub-

licly denounced as unjust and adulterous certain marriages which had been sanctioned by imperial law.

22. Futhermore, after all power had devolved upon the Christian emperors, the supreme pontiffs and bishops assembled in council persisted with the same independence and consciousness of their right in commanding or forbidding in regard to marriage whatever they judged to be profitable or expedient for the time being, however much it might seem to be at variance with the laws of the State. It is well known that, with respect to the impediments arising from the marriage bond, through vow, disparity of worship, blood relationship, certain forms of crime, and from previously plighted troth, many decrees were issued by the rulers of the Church at the Councils of Granada,[40] Arles,[41] Chalcedon,[42] the second of Milevum,[43] and others, which were often widely different from the decrees sanctioned by the laws of the empire. Futhermore, so far were Christian princes from arrogating any power in the matter of Christian marriage that they on the contrary acknowledged and declared that it belonged exclusively in all its fullness to the Church. In fact, Honorius, the younger Theodosius, and Justinian,[44] also, hesitated not to confess that the only power belonging to them in relation to marriage was that of acting as guardians and defenders of the holy canons. If at any time they enacted anything by their edicts concerning impediments of marriage, they voluntarily explained the reason, affirming that they took it upon themslves so to act, by leave and authority of the Church,[45] whose judgment they were wont to appeal to and reverently to accept in all questions that concerned legitimacy[46] and divorce;[47] as also in all those points which in any way have a necessary connection with the marriage bond.[48] The Council of Trent, therefore, had the clearest right to define that it is in the Church's power "to establish diriment impediments of matrimony,"[49] and that "matrimonial causes pertain to ecclesiastical judges."[50]

23. Let no one, then, be deceived by the distinction which some civil jurists have so strongly insisted upon – the distinction, namely, by virtue of which they sever the matrimonial contract from the sacrament, with intent to hand over the contract to the power and will of the rulers of the State, while reserving questions concerning the sacrament of the Church. A distinction, or rather severance, of this kind cannot be approved; for certain it is that in Christian marriage the contract is inseparable from the sacrament, and that, for this reason, the contract cannot be true and legitimate without being a sacrament as well. For Christ our Lord added to marriage the dignity of a sacrament; but marriage is the contract itself, whenever that contract is lawfully concluded.

24. Marriage, moreover, is a sacrament, because it is a holy sign which gives grace, showing forth an image of the mystical nuptials of Christ with the Church. But the form and image of these nuptials is shown precisely by the very bond of that most close union in which man and woman are bound together in one; which bond is nothing else but the marriage itself. Hence it is clear that among Christians every true marriage is, in itself and by itself, a sacrament; and that nothing can be further from the truth than to say that the sacrament is a certain added ornament, or

outward endowment, which can be separated and torn away from the contract at the caprice of man. Neither, therefore, by reasoning can it be shown, nor by any testimony of history be proved, that power over the marriages of Christians has ever lawfully been handed over to the rulers of the State. If, in this matter, the right of anyone else has ever been violated, no one can truly say that it has been violated by the Church. Would that the teaching of the naturalists, besides being full of falsehood and injustice, were not also the fertile source of much detriment and calamity! But it is easy to see at a glance the greatness of the evil which unhallowed marriages have brought, and ever will bring, on the whole of human society.

25. From the beginning of the world, indeed, it was divinely ordained that things instituted by God and by nature should be proved by us to be the more profitable and salutary the more they remain unchanged in their full integrity. For God, the Maker of all things, well knowing what was good for the institution and preservation of each of His creatures, so ordered them by His will and mind that each might adequately attain the end for which it was made. If the rashness or the wickedness of human agency venture to change or disturb that order of things which has been constituted with fullest foresight, then the designs of infinite wisdom and usefulness begin either to be hurtful or cease to be profitable, partly because through the change undergone they have lost their power of benefiting, and partly because God chooses to inflict punishment on the pride and audacity of man. Now, those who deny that marriage is holy, and who relegate it, stripped of all holiness, among the class of common secular things, uproot thereby the foundations of nature, not only resisting the designs of Providence, but, so far as they can, destroying the order that God has ordained. No one, therefore, should wonder if from such insane and impious attempts there spring up a crop of evils pernicious in the highest degree both to the salvation of souls and to the safety of the commonwealth.

26. If, then, we consider the end of the divine institution of marriage, we shall see very clearly that God intended it to be a most fruitful source of individual benefit and of public welfare. Not only, in strict truth, was marriage instituted for the propagation of the human race, but also that the lives of husbands and wives might be made better and happier. This comes about in many ways: by their lightening each other's burdens through mutual help; by constant and faithful love; by having all their possessions in common; and by the heavenly grace which flows from the sacrament. Marriage also can do much for the good of families, for, so long as it is conformable to nature and in accordance with the counsels of God, it has power to strengthen union of heart in the parents; to secure the holy education of children; to temper the authority of the father by the example of the divine authority; to render children obedient to their parents and servants obedient to their masters. From such marriages as these the State may rightly expect a race of citizens animated by a good spirit and filled with reverence and love for God, recognizing it their duty to obey those who rule justly and lawfully, to love all, and to injure no one.

27. These many and glorious fruits were ever the product of marriage, so long as it retained those gifts of holiness, unity, and indissolubility from which proceeded all its fertile and saving power; nor can anyone doubt but that it would always have brought forth such fruits, at all times and in all places, had it been under the power and guardianship of the Church, the trustworthy preserver and protector of these gifts. But, now, there is a spreading wish to supplant natural and divine law by human law; and hence has begun a gradual extinction of that most excellent ideal of marriage which nature herself had impressed on the soul of man, and sealed, as it were, with her own seal; nay, more, even in Christian marriages this power, productive of so great good, has been weakened by the sinfulness of man. Of what advantage is it if a state can institute nuptials estranged from the Christian religion, which is the mother of all good, cherishing all sublime virtues, quickening and urging us to everything that is the glory of a lofty and generous soul? When the Christian religion is reflected and repudiated, marriage sinks of necessity into the slavery of man's vicious nature and vile passions, and finds but little protection in the help of natural goodness. A very torrent of evil has flowed from this source, not only into private families, but also into States. For, the salutary fear of God being removed, and there being no longer that refreshment in toil which is nowhere more abounding than in the Christian religion, it very often happens, as indeed is natural, that the mutual services and duties of marriage seem almost unbearable; and thus very many yearn for the loosening of the tie which they believe to be woven by human law and of their own will, whenever incompatibility of temper, or quarrels, or the violation of the marriage vow, or mutual consent, or other reasons induce them to think that it would be well to be set free. Then, if they are hindered by law from carrying out this shameless desire, they contend that the laws are iniquitous, inhuman, and at variance with the rights of free citizens; adding that every effort should be made to repeal such enactments, and to introduce a more humane code sanctioning divorce.

28. Now, however much the legislators of these our days may wish to guard themselves against the impiety of men such as we have been speaking of, they are unable to do so, seeing that they profess to hold and defend the very same principles of jurisprudence; and hence they have to go with the times, and render divorce easily obtainable. History itself shows this; for, to pass over other instances, we find that, at the close of the last century, divorces were sanctioned by law in that upheaval or, rather, as it might be called, conflagration in France, when society was wholly degraded by the abandoning of God. Many at the present time would fain have those laws reenacted, because they wish God and His Church to be altogether exiled and excluded from the midst of human society, madly thinking that in such laws a final remedy must be sought for that moral corruption which is advancing with rapid strides.

29. Truly, it is hardly possible to describe how great are the evils that flow from divorce. Matrimonial contracts are by it made variable; mutual kindness is weakened; deplorable inducements to unfaithfulness are supplied; harm is done to

the education and training of children; occasion is afforded for the breaking up of homes; the seeds of dissension are sown among families; the dignity of womanhood is lessened and brought low, and women run the risk of being deserted after having ministered to the pleasures of men. Since, then, nothing has such power to lay waste families and destroy the mainstay of kingdoms as the corruption of morals, it is easily seen that divorces are in the highest degree hostile to the prosperity of families and States, springing as they do from the depraved morals of the people, and, as experience shows us, opening out a way to every kind of evil-doing in public and in private life.

30. Further still, if the matter be duly pondered, we shall clearly see these evils to be the more especially dangerous, because, divorce once being tolerated, there will be no restraint powerful enough to keep it within the bounds marked out or presurmised. Great indeed is the force of example, and even greater still the might of passion. With such incitements it must needs follow that the eagerness for divorce, daily spreading by devious ways, will seize upon the minds of many like a virulent contagious disease, or like a flood of water bursting through every barrier. These are truths that doubtlessly are all clear in themselves, but they will become clearer yet if we call to mind the teachings of experience. So soon as the road to divorce began to be made smooth by law, at once quarrels, jealousies, and judicial separations largely increased; and such shamelessness of life followed that men who had been in favor of these divorces repented of what they had done, and feared that, if they did not carefully seek a remedy by repealing the law, the State itself might come to ruin. The Romans of old are said to have shrunk with horror from the first example of divorce, but ere long all sense of decency was blunted in their soul; the meager restraint of passion died out, and the marriage vow was so often broken that what some writers have affirmed would seem to be true – namely, women used to reckon years not by the change of consuls, but of their husbands. In like manner, at the beginning, Protestants allowed legalized divorces in certain although but few cases, and yet from the affinity of circumstances of like kind, the number of divorces increased to such extent in Germany, America, and elsewhere that all wise thinkers deplored the boundless corruption of morals, and judged the recklessness of the laws to be simply intolerable.

31. Even in Catholic States the evil existed. For whenever at any time divorce was introduced, the abundance of misery that followed far exceeded all that the framers of the law could have foreseen. In fact, many lent their minds to contrive all kinds of fraud and device, and by accusations of cruelty, violence, and adultery to feign grounds for the dissolution of the matrimonial bond of which they had grown weary; and all this with so great havoc to morals that an amendment of the laws was deemed to be urgently needed.

32. Can anyone, therefore, doubt that laws in favor of divorce would have a result equally baneful and calamitous were they to be passed in these our days? There exists not, indeed, in the projects and enactments of men any power to change the character and tendency with things have received from nature. Those

men, therefore, show but little wisdom in the idea they have formed of the well-being of the commonwealth who think that the inherent character of marriage can be perverted with impunity; and who, disregarding the sanctity of religion and of the sacrament, seem to wish to degrade and dishonor marriage more basely than was done even by heathen laws. Indeed, if they do not change their views, not only private families, but all public society, will have unceasing cause to fear lest they should be miserably driven into that general confusion and overthrow of order which is even now the wicked aim of socialists and communists. Thus we see most clearly how foolish and senseless it is to expect any public good from divorce, when, on the contrary, it tends to the certain destruction of society.

33. It must consequently be acknowledged that the Church has deserved exceedingly well of all nations by her ever watchful care in guarding the sanctity and the indissolubility of marriage. Again, no small amount of gratitude is owing to her for having, during the last hundred years, openly denounced the wicked laws which have grievously offended on this particular subject;[51] as well as for her having branded with anathema the baneful heresy obtaining among Protestants touching divorce and separation;[52] also, for having in many ways condemned the habitual dissolution of marriage among the Greeks;[53] for having declared invalid all marriages contracted upon the understanding that they may be at some future time dissolved;[54] and, lastly, for having, from the earliest times, repudiated the imperial laws which disastrously favored divorce.[55]

34. As often, indeed, as the supreme pontiffs have resisted the most powerful among rulers, in their threatening demands that divorces carried out by them should be confirmed by the Church, so often must we account them to have been contending for the safety, not only of religion, but also of the human race. For this reason all generations of men will admire the proofs of unbending courage which are to be found in the decrees of Nicholas I against Lothair; of Urban II and Paschal II against Philip I of France; of Celestine III and Innocent III against Alphonsus of Leon and Philip II of France; of Clement VII and Paul III against Henry VIII; and, lastly, of Pius VII, that holy and courageous pontiff, against Napoleon I, when at the height of his prosperity and in the fulness of his power. This being so, all rulers and administrators of the State who are desirous of following the dictates of reason and wisdom, and anxious for the good of their people, ought to make up their minds to keep the holy laws of marriage intact, and to make use of the proffered aid of the Church for securing the safety of morals and the happiness of families, rather than suspect her of hostile intention and falsely and wickedly accuse her of violating the civil law.

35. They should do this the more readily because the Catholic Church, though powerless in any way to abandon the duties of her office or the defence of her authority, still very greatly inclines to kindness and indulgence whenever they are consistent with the safety of her rights and the sanctity of her duties. Wherefore she makes no decrees in relation to marriage without having regard to the state of the body politic and the condition of the general public; and has besides more than

once mitigated, as far as possible, the enactments of her own laws when there were just and weighty reasons. Moreover, she is not unaware, and never calls in doubt, that the sacrament of marriage, being instituted for the preservation and increase of the human race, has a necessary relation to circumstances of life which, though connected with marriage, belong to the civil order, and about which the State rightly makes strict inquiry and justly promulgates decrees.

36. Yet, no one doubts that Jesus Christ, the Founder of the Church, willed her sacred power to be distinct from the civil power, and each power to be free and unshackled in its own sphere: with this condition, however – a condition good for both, and of advantage to all men – that union and concord should be maintained between them; and that on those questions which are, though in different ways, of common right and authority, the power to which secular matters have been entrusted should happily and becomingly depend on the other power which has in its charge the interests of heaven. In such arrangement and harmony is found not only the best line of action for each power, but also the most opportune and efficacious method of helping men in all that pertains to their life here, and to their hope of salvation hereafter. For, as We have shown in former encyclical letters,[56] the intellect of man is greatly ennobled by the Christian faith, and made better able to shun and banish all error, while faith borrows in turn no little help from the intellect; and in like manner, when the civil power is on friendly terms with the sacred authority of the Church, there accrues to both a great increase of usefulness. The dignity of the one is exalted, and so long as religion is its guide it will never rule unjustly; while the other receives help of protection and defence for the public good of the faithful.

37. Being moved, therefore, by these considerations, as We have exhorted rulers at other times, so still more earnestly We exhort them now, to concord and friendly feeling; and we are the first to stretch out Our hand to them with fatherly benevolence, and to offer to them the help of Our supreme authority, a help which is the more necessary at this time when, in public opinion, the authority of rulers is wounded and enfeebled. Now that the minds of so many are inflamed with a reckless spirit of liberty, and men are wickedly endeavoring to get rid of every restraint of authority, however legitimate it may be, the public safety demands that both powers should unite their strength to avert the evils which are hanging, not only over the Church, but also over civil society.

38. But, while earnestly exhorting all to a friendly union of will, and beseeching God, the Prince of peace, to infuse a love of concord into all hearts, We cannot, venerable brothers, refrain from urging you more and more to fresh earnestness, and zeal, and watchfulness, though we know that these are already very great. With every effort and with all authority, strive, as much as you are able, to preserve whole and undefiled among the people committed to your charge the doctrine which Christ our Lord taught us; which the Apostles, the interpreters of the will of God, have handed down; and which the Catholic Church has herself scrupulously guarded, and commanded to be believed in all ages by the faithful of Christ.

39. Let special care be taken that the people be well instructed in the precepts of Christian wisdom, so that they may always remember that marriage was not instituted by the will of man, but, from the very beginning, by the authority and command of God; that it does not admit of plurality of wives or husbands; that Christ, the Author of the New Covenant, raised it from a rite of nature to be a sacrament, and gave to His Church legislative and judicial power with regard to the bond of union. On this point the very greatest care must be taken to instruct them, lest their minds should be led into error by the unsound conclusions of adversaries who desire that the Church should be deprived of that power.

40. In like manner, all ought to understand clearly that, if there be any union of a man and a woman among the faithful of Christ which is not a sacrament, such union has not the force and nature of a proper marriage; that, although contracted in accordance with the laws of the State, it cannot be more than a rite or custom introduced by the civil law. Further, the civil law can deal with and decide those matters alone which in the civil order spring from marriage, and which cannot possibly exist, as is evident, unless there be a true and lawful cause of them, that is to say, the nuptial bond. It is of the greatest consequence to husband and wife that all these things should be known and well understood by them, in order that they may conform to the laws of the State, if there be no objection on the part of the Church; for the Church wishes the effects of marriage to be guarded in all possible ways, and that no harm may come to the children.

41. In the great confusion of opinions, however, which day by day is spreading more and more widely, it should further be known that no power can dissolve the bond of Christian marriage whenever this has been ratified and consummated; and that, of a consequence, those husbands and wives are guilty of a manifest crime who plan, for whatever reason, to be united in a second marriage before the first one has been ended by death. When, indeed, matters have come to such a pitch that it seems impossible for them to live together any longer, then the Church allows them to live apart, and strives at the same time to soften the evils of this separation by such remedies and helps as are suited to their condition; yet she never ceases to endeavor to bring about a reconciliation, and never despairs of doing so. But these are extreme cases; and they would seldom exist if men and women entered into the married state with proper dispositions, nor influenced by passion, but entertaining right ideas of the duties of marriage and of its noble purpose; neither would they anticipate their marriage by a series of sins drawing down upon them the wrath of God.

42. To sum up all in a few words, there would be a calm and quiet constancy in marriage if married people would gather strength and life from the virtue of religion alone, which imparts to us resolution and fortitude; for religion would enable them to bear tranquilly and even gladly the trials of their state, such as, for instance, the faults that they discover in one another, the difference of temper and character, the weight of a mother's cares, the wearing anxiety about the education of children, reverses of fortune, and the sorrows of life.

43. Care also must be taken that they do not easily enter into marriage with those who are not Catholics; for, when minds do not agree as to the observances of religion, it is scarcely possible to hope for agreement in other things. Other reasons also proving that persons should turn with dread from such marriages are chiefly these: that they give occasion to forbidden association and communion in religious matters; endanger the faith of the Catholic partner; are a hindrance to the proper education of the children; and often lead to a mixing up of truth and falsehood, and to the belief that all religions are equally good.

44. Lastly, since We well know that none should be excluded from Our charity, We commend, venerable brothers, to your fidelity and piety those unhappy persons who, carried away by the heat of passion, and being utterly indifferent to their salvation, live wickedly together without the bond of lawful marriage. Let your utmost care be exercised in bringing such persons back to their duty; and, both by your own efforts and by those of good men who will consent to help you, strive by every means that they may see how wrongly they have acted; that they may do penance; and that they may be induced to enter into a lawful marriage according to the Catholic rite.

45. You will at once see, venerable brothers, that the doctrine and precepts in relation to Christian marriage, which We have thought good to communicate to you in this letter, tend no less to the preservation of civil society than to the everlasting salvation of souls. May God grant that, by reason of their gravity and importance, minds may everywhere be found docile and ready to obey them! For this end let us all suppliantly, with humble prayer, implore the help of the Blessed and Immaculate Virgin Mary, that, our hearts being quickened to the obedience of faith, she may show herself our mother and our helper. With equal earnestness let us ask the princes of the Apostles, Peter and Paul, the destroyers of heresies, the sowers of the seed of truth, to save the human race by their powerful patronage from the deluge of errors that is surging afresh. In the meantime, as an earnest of heavenly gifts, and a testimony of Our special benevolence, We grant to you all, venerable brothers, and to the people confided to your charge, from the depths of Our heart, the apostolic benediction.

Given at St. Peter's in Rome, the tenth day of February, 1880, the third year of Our pontificate.

---

[1] Eph. 1:9-10.

[2] Matt. 19:5-6.

[3] Matt. 19:8.

[4] Jerome, *Epist.* 77, 3 (*PL* 22, 691).

[5] Arnobius, *Adversus Gentes,* 4 (*sic,* perhaps 1, 64).

[6] Dionysius Halicarnassus, lib, II, chs. 26-27 (see *Roman Antiquities,* tr. E. Cary, Loeb Classical Library, Harvard University Press, 1948, Vol. I, pp. 386-393).

[7] John 2.

[8] Matt. 19:9.

[9] Trid., sess. xxiv, *in principio* (that is, Council of Trent, *Canones et decreta*; the text is divided into sessions, chapters, and canons, i.e., decrees).

[10] Trid., sess. xxiv, cap. I, *De reformatione matrimonii.*

[11] Eph. 5:25-32.

[12] 1 Cor. 7:10-11.

[13] 1 Cor. 7:39.

[14] Eph. 5:32.

[15] Heb. 13:4.

[16] Eph. 2:19.

[17] *Catech. Rom.,* ch. 8.

[18] Eph. 5:23-24.

[19] Eph. 6:4.

[20] Acts 15:29.

[21] 1 Cor. 5:5.

[22] *Gnostics:* common name for several early sects claiming a Christian knowledge (gnosis) higher than faith. *Manichaeans:* disciples of the Persian Mani (or Manes, *c.* 216–276) who taught that everything goes back to two first principles, light and darkness, or good and evil. *Montanists:* disciples of Montanus (in Phrygia, last third of the second century), condemned marriage as a sinful institution. *Mormons:* sect founded in 1830 by Joseph Smith, which favored polygamy. *Saint-Simonians:* disciples of the French philosopher Saint-Simon (1760–1825) founder of a "new Christianity" based upon science instead of faith. *Phalansterians:* members of a phalanstery, that is, of a socialist community after the principles of Charles Fourier (1772–1837). *Communists:* supporters of a regime in which property belongs to the body politic, each member being supposed to work according to his capacity and to receive according to his wants; communism is usually associated with the name of Karl Marx (1818–1893).

[23] Cap. 1, *De conjug. serv. Corpus juris canonici,* ed. Friedberg (Leipzig, 1884), Part 2, cols. 691-692.

[24] Jerome, *Epist.* 77 (*PL* 22, 691).

[25] Can. *Intesfectores* and Canon *Admonere,* quaest. 2 *Corpus juris canonici* (Leipzig, 1879), Part 1, cols. 1152-1154.

[26] Saus. 30, quaest. 3, cap. 3, *De cognat. spirit.* (op. cit., Part 1, col. 1101).

[27] Cap. 8, *De consang. et affin.* (op. cit., Part 2, col. 703); cap 1, *De cognat. legali* (col. 696).

[28] Cap. 26, *De sponsal.* (op. cit., Part 2, col. 670); cap. 13 (col. 665); cap. 15 (col. 666); cap. 29 (col. 671); *De sponsalibus et matrimonio et alibi.*

[29] Cap. 1, *De convers. infid.* (op. cit., Part 2, col. 587); cap. 5, 6, *De eo qui duxit in matrim.* (cols. 688-689).

[30] Cap. 3, 5, 8, *De sponsal. et matr.* (op. cit., Part 2, cols. 661, 663). Trid., sess. xxiv, cap. *De reformatione matrimonii.*

[31] Cap. 7, *De divort.* (op. cit., Part 2, col. 722).

[32] Maintain the self-sufficiency of the natural order.

[33] Concerning Innocent III, see *Corpus juris canonici,* cap. 8, *De divort.,* ed. cit., Part 2, col. 723. Innocent III refers to 1 Cor. 7:13. Concerning Honorius III, see cap. ii, *De transact.,* (op. cit., Part 2, cal. 210).

[34] *Canones Apostolorum,* 16, 17, 18, ed. Fr. Lauchert, J.C.B. Mohr (Leipzig, 1896) p. 3.

[35] *Philosophumena* (Oxford, 1851), i.e., Hippolytus, *Refutation of All Heresies,* 9, 12 *(PG* 16, 3386D-3387A).

[36] *Epistela ad Polycarpum,* cap. 5 *(PG* 5, 723-724).

[37] *Apolog. Maj.,* 15 *(PG* 6, 349A, B).

[38] *Legat. pro Christian.,* 32, 33 *(PG* 6, 963-968).

[39] *De coron. milit.,* 13 *(PL* 2, 116).

[40] De Aguirre, *Conc. Hispan.,* Vol. 1, can. 11.

[41] Harduin, *Act. Concil.,* Vol. 1, can. 11.

[42] Ibid., can. 16.

[43] Ibid., can. 17.

[44] *Novel.,* 137 Justinianus, *Novellae,* ed. C.E.Z. Lingenthal, Leipzig, 1881, Vol. 2, p. 206).

[45] Fejer, *Matrim. es instit. Chris.* (Pest, 1835).

[46] Cap. 3, *De ord. cogn. (Corpus juris canonici,* ed. cit., Part 2, col. 276).

[47] Cap. 3, *De divort.* (ed. cit., Part 2, col. 720).

[48] Cap. 13, *Qui filii sint legir. legit.* Part 2, col. 716).

[49] Trid., sess. xxiv, can. 4.

[50] Ibid., can. 12.

[51] Pius VI, *Epist. ad episc. Lucion.,* May 20, 1793; Pius VII, encycl. letter, Feb. 17, 1809, and constitution given July 19, 1817; Pius VIII, encycl. letter, May 29, 1829; Gregory XVI, constitution given August 15, 1832; Pius IX, address, Sept. 22, 1852.

[52] Trid., sess. xxiv, can. 5, 7.

[53] Council of Florence and instructions of Eugene IV to the Armenians; Benedict XIV, constitution *Etsi Pastoralis,* May 6, 1742.

[54] Cap. 7, *De condit. appos. (Corpus juris canonici,* ed. cit., Part 2, col. 684).

[55] Jerome, *Epist. 69, ad Oceanum (PL* 22, 657); Ambrose, Lib. 8 in cap. 16 Lucae, n. 5 *(PL* 15, 1857); Augustine, De nuptiis, 1, 10, 11 *(PL* 44, 420). Fifty years after the publication of *Arcanum,* Pope Pius XI published his own encyclical *Casti Connubii* (December 31, 1930), which may be found translated, with notes and bibliography, in J. Husslein, S.J., *Social Wellsprings,* Vol. II, pp. 122-173; also in pamphlet form, translated by Canon G.D. Smith, Catholic Truth Society of London; Paulist Press, New York; with a discussion club outline by Gerald C. Treacey, S.J.; National Catholic Welfare Conference, Washington, 1939. These pontifical acts should be completed by two addresses given by Pope Pius XII (October 29, 1951, and November 26, 1951), English translation published in pamphlet form by the National Catholic Welfare Conference under the title, *Moral Questions Affecting Married Life,* with a discussion outline by Edgar Schmiedeler, O.S.B.

[56] *Aeterni Patris,* above, pp. 38-39.

13.

CASTI CONNUBII

Encyclical Letter on Christian Marriage
Pope Pius XI
December 31, 1930

To Our Venerable Brethren, Patriarchs, Primates, Archbishops, Bishops, and Other Local Ordinaries Enjoying Peace and Communion with the Apostolic See

In View of the Present Conditions, Needs, Errors and Vices That Affect the Family and Society

Venerable Brethren and Beloved Children

Health and Apostolic Benediction

1. How great is the dignity of chaste wedlock, Venerable Brethren, may be judged best from this that Christ our Lord, Son of the Eternal Father, having assumed the nature of fallen man, not only, with His loving desire of compassing the redemption of our race, ordained it in an especial manner as the principle and foundation of domestic society and therefore of all human intercourse, but also raised it to the rank of a truly and great sacrament of the New Law, restored it to the original purity of its divine institution, and accordingly entrusted all its discipline and care to His spouse the Church.

2. In order, however, that amongst men of every nation and every age the desired fruits may be obtained from this renewal of matrimony, it is necessary, first of all, that men's minds be illuminated with the true doctrine of Christ regarding it; and secondly, that Christian spouses, the weakness of their wills strengthened by the internal grace of God, shape all their ways of thinking and of acting in conformity with that pure law of Christ so as to obtain true peace and happiness for themselves and for their families.

3. Yet not only do We, looking with paternal eye on the universal world from this Apostolic See as from a watchtower, but you, also, Venerable Brethren, see, and seeing deeply grieve with Us that a great number of men, forgetful of that divine work of redemption, either entirely ignore or shamelessly deny the great sanctity of Christian wedlock, or relying on the false principles of a new and utterly perverse morality, too often trample it under foot. And since these most pernicious errors and depraved morals have begun to spread even amongst the faithful and are

gradually gaining ground, in Our office as Christ's Vicar upon earth and Supreme Shepherd and Teacher We consider it Our duty to raise Our voice to keep the flock committed to Our care from poisoned pastures and, as far as in Us lies, to preserve it from harm.

4. We have decided therefore to speak to you, Venerable Brethren, and through you to the whole Church of Christ and indeed to the whole human race, on the nature and dignity of Christian marriage, on the advantages and benefits which accrue from it to the family and to human society itself, on the errors contrary to this most important point of the Gospel teaching, on the vices opposed to conjugal union, and lastly on the principal remedies to be applied. In so doing We follow the footsteps of Our Predecessor, Leo XIII, of happy memory, whose Encyclical *Arcanum,*[1] published fifty years ago, We hereby confirm and make Our own, and while We wish to expound more fully certain points called for by the circumstances of our times, nevertheless We declare that, far from being obsolete, it retains its full force at the present day.

Divine Institution of Matrimony

5. And to begin with that same Encyclical, which is wholly concerned in vindicating the divine institution of matrimony, its sacramental dignity, and its perpetual stability, let it be repeated as an immutable and inviolable fundamental doctrine that matrimony was not instituted or restored by man but by God; not by man were the laws made to strengthen and confirm and elevate it but by God, the Author of nature, and by Christ our Lord by whom nature was redeemed, and hence these laws cannot be subject to any human decrees or to any contrary pact even of the spouses themselves. This is the doctrine of Holy Scripture;[2] this is the constant tradition of the Universal Church; this the solemn definition of the sacred Council of Trent, which declares and establishes from the words of Holy Writ itself that God is the Author of the perpetual stability of the marriage bond, its unity and its firmness.[3]

Nature of the Contact

6. Yet, although matrimony is of its very nature of divine institution, the human will, too, enters into it and performs a most noble part. For each individual marriage, inasmuch as it is a conjugal union of a particular man and woman, arises only from the free consent of each of the spouses; and this free act of the will, by which each party hands over and accepts those rights proper to the state of marriage,[4] is so necessary to constitute true marriage that it cannot be supplied by any human power.[5] This freedom, however, regards only the question whether the contracting parties really wish to enter upon matrimony or to marry this particular person; but the nature of matrimony is entirely independent of the free will of man, so that if one has once contracted matrimony he is thereby subject to its divinely made laws and its essential properties. For the Angelic Doctor, writing on conjugal honor and on the offspring which is the fruit of marriage, says: "These things are so contained in matrimony by the marriage pact itself that, if anything to the contrary

were expressed in the consent which makes the marriage, it would not be a true marriage."[6]

7. By matrimony, therefore, the souls of the contracting parties are joined and knit together more directly and more intimately than are their bodies, and that not by any passing affection of sense or spirit, but by a deliberate and firm act of the will; and from this union of souls by God's decree, a sacred and inviolable bond arises. Hence the nature of this contract, which is proper and peculiar to it alone, makes it entirely different both from the union of animals entered into by the blind instinct of nature alone in which neither reason nor free will plays a part, and also from the haphazard unions of men, which are far removed from all true and honorable unions of will and enjoy none of the rights of family life.

8. From this it is clear that legitimately constituted authority has the right and therefore the duty to restrict, to prevent, and to punish those base unions which are opposed to reason and to nature; but since it is a matter which flows from human nature itself, no less certain is the teaching of Our Predecessor, Leo XIII, of happy memory:[7] "In choosing a state of life there is no doubt but that it is in the power and discretion of each one to prefer one or the other: either to embrace the counsel of virginity given by Jesus Christ, or to bind himself in the bonds of matrimony. To take away from man the natural and primeval right of marriage, to circumscribe in any way the principles of marriage laid down in the beginning by God Himself, the words 'Increase and multiply,'[8] is beyond the power of any human law."

9. Therefore the sacred partnership of true marriage is constituted both by the will of God and the will of man. From God comes the very institution of marriage, the ends for which it was instituted, the laws that govern it, the blessings that flow from it; while man, through generous surrender of his own person made to another for the whole span of life, becomes, with the help and co-operation of God, the author of each particular marriage, with the duties and blessings annexed thereto from divine institution.

I

Blessings of Matrimony

10. Now when We come to explain, Venerable Brethren, what are the blessings that God has attached to true matrimony, and how great they are, there occur to Us the words of that illustrious Doctor of the Church whom We commemorated recently in Our Encyclical *Ad salutem* on the occasion of the fifteenth centenary of his death:[9] "These," says St. Augustine, "are all the blessings of matrimony on account of which matrimony itself is a blessing; offspring, conjugal faith and the sacrament."[10] And how under these three heads is contained a splendid summary of the whole doctrine of Christian marriage, the holy Doctor himself expressly declares when he said: "By conjugal faith it is provided that there should be no carnal intercourse outside the marriage bond with another man or woman; with regard to offspring, the children should be begotten of love, tenderly cared for and educated in a religious atmosphere; finally, in its sacramental aspect that the

marriage bond should not be broken and that a husband and wife, if separated, should not be joined to another even for the sake of offspring. This we regard as the law of marriage by which the fruitfulness of nature is adorned and the evil of incontinence is restrained."[11]

The Child

11. Thus amongst the blessings of marriage, the child holds the first place. And indeed the Creator of the human race Himself, who in His goodness wished to use men as His helpers in the propagation of life, taught this when, instituting marriage in Paradise, He said to our first parents, and through them to all future spouses: "Increase and multiply, and fill the earth."[12] As St. Augustine admirably deduces from the words of the holy Apostle Saint Paul to Timothy[13] when he says: "The Apostle himself is therefore a witness that marriage is for the sake of generation: 'I wish,' he says, 'young girls to marry.' And, as if someone said to him, 'Why?,' he immediately adds: 'To bear children, to be mothers of families.'"[14]

12. How great a boon of God this is, and how great a blessing of matrimony is clear from a consideration of man's dignity and of his sublime end. For man surpasses all other visible creatures by the superiority of his rational nature alone. Besides, God wishes men to be born not only that they should live and fill the earth, but much more that they may be worshipers of God, that they may know Him and love Him and finally enjoy Him forever in heaven; and this end, since man is raised by God in a marvelous way to the supernatural order, surpasses all that eye hath seen, and ear heard, and all that hath entered into the heart of man.[15] From which it is easily seen how great a gift of divine goodness and how remarkable a fruit of marriage are children born by the omnipotent power of God through the co-operation of those bound in wedlock.

13. But Christian parents must also understand that they are destined not only to propagate and preserve the human race on earth, indeed, not only to educate any kind of worshipers of the true God, but children who are to become members of the Church of Christ, to raise up fellow citizens of the Saints, and members of God's household,[16] that the worshipers of God and Our Saviour may daily increase.

14. For, although Christian spouses even if sanctified themselves cannot transmit sanctification to their progeny, nay, although the very natural process of generating life has become the way of death by which original sin is passed on to posterity, nevertheless, they share to some extent in the blessings of that primeval marriage of Paradise, since it is theirs to offer their offspring to the Church in order that by this most fruitful Mother of the children of God they may be regenerated through the layer of Baptism unto supernatural justice and finally be made living members of Christ, partakers of immortal life, and heirs of that eternal glory to which we all aspire from our inmost heart.

15. If a true Christian mother weigh well these things, she will indeed understand with a sense of deep consolation that of her the words of Our Saviour were spoken: "A woman . . . when she hath brought forth the child remembereth no

more the anguish, for joy that a man is born into the world";[17] and proving herself superior to all the pains and cares and solicitudes of her maternal office with a more just and holy joy than that of the Roman matron, the mother of the Gracchi, she will rejoice in the Lord crowned as it were with the glory of her offspring. Both husband and wife, however, receiving these children with joy and gratitude from the hand of God, will regard them as a talent committed to their charge by God, not only to be employed for their own advantage or for that of an earthly commonwealth, but to be restored to God with interest on the day of reckoning.

Education of Children

16. The blessing of offspring, however, is not completed by the mere begetting of them, but something else must be added, namely the proper education of the offspring. For the most wise God would have failed to make sufficient provision for children that had been born, and so for the whole human race, if He had not given to those to whom He had entrusted the power and right to beget them, the power also and the right to educate them. For no one can fail to see that children are incapable of providing wholly for themselves, even in matters pertaining to their natural life, and much less in those pertaining to the supernatural, but require for many years to be helped, instructed, and educated by others. Now it is certain that both by the law of nature and of God this right and duty of educating their offspring belongs in the first place to those who began the work of nature by giving them birth, and they are indeed forbidden to leave unfinished this work and so expose it to certain ruin. But in matrimony provision has been made in the best possible way for this education of children that is so necessary, for, since the parents are bound together by an indissoluble bond, the care and mutual help of each is always at hand.

17. Since, however, We have spoken fully elsewhere on the Christian education of youth,[18] let Us sum it all up by quoting once more the words of St. Augustine: "As regards the offspring it is provided that they should be begotten lovingly and educated religiously,"[19] – and this is also expressed succinctly in the Code of Canon Law – "The primary end of marriage is the procreation and the education of children."[20]

18. Nor must We omit to remark, in fine, that since the duty entrusted to parents for the good of their children is of such high dignity and of such great importance, every use of the faculty given by God for the procreation of new life is the right and the privilege of the married state alone, by the law of God and of nature, and must be confined absolutely within the sacred limits of that state.

19. The second blessing of matrimony which We said was mentioned by St. Augustine, is the blessing of conjugal honor which consists in the mutual fidelity of the spouses in fulfilling the marriage contract, so that what belongs to one of the parties by reason of this contract sanctioned by divine law, may not be denied to him or permitted to any third person; nor may there be conceded to one of the parties anything which, being contrary to the rights and laws of God and entirely opposed to matrimonial faith, can never be conceded.

20. Wherefore, conjugal faith, or honor, demands in the first place the complete unity of matrimony which the Creator Himself laid down in the beginning when He wished it to be not otherwise than between one man and one woman. And although afterwards this primeval law was relaxed to some extent by God, the Supreme Legislator, there is no doubt that the law of the Gospel fully restored that original and perfect unity, and abrogated all dispensations as the words of Christ and the constant teaching and action of the Church show plainly. With reason, therefore, does the Sacred Council of Trent solemnly declare: "Christ Our Lord very clearly taught that in this bond two persons only are to be united and joined together when He said: 'Therefore they are no longer two, but one flesh'."[21]

21. Nor did Christ Our Lord wish only to condemn any form of polygamy or polyandry, as they are called, whether successive or simultaneous, and every other external dishonorable act, but, in order that the sacred bonds of marriage may be guarded absolutely inviolate, He forbade also even willful thoughts and desires of such like things: "But I say to you, that whosoever shall look on a woman to lust after her hath already committed adultery with her in his heart."[22] Which words of Christ Our Lord cannot be annulled even by the consent of one of the partners of marriage for they express a law of God and of nature which no will of man can break or bend.[23]

22. Nay, that mutual familiar intercourse between the spouses themselves, if the blessing of conjugal faith is to shine with becoming splendor, must be distinguished by chastity so that husband and wife bear themselves in all things with the law of God and of nature, and endeavor always to follow the will of their most wise and holy Creator with the greatest reverence toward the work of God.

23. This conjugal faith, however, which is most aptly called by St. Augustine the "faith of chastity" blooms more freely, more beautifully and more nobly, when it is rooted in that more excellent soil, the love of husband and wife which pervades all the duties of married life and holds pride of place in Christian marriage. For matrimonial faith demands that husband and wife be joined in an especially holy and pure love, not as adulterers love each other, but as Christ loved the Church. This precept the Apostle laid down when he said: "Husbands, love your wives as Christ also loved the Church,"[24] that Church which of a truth He embraced with a boundless love not for the sake of His own advantage, but seeking only the good of His Spouse.[25] The love, then, of which We are speaking is not that based on the passing lust of the moment nor does it consist in pleasing words only, but in the deep attachment of the heart which is expressed in action, since love is proved by deeds.[26] This outward expression of love in the home demands not only mutual help but must go further; must have as its primary purpose that man and wife help each other day by day in forming and perfecting themselves in the interior life, so that through their partnership in life they may advance ever more and more in virtue, and above all that they may grow in true love toward God and their neighbor, on which indeed "dependeth the whole Law and the Prophets."[27] For all men of every condition, in whatever honorable walk of life they may be, can and

ought to imitate that most perfect example of holiness placed before man by God, namely Christ Our Lord, and by God's grace to arrive at the summit of perfection, as is proved by the example set us of many saints.

24. This mutual inward moulding of husband and wife, this determined effort to perfect each other, can in a very real sense, as the Roman Catechism teaches, be said to be the chief reason and purpose of matrimony, provided matrimony be looked at not in the restricted sense as instituted for the proper conception and education of the child, but more widely as the blending of life as a whole and the mutual interchange and sharing thereof.

25. By this same love it is necessary that all the other rights and duties of the marriage state be regulated as the words of the Apostle: "Let the husband render the debt to the wife, and the wife also in like manner to the husband,"[28] express not only a law of justice but of charity.

26. Domestic society being confirmed, therefore, by this bond of love there should flourish in it that "order of love," as St. Augustine calls it. This order includes both the primacy of the husband with regard to the wife and children, the ready subjection of the wife and her willing obedience, which the Apostle commends in these words: "Let women be subject to their husbands as to the Lord, because the husband is the head of the wife, as Christ is the head of the Church."[29]

27. This subjection however does not deny or take away the liberty which fully belongs to the woman both in view of her dignity as a human person and in view of her most noble office as a wife and mother and companion; nor does it bid her obey her husband's every request if not in harmony with right reason or with the dignity due to wife; nor, in fine, does it imply that the wife should be put on a level with those persons who in law are called minors, to whom it is not customary to allow free exercise of their rights on account of their lack of mature judgment, or of their ignorance of human affairs. But it forbids that exaggerated liberty which cares not for the good of the family; it forbids that in this body which is the family, the heart be separated from the head to the great detriment of the whole body and the proximate danger of ruin. For if the man is the head, the woman is the heart, and as he occupies the chief place in ruling, so she may and ought to claim for herself the chief place in love.

28. Again, this subjection of wife to husband in its degree and manner may vary according to the different conditions of persons, place and time. In fact, if the husband neglect his duty, it falls to the wife to take his place in directing the family. But the structure of the family and its fundamental law, established and confirmed by God, must always and everywhere be maintained intact.

29. With great wisdom Our Predecessor Leo XIII, of happy memory, in the Encyclical on *Christian Marriage* which We have already mentioned, speaking of this order to be maintained between man and wife, teaches: "The man is the ruler of the family, and the head of the woman; but because she is flesh of his flesh and bone of his bone, let her be subject and obedient to the man, not as a servant but as

a companion, so that nothing be lacking of honor or of dignity in the obedience which she pays. Let divine charity be the constant guide of their mutual relations, both in him who rules and in her who obeys, since each bears the image, the one of Christ, the other of the Church."[30]

30. These, then, are the elements which compose the blessing of conjugal faith: unity, chastity, honorable noble obedience, which are at the same time an enumeration of the benefits which are bestowed on husband and wife in their married state, benefits by which the peace, the dignity and the happiness of matrimony are securely preserved and fostered. Wherefore it is not surprising that this conjugal faith has always been counted amongst the most priceless and special blessings of matrimony.

Indissolubility

31. But this accumulation of benefits is completed and, as it were, crowned by that blessing of Christian marriage which in the words of St. Augustine we have called the sacrament, by which is denoted both the indissolubility of the bond and the raising and hallowing of the contract by Christ Himself, whereby He made it an efficacious sign of grace.

32. In the first place Christ Himself lays stress on the indissolubility and firmness of the marriage bond when He says: "What God hath joined together let no man put asunder,"[31] and: "Everyone that putteth away his wife and marrieth another committeth adultery, and he that marrieth her that is put away from her husband committeth adultery."[32]

33. And St. Augustine clearly places what he calls the blessing of matrimony in this indissolubility when he says: "In the sacrament it is provided that the marriage bond should not be broken, and that a husband or wife, if separated, should not be joined to another even for the sake of offspring."[33]

34. And this inviolable stability, although not in the same perfect measure in every case, belongs to every true marriage, for the words of the Lord: "What God hath joined together let no man put asunder," must of necessity include all true marriages without exception, since it was spoken of the marriage of our first parents, the prototype of every future marriage. Therefore, although before Christ, the sublimeness and the severity of the primeval law was so tempered that Moses permitted to the chosen people of God on account of the hardness of their hearts that a bill of divorce might be given in certain circumstances, nevertheless, Christ, by virtue of His supreme legislative power, recalled this concession of greater liberty and restored the primeval law in its integrity by those words which must never be forgotten, "What God hath joined together let no man put asunder." Wherefore, Our Predecessor Pius VI, of happy memory, writing to the Bishop of Agria, most wisely said: "Hence it is clear that marriage even in the state of nature, and certainly long before it was raised to the dignity of a sacrament, was divinely instituted in such a way that it should carry with it a perpetual and indissoluble bond which cannot therefore be dissolved by any civil law. Therefore, although the

sacramental element may be absent from a marriage as is the case among unbelievers, still in such a marriage, inasmuch as it is a true marriage there must remain and
indeed there does remain that perpetual bond which by divine right is so bound up
with matrimony from its first institution that it is not subject to any civil power.
And so, whatever marriage is said to be contracted, either it is so contracted that it
is really a true marriage, in which case it carries with it that enduring bond which by
divine right is inherent in every true marriage; or it is thought to be contracted
without that perpetual bond, and in that case there is no marriage, but an illicit
union opposed of its very nature to the divine law, which therefore cannot be
entered into or maintained."[34]

A Perpetual Bond

35. And if this stability seems to be open to exception, however rare the
exception may be, as in the case of certain natural marriages between unbelievers,
or amongst Christians in the case of those marriages which though valid have not
been consummated, that exception does not depend on the will of men nor on that
of any merely human power, but on divine law, of which the only guardian and
interpreter is the Church of Christ. However, not even this power can ever affect for
any cause whatsoever a Christian marriage which is valid and has been consummated, for as it is plain that here the marriage contract has its full completion, so, by
the will of God, there is also the greatest firmness and indissolubility which may
not be destroyed by any human authority.

36. If we wish with all reverence to inquire into the intimate reason of this
divine decree, Venerable Brethren, we shall easily see it in the mystical signification of Christian marriage which is fully and perfectly verified in consummated
marriage between Christians. For, as the Apostle says in his Epistle to the
Ephesians,[35] the marriage of Christians recalls that most perfect union which exists
between Christ and the Church: "Sacramentum hoc magnum est, ego autem dico,
in Christo et in ecclesia"; which union, as long as Christ shall live and the Church
through Him, can never be dissolved by any separation. And this St. Augustine
clearly declares in these words: "This is safeguarded in Christ and the Church,
which, living with Christ who lives forever, may never be divorced from Him. The
observance of this sacrament is such in the City of God . . . that is, in the Church of
Christ, that when for the sake of begetting children, women marry or are taken to
wife, it is wrong to leave a wife that is sterile in order to take another by whom
children may be had. Anyone doing this is guilty of adultery, just as if he married
another, guilty not by the law of the day, according to which when one's partner is
put away another may be taken, which the Lord allowed in the law of Moses
because of the hardness of hearts of the people of Israel; but by the law of the
Gospel."[36]

Benefits Derived

37. Indeed, how many and how important are the benefits which flow from the
indissolubility of matrimony cannot escape anyone who gives even a brief consid-

eration either to the good of the married parties and the offspring or to the welfare of human society. First of all, both husband and wife possess a positive guarantee of the endurance of this stability which that generous yielding of their persons and the intimate fellowship of their hearts by this nature strongly require, since true love never falls away.[37] Besides, a strong bulwark is set up in defense of a loyal chastity against incitements to infidelity, should any be encountered either from within or from without; any anxious fear lest in adversity or old age the other spouse would prove unfaithful is precluded and in its place there reigns a calm sense of security. Moreover, the dignity of both man and wife is maintained and mutual aid is most satisfactorily assured, while through the indissoluble bond, always enduring, the spouses are warned continuously that not for the sake of perishable things nor that they may serve their passions, but that they may procure one for the other high and lasting good have they entered into the nuptial partnership, to be dissolved only by death. In the training and education of children, which must extend over a period of many years, it plays a great part, since the grave and long enduring burdens of this office are best borne by the united efforts of the parents. Nor do lesser benefits accrue to human society as a whole. For experience has taught that unassailable stability in matrimony is a fruitful source of virtuous life and of habits of integrity. Where this order of things obtains, the happiness and well-being of the nation is safely guarded; what the families and individuals are, so also is the State, for a body is determined by its parts. Wherefore, both for the private good of husband, wife and children, as likewise for the public good of human society, they indeed deserve well who strenuously defend the inviolable stability of matrimony.

Sacramental Grace

38. But considering the benefits of the sacrament, besides the firmness and indissolubility, there are also much higher emoluments as the word "sacrament" itself very aptly indicates; for to Christians this is not a meaningless and empty name. Christ the Lord, the Institutor and "Perfecter" of the holy sacraments,[38] by raising the matrimony of His faithful to the dignity of a true sacrament of the New Law, made it a sign and source of that peculiar internal grace by which "it perfects natural love, it confirms an indissoluble union, and sanctifies both man and wife."[39]

39. And since the valid matrimonial consent among the faithful was constituted by Christ as a sign of grace, the sacramental nature is so intimately bound up with Christian wedlock that there can be no true marriage between baptized persons "without it being by that very fact a sacrament."[40]

40. By the very fact, therefore, that the faithful with sincere mind give such consent, they open up for themselves a treasure of sacramental grace from which they draw supernatural power for the fulfilling of their rights and duties faithfully, holily, perseveringly even unto death. Hence this sacrament not only increases sanctifying grace, the permanent principle of the supernatural life, in those who, as the expression is, place no obstacle *(obex)* in its way, but also adds particular gifts,

dispositions, seeds of grace, by elevating and perfecting the natural powers. By these gifts the parties are assisted not only in understanding, but in knowing intimately, in adhering to firmly, in willing effectively, and in successfully putting into practice, those things which pertain to the marriage state, its aims and duties, giving them in fine right to the actual assistance of grace, whensoever they need it for fulfilling the duties of their state.

41. Nevertheless, since it is a law of divine Providence in the supernatural order that men do not reap the full fruit of the sacraments which they receive after acquiring the use of reason unless they co-operate with grace, the grace of matrimony will remain for the most part an unused talent hidden in the field unless the parties exercise these supernatural powers and cultivate and develop the seeds of grace they have received. If, however, doing all that lies within their power, they co-operate diligently, they will be able with ease to bear the burdens of their state and to fulfill their duties. By such a sacrament they will be strengthened, sanctified and in a manner consecrated. For, as St. Augustine teaches, just as by Baptism and Holy Orders a man is set aside and assisted either for the duties of Christian life or for the priestly office and is never deprived of their sacramental aid, almost in the same way (although not by a sacramental character), the faithful once joined by marriage ties can never be deprived of the help and the binding force of the sacrament. Indeed, as the Holy Doctor adds, even those who commit adultery carry with them that sacred yoke, although in this case not as a title to the glory of grace but for the ignominy of their guilty action, "as the soul by apostasy, withdrawing as it were from marriage with Christ, even though it may have lost its faith, does not lose the sacrament of Faith which it received at the laver of regeneration."[41]

42. These parties, let it be noted, not fettered but adorned by the golden bond of the sacrament, not hampered but assisted, should strive with all their might to the end that their wedlock, not only through the power and symbolism of the sacrament, but also through their spirit and manner of life, may be and remain always the living image of that most fruitful union of Christ with the Church, which is to be venerated as the sacred token of most perfect love.

43. All of these things, Venerable Brethren, you must consider carefully and ponder over with a lively faith if you would see in their true light the extraordinary benefits of matrimony on offspring, conjugal faith, and the sacrament. No one can fail to admire the divine Wisdom, Holiness and Goodness which, while respecting the dignity and happiness of husband and wife, has provided so bountifully for the conservation and propagation of the human race by a single, chaste and sacred fellowship of nuptial union.

II

Modern Fallacies

44. When we consider the great excellence of chaste wedlock, Venerable Brethren, it appears all the more regrettable that particularly in our day we should witness this divine institution often scorned and on every side degraded.

45. For now, alas, not secretly nor undercover, but openly, with all sense of shame put aside, now by word again by writings, by theatrical productions of every kind, by romantic fiction, by amorous and frivolous novels, by cinematographs portraying in vivid scene, in addresses broadcast by radio telephony, in short by all the inventions of modern science, the sanctity of marriage is trampled upon and derided, divorce, adultery, all the basest vices either are extolled or at least are depicted in such colors as to appear to be free of all reproach and infamy. Books are not lacking which dare to pronounce themselves as scientific but which in truth are merely coated with a veneer of science in order that they may the more easily insinuate their ideas. The doctrines defended in these are offered for sale as the productions of modern genius, of that genius namely, which, anxious only for truth, is considered to have *emancipated* itself from all those old-fashioned and immature opinions of the ancients; and to the number of these antiquated opinions they relegate the traditional doctrine of Christian marriage.

46. These thoughts are instilled into men of every class, rich and poor, masters and workers, lettered and unlettered, married and single, the godly and godless, old and young, but for these last, as easiest prey, the worst snares are laid.

47. Not all the sponsors of these new doctrines are carried to the extremes of unbridled lust; there are those who, striving as it were to ride a middle course, believe nevertheless that something should be conceded in our times as regards certain precepts of the divine and natural law. But these likewise, more or less wittingly, are emissaries of the great enemy who is ever seeking to sow cockle among the wheat.[42] We, therefore, whom the Father has appointed over His field, We who are bound by Our most holy office to take care lest the good seed be choked by the weeds, believe it fitting to apply to Ourselves the most grave words of the Holy Ghost with which the Apostle Paul exhorted his beloved Timothy: "Be thou vigilant . . . Fulfill thy ministry . . . Preach the word, be instant in season, out of season, reprove, entreat, rebuke in all patience and doctrine."[43]

Invention of Man

48. And since, in order that the deceits of the enemy may be avoided, it is necessary first of all that they be laid bare; since much is to be gained by denouncing these fallacies for the sake of the unwary, even though We prefer not to name these iniquities "as becometh saints,"[44] yet for the welfare of souls We cannot remain altogether silent.

49. To begin at the very source of these evils, their basic principle lies in this, that matrimony is repeatedly declared to be not instituted by the Author of nature nor raised by Christ the Lord to the dignity of a true sacrament, but invented by man. Some confidently assert that they have found no evidence for the existence of matrimony in nature or in her laws, but regard it merely as the means of producing life and gratifying in one way or another a vehement impulse; on the other hand, others recognize that certain beginnings or, as it were, seeds of true wedlock are found in the nature of man since, unless men were bound together by some form of

permanent tie, the dignity of husband and wife or the natural end of propagating and rearing the offspring would not receive satisfactory provision. At the same time they maintain that in all beyond this germinal idea matrimony, through various concurrent causes, is invented solely by the mind of man, established solely by his will.

50. How grievously all these err and how shamelessly they leave the ways of honesty is already evident from what We have set forth here regarding the origin and nature of wedlock, its purposes and the good inherent in it. The evil of this teaching is plainly seen from the consequences which its advocates deduce from it, namely, that the laws, institutions and customs by which wedlock is governed, since they take their origin solely from the will of men, are subject entirely to him, hence can and must be founded, changed and abrogated according to human caprice and the shifting circumstances of human affairs; that the generative power which is grounded in nature itself is more sacred and has wider range than matrimony – hence it may be exercised both outside as well as within the confines of wedlock, and though the purpose of matrimony be set aside, as though to suggest that the license of a base fornicating woman should enjoy the same rights as the chaste motherhood of a lawfully wedded wife.

Companionate Marriage

51. Armed with these principles, some men go so far as to concoct new species of unions, suited, as they say, to the present temper of men and the times, which various new forms of matrimony they presume to label "temporary," "experimental," and "companionate." These offer all the indulgence of matrimony and its rights without however, the indissoluble bond, and without offspring, unless later the parties alter their cohabitation into a matrimony in the full sense of the law.

52. Indeed there are some who desire and insist that these practices be legitimized by the law or, at least, excused by their general acceptance among the people. They do not seem even to suspect that these proposals partake of nothing of the modern "culture" in which they glory so much, but are simply hateful abominations which beyond all question reduce our truly cultured nations to the barbarous standards of savage peoples.

Birth Control

53. And now, Venerable Brethren, We shall explain in detail the evils opposed to each to the benefits of matrimony. First, consideration is due to the offspring, which many have the boldness to call the disagreeable burden of matrimony and which they say is to be carefully avoided by married people not through virtuous continence (which Christian law permits in matrimony when both parties consent) but by frustrating the marriage act. Some justify this criminal abuse on the ground that they are weary of children and wish to gratify their desires without their consequent burden. Others say that they cannot on the one hand remain continent nor on the other can they have children because of the difficulties whether on the part of the mother or on the part of family circumstances.

54. But no reason, however grave may be put forward by which anything intrinsically against nature may become conformable to nature and morally good. Since, therefore, the conjugal act is destined primarily by nature for the begetting of children, those who in exercising it deliberately frustrate its natural power and purpose sin against nature and commit a deed which is shameful and intrinsically vicious.

55. Small wonder, therefore, if Holy Writ bears witness that the Divine Majesty regards with greatest detestation this horrible crime and at times has punished it with death. As St. Augustine notes, "Intercourse even with one's legitimate wife is unlawful and wicked where the conception of the offspring is prevented. Onan, the son of Juda, did this and the Lord killed him for it."[45]

A Grave Sin

56. Since, therefore, openly departing from the uninterrupted Christian tradition some recently have judged it possible solemnly to declare another doctrine regarding this question, the Catholic Church, to whom God has entrusted the defense of the integrity and purity of morals, standing erect in the midst of the moral ruin which surrounds her, in order that she may preserve the chastity of the nuptial union from being defiled by this foul stain, raises her voice in token of her divine ambassadorship and through Our mouth proclaims anew: any use whatsoever of matrimony exercised in such a way that the act is deliberately frustrated in its natural power to generate life is an offense against the law of God and of nature, and those who indulge in such are branded with the guilt of a grave sin.

57. We admonish, therefore, priests who hear confessions and others who have the care of souls, in virtue of Our supreme authority and in Our solicitude for the salvation of souls, not to allow the faithful entrusted to them to err regarding this most grave law of God; much more, that they keep themselves immune from such false opinions, in no way conniving in them. If any confessor or pastor of souls, which may God forbid, lead the faithful entrusted to him into these errors or should at least confirm them by approval or by guilty silence, let him be mindful of the fact that he must render a strict account to God, the Supreme Judge, for the betrayal of his sacred trust, and let him take to himself the words of Christ: "They are blind and leaders of the blind: and if the blind lead the blind, both fall into the pit."[46]

58. As regards the evil use of matrimony, to pass over the arguments which are shameful, not infrequently others that are false and exaggerated are put forward. Holy Mother Church very well understands and clearly appreciates all that is said regarding the health of the mother and the danger to her life. And who would not grieve to think of these things? Who is not filled with the greatest admiration when he sees a mother risking her life with heroic fortitude, that she may preserve the life of the offspring which she has conceived? God alone, all bountiful and all merciful as He is, can reward her for the fulfillment of the office allotted to her by nature, and will assuredly repay her in a measure full to overflowing.[47]

59. Holy Church knows well that not infrequently one of the parties is sinned against rather than sinning, when for a grave cause he or she reluctantly allows the perversion of the right order. In such a case, there is no sin, provided that, mindful of the law of charity, he or she does not neglect to seek to dissuade and to deter the partner from sin. Nor are those considered as acting against nature who in the married state use their right in the proper manner, although on account of natural reasons either of time or of certain defects, new life cannot be brought forth. For in matrimony as well as in the use of the matrimonial rights there are also secondary ends, such as mutual aid, the cultivating of mutual love, and the quieting of concupiscence which husband and wife are not forbidden to consider so long as they are subordinated to the primary end and so long as the intrinsic nature of the act is preserved.

No Possible Excuse

60. We are deeply touched by the sufferings of those parents who, in extreme want, experience great difficulty in rearing their children.

61. However, they should take care lest the calamitous state of their external affairs should be occasion for a much more calamitous error. No difficulty can arise that justifies the putting aside of the law of God which forbids all acts intrinsically evil. There is no possible circumstance in which husband and wife cannot, strengthened by the grace of God, fulfill faithfully their duties and preserve in wedlock their chastity unspotted. This truth of Christian Faith is expressed by the teaching of the Council of Trent. "Let no one be so rash as to assert that which the Fathers of the Council have placed under anathema, namely, that there are precepts of God impossible for the just to observe. God does not ask the impossible, but by His commands, instructs you to do what you are able, to pray for what you are not able that He may help you."[48]

62. This same doctrine was again solemnly repeated and confirmed by the Church in the condemnation of the Jansenist heresy which dared to utter this blasphemy against the goodness of God: "Some precepts of God are, when one considers the powers which man possesses, impossible of fulfillment even to the just who wish to keep the law and strive to do so; grace is lacking whereby these laws could be fulfilled."[49]

"Thou Shalt Not Kill"

63. But another very grave crime is to be noted, Venerable Brethren, which regards the taking of the life of the offspring hidden in the mother's womb. Some wish it to be allowed and left to the will of the father or the mother; others say it is unlawful unless there are weighty reasons which they call by the name of medical, social, or eugenic "indication." Because this matter falls under the penal laws of the State by which the destruction of the offspring begotten but unborn is forbidden, these people demand that the "indication," which in one form or another they defend, be recognized as such by the public law and in no way penalized. There are those, moreover, who ask that the public authorities provide aid for these death-

dealing operations, a thing which, sad to say, everyone knows is of very frequent occurrence in some places.

64. As to the "medical and therapeutic indication" to which, using their own words, we have made reference, Venerable Brethren, however much we may pity the mother whose health and even life is gravely imperiled in the performance of the duty allotted to her by nature, nevertheless what could ever be a sufficient reason for excusing in any way the direct murder of the innocent? This is precisely what we are dealing with here. Whether inflicted upon the mother or upon the child, it is against the precept of God and the law of nature: "Thou shalt not kill";[50] The life of each is equally sacred, and no one has the power, not even the public authority, to destroy it. It is of no use to appeal to the right of taking away life for here it is a question of the innocent, whereas that right has regard only to the guilty; nor is there here question of defense by bloodshed against an unjust aggressor (for who would call an innocent child an unjust aggressor?); again there is no question here of what is called the "law of extreme necessity" which could never extend to the direct killing of the innocent. Upright and skillful doctors strive most praiseworthily to guard and preserve the lives of both mother and child; on the contrary, those show themselves most unworthy of the noble medical profession who encompass the death of one or the other, through a pretense at practicing medicine or through motives of misguided pity.

65. All of which agrees with the stern words of the Bishop of Hippo in denouncing those wicked parents who seek to remain childless, and failing in this, are not ashamed to put their offspring to death: "Sometimes this lustful cruelty or cruel lust goes so far as to seek to procure a baneful sterility, and if this fails the foetus conceived in the womb is in one way or another smothered or evacuated, in the desire to destroy the offspring before it has life, or if it already lives in the womb, to kill it before it is born. If both man and woman are party to such practices they are not spouses at all; and if from the first they have carried on thus they have come together not for honest wedlock, but for impure gratification; if both are not party to these deeds, I make bold to say that either the one makes herself a mistress of the husband, or the other simply the paramour of his wife."[51]

66. What is asserted in favor of the social and eugenic "indication" may and must be accepted, provided lawful and upright methods are employed within the proper limits; but to wish to put forward reasons based upon them for the killing of the innocent is unthinkable and contrary to the divine precept promulgated in the words of the Apostle: Evil is not to be done that good may come of it.[52]

67. Those who hold the reins of government should not forget that it is the duty of public authority by appropriate laws and sanctions to defend the lives of the innocent, and this all the more so since those whose lives are endangered and assailed cannot defend themselves. Among whom We must mention in the first place infants hidden in the mother's womb. And if the public magistrates not only do not defend them, but by their laws and ordinances betray them to death at the

hands of doctors or of others, let them remember that God is the Judge and Avenger of innocent blood which cries from earth to Heaven.[53]

Sterilization

68. Finally, that pernicious practice must be condemned which closely touches upon the natural right of man to enter matrimony but affects also in a real way the welfare of the offspring. For there are some who oversolicitous for the cause of eugenics, not only give salutary counsel for more certainly procuring the strength and health of the future child – which, in deed, is not contrary to right reason – but put eugenics before aims of a higher order, and by public authority wish to prevent from marrying all those whom, even though naturally fit for marriage, they consider, according to the norms and conjectures of their investigations, would, through hereditary transmission, bring forth defective offspring. And more, they wish to legislate to deprive these of that natural faculty by medical action despite their unwillingness; and this they do not propose as an inflection of grave punishment under the authority of the State for a crime committed, nor to prevent future crimes by guilty persons, but against every right and good they wish the civil authority to arrogate to itself a power over a faculty which it never had and can never legitimately possess.

69. Those who act in this way are at fault in losing sight of the fact that the family is more sacred than the State and that men are begotten not for the earth and for time, but for Heaven and eternity. Although often these individuals are to be dissuaded from entering into matrimony, certainly it is wrong to brand men with the stigma of crime because they contract marriage, on the ground that, despite the fact that they are in every respect capable of matrimony, they will give birth only to defective children, even though they use all care and diligence.

70. Public magistrates have no direct power over the bodies of their subjects; therefore, where no crime has taken place and there is no cause present for grave punishment, they can never directly harm, or tamper with the integrity of the body, either for the reasons of eugenics or for any other reason. St. Thomas teaches this when, inquiring whether human judges for the sake of preventing future evils can inflict punishment, he admits that the power indeed exists as regards certain other forms of evil, but justly and properly denies it as regards the maiming of the body. "No one who is guiltless may be punished by a human tribunal either by flogging to death, or mutilation, or by beating."[54]

71. Furthermore, Christian doctrine establishes, and the light of human reason makes it most clear, that private individuals have no other power over the members of their bodies than that which pertains to their natural ends; and they are not free to destroy or mutilate their members, or in any other way render themselves unfit for their natural functions, except when no other provision can be made for the good of the whole body.

72. We may now consider another class of errors concerning conjugal faith. Every sin committed as regards the offspring becomes in some way a sin against

conjugal faith, since both these blessings are essentially connected. However, We must mention briefly the sources of error and vice corresponding to those virtues which are demanded by conjugal faith, namely the chaste honor existing between man and wife, the due subjection of wife to husband, and the true love which binds both parties together.

Adultery Forbidden

73. It follows therefore that they are destroying mutual fidelity, who think that the ideas and morality of our present time concerning a certain harmful and false friendship with a third party can be countenanced, and who teach that a great freedom of feeling and action in such external relations should be allowed to man and wife, particularly as many (so they consider) are possessed of an inborn sexual tendency which cannot be satisfied within the narrow limits of monogamous marriage. That rigid attitude which condemns all sensual affections and actions with a third party they imagine to be a narrowing of mind and heart, something obsolete, or an abject form of jealousy, and as a result they look upon whatever penal laws are passed by the State for the preserving of conjugal faith as void or to be abolished. Such unworthy and idle opinions are condemned by that noble instinct which is found in every chaste husband and wife, and even by the light of the testimony of nature alone – a testimony that is sanctioned and confirmed by the command of God: "Thou shalt not commit adultery,"[55] and the words of Christ: "Whosoever shall look on a woman to lust after her hath already committed adultery with her in his heart."[56] The force of this divine precept can never be weakened by any merely human custom, bad example or pretext of human progress, for just as it is the one and the same "Jesus Christ, yesterday and today and the same forever,"[57] so it is the one and the same doctrine of Christ that abides and of which not one jot or tittle shall pass away till all is fulfilled.[58]

Emancipation of Women

74. The same false teachers who try to dim the luster of conjugal faith and purity do not scruple to do away with the honorable and trusting obedience which the woman owes to the man. Many of them even go further and assert that such a subjection of one party to the other is unworthy of human dignity, that the rights of husband and wife are equal; wherefore, they boldly proclaim, the emancipation of women has been or ought to be effected. This emancipation in their ideas must be threefold, in the ruling of the domestic society, in the administration of family affairs and in the rearing of the children. It must be social, economic, physiological: – physiological, that is to say, the woman is to be freed at her own good pleasure from the burdensome duties properly belonging to a wife as companion and mother (We have already said that this is not an emancipation but a crime); social, inasmuch as the wife being freed from the care of children and family, should, to the neglect of these, be able to follow her own bent and devote herself to business and even public affairs; finally economic, whereby the woman even without the knowledge and against the wish of her husband may be at liberty to conduct and

administer her own affairs, giving her attention chiefly to these rather than to children, husband and family.

75. This, however, is not the true emancipation of woman, nor that rational and exalted liberty which belongs to the noble office of a Christian woman and wife; it is rather the debasing of the womanly character and the dignity of motherhood, and indeed of the whole family, as a result of which the husband suffers the loss of his wife, the children of their mother, and the home and the whole family of an ever watchful guardian. More than this this false liberty and unnatural equality with the husband is to the detriment of the woman herself, for if the woman descends from her truly regal throne to which she has been raised within the walls of the home by means of the Gospel, she will soon be reduced to the old state of slavery (if not in appearance, certainly in reality) and become as amongst the pagans the mere instrument of man.

76. This equality of rights which is so much exaggerated and distorted, must indeed be recognized in those rights which belong to the dignity of the human soul and which are proper to the marriage contract and inseparably bound up with wedlock. In such things undoubtedly both parties enjoy the same rights and are bound by the same obligations; in other things there must be a certain inequality and due accommodation, which is demanded by the good of the family and the right ordering and unity and stability of home life.

77. As, however, the social and economic conditions of the married woman must in some way be altered on account of the changes in social intercourse, it is part of the office of the public authority to adapt the civil rights of the wife to modern needs and requirements, keeping in view what the natural disposition and temperament of the female sex, good morality, and the welfare of the family demands, and provided always that the essential order of the domestic society remain intact, founded as it is on something higher than human authority and wisdom, namely on the authority and wisdom of God, and so not changeable by public laws or at the pleasure of private individuals.

Incompatibility

78. These enemies of marriage go further, however, when they substitute for that true and solid love, which is the basis of conjugal happiness, a certain vague compatibility of temperament. This they call sympathy and assert that, since it is the only bond by which husband and wife are linked together, when it ceases the marriage is completely dissolved. What else is this than to build a house upon sand? – a house that in the words of Christ would forthwith be shaken and collapse, as soon as it was exposed to the waves of adversity "and the winds blew and they beat upon that house. And it fell: and great was the fall thereof."[59] On the other hand, the house built upon a rock, that is to say on mutual conjugal chastity and strengthened by a deliberate and constant union of spirit, will not only never fall away but will never be shaken by adversity.

79. We have so far, Venerable Brethren, shown the excellency of the first two blessings of Christian wedlock which the modern subverters of society are attacking. And now considering that the third blessing, which is that of the sacrament, far surpasses the other two, we should not be surprised to find that this, because of its outstanding excellence, is much more sharply attacked by the same people. They put forward in the first place that matrimony belongs entirely to the profane and purely civil sphere, that it is not to be committed to the religious society, the Church of Christ, but to civil society alone. They then add that the marriage contract is to be freed from any indissoluble bond, and that separation and divorce are not only to be tolerated but sanctioned by the law; from which it follows finally that, robbed of all its holiness, matrimony should be enumerated amongst the secular and civil institutions. The first point is contained in their contention that the civil act itself should stand for the marriage contract (civil matrimony, as it is called), while the religious act is to be considered a mere addition, or at most a concession to a too superstitious people. Moreover they want it to be no cause for reproach that marriages be contracted by Catholics with non-Catholics without any reference to religion or recourse to the ecclesiastical authorities. The second point, which is but a consequence of the first is to be found in their excuse for complete divorce and in their praise and encouragement of those civil laws which favor the loosening of the bond itself. As the salient features of the religious character of all marriage and particularly of the sacramental marriage of Christians have been treated at length and supported by weighty arguments in the encyclical letters of Leo XIII, letters which We have frequently recalled to mind and expressly made Our own. We refer you to them, repeating here only a few points.

Sacredness of Marriage

80. Even by the light of reason alone and particularly if the ancient records of history are investigated, if the unwavering popular conscience is interrogated and the manners and institutions of all races examined, it is sufficiently obvious that there is a certain sacredness and religious character attaching even to the purely natural union of man and woman, "not something added by chance but innate, not imposed by men but involved in the nature of things," since it has "God for its author and has been even from the beginning a foreshadowing of the Incarnation of the Word of God." [60] This sacredness of marriage which is intimately connected with religion and all that is holy, arises from the divine origin we have just mentioned, from its purpose which is the begetting and educating of children for God, and the binding of man and wife to God through Christian love and mutual support; and finally it arises from the very nature of wedlock, whose institution is to be sought for in the farseeing Providence of God, whereby it is the means of transmitting life, thus making the parents the ministers, as it were, of the Divine Omnipotence. To this must be added that new element of dignity which comes from the sacrament, by which the Christian marriage is so ennobled and raised to such a level, that it appeared to the Apostle as a great sacrament, honorable in every way.[61]

81. This religious character of marriage, its sublime signification of grace and the union between Christ and the Church, evidently requires that those about to marry should show a holy reverence toward it, and zealously endeavor to make their marriage approach as nearly as possible to the archetype of Christ and the Church.

Mixed Marriage

82. They, therefore, who rashly and heedlessly contract mixed marriages, from which the maternal love and providence of the Church dissuades her children for very sound reasons, fail conspicuously in this respect, sometimes with danger to their eternal salvation. This attitude of the Church to mixed marriages appears in many of her documents, all of which are summed up in the Code of Canon Law: "Everywhere and with the greatest strictness the Church forbids marriages between baptized persons, one of whom is a Catholic and the other a member of a schismatical or heretical sect; and if there is, add to this, the danger of the falling away of the Catholic party and the perversion of the children, such a marriage is forbidden also by the divine law."[62] If the Church occasionally on account of circumstances does not refuse to grant a dispensation from these strict laws (provided that the divine law remains intact and the dangers above mentioned are provided against by suitable safeguards), it is unlikely that the Catholic party will not suffer some detriment from such a marriage.

83. Whence it comes about not unfrequently, as experience shows, that deplorable defections from religion occur among the offspring, or at least a headlong descent into that religious indifference which is closely allied to impiety. There is this also to be considered that in these mixed marriages it becomes much more difficult to imitate by a lively conformity of spirit the mystery of which We have spoken, namely that close union between Christ and His Church.

84. Assuredly, also, will there be wanting that close union of spirit which as it is the sign and mark of the Church of Christ, so also should be the sign of Christian wedlock, its glory and adornment. For, where there exists diversity of mind, truth and feeling, the bond of union of mind and heart is wont to be broken, or at least weakened. From this comes the danger lest the love of man and wife grow cold and the peace and happiness of family life, resting as it does on the union of hearts, be destroyed. Many centuries ago indeed, the old Roman law had proclaimed: "Marriages are the union of male and female, a sharing of life – and the communication of divine and human rights."[63] But especially, as We have pointed out, Venerable Brethren, the daily increasing facility of divorce is an obstacle to the restoration of marriage to that state of perfection which the divine Redeemer willed it should possess.

Divorce

85. The advocates of the neopaganism of today have learned nothing from the sad state of affairs but instead, day by day, more and more vehemently, they continue by legislation to attack the indissolubility of the marriage bond, proclaim-

ing that the lawfulness of divorce must be recognized, and that the antiquated laws should give place to a new and more humane legislation. Many and varied are the grounds put forward for divorce, some arising from the wickedness and the guilt of the persons concerned, others arising from the circumstances of the case; the former they describe as subjective, the latter as objective; in a word, whatever might make married life hard or unpleasant. They strive to prove their contentions regarding these grounds for the divorce legislation they would bring about, by various arguments. Thus, in the first place, they maintain that it is for the good of either party that the one who is innocent should have the right to separate from the guilty, or that the guilty should be withdrawn from a union which is unpleasing to him and against his will. In the second place, they argue, the good of the child demands this, for either it will be deprived of a proper education or the natural fruits of it, and will too easily be affected by the discords and shortcomings of the parents, and drawn from the path of virtue. And thirdly the common good of society requires that these marriages should be completely dissolved, which are now incapable of producing their natural results, and that legal separations should be allowed when crimes are to be feared as the result of the common habitation and intercourse of the parties. This last, they say must be admitted to avoid the crimes being committed purposely with a view to obtaining the desired sentence of divorce for which the judge can legally loose the marriage bond, as also to prevent people from coming before the courts when it is obvious from the state of the case that they are lying and perjuring themselves – all of which brings the court and the lawful authority into contempt. Hence the civil laws, in their opinion, have to be reformed to meet these new requirements, to suit the changes of the times and the changes in men's opinions, civil institutions and customs. Each of these reasons is considered by them as conclusive, so that all taken together offer a clear proof of the necessity of granting divorce in certain cases.

86. Others, taking a step further, simply state that marriage, being a private contract, is, like other private contracts, to be left to the consent and good pleasure of both parties, and so can be dissolved for any reason whatsoever.

Unalterable Law of God

87. Opposed to all these reckless opinions, Venerable Brethren, stands the unalterable law of God, fully confirmed by Christ, a law that can never be deprived of its force by the decrees of men, the ideas of a people or the will of any legislator: "What God hath joined together, let no man put asunder." [64] And if any man, acting contrary to this law, shall have put asunder, his action is null and void, and the consequence remains, as Christ Himself has explicitly confirmed: "Everyone that putteth away his wife and marrieth another, committeth adultery; and he that marrieth her that is put away from her husband committeth adultery." [65] Moreover, these words refer to every kind of marriage, even that which is natural and legitimate only; for, as has already been observed, that indissolubility by which the loosening of the bond is once and for all removed from the whim of the parties and from every secular power, is a property of every true marriage.

88. Let that solemn pronouncement of the Council of Trent be recalled to mind in which, under the stigma of anathema, it condemned these errors: "If anyone should say that on account of heresy or the hardships of cohabitation or a deliberate abuse of one party by the other the marriage tie may be loosened, let him be anathema;"[66] and again: "If anyone should say that the Church errs in having taught or in teaching that, according to the teaching of the Gospel and the Apostles, the bond of marriage cannot be loosed because of the sin of adultery of either party; or that neither party, even though he be innocent, having given no cause for the sin of adultery, can contract another marriage during the lifetime of the other; and that he commits adultery who marries another after putting away his adulterous wife, and likewise that she commits adultery who puts away her husband and marries another: let him be anathema."[67]

89. If, therefore, the Church has not erred and does not err in teaching this, and consequently it is certain that the bond of marriage cannot be loosed even on account of the sin of adultery, it is evident that all the other weaker excuses that can be, and are usually brought forward, are of no value whatsoever. And the objections brought against the firmness of the marriage bond are easily answered. For, in certain circumstances, imperfect separation of the parties is allowed, the bond not being severed. This separation, which the Church herself permits, and expressly mentions in her Canon Law in those canons which deal with the separation of the parties as to marital relationship and cohabitation, removes all the alleged inconveniences and dangers.[68] It will be for the sacred law and, to some extent, also the civil law, in so far as civil matters are affected, to lay down the grounds, the conditions, the method and precautions to be taken in a case of this kind in order to safeguard the education of the children and the well-being of the family, and to remove all those evils which threaten the married persons, the children and the State. Now all those arguments that are brought forward to prove the indissolubility of the marriage tie, arguments which have already been touched upon, can equally be applied to excluding not only the necessity of divorce, but even the power to grant it; while for all the advantages that can be put forward for the former, there can be adduced as many disadvantages and evils which are a formidable menace to the whole of human society.

Divorce, a Menace to Society

90. To revert again to the expressions of Our Predecessor, it is hardly necessary to point out what an amount of good is involved in the absolute indissolubility of wedlock and what a train of evil follows upon divorce. Whenever the marriage bond remains intact, then we find marriages contracted with a sense of safety and security, while, when separations are considered and the dangers of divorce are present, the marriage contract itself becomes insecure, or at least gives ground for anxiety and surprises. On the one hand we see a wonderful strengthening of good will and co-operation in the daily life of husband and wife, while, on the other, both of these are miserably weakened by the presence of a facility for divorce. Here we have at a very opportune moment a source of help by which both parties are

enabled to preserve their purity and loyalty; there we find harmful inducements to unfaithfulness. On this side we find the birth of children and their tuition and upbringing effectively promoted, many avenues of discord closed amongst families and relations, and the beginnings of rivalry and jealousy easily suppressed; on that, very great obstacles to the birth and rearing of children and their education, and many occasions of quarrels, and seeds of jealousy sown everywhere. Finally, but especially, the dignity and position of women in civil and domestic society is reinstated by the former; while by the latter it is shamefully lowered and the danger is incurred "of their being considered outcasts, slaves of the lust of men."[69]

91. To conclude with the important words of Leo XIII, since the destruction of family life "and the loss of national wealth is brought about more by the corruption of morals than by anything else, it is easily seen that divorce, which is born of the perverted morals of a people, and leads, as experiments show to vicious habits in public and private life, is particularly opposed to the well-being of the family and of the State. The serious nature of these evils will be the more clearly recognized, when we remember that, once divorce has been allowed, there will be no sufficient means of keeping it in check within any definite bounds. Great is the force of example, greater still that of lust; and with such incitements it cannot but happen that divorce and its consequent setting loose of the passions should spread daily and attack the souls of many like a contagious disease or a river bursting its banks and flooding the land."[70]

92. Thus, as we read in the same letter, "unless things change, the human family and State have every reason to fear lest they should suffer absolute ruin."[71] All this was written fifty years ago, yet it is confirmed by the daily increasing corruption of morals and the unheard of degradation of the family in those lands where Communism reigns unchecked.

III

Suitable Remedies

93. Thus far, Venerable Brethren, We have admired with due reverence what the all wise Creator and Redeemer of the human race has ordained with regard to human marriage; at the same time We have expressed Our grief that such a pious ordinance of the divine Goodness should today, and on every side, be frustrated and trampled upon by the passions, errors and vices of men.

94. It is then fitting that with all fatherly solicitude, We should turn Our minds to seek out suitable remedies whereby those most detestable abuses which We have mentioned, may be removed, and everywhere marriage may again be revealed. To this end, it behooves Us, above all else, to call to mind that firmly established principle, esteemed alike in sound philosophy and sacred theology: namely, that whatever things have deviated from their right order, cannot be brought back to that original state which is in harmony with their nature except by a return to the divine plan which, as the Angelic Doctor teaches,[72] is the exemplar of all right order.

95. Wherefore, Our Predecessor of happy memory, Leo XIII, attacked the doctrine of the naturalists in these words: "It is a divinely appointed law that whatsoever things are constituted by God, the Author of nature, these we find the more useful and salutary, the more they remain in their natural state, unimpaired and unchanged; inasmuch as God, the Creator of all things, intimately knows what is suited to the constitution and the preservation of each, and by His will and mind has so ordained all things that each may duly achieve its purpose. But if the boldness and wickedness of men change and disturb this order of things, so providentially disposed, then, indeed, things so wonderfully ordained, will begin to be injurious, or will cease to be beneficial, either because, in the change, they have lost their power to benefit, or because God Himself is thus pleased to draw down chastisement on the pride and presumption of men."[73]

96. In order, therefore, to restore due order in this matter of marriage, it is necessary that all should bear in mind what is the divine plan and strive to conform to it.

The Divine Plan

97. Wherefore, since the chief obstacle to this study is the power of unbridled lust, which indeed is the most potent cause of sinning against the sacred laws of matrimony, and since man cannot hold in check his passions, unless he first subject himself to God, this must be his primary endeavor, in accordance with the plan divinely ordained. For it is a sacred ordinance that whoever shall have first subjected himself to God will, by the aid of divine grace, be glad to subject to himself his own passions and concupiscence; while he who is a rebel against God will, to his sorrow, experience within himself the violent rebellion of his worst passions.

98. And how wisely this has been decreed, St. Augustine thus shows: "This indeed is fitting; that the lower be subject to the higher, so that he who would have subject to himself whatever is below him, should himself submit to whatever is above him. Acknowledge order, seek peace. Be thou subject to God, and thy flesh subject to thee. What more fitting! What more fair! Thou art subject to the higher and the lower is subject to thee. Do thou serve Him who made thee, so that that which was made for thee may serve thee. For we do not commend this order, namely, 'The flesh to thee and thou to God,' but 'Thou to God, and the flesh to thee.' If, however, thou despisest the subjection of thyself to God, thou shalt never bring about the subjection of the flesh to thyself. If thou dost not obey the Lord, thou shalt be tormented by thy servant."[74] This right ordering on the part of God's wisdom is mentioned by the holy Doctor of the Gentiles, inspired by the Holy Ghost, for in speaking of those ancient philosophers who refused to adore and reverence Him whom they knew to be the Creator of the universe, he says: "Wherefore God gave them up to the desires of their heart, unto uncleanness, to dishonor their own bodies among themselves"; and again: "For this same God delivered them up to shameful affections."[75] And St. James says: "God resisteth the

proud and giveth grace to the humble,"[76] without which grace, as the same Doctor of the Gentiles reminds us, man cannot subdue the rebellion of his flesh.[77]

99. Consequently, as the onslaughts of these uncontrolled passions cannot in any way be lessened, unless the spirit first shows a humble compliance of duty and reverence toward its Maker, it is above all and before all needful that those who are joined in the bond of sacred wedlock should be wholly imbued with a profound and genuine sense of duty toward God, which will shape their whole lives, and fill their minds and wills with a very deep reverence for the majesty of God.

Supernatural Means

100. Quite fittingly, therefore, and quite in accordance with the defined norm of Christian sentiment, do those pastors of souls act who, to prevent married people from failing in the observance of God's law, urge them to perform their duty and exercise their religion so that they should give themselves to God, continually ask for His divine assistance, frequent the sacraments, and always nourish and preserve a loyal and thoroughly sincere devotion to God.

101. They are greatly deceived who having underestimated or neglected these means which rise above nature, think that they can induce men by the use and discovery of the natural sciences, such as those of biology, the science of heredity, and the like, to curb their carnal desires. We do not say this in order to belittle those natural means which are not dishonest; for God is the Author of nature as well as of grace, and He has disposed the good things of both orders for the beneficial use of men. The faithful, therefore, can and ought to be assisted also by natural means. But they are mistaken who think that these means are able to establish chastity in the nuptial union, or that they are more effective than supernatural grace.

Obedience Toward the Church

102. This conformity of wedlock and moral conduct with the divine laws respective of marriage, without which its effective restoration cannot be brought about, supposes, however, that all can discern readily, with real certainty, and without any accompanying error, what those laws are. But everyone can see to how many fallacies an avenue would be opened up and how many errors would become mixed with the truth, if it were left solely to the light of reason of each to find it out, or if it were to be discovered by the private interpretation of the truth which is revealed. And if this is applicable to many other truths of the moral order, we must all the more pay attention to those things, which appertain to marriage where the inordinate desire for pleasure can attack frail human nature and easily deceive it and lead it astray; this is all the more true of the observance of the divine law, which demands sometimes hard and repeated sacrifices, for which, as experience points out, a weak man can find so many excuses for avoiding the fulfillment of the divine law.

103. On this account, in order that no falsification or corruption of the divine law but a true genuine knowledge of it may enlighten the minds of men and guide

their conduct, it is necessary that a filial and humble obedience toward the Church should be combined with devotedness to God and the desire of submitting to Him. For Christ Himself made the Church the teacher of truth in those things also which concern the right regulation of moral conduct, even though some knowledge of the same is not beyond human reason. For just as God, in the case of the natural truths of religion and morals, added revelation to the light of reason so that what is right and true, "in the present state also of the human race may be known readily with real certainty without any admixture of error," [78] so for the same purpose He has constituted the Church the guardian and the teacher of the whole of the truth concerning religion and moral conduct; to her, therefore, should the faithful show obedience and subject their minds and hearts so as to be kept unharmed and free from error and moral corruption, and so that they shall not deprive themselves of that assistance given by God with such liberal bounty, they ought to show this due obedience not only when the Church defines something with solemn judgment, but also, in proper proportion, when by the constitutions and decrees of the Holy See, opinions are prescribed and condemned as dangerous or distorted.[79]

104. Wherefore, let the faithful also be on their guard against the overrated independence of private judgment and that false autonomy of human reason. For it is quite foreign to everyone bearing the name of a Christian to trust his own mental powers with such pride as to agree only with those things which he can examine from their inner nature, and to imagine that the Church, sent by God to teach and guide all nations, is not conversant with present affairs and circumstances; or even that they must obey only in those matters which she has decreed by solemn definition as though her other decisions might be presumed to be false or putting forward insufficient motive for truth and honesty. Quite to the contrary, a characteristic of all true followers of Christ, lettered or unlettered, is to suffer themselves to be guided and led in all things that touch upon faith or morals by the Holy Church of God through its Supreme Pastor the Roman Pontiff, who is himself guided by Jesus Christ Our Lord.

Oppose Error

105. Consequently, since everything must be referred to the law and mind of God, in order to bring about the universal and permanent restoration of marriage, it is indeed of the utmost importance that the faithful should be well instructed concerning matrimony; both by word of mouth and by the written word, not cursorily but often and fully, by means of plain and weighty arguments, so that these truths will strike the intellect and will be deeply engraved on their hearts. Let them realize and diligently reflect upon the great wisdom, kindness and bounty God has shown toward the human race, not only by the institution of marriage, but also, and quite as much, by upholding it with sacred laws; still more, in wonderfully raising it to the dignity of a Sacrament by which such an abundant fountain of graces has been opened to those joined in Christian wedlock, that these may be able to serve the noble purposes of wedlock for their own welfare and for that of their children, of the community and also for that of human relationship.

106. Certainly, if the latter day subverters of marriage are entirely devoted to misleading the minds of men and corrupting their hearts, to making a mockery of matrimonial purity and extolling the filthiest of vices by means of books and pamphlets and other innumerable methods, much more ought you, Venerable Brethren, whom "the Holy Ghost has placed as bishops, to rule the Church of God, which He hath purchased with His own blood,"[80] to give yourselves wholly to this, that through yourselves and through the priests subject to you, and, moreover, through the laity welded together by Catholic Action, so much desired, and recommended by Us, into a power of hierarchial apostolate, you may, by every fitting means, oppose error by truth, vice by the excellent dignity of chastity, the slavery of covetousness by the liberty of the sons of God,[81] that disastrous ease in obtaining divorce by an enduring love in the bond of marriage and by the inviolate pledge of fidelity given even to death.

107. Thus will it come to pass that the faithful will whole-heartedly thank God that they are bound together by His command and led by gentle compulsion to fly as far as possible from every kind of idolatry of the flesh and from the base slavery of the passions. They will, in a great measure, turn and be turned away from these abominable opinions which to the dishonor of man's dignity are now spread about in speech and in writing and collected under the title of "perfect marriage" and which indeed would make that perfect marriage nothing better than "depraved marriage," as it has been rightly and truly called.

Wholesome Instruction

108. Such wholesome instruction and religious training in regard to Christian marriage will be quite different from that exaggerated physiological education by means of which, in these times of ours, some reformers of married life make pretense of helping those joined in wedlock, laying much stress on these physiological matters, in which is learned rather the art of sinning in a subtle way than the virtue of living chastely.

109. So, Venerable Brethren, We make entirely Our own the words which Our Predecessor of happy memory, Leo XIII, in his encyclical letter on *Christian Marriage* addressed to the bishops of the whole world: "Take care not to spare your efforts and authority in bringing about that among the people committed to your guidance that doctrine may be preserved whole and unadulterated which Christ the Lord and the apostles, the interpreters of the divine will, have handed down, and which the Catholic Church herself has religiously preserved, and commanded to be observed by the faithful of every age."[82]

Steadfast Determination

110. Even the very best instruction given by the Church, however, will not alone suffice to bring about once more conformity of marriage to the law of God; something more is needed in addition to the education of the mind, namely, a steadfast determination of the will, on the part of husband and wife, to observe the sacred laws of God and of nature in regard to marriage. In fine, in spite of what

others may wish to assert and spread abroad by word of mouth or in writing, let husband and wife resolve: to stand fast to the commandments of God in all things that matrimony demands; always to render to each other the assistance of mutual love; to preserve the honor of chastity; not to lay profane hands on the stable nature of the bond; to use the rights given them by marriage in a way that will be always Christian and sacred, more especially in the first years of wedlock, so that should there be need of continency afterwards, custom will have made it easier for each to preserve it. In order that they may make this firm resolution, keep it and put it into practice, an oft-repeated consideration of their state of life, and a diligent reflection on the sacrament they have received, will be of great assistance to them. Let them constantly keep in mind, that they have been sanctified and strengthened for the duties and for the dignity of their state by a special sacrament, the efficacious power of which, although it does not impress a character, is undying. To this purpose we may ponder over the words in full of real comfort of holy Cardinal Robert Bellarmine, who with other well-known theologians with devout conviction thus expresses himself: "The sacrament of matrimony can be regarded in two ways: first, in the making, and then in its permanent state. For it is a sacrament like to that of the Eucharist, which not only when it is being conferred, but also whilst it remains, is a sacrament; for as long as the married parties are alive, so long is their union a sacrament of Christ and the Church."[83]

Observance of Duties

111. Yet in order that the grace of this sacrament may produce its full fruit, there is need, as we have already pointed out, of the co-operation of the married parties; which consists in their striving to fulfill their duties to the best of their ability and with unwearied effort. For just as in the natural order men must apply the powers given them by God with their own toil and diligence that these may exercise their full vigor, failing which, no profit is gained, so also men must diligently and unceasingly use the powers given them by the grace which is laid up in the soul by this sacrament. Let not, then, those who are joined in matrimony neglect the grace of the sacrament which is in them;[84] for, in applying themselves to the careful observance, however, laborious, of their duties they will find the power of that grace becoming more effectual as time goes on. And if ever they should feel themselves to be overburdened by the hardships of their condition of life, let them not lose courage, but rather let them regard in some measure as addressed to them that which St. Paul the Apostle wrote to his beloved disciple Timothy regarding the sacrament of Holy Orders when the disciple was dejected through hardship and insults: "I admonish thee that thou stir up the grace which is in thee by the imposition of my hands. For God hath not given us the spirit of fear; but of power, and of love, and of sobriety."[85]

Due Preparation for Marriage

112. All these things, however, Venerable Brethren, depend in large measure on the due preparation remote and proximate, of the parties for marriage. For it

cannot be denied that the basis of a happy wedlock, and the ruin of an unhappy one, is prepared and set in the souls of boys and girls during the period of childhood and adolescence. There is danger that those who before marriage sought in all things what is theirs, who indulged even their impure desires, will be in the married state what they were before, that they will reap that which they have sown;[86] indeed, within the home there will be sadness, lamentation, mutual contempt, strifes, estrangements, weariness of common life, and, worst of all, such parties will find themselves left alone with their own unconquered passions.

113. Let then those, who are about to enter on married life, approach that state well disposed and well prepared, so that they will be able, as far as they can, to help each other in sustaining the vicissitudes of life, and yet more in attending to their eternal salvation and in forming the inner man unto the fullness of the age of Christ.[87] It will also help them, if they behave toward their cherished offspring as God wills: that is, that the father be truly a father, and the mother truly a mother; through their devout love and unwearying care, the home, though it suffer the want and hardship of this valley of tears, may become for the children in its own way a foretaste of that paradise of delight in which the Creator placed the first men of the human race. Thus will they be able to bring up their children as perfect men and perfect Christians; they will instill into them a sound understanding of the Catholic Church, and will give them such a disposition and love for their fatherland as duty and gratitude demand.

114. Consequently, both those who are now thinking of entering upon this sacred married state, as well as those who have the charge of educating Christian youth, should, with due regard to the future, prepare that which is good, obviate that which is bad, and recall those points about which We have already spoken in Our encyclical letter concerning education: "The inclinations of the will, if they are bad, must be repressed from childhood, but such as are good must be fostered, and the mind, particularly of children, should be imbued with doctrines which begin with God, while the heart should be strengthened with the aids of divine grace, in the absence of which, no one can curb evil desires, nor can his discipline and formation be brought to complete perfection by the Church. For Christ has provided her with heavenly doctrines and divine sacraments, that He might make her an effectual teacher of men."[88]

Choosing a Partner

115. To the proximate preparation of a good married life belongs very specially the care in choosing a partner; on that depends a great deal whether the forthcoming marriage will be happy or not, since one may be to the other either a great help in leading a Christian life, or, a great danger and hindrance. And so that they may not deplore for the rest of their lives the sorrows arising from an indiscreet marriage, those about to enter into wedlock should carefully deliberate in choosing the person with whom henceforward they must live continually: they should, in so deliberating, keep before their minds the thought first of God and of

the true religion of Christ, then of themselves, of their partner, of the children to come, as also of human and civil society, for which wedlock is a fountainhead. Let them diligently pray for divine help, so that they make their choice in accordance with Christian prudence, not indeed led by the blind and unrestrained impulse of lust, nor by any desire of riches or other base influence, but by a true and noble love and by a sincere affection for the future partner; and then let them strive in their married life for those ends for which the State was constituted by God. Lastly, let them not omit to ask the prudent advice of their parents with regard to the partner, and let them regard this advice in no light manner, in order that by their mature knowledge and experience of human affairs they may guard against a disastrous choice, and, on the threshold of matrimony, may receive more abundantly the divine blessing of the fourth commandment: "Honor thy father and thy mother (which is the first commandment with a promise) that it may be well with thee and thou mayest be long-lived upon the earth." [89]

116. Now since it is no rare thing to find that the perfect observance of God's commands and conjugal integrity encounter difficulties by reason of the fact that the man and wife are in straitened circumstances, their necessities must be relieved as far as possible.

Temporal Necessities

117. And so, in the first place, every effort must be made to bring about that which Our Predecessor Leo XIII, of happy memory, has already insisted upon,[90] namely, that in the State such economic and social methods should be adopted as will enable every head of a family to earn as much as, according to his station in life, is necessary for himself, his wife, and for the rearing of his children, for "the laborer is worthy of his hire." [91] To deny this, or to make light of what is equitable, is a grave injustice and is placed among the greatest sins by Holy Writ;[92] nor is it lawful to fix such a scanty wage as will be insufficient for the upkeep of the family in the circumstances in which it is placed.

118. Care, however, must be taken that the parties themselves, for a considerable time before entering upon married life, should strive to dispose of, or at least to diminish, the material obstacles in their way. The manner in which this may be done effectively and honestly must be pointed out by those who are experienced. Provision must be made also, in the case of those who are not self-supporting, for joint aid by private or public guilds.[93]

119. When these means which We have pointed out do not fulfill the needs, particularly of a larger or poorer family, Christian charity toward our neighbor absolutely demands that those things which are lacking to the needy should be provided; hence it is incumbent on the rich to help the poor, so that, having an abundance of this world's goods, they may not expend them fruitlessly or completely squander them, but employ them for the support and well-being of those who lack the necessities of life. They who give of their substance to Christ in the person of His poor will receive from the Lord a most bountiful reward when He

shall come to judge the world; they who act to the contrary will pay the penalty.[94] Not in vain does the Apostle warn us: "He that hath the substance of this world and shall see his brother in need, and shall shut up his bowels from him: how doth the charity of God abide in him?"[95]

Civil Obligation

120. If, however, for this purpose, private resources do not suffice, it is the duty of the public authority to supply for the insufficient forces of individual effort, particularly in a matter which is of such importance to the common weal, touching as it does the maintenance of the family and married people. If families, particularly those in which there are many children, have not suitable dwellings; if the husband cannot find employment and means of livelihood; if the necessities of life cannot be purchased except at exorbitant prices; if even the mother of the family to the great harm of the home, is compelled to go forth and seek a living by her own labor; if she, too, in the ordinary or even extraordinary labors of childbirth, is deprived of proper food, medicine, and the assistance of a skilled physician, it is patent to all to what an extent married people may lose heart, and how home life and the observance of God's commands are rendered difficult for them; indeed it is obvious how great a peril can arise to the public security and to the welfare and very life of civil society itself when such men are reduced to that condition of desperation that, having nothing which they fear to lose, they are emboldened to hope for chance advantage from the upheaval of the State and of established order.

121. Wherefore, those who have the care of the State and of the public good cannot neglect the needs of married people and their families, without bringing great harm upon the State and on the common welfare. Hence, in making the laws and in disposing of public funds they must do their utmost to relieve the needs of the poor, considering such a task as one of the most important of their administrative duties.

122. We are sorry to note that not infrequently nowadays it happens that through a certain inversion of the true order of things, ready and bountiful assistance is provided for the unmarried mother and her illegitimate offspring (who, of course must be helped in order to avoid a greater evil) which is denied to legitimate mothers or given sparingly or almost grudgingly.

123. But not only in regard to temporal goods, Venerable Brethren, is it the concern of the public authority to make proper provision for matrimony and the family, but also in other things which concern the good of souls. Just laws must be made for the protection of chastity, for reciprocal conjugal aid, and for similar purposes, and these must be faithfully enforced, because, as history testifies, the prosperity of the State and the temporal happiness of its citizens cannot remain safe and sound where the foundation on which they are established, which is the moral order, is weakened and where the very fountainhead from which the State draws its life, namely, wedlock and the family, is obstructed by the vices of its citizens.

Religious Authority

124. For the preservation of the moral order neither the laws and sanctions of the temporal power are sufficient, nor is the beauty of virtue and the expounding of its necessity. Religious authority must enter in to enlighten the mind, to direct the will, and to strengthen human frailty for the assistance of divine grace. Such an authority is found nowhere save in the Church instituted by Christ the Lord. Hence We earnestly exhort in the Lord all those who hold the reins of power that they establish and maintain firmly harmony and friendship with this Church of Christ so that through the united activity and energy of both powers the tremendous evils, fruits of those wanton liberties which assail both marriage and the family and are a menace to both Church and State, may be effectively frustrated.

125. Governments can assist the Church greatly in the execution of its important office, if, in laying down their ordinances, they take account of what is prescribed by divine and ecclesiastical law, and if penalties are fixed for offenders. For as it is, there are those who think that whatever is permitted by the laws of the State, or at least is not punished by them, is allowed also in the moral order, and, because they neither fear God nor see any reason to fear the laws of man, they act even against their conscience, thus often bringing ruin upon themselves and upon many others. There will be no peril to or lessening of the rights and integrity of the State from its association with the Church. Such suspicion and fear is empty and groundless, as Leo XIII has already so clearly set forth: "It is generally agreed," he says, "that the Founder of the Church, Jesus Christ, wished the spiritual power to be distinct from the civil, and each to be free and unhampered in doing its own work, not forgetting, however, that it is expedient to both, and in the interest of everybody, that there be a harmonious relationship.... If the civil power combines in a friendly manner with the spiritual power of the Church, it necessarily follows that both parties will greatly benefit. The dignity of the State will be enhanced, and with religion as its guide, there will never be a rule that is not just; while for the Church there will be at hand a safeguard and defense which will operate to the public good of the faithful." [96]

The Lateran Pact

126. To bring forward a recent and clear example of what is meant, it has happened quite in consonance with right order and entirely according to the law of Christ, that in the solemn Convention happily entered into between the Holy See and the Kingdom of Italy, also in matrimonial affairs a peaceful settlement and friendly co-operation has been obtained, such as befitted the glorious history of the Italian people and its ancient and sacred traditions. These decrees are to be found in the Lateran Pact: "The Italian State, desirous of restoring to the institution of matrimony, which is the basis of the family, that dignity conformable to the traditions of its people, assigns as civil effects of the sacrament of matrimony all that is attributed to it in Canon Law." [97] To this fundamental norm are added further clauses in the common pact.

127. This might well be a striking example to all of how, even in this our own day (in which, sad to say, the absolute separation of the civil power from the Church, and indeed from every religion, is so often taught), the one supreme authority can be united and associated with the other without detriment to the rights and supreme power of either thus protecting Christian parents from pernicious evils and menacing ruin.

128. All these things which, Venerable Brethren, prompted by Our past solicitude We put before you, We wish according to the norm of Christian prudence to be promulgated widely among all Our beloved children committed to your care as members of the great family of Christ, that all may be thoroughly acquainted with sound teaching concerning marriage, so that they may be ever on their guard against the dangers advocated by the teachers of error, and most of all, that "denying ungodliness and worldly desires, they may live soberly and justly, and godly in this world, looking for the blessed hope and coming of the glory of the great God and Our Saviour Jesus Christ."[98]

129. May the Father, "of whom all paternity in heaven and earth is named," [99] who strengthens the weak and gives courage to the pusilanimous and faint-hearted; and Christ Our Lord and Redeemer, "the Institutor and Perfecter of the holy sacraments."[100] Who desired marriage to be and made it the mystical image of His own ineffable union with the Church; and the Holy Ghost, Love of God, the Light of hearts and the Strength of the mind, grant that all will perceive, will admit with a ready will, and by the grace of God will put into practice, what We by this letter have expounded concerning the holy Sacrament of Matrimony, the wonderful law and will of God respecting it, the errors and impending dangers, and the remedies with which they can be counteracted, so that that fruitfulness dedicated to God will flourish again vigorously in Christian wedlock.

130. We must humbly pour forth Our earnest prayer at the Throne of His Grace, that God, the Author of all graces, the inspirer of all good desires and deeds,[101] may bring this about, and deign to give it bountifully according to the greatness of His liberality and omnipotence, and as a token of the abundant blessing of the same Omnipotent God, We most lovingly grant to you, Venerable Brethren, and to the clergy and people committed to your watchful care, the Apostolic Benediction.

131. Given at Rome, in St. Peter's, the 31st day of December, of the year 1930, the ninth of Our Pontificate.

PIUS PP. XI.

---

[1] Encycl. *Arcanum divinae sapientiae,* Febr. 10, 1880.

[2] Gen. i. 27, 28; ii. 22, 23; Matt. *xix.* 3 sqq.; Eph,.v. *23* sqq.

[3] Conc. Trid., Sess. XXIV.

[4] Cod, iur. can., c. 1081. § 2.

[5] Cod, iur, can. 1081. § 1.

[6] St. Th., *Summa theol.,* p. iii., Supplem. 9, XLIX art. 3.

[7] Encycl. *Rerum novarum,* May 15, 1891.

[8] Gen. i, 28.

[9] Encycl. *Ad salutem,* April 20, 1930.

[10] St. August., *De bono coniug.,* cap. 24, n. 32.

[11] St. August., *De Gen, ad Litt.,* lib. IX, cap. 7, n. 12.

[12] Gen. i. 28.

[13] 1 Tim. v. 14.

[14] St. August., *De bono coniug.,* cap. 24, n. 32.

[15] i Cor. ii. 9.

[16] Eph. ii. 19.

[17] John xvi. 21.

[18] Encycl. *Divini illius Magistri,* 31 Dec. 1929.

[19] St. August., *De Gen. ad litt.,* lib. IX, cap. 7, n. 12.

[20] Cod. iur. can., c. 1013 p 7.

[21] Conc. Trid., Sess. XXIV.

[22] Matt., V, 28.

[23] Decr. S. Officii, 2 March 1679, propos. 50.

[24] Eph., V, 25; Col., III, 19.

[25] *Catech. Rom.,* II, cap. VIII q. 24.

[26] St Greg the Great, *Homii.* XXX in Evang (John XIV, 23-31), n.1.

[27] Matt. xxii. 40.

[28] 1 Cor. vii. 3.

[29] Eph. v. 22, 23.

[30] Encycl. *Arcanum divinae sapientiae,* 10 Febr. 1880.

[31] Matt. xix. 6.

[32] Luke xvi. 18.

[33] St. August., *De Gen. ad litt.,* lib. IX, cap. 7, n. 12.

[34] Pius VI, *Rescript, ad Episc. Agriens.,* July 11, 1789.

[35] Eph. v. 32.

[36] St. August., *De nupt. et concup.,* lib. I, cap. 10.

[37] 1 Cor. xiii. 8.

[38] Conc. Trid., Sess. XXIV.

[39] Conc. Trid., Sess. XXIV.

[40] Cod. iur. can., c. 1012.

[41] St. August., *De nupt. et concup.,* lib. I, cap. 10.

[42] Matt. xiii. 25.

[43] 2 Tim. iv. 2-5.

[44] Eph. v. 3.

[45] St. August., *De nupt. et concup.,* lib. II n. 12.; Gen. xxxviii. 8-10.

[46] Matt. xv. 14.

[47] Luke vi. 38.

[48] Conc. Trid., Sess. VI, cap. 11.

[49] Const. Apost., *Cum occasione,* May 31, 1653, prop. 1.

[50] Exod. xx. 13; cfr. Decr. S. Offic. May 4, 1897; July 24, 1895; May 31, 1884.

[51] St. August., *De nupt. et concupisc.,* cap. XV.

[52] Rom. iii. 8.

[53] Gen. iv. 10.

[54] *Summ. theol.,* 2a, 2ae, q. 108 a 4 ad 2um.

[55] Exod. xx. 14.

[56] Matt. v. 28.

[57] Heb. xiii. 8.

[58] Matt. v. 18.

[59] Matt. vii. 27.

[60] Leo XIII, Encycl. *Arcanum,* Febr. 10, 1880.

[61] Eph. v. 32: Heb. xiii. 4.

[62] Cod. iur. can., c. 1060.

[63] Modestinus, in Dig. (Lib. XXIII, II: *De ritu nuptiarum),* lib. I, Regularum.

[64] Matt. xix. 6.

[65] Luke xvi. 18.

[66] Conc. Trid., Sess. XXIV, cap. 5.

[67] Conc. Trid., Sess. XXIV, cap. 7.

[68] Cod. iur. can., c. 1128 sqq.

[69] Leo XIII, Encycl. *Arcanum divinae sapientiae,* Feb. 10, 1880.

[70] Encycl. *Arcanam,* Febr. 10, 1880.

[71] Encycl. *Arcanum,* Febr. 10, 1880.

[72] S. Th., *Summ. theolog.,* 1a. 2ae. q. 91, a. 1-2.

[73] Encycl. *Arcanum divinae sapientiae,* Feb. 10, 1880.

[74] St. August., *Enarrt. in Ps. 143.*

[75] Rom. i. 24, 26.

[76] James iv. 6.

[77] Rom. vii., viii.

[78] Conc. Vat., Sess. III, cap. 2.

[79] Conc. Vat., Sess. III, cap 4; Cod. iur. can., c 1324.

[80] Acts xx. 28.

[81] John viii. 32 sqq.; Gal. v. 13.

[82] Encycl. *Arcanum,* Feb. 10, 1880.

[83] St. Rob. Bellarmin, *De controversiis,* tom. III, *De Matr.* controvers. II, cap. 6.

[84] 1 Tim. iv. 14.

[85] 2 Tim. i. 6, 7.

[86] Gal. vi. 9.

[87] Eph iv. 13.

[88] Encycl. *Divini illius Magistri,* Dcc. 31, 1929.

[89] Eph. vi. 2, 3; Exod. xx. 12.

[90] Encycl. *Rerum Novarum,* May 15, 1891.

[91] Luke x. 7.

[92] Deut. xxiv. 14, 15.

[93] Leo XIII, Encycl. *Rerum Novarum,* May 15, 1891.

[94] Matt. xxv. 34 sqq.

[95] 1 John iii, 17.

[96] Encycl. *Arcanum Divinae Sapientiae,* Feb. 10, 1880.

[97] Concord., art. 34; *Act. Apost. Sed.* XXI (1929), p. 290.

[98] Tit. ii. 12, 13.

[99] Eph. iii. 15.

[100] Conc. Trid., Sess. XXIV.

[101] Phil. ii. 13.

14.

HUMANAE VITAE AND
THE STRUGGLE OVER PERSONAL CONSCIENCE
Michael W. Higgins and Douglas R. Letson

When *Humanae vitae* appeared in 1968, reaffirming Catholicism's traditional ban on artificial means of contraception, [Emmett Cardinal] Carter says "it was one of the most crucial moments of my life as a bishop."

Although Pius XII had addressed birth control issues in a number of his allocutions in the 1950s, the last detailed papal document was *Casti connubii,* issued by his predecessor, Pius XI, in 1930. This encyclical was occasioned by the Anglican Church's Lambeth Conference of the same year, which decided that contraception could be permitted in certain circumstances, although it was never the normal or preferred course. *Casti connubii* was, in contrast, blunt and categorical, condemning contraception "as an offense against the law of God and of nature." T.S. Eliot summed up the difference between the Roman and the Anglican approaches in a way wholly appropriate to its time: "To put it frankly, but I hope not offensively, the Roman view in general seems to me to be that a principle must be affirmed without exception; and that thereafter exceptions can be dealt with, without modifying the principle. The view natural to the English mind, I believe, is rather that a principle must be framed in such a way as to include all allowable exceptions. It follows inevitably that the Roman Church must profess to be fixed, while the Anglican Church must profess to take account of changed conditions."[1]

But Rome's position appeared increasingly less fixed, despite papal utterances to the contrary. Pope John XXIII established a six-man commission to advise him on the birth control question. It consisted of the French Jesuit sociologist Stanislaus de Lestapis; British neurologist John Marshall; the Belgian Jesuit demographer Clement Mertens; Swiss Dominican and Vatican observer at the United Nations in Geneva, Henri de Riedmatten; Belgian physician Pierre Van Rossum; and Louvain professor Jacques Mertens de Wilmars.

Before they could meet, John died, but his successor, rather than disbanding the Johannine commission, greatly augmented it. It became known as the Pontifical Commission on Population, Family and Birth and was broadly representative of the Catholic world: it included lay and clerical members, ethicists, psychiatrists, gynecologists, theologians, philosophers, lawyers and population experts. The church seemed to be poised for a change.

And people did expect a change, or at least some clarification. Research on oral contraceptives and rising disagreement among moral theologians on the morality of artifical contraception contributed to Catholic confusion. Catholic physicians and lawyers were no longer of one mind. Rome had to do something.

Lawyer and eventual Ontario Supreme Court Justice John O'Driscoll made a statement typical of an increasingly restive Canadian laity when he reminded the hierarchy that "as a layman I feel that . . . an immediate and definitive statement should be made so that those in the married state will know right from wrong. I feel that such a statement should issue only after a full discussion with Catholic laymen living in the married state; it should not be a document on marriage issued by celibates."[2]

The pressure on Rome mounted throughout the 1960s, and when the Report of the Pontifical Commission was clandestinely published in 1967 by *The Tablet* of London and the *National Catholic Reporter* of Kansas City, revealing that the majority opinion of the Pope's own high-level consultative body recommended a change in the church's teaching on contraception, expectations reached a pitch. The report was unambiguous in its respect for the church's long tradition regarding conjugal relations and the transmission of life, but it was also unambiguous in its argument in favour of a rightful evolution of that teaching: "The large amount of knowledge and facts which throw light on today's world suggest that it is not to contradict the genuine sense of this tradition and the purpose of the previous doctrinal condemnations if we speak of the regulation of conception by using means, human and decent, ordered to favoring fecundity in the totality of married life and toward the realization of the authentic values of a fruitful matrimonial community. The reasons in favor of this affirmation are of several kinds: social changes in matrimony and the family, especially in the role of the woman; lowering of the infant mortality rate; new bodies of knowledge in biology, psychology, sexuality and demography; a changed estimation of the value and meaning of human sexuality and of conjugal relations; most of all, a better grasp of the duty of man to humanize and to bring to greater perfection for the life of man what is given in nature. Then must be considered the sense of the faithful: according to it, condemnation of a couple to a long and often heroic abstinence as the means to regulate conception, cannot be founded on the truth .... The doctrine on marriage and its essential values remains the same and whole, but it is now applied differently out of a deeper understanding."[3]

Pope Paul was unpersuaded. When he issued *Humanae vitae,* the Roman Catholic Church went into a state of crisis. Emmett Carter would later observe that "the tragedy of *Humanae vitae* was not that the pope spoke alone, but that, apparently, he thought he had to."[4]

When Carter received news of the encyclical's release, he was with his brother Alex and three other bishops: Plourde of Ottawa; Gerard-Marie Coderre, Bishop of Saint-Jean Longueuil; and Pocock of Toronto. They were at a meeting in Plourde's chalet just north of Ottawa when the papal nuncio, Archbishop Emmanuele

Clarizio, arrived with suitable gravity of purpose and demeanour, although, as Carter recalls, he introduced them to the most controversial papal document of the century "in a way that was funny. He said, 'I am very sorry but here is the pope's statement.' He had, of course, already examined the pertinent parts. So, we promptly dropped everything else we were doing and pored over the encyclical. It was with a certain sense of dismay that we read the vital passages in it. He had clearly taken a position that was contrary to the majority position of his own Commission. We felt that this was going to be a major problem."

Indeed they did have a major problem on their hands. Article 14 of the encyclical categorically condemned "any action, which either before, at the moment of, or after sexual intercourse, is specifically intended to prevent procreation—whether as an end or as a means." The document went on to argue that by retaining the ban on all means of artifical contraception the church was upholding the integrity of sexual love and resisting the "general lowering of moral standards." In Article 18, the church was portrayed in heroic terms as engaged in no less vital a task than the "creation of a truly human civilization." The church, it said, "urges man not to betray his personal responsibilities by putting all his faith in technical expedients. In this way [the church] defends the dignity of husband and wife."

The moral and theological argumentation of *Humanae vitae,* specifically in the light of the unofficially released Final Report of the Pontifical Commission, was far from persuasive for the majority of Catholic people, lay and cleric alike. In fact, *Humanae vitae* ushered in a whole new set of problems for the post-Vatican II church. The Mill Hill missionary and demographer Father Arthur McCormack observed in an article in *The Tablet* that although the Pope was convinced that papal authority and the very credibility of the church were on the line in 1968, "nothing has done more harm than *Humanae vitae* to that authority, which reached its lowest ebb as the protest mounted and the motivation for the encyclical became clear. Few documents in the course of the long and turbulent history of the Catholic church have caused such widespread and immediate consternation and opposition."[5]

Popular and critical attention soon moved from the controverted debates about sexual morality and natural law to an examination of the legitimate role and exercise of papal authority. Priests throughout the world wrote letters of dissent to secular and religious publications, acting out of their conviction that quiet submission to a teaching they considered in error did violence to their spiritual integrity. But the price of public dissent was high. Brocard Sewell, a British Carmelite friar and literary biographer, signed his name to a letter of dissent submitted to *The Times,* and was publicly censured as a result. In *The Vatican Oracle,* a work he concluded in 1970 while teaching at St. Francis Xavier University in Nova Scotia, he spoke for many a suspended cleric when he said that "while not presuming to judge the consciences of others, those priests who made some kind of public protest did so lest, by seeming to support the teaching of the encyclical, they should incur the judgement that awaits those who knowingly impose on others burdens from which they are free themselves, and which they do nothing to help others to bear. In so doing it was not in their minds to make any criticism of their fellow clergy who conscientiously accepted the teaching of *Humanae vitae*."[6]

Tortured by the irony that through his efforts to affirm the authority of the church by disallowing any possibility of deviation from previous papal teaching, he had seriously undermined that authority, Pope Paul chose the road of gentle correction rather than blatant repudiation when it came to rebellious clerics and uncomprehending or unreceptive laypeople. While some hierarchs, like Cardinal O'Boyle of Washington and Bishop McNulty of Buffalo, were severe in meting out disciplinary penalties to recalcitrant priests (some of McNulty's priests sought exile in Pocock's Toronto, including Tom Dailey, a prominent and respected moral theologian), the Pope did not indulge in such summary condemnations and suspensions himself. "While he seemed to feel a mystical need to uphold the Church's pro-natalist position," wrote one observer in later years, "he did little to curb the conferences of bishops who interpreted the pastoral teaching of the encyclical broadly, telling their people that the pope proposed a high ideal; but that if, in conscience, they could not live up to that ideal, they should not consider themselves in sin."[7]

One of these conferences of bishops was the Canadian Catholic Conference, composed of bishops who were often compared to the avant-garde Dutch bishops, and their Winnipeg Statement in the fall of 1968 was widely recognized as one of the boldest in the Catholic world.

From the very moment that Clarizio arrived at the doors of Plourde's chalet, Carter and the others knew that they would have to issue a statement that, in Emmett's words, would give them some manoeuvring room in dealing with the people of Canada. And so to Winnipeg from September 23 to 27, the city chosen that year to host the Canadian bishops' annual assembly (the Archdiocese of St. Boniface was holding anniversary celebrations). But it wasn't the anniversary celebrations that dominated the meeting.

The President of the Conference in that fateful year was Alexander Carter, and sitting on the Theological Commission was the man who, during Emmett Carter's Toronto years, would often function as his bête noir—the Bishop of Victoria, British Columbia, Remi De Roo. Trained at Rome's Angelicum University, De Roo had demonstrated competence in systematic theology, but the Theological Commission was going to have to rely on the professional assistance of numerous experts to draft the particular episcopal statement required by *Humanae vitae*. The Winnipeg periti included the Jesuit moralist Edward Sheridan; Father Ora McManus, Chairman of the Western Canadian Conference of Priests; Father Andre Naud, President of the Canadian Institute of Theology; Mr. Bernard Daly, the Director of the Family Life Bureau (English) of the Canadian Catholic Conference; and Father Charles St. Onge, the French Director of the Family Life Bureau. It did not appear on the face of it that Emmett Carter would have a role to play in Winnipeg, but such was not to be the case.

Returning to his room for a nightcap after a dinner with Alex, he discovered a note from Pocock imploring him to join his brother bishops of the Theological Commission immediately. He went down to the room where they were closeted, and found Emmett Doyle (Bishop of Nelson, B.C.) banging on a typewriter and surrounded by the Theological Commission. He was working on the draft of a declaration for the Conference and they were a little panicky. It was late Wednesday evening and their deadline was noon on Friday. They were totally at a loss; they hadn't even got past the first paragraph. Carter relates the story: "So Pocock says, 'Well, we thought you could help us put this thing together.' I demurred at first, but I eventually relented, told them that I wouldn't type anything. They agreed. The system I worked out proved satisfactory: I would take notes point by point, and while they were making up their minds as to what it was that should be included in the next paragraph, I would go into an adjacent room and compose in paragraph form the points they had made to date. When I came back into their room, I would pick up where I left off after we examined the paragraph I had just composed."

In addition to this rather rough drafting procedure, they had to consult with their periti and translators and they ended up working well into the morning hours. At about 3:00 A.M. Carter dispatched them to bed and promised them a statement that they could either approve or send back for revisions by the next morning. At about 5:00 A.M. he slipped the completed draft under the secretariat's door for typing and went to bed himself.

It is not surprising that Pocock should have asked Carter for his help; Winnipeg's Archbishop Flahiff had requested as early as 1964 that Carter prepare (*sub secreto*) the Canadian response to a questionnaire issued by the Holy See, which had been designed to test the waters regarding contemporary attitudes and expectations about birth regulation in the Catholic world. His report (April 11,1964) does not make light of the contemporary unhappiness over the official position and the turmoil compounded by Roman indecision. It was characteristically forthright. Something had to be done, something "sympathetic and comprehensible." *Humanae vitae* wasn't what he had had in mind. And so he accepted Pocock's invitation.

The draft was thoroughly debated on Thursday, and that evening proved to be a replay of the previous night's activities. Carter was up all night again, and when he took his corrected draft down to the secretariat his room was rifled, but because he hadn't made a carbon copy of his draft the morass of notes and files clearly flummoxed the would-be thief, and nothing of consequence was stolen. It was a measure of the interest, not to say the desperation, inspired by the Winnipeg proceedings.

On Friday morning the debate continued. Archbishop Joseph Wilhelm of Kingston and Bishop Joseph Ryan of Hamilton provided what little opposition there was. That afternoon, as scheduled, the Canadian Catholic hierarchy issued its pastoral statement on *Humanae vitae*. Carter felt that his efforts as editor/ amanuensis ("It was my authorship but not my substance.") and the intention of the

Canadian bishops were fully realized: "Our statement was definitely meant to indicate to the people of Canada that if they found, as we anticipated, and God knows history has proven us to be correct, that they couldn't follow the directives of the encyclical, then they were not to consider themselves as cut off from the church. We were trying to create a situation wherein Catholics would not feel that they were alienated from the church although on the issue of birth control they could not follow the teaching of the pope." Carter believed that they had succeeded, and thereby avoided the strife that some nations, especially the United States, experienced.

Emmett's labours, to a considerable extent, went unnoticed in Winnipeg. Alex, by contrast, was more visible. As President of the CCC and Chairman of the Plenary Assembly, he was the one who had to rule Kingston's Wilhelm out of order when he attempted to scuttle the statement, and he was the one saddled with the unhappy task of providing the nuncio with a copy of the finalized and approved Winnipeg Statement for His Holiness. Along with De Roo and Archbishop Baudoux of St. Boniface, Alex handled the press conference that launched their document. "Each insisted that the bishops had not intended to make a doctrinal statement, but that they had attempted to help the People of God in Canada to face the agonizing situation in which they found themselves after the encyclical.... The bishops had rejected *simpliste* attitudes either ignoring the encyclical or regarding it as a legalistic document, and they had, above all, rejected the 'contraceptive attitude' within marriage."[8]

The Statement acknowledges, from the very beginning, Canadian episcopal solidarity with the pontiff and proceeds to outline the role of the Christian conscience and the divine law in a way wholly consonant with the best of the Catholic tradition. The Statement is respectful of official church teaching but recognizes the pastoral necessity that must sometimes mollify abstract moral principles in the light of concrete human behaviour. It concludes by pledging loyalty to the institutional church, yet acknowledging the very status of that church as a pilgrim, a people in process. "We stand in union with the Bishop of Rome, the successor of Peter, the sign and contributing cause of our unity with Christ and with one another. But this very union postulates such a love of the Church that we can do no less than to place all of our love and all of our intelligence at its service. If this sometimes means that in our desire to make the Church more intelligible and more beautiful we must, as pilgrims do, falter in the way or differ as to the way, no one should conclude that our common faith is lost or our loving purpose blunted. The great Cardinal Newman once wrote: 'Lead kindly light amidst the encircling gloom.' We believe that the Kindly Light will lead us to a greater understanding of the ways of God and the love of men."

Alex Carter was informed by Clarizio that Pope Paul said of the Canadian Statement, "*L'accettiamo con soddisfucione*" (We accept it with satisfaction). Similarly, when Emmett had occasion to be in Rome on Consilium business shortly after the Statement appeared, he was cautioned by Cardinal Gray that some of it was "strong meat, my Lord," although Carter reports that when he met Pope Paul the pontiff assured him that he had no objection to the Statement.

Carter must have been puzzled, if not a little pained, by the strikingly different direction his friend John Wright chose to take on the issue. Pittsburgh and London did not see eye to eye on this one.

If Carter moved carefully, choosing nuance over exhortation, demonstrating the need for universal consultation and the reasonable application of the principle of collegiality, it is because that was his preferred way of operating. He courted Rome's attention; he had no desire to emulate its procedures. The Roman mentality was irksome, a puzzle, a thing to be avoided. But not so with Wright. He argued, in sharp contrast to the conciliatory and progressive Statement of the Canadians, that what "Pope Paul has done, what he had to do, is recall to a generation that does not like the word the fact that sin exists; that artificial contraception is objectively sinful; that those who impose it, foster it, counsel it, whether they be governments, experts, or—God forgive them!—spiritual directors impose, foster and counsel objective sin, just as they would if they taught racism, hatred, fraud, injustice or impiety."[9] Wright was never inclined to ambiguity.

Carter, who chose to accentuate the positive rather than the negative and to respect the individual's personal obligations of conscience, Carter, Gaunt John's old friend, could not have been impressed by this legalistic rebuke of error. It conveyed little in the way of compassion. The statement that Wright chose to issue did not represent him at his best. Within a year, Wright was named a Cardinal.

Carter has never been partial to ambiguity either, and when various readings of the Winnipeg Statement called into question the Canadian bishops' loyalty to the Holy See and the universal magisterium, he appreciated the necessity of releasing a "clarifying statement." He wrote this one entirely himself, though the bishops saw it before it went out. "It was not one of the 'ethical statements' as was issued in 1983 with no consultation. They'd all seen it and they'd all had the chance to talk about it. There was no hidden ballplay; I wrote it." It was released following the plenary assembly of the Canadian bishops in Ottawa on April 18, 1969.

But it did not appease critic Anne Roche Muggeridge, a formidable polemicist with a taste for apocalyptic prose and easy judgements. Muggeridge excoriated the Winnipeg prelates and their *periti* in a way that still smarts. For her, the Winnipeg Statement illustrated the triumph in Canada of that spirit of Vatican II which, in her estimation, disguises the Protestantizing tendencies of the liberal theologians and their witless dupes, the *episkopoi*, the shepherds of the church. In *Gates of Hell: The Struggle for the Catholic Church* she moves in for the kill: "The bishops had spent the two months between the publication of the encyclical and their Winnipeg meeting (according to the *Western Catholic Reporter* and Douglas Roche) listening: to the Catholic Physicians' Guild of Manitoba, to 551 members of the Western Canadian Conference of Priests, to fifteen directors of departments within the Canadian Catholic Conference, to eighty-two Catholics in Dialogue [a group of academics originating at the Basilian Fathers' St. Michael's College, University of Toronto, with leadership by such liberal notables as Gregory Baum and Leslie Dewart], to the 'allimportant Canadian Institute of Theology', and to fifty-eight of the 'Cream of Antigonish' [dissenting Catholic priests and lay academics attached to St. Francis Xavier University], all of whom disagreed violently with the encyclical. This listening apparently left them no choice, for as the *Western Catholic Reporter* remarked, 'with the integrity of so many of the protesters irreproachable, the progressive bishops were able to discern the Holy Spirit speaking to them through the people.' That sentence is the most perfect definition of the liberal elitist 'spirit of Vatican II' mentality ever written."[10]

The very integrity of the Catholic Church itself, argues Muggeridge, was thus sundered by its own chief protectors. Eager to pacify a disaffected and highly vocal Catholic laity infected by a doctrinally spineless liberalism, and eager to accommodate the new darlings of the post-conciliar era, the *periti,* the bishops so qualified *Humanae vitae* that its punch was reduced to a gentle slap. Some leadership, she said. And the Carter brothers, she contended, were in the forefront of this betrayal. They had capitulated to the clever stratagems of the *periti* and they had outmanoeuvred the bishops who opposed them. That was her line; the Carters vigorously disputed it.

Convinced of the scandalous liberalism of Alexander Carter and ever fearful of the wily Emmett, Muggeridge persists in seeing the Winnipeg Statement as the product of a cabal of theologians and obliging bishops determined to undo the perceived damage of *Humanae vitae* and pledged to continue the Protestantizing of the Roman Church in Canada. In her 1986 book, *The Desolate City: The Catholic Church in Ruins,* Muggeridge recalls that from the very "beginning of the fall 1968 assembly of the Canadian Conference of Catholic Bishops [the name was changed in 1977], the deck was stacked against those who wished to accept the traditional position. Canada's leading progressive bishops, in particular Remi De Roo, head of the theological commission, and Alexander Carter, then president of the CCCB, obtained a consensus of sorts on the Winnipeg Statement.... The Canadian bishops, like the Protestant reformers, reversed the order of importance in moral judgement, that is, they put the private, subjective elements of morality before the universal and objective."[11]

What is anathema to Muggeridge is revisionism to Emmett Carter. In Carter's memory there was no "consensus of sorts," but a majority vote with minimal dissent among the bishops. There was no railroading by Alexander, but an open and free exchange of ideas directed by acceptable parliamentary procedure: "The Winnipeg Statement has been totally misread and misrepresented by our dear Anne Roche. Her account of the assembly and the process of composition is comic, fantastic." That may be. But the perception was that the Canadian hierarchy was ambivalent in its treatment of the encyclical persists, even in quarters not constricted by reactionary fever.

As late as five years after the Winnipeg Statement, Carter still felt called to defend the document and its fidelity to Rome. In an article sent to the *Catholic Register* on March 29, 1973, Carter invited Catholics to read the Winnipeg Statement analytically, and defied anyone to find the slightest disloyalty to the Holy Father in a statement that was a pastoral one, meant to help the consciences of the faithful either in their acceptance of the papal teaching or with their struggle where acceptance was difficult. But these kinds of defences and explanations were insufficient. Something more substantive was necessary, something more than what the pastoral statement, the clarifying statement and countless columns in newspapers could provide. And so the 1973 "Statement on the Formation of Conscience" came to birth, and Carter was its midwife.

The conference of bishops had promised the conscience document for some time, and because Carter had served as Vice-President of the Faith and Doctrine Department (as it was then called) of the CCC since 1969, and since he had been so crucial a figure in the drafting of the previous statements, it was not unreasonable to see his hand directly in this one. And so it happened that after countless committee sessions and consultations between bishops and theologians, a frustrated James Carney, Archbishop of Vancouver, implored Carter to do something. In the spring of 1973 Carney reminded Carter of the long-promised statement and warned him that with all the committees and sub-committees that were working on various pieces of it, it would never come together. Carter looked ahead at the leisurely summer he had planned, and declined. Carney persisted and told him flatly, "If you don't do it, it won't get done."

Carter concluded that Carney was right. He took all the documentation to his cottage, put the statement together and presented it to the bishops at their fall assembly. The bishops argued, interpolated, deleted and added. But it went back to a delighted Carter, who felt that his statement "was much better after they got through with it." The end result was a well-reasoned, if somewhat dry, examination of the various types of conscience and the processes involved in the formation of a mature conscience. Its references to Scripture are bountiful and it contains ample allusions to the Church Fathers and conciliar documents. It is a careful and intelligent document.

The kind of conscience that today's society needs, the "Statement on the Formation of Conscience" argues in Article 22, is a "dynamic Christian conscience. This is the conscience which leads us to have a responsible attitude to someone, to Jesus, to the community, to the Church, etc. Every person who fits into this category feels a responsibility for a progressive search and striving to live out a life ideal according to the mind of Christ (Phil. 2:5)."

Having affirmed the role of freedom and the individual conscience, the statement proceeds to remind believing Catholics in Article 28 that, in their tradition, the magisterium is "the definitive cornerstone upon which the whole edifice of conscientious judgement must be built." Catholics must realize that "'to follow one's conscience' and to remain a Catholic, one must take into account first and foremost the teaching of the magisterium." The authority of the magisterium must be clearly distinguished from that of individual theologians and priests. There is nothing brazen or revolutionary in these arguments. They are as conservative as John Henry Newman, the principal force behind Carter's thinking on conscience. But it was this very same Newman who also upheld the priority of conscience over papal authority and who articulated the church's current thinking on consulting the laity on doctrinal matters. There is something of this Newman in the conscience statement as well.

The bishops overwhelmingly approved the Statement, and it was released on December 1, 1973.

Within two weeks Carter wrote to his close friend and neighbour, the progressive Archbishop of Detroit, John Cardinal Dearden, claiming that "it is, between us, largely my own brainchild and I am perhaps unduly proud of it."[12] Not surprisingly, under the seal "Personal and Confidential", he forwarded a copy of the Statement to the far less progressive John Wright, the Cardinal Prefect. "This Document on the Formation of Conscience, which has now been accepted and promulgated by the Catholic Bishops, represents something of a mammoth struggle. It took several years to prepare and, at one point, when it was mainly the work of a group of theologians, it appeared to be doomed. It was at that juncture that I was approached by my brother bishops with the proposal that I take it under my wing and rewrite the whole thing.... [T]he end result, now that it has been studied and improved by the contributions of a number of bishops is, I believe, worthwhile. I am rather proud of it and I wanted you to have a copy as soon as possible."[13]

If Rome was wary of the Canadian hierarchy as a consequence of the 1968 statement, perhaps the 1973 document would go some way to assuage her fears. The latter statement was not a repudiation of the earlier one but a careful amplification. It might appease Rome; it was good theology based on sturdy argumentation. But would it appease the homefront critics?

---

[1] T.S. Eliot, "Thoughts after Lambeth," *Selected Essays* (London: Faber and Faber, 1969), p. 375.

[2] John G.J. O'Driscoll, "Divorce, Abortion, and Birth Control," in Brief to the Bishops: *Canadian Catholic Laymen Speak Their Minds,* ed. Paul T. Harris (Toronto: Longmans, 1965), p. 38.

[3] "Final Report of the Pontifical Commission on Population, Family and Birth," included in Robert Blair Kaiser's *The Encyclical that Never Was* (London: Sheed and Ward, 1987), p. 10.

[4] "Statement on the Synod of Bishops, issued October 19, 1969.

[5] Arthur McCormack, "Light on Humanae Vitae," *The Tablet,* December 12, 1987, p. 1346.

[6] Brocard Sewell, *The Vatican Oracle* (London: Duckworth, 1970), p. 97.

[7] Francis X. Murphy, *The Papacy Today* (New York: Macmillan, 1981), p. 131.

[8] John Horgan, ed., Humanae Vitae *and the Bishops: The Encyclical and the Statements of the National Hierarchies* (Shannon: Irish University Press, 1972), p. 8.

[9] As quoted in *The Encyclical that Never Was*, p. 48.

[10] Anne Roche, *The Gates of Hell : The Struggle for the Catholic Church* (Toronto: McClelland and Stewart, 1986), pp. 97-98.

[11] Anne Roche Muggeridge, *The Desolate City: The Catholic Church in Ruins* (Toronto: McClelland and Stewart, 1986), pp. 97-98.

[12] Letter to John Cardinal Dearden, December 14, 1973.

[13] Letter to John Cardinal Wright, December 14, 1973.

15.

FINAL REPORT OF THE PONTIFICAL COMMISSION ON POPULATION, FAMILY AND BIRTH

I: The Majority View

The pastoral constitution on the Church in the modern world *(Gaudium et Spes)* has not explained the question of responsible parenthood under all its aspects. To those problems as yet unresolved, a response is to be given in what follows. This response, however, can only be understood if it is grasped in an integrated way within the universal concept of salvation history.

In creating the world, God gave man the power and the duty to form the world in spirit and freedom and, through his creative capacity, to actuate his own personal nature. In his Word, God himself, as the first efficient cause of the whole evolution of the world and of man, is present and active in history. The story of God and of man, therefore, should be seen as a shared work. And it should be seen that man's tremendous progress in control of matter by technical means, and the universal and total 'intercommunication' that has been achieved, correspond perfectly to the divine decrees (cf. *Gaudium et Spes* [GS], I, c. 3).

In the fullness of time, the Word of the eternal Father entered into history and took his place within it, so that by his work humanity and the world might become sharers in salvation. After his ascension to the Father, the Lord continues to accomplish his work through the church. As God became man, so his church is really incarnate in the world. But because the world, to which the church ought to represent the mystery of Christ, always undergoes changes, the church itself necessarily and continually is in pilgrimage. Its essence and fundamental structures remain immutable always; and yet no one can say of the church that at any time it is sufficiently understood or bounded by definition (cf. Paul VI *Ecclesiam Suam* and in his opening speech to the second session of Vatican Council II).

The church was constituted in the course of time by Christ, its principle of origin is the Word of creation and salvation. For this reason the church draws understanding of its own mystery not only from the past, but standing in the present time and looking to the future, assumes within itself the whole progress of the human race. The church is always being made more sure of this. What John XXIII wished to express by the word 'aggiornamento,' Paul VI took up, using the phrase 'dialogue with the world,' and in his encyclical *Ecclesiam Suam* has the following: 'The world cannot be saved from the outside. As the Word of God became man, so must a man to a certain degree identify with the forms of life of those to whom he wishes to bring the message of Christ. Without invoking privileges, which would but widen the separation, without employing unintelligible terminology, he must share the common way of life – provided that it is human and honorable especially of the most humble, if he wishes to be listened to and understood' (par. 87).

In response to the many problems posed by the changes occurring today in almost every field, the church in Vatican Council II has entered into the way of dialogue. 'The church guards the heritage of God's Word and draws from it religious and moral principles, without always having at hand the solution to particular problems. She desires thereby to add the light of revealed truth to mankind's store of experience, so that the path which humanity has taken in recent times will not be a dark one' (GS, I, c. 3, § 33).

In its fulfillment of its mission the church must propose obligatory norms of human and Christian life from the deposit of faith in an open dialogue with the world. But since moral obligations can never be detailed in all their concrete particularities, the personal responsibility of each individual must always be called into play. This is even clearer today because of the complexity of modern life: the concrete moral norms to be followed must not be pushed to an extreme.

In the present study, dealing with problems relating to responsible parenthood, the Holy Father through his willingness to enter into dialogue has given it an importance unprecedented in history. After several years of study, a commission of experts called together by him, made up for the most part of laymen from various fields of competency, has prepared material for him, which was lastly examined by a special group of bishops.

PART 1: FUNDAMENTAL PRINCIPLES

Chapter I: The Fundamental Values of Marriage

'The well-being of the individual person and of human and Christian society is intimately linked with the healthy condition of that community produced by marriage and the family. Hence Christians and all men who hold this community in high esteem sincerely rejoice in the various ways by which men today find help in fostering this community of love and perfecting its life, and by which spouses and parents are assisted in their lofty calling. Those who rejoice in such aid look for additional benefits from them and labour to bring them about.' (GS, II, c. 1, § 47).

Over the course of centuries the church, with the authority conferred it by Christ our Lord, has constantly protected the dignity and essential values of this institution whose author is God himself, who had made man to his image and raised him to share in his love. It has always taught this to its faithful and to all men. In our day it again intends to propose to those many families who are seeking a right way how they are able, in the conditions of our times, to live and develop fully the higher gifts of this community.

A couple *(unio conjugum)* ought to be considered above all a community of persons which has in itself the beginning of new human life. Therefore those things which strengthen and make more profound the union of persons within this community must never be separated from the procreative finality which specifies the conjugal community. Pius XI, in *Casti Connubii* already, referring to the tradition expressed in the Roman Catechism, said: 'This mutual inward molding of a husband and wife, this determined effort to perfect each other, can in a very real sense be said to be the chief reason and purpose of matrimony, provided matrimony be looked at not in the restricted sense as instituted for the conception and education of the child, but more widely as the blending of life as a whole and the mutual interchange and sharing thereof' (AAS., XXII, 1930, page 547).

But conjugal love, without which marriage would not be a true union of persons, is not exhausted in the simple mutual giving in which one party seeks only the other. Married people know well that they are only able to perfect each other and establish a true community if their love does not end in a merely egotistic union but according to the condition of each is made truly fruitful in the creation of new life. Nor on the other hand can the procreation and education of a child be considered a truly human fruitfulness unless it is the result of a love existing in a family community. Conjugal love and fecundity are in no way opposed, but complement one another in such a way that they constitute an almost indivisible unity.

Unfolding the natural and divine law, the church urges all men to be true dispensers of the divine gifts, to act in conformity with their own personal nature and to shape their married life according to the dictates of the natural and divine law. God created man male and female so that, joined together in the bonds of love, they might perfect one another through a mutual, corporal and spiritual giving and that they might carefully prepare their children, the fruit of this love, for a truly human life. Let them regard one another always as persons and not as mere objects. Therefore everything should be done in marriage so that the goods conferred on this institution can be attained as perfectly as possible and so that fidelity and moral rightness can be served.

Chapter II: Responsible Parenthood and the Regulation of Conception

To cultivate and realize all the essential values of marriage, married people should become ever more deeply aware of the profundity of their vocation and the breadth of their responsibilities. In this spirit and with this awareness let married people seek how they might better be 'co-operators with the love of God and Creator and be, so to speak, the interpreters of that love' for the task of procreation and education (GS, II, c. 1, § 50).

1. *Responsible parenthood* (that is, generous and prudent parenthood) is a fundamental requirement of a married couple's true mission. Illumined by faith, the spouses understand the scope of their whole task; helped by divine grace, they try to fulfill it as a true service, carried out in the name of God and Christ, oriented

to the temporal and eternal good of men. To save, protect and promote the good of the offspring, and thus of the family community and of human society, the married couple will take care to consider all values and seek to realize them harmoniously in the best way they can, with proper reverence towards each other as persons and according to the concrete circumstances of their life. They will make a judgment in conscience before God about the number of children to have and educate according to the objective criteria indicated by Vatican Council II (GS, II, c. 1, § 50 and c. 5, § 80).

This responsible, generous and prudent parenthood always carries with it new demands. In today's situations, both because of new difficulties and because of new possibilities for the education of children, couples are hardly able to meet such demands unless with generosity and sincere deliberation.

With a view to the education of children, let couples more and more build the community of their whole life on a true and magnanimous love, under the guidance of the spirit of Christ (I Cor. 12, 31–13, 13). For this stable community between man and woman shaped by conjugal love, is the true foundation of human fruitfulness. This community between married people through which an individual finds himself by opening himself to another, constitutes the optimum situation in which children can be educated in an integrated way. Through developing their communion and intimacy in all its aspects, a married couple is able to provide that environment of love, mutual understanding and humble acceptance which is the necessary condition of authentic human education and maturation.

Responsible parenthood – through which married persons intend to observe and cultivate the essential values of matrimony with a view to the good of persons (the good of the child to be educated, of the couples themselves and of the whole of human society) – is one of the conditions and expressions of a true conjugal chastity. For genuine love, rooted in faith, hope and charity, ought to inform the whole life and every action of a couple. By the strength of this chastity the couple tend to the actuation of that true love precisely inasmuch as it is conjugal and fruitful. They accept generously and prudently their task with all its values, combining them in the best way possible according to the particular circumstances of their life and in spite of difficulties.

Married people know well that very often they are invited to abstain, and sometimes not just for a brief time, because of the habitual conditions of their life, for example, the good of one of the spouses (physical or psychic well-being), or because of what are called professional necessities. This abstinence a chaste couple know and accept as a condition of progress into a deeper mutual love, fully conscious that the grace of Christ will sustain and strengthen them for this.

Seeing their vocation in all its depth and breadth and accepting it, the couple follows Christ and tries to imitate Him in a true evangelical spirit (Mt. 5, 1-12). Comforted by the spirit of Christ according to the inner man and rooted in faith and charity (Eph. 3, 16-17), they try to build up a total life community, 'bearing with one another charitably, in complete selflessness, gentleness and patience' (Eph. 4, 2-3, cf. Col. 3, 12-17). They will have the peace of Christ in their hearts and give thanks to God the Father as his holy and elected sons.

A couple then is able to ask and expect that they will be helped by all in such a way that they are progressively able to approach more and more responsible parenthood. They need the help of all in order to fulfill their responsibilities with full liberty and in the most favorable material, psychological, cultural and spiritual conditions. By the development of the family, then, the whole society is built up with regard to the good of all men in the whole world.

2. The *regulation of conception* appears necessary for many couples who wish to achieve a responsible, open and reasonable parenthood in today's circumstances. If they are to observe and cultivate all the essential values of marriage, married people need decent and human means for the regulation of conception. They should be able to expect the collaboration of all, especially from men of learning and science, in order that they have at their disposal means agreeable and worthy of man in the fulfilling of his responsible parenthood.

It is proper to man, created in the image of God, to use what is given in physical nature in a way that he may develop it to its full significance with a view to the good of the whole person. This is the cultural mission which the Creator has commissioned to men, whom he had made his co-operators. According to the exigencies of human nature and with the progress of the sciences, men should discover means more and more apt and adequate so that the 'ministry which must be fulfilled in a manner which is worthy of man' (GS, II, c. 1, § 51) can be fulfilled by married people.

This intervention of man in physiological processes, an intervention ordained to the essential values of marriage and first of all to the good of children, is to be judged according to the fundamental principles and objective criteria of morality, which will be treated below (in Chap. 4).

'Marriage and conjugal love are by their nature ordained towards the begetting and educating of children' (GS II, c. 1, § 50). A right ordering toward the good of the child within the conjugal and familial community pertains to the essence of human sexuality. Therefore the morality of sexual acts between married people takes its meaning first of all and specifically from the ordering of their actions in a fruitful married life, that is one which is practised with responsible, generous and prudent parenthood. It does not then depend upon the direct fecundity of each and every particular act. Moreover, the morality of every marital act depends upon the requirements of mutual love in all its aspects. In a word, the morality of sexual actions is thus to be judged by the true exigencies of the nature of human sexuality, whose meaning is maintained and promoted especially by conjugal chastity, as we have said previously.

More and more clearly, for a conscience correctly formed, a willingness to raise a family with full acceptance of the various human and Christian responsibilities is altogether distinguished from a mentality and way of married life which in its totality is egotistically and irrationally opposed to fruitfulness. This truly 'contraceptive' mentality and practice has been condemned by the traditional doctrine of the Church and will always be condemned as gravely sinful.

Chapter III: On the Continuity of Doctrine and Its Deeper Understanding

The tradition of the Church which is concerned with the morality of conjugal relations began with the beginning of the Church. It should be observed, however, that the tradition developed in the argument and conflict with heretics such as the Gnostics, the Manichaeans and later the Cathari, all of whom condemned procreation or the transmission of life as something evil, and nonetheless indulged in moral vices. Consequently this tradition always, albeit with various words, intended to protect two fundamental values: the good of procreation and the rectitude of marital intercourse. Moreover, the Church always taught another truth equally fundamental, although hidden in a mystery, namely original sin. This had wounded man in his various faculties, including sexuality. Man could only be healed of this wound by the grace of a Saviour. This is one of the reasons why Christ took marriage and raised it to a sacrament of the New Law.

It is not surprising that in the course of centuries this tradition was always interpreted in expressions and formulas proper to the times and that the words with which it was expressed and the reasons on which it was based were changed by knowledge which is now obsolete. Nor was there maintained always a right equilibrium of all the elements. Some authors even used expressions which depreciated the matrimonial state. But what is of real importance is that the same values were again and again reaffirmed. Consequently, an egotistical, hedonistic and contraceptive way which turns the practice of married life in an arbitrary fashion from its ordination to a human, generous and prudent fecundity is always against the nature of man and can never be justified.

The large amount of knowledge and facts which throw light on today's world suggest that it is not to contradict the genuine sense of this tradition and the purpose of the previous doctrinal condemnations if we speak of the regulation of conception by using means, human and decent, ordered to favoring fecundity in the totality of married life and toward the realization of the authentic values of a fruitful matrimonial community.

The reasons in favour of this affirmation are of several kinds: social changes in matrimony and the family, especially in the role of the woman; lowering of the infant mortality rate; new bodies of knowledge in biology, psychology, sexuality and demography; a changed estimation of the value and meaning of human sexuality and of conjugal relations; most of all, a better grasp of the duty of man to humanize and to bring to greater perfection for the life of man what is given in nature. Then must be considered the sense of the faithful: according to it, condemnation of a couple to a long and often heroic abstinence as the means to regulate conception, cannot be founded on the truth.

A further step in the doctrinal evolution, which it seems now should be developed, is founded less on these facts than on a better, deeper and more correct understanding of conjugal life and of the conjugal act when these other changes occur. The doctrine on marriage and its essential values remains the same and whole, but it is now applied differently out of a deeper understanding.

This maturation has been prepared and has already begun. The magisterium itself is in evolution. Leo XIII spoke less explicitly in his encyclical *Arcanum* than did Pius XI in his wonderful doctrinal synthesis of *Casti Connubii* of 1930 which gave a fresh start to so many beginnings in a living conjugal spirituality. He proclaimed, using the very words of the Roman Catechism, the importance, in a true sense the primary importance, of true conjugal love for the community of matrimony. The notion of responsible parenthood which is implied in the notion of a prudent and generous regulation of conception advanced in Vatican Council II, had already been prepared by Pius XII. The acceptance of a lawful application of the calculated sterile periods of the woman – that the application is legitimate presupposes right motives – makes a separation between the sexual act which is explicitly intended and its reproductive effect which is intentionally excluded.

The tradition has always rejected seeking this separation with a contraceptive intention for motives spoiled by egoism and hedonism, and such seeking can never be admitted. The true opposition is not sought between some material conformity to the physiological processes of nature and some artificial intervention. For it is natural to man to put under human control what is given by physical nature. The opposition is really to be sought between one way of acting which is contraceptive and opposed to a prudent and generous fruitfulness, and another way which is in an ordered relationship to responsible fruitfulness and which has a concern for education and all the essential, human and Christian values.

In such a conception the substance of tradition stands in continuity and is respected. The new elements which today are discerned in tradition under the influence of new knowledge and facts were found in it before; they were undifferentiated but not denied; so that the problem in today's terms is new and has not been proposed before in this way. In light of the new data these elements are being explained and made more precise. The moral obligation of following fundamental norms and fostering all the essential values in a balanced fashion is strengthened not weakened. The virtue of chastity by which a couple positively regulates the practice of sexual relations is all the more demanded. The criteria of morality, therefore, which are human and Christian, demand and at the same time foster a spirituality which is more profound in married life, with faith, hope and charity informed according to the spirit of the Gospel.

Chapter IV: The Objective Criteria of Morality

The question comes up which many men rightly think to be of great importance, at least practically: what are the objective criteria by which to choose a method of reconciling the needs of marital life with a right ordering of this life to fruitfulness in the procreation and education of offspring?

It is obvious that the method is not to be left to purely arbitrary decision.

1. In resolving the similar problem of responsible parenthood and the appropriate determination of the size of the family, Vatican Council II has shown the way. The objective criteria are the various values and needs duly and harmoniously evaluated. These objective criteria are to be applied by the couples, acting from a rightly formed conscience and according to their concrete situation. In the words of the Council: 'Thus they will fulfill their task with human and Christian responsibility. With docile reverence towards God, they will come to the right decision by common counsel and effort. They will thoughtfully take into account both their own welfare and that of their children, those already born and those which may be foreseen. For this accounting they will reckon with both the material and spiritual conditions of the times as well as of their state in life. Finally they will consult the interests of the family community, of temporal society, and of the Church herself.... But in their manner of acting, spouses should be aware that they cannot proceed arbitrarily. They must always be governed according to a conscience dutifully conformed to the Divine Law itself, and should be submissive toward the Church's teaching office, which authentically interprets that law in the light of the gospel' (GS 11 c. I § 50; cf. c. 5, § 87).

In other questions of conjugal life, one should proceed in the same way. There are various objective criteria which are concretely applied by couples themselves acting with a rightly formed conscience. All, for example, know that the objective criteria prohibit that the intimate acts of conjugal life, even if carried out in a way which could be called 'natural,' be practiced if there is a loss of physical or psychic health or if there is neglect of the personal dignity of the spouses or if they are carried out in an egotistic or hedonistic way. These objective criteria are the couples', to be applied by them to their concrete situation, avoiding pure arbitrariness in forming their judgment. It is impossible to determine exhaustively by a general judgment and ahead of time for each individual case what these objective criteria will demand in the concrete situation of a couple.

2. Likewise, there are objective criteria as to the means to be chosen for responsibly determining the size of the family: if they are rightly applied, the couples themselves will find and determine the way of proceeding.

In grave language, Vatican Council II has reaffirmed that abortion is altogether to be excluded from the means of responsibly preventing birth. Indeed, abortion is not a method of preventing conception but of eliminating offspring already conceived. This affirmation about acts which do not spare an offspring already conceived is to be repeated in regard to those interventions as to which there is serious grounds to suspect that they are abortive.

Sterilization, since it is a drastic and irreversible intervention in a matter of great importance, is generally to be excluded as a means of responsibly avoiding conception.

Moreover, the natural law and reason illuminated by Christian faith dictate that a couple proceed in choosing means not arbitrarily but according to objective criteria. These objective criteria for the right choice of methods are the conditions for keeping and fostering the essential values of marriage as a community of fruitful love. If these criteria are observed, then a right ordering of the human act according to its object, end and circumstances is maintained.

Among these criteria, this must be put first: the action must correspond to the nature of the person and of his acts so that the whole meaning of the mutual giving and of human procreation is kept in a context of true love (cf. GS, II, c. 1, § 51). *Secondly,* the means which are chosen should have effectiveness proportionate to the degree of right or necessity of averting a new conception temporarily or permanently. *Thirdly,* every method of preventing conception – not excluding either periodic or absolute abstinence – carries with it some negative element of physical evil which the couple more or less seriously feels. This negative element or physical evil can arise under different aspects: account must be taken of the biological, hygienic and psychological aspects, and personal dignity of the spouses, and the possibility of expressing sufficiently and aptly the interpersonal relation or conjugal love. The means to be chosen, where several are possible, is that which carries with it the least possible negative element, according to the concrete situation of the couple. *Fourthly,* then, in choosing concretely among means, much depends on what means may be available in a certain region or at a certain time or for a certain couple; and this may depend on the economic situation.

Therefore not arbitrarily, but as the law of nature and of God commands, let couples form a judgment which is objectively founded, with all the criteria considered. This they may do without major difficulty, and with peace of mind, if they take common and prudent counsel before God. They should, however, to the extent possible, be instructed about the criteria by competent persons and be educated as to the right application of the criteria. Well instructed and prudently educated as Christians, they will prudently and serenely decide what is truly for the good of the couple and of the children, and does not neglect their own personal Christian perfection, and is, therefore, what God revealing himself through the natural law and Christian revelation, sets before them to do.

PART II: PASTORAL NECESSITIES

Chapter I: The Task and Fundamental Conditions of Educational Renewal

Sometimes when a new aspect of human life obtains a special place in the area of man's responsibility, a task of educational renewal is imposed in a seriously binding way.

In order that spouses may take up the duty of responsible parenthood, they must grasp, more than in the past, the meaning of fruitfulness and experience a desire for it. In order that they may give to married life its unitive value, and do so in service of its procreative function, they must develop an increasingly purer respect for their mutual needs, the sense of community and the acceptance of their common Christian vocation.

It will not be a surprise that this conviction of a greater responsibility will come about as the effect and crown of a gradual development of the meaning of marriage and conjugal spirituality. For several generations, in an always increasing number, couples have sought to live their proper married vocation in a more profound and more conscientious way. The doctrine of the magisterium and especially the encyclical *Casti Connubii* notably contributed and strengthened this formation of conscience by giving to it its full meaning.

The more urgent the appeal is made to observe mutual love and charity in every expression of married life, the more urgent is the necessity of forming consciences, of educating spouses to a sense of responsibility and of awakening a right sense of values. This new step in the development of conjugal life cannot bear all its fruits, unless it is accompanied by an immense educational activity. No one will regret that these new demands stirred by the Holy Spirit call the entire human race to this profound moral maturity.

Couples who might think they find in the doctrine, as it has just been proposed, an open door to laxism or easy solutions make a grave mistake, of which they will be the first victims. The conscientious decision to be made by spouses about the number of children is not a matter of small importance. On the contrary, it imposes a more conscientious fulfilling of their vocation to fruitfulness in the consideration of a whole complex of values which are involved here. The same is true of the responsibility of the spouses for the development of their common life in such a way that it will be a source of continual progress and perfection.

The God who created male and female, in order that they might be two in one flesh, in order that they might bring the world under their control, in order that they might increase and multiply (Gen. 1–2), is the God who has elevated their union to the dignity of a sacrament and so disposed that in this world it is a special sign of His own love for His people. He Himself will gird the spouses with His strength, His light, His love and His joy in the strength of the spirit of Christ. Who then would doubt that couples, all couples, will not be able to respond to the demands of their vocation?

Chapter II: Further Consideration: Application of the Doctrine of Matrimony to Different Parts of the World

1. It seems very necessary to establish some pontifical institute or secretariat for the study of the sciences connected with married life. In this commission there could be continual collaboration in open dialogue among experts competent in various areas. The aim of this institute (or secretariat) would be, among other duties, to carry further the research and reflection begun by the commission. The various studies which the commission has already done could be made public. It would be in a special way for this institute to study how the doctrine of matrimony should be applied to different parts of the world and to contribute to the formation of priests and married couples dedicated to the family apostolate by sending experts to them (cf. GS 11, c. 1, § 52).

2. Universal principles and the essential values of matrimony and married life become actual in ways which partially differ according to different cultures and different mentalities. Consequently there is a special task for episcopal conferences to institute organizations for investigation and dialogue between families, between representatives of the different sciences and pastors of souls. They would also have the task of judging which may be in practice the more apt pastoral means in each region to promote the health formation of consciences and education to a sense of responsibility.

Episcopal conferences should be particularly concerned that priests and married lay persons be adequately formed in a more spiritual and moral understanding of Christian matrimony. Thus they will be prepared to extend pastoral action to the renewal of families in the spirit of 'aggiornamento' initiated by the constitution on the church in the modern world.

Under their guidance there should also be action to start in each region the genuine fostering of all families in a context of social evolution which should be truly human. The fostering of the role of woman is of special importance here.

There are many reforms and initiatives which are needed to open the way to decent and joyful living for all families. Together with all men of goodwill, Christians must approach this great work of human development, without which the elevation of families can never become actual. Christianity does not teach some ideal for a small number of elect, but the vocation of all to the essential values of human life. It cannot be that anyone would wish to elevate his own family without at the same time actively dedicating himself to opening a way for similar elevation for all families in all parts of the world.

Chapter III: Demographic Fact and Policy

The increase of inhabitants cannot in any way be said to be something evil or calamitous for the human race. As children are 'the most excellent gift of matrimony' (GS II, c. 1, § 50) and the object of the loving care of the parents, which demands from them many sacrifices, so the great number of men pertaining to a certain nation and constituting the whole human race spread over the globe is the foundation of all social sharing and cultural progress. Thus there should be afforded to it all those things which according to social justice are due to men as persons.

The church is not ignorant of the immense difficulties and profound transformations which have arisen from the conditions of contemporary life throughout the world and especially in certain regions where there has been a rapid rise in population. That is why she again and again raises her voice to urge various nations and the whole human family to help one another in truly human progress united in true solidarity and excluding every intention of domination. Then they might avoid all those things both in the political and in the social order which restrict or dissipate in an egotistical way the full utilization of the goods of the earth which are destined for all men.

The church, by her doctrine and by her supernatural aids, intends to help all families so that they might find the right way in undertaking their generous and prudent responsibility. Governments which have the care of the common good should look with great concern on subhuman conditions of families and 'beware of solutions contradicting the moral law, solutions which have been promoted publicly or privately, and sometimes actually imposed' (Constitution on the Church in the Modern World, II, c. 5, § 87). These solutions have contradicted the moral law in particular by propagating abortion or sterilization. Political demography can be called human only if the rights of parents with regard to the procreation and education of children are respected and conditions of life are fostered with all vigor so that parents are enabled to exercise their responsibilities before God and society.

Chapter IV: The Inauguration and Further Development of Means for Education of Couples and Youth

1. Couples are burdened by multiple responsibilities throughout the whole of life; they seek light and aid. With the favor of God there will develop in many regions what has already been initiated often by the married couples themselves, to sustain families in their building and continual development.

Maximum help is to be given to parents in their educational task. They strongly desire to provide the best for their children. The more parents are conscious of their office of fruitfulness, which is extended over the whole time in which the education of their children is accomplished, so much the more do they seek a way of acquiring better preparation to carry out this responsibility.

Moreover, in exercising this educational office, the spouses mature more deeply in it themselves, create a unity, become rich in love and apply themselves with the high task of giving themselves with united energies to the high task of giving life and education.

2. The building up of the conjugal and family community does not happen without thought. Therefore it is fitting everywhere to set up and work out many better means of remote and immediate preparation of youth for marriage. This requires the collaboration of everyone. Married people who are already well educated will have a great and indispensable part in this work. In these tasks of providing help to spouses and to the young who are preparing to build and develop a conjugal and family community, priests and religious will cooperate closely with the families. Without this cooperation, in which each one has his own indispensable part, there will never be apt methods of education to those responsibilities of the vocation which places the sacrament in clear light so that its full and profound meaning shines forth.

The church, which holds the deposit of the Gospel, has to bring this noble message to all men in the entire world. This announcing of the Gospel, grounded in love, illumines every aspect of married and family life. Every aspect, every task and responsibility of the conjugal and family community shines with a clear light, in love toward one's neighbor – a love which is rich with human values and is formed by the divine interpersonal love of Father, Son and Holy Spirit. May the spirit of Christ's love more and more penetrate families everywhere so that together with John, the beloved disciple of Jesus, married couples, parents and children may always understand more deeply the wonderful relation between love of God and love of one another (1 John 4, 7–5, 4).

II. THE CONSERVATIVE CASE

I : The Strength of the Tradition

A. THE STATE OF THE QUESTION

The central question to which the Church must now respond is this: *Is contraception always seriously evil?* All other questions discussed are reduced in the final analysis to this simple and central question. If a clear answer is given to this question, other questions can be solved without great theological difficulty. The whole world, the faithful as well as the non-believers, wish to know what the Church will now have to say on this question.

Contraception is understood by the Church as any use of the marriage right in the exercise of which the act is deprived of its natural power for the procreation of life through human intervention. *Contraceptive sterilization* is related to the definition of contraception just given. It may be defined theologically as any physical intervention in the generative process *(opus naturae)* which, before or after the proper placing of generative acts *(opus hominis),* causes these acts to be deprived of their natural power for the procreation of life by human intervention.

Always evil. Something which can never be justified by any motive or any circumstance is always evil because it is intrinsically evil. It is wrong not because of a precept of positive law, but of reason of the natural law. It is not evil because it is prohibited, but it is prohibited because it is evil. Homicide may be used as an example, inasmuch as the direct killing of an innocent person can be justified by no motive and no circumstance whatsoever. Understanding "something which is always evil" in this sense, the faithful are now asking the Church: is contraception always seriously evil?

B. WHAT ANSWER HAS THE CHURCH GIVEN TO THIS QUESTION UP TO NOW?

A constant and perennial affirmative answer is found in the documents of the magisterium and in the whole history of teaching on the question.

1. First of all, some more recent documents of the pontifical teaching authority may be cited, namely, the encyclical *Casti Connubii* of Pius XI (1930); the *Allocution to Midwives* of Pius XII (1951); the encyclical *Mater et Magistra* of John XXIII (1961).

Pius XI, *Casti Connubii* (§§ 54, 56, 57): "But no reason, however grave, may be put forward by which anything *intrinsically* against nature may become conformable to nature and morally good. Since, therefore, the *conjugal act* is destined primarily *by nature* for the begetting of children, those who in exercising it deliberately frustrate its natural power and purpose sin against nature and commit a deed which is shameful and *intrinsically vicious*...

"Since, therefore, openly departing from the *uninterrupted Christian tradition* some recently have judged it possible solemnly to declare another doctrine regarding this question, the Catholic Church, to whom God has entrusted the defense of the integrity and purity of morals, standing erect in the midst of the moral ruin which surrounds her, in order that she may *preserve the chastity of the nuptial union from being defiled by this foul stain,* raises her voice in token of her divine ambassadorship and *through our mouth proclaims anew: any use whatsoever of matrimony exercised in such a way that the act is deliberately frustrated in its natural power to generate life is an offence against the law of God and of nature,* and those who indulge in such are branded with the guilt of a grave sin...

"If any confessor or pastor of souls, which may God forbid, leads the faithful entrusted to him into these errors or should at least confirm them by approval or by guilty silence, let him be mindful of the fact that he must render a strict account to God, the Supreme Judge, for the betrayal of his sacred trust, and let him take to himself the words of Christ: 'They are blind and leaders of the blind'; and if the blind lead the blind, both fall into the pit.'"

Pius XII, *Allocution to Midwives,* 1951: "In his encyclical *Casti Connubii* of December 31, 1930, our predecessor, Pius XII, of happy memory, solemnly restated the basic law of the conjugal act and conjugal relations: 'Every attempt on the part of the married couple during the conjugal act or during the development of its natural consequences, to deprive it of its inherent power and to hinder the procreation of a new life is immoral. No "indication" or need can change an action that is intrinsically immoral into an action that is moral and lawful.'

"This prescription holds good today just as much as it did yesterday. It will hold tomorrow and always, for it is not a mere precept of human right but the expression of a natural and Divine Law...

"Let our words be for you equivalent to a sure norm in all those things in which your profession and apostolic task demands that you work with a certain and firm opinion...

"Direct sterilization, that which aims at making procreation impossible as both means and end, is a grave violation of the moral law, and therefore illicit. Even public authority has no right to permit it under the pretext of any 'indication' whatsoever, and still less to prescribe it or to have it carried out to the harm of the innocent..."

Other addresses of Pius XII should be noted in which till the end of his life he explicitly and implicitly reiterated that contraception was always gravely evil. Note, for example, his address to the Roman Rota (1941); to Catholic doctors (1949); to families (1951); to histopathologists (1952); to the Society of Urologists (1953); to a symposium of geneticists (1953); to the Congress for Fertility and Sterility (1956); to the Society of Haematologists (1958).

John XXIII, *Mater et Magistra,* 1961, writes as follows: "Hence, the real solution of the problem (over-population) is not to be found in expedients which offend against the divinely established moral order or which attack human life at its very source, but in a renewed, scientific and technical effort on man's part to deepen and extend his dominion over nature... The transmission of human life is the result of a personal and conscious act, and, as such, is subject to the all-holy, inviolable and immutable laws of God, which no man may ignore or disobey. He is not therefore, permitted to use certain ways and means which are allowable in the propagation of plant and animal life. Human life is sacred – all men must recognize that fact. From its inception it reveals the creating hand of God. Those who violate his laws not only offend the Divine Majesty and degrade themselves and humanity, they also sap the vitality of the political community of which they are the members" (§§189, 193, 194).

2.   The answer of the Church in the present century is also illustrated by *declarations of the bishops* either (a) *collectively* speaking in a particular region or (b) speaking *individually* in their own diocese.

(a) The German bishops, 1913 (and from this followed their "instruction for Confessors" several years later); the French bishops, 1919; the bishops of the United States of America, 1920; the Belgian bishops, 1920; the bishops of India, 1960; the bishops of the United States of America, 1959; the bishops of England, 1964; the bishops of Honduras, 1966. In Spain (1919) there were eight dioceses in which conjugal onanism was a reserved sin.

(b) Here are several examples of pastoral letters of this century; Rutten, Liége, 1907; Mercier, Malines, 1909; Cologne, 1913; Cardinal Bourne, Westminster, 1930; Cardinal Montini, Milan, 1960; Cardinal Gracias, Bombay, 1961. More notable was the declaration of Cardinal Bourne, immediately after the Lambeth Conference of 1930, because of the fact that he publicly denounced the (Anglican) bishops of the Lambeth Conference as if they had abdicated all title whereby they could pretend to be "authoritative interpreters of Christian morality."

It must be noted that the Holy See between 1816 and 1929, through the Roman curia, answered questions in this matter 19 times. Since then it has spoken almost as many times. In the responses given, it was at least implicitly supposed that contraception was always seriously evil.

3. History provides fullest evidence (cf especially the excellent work of Professor John T. Noonan, *Contraception,* Harvard University Press, 1965) that the answer of the Church has always and everywhere been the same, from the beginning up to the present decade. One can find no period of history, no document of the Church, no theological school, scarcely one Catholic theologian, who ever denied that contraception was always seriously evil. The teaching of the Church in this matter is absolutely constant. Until the present century this teaching was peacefully possessed by all other Christians, whether Orthodox or Anglican or Protestant. The Orthodox retain this as common teaching today.

The theological history of the use of matrimony is very complicated. It evolved very much in the course of the centuries up to the Second Vatican Council. Teachings which have slowly evolved this way are especially: concerning the nature of sexual concupiscence; the teaching of the malice (venial) of the use of matrimony without the procreative intention or from motives of concupiscence; the teaching about the positive value of the sexual element in the use of matrimony, and as it involves conjugal love. Then, too, human sexuality and its genuine value is now being treated more positively. The history of this evolution is by no means simple.

On the contrary, the theological history of contraception, comparatively speaking, is sufficiently simple, at least with regard to the central question : Is contraception always seriously evil? For in answer to this question there has never been any variation and scarcely any evolution in the teaching. The ways of formulating and explaining this teaching have evolved, but not the doctrine itself.

Therefore it is not a question of a teaching proposed in 1930 which because of new physiological facts and new theological perspectives ought to be changed. It is a question rather of a teaching which until the present decade was constantly and authentically taught by the Church.

C. UNSATISFACTORY EXPLANATIONS OF THE ORIGIN AND EVOLUTION OF THE CHURCH'S TEACHING

Among those who wish to change the doctrine (or who declare that it has already evolved) are those who appeal to various past circumstances, as if the malice of contraception was rooted in these circumstances and was to be explained by them. Further, they argue that since these circumstances have entirely changed, the teaching itself can legitimately be changed. Examples of this kind of argumentation follow.

1. Some say that the foundation of this teaching was the following biblical text: "Increase and multiply." The malice of contraception would then be in the violation of this affirmative precept. But theologians and the Church have considered

contraception as a violation not of an affirmative precept, but of a negative precept which obliges always and everywhere: "Let no one impede human life in its proximate causes," or: "Let no one violate the ordination of this act and processes to the good of the species."

Theologians have never said: "Homicide is always evil because God has said, 'Increase and multiply'; but because He has said, 'You may not kill the innocent.'" "Similarly they have not said that contraception is evil because God has said, "Increase and multiply"; but because they have considered it in some way analogous to homicide. This analogy was constant in tradition up until the eighteenth century and still more recently it was invoked by the hierarchy of Germany (1913) and India (1960). Through the course of the centuries the malice of contraception has lain in the violation of the essential ordination of the generative faculty to the good of the species. It has been expressed in various formulations. But in every age it is clearly evident that contraception essentially offends against the negative precept: "One may not deprive the conjugal act of its natural power for the procreation of new life."

2. Some say that the Church condemned contraception because of demographic needs, the necessity among rural people for larger families, the high mortality rate among the newborn, etc. So they argue: since these situations no longer exist, the foundation of the teaching has been removed and the teaching itself ought to be set aside.

As an answer to this, it must be said that both St. Augustine and St. Thomas taught that our earth was already sufficiently populated. There is no proof that such considerations as those cited in this paragraph have had any effect on the teaching of the Fathers, or theologians, or the magisterium.

3. Some say that older theologians had prohibited contraception because they falsely supposed that the procreative intention is always required in order that the use of matrimonial rights might not be considered sinful. In answer clearly the necessity of procreative intention was regularly insisted upon, lest there be committed a *venial* sin of sexual concupiscence, and without a doubt this teaching confirmed the condemnation of contraception. But it is impossible to understand how the *serious evil of* contraception could then be cited as an insignificant failure in the matter of chastity. Among theologians contraception was a damnable vice, an anticipated homicide, a serious and unnatural sin. Now to explain its malice by appealing to a defect in the procreative intention would be as inept as to say that a murderer merits capital punishment *because* he used another's instrument without permission in committing the homicide. It is not the teaching concerning the malice of contraception which has evolved now but rather the teaching of sexual concupiscence in the use of matrimony.

4. Some say that the teaching of the Church was founded on the false supposition that all conjugal acts are procreative by their very nature, whereas the facts of physiology show that very few of them are actually fertile or productive of

new life. In answer to this, it must be said that the older thinkers knew that many conjugal acts are actualy sterile, e.g., during pregnancy and old age. Moreover, a legitimate conclusion from the facts now known would be this: there are fewer acts which are as a matter of fact capable of producing new life; therefore, there are fewer acts against which a person in acting contraceptively would incur the specific malice of contraception. But the facts do not invite us to intervene contraceptively, now that we have a more accurate knowledge about fertility; rather they invite us to have a greater respect for them.

5. Others say that the teaching of the Church is based on an obsolete mediaeval notion of "nature," according to which nature would order its own processes to its own natural ends, fixed by the "intention of nature," and of God. Contraception, as something going against the order established by nature, would be considered intrinsically evil because it is "contrary to nature."

In answer to this: the teaching of the Church was first fully formulated and handed down constantly for several centuries before scholastic philosophy was refined. Secondly, in no way does it derive from any philosophy of nature (of the scholastics, Stoics or others) in which the natural physical order is the *general criterion* of morality for man. Thirdly, theology (just as scholastic philosophy) does not say that the physical ordering of things to their natural end is inviolable with respect to being "natural." It does attribute a special inviolability to this act and to the generative process precisely because they are generative of new *human life,* and life is not under man's dominion. It is not because of some philosophy which would make the physical order of nature as such the criterion of the morality of human acts.

D. WHY DOES THE CHURCH TEACH THAT CONTRACEPTION IS ALWAYS SERIOUSLY EVIL?

If we could bring forward arguments which are clear and cogent based on reason alone, it would not be necessary for our commission to exist, nor would the present state of affairs exist in the Church as it is.

1. The Fathers, theologians, and the Church herself has always taught that certain acts and the generative processes are in some way specially inviolable precisely because they are generative. This inviolability is attributed to the act and to the process, which are biological; not inasmuch as they are biological, but inasmuch as they are human, namely inasmuch as they are the object of human acts, and are destined by their nature to the good of the human species.

2. This inviolability was explained for many centuries by the Fathers, the theologians and in canon law as analogous to the inviolability of human life itself. This analogy is not merely rhetorical or metaphorical, but it expressed a fundamental moral truth. Human life already existing *(in facto esse)* is inviolable. Likewise, it is also in some sense inviolable in its proximate causes *(vita in fieri)*. To put it in another way; just as already existing human life is removed from the dominion of

man, so also in some similar way is human life as it comes to be; that is, the act and the generative process, inasmuch as they are generative, are removed from his dominion, in the course of centuries, scholastic philosophy explained this inviolability further and grounded it in the essential ordination of the act and the generative process to the good of the species.

3. The substratum of this teaching would seem to presuppose various Christian conceptions concerning the nature of God and of man, the union of the soul and the body which creates *one* human person, God as the Supreme Lord of human life, the special creation of each individual human soul. Moreover, the value of human life is presupposed as a fundamental good, which has in itself the reason for its inviolability, not because it is of man but because it is of God. This quasi-sacredness of natural human life (recall the quotation from John XXIII) is extended in the teaching of the Church to the acts and generative processes inasmuch as they are such. At least this is the way the matter must be conceived if we wish to understand the ancient traditional analogy to homicide and the severity with which the Fathers, the theologians and all faithful Christians have constantly rejected contraception.

Nor should one exclude from this view that malice in contraception which is derived precisely from violated chastity: first, because chastity is understood as regulating the total generative process; and secondly, because (especially in antiquity) the conjugal act which proceeded from unexcused concupiscence was considered for this reason to be venially sinful.

4. The philosophical arguments by which the teaching of the Church is attacked are diversely proposed by diverse people. Some see the malice principally in the fact that procreation itself (that is, the act and the generative process) is a certain fundamental human good (as truth, as life itself is such a good). To destroy it voluntarily is therefore evidently evil. For to have an intention, directly and actively contrary to a fundamental human good, is something intrinsically evil. St. Thomas spoke of this good, in discussing the matter, referring to "man in his proximate potency."

Others derive its malice also from the disorientation, whereby the act and the process, which are destined for the good of the species, are essentially deprived of their relation to this good of the species, and are subordinated to the good of the individual. Plus XII developed this argument.

5. But note: first, the question is not merely or principally philosophical. It depends on the nature of human life and human sexuality, as understood theologically by the Church. Secondly, in this matter men need the help of the teaching of the Church, explained and applied under the leadership of the magisterium so that they can with certitude and security embrace the way, the truth and the life.

Pius XI spoke to the point in *Casti Connubii*: "But everyone can see to how many fallacies an avenue would be opened up and how many errors would become mixed with the truth, if it were left solely to the light of reason of each to find it out, or if it were to be discovered by the private interpretation of the truth which is revealed. And if this is applicable to many other truths of moral order, we must all the more pay attention to those things which appertain to marriage where the inordinate desire for pleasure can attack frail human nature and easily deceive it and lead it astray...

"For Christ Himself made the Church the teacher of truth in those things also which concern the right regulation of moral conduct, even though some knowledge of the same is not beyond human reason."

E. WHY CANNOT THE CHURCH CHANGE HER ANSWER TO THIS CENTRAL QUESTION?

1. The Church cannot change her answer *because this answer is true.* Whatever may pertain to a more perfect formulation of the teaching or its possible genuine development, the teaching itself cannot not be substantially true. It is true because the Catholic Church, instituted by Christ to show men a secure way to eternal life, could not have so wrongly erred during all those centuries of its history. The Church cannot substantially err in teaching doctrine which is most serious in its import for faith and morals, throughout all centuries or even one century, if it has been constantly and forcefully proposed as necessarily to be followed in order to obtain eternal salvation. The Church could not have erred through so many centuries, even through one century, by imposing under serious obligation very grave burdens in the name of Jesus Christ, if Jesus Christ did not actually impose these burdens. The Catholic Church could not have furnished in the name of Jesus Christ to so many of the faithful everywhere in the world, through so many centuries the occasion for formal sin and spiritual ruin, because of a false doctrine promulgated in the name of Jesus Christ.

If the Church could err in such a way, the authority of the ordinary magisterium in moral matters would be thrown into question. The faithitil could not put their trust in the magisterium's presentation of moral teaching, especially in sexual matters.

2. *Our question is not about the irreformability of Casti Connubii.* The teaching of the Church did not have its beginning in *Casti Connubii,* nor does it depend on the precise degree of authority with which Pius XI wished to teach the Church in that document. The teaching of the Church in this matter would have its own validity and truth even if *Casti Connubii* had never been written. (When it was published, all saw in it not something new but the true teaching of the Church.) Our question is a question of the *truth* of this proposition: contraception is always seriously evil. The truth of this teaching stems from the fact that it has been proposed with such constancy, with such universality, with such obligatory force, always and everywhere, as something to be held and followed by the faithful. Technical and juridical investigation into the irreformability and infallibility of *Casti Connubii* (as if once this obstacle had been removed, the true doctrine could

be found and taught) distracts from the central question and even prejudices the question.

3. One can subtly dispute about many questions: e.g., whether the teaching is infallible by reason of the wording of *Casti Connubii;* whether the Church can teach something infallibly or define what is not formally revealed; whether the Church can teach authoritatively and in an obligatory fashion the principles of the natural law, whether infallible or not. But after all this, in practice we know what the Church can do from the things which she has always done, either implicitly by some action, or explicitly by invoking her power, derived from Christ Himself, of teaching the faithful in moral matters.

In dealing with this question, to dispute in a subtle way whether the teaching is technically "infallible by a judgment of the magisterium" is empty-headed *(supervacaneum.)* For if this doctrine is not substantially true, the magisterium itself will seem to be empty and useless in any moral matter.

F. NEW NOTIONS OF THE MAGISTERIUM AND ITS AUTHORITY

1. What has been commonly held and handed down concerning the nature, function and authority of the magisterium does not seem to be accepted by everyone today. For among those who say that the teaching of *Casti Connubii* is reformable and who say that contraception is not always intrinsically evil, some seem to have a concept which is radically different about the nature and function of the magisterium, especially in moral matters. Thus, in the report of our commission's general session (plenary), March 25th-28th, 1965, pages 52-53, we read the following presentation of certain members opinions:

"I. Nature is not something totally complete, but is in some sense 'making itself.' We cannot attain it except by taking an overall view, because a fixed concept of nature does not exist...

"II. The principle of continuity does not refer to precise judgments about the manner of acting (*'comportements'*) as if they were once and for all determined for everyone. Rather it refers to the permanent values which must be protected, discovered and realised. Consequently, continuity refers neither to the formulations nor to concrete solutions. It suffices in a particular moment if the judgment on a moral matter is true 'for the moment' (*geschichtsgerecht,* historically valid)...

"IV. The function of the magisterium, therefore, does not consist in defining ways of acting (*'comportements'*) in moral matters, unless one is speaking of prudential guidance. For its proper role, as for the Gospel, is to provide those broader clarifications which are needed. But it could not publish edicts of such a nature that they would bind consciences to precise ways of acting; that would be to proceed against that respect for life which is an absolute value..."

It is no surprise, then, if some theologians in the contemporary Church have no difficulty either in acknowledging the Church to have erred or in explaining what now they call erroneous as something historically true and valid for the time in which it took place, or even in denying to the magisterium of the Church the power of binding the consciences of the faithful in current concrete cases, especially touching on the question of natural law.

2. Those who proceed along the more traditional way in this matter cite various documents of the Holy See. Here are a few examples:

(a) Pius XII in his address *Magnificate Dominum* (1954): "The power of the Church is never limited to matters of 'strictly religious concern,' as they say. Rather the entire matter of the natural law, its institutions, interpretation, application, inasmuch as it is a question of moral concern, are in her power. For the observance of the natural law out of respect for the ordination of God looks to the way by which man must move along to his final supernatural end. The Church is already in this way the guardian and leader of men toward this end which is above nature. The Church, from the Apostles down to our times, has always maintained this manner of acting and will today, not just by way of guide and private council, but by the mandate and authority of the Lord."

(b) John XXIII, in his encyclical *Pacem in Terris* (1963), where he is speaking of social matters and the authority of the Church to apply the principles of the natural law: "Let no one object to the fact that it is the right and duty of the Church, not only to safeguard the teaching of faith and morals, but also to interpose her authority among her sons in the area of external affairs when it is necessary to determine how that teaching may be made effective."

(c) The Second Vatican Council, in the constitution on the Church, § 25, reaffirms the obligatory character of the teaching authority of the Supreme Pontiff when he teaches authentically, even if not infallibly.

Furthermore, among those who think that the Church today can now say "contraception is not seriously evil," there seem to be some who conceive human nature as something continually and essentially evolving. There are some who will admit no intrinsic evil as necessarily connected with any external human action. There are some who permit suicide, abortion, fornication and even adultery in certain circumstances. There are some who, equivalently at least in these matters, defend the principle that the end justifies the means. There are some who promote situation morality, and a morality of relativism, or the "new morality." There are some who deny or doubt that the teaching authority of the Church can teach moral truths of the natural law infallibly. There are some who seem to deny that the teaching authority of the Church can oblige the consciences of the faithful in a concrete and individual case in any moral matter. The conclusions in our area of interest, derived from such principles, must be examined accurately, so that we may see to what further conclusions they will finally push us.

G. A BRIEF SUMMARY OF RECENT DOCTRINAL DEVELOPMENT

1. With regard to sexual acts and their natural consequences, it is possible to do the following:

(a) practice *continence;*

(b) an imperfect or incomplete act, including *amplexus reservatus;*

(c) intervene in the *operation of nature without a mutilation,* for example, by using the pill for contraception;

(d) intervene in the *operation of nature by an irreversible surgery,* for instance, through sterilization;

(e) intervene in *man's operation (opus hominis)* by depriving the act itself of procreative power, as through onanism;

(f) intervene against the embryo, considering it not yet animated by a rational soul;

(g) intervene against the foetus, animated by a rational soul, by abortion properly so-called;

(h) intervene against a newly born deformed child.

2. Interventions (a) to (d) do not corrupt the act in itself; (c) and (d) intervene in the natural operation *(opus naturae),* but before the beginning of *any kind* of new life. Intervention (e) has to do with *man's operation (opus hominis),* namely, through onanism which is against the operation of the spermata. Interventions (f) and (g) touch on the *fertilized ovum.* The mediaeval doubt now reappears when a person asks whether it is animated by a rational soul at the moment of fertilization or later; or perhaps when the differentiation of the placenta and the embryo begins after nidation.

3. Until now the Church has condemned human interventions in genital activity from (c) on, whether it was a question of impeding or frustrating the natural power of conjugal intercourse. After a few years, some theologians allowed intervention (c). Then some allowed (d) for special cases. Many with ease allow even (e) at least when it is not a question of a condom impeding intimate union. Some seem prepared to admit (f) if it can be established with certainty that the rational soul does not come into existence at the moment of fertilization. Further it would seem that (g) is *not absolutely* excluded by all. And indeed, this seems logical. On that account there should be a careful indication of the previous steps just described.

II: Philosophical Foundations and Arguments of Others and Critique

(Not all approved everything, or proposed things in the same way.)

A. SYNTHETIC PRESENTATION

1. The *immutable principles of the natural law seem to come down to:*

(a) subjection to God;

(b) reverence for the human person – often only in its spiritual element, and in a partial fashion;

(c) the duty of promoting earthly culture by humanizing nature.

When these values are preserved, man's intervention in nature is not limited *a priori* by any absolute boundaries. This holds for one's own organism, when all superstitious reverence for biological integrity has been eliminated. Parts, organs, functions of man are conceived as contra-distinct from him. They are subordinated to him because of cultural values, almost as are plants and animals. So now they approve masturbation as being useful therapeutically; sterilization to avoid danger to life from use of the genital function in marriage; and action taken against the foetus so that at least the one giving birth will live. Their *basic reasoning:* in the complexity of these interventions, true existential values are sought through the best method available at the time.

2. *Human nature and the particular norms of morality* are conceived of as adaptable and perfectible historically, so that they admit of *true changes.* They do not mean merely new applications and new modes of proceeding where the natural quality of such actions may depend on extrinsic conditions. Then, when man's fecundity and mortality have been modified, his sexual activity ought not to be changed, but rather the moral norm laid down for it in *Casti Connubii,* by taking away natural procreativity from generative acts. To the extent that this frustration affords personal utility, it bestows value and is considered rightly ordered.

3. *The teaching authority of the Church ought not to impede the development of culture* by limiting the control of nature or by defining methods of action. Experience will show what is good, or what is evil, in the concrete situations, as the experiencing subject here and now discovers. So then (a) the magisterium, taught by the experience of past errors, may not propose as infallible whatever is not clearly in revelation; (b) conscious of its limitations, it will not impose as the norm of the natural law what the greater number of the faithful sense as uncertain but it will dictate reasonable criteria for a given time (this is the way to interpret the declaration of *Casti.Connubii).* These criteria are changeable and should be changed according to the progress of culture; (c) in the study of nature the magisterium will leave methods of action up to the discretion and responsibility of scientists, by not impeding the investigation of Catholics as it has often done in the past, with the loss of some influence in the world. ("Methods" they understand not merely in their technical aspect, but inasmuch as science show them to be more apt

for humanitarian ends, and thus moralizes them through the intention, for example, as it moralizes conception by ordering it to the regulation of births.)

4. *As moral criteria of the methods for exploring nature,* for bettering them and making them more humane, the *following* should be considered:

(a) the basic intention of the person acting, which must be worthy of man and enriching his values. This is to be considered in the total complex of his action – not necessarily in single action, standing by themselves, but subordinated to a higher finality.

(b) The means to accomplish this are not to harm immediately the dignity or the rights of others, that is, they are not to use others as a means to bring about what they value. Otherwise means are morally indifferent and are to be specified by the intention of the person acting.

(c) Damage which might be caused by physical necessity, in interventions whose effects can be known and decided in advance should be as minimal as possible.

(d) That method of action should be used which is the more humanitarian for a given situation.

5. *The signiftcance and morality of sexuality in marriage.*

I. The following points, acknowledged by everyone, do not enter into the present discussion:

(a) The importance of sexuality for the perfecting and ordering of human existence, inasmuch as it is sexual;

(b) the dignity of conjugal love and its beneficial influence on the procreative society;

(c) the fittingness and definite moral necessity of more frequent carnal acts for couples to keep up their conjugal harmony and enthusiasm for having and educating offspring;

(d) the nobility of this act, holding a mean between its contemporary exaltation and the pessimistic evaluation of it in the past;

(e) the obligation of responsible paternity, attentive to the future education of children according to the condition of the family and of society;

(f) any judgment about the number of children to be made personally by the spouses themselves.

II. The question is whether frequent copulation in marriage is necessary, even obligatory, to bring about and maintain the maximum values of the couple, the children and the family – not out of any egoistic hedonism, nor from a lack of moral generosity or continence, but from an incompatibility between their duty and need of expressing conjugal love and at the same time of avoiding children in that very expression. The existence of sterile days does not afford a sufficient solution for modern society – because of the conditions of life, biological anomalies, psychological disturbances, the repression of spontaneity, the dangers to fidelity, etc. Recourse must be had to artificial ways of frustrating the natural generative power, by limiting its specific natural power, even if, normally and deliberately, it is ordered to the species and granted in marriage for the species. Therefore the use of contraceptives in marriage for the purpose of regulating children is presumed to be moral because it is specified by an honest intention, harmonises the psychosomatic relationships between the spouses, is beneficial for their moral life and is of service to the procreative society. Some think it is evil, because it detracts something from the powers of nature, but it is a lesser evil, to be accepted humbly by fallen man rising with difficulty towards perfection. Others think it simply is good, indeed the optimum existential good possible for the present, fully legitimate because of the values and complex intention indicated above.

6. *The concrete application to contraception* is made in this manner. Considered in itself contraception does not attain the ideal fullness of values. But it is not intrinsicaly evil. (Intrinsic evils are denied to creatures in man's horizontal plane.) In the concrete it is commonly licit and obligatory in marriage where the necessity of regulating children exists. No means and methods of obtaining this regulation are *a priori* immoral. In practice those are to be preferred which here and now better respect the complex finality of the action in humanitarian and existential values (the expression of love, the service to the procreative society, the more secure exclusion of undesired children, the intimacy and spontaneity of carnal gestures, the liberation of one's self or one's spouse's from distress, tension, etc.).

7. The *principal arguments to legitimise contraception.* These vary from one to another whenever something new is proposed.

(a) In order *to supersede the traditional teaching,* they say that the traditional teaching, from an ignorance of biology, supposed that each individual conjugal act was by its nature ordained to children, and therefore erroneously thought that the order of nature was violated through use of an artificial means. They argue that Pius XI would not condemn such resort to artifice except when used for an arbitrary, egoistic-hedonistic reason vitiating the acts of nature; not when used for legitimate motives of expressing conjugal love in union, which contemporary investigations reveal prevails. They argue that this same Pontiff was not dealing with individual actions destined to the service of biological life of a future offspring but with the whole complex of conjugal life. About this, what he said is most rightly affirmed. They argue that the traditional teaching concerning contraception, since it was never defined (and cannot be defined because it is not a revelation), must be reformed, once the falsity has been demonstrated of its foundation with regard to children, as to the primary end of marriage (one out of every two hundred acts can be said to be generative) and with regard to false interpretation of Genesis 38, 8-10, and once its pessimism, stemming from an ignorance or a poor interpretation of sexual values, has been overcome.

(b) *On the level of experience,* they argue that, by the testimony of the best doctors and married couples in modern life, periodic continence has been demonstrated to be impossible in itself, uncertain of biological regulation, harmful for the psychological life of the spouses, dangerous for conjugal fidelity and for the efficient regulation of offspring.

(c) *In the order of arguments from reason,* some insist on a dispensation from the principle of the lesser evil which often permits man in his fallen condition not only to consider but even to choose the lesser evil, even without physical necessity but with great moral fittingness. Others reject this prior consideration as injurious to the generosity of many couples and speak rather of the perplexity which persuades many to save the greater conjugal-family good by sacrificing the lesser good of the psychological integrity of the act, as often and as easily as this can be repeated. Others, more generally, apply the principle of totality which permits the renunciation even of members and functions of organic life *(a fortiori,* therefore of their particular acts), not only for the health of the body or its functions, but even for the greater good of the person, both in the physical order and in the psychic order (cf. lobotomy). It follows that in conjugal life, through the physical evil of contraception, a psychic good may be obtained – the good of eliminating anxiety over a dangerous maternity, various obsessions, the inhibition of spontaneous love, etc. Some think that this principle probably applies also to the quasi-personal husband-wife union, so that the husband for the good of the wife, may impede the natural generative power of free genital action – for example, if she might conceive when she is weak or sick. And vice versa, the wife may do so, lest her husband suffer tension by reason of conjugal continence, etc.

B. A CRITIQUE OF THIS POSITION

1. The *notion of the natural law* remains uncertain, changeable, withdrawn from the magisterium. For some, it may never be revealed; to others, only for a very special reason, in the rarest of cases, it proposes some relationship of man to God or to other men in acceptable arguments as definitive. (It is asserted that this never happened in history, certainly not in the solemn declaration of *Casti Connubii.)* This view does not do justice to or protect either the competence which the Church has so many times vindicated for herself for the interpretation of the natural law, nor the Church's effective capacity of discerning the moral order established by God, which is so often obscure to fallen man.

2. *Nature* seems to be understood as a complex of physical and psychic powers in the world, granted to the dominion of man, so that he can experience them, foster change, or frustrate them for his own earthly convenience. Numbered among these are the organs, powers, acts of man himself, without excepting such "superpersonal" functions, as the specifically genital actions ordered to the species. All these things, and in particular man's own psycho-physical parts, are conceived of as having been entrusted to the "embodied spirit" which is man, so that he may humanize them through his culture in a given set of physical possibilities. Therefore he can frustrate his own biological sexual function, even when voluntarily aroused, because it is subject to reason for the bettering of the human condition. Such earthly, cultural naturalism and utilitarian, exceedingly humanistic altruism,

seem to allow insufficient place in human life for the action of the Holy Spirit and for his mission of healing sin. Neither is it evident what are the great demands on virtue which are often affirmed in this new tendency.

3. Many things seem to be mixed up and confused when there is affirmed the mutability of nature in the human person according to the evolution of history. The essential distinction between mutations which are dependent on extrinsic conditions and the stability of principles deduced by right reason is ignored. Changes which are dependent on extrinsic conditions may permit or require contradictory moral actions in diverse situations, though under the same moral principle. One may cite, for example, heart surgery, which is now licit, but which once amounted to homicide. But the principles of right reason are deduced from a consideration of the essential relations of human nature, which constitute the norm of morality. For example, the different and complementary genitality of the sexes determines the right use of the generative function in Adam and Eve as in Titus and Sempronia. Many of the alleged changes in human nature are brought out by false reasoning and false interpretations of history, we can show; for example, that slavery became intrinsically evil or usury was permitted.

4. The *authenticity of the magisterium* seems to be substantially violated:

(a) By *restricting its mission and power* beyond the limits vindicated by the Church for herself through the actions of several Pontiffs and through the First and Second Vatican Councils; and by reducing her competence so that she is deprived of her necessary authority to remain a light to the nations, teaching effectively the moral order established by God even when this is not clearly shown in Sacred Scripture and in apostolic tradition. Such is now claimed about onanism. Why should their contemporary solution be admitted any more than the statements of Pius XI or XII?

(b) By *confusing the consensus of the faithful* (of the Universal Church), of all who profess the common faith existing in all people of God, with the belief of the faithful *(Ecclesia discens,* the Church learning) which works together to illumine the hierarchy *(Ecllesia docens,* the Church teaching) in the quest for religious truths and in judging obscure and uncertain matters.

(c) By *taking away from the magisterium the authority* to discern the requirements of the natural law and to teach authoritatively when a large part of the faithful are in doubt. In this they approach the mentality of other Christian Churches and offend against the genuine hierarchical constitution of the Church of Christ.

(d) By *not recognising the differences* among the assents (to be given to truth) other than the difference between the infallible faith concerning things which have been revealed, and the assent of prudence concerning declarations reformable according to the developments of time, as is often the case in social matters. Thereby they ignore Catholic doctrines in the area of human actions which are plainly certain and morally irreformable, not to speak of theological conclusions constantly proved valid and of those things which some call "ecclesiastical faith." If contraception were declared not intrinsically evil, in honesty it would have to be acknowledged that the Holy Spirit in 1930, in 1951 and 1958, assisted Protestant Churches, and that for half a century Pius XI, Plus XII and a great part of the Catholic hierarchy did not protest against a very serious error, one most pernicious to souls; for it would thus be suggested that they condemned most imprudently, under the pain of eternal punishment, thousands upon thousands of human acts which are now approved. Indeed, it must be neither denied nor ignored that these acts would be approved for the same fundamental reasons which Protestantism alleged and which they (Catholics) condemned or at least did not recognise. Therefore one must very cautiously inquire whether the change which is proposed would not bring along with it a definitive depreciation of the teaching of the moral direction of the hierarchy of the Church and whether several very grave doubts would not be opened up about the very history of Christianity.

5. As for the *reasoning used* to justify contraception, among other things it seems: (a) To lack the fundamental distinction between the sexual condition of man and the free and voluntary use of the genital faculty. This latter is a particular aspect of man's sexual condition, about which in marriage a determined right is obtained. In theological tradition, this right is limited according to the natural ends of the generative faculties.

(b) If the specific use of this faculty can be turned aside in marriage from the generative finality, in the service of either the individual spouses, or of the family itself, or of a consort, why not outside of marriage? More of this later.

(c) Biology is said to have revealed both the falsity of the ordering of each and every conjugal act toward generation, and the constant natural unitive quality of this act (which from the very beginning has been clear enough!), so that one might conclude that it is licit to contradict the generative power in order to satisfy the unitive tendency.

But (I) this conclusion is not at all apparent. For if an act is rarely generative, then one must exert care that it might produce its effect, while the expression of union which is constantly present could be more easily omitted in particular cases (for example, to procure fecundation artificially if it could not otherwise be obtained). There is a confusion between *inchoate procreativity,* which man actuates through a deliberative act, and *effective procreation,* which depends upon nature and has been removed from human deliberation by the creator.

(II) There can be no contiadiction between what Catholic teaching wished to signify through the term "procreation-education" which from the sixteenth century was commonly designated as a primary end of marriage, and the biology and physiology of the sexual act freely exercised. Any other finality, legitimately determining its use, must observe that integrity.

(III) Finally, it is not apparent how a freely placed act can be perfective of human nature, but at the same time be voluntarily mutilated and changed in its natural power, even if that frustration be for another good end. Indeed, that good can be obtained in another way – this is something which the contraceptive theory is always silent about – for conjugal love is above all spiritual (if the love is genuine) and it requires no specific carnal gesture, much less its repetition in some determined frequency. Consequently, the affirmed sense of generosity and the absence of hedonism are suspect, when we find the intimate love of the whole person between a father and daughter, a brother and sister, without the necessity of carnal gestures.

One final question might be asked: are not these men essentially limited by the influence of their time and culture and region and by organized propaganda so that they bring to the problem only a partial, transitory and vitiated vision, one that even now is not a fair response to the mind of very many people?

III : Consequences if the Teaching of the Church is Changed

A. AS IT WOULD PERTAIN TO MORAL TEACHING IN SEXUAL MATTERS

The great majority of theologians who argue that contraception is not absolutely illicit in individual conjugal acts posit the *principle of totality* as the basis for this opinion. This means that every partial good must be ordered to the good of the whole, and in a case of a conflict of interest a partial good must be sacrificed, for the good of the whole. However, this principle is applied to the case differently by different people.

1. A great number seem to admit that each and every sexual act is ordered by nature and ought to be ordered by man to procreation in its total complexity, i.e., understood as to include education. But education, in order that this might take place in a human way, requires a harmonious and balanced way of life by the parents and the whole family. This, in turn, requires an undisturbed and spontaneous sexual life between the spouses. Therefore, individual conjugal acts ought to be ordered to this whole complex. A partial good, namely, the ordering of individual acts to procreation, can be sacrificed for the good of the whole, even if this does positively remove their procreative force.

Traditional teaching obviously admits the principle of totality and demands that the sexual act not take place except in relation to the whole reality of procreation and education. However, it maintains that each and every conjugal act of its very nature has a certain *specific, intrinsic, proper order,* inasmuch as by its nature it is both ordered to the whole reality of procreation, and in that way is ordered as an act of *bestowing life* (a creative action in the strict sense). To place an action which removes this specific ordination, intrinsically proper to it, even for the sake of a higher good, is to act contrary to the nature of things.

Once one has set aside this traditional principle, one would also be setting aside a *fundamental* criterion, up until the present time unshaken in its application to many acts which have always been considered by the Church to be serious sins against chastity.

(a) The case of *extra-marital sexual relationships* of those whose living together is ordered to the good of procreation understood as a total complex. So demanding might be those who are close to marriage but could not contract it at the moment because of difficulties, yet nevertheless feel bound to foster and make as secure as possible their future harmonious conjugal life together. Similarly demanding might be those who wish to test their mutual adaptability and their sexual compatibility for the good of the family. So also might be those in concubinage who can neither marry nor be separated from one. another because of the children to be educated. This education also demands the harmonious home life of the parents and, of course, a peaceful sexual life.

It should be noted that these consequences are not imaginary, but actually are being defended by some Catholics in speech and in writing. It would seem that they are not illogical, once one abandons the principle of the specific ordering of each free, generative action to procreation in the strict sense.

(b) The *case of sexual acts in marriage,* for example, oral and anal copulation. They object that such acts as these will remain evil because they do not observe the intrinsic ordination of the conjugal act to a loving union. It could be answered, first of all, that it is not apparent why an ordination to procreation in the strict sense would not be required in every act, but nevertheless there would be required an ordination to loving union, as a good never to be sacrificed in single acts for the good of the whole. Then too, it stands to reason that some spouses experience the above described forms of intercourse as true amorous union. Nor is it apparent in this opinion why a loving union must be realized uniquely through the sexual organs of each. The same ought to be applied to mutual masturbation between the spouses, at least in the case where they cannot have intercourse. Or to the solitary masturbation of one spouse in the absence of the other, yet done with a certain marital affection, or as a means of releasing nervous pressure because of a long imposed abstinence with possible damage to the peace and education of the family (for example in the case of the illness of one spouse).

(c) Even further *the door is opened easily to the licitness of masturbation* among youths on the ground that it could be a remote preparation for realizing a harmonious sexual life in marriage. Many psychologists judge this to be a normal phase in adolescence for sound sexual formation and maintain that its forced suppression could cause much wrong in such formation.

(d) It is *equally logical that direct sterilization would be permitted* as well. For although sterilization in the strict sense is commonly judged as a more serious intervention than the use of certain preventive means, nevertheless several newer theologians (and it seems quite logical) already admit the licitness even of this kind of intervention for a contraceptive end, in the case where the definitive removal of the fecundity of conjugal acts through the use of merely contraceptive media would not allow the couple to have sufficient security and tranquility.

We admit that the illicity of several of the abuses mentioned above is evident from Sacred Scriptures (as also for several of those to be spoken of later). However, the exegetes generally agree that in those places there is not being stated the positive law for Christians, but simply the restatement of precepts of the natural law. Therefore we return to the same question: on what kind of basis does the prohibition of the natural law rest? In other wards, by the law set forth in Sacred Scripture, is not a general prohibition for acting sexually against the good of procreation included?

2. However, many theologians, who maintain that contraception is not intrinsically evil, seem to come to this conclusion from a more general principle: that, namely, which denies *all absolute intrinsic morality* to external human acts, in such a way that there is no human act which is so intrinsically evil that it cannot be justified because of a higher good of man. In stating this, they apply the principle that "the end specifies the means" and that "between two evils the lesser is to be chosen." They say that this specification and choice also include those things which are commonly called intrinsically evil.

If this principle is admitted, it would seem that more serious evils can yet be expected. Perhaps the promoters of the principle do not intend this. Nevertheless, these conclusions are actually drawn by others. Thus, for example, it could be concluded that masturbation is for the good of personal equilibrium, or homosexuality good for those who are affected with abnormal inclinations and seek only friendship with the same sex for their balance. The same could be done for the use of abortives or of abortion directly induced to save the life of the mother.

B. THE VALUE AND DIGNITY OF THE CHURCH'S TEACHING AUTHORITY

If the Church should now admit that the teaching passed on is no longer of value, teaching which has been preached and stated with ever more insistent solemnity until very recent years, it must be feared greatly that its authority in almost all moral and dogmatic matters will be seriously harmed. For there are few moral truths so constantly, solemnly and, as it has appeared, definitively stated as this one for which it is now so quickly proposed tha it be changed to the contrary.

What is more, however, this change would inflict a grave blow on the teaching about the assistance of the Holy Spirit, promised to the Church to lead the faithful on the right way toward their salvation. For, as a matter of fact, the teaching of *Casti Connubii* was solemnly proposed in opposition to the doctrine of the Lambeth Conference of 1930, by the Church "to whom God has entrusted the defense of the integrity and purity of morals...in token of her divine ambassadorship...and through Our mouth." Is it nevertheless now to be admitted that the Church erred in this her work, and that the Holy Spirit rather assists the Anglican Church?

Some who fight for a change say that the teaching of the Church was not false for those times. Now, however, it must be changed because of changed historical conditions. But this seems to be something that one cannot propose, for the Anglican Church was teaching precisely that and for the very reasons which the Catholic Church solemnly denied, but which it would now admit. Certainly such a manner of speaking would be unintelligible to the people and would seem to be a specious pretext.

Others claim that the Church would be better off to admit her error, just as recently she has done in other circumstances. But this is no question of peripheral matters (as, for example, the case of Galileo), or of an excess in the way a thing is done (the excommunication of Photius). This is a most significant question which profoundly enters into the practical lives of Christians in such a way that innumerable faithful would have been thrown by the magisterium into formal sin without material sin. But let there be consulted the serious words of Pius XI in his "Directive to priests who are confessors and who have the care of souls" (1930). Also let there be consulted the worft of Pius XII in his "Address to the cardinals and bishops on the occasion of the definition of the dogma of the Assumption of the Blessed Virgin Mary" (1950):

"This way (namely, of liberation from the law of God) can never be taken because it is hurtful and harmful even when it is a question of someone who wishes to bring help to men in difficult situations of conjugal life. Therefore it would be pernicious to the Church and to civil society, if those who had care of souls, in teaching and in their way of life, would knowingly remain silent when the laws of God are violated in marriage. These laws always flourish whatsoever the case may be."

For the Church to have erred so gravely in its grave responsibility of leading souls would be tantamount to seriously suggesting that the assistance of the Holy Spirit was lacking to her.

III: THE ARGUMENT FOR REFORM

1. The Past Teaching of the Church is not Decisive

1: THE IMPORTANCE OF THE ENCYCLICAL *CASTI CONNUBII*

The encyclical *Casti Connubii* has special importance in solving the question of the reasonable regulation of births precisely because of its solemn condemnation of every contraceptive intervention in the conjugal act. But the encyclical did nothing other than reaffirm the common teaching at that time. The solemnity of the condemnation of every contraceptive intervention is especially understandable as a reaction to the declaration of the Lambeth Conference. But to this must be added the fear prevalent at that time among many peoples that contraceptive practice could lead to an undesired reduction of (the world) population.

Today no one holds that the solemn declaration of the encyclical *Casti Connubii* constitutes a true doctrinal definition. Nor does the reference of the encyclical to Genesis chapter 38 (concerning the sin of Onan) prove that the teaching of the encyclical is divinely revealed. For the reference is made only incidentally and only because of the well-known exegesis of St. Augustine. Augustine, with only one or two other Fathers, saw in the scriptural text a condemnation of onanism, whereas contemporary exegetes, Protestant and Catholic, are rather inclined to another interpretation, or, at least, are uncertain. The encyclical offers no other text from the Old or New Testament which condemns contraceptive intervention, nor can one be found. Finally, the reference of the encyclical to an uninterrupted tradition does not make its teaching infallible, since the assertion of the encyclical of such an existent tradition is not infallible.

The reference of the encyclical to the argument from reason or the natural law is vague and imprecise, especially since this argument does not consider sufficiently man, God's creature, as the prudent administrator and steward of the gifts of nature.

2: THE TRADITION TO WHICH *CASTI CONNUBII* REFERS

Casti Connubii is of greater importance if it is considered as a *particular* and even solemn part of the total tradition, including the explicit teaching of the past two centuries. For in this tradition contraceptive intervention is never approved, but when the question arises it is condemned. This has occurred many times in the last few centuries. However, this is by no means an apostolic tradition or an attestation of faith but merely the tradition of a teaching formulated in diverse ways at diverse times.

In this tradition there is a constant concern for protecting the goodness of procreation, especially in opposition to the Gnostics, Manichees and, later, the Cathari. But the necessity of multiplying the human race and therefore of increasing the number of children in families was denied through the centuries on theological grounds. The protection of the goodness of procreation as such through the prohibition of contraceptive intervention is more rarely proved from Scripture (Gen. 38), than from reason or natural law and not without the influence of philosophies and medical science of the three prior centuries. But the reasons alleged are generally quite vague and lack precision, nor do they always refer to the avoidance of children in marriage specifically, but from adulterous unions and fornication. Likewise today many of the best theologians who defend the illicitness of every contraceptive intervention because of the past teaching of the Church, concede that they do not have a convincing argument based on reason or natural law,

For the rest, the concept of the natural law, as it is found in traditional discussion of this question, is insufficient; for the gifts of nature are considered to be immediately the expression of the will of God, preventing man, also a creature of God, from being understood as called to receive material nature and to perfect its potentiality. Churchmen have been slower than the rest of the world in clearly seeing this as man's vocation.

3: THE OFFICIAL TEACHING IS IN EVOLUTION

Little by little, however, the Church has freed herself from this inadequate concept of nature and the natural law. A first intimation of this is already found in the notion of conjugal love expressed in reference to the physical act of marriage. Thus stated, it is found both in the writings of Pius XI *(Casti Connubii)* and more frequently in the writings of Pius XII. The teaching of Pius XII on the regulation of birth through rhythm follows this direction even more (1951). Finally the teaching of the Second Vatican Council affirmed the great importance of the expression of conjugal love through intercourse and especially the virtuous exercise of responsibility in determining the number of children. And this teaching was felt at that time by certain Fathers of the Council to be "pregnant" in terms of the licitness of diverse contraceptive interventions. They showed this by pointing out the difficulty in arriving at a conciliar consensus on the former position. Hence the council proceeded very cautiously in simply reaffirming the traditional teaching on this matter. It is easily understood, then, why a widely felt doubt on the truth of the teaching of the encyclical *Casti Connubii* in the matter of contraceptive intervention could have arisen, notwithstanding the teaching of the ordinary magisterium.

This issue is a matter of real concern not only among husbands and wives but also among priests and the hierarchy itself. With all this in mind it becomes evident that the official teaching with regard to the manner of protecting the good of procreation has been evolving in recent decades, and that the position stated in the text of the encyclical *Casti Connubii* has not yet been found to be definitive.

4 : REASONS FOR THIS EVOLUTION

The reason – or, if you will, the forceful occasion – for seriously rethinking the traditional teaching on the illicit contraceptive intervention as regards each and every conjugal act is based on various things: the social change in marriage, in the family, in the position of woman; the diminution of infant mortality; advances in physiological, biological, psychological and sexological knowledge; a changed estimation of the meaning of sexuality and of conjugal relations; but especially a better perception of the responsibility of man for humanising the gifts of nature and using them to bring the life of man to greater perfection. Finally, one must consider the consensus of the faithful, according to which a condemnation of spouses to a prolonged and heroic abstinence from the helpful and appropriate expressions of conjugal life must be erroneous.

A later development of such a position (which seems to be prevalent) is based less on these changes than on a better, more profound and more correct perspective on married life and intercourse which the changes have brought about.

5. THE IMPORTANCE OF THE DEVELOPING OFFICIAL TEACHING

Not a few theologians and faithful fear that a change in the official teaching could damage the confidence of Catholics in the teaching authority of the Church. For they ask how the assistance of the Holy Spirit could permit such an error for so many centuries, and one that has had so many consequences, especially in recent centuries. But the criteria for discerning what the Spirit could or could not permit in the Church can scarcely be determined *a priori.* In point of fact, we know that there have been errors in the teaching of the magisterium and of tradition. With regard to intercourse one should note that for so many centuries in the Church, with the active concurrence of the Popes, it was all but unanimously taught that marital intercourse was illicit unless accompanied by the intention to procreate – or at least (because of the words of I Cor. 7) to offer an outlet for the other partner; and yet no theologians hold to this teaching today, nor is it the official position. In recent decades there has been an increasing tendency to consider the authentic non-infallible magisterium infallible in practice, whereas in reality it must be expected that the non-infallible magisterium is sometimes mistaken. There is, then, no sound basis for fearing that a change in this particular point would cause a loss of trust in the Church's teaching authority or would make it possible to raise doubts on every other doctrine. Such a change is to be seen rather as a step toward a more mature comprehension of the whole doctrine of the Church. For doubt and reconsideration are quite reasonable when proper reasons for doubt and reconsideration occur with regard to some specific question. This is part and parcel of the accepted teaching of fundamental theology.

II. A Systematic Examination of the Arguments from the Law of Nature

(1) *The arguments based on the law of nature are not persuasive.* The principal argument is founded on the inviolability of the sources of life – like human life itself, it is said, they do not fall under the dominion of man but pertain to the dominion of God.

But an unconditional respect for nature as it is in itself (as if nature in its physical existence were the expression of the will of God) pertains to a vision of man which sees something mysterious and sacred in nature, and because of this fears that any human intervention tends to destroy rather than perfect this very nature. In past centuries, because of this mentality, many interventions of the art of medicine were prohibited, and only little by little, with the progress of medicine and science, have the possibilities of intervention for the good of the person and sometimes even for the good of the community been acknowledged.

The sources of life, just as existent life itself, are not more of God than is the totality of created nature, of which he is the Creator. The very dignity of man created to the image of God consists in this : that God wishes man to share in his dominion. God has left man in the hands of his own counsel. To take his own or another's life is a sin not because life is under the exclusive dominion of God but because it is contrary to right reason unless there is question of a good or a higher order. It is licit to sacrifice a life for the good of the community. It is licit to take a life in capital punishment for the sake of the community, and therefore from a motive of charity for others. Suicide is a sin because it is contrary to right reason and opposed to man's destiny.

In the course of his life man must attain his perfection in difficult and adverse conditions, he must accept the consequences of his responsibility, etc. Therefore the dominion of God is exercised through man, who can use nature for his own perfection according to the dictates of right reason.

In the matter at hand, then, there is a certain change in the mind of contemporary man. He feels that he is more conformed to his rational nature, created by God with liberty and responsibility, when he uses his skill to intervene in the biological processes of nature so that he can achieve the ends of the institution of matrimony in the conditions of actual life, than if he would abandon himself to chance.

(2) *The principle of moral criterion* for his action remains the same: it is conformity to his own rational nature created by God and redeemed by Christ, even in those matters which pertain to Christian matrimony. The order impressed on things by the Creator is preserved; Christian matrimony is fashioned according to the teaching of the New Testament. However (since at this point we are speaking of matrimony as a natural institution), man too belongs to created nature, just as subhuman nature and man's relationship to it. The order of creation does not require that all things be left untouchable just as they are, but that they reach the ends to which they have been ordered. Nature is understood by St. Thomas from the finalities which make up the dynamic element of nature. The decision about the manner of intervention therefore must be formulated according to the finalities which can be discovered from human nature.

(3) *The sources of life* are *persons* in and through their voluntary and responsible conjugal acts. The pastoral constitution *Gaudium et Spes* recognises that the decision about the number of children rests ultimately with the parents and is their exclusive right. The parents must be guided in this decision by objective criteria, or, to say it in another way, by the objective finality of the institution of matrimony. But it is up to them to determine, in view of their personal and social situation, how to achieve this purpose of marriage, as one essential element among diverse goods, and how to bring about a perfect balance between conjugal love and harmonious fecundity. In virtue of this decision they use the sexual organs to gain the predetermined goal, but the organs themselves are not *per se* the sources of life. The biological process in man is not some separated part (animality) but is integrated into the total personality of man.

(4) *It is more and more evident today* that in man sexual relations in marriage are raised to the expression of a mutual personal giving (herein lies the change of object). Intercourse materially considered carries with it some orientation toward fecundation, but this finality must be rationally directed by man according to the

measure and conditions of human love, size of the family, educational need, etc. The mutual giving of self perdures throughout the entire life, biological fecundity is not continuous and is subject to many irregularities and therefore ought to be assumed into the human sphere and be regulated within it. Finalisation towards fecundity can formally come only from man, though this finality is found materially in the organs. Fecundation must be a personal human act (deliberate, responsible for its effects, etc.). With the progress of knowledge, man can exercise this dominion and ought to exercise it with responsibility.

(5) *From this point of view there is no difference between acts* which happen in a fertile or unfertile period. For either it is permissible for man to use his sexual organs both to foster love and to achieve fertilisation (with the result that the conjugal community is filled with the goods of matrimony and then it makes no difference whether the intervention of man happens in a fertile or infertile period); or it is permissible to use his organs for fostering love in infertile periods, but in fertile periods he is given no alternative other than fertilisation or abstinence. This, however, seems to have no foundation in the law of nature.

III. Intervention is Well Explained
within the Limits of the Classic Doctrine

What are the limits of the dominion of man with regard to the rational determination of his fecundity ?

The general principle can be formulated in this manner. It is the duty of man to perfect nature (or to order it to the human good expressed in matrimony) but not to destroy it. Even if the absolute untouchability of the fertile period cannot be maintained, neither can complete dominion be affirmed. Besides, when man intervenes in the procreative process, he does this with the intention of regulating and not excluding fertility. Then he unites the material finality toward fecundity which exists in intercourse with the formal finality of the person and renders the entire process "human." Conjugal acts which by intentions are infertile (or which are rendered infertile) are ordered to the expression of the union of love; that love, however, reaches its culmination in fertility responsibly accepted. For that reason other acts of union in a certain sense are incomplete and they receive their full moral quality with ordination toward the fertile act. If this act is deliberately and without sufficient reason excluded, then these "incomplete" acts receive their proper moral specification from some other end (which is outside the order of the goods of matrimony) and then it is a question of an intervention which is illicitly "anti-conceptional." Infertile conjugal acts constitute a totality with fertile acts and have a single moral specification.

Explanatory Note: Not every act which proceeds from man is a complete human act. The subject of morality for St. Thomas is always the human act whose master is man (determined from a knowledge of the object or end). But this human act which has one moral specification can be composed of several particular acts if these partial acts do not have some object in itself already morally specified. And this is the case for matrimonial acts which are composed of several fertile and unfertile acts; they constitute one totality because they are referred to one deliberate choice.

IV. Moral Criteria with Regard to Human Intervention in Conception

I : GENERAL REMARKS

Up to this time the simple biological conformity of the acts has been adhered to as the determining criterion or morality in this matter. A renunciation of this (*Gaudium et Spes,* § 51) does not abandon Christians to subjectivism or laxism. There are other criteria, more strict from one point of view, concerned no longer with the materiality of the acts but pertaining to the meaning of the action. Christian ethics confirms this in many other areas – for example, in the use of arms which are good when used in defence but evil when used to take away life unjustly or to steal.

What are these objective criteria?

Gaudium et Spes § 51 treats of these: "Therefore when there is question of harmonising conjugal love with the responsible transmission of life, the moral aspect of any procedure does not depend solely on sincere intentions or on an evaluation of motives. It must be determined by objective standards. These, based on the nature of the human person and his acts, preserve the full sense of mutual self-giving, and human procreation in the context of true love. Such a goal cannot be achieved unless the virtue of conjugal chastity is sincerely practised. Relying on these principles, sons of the Church may not undertake methods of regulating procreation which are found blameworthy by the teaching authority of the Church in its unfolding of the divine law."

EXPLANATION AND SYNTHESIS OF THESE OBJECTIVE CRITERIA

(a) *The meaning of sexuality in marriage.* "The responsible procreative community" is always ordered towards procreation; this is the objective and authentic meaning of sexuality and of those things which refer to sexuality (affectivity, unity, the ability to educate). So we can speak of the "procreative end" as the essential end of sexuality and of conjugal life.

But this procreative end does not have to be realised by a fertile act when, for instance, parents already have children to educate or they are not prepared to have a child. *This obligation of conscience* for not generating springs from the rights of the already existing child or the rights of a future child. *A child has a right* to a "community of life and unity" so that it can be formed and educated. Therefore the procreative end is substantially and really preserved even when here and now a fertile act is excluded; for infecundity is ordered to a new life well and humanly possessed. Man is the administrator of life and consequently of his own fecundity.

(b) *The meaning of mutual giving.* On the other hand, sexuality is not ordered only to procreation. Sacred Scripture says not only "increase and multiply" but "they shall be two in one flesh," and it shows the partner as another helpful self. In some cases intercourse can be required as a manifestation of self-giving love, directed to the good of the other person or of the community, while at the same time a new life cannot be received. This is neither egocentricity nor hedonism but a legitimate communication of persons through gestures proper to beings composed of body and soul with sexual powers. Here intervention is a material privation since love in this case cannot be fertile; but it receives its moral specification from the other finality, which is good in itself, and from the fertility of the whole conjugal life.

3: OBJECTIVE CRITERIA FOR THE MORAL DECISION CONCERNING METHODS

Now if we come more precisely to a decision as to methods, it helps to recall these principles which must simultaneously be considered.

(1) Infecundity of the act, when this is required by right reason, should be accomplished by an intervention with lesser inconveniences to the subject. Man can use his body in such a way as to render it more apt to attain its proper ends but he cannot manipulate his body and organs in an arbitrary fashion.

(2) If nature ought to be perfected, then it should be perfected in the manner more fitting and connatural.

(3) On the other hand, this intervention ought to be done in a way more conformed to the expression of love and to respect for the dignity of the partner.

(4) Finally, efficacity should also be considered. If there is a privation of conception for the sake of procuring other goods, these must be sought in a more secure and apt manner.

In this matter the rhythm method is very deficient. Besides, only 60 per cent of women have a regular cycle.

4: CONCERNING THE ALLEGED RELATION BETWEEN INTERVENTION IN CONCEPTION AND OTHER SINS

Some argue that to legitimise contraception will prepare the way for indulgence with regard to certain sins such as abortion, fellation, anal intercourse, fornication, adultery and masturbation. How far this is from the truth is clearly evident from the following remarks.

(a) Abortion is entirely different from contraception because it concerns human life already in existence. Thousands upon thousands of male sperm become useless and are lost in every act of intercourse; from approximately 200 ova present in a woman, perhaps 15 can be raised to the dignity of human life while the others are eliminated during menstrual periods. The right of an offspring already conceived and living is absolute and must be regarded with the same respect as every human life. From a sociological point of view it is interesting to note that abortions are more numerous in areas where contraception is neglected.

(b) The so-called new theory is extremely strict, as is that of the casuists, with regards to oral and anal copulation, since it does not permit them. For in these acts there is preserved neither the dignity of love nor the dignity of the spouses as human persons created according to the image of God.

(c) Human intervention in the process of conception is not permitted, as we have said, unless it favours the stability of the family. Therefore there is no parity with the question of extra-marital relations. These relations lack the sense of complete and irrevocable giving and the possibility of normally accepting and educating children. These extra-marital relations contradict the norms already given concerning the habitual ordination of the institution of marriage towards offspring and love.

(d) The affirmation of the permissibility of intervention does not lead to an indulgent attitude toward masturbation since intervention preserves the intersubjectivity of sexuality ("they shall be two in one flesh"). Masturbation rather negates that intersubjectivity. Masturbation, in as much as it turns the individual on himself and seeks mere egocentric satisfaction, totally perverts the essential intentionality of sexuality whereby man is directed out of himself towards another. For intercourse even with intervention is self-offering and heterosexual. If a question is to be raised about masturbation, this should be done independently of the question of the regulation of birth, even should the classic teaching on this matter remain in force.

16.

HUMANAE VITAE [OF HUMAN LIFE]

Encyclical Letter of His Holiness Pope Paul VI
on the Regulation Of Birth

Issued July 25, 1968

To the venerable Patriarchs, Archbishops and Bishops and other local ordinaries in peace and communion with the Apostolic See, to priests, the faithful and to all men of good will.

Venerable brothers and beloved sons:

The Transmission of Life

1. The most serious duty of transmitting human life, for which married persons are the free and responsible collaborators of God the Creator, has always been a source of great joys to them, even if sometimes accompanied by not a few difficulties and by distress.

At all times the fulfillment of this duty has posed grave problems to the conscience of married persons, but, with the recent evolution of society, changes have taken place that give rise to new questions which the Church could not ignore, having to do with a matter which so closely touches upon the life and happiness of men.

I. New Aspects of the Problem and Competency of the Magisterium

New Formulation of the Problem

2. The changes which have taken place are in fact noteworthy and of varied kinds. In the first place, there is the rapid demographic development. Fear is shown by many that world population is growing more rapidly than the available resources, with growing distress to many families and developing countries, so that the temptation for authorities to counter this danger with radical measures is great. Moreover, working and lodging conditions, as well as increased exigencies both in the economic field and in that of education, often make the proper education of an elevated number of children difficult today. A change is also seen both in the manner of considering the person of woman and her place in society, and in the value to be attributed to conjugal love in marriage, and also in the appreciation to be made of the meaning of conjugal acts in relation to that love.

Finally and above all, man has made stupendous progress in the domination and rational organization of the forces of nature; such that he tends to extend this domination to his own total being: to the body, to psychical life, to social life and even to the laws which regulate the transmission of life.

3. This new state of things gives rise to new questions. Granted the conditions of life today, and granted the meaning which conjugal relations have with respect to the harmony between husband and wife and to their mutual fidelity, would not a revision of the ethical norms, in force up to now, seem to be advisable, especially when it is considered that they cannot be observed without sacrifices, sometimes heroic sacrifices?

And again: by extending to this field the application of the so-called "principle of totality," could it not be admitted that the intention of a less abundant but more rationalized fecundity might transform a materially sterilizing intervention into a licit and wise control of birth? Could it not be admitted, that is, that the finality of procreation pertains to the ensemble of conjugal life, rather than to its single acts? It is also asked whether, in view of the increased sense of responsibility of modern man, the moment has not come for him to entrust to his reason and his will, rather than to the biological rhythms of his organism, the task of regulating birth.

Competency of the Magisterium

4. Such questions required from the teaching authority of the Church a new and deeper reflection upon the principles of the moral teaching on marriage: a teaching founded on the natural law, illuminated and enriched by divine revelation.

No believer will wish to deny that the teaching authority of the Church is competent to interpret even the natural moral law. It is, in fact, indisputable, as our predecessors have many times declared,[1] that Jesus Christ, when communicating to Peter and to the apostles His divine authority and sending them to teach all nations His commandments[2] constituted them as guardians and authentic interpreters of all the moral law, not only, that is, of the law of the Gospel, but also of the natural law, which is also an expression of the will of God, the faithful fulfillment of which is equally necessary for salvation.[3]

Conformably to this mission of hers, the Church has always provided – and even more amply in recent times – a coherent teaching concerning both the nature of marriage and the correct use of conjugal rights and the duties of husband and wife.[4]

Special Studies

5. The consciousness of that same mission induced us to confirm and enlarge the study commission which our predecessor Pope John XXIII of happy memory had instituted in March, 1963. That commission which included, besides several experts in the various pertinent disciplines, also married couples, had as its scope the gathering of opinions on the new questions regarding conjugal life, and in particular on the regulation of births, and of furnishing opportune elements of

information so that the magisterium could give an adequate reply to the expectation not only of the faithful, but also of world opinion.[5]

The work of these experts, as well as the successive judgments and counsels spontaneously forwarded by or expressly requested from a good number of our brothers in the episcopate, have permitted us to measure more exactly all the aspects of this complex matter. Hence with all our heart we express to each of them our lively gratitude.

Reply of the Magisterium

6. The conclusions at which the commission arrived could not, nevertheless, be considered by us as definitive, nor dispense us from a personal examination of this serious question; and this also because, within the commission itself, no full concordance of judgments concerning the moral norms to be proposed had been reached, and above all because certain criteria of solutions had emerged which departed from the moral teaching on marriage proposed with constant firmness by the teaching authority of the Church.

Therefore, having attentively sifted the documentation laid before us, after mature reflection and assiduous prayers, we now intend, by virtue of the mandate entrusted to us by Christ, to give our reply to these grave questions.

II. Doctrinal Principles

A Total Vision of Man

7. The problem of birth, like every other problem regarding human life, is to be considered, beyond partial perspectives – whether of the biological or psychological, demographic or sociological orders – in the light of an integral vision of man and of his vocation, not only his natural and earthly, but also his supernatural and eternal vocation. And since, in the attempt to justify artificial methods of birth control, many have appealed to the demands both of conjugal love and of "responsible parenthood" it is good to state very precisely the true concept of these two great realities of married life, referring principally to what was recently set forth in this regard, and in a highly authoritative form, by the Second Vatican Council in its pastoral constitution *Gaudium et Spes* (Constitution on the Church in the Modern World).

8. Conjugal love reveals its true nature and nobility when it is considered in its supreme origin, God, who is love,[6] "the Father, from whom every family in Heaven and on earth is named."[7]

Marriage is not, then, the effect of chance or the product of evolution of unconscious natural forces; it is the wise institution of the Creator to realize in mankind His design of love. By means of the reciprocal personal gift of self, proper and exclusive to them, husband and wife tend towards the communion of their beings in view of mutual personal perfection, to collaborate with God in the generation and education of new lives.

For baptized persons, moreover, marriage invests the dignity of a sacramental sign of grace, inasmuch as it represents the union of Christ and of the Church.

Its Characteristics

9. Under this light, there clearly appear the characteristic marks and demands of conjugal love, and it is of supreme importance to have an exact idea of these.

This love is first of all fully human, that is to say, of the senses and of the spirit at the same time. It is not, then, a simple transport of instinct and sentiment, but also, and principally, an act of the free will, intended to endure and to grow by means of the joys and sorrows of daily life, in such a way that husband and wife become one only heart and one only soul, and together attain their human perfection.

Then, this love is total, that is to say, it is a very special form of personal friendship, in which husband and wife generously share everything, without undue reservations or selfish calculations. Whoever truly loves his marriage partner loves not only for what he receives, but for the partner's self, rejoicing that he can enrich his partner with the gift of himself.

Again, this love is faithful and exclusive until death. Thus in fact do bride and groom conceive it to be on the day when they freely and in full awareness assume the duty of the marriage bond. A fidelity, this, which can sometimes be difficult, but is always possible, always noble and meritorious, as no one can deny. The example of so many married persons down through the centuries shows, not only that fidelity is according to the nature of marriage, but also that it is a source of profound and lasting happiness and finally, this love is fecund for it is not exhausted by the communion between husband and wife, but is destined to continue, raising up new lives. "Marriage and conjugal love are by their nature ordained toward the begetting and educating of children. Children are really the supreme gift of marriage and contribute very substantially to the welfare of their parents."[8]

Responsible Parenthood

10. Hence conjugal love requires in husband and wife an awareness of their mission of "responsible parenthood," which today is rightly much insisted upon, and which also must be exactly understood. Consequently it is to be considered under different aspects which are legitimate and connected with one another.

In relation to the biological processes, responsible parenthood means the knowledge and respect of their functions; human intellect discovers in the power of giving life biological laws which are part of the human person.[9]

In relation to the tendencies of instinct or passion, responsible parenthood means that necessary dominion which reason and will must exercise over them.

In relation to physical, economic, psychological and social conditions, responsible parenthood is exercised, either by the deliberate and generous decision to raise a numerous family, or by the decision, made for grave motives and with due respect for the moral law, to avoid for the time being, or even for an indeterminate period, a new birth.

Responsible parenthood also and above all implies a more profound relationship to the objective moral order established by God, of which a right conscience is the faithful interpreter. The responsible exercise of parenthood implies, therefore, that husband and wife recognize fully their own duties towards God, towards themselves, towards the family and towards society, in a correct hierarchy of values.

In the task of transmitting life, therefore, they are not free to proceed completely at will, as if they could determine in a wholly autonomous way the honest path to follow; but they must conform their activity to the creative intention of God, expressed in the very nature of marriage and of its acts, and manifested by the constant teaching of the Church."[10]

Respect for the Nature and Purpose of the Marriage Act

11. These acts, by which husband and wife are united in chaste intimacy, and by means of which human life is transmitted, are, as the council recalled, "noble and worthy,"[11] and they do not cease to be lawful if, for causes independent of the will of husband and wife, they are foreseen to be infecund, since they always remain ordained towards expressing and consolidating their union. In fact, as experience bears witness, not every conjugal act is followed by a new life. God has wisely disposed natural laws and rhythms of fecundity which, of themselves, cause a separation in the succession of births. Nonetheless the Church, calling men back to the observance of the norms of the natural law, as interpreted by its constant doctrine, teaches that each and every marriage act *(quilibet matrimonii usus)* must remain open to the transmission of life.[12]

Two Inseparable Aspects: Union and Procreation

12. That teaching, often set forth by the magisterium, is founded upon the inseparable connection, willed by God and unable to be broken by man on his own initiative, between the two meanings of the conjugal act: the unitive meaning and the procreative meaning. Indeed, by its intimate structure, the conjugal act, while most closely uniting husband and wife, capacitates them for the generation of new lives, according to laws inscribed in the very being of man and of woman. By safeguarding both these essential aspects, the unitive and the procreative, the conjugal act preserves in its fullness the sense of true mutual love and its ordination towards man's most high calling to parenthood. We believe that the men of our day are particularly capable of seizing the deeply reasonable and human character of this fundamental principle.

Faithfulness to God's Design

13. It is in fact justly observed that a conjugal act imposed upon one's partner without regard for his or her condition and lawful desires is not a true act of love, and therefore denies an exigency of right moral order in the relationships between

husband and wife. Hence, one who reflects well must also recognize that a reciprocal act of love, which jeopardizes the responsibility to transmit life which God the Creator, according to particular laws, inserted therein, is in contradiction with the design constitutive of marriage, and with the will of the Author of life. To use this divine gift destroying, even if only partially, its meaning and its purpose is to contradict the nature both of man and of woman and of their most intimate relationship, and therefore it is to contradict also the plan of God and His will. On the other hand, to make use of the gift of conjugal love while respecting the laws of the generative process means to acknowledge oneself not to be the arbiter of the sources of human life, but rather the minister of the design established by the Creator. In fact, just as man does not have unlimited dominion over his body in general, so also, with particular reason, he has no such dominion over his generative faculties as such, because of their intrinsic ordination towards raising up life, of which God is the principle. "Human life is sacred," Pope John XXIII recalled; "from its very inception it reveals the creating hand of God."[13]

Illicit Ways of Regulating Birth

14. In conformity with these landmarks in the human and Christian vision of marriage, we must once again declare that the direct interruption of the generative process already begun, and, above all, directly willed and procured abortion, even if for therapeutic reasons, are to be absolutely excluded as licit means of regulating birth.[14]

Equally to be excluded, as the teaching authority of the Church has frequently declared, is direct sterilization, whether perpetual or temporary, whether of the man or of the woman.[15] Similarly excluded is every action which, either in anticipation of the conjugal act, or in its accomplishment, or in the development of its natural consequences, proposes, whether as an end or as a means, to render procreation impossible.[16]

To justify conjugal acts made intentionally infecund, one cannot invoke as valid reasons the lesser evil, or the fact that such acts would constitute a whole together with the fecund acts already performed or to follow later, and hence would share in one and the same moral goodness. In truth, if it is sometimes licit to tolerate a lesser evil in order to avoid a greater evil or to promote a greater good,[17] it is not licit, even for the gravest reasons, to do evil so that good may follow therefrom,[18] that is, to make into the object of a positive act of the will something which is intrinsically disorder, and hence unworthy of the human person, even when the intention is to safeguard or promote individual, family or social well-being. Consequently it is an error to think that a conjugal act which is deliberately made infecund and so is intrinsically dishonest could be made honest and right by the ensemble of a fecund conjugal life.

Licitness of Therapeutic Means

15. The Church, on the contrary, does not at all consider illicit the use of those therapeutic means truly necessary to cure diseases of the organism, even if an

impediment to procreation, which may be foreseen, should result therefrom, provided such impediment is not, for whatever motive, directly willed.[19]

Licitness of Recourse to Infecund Periods

16. To this teaching of the Church on conjugal morals, the objection is made today, as we observed earlier (no. 3), that it is the prerogative of the human intellect to dominate the energies offered by irrational nature and to orientate them towards an end conformable to the good of man. Now, some may ask: in the present case, is it not reasonable in many circumstances to have recourse to artificial birth control if, thereby, we secure the harmony and peace of the family, and better conditions for the education of the children already born? To this question it is necessary to reply with clarity: the Church is the first to praise and recommend the intervention of intelligence in a function which so closely associates the rational creature with his Creator; but she affirms that this must be done with respect for the order established by God.

If, then, there are serious motives to space out births, which derive from the physical or psychological conditions of husband and wife, or from external conditions, the Church teaches that it is then licit to take into account the natural rhythms immanent in the generative functions, for the use of marriage in the infecund periods only, and in this way to regulate birth without offending the moral principles which have been recalled earlier.[20]

The Church is coherent with herself when she considers recourse to the infecund periods to be licit, while at the same time condemning, as being always illicit, the use of means directly contrary to fecundation, even if such use is inspired by reasons which may appear honest and serious. In reality, there are essential differences between the two cases; in the former, the married couple make legitimate use of a natural disposition; in the latter, they impede the development of natural processes. It is true that, in the one and the other case, the married couple are concordant in the positive will of avoiding children for plausible reasons, seeking the certainty that offspring will not arrive; but it is also true that only in the former case are they able to renounce the use of marriage in the fecund periods when, for just motives, procreation is not desirable, while making use of it during infecund periods to manifest their affection and to safeguard their mutual fidelity. By so doing, they give proof of a truly and integrally honest love.

Grave Consequences of Methods of Artificial Birth Control

17. Upright men can even better convince themselves of the solid grounds on which the teaching of the Church in this field is based, if they care to reflect upon the consequences of methods of artificial birth control. Let them consider, first of all, how wide and easy a road would thus be opened up towards conjugal infidelity and the general lowering of morality. Not much experience is needed in order to know human weakness, and to understand that men – especially the young, who are so vulnerable on this point – have need of encouragement to be faithful to the moral law, so that they must not be offered some easy means of eluding its observance. It

is also to be feared that the man, growing used to the employment of anticonceptive practices, may finally lose respect for the woman and, no longer caring for her physical and psychological equilibrium, may come to the point of considering her as a mere instrument of selfish enjoyment, and no longer as his respected and beloved companion.

Let it be considered also that a dangerous weapon would thus be placed in the hands of those public authorities who take no heed of moral exigencies. Who could blame a government for applying to the solution of the problems of the community those means acknowledged to be licit for married couples in the solution of a family problem? Who will stop rulers from favoring, from even imposing upon their peoples, if they were to consider it necessary, the method of contraception which they judge to be most efficacious? In such a way men, wishing to avoid individual, family, or social difficulties encountered in the observance of the divine law, would reach the point of placing at the mercy of the intervention of public authorities the most personal and most reserved sector of conjugal intimacy.

Consequently, if the mission of generating life is not to be exposed to the arbitrary will of men, one must necessarily recognize unsurmountable limits to the possibility of man's domination over his own body and its functions; limits which no man, whether a private individual or one invested with authority, may licitly surpass. And such limits cannot be determined otherwise than by the respect due to the integrity of the human organism and its functions, according to the principles recalled earlier, and also according to the correct understanding of the "principle of totality" illustrated by our predecessor Pope Pius XII.[21]

The Church, Guarantor of True Human Values

18. It can be foreseen that this teaching will perhaps not be easily received by all: Too numerous are those voices – amplified by the modern means of propaganda – which are contrary to the voice of the Church. To tell the truth, the Church is not surprised to be made, like her divine founder, a "sign of contradiction,"[22] yet she does not because of this cease to proclaim with humble firmness the entire moral law, both natural and evangelical. Of such laws the Church was not the author, nor consequently can she be their arbiter; she is only their depositary and their interpreter, without ever being able to declare to be licit that which is not so by reason of its intimate and unchangeable opposition to the true good of man.

In defending conjugal morals in their integral wholeness, the Church knows that she contributes towards the establishment of a truly human civilization; she engages man not to abdicate from his own responsibility in order to rely on technical means; by that very fact she defends the dignity of man and wife. Faithful to both the teaching and the example of the Savior, she shows herself to be the sincere and disinterested friend of men, whom she wishes to help, even during their earthly sojourn, "to share as sons in the life of the living God, the Father of all men."[23]

III. Pastoral Directives

The Church, Mater et Magistra

19. Our words would not be an adequate expression of the thought and solicitude of the Church, mother and teacher of all peoples, if, after having recalled men to the observance and respect of the divine law regarding matrimony, we did not strengthen them in the path of honest regulation of birth, even amid the difficult conditions which today afflict families and peoples. The Church, in fact, cannot have a different conduct towards men than that of the Redeemer. She knows their weaknesses, has compassion on the crowd, receives sinners; but she cannot renounce the teaching of the law which is, in reality, that law proper to a human life restored to its original truth and conducted by the spirit of God.[24]

Possibility of Observing the Divine Law

20. The teaching of the Church on the regulation of birth, which promulgates the divine law, will easily appear to many to be difficult or even impossible of actuation. And indeed, like all great beneficent realities, it demands serious engagement and much effort, individual, family and social effort. More than that, it would not be practicable without the help of God, who upholds and strengthens the good will of men. Yet, to anyone who reflects well, it cannot but be clear that such efforts ennoble man and are beneficial to the human community.

Mastery of Self

21. The honest practice of regulation of birth demands first of all that husband and wife acquire and possess solid convictions concerning the true values of life and of the family, and that they tend towards securing perfect self-mastery. To dominate instinct by means of one's reason and free will undoubtedly requires ascetical practices, so that the affective manifestations of conjugal life may observe the correct order, in particular with regard to the observance of periodic continence. Yet this discipline which is proper to the purity of married couples, far from harming conjugal love, rather confers on it a higher human value. It demands continual effort yet, thanks to its beneficent influence, husband and wife fully develop their personalities, being enriched with spiritual values. Such discipline bestows upon family life fruits of serenity and peace, and facilitates the solution of other problems; it favors attention for one's partner, helps both parties to drive out selfishness, the enemy of true love; and deepens their sense of responsibility. By its means, parents acquire the capacity of having a deeper and more efficacious influence in the education of their offspring; little children and youths grow up with a just appraisal of human values, and in the serene and harmonious development of their spiritual and sensitive faculties.

Creating an Atmosphere Favorable to Chastity

22. On this occasion, we wish to draw the attention of educators, and of all who perform duties of responsibility in regard to the common good of human society, to

the need of creating an atmosphere favorable to education in chastity, that is, to the triumph of healthy liberty over license by means of respect for the moral order.

Everything in the modern media of social communications which leads to sense excitation and unbridled customs, as well as every form of pornography and licentious performances, must arouse the frank and unanimous reaction of all those who are solicitous for the progress of civilization and the defense of the common good of the human spirit. Vainly would one seek to justify such depravation with the pretext of artistic or scientific exigencies,[25] or to deduce an argument from the freedom allowed in this sector by the public authorities.

Appeal to Public Authorities

23. To rulers, who are those principally responsible for the common good, and who can do so much to safeguard moral customs, we say: Do not allow the morality of your peoples to be degraded; do not permit that by legal means practices contrary to the natural and divine law be introduced into that fundamental cell, the family. Quite other is the way in which public authorities can and must contribute to the solution of the demographic problem: namely, the way of a provident policy for the family, of a wise education of peoples in respect of moral law and the liberty of citizens.

We are well aware of the serious difficulties experienced by public authorities in this regard, especially in the developing countries. To their legitimate preoccupations we devoted our encyclical letter *Populorum Progressio* (The Development of Peoples). But with our predecessor Pope John XXIII, we repeat: no solution to these difficulties is acceptable "which does violence to man's essential dignity" and is based only on an utterly materialistic conception of man himself and of his life. The only possible solution to this question is one which envisages the social and economic progress both of individuals and of the whole of human society, and which respects and promotes true human values.[26] Neither can one, without grave injustice, consider divine providence to be responsible for what depends, instead, on a lack of wisdom in government, on an insufficient sense of social justice, on selfish monopolization, or again on blameworthy indolence in confronting the efforts and the sacrifices necessary to ensure the raising of living standards of a people and of all its sons.[27]

May all responsible public authorities – as some are already doing so laudably – generously revive their efforts. And may mutual aid between all the members of the great human family never cease to grow: This is an almost limitless field which thus opens up to the activity of the great international organizations.

To Men of Science

24. We wish now to express our encouragement to men of science, who "can considerably advance the welfare of marriage and the family, along with peace of conscience, if by pooling their efforts they labor to explain more thoroughly the various conditions favoring a proper regulation of births.[28] It is particularly desir-

able that, according to the wish already expressed by Pope Pius XII, medical science succeed in providing a sufficiently secure basis for a regulation of birth, founded on the observance of natural rhythms.[29] In this way, scientists and especially Catholic scientists will contribute to demonstrate in actual fact that, as the Church teaches, "a true contradiction cannot exist between the divine laws pertaining to the transmission of life and those pertaining to the fostering of authentic conjugal love."[30]

To Christian Husbands and Wives

25. And now our words more directly address our own children, particularly those whom God calls to serve Him in marriage. The Church, while teaching imprescriptible demands of the divine law, announces the tidings of salvation, and by means of the sacraments opens up the paths of grace, which makes man a new creature, capable of corresponding with love and true freedom to the design of his Creator and Savior, and of finding the yoke of Christ to be sweet.[31]

Christian married couples, then, docile to her voice, must remember that their Christian vocation, which began at baptism, is further specified and reinforced by the sacrament of matrimony. By it husband and wife are strengthened and as it were consecrated for the faithful accomplishment of their proper duties, for the carrying out of their proper vocation even to perfection, and the Christian witness which is proper to them before the whole world.[32] To them the Lord entrusts the task of making visible to men the holiness and sweetness of the law which unites the mutual love of husband and wife with their cooperation with the love of God, the author of human life.

We do not at all intend to hide the sometimes serious difficulties inherent in the life of Christian married persons; for them as for everyone else, "the gate is narrow and the way is hard, that leads to life."[33] But the hope of that life must illuminate their way, as with courage they strive to live with wisdom, justice and piety in this present time,[34] knowing that the figure of this world passes away.[35]

Let married couples, then, face up to the efforts needed, supported by the faith and hope which "do not disappoint...because God's love has been poured into our hearts through the Holy Spirit, who has been given to us."[36] Let them implore divine assistance by persevering prayer; above all, let them draw from the source of grace and charity in the Eucharist. And if sin should still keep its hold over them, let them not be discouraged, but rather have recourse with humble perseverance to the mercy of God, which is poured forth in the sacrament of Penance. In this way they will be enabled to achieve the fullness of conjugal life described by the Apostle: "husbands, love your wives, as Christ loved the Church... husbands should love their wives as their own bodies. He who loves his wife loves himself. For no man ever hates his own flesh, but nourishes and cherishes it, as Christ does the Church... this is a great mystery, and I mean in reference to Christ and the Church. However, let each one of you love his wife as himself, and let the wife see that she respects her husband."[37]

Apostolate in Homes

26. Among the fruits which ripen forth from a generous effort of fidelity to the divine law, one of the most precious is that married couples themselves not infrequently feel the desire to communicate their experience to others. Thus there comes to be included in the vast pattern of the vocation of the laity a new and most noteworthy form of the apostolate of like to like; it is married couples themselves who become apostles and guides to other married couples. This is assuredly, among so many forms of apostolate, one of those which seem most opportune today.[38]

To Doctors and Medical Personnel

27. We hold those physicians and medical personnel in the highest esteem who, in the exercise of their profession, value above every human interest the superior demands of their Christian vocation. Let them persevere, therefore, in promoting on every occasion the discovery of solutions inspired by faith and right reason, let them strive to arouse this conviction and this respect in their associates. Let them also consider as their proper professional duty the task of acquiring all the knowledge needed in this delicate sector, so as to be able to give to those married persons who consult them wise counsel and healthy direction, such as they have a right to expect.

To Priests

28. Beloved priest sons, by vocation you are the counselors and spiritual guides of individual persons and of families. We now turn to you with confidence. Your first task – especially in the case of those who teach moral theology – is to expound the Church's teaching on marriage without ambiguity. Be the first to give, in the exercise of your ministry, the example of loyal internal and external obedience to the teaching authority of the Church. That obedience, as you know well, obliges not only because of the reasons adduced, but rather because of the light of the Holy Spirit, which is given in a particular way to the pastors of the Church in order that they may illustrate the truth.[39] You know, too, that it is of the utmost importance, for peace of consciences and for the unity of the Christian people, that in the field of morals as well as in that of dogma, all should attend to the magisterium of the Church, and all should speak the same language. Hence, with all our heart we renew to you the heartfelt plea of the great Apostle Paul: "I appeal to you, brethren, by the name of Our Lord Jesus Christ, that all of you agree and that there be no dissensions among you, but that you be united in the same mind and the same judgment."[40]

29. To diminish in no way the saving teaching of Christ constitutes an eminent form of charity for souls. But this must ever be accompanied by patience and goodness, such as the Lord himself gave example of in dealing with men. Having come not to condemn but to save,[41] He was intransigent with evil, but merciful toward individuals.

In their difficulties, may married couples always find, in the words and in the heart of a priest, the echo of the voice and the love of the Redeemer.

And then speak with confidence, beloved sons, fully convinced that the spirit of God, while He assists the magisterium in proposing doctrine, illumines internally the hearts of the faithful inviting them to give their assent. Teach married couples the indispensable way of prayer; prepare them to have recourse often and with faith to the sacraments of the Eucharist and of Penance, without ever allowing themselves to be discouraged by their own weakness.

To Bishops

30. Beloved and venerable brothers in the episcopate, with whom we most intimately share the solicitude of the spiritual good of the people of God, at the conclusion of this encyclical our reverent and affectionate thoughts turn to you. To all of you we extend an urgent invitation. At the head of the priests, your collaborators, and of your faithful, work ardently and incessantly for the safeguarding and the holiness of marriage, so that it may always be lived in its entire human and Christian fullness. Consider this mission as one of your most urgent responsibilities at the present time.

As you know, it implies concerted pastoral action in all the fields of human activity, economic, cultural and social; for, in fact, only a simultaneous improvement in these various sectors will make it possible to render the life of parents and of children within their families not only tolerable, but easier and more joyous, to render the living together in human society more fraternal and peaceful, in faithfulness to God's design for the world.

Final Appeal

31. Venerable brothers, most beloved sons, and all men of good will, great indeed is the work of education, of progress and of love to which we call you, upon the foundation of the Church's teaching, of which the successor of Peter is, together with his brothers in the episcopate, the depositary and interpreter. Truly a great work, as we are deeply convinced, both for the world and for the Church, since man cannot find true happiness – towards which he aspires with all his being – other than in respect of the laws written by God in his very nature, laws which he must observe with intelligence and love. Upon this work, and upon all of you, and especially upon married couples, we invoke the abundant graces of the God of holiness and mercy, and in pledge thereof we impart to you all our apostolic blessing.

Given at Rome, from St. Peter's, this 25th day of July, feast of St. James the Apostle, in the year 1968, the sixth of our pontificate.

PAULUS PP.VI.

[1] Cf. Pius IX, encyclical Qui Pluribus, Nov. 9, 1846; in PII IX P.M. Acta, I, pp. 9-10; St. Pius X, encyc. Singulari Quadam, Sept. 24, 1912; in AASIV (1912), p. 658; Pius XI, encyc. Casti Connubii, Dec. 31, 1930; in AAS XXII (1930), pp. 579-581; Pius XII, allocution Magnificate Dominum to the episcopate of the Catholic world, Nov. 2, 1954;in AAS XLVI (1954), pp. 671-672; John XXIII, encyc. Mater et Magistra, May 15, 1961; in AAS LIII (1961), p. 457.

[2] Cf. Matt. 28:18-19.

[3] Cf. Matt. 7:21.

[4] Cf. Catechismus Romanus Concilii Tridentini, part II. ch. VIII; Leo XIII, encyc. Arcanum, Feb. 19, 1880; in Acta Leonis XIII, II (1881), pp. 26-29; Pius XI, encyc. Divini Illius Magistri, Dec. 31, 1929, in AAS XXII (1930), pp. 58-61; encyc. Casti Connubii, in AAS XXII (1930), pp. 545-546; Pius XII, alloc. to the Italian medico-biological union of St. Luke, Nov. 12, 1944, in Discorsi e Radiomessaggi, VI, pp. 191-192; to the Italian Catholic union of midwives Oct. 29, 1951, in AAS XLIII (1951), pp. 857-859; to the seventh Congress of the International Society of Hoematology, Sept. 12, 1958, in AAS L (1958), pp. 734-735; John XXIII, encyc. Mater et Magistra, in AAS LIII (1961), pp. 446-447; Codex Iuris Canonici, Canon 1067; Can. 1968, S 1, Can. 1066 S 1-2, Second Vatican Council, Pastoral constitution Gaudium et Spes, nos. 47-52.

[5] Cf. Paul VI, atlocution to the Sacred College, June 23, 1964, in AAS LVI (1964), p. 588; to the Commission for Study of Problems of Population, Family and Birth, March 27, 1965, in AAS LVII (1965), p. 388, to the National Congress of the Italian Society of Obstetrics and Gynecology, Oct. 29, 1966, in AAS LVIII (1966), p. 1168.

[6] Cf. 1 John 4:8.

[7] Cf. Eph. 3:15.

[8] Cf. Second Vatican Council, Pastoral constitution Gaudium at Spes, no. 50.

[9] Cf. St. Thomas, Summa Theologica, I-II, q. 94, art. 2.

[10] Cf. Pastoral constitution Gaudium et Spes, nos. 50, 51.

[11] Ibid., no. 49.

[12] Cf. Pius XI, encyc. Casti Connubii, in AAS XXII (1930), p. 560; Pius XII, in AAS XLIII (1951), p. 843.

[13] Cf. John XXIII, encyc. Mater et Magistra, in AAS LIII (1961), p. 447.

[14] Cf. Catechismus Romanus Concilii Tridentini, part. II, Ch. VIII; Pius XI, encyc. Casti Connubii, in AAS XXII (1930), pp. 562-564; Pius XII, discorsi e Radiomessaggi, VI (1944), pp. 191-192; AAS XLIII (1951), pp. 842-843; pp. 857-859; John XXIII, encyc. Pacem in Terris, Apr. 11, 1963, in AAS LV (1963), pp. 259-260; Gaudium at Spes, no. 51.

[15] Cf. Pius XI, encyc. Casti Connubii, in AAS XXII (1930) p. 565; decree on the Holy Office, Feb. 22, 1940, in AAS L (1958), pp. 734-735.

[16] Cf. Catechismus Romanus Concilii Tridentini, part. II. Ch. VIII; Pius XI, encyc. Casti Connubii, in AAS XXII (1930), pp. 559-561; Pius XII, AAS XLIII (1951), p. 643; AAS L (1958), pp. 734-735; John XXIII, encyc. Mater et Magistra, in AAS LIII (1961), p. 447.

[17] Cf Pius XII, alloc. to the National Congress of the Union of Catholic Jurists, Dec. 6, 1953, in AAS XLV (1953), pp. 798-799.

[18] Cf. Rom. 3:8.

[19] Cf. Pius XII, alloc. to Congress of the Italian Association of Urology, Oct. 8, 1953, in AAS XLV (1953), pp. 674-675; AAS L (1958), pp. 734-735.

[20] Cf. Pius XII, AAS XLIII (1951), p. 846.

[21] Cf. AAS XLV (1953), pp. 674-675; AAS XLVIII (1956), pp. 461-462.

[22] Cf. Luke 2:34.

[23] Cf. Paul VI, encyc. Populorum Progressio, March 26, 1967, no. 21.

[24] Cf. Rom. 8.

[25] Cf. Second Vatican Council, decree Inter Mirifica on the Media of Social Communication, nos. 6-7.

[26] Cf. encyc. Mater et Magistra, in AAS LIII (1961), p. 447.

[27] Cf. encyc. Populorum Progressio, nos. 48-55.

[28] Cf. Pastoral constitution Gaudium et Spes, no. 52.

[29] Cf. AAS XLIII (1951), p. 859.

[30] Cf. Pastoral constitution Gaudium et Spes, no. 51.

[31] Cf. Matt. 11:30.

[32] Cf. Pastoral constitution Gaudium et Spes, no. 48; Second Vatican Council, Dogmatic constitution Lumen Gentium, no. 35.

[33] Matt. 7:14; cf. Heb. 11:12.

[34] Cf. Tit. 2:12.

[35] Cf. 1 Cor. 7:31.

[36] Cf. Rom. 5:5.

[37] Eph. 5:25, 28-29, 32-33.

[38] Cf. Dogmatic constitution Lumen Gentium, nos. 35 and 41; Pastoral constitution Gaudium et Spes, nos. 48-49; Second Vatican Council, decree Apostolicam Actuositatem, no. 11.

[39] Cf. Dogmatic constitution Lumen Gentium, no. 25.

[40] Cf. 1 Cor. 1:10.

[41] Cf. John 3:17.

17.

STATEMENT ON THE ENCYCLICAL *HUMANAE VITAE*[1]

The Plenary Assembly, Canadian Catholic Conference
September 27, 1968

1. Pope Paul VI in his recent encyclical *On Human Life* has spoken on a profound human problem as is clearly evidenced by the immediate and universal reaction to his message. It is evident that he has written out of concern and love, and in a spirit of service to all humanity. Conscious of the current controversy and deep differences of opinion as to how to harmonize married love and the responsible transmission of life, we, the Canadian bishops, offer our help to our priests and Catholic people, believing it to be our pastoral duty.

I – SOLIDARITY WITH THE POPE

2. We are in accord with the teaching of the Holy Father concerning the dignity of married life and the necessity of a truly Christian relationship between conjugal love and responsible parenthood. We share the pastoral concern which has led him to offer counsel and direction in an area which, while controverted, could hardly be more important to human happiness.

3. By divine commission, clarification of these difficult problems of morality is required from the teaching authority of the Church.[2] The Canadian Bishops will endeavour to discharge their obligation to the best of their ability. In this pursuit we are acting consistently with our recent submissions to the federal government on contraception, divorce and abortion, nor is there anything in those submissions which does not harmonize with the encyclical.

II – SOLIDARITY WITH THE FAITHFUL

4. In the same spirit of solidarity we declare ourselves one with the People of God in the difficulties they experience in understanding, making their own and living this teaching.

5. In accord with the teaching of the Second Vatican Council, the recent encyclical[3] recognizes the nobility of conjugal love which is "uniquely expressed and perfected through the marital act."[4] Many married people experience a truly

agonizing difficulty in reconciling the need to express conjugal love with the responsible transmission of human life.[5]

6. This difficulty is recognized in deep sympathy and is shared by bishops and priests as counsellors and confessors in their service of the faithful. We know that we are unable to provide easy answers to this difficult problem, a problem made more acute by the great variety of solutions proposed in an open society.

7. A clearer understanding of these problems and progress toward their solution will result from a common effort in dialogue, research and study on the part of all, laity, priests and bishops, guided by faith and sustained by grace. To this undertaking the Canadian bishops pledge themselves.

III – CHRISTIAN CONSCIENCE AND DIVINE LAW

8. Of recent years many have entertained doubts about the validity of arguments proposed to forbid any positive intervention which would prevent the transmission of human life. As a result there have arisen opinions and practices contrary to traditional moral theology. Because of this many had been expecting official confirmation of their views. This helps to explain the negative reaction the encyclical received in many quarters. Many Catholics face a grave problem of conscience.

9. Christian theology regarding conscience has its roots in the teaching of St. Paul (Rom. 14:23 and 1 Cor. 10). This has been echoed in our day by the Second Vatican Council: "Conscience is the most secret core and sanctuary of a man. There he is alone with God, whose voice echoes in his depths".[6] On his part, man perceives and acknowledges the imperatives of the divine law through the mediation of conscience. In all activity a person is bound to follow conscience faithfully, to come to God, the final end of each."[7] The dignity of the person consists precisely in this ability to achieve fulfillment in God through the exercise of a knowing and free choice.

10. This does not however, exempt one from the responsibility of forming conscience according to truly Christian values and principles. This implies a spirit of openness to the teaching of the Church which is an essential aspect of the Christian's baptismal vocation. It likewise implies sound personal motivation free from selfishness and undue external pressure which are incompatible with the spirit of Christ. Nor can one succeed in this difficult task without the help of God. We are all prone to sin and evil and unless we humbly ask and gratefully receive the grace of God this basic freedom will inevitably lead to abuse.

IV – TEACHING OFFICE OF THE CHURCH

11. Belief in the Church which is the prolongation of Christ in the world, belief in the Incarnation, demands a cheerful readiness to hear that Church to whose first apostles Christ said: "He who hears you hears me" (Lk. 10:16).

12. True freedom of conscience does not consist, then, in the freedom to do as one likes, but rather to do as a responsible conscience directs. The Second Vatican Council applies this concept forcefully. Christians therefore must always be governed according to a conscience dutifully conformed to the divine law itself, and should be submissive towards the Church's teaching office, which authentically interprets that law in the light of the gospel. That divine law reveals and protects the integral meaning of conjugal love, and impels it towards truly human fulfillment.[8]

13. Today, the Holy Father has spoken on the question of morally acceptable means to harmonize conjugal love and responsible parenthood. Christians must examine in all honesty their reaction to what he has said.

14. The Church is competent to hand on the truth contained in the revealed word of God and to interpret its meaning. But its role is not limited to this function. In our pilgrimage to salvation, we achieve final happiness by all our responsible conduct and whole moral life. Since the Church is our guide in this pilgrimage, she is called upon to exercise her role as teacher, even in those matters which do not demand the absolute assent of faith.

15. Of this sort of teaching Vatican II wrote:

This religious submission of will and of mind must be shown in a special way to the authentic teaching authority of the Roman Pontiff, even when he is not speaking *ex cathedra*. That is, it must be shown in such a way that his supreme teaching authority is acknowledged with reverence, the judgments made by him are sincerely adhered to, according to his manifest mind and will.[9]

16. It follows that those who have been commissioned by the Church to teach in her name will recognize their responsibility to refrain from public opposition to the encyclical; to do otherwise would compound confusion and be a source of scandal to God's people. This must not be interpreted however, as a restriction on the legitimate and recognized freedom of theologians to pursue loyally and conscientiously their research with a view to greater depth and clarity in the teaching of the Church.

17. It is a fact that a certain number of Catholics, although admittedly subject to the teaching of the encyclical, find it either extremely difficult or even impossible to make their own all elements of this doctrine. In particular the argumentation and rational foundation of the encyclical, which are only briefly indicated, have failed in some cases to win the assent of scientists, or indeed of some people of culture and education who share in the contemporary empirical and scientific mode of thought. We must appreciate the difficulty experienced by contemporary minds in understanding and appropriating some of the points of this encyclical, and must make every effort to learn from the insights of Catholic scientists and intellectuals, who are of undoubted loyalty to Christian truth, to the Church and to the authority of the Holy See. Since they are not denying any point of divine and Catholic faith nor rejecting the teaching authority of the Church, these Catholics should not be considered, or consider themselves, shut off from the body of the faithful. But they

should remember that their good faith will be dependent on a sincere self-examination to determine the true motives and grounds for such suspension of assent and on continued effort to understand and deepen their knowledge of the teaching of the Church.

18. The difficulties of this situation have been felt by the priests of the Church, and by many others. We have been requested to provide guidelines to assist them. This we will endeavour to do in a subsequent document. We are conscious that continuing dialogue, study and reflection will be required by all members of the Church in order to meet as best we can the complexities and exigencies of the problem.

19. We point out that the particular norms which we may offer will prove of little value unless they are placed in the context of our human and Christian vocations and of all the values of Christian marriage. This formation of conscience and this education in true love will be achieved only by a well balanced pastoral insistence upon the primary importance of a love which is human, total, faithful and exclusive as well as generously fruitful.[10]

V – PRELIMINARY PASTORAL GUIDANCE

20. For the moment, in conformity with traditional Christian morality, we request priests and all who may be called to guide or counsel the consciences of others to give their attention to the following considerations.

21. The pastoral directives given by Pope Paul VI in the encyclical are inspired by a positive sacramental approach. The Eucharist is always the great expression of Christian love and union. Married couples will always find in this celebration a meeting place with the Lord which will never fail to strengthen their own mutual love. With regard to the sacrament of penance the spirit is one of encouragement both for penitents and confessors and avoids both extremes of laxity and rigorism.

22. The encyclical suggests an attitude towards the sacrament of penance which is at once less juridical, more pastoral and more respectful of persons. There is real concern for their growth, however slow at times, and for the hope of the future.

23. Confession should never be envisaged under the cloud of agonizing fear of severity. It should be an exercise in confidence and respect of consciences. Paul VI invited married couples to "have recourse with humble perseverance to the mercy of God, which is poured forth in the Sacrament of Penance."[11] Confession is a meeting between a sincere conscience and Christ Our Lord who was "indeed intransigent with evil, but merciful towards individuals."[12]

24. Such is the general atmosphere in which the confessor and counsellor must work. We complete the concept with a few more particular applications.

25. In the situation we described earlier in this statement (n. 17) the confessor or counsellor must show sympathetic understanding and reverence for the sincere good faith of those who fail in their effort to accept some point of the encyclical.

26. Counsellors may meet others who, accepting the teaching of the Holy Father, find that because of particular circumstances, they are involved in what seems to them a clear conflict of duties; e.g., the reconciling of conjugal love and responsible parenthood with the education of children already born or with the health of the mother. In accord with the accepted principles of moral theology, if these persons have tried sincerely but without success to pursue a line of conduct in keeping with the given directives, they may be safely assured that whoever honestly chooses that course which seems right does so in good conscience.

27. Good pastoral practice for other and perhaps more difficult cases will be developed in continuing communication among bishops, priests and laity, and in particular in the document we have promised to prepare. In the meantime we earnestly solicit the help of medical scientists and biologists in their research into human fertility. While it would be an illusion to hope for the solution of all human problems through scientific technology, such research can bring effective help to the alleviation and solution of problems of conscience in this area.

VI – INVITATION TO SOCIAL PASTORAL ACTION

28. The whole world is increasingly preoccupied with the social impact of people's thoughts, words and actions. Sexuality in all its aspects is obviously an area of the greatest human and social impact. The norms and values which govern this so vital human concern merit the attention and reflection of all. Our world evolves at a frightening rate, creating at once a vivid sense of unity and a set of conflicting forces which could destroy us.

29. This concern will be fruitful only if it leads all of us to recognize our true human worth in the possession of our inner powers by which we are distinctively ourselves with the full recognition of our complementary sexual differences on the physical, the psychological and the spiritual plane. Only in this manner will we achieve marriages that are truly unions of love in the service of life.

30. To this end there must be a mobilization of all the positive energies of the family, the school, the state, the Church. No one may stand aloof, nor are there really national boundaries in a matter of such universal application. With this in mind we call on all members of the Church to realize the importance of the process of education for marriage on every level from the very youngest to the various possibilities of adult education.

31. Without wishing to specify in detail we single out for special mention a few aspects which may have richer possibilities. We place first the dialogue and cooperation, which have been so encouraging, among all members of the Church and, through the ecumenical movement, with other Churches.

32. We note with deep satisfaction the spread and strength of so many activities calculated to prepare for marriage or to deepen the appreciation by married persons of this sublime state. For example, marriage preparation courses, family apostolates, discussion groups, etc.

33. Educators, too, are to be commended for their growing attention to the question. Everywhere the problems of sex education and family life are being studied. And this education is happily being deepened by scientific research and diffused through the creative use of mass media. Nothing less than this mobilization of all human forces will suffice to meet the challenge of divisive and destructive forces which begin deep in willful human selfishness and inhibit the true expression of human love. We pledge ourselves to the pastoral priority of encouraging and promoting these programs whenever and wherever possible.

34. We conclude by asking all to pray fervently that the Holy Spirit will continue to guide His Church through all darkness and suffering. We, the People of God, cannot escape this hour of crisis but there is no reason to believe that it will create division and despair. The unity of the Church does not consist in a bland conformity in all ideas, but rather in a union of faith and love, in submission to God's will and in a humble but honest and ongoing search for the truth. That unity of love and faith is founded in Christ and as long as we are true to Him nothing can separate us. We stand in union with the Bishop of Rome, the successor of Peter, the sign and contributing cause of our unity with Christ and with one another. This very union postulates such a love of the Church that we can do no less than to place all our love and intelligence at her service. If this sometimes means that in our desire to make the Church more intelligible and more beautiful we must, as pilgrims do, falter in the way or differ as to the way, no one should conclude that our common faith is lost or our loving purpose blunted. It was the great theologian, John Henry Cardinal Newman, who penned the comforting lines of the well known "Lead kindly light amid the encircling gloom." We believe that the kindly Light will lead us to a greater understanding of God and of human love.

---

[1] The initial Latin words of Pope Paul IV's encyclical letter, variously named *On Human Life* or *On the Regulation of Birth,* July 5, 1968, cf. *The Papal Encyclicals,* edit. Claudia Carlen, IHM (Wilmington, NC., McGrath Publishing. 1981), V, 223.

[2] Vatican II, The Church in the Modern World, nn. 4 and 18.

[3] *On Human Life,* n. 8, cf. note 1.

[4] Vatican II, *The Church in the Modern World,* n. 49.

[5] *Ibid.,* n. 51.

[6] *Ibid.,* n. 16.

[7] Vatican II, *Declaration on Religious Freedom,* n. 3; *The Church in the Modern World,* nn. 16f.

[8] Vatican II, The Church in the Modern World, n. 50.

[9] Vatican II, *Dogmatic Constitution on the Church,* 1964, n. 25. The Holy Father speaks *ex cathedra* – "from the chair" (of Peter) – when he intends to teach authoritatively, revealed truth demanding the assent of faith.

[10] *On Human Life,* n. 9; cf. note 1.

[11] *Ibid.,* n. 25.

[12] *Ibid.,* n. 29.

18.

STATEMENT ON THE FORMATION OF CONSCIENCE

Canadian Catholic Conference
December 1, 1973

PROLOGUE

1. In all creation man alone of the visible world is called by God to accept the responsibility of his actions. Yet God did not desert him in a world of mystery where good and evil are often interwoven and frequently filled with complexities. We who are Christians believe that not only did God give us his guidance "engraved on their hearts" (Rom. 2:1f) showing us in the very depth of our being the things which are for our good, he also intervened in history to reveal himself in his Son, our Lord Jesus. Henceforth, Jesus and the Spirit he was to send from the Father would be the focal point of our life and of our doing, "I am the Way, the Truth and the Life. No one comes to the Father except through me" (Jn. 14:6).

2. Man, then, has God's clear teaching to guide him, found in Scripture and tradition, protected and authenticated by the teaching Church. God speaks to us also through concrete situations, the providential framework of our existence, our times, our vicissitudes, events, happenings, circumstances. "The People of God believes that it is led by the Spirit of the Lord, who fills the earth". (*Gaudium et Spes,* #11).

3. Above all, we believe that we live now in the time of the fullness of Christ, the law of love. The responsibility of the Christian is not only to fight against his sinful nature in which he is assisted by his obedience to all legitimate laws. It is also to respond to God's call to conversion in a movement towards Christ and his Spirit. It is the realization of what it means to be a Christian, a son of God. "Christian, acknowledge your dignity. Become what you are, another Christ" (St. Leo the Great, First Christmas Sermon).

It is in this context that we wish to present these considerations on conscience. We must of necessity at times leave this high ground because man is frail and loses himself readily. But we do so always with the serenity and joy of those who know that we have already triumphed in our Risen Lord.

PART ONE

1. THE MEANING OF CONSCIENCE

The Basic Concept

5. The signs of our times have much to say to us even when they point to negative and harmful dimensions. The most optimistic person could hardly deny that our times are characterized by a frightening confusion in regard to man's moral life and the understanding of values which for many centuries were taken for granted. It is to this confusion of mind that we would like to address ourselves at the present moment in order to provide certain pastoral guidelines which are meant primarily for our Catholic people, but to which we invite the attention of all people of good will interested in preserving the best elements of our civilization and culture. We appeal in a special manner to those who share with us our faith in Christ as Redeemer and as guide of our lives.

6. To be consistent, since we openly admit the existence of confusion, we cannot even take the idea of "conscience" for granted. It has always been a somewhat ambiguous term and has frequently been presented with more poetry than clarity. Conscience is not simply some "still small voice" which is evoked by some mysterious mechanism within us when we are faced with a practical decision as to whether a given course of action is acceptable or not. Conscience is that ultimate judgment that every man is called to make as to whether this or that action is acceptable to him without which he is prepared to admit as governing him. If he goes against those principles, he is said to be acting "against his conscience".

Different Connotations

7. It follows that conscience has different connotations for different persons. We will develop this concept further in the following section on the "Formation of Conscience". For the moment it suffices to point out that for some people, the very existence of a conscience will be denied. These are the men and women who refuse to accept that man is subject to any laws outside himself; in a word, they maintain that he is his own Lord and Master. In a strict logical sense these people are consistent even though it is hard to digest their premises that man is supreme in a universe which he has not made.

8. For anyone to accept the idea of conscience, as we here present it, he must begin by agreeing that man is not Lord of the Universe and that man is subject to a law-giver who is greater than he is. In a word, we must begin with that very first basis of any moral life and of any question of responsible judgement in our actions, the acceptance of God. And not a God who is remote and unconcerned but a God who is our Father, who made the Universe, who made each one of us and who has lovingly cast our lives in a certain framework. (Gen. 1:26-27).

9. In that same love, he has made us not automata who are led by the blind forces of the universe, but free intelligent beings and his adoptive sons to whom the challenge has come to adapt our conduct to our dignity. Man, as a consequence,

must search out what is that dignity and what are the results of it in terms of how he must accept the responsibility that stems from it.

2. THE FORMATION OF CONSCIENCE

10. This never-ending search which every man must undertake for himself in order to find out what is worthy of a man and what is not worthy of a man is what we call the "formation" of his conscience. And this too will be qualified by the various assumptions which he makes at any period in his life. For example, the formation of conscience in a person who simply believes in God will be different from the formation of conscience in a man who accepts that God did intervene in history and did send us a Saviour in the person of our Lord Jesus Christ who as our Brother was to rehabilitate mankind, give it a new life and lay down for us certain revealed principles showing the way in which God expects us to act. (Jn. 3:16; 8:12).

11. Further, a Christian who is also an adherent of the Catholic faith and a member of the Catholic Church must probe deeper in the refinement of what God has revealed as our norm of conduct. As Catholics we accept that Jesus committed to his disciples his own power saying, "As the Father has sent Me, now also I send you..." (Jn. 20:21), "Whatever you bind on earth shall be considered bound in heaven; whatever you loose on earth shall be considered loosed in heaven" (Mt. 18:18). We believe that this power transmitted to his disciples was meant to endure in the Church and now resides in the College of Bishops under the presiding direction of the successor of Peter. This is what we call "the magisterium" or teaching service of the Church and in matters of guiding our conduct, a binding rule for those who call themselves Catholic. (See also Mt. 28:18-20 and Jn. 14:25-26).

12. Nor must this be considered as some sort of inhibition or limiting force. It would be wrong to think that the persons most free are those who do not believe at all and that we go in a descending scale of freedom till we meet the Catholic. We believe that the reverse is true. We believe that knowing what God has established for the fulfillment of man is a freeing principle, not a principle of enslavement. The more we know about God's will for us, the more fulfilled we are, the surer we are that we will not destroy ourselves and wander into paths which will not enhance our liberty but take it away entirely. "The truth will make you free" (Jn. 8:32; Ps. 1).

13. This is the basic context in which we would like to talk about some of the problems of our times.

PART TWO

PROBLEMS OF OUR TIMES

Confusion in the Church

14. Although we admit that it would be fallacious to postulate that the changes within the Church during the past quarter century have been unrelated to the even

greater upheavals in the world, for clarity sake, we distinguish between the two areas.

15. The faithful Catholic has been disturbed and sometimes confused during the past years by a multiplicity of changes which have been unparalleled in modern history. These changes have often had implications which relate to his day-by-day actions and conduct and consequently, at least to him, appear to affect the very norms of that conduct. A few years ago, the Catholic was distinguished by external practices such as abstinence on Fridays, fasting and various penitential disciplines, a number of holy days of obligation, etc. The liturgy was an unchanging structure which had remained the same for hundreds of years. Devotions of various sorts seemed also to be immovable and irreplaceable and a necessary part of the practice of the faithful. The priest appeared as the conscience of the community and interpreted the teaching of the Church with a voice that was considered authoritative and usually unchallengeable.

16. Today much of this has changed. Many of the penitential disciplines such as fasting and abstinence are left to the judgement of the individual, the emphasis on the liturgy is one of participation and commitment, and a biblical renewal has pushed a certain number of traditional devotions into the background. As far as the priest is concerned, his role is not less important but it is less overwhelming. He still has the duty of teaching his community the way of God and of morality, but he understands better that this judgement must ultimately be made by the person himself, as we will try to describe later.

Confusion in the World

17. It is rare that changes take place in the world without influencing the Church or that changes take place in the Church without influencing the world. During this period of confusion, popular morality has been shaken to the ground roots. There is a general attitude that "I can do pretty much anything which doesn't hurt somebody else". A permissiveness sweeps our society. Practices which would previously have been repudiated as absolutely unacceptable are becoming the general rule of conduct. We have only to look at the practice of abortion, at a growing pressure for euthanasia and the other manifestations against life itself to see the truth of the statement. In the midst of this, legislators are making the distinction between that which is legal and that which may or may not be evil in the mind of an individual. Even Catholic legislators frequently take the attitude that the law should not be guided by principles that derive from religious conviction. (Many Christians are influenced by this and fall into the trap of thinking that if a thing is legal, it must be morally acceptable.)

18. Another factor is the widespread propaganda which makes all aspects of family planning and sexual permissiveness a matter of private concern and individualistic ethics (*Gaudium et Spes,* #30). The idea has been abroad that "everybody is doing it" and that if everybody is doing it, it must be acceptable. Finally, the economic and political conditions of our society are tending to bring down our

moral sense. The calm acceptance by some of economic inequality by which some have so much and so many have so little is combined with the depersonalizing of society and the exploitation of man. All of these and other factors have tended to bring about a reversal of traditional morality or, at the least, a great questioning of moral values.

Reaction to Confusion: Types of Conscience

19. From these factors has stemmed the confusion of conscience to which we alluded in the first lines of this Statement. Although it may represent some species of oversimplification, we feel that something can be gained by placing the types of reaction to the general situation in three categories. These are not totally exclusive categories but they do sum up, pretty well, the general possible attitudes of the Catholic today.

20. a. In the first category are those who have developed a static or complacent conscience. These persons have not accepted the dynamics behind the changes in the Church and in society, and have not seen the positive value which can come from personal acceptance of moral responsibility. They insist that the Church must spell out for them every obligation down to the last detail. This attitude of conscience is of course a denial of responsibility and can result in negating the whole positive value of the movement of the Spirit at the present time.

21. b. At the opposite extreme we have the excessively dynamic and revolutionary conscience. This characterizes the person who has totally misread the idea that everyone must ultimately be the judge, before God, of his actions and that in the ultimate decision he must make up his own mind. The persons in this category have distorted an appeal to intelligent decision into a destruction of law, objective structures, and have arrived at the conclusion that no one can tell them what to do, including the Church. It is seldom stated this way but it is where this type of exaggerated objectivism necessarily leads.

22. c. In the middle position is the conscience which we consider to be the proper attitude of any human being in today's society, and particularly of the Catholic Christian. We can qualify this as the dynamic Christian conscience which leads us to have a responsible attitude to someone, to Jesus, to the community, to the Church, etc. Every person who fits into this category feels a responsibility for a progressive search and striving to live out a life ideal according to the mind of Christ (Phil. 2:5).

PART THREE

FUNDAMENTAL BASIS FOR MATURE CONSCIENCE

23. In support of this type of conscience, we offer the following considerations.

Human Dignity

24. In the first place, this category represents a truly acceptable and dignified human position. Vatican Council II has clearly placed great emphasis upon the basic dignity and value of the human being and upon his responsibility as the ultimate judge under God of the value of his action. "For its part, authentic freedom is an exceptional sign of the divine image within man. For God has willed that man be left 'in the hand of his own counsel' (Ecclesiasticus 15:14) so that he can seek his Creator spontaneously, and come freely to utter and blissful perfection through loyalty to Him. Hence man's dignity demands that he act according to a knowing and free choice. Such a choice is personally motivated and prompted from within. It does not result from blind internal impulse nor from more external pressure" (*Gaudium et Spes,* #17). Consequently, it is the proper dignity of every human being to feel the responsibility which is postulated by God himself in the manner in which He has created us. This is the basis for the argument which St. Paul presented in his letter to the Romans, where he so clearly enunciates the fact that every human being, in coming into the world, has God's law in his heart. By this he means two things. First, that man is responsible for his acts, and secondly, that he cannot take it upon himself to act according to the whims of the moment without reference to his creator, to his fellowmen and to himself (Rom. 2:14-16).

Responsibility

25. In our times we welcome the growing maturity of our people who understand this first element, but we remind them that so to judge does not dispense them from the second element of referring to God's presence, variously but truly manifested in their lives and guiding their judgements.

26. "In the depths of his conscience, man detects a law which he does not impose upon himself, but which holds him to obedience. Always summoning him to love good and avoid evil, the voice of conscience can when necessary speak to his heart more specifically: do this, shun that. For man has in his heart a law written by God. To obey it is the very dignity of man; according to it he will be judged." (*Gaudium et Spes*, #16).

Antidote to Denial of Sin

27. We feel that this type of mature conscience will be the greatest antidote to the growing attack, both explicit and implicit, upon the concept of man's sinfulness. The exaggerated and pseudo-autonomy of man has led us into a frame of mind in which we have played down the concept of sin and redemption, and have deliberately turned our backs upon the clear teaching of God and of our Lord Jesus Christ that while God is a loving Father, he cannot be mocked. This does not postulate the ancient erroneous idea that God is some sort of a tyrant who is looking for an opportunity to punish us. On the other hand, the very gift of our freedom indicates that when we misuse it, we ourselves will suffer. In this sense, possible punishment is the necessary concomitant of the law of love. Love cannot be forced

upon anyone, but as a modern writer has put it, "He who rejects love is in turn rejected by it and lies howling at the threshold".

The "howling at the threshold" could hardly be blamed upon the person who has offered love and has been rejected. The suffering of those who reject God's norms of life is their own doing. Hence, we feel that a dynamic Christian conscience is one which recognizes all of these facts and is freed by it. It is therefore freed from the necessity of pretending that sin is not there and that the eventual result of sin is not there.

Faith Dimension

28. We have already pointed out that the basic responsibility of every human being lies in the fact that he is God's creature and that, as a result, he must assume responsibility for his actions over which God has given him direct stewardship. But, we have also pointed out that for the Christian and for the Catholic Christian, in particular, there are guides which he has freely accepted which are meant to help him to discover that light of God's guidance within him.

29. In this context, we necessarily insist first and foremost upon the working of the Spirit in the hearts of men (Jn. L5:26; 16:7-13). Vatican II brought us from a somewhat widespread opinion that the Catholic Church constituted a monolithic arrangement in which the very voice of the Spirit was controlled and channelled. Everything was supposed to come from above, with the faithful, as it were, the ultimate recipients of the straining of the Spirit through the upper echelons. It is obvious that nothing so crass was ever officially taught by the Church, but impressions are sometimes more lasting and more universal than teachings. The insistence of the Council on the importance of the people of God and of their personal and direct relationship to the Spirit is a clarification which must never be lost to sight. (*Lumen Gentium,* #4 and #12).

30. It is under this heading that we recognize the need of the personal conversion and acceptance of salvation by every human being. The Council (*Lumen Gentium,* #13 and #48) has explicitly upheld the scriptural teaching that God wills the salvation of all men, but there is always the second movement to this symphony of love and that is that man cannot be saved without himself. Every man must turn freely to God. For us who believe in an order over and above that of the temporal and the temporary, this turning to God and the acceptance of his loving will for man, even though he has revealed himself in an obscure fashion, is called an act of faith. It is the free decision of a man to accept as true that God has spoken to us "...in former times... in fragmentary and varied fashions through the prophets. But in this the final age He has spoken to us in the Son..." (Heb. 1:1-2). The guidance of the Church is a part of that revelation.

PART FOUR

GUIDES FOR CHRISTIAN CONSCIENCE

31. We are now in a position where we can lay down certain norms for the guidance of the conscience of the Catholic Christian. If our positions up to this point have been accepted, it follows that an act of conscience is an individual thing but must be based upon certain accepted principles and positions. It becomes, therefore, the duty of the individual to acquire the necessary information and attitude in order to make the right decision.

Human Balance

32. Certain human conditions undoubtedly aid in the balanced performance which one requires from a Christian. Sound emotional stability, a cultivation of self-knowledge and clear objective judgement, even education itself, will undoubtedly help, although we must not postulate a certain elitism which would expect only the educated to have sound conscience. The assistance of sound communal attitudes and of cultural and social influences – all of these things are sound human contributions to the acquisition of knowledge and, above all, of proper attitude.

33. But these fall far short of the total necessary conditions for the formation of conscience and their ultimate application in life.

Presence of Christ

34. For the man who has made his act of faith, the prime factor in the formation of his conscience and in his moral judgement is to be found in the existence and the role of Christ in his life. (Jn. 14:6-8; 12:46). A person who wishes to have a true Christian conscience must be faithfully in communication with his Lord in all of his life, particularly through his own prayer and the prayer of the Church. Indeed, properly understood, the presence of Christ in his life is all-pervasive and all-embracing. All the other aspects of conscience formation are based on this one and stem from it. This does not make them unnecessary or superfluous, but simply puts them in their place. (1 Jn. 4:1).

Scripture and Tradition

35. With this in mind, the man of faith draws his inspiration from the Scripture, the very Word of God in which he finds revealed not only the designs of the Father in the historical context of the world, but a refined series of ideals, precepts and examples given to us by the same Lord Jesus. This is communicated to him not only in the words of the Scripture but in the Spirit of Jesus which continues to live with us and which makes us "a chosen race and a royal priesthood, a consecrated nation and a people set apart". (1 Pet. 2:9).

The Magisterium

36. It is in this context that the teaching of the Church finds its full force. We have seen through sad historical example, the kind of confusion that can arise from an unguided and overly subjective reading of the Scriptures and interpretation of

tradition. The Church makes sure that the Word of God contained in the Scriptures and illustrated to us in the Spirit can be authenticated in the community of believers.

37. In this one Spirit of which we speak, we have the service of the apostles and of their successors, the College of Bishops, united with their head, the Pope. The role of the apostles and their successors was and is to bear witness to Christ, the revealer of the Father's Will. It was and is their duty to transmit the testimony of the original apostles concerning Christ, to celebrate the new covenant and to guide the people of God in the living of the new creation of Christ (Mt. 28:18-20, Mk. 16:15-16). Guided by the Spirit, the Church has sought to do precisely this in the past and continues to do so in the present world while turned toward the second coming of Christ. The doctrinal service of the successors of the apostles includes the Scriptures and tradition as described above. In the fulfillment of this task, they do not seek to suppress the other gifts of the Spirit but encourage all to test the gifts according to the criteria found in Scripture and tradition.

38. For a believer, this teaching of the magisterium as outlined above cannot be just one element among others in the formation of his conscience. It is the definitive cornerstone upon which the whole edifice of conscientious judgement must be built. "You are built upon the foundation laid by the apostles and prophets, and Christ Jesus himself is the foundation stone" (Eph. 2:20). "You are Peter and upon this rock I will build my Church" (Mt. 16:18). What must be kept in mind is that we are in the dimension of faith. And we should be encouraged and hopeful because we can count on the continued assistance of the Holy Spirit in a manner which pure reason could never give.

39. The responsible person, as defined above, must weigh the facts before acting. This is far removed from saying that he may act in accordance with his whims and wishes. A believer has the absolute obligation of conforming his conduct first and foremost to what the Church teaches, because first and foremost for the believer is the fact that Christ, through his Spirit, is ever present in his Church, in the whole Church to be sure, but particularly with those who exercise services within the Church and for the Church, the first of which services is that of the apostles.

40. Furthermore, even in matters which have not been defined ex cathedra, i.e. infallibly, the believer has the obligation to give full priority to the teaching of the Church in favor of a given position, to pray for the light of the Spirit, to refer to Scripture and tradition and to maintain a dialogue with the whole Church, which he can do only through the source of unity which is the collectivity of the bishops. The reality itself, for example, sex, marriage, economics, politics, war, must be studied in detail. In this study, he should make an effort to become aware of his own inevitable presuppositions as well as his cultural background which leads him to act for or react against any given position. If his ultimate practical judgement to do this or avoid that does not take into full account the teaching of the Church, an

account based not only on reason but on the faith dimension, he is deceiving himself in pretending that he is acting as a true Catholic must.

41. For a Catholic "to follow one's conscience" is not, then, simply to act as his unguided reason dictates. "To follow one's conscience" and to remain a Catholic, one must take into account first and foremost the teaching of the magisterium. When doubt arises due to a conflict of their views and those of the magisterium, the presumption of truth lies on the part of the magisterium. "In matters of faith and morals, the bishops speak in the name of Christ and the faithful are to accept their teaching and adhere to it with a religious assent of soul. This religious submission of will and of mind must be shown in a special way to the authentic teaching authority of the Roman Pontiff, even when he is not speaking ex cathedra" (*Lumen Gentium,* #25). And this must be carefully distinguished from the teaching of individual theologians or individual priests, however intelligent or persuasive.

PART FIVE

LAW AND CONSCIENCE

42. These positions bring us now to the delicate question of law, which is a regulating force in human and Christian action. The word itself is frequently used in various senses and we recognize the complexity of the subject.

Distinction of "Law" as Spirit and as Precept

43. Any Christian reflection on law must take into consideration the crucial distinction between law as precept and law as the dynamic structure of personal being.

44. With regard to the latter concept of law, the passage of St. Paul to the Romans quoted above (Rom. 2:12-15) illustrates this distinction by contrasting the impotence of the precepts of the Mosaic Law with the fundamental belief of Christians that sinful rebellion has been radically – though not completely – healed. All forms of preceptive law stand under the Spirit of love released when Christ, by suffering in himself the consequences of the law, passed from death to life. As we have already stated (Rom. 8:1-5), any law is ultimately subject to that influx of the Spirit by which the redeemed are transformed into brothers of Christ enjoying the freedom of the children of God in his Spirit (Rom. 8:15-17). This operation of the indwelling Spirit of Christ, this conformity of our nature to Christ's word in our hearts, is the New Law. It is discipleship to this word which makes us free (Jn. 8:31-32).

45. This note of the freedom of the sons of God is crucial because it establishes the ultimate priority of personal concience informed by the Spirit of Christ in the case of possible conflict with extrinsic law. God had promised that the New Law would be written in the person's heart, not on tablets of stone (Jer. 31:31; Ez. 36:25). Jesus teaches that the spirit of God's laws takes priority over the letter (Mt. 5:20-48). The great teachers of the Christian tradition have re-echoed this central-

ity of the interior law of grace. "There on Sinai the finger of God wrote on stone tablets, here in the hearts of men with the sending of the Spirit and Pentecost" (Augustine, *De Spiritu et Littera,* XVII). The whole strength of the New Law and its specifically Christian meaning consists in its being written in the heart of man by the Spirit which is given through faith in Christ" (Aquinas, S. T., I-II, 106, 1 and 2; Gal. 3:21-22). In our day the supremacy of the voice of God making himself heard in the depths of the personal conscience has been reaffirmed, as already stated, by the Second Vatican Council (*The Pastoral Constitution on the Church in the Modern World,* #16; The Declaration on Religious Freedom, #3).

Preceptive Law

46. Having established this as a fundamental principle, we can ask how preceptive laws are to be judged by the conscience conformed to the indwelling Spirit which gives life. The new life of Christ in us is not yet fully accomplished. The preceptive law of legitimate authority must be taken into account in every moral decision because it has the right to command our assent and stands as a constant reminder of our sinfulness and of our dependence upon a source of life which transcends our individual selves. Moreover, it would be unthinkable that the Spirit, speaking in the heart of the redeemed Christian, would be in opposition to himself teaching in the authority established by Jesus.

47. It is in this context that we offer some considerations on preceptive "law" in our lives.

48. In a society which finds it extremely difficult to accept any limitations upon even the grossest perversions of freedom, law has become a sort of whipping boy. Yet it can be said that the law is nothing more or less than the expression of conditions which must exist if man is to be free. Scripture has told us, "The truth shall make you free" (Jn. 8:32). This idea could be extended to law when it is a good law since we are thus led to our best, liberating interests.

49. In particular, the presence of evil within us and the ability we have to explain away our most bizarre actions easily incline us to ignore facts and assume a false sense of values. It is precisely as an antidote to this soft deception that laws have been formulated. In a statement of this necessarily limited scope, it is impossible for us to make all the necessary distinctions between divine law and natural law, civil and ecclesiastical law. We limit ourselves to saying that any law set up by legitimate authority and in conformity with divine law must be taken into account in every moral action.

50. Some, set by God in the very manner in which he has created us and the universe, are immutable and not subject to any exception. Such are the prohibitions against killing the innocent, adultery, theft, etc. Nor has basic morality changed over the years. The fundamental points of the ten commandments are as valid today as they were when Moses received them on Mount Sinai. Others are established by legitimate human authority to regulate and regularize our human relationships and

to govern society whether civil or ecclesiastical. These presume the great laws of God and take them for granted as a basis for this obligatory nature.

51. In the same context, laws made for the proper government of the Church are required for the inter-relationships of the people of God and for the guidance of believers. In every case, they should postulate the law of love and be designed to assist us in its realization. A totally mature and saintly people would require a minimum of laws. But the Church is a pilgrim Church and a Church sent precisely to redeem sinners. The laws it promulgates are specifically to guide our feet away from the traps set by our sinfulness and our own tendencies to sin.

The Use of Exceptions

52. In particular, we warn our faithful people about the misuse of exceptions to the law in particular cases (called by moralists "*epikeia*"), a misuse which has now become so widespread as to threaten the whole structure of our moral lives. This misuse is very akin to the condition described above where some feel exempt from being told anything by anybody, an exaggeration and flagrant abuse of "I must form my own conscience".

53. It is understood that every law is for a general condition and there may be situations in which a person not only is not bound to respond to the law but may not be able to do so. (We refer, of course, to matters which are covered by ecclesiastical law, by positive law, not to the great moral laws that have been given to us by God and, as stated, are without exception.) In exceptional circumstances, the true believer, understanding the law of love, has no feelings of guilt, but a certain regret in not being able to fulfill the law in this particular instance.

54. But the use of exceptions ("*epikeia*") has its requirements. And, as we have already intimated, the truly sincere person uses such a device only when absolutely necessary and regrets the need to be an exception in the community in this particular regard. One who understands that he has been commanded in love will respond in love and will not be a seeker of exceptions

CONCLUSION

55. Such, we feel to be the major points upon which our present concern should bear. There is, of course, a great deal more that could be said about the conscience of man. Much, indeed, has been said and we refer our faithful people to the various pronouncements of the Pope, particularly in recent years, to the statements of a number of national hierarchies, and to the teaching of reliable theologians. In the present text we have striven only to place the problem of the formation of conscience in the contemporary situation and to deal with the major problems facing our people here.

56. We have tried to avoid legalism and to make as basis of our considerations, the person of Christ, his teachings and his Spirit. Hence, the true Christian

will far transcend these minimal observations and go deep into that country whose guide is the Spirit and whose sole law is love. But he will not go there against the mind of the Catholic Church but only in accordance with it and after he has been freed by it for the journey ahead. (1 Jn. 4:16).

19.

HUMANAE VITAE REVISITED

(1) The argument goes on
Jack Dominian

The Tablet, 27 October 1984

It is 16 years since *Humanae Vitae* was promulgated. An encyclical of such importance should have settled the uncertainty over contraception once and for all. But it has not. So we see on the one hand, continual interventions by the teaching authority of the Church, repeated calls to the faithful to heed the rule, and, on the other hand, the widespread refusal of married couples to do so. Individual bishops, priests and laity hope that the matter will go away, but it does not. In a series of articles, I propose to examine the main arguments of each side, to sketch the history of how we have reached the present position, to present evidence which shows that we cannot stay as we are, and finally to propose a solution.

After an introduction which owes much to the second Vatican Council, the encyclical states: "The Church, nevertheless, urging men to the observance of the precepts of the natural law, which it interprets by its constant doctrine, teaches as absolutely required that any use whatever of marriage must retain its natural potential to procreate human life." The objection is that such an interpretation of sexual intercourse never leaves the biological level.

The teaching of *Humanae Vitae* is profound and carries full papal authority, and there are some who maintain that the continuous teaching of the Church against contraception renders the document infallible. This is clearly mistaken. No claim to infallibility was made at the time. But, comes back the voice of authority, Vatican II says: 'In matters of faith and morals, the bishops speak in the name of Christ and the faithful are to accept their teaching and to adhere to it with a religious assent of the soul. This religious submission of will and of mind must be shown in a special way to the authentic teaching authority of the Roman pontiff, even when he is not speaking *ex cathedra*."

The facts are, however, that the majority have not given this assent. The teaching has been declared but not received. It concerns especially married people, yet they had no say in this decision, and they have not accepted it. Of course, it is not necessary to be married to be able to discern truth. It is fair comment, nevertheless, to ask whether celibates can truly say that they entirely understand the full implications of sexual intercourse.

But, it is argued, authority has spoken and it is unbelievable that it could have been mistaken. The decision should therefore be accepted and not challenged – even if that challenge is made with love and concern. It would be a nightmare if the Church had got it wrong.

One can understand why there is an impulse to uphold this teaching blindly, on arguments of authority alone. But it is surely possible for the Church, protected by the Spirit, to develop the truth further, particularly since in this case the origins of the teaching are not to be found in the Scriptures. There is ample historical evidence for teaching which has been modified. The usual example given is that of usury, but in the theology of marriage itself there have been major changes from Augustine to Aquinas and from Aquinas to the present day. The obsession with authority is a comparatively recent phenomenon in the life of the Church and risks distorting the tradition of freedom and constant dialogue over matters where there is contention.

Doubts and fears

The encyclical rules out all artificial methods of birth control. Many opponents of its teaching decry the efficiency of the safe period, but the method has its defendants and for some people it works. On the other hand, enthusiasts for the method proclaim results which are possibly too optimistic, for many have experienced failure. The safe period has its use, its advantages and disadvantages, but it is no panacea.

Proponents of the method assert that use of the safe period is more natural, because the couple do not interfere in any way with the marriage act. This is true. But, reply opponents of *Humanae Vitae,* the spontaneity of sexual intercourse is inhibited by the restrictions which are imposed by observance of the safe period. This point, however, can be argued in the opposite sense. If the couple use the safe period, the restrictions that are imposed on them at the time when they should avoid intercourse are an opportunity for self-control over instinct and passion. This ideal has great historical attraction, because it stands in a continuous tradition. It is however opposed by the whole of modern thinking which sees sexual intercourse as a powerful expression of love to be controlled by considerations not of biology, but of care and concern for the other spouse.

In any case, couples using the safe period have exactly the same aim as couples using artificial contraception – to avoid children. What, then, ask the critics of *Humanae Vitae,* is really the difference?

The central argument of the encyclical is that "each and every marriage act must remain open to the transmission of life" (no. 11). But we know now for certain that during most of the lifetime of the couple, even during the reproductive years, nature is not trying to make a baby. It is clear that, in man, intercourse transcends the exigencies of biology.

Elsewhere, there are fears – not unjustified – that the use of contraception has opened the floodgates to promiscuity. There is no doubt that in the last 25 years there has been an increase in sexual activity among all sections of the community, particularly the young, and undoubtedly contraception has played a part in bringing this about. However, it should not be forgotten that contraception has been used since ancient times, and that periods of sexual laxity have come and gone. Promiscuity results from complex social and psychological factors, and cannot be stemmed simply by condemning contraception.

The Church is also concerned that contraception will be used as a forced method of birth control. It is absolutely correct that it would be simplistic to try to rely on contraception to resolve human problems by itself, without any accompanying progress in development. But that does not mean that contraception has no part to play in population control

A related fear is that contraception may be linked with abortion in population control. Here again the Church is absolutely correct. But one cannot emphasise too strongly that contraception and abortion are two separate issues.

The witness of ecumenism also raises doubts about *Humanae Vitae,* for the encyclical is addressed to everyone – it is not directed to Catholics alone. Yet all major Christian denominations in the West have accepted contraception. Can it be that in this matter everybody is wrong except the Catholics?

There is no single argument in favour of *Humanae Vitae* which cannot be contradicted. This is the reason why millions of words have been poured out over this topic without any definite conclusion being reached. The situation is totally unsatisfactory. More and more people find the teaching unacceptable, and yet at the same time the supreme teaching authority of the Church reiterates it. Every time artificial contraception is condemned, those who find the pronouncements of authority comforting are reassured, while those who find the teaching unacceptable shudder. In the meantime, many of the young and most of the world around us look on in sheer wonder that we should be in such a predicament. How did it happen? That will be the theme of my next article.

(2) The flaw in the tradition
Jack Dominian

***The Tablet,* 3 November 1984**

My first article showed that the teaching on contraception is fraught with ambiguity. The clear message of *Humanae Vitae* that "any use whatever of marriage must retain its natural potential to procreate human life" has not been received, understood or accepted by many of the faithful who have articulated an opinion. The question then arises how the teaching authority of the Church finds itself so isolated from so many married people on whose behalf it purports to speak.

The seriousness of the position is beyond doubt. The Church claims to teach truths which are evident, which are understood by the faithful and accepted with a religious assent of the soul. Is it sheer bad will or stubbornness that makes them oppose this teaching, or is it that they feel deep inside them that it does not correspond fully to the truth? If the latter is the case, how is it that the Church keeps on proclaiming this teaching?

The explanation can only be found if we trace the antecedents of this teaching historically. No book has done this so well as Noonan's *Contraception* to which all of us are in debt. In it, the teaching of the Church on contraception, sexual love and sexual pleasure is examined in detail right up to the eve of *Humanae Vitae.* If we consider the details carefully, we find that, throughout the history of Christianity, the teaching in the West has been unbalanced.

An emphasis on the procreative potential of intercourse has been consistent, as has the condemnation of contraception. By contrast the value of sexual love in itself was neither understood nor taught in anything but hesitant terms, accompanied by much criticism and condemnation. At the heart of the debate on contraception lies a good deal more than whether it is right to use contraceptives. What is basically at issue is the meaning of sexual intercourse. In this article I want to show that the basic human experience of sexual love was neither understood nor appreciated, indeed was found for a long time to be dangerous, and procreation was seen as the safeguard. As a result, theology has yet to assimilate the deep meaning of sexual love.

The Jewish tradition out of which Christianity sprang held sexual pleasure to be good, as is evident in the teaching of the Song of Songs, linking it intimately with procreation. Very quickly Christianity spread beyond the confines of Judaism and met the Stoic philosophy of Greece. This philosophy mistrusted passion and sought the ideal of self-control and *ataraxia,* freedom from instinctual impulses. This was a concept which proved attractive to the early fathers. The other religious philosophy widespread in these early centuries was Gnosticism, which attacked creation, marriage and procreation. Against it, the early Church protected all three.

Within Christianity itself there were two elements. First, the marriage of Mary and Joseph was seen as a proper marriage but traditionally was held not to have been consummated. Secondly, the personality and attitude of individual fathers of the Church were very influential.

As the unmarried state gradually became the norm for the priesthood, those who formulated theology were at one remove from the existential reality of sexual love which became a dark, dangerous and prohibited entity. It is common psychological knowledge that one way of protecting ourselves from the anxiety of the forbidden is to diminish and deny its importance. This makes it less attractive and we can live with its absence. There is no doubt in my mind that a defence mechanism of this sort has operated collectively among the celibate priesthood of the Church. Furthermore, individuals who have difficult struggles with their own sexuality are likely to take a very severe view of its danger when they come to control it at a later stage of their life.

The innumerable sayings of the fathers about sex are favourite material for those who desire to mock Christianity. Sexual pleasure was condemned savagely. Jerome spelled out that too ardent a lover was an adulterer. In the West, the greatest theologian of the patristic period, who left an indelible mark on sexuality, was Augustine. He wrote frankly about the personal crisis in his life as he sought to exercise control over his sexual appetite. For him, intercourse was accompanied by concupiscence and concupiscence transmitted original sin. Concupiscence was very close to "lust". Augustine was obsessed with the fact that sexual desire and pleasure seemed to overcome mental control and therefore considered concupiscence as the loss of an effective ordering of man's passions. In this way, he reached the conclusion that the sexual act was always accompanied by sin unless performed solely for the procreation of children.

Aquinas was far more positive about sexual love and taught that the essential element of original sin was the loss of sanctifying grace. But many of the theologians of the medieval period continued to see sin in intercourse if pursued for pleasure or if the position with the man above was not followed.

The majority opinion of the Middle Ages was that intercourse for the sake of avoiding fornication was venial sin but that intercourse for pleasure was a mortal sin. Two theologians opposed these views: Le Maistre and Major in the 15th and 16th centuries. Their opinion did not prevail, and in fact pleasure has never been accepted as an independent value. Gradually, however, the connection with sin disappeared, and then the justification of intercourse was extended until finally the connection with love was reached.

But even in the second Vatican Council, where sexual love is totally and unconditionally accepted, there is little examination of its meaning, and the link between procreation and intercourse remains the dominant theme. Thus the alienation between experience and teaching continues.

The teaching

Love is the principle which distinguishes Christian life. It would naturally be expected, then, that love and marriage would be seen as belonging together, but this is not the case. The early fathers, with the exception of Chrysostom, made no such connection. According to Noonan, the first time an ecumenical council spoke of love in marriage was as late as 1563, and even then no connection was made between love and intercourse. That had to wait till the 19th century, when the link was made but in a most simplistic way.

After the First World War, the connection between love and intercourse was rapidly developed. In 1925 von Hildebrand proposed: "The marital act has not only a function, the generation of children, it also possesses a significance for man as a human being, namely to be the expression and fulfillment of wedded love and community of life." In the 1940s, Doms stressed the relationship between love and intercourse without reference to procreation.

The first link between intercourse and love in a papal document came in 1930 in the famous encyclical, *Casti Connubii,* but once again no development of the idea took place. It was the second Vatican Council that joined love and intercourse in strong terms. "Marital love is uniquely expressed and perfected through the marital act. The actions within marriage by which the couple are united intimately and chastely are noble and worthy ones. Expressed in a manner which is truly human, these actions signify and promote that mutual self-giving by which spouses enrich each other with a joyful and thankful will."

Humanae Vitae speaks a great deal about love. But when referring to the unitive and procreative significance which are considered inherent in the sexual act, the encyclical sees the procreative element as the dominant one and there is no detailed examination of the nature of unitive love.

But if the poverty of the tradition is evident where sexual love and sexual pleasure are concerned, the continuous and powerful condemnation of contraception is fully documented. It is not difficult to fathom the reasons for this. Sexual intercourse was only justifiable in the mind of the early Church if engaged in for the purpose of procreation. Anything which attacked life was seriously sinful. Contraception was seen as unnatural because the inseminating function of the sexual act was frustrated.

Augustine was deeply involved in a battle against the Manichaean heresy. The Manichaeans vigorously condemned procreation and separated it from intercourse. Augustine attacked them: "What food is to the health of man, intercourse is to the health of the race." He rules out contraception in the phrase: "Sometimes *(Aliquando)* this lustful cruelty, or cruel lust, comes to this, that they even procure poisons of sterility, and, if these do not work, extinguish and destroy the fetus in some way in the womb, preferring that their offspring die before it lives, or, if it was already alive in the womb, to kill it before it was born. Assuredly, if both husband and wife are like this, they are not married and if they were like this from the beginning, they come together not joined in matrimony but in seduction. If both are not like this, I dare to say that either the wife is in the fashion of a harlot of her husband or he is an adulterer with his own wife."

In this passage, whose impact endures to this very day, the vehemence with which contraception is treated could hardly be stronger. For Augustine, contraception was evil because, when procreation is frustrated, then pleasure runs rampant. The other point to be noted is the close approximation made between contraception and abortion. Both are seen as killers of life. This equation could not be justified in Augustine's day or at any time. The prevention of life is one thing, the killing of life another. It is a distinction which is very clear but one that many people prefer to ignore.

The condemnation of contraception was developed by Regino of Prom, who to Augustine's *Aliquando* added the *Si aliquis.* "If someone *(Si aliquis)* to satisfy his lust or in deliberate hatred does something to a man or a woman so that no children be born to him or her, or gives them to drink, so that he cannot generate or she conceive, let it be held as homicide." The *Aliquando* and the *Si aliquis* remained forceful background pronouncements throughout the Middle Ages and subsequently.

By the 18th and 19th centuries, contraception began to spread rapidly. The Church maintained its condemnation. In the 20th century, however, the Christian churches one by one began to allow contraception and finally the Church of England also accepted it in 1930. The response to this from the Catholic Church came in *Casti Connubii,* which once again condemned contraception unequivocally. In the meantime, developments took place in the understanding of the infertile period. In 1951 Pius XII, addressing the Italian midwives, made it clear that this method of regulating birth could be used. "Serious reasons often put forward on medical, eugenic, economic and social grounds can exempt from that obligatory service for a considerable period of time, even for the entire duration of marriage. It follows from this that the use of the infertile period can be lawful from the moral point of view and, in the circumstances mentioned, it is indeed lawful."

Unequal

Approval of the safe period as morally licit took the Church by surprise, it was some time before this possibility was accepted and developed. When the shock was over and use of the method began to spread, Catholics began to have real difficulties in seeing the difference between it and artificial contraception. It soon became clear that an end to the prohibition of contraception was a distinct possibility. Expectations rose.

Vatican II did not pronounce on the matter. A commission was set up which favoured a change of teaching. But in 1968 *Humanae Vitae* gave its ruling: the teaching against artificial contraception was to be maintained. Despite being qualified by a number of hierarchies for pastoral reasons, the encyclical met deep opposition from many married people, whose disappointment continues to this day.

Why did Paul VI write *Humanae Vitae?* It seems to me that he could not have done anything else. The position in which he found himself was precise and unequivocal. There was a continuous condemnation of contraception from the early days of the Church right up to recent times. The only possible grounds for altering the teaching would have been if the positive qualities of sexual love had become equally accepted as fostering married life. As this was not the case, *Humanae Vitae* was tragically inevitable and has led to continuous problems inside the Church.

Condemnation had to win. It had always been taught that sexual intercourse was for procreation. The ordinary everyday experience of the married, of the value of sexual love and pleasure, had not been appreciated till the last 50 years and then only partially. The contest was unequal. The voice of the married never played a part in official teaching. Their experience was excluded and they remained unheard.

This is the paradox which confronts the Church. The teaching is clear: there has been an uninterrupted condemnation of contraception. But this clarity depends on the most incomplete and unsatisfactory understanding of sexual intercourse. It is the married who know and appreciate the bias of this teaching and it is they who must make their insights clear. In the next article, these insights will be spelled out.

(3) Beyond biology
Jack Dominian

The Tablet, 10 November 1984

Men and women are sexual beings. Their sexuality is directed towards sexual intimacy, which results from two persons finding meaning, fulfilment, solace and comfort in their social, emotional, intellectual, physical and spiritual encounter.

Sexual intimacy is expressed in the formation of a bond. The evidence is overwhelming that in nature, bond formation is the key not only to procreation but also to the fostering of a community. In the human species, bond formation leads to a man and woman pairing for the exchange of a sexual life which pervades all their being. Sexual intimacy, which is the key to the pairing, finds its ultimate expression in sexual intercourse, the act that sums up the whole expression of the complementary role of the sexes.

The secular reality of marriage – the pairing and bond formation of man and woman – thus has its roots deep in the origin and development of mankind. Christianity took up this secular reality and integrated it into the divine order and in the Middle Ages acknowledged it to be a sacrament.

Sexual intercourse is central to this sacrament. Just as the pouring of water is the sign in baptism of the washing away of sin, so sexual intercourse is the sign of sexual intimacy in marriage. It is the act that affirms and confirms the initiation and maintenance of marriage. In the history of the Church's teaching on marriage, the central significance of sexual intercourse has never been lost, however much the act may have been devalued. A marriage which has not been consummated is capable of being annulled.

For a very long time, and even today, the sexual act was only regarded as properly carried out if semen was deposited inside the vagina so that the procreative purpose could be fulfilled. In other words, the biological component of intercourse was thought to be its chief characteristic. The reality is otherwise. Sexual intercourse is first and foremost an encounter of persons. It is the fulfilment of sexual intimacy at the social, emotional, intellectual, physical and spiritual level. Personal love and sexual pleasure together form the essence of the sexual act, not the biological potential. This is how intercourse is experienced by the couple and the attempt to make the procreative element supreme is a violation of its true meaning. Implicitly, the Church has always acknowledged this, giving permission for the sterile and the old to marry, and gradually allowing that intercourse may take place during pregnancy.

Spiritually, the sexual act is the central pivot that sustains the bond of the couple and, as the Scriptures affirm, is analogous to the covenant between God and man and the union between Christ and the Church. In the act of intercourse, the two persons donate the totality of themselves to each other. Male and female, as Genesis states, were created in the image of God for the purpose of sexual intimacy in order to overcome their aloneness and finally to become one. The means of becoming one in marriage is sexual intercourse, which becomes a recurrent act of prayer of the couple.

There are at least five meanings to the act of sexual intercourse which is a body language whose articulation is pleasure.

The first is that of thanksgiving. In the course of sexual intercourse, the couple donate themselves to each other. In the past this was understood as the payment of the sexual debt. The man had rights over his wife's body and vice versa and the act was seen as rendering the debt. But that is not the way of love. Love-making springs from a recurrent act of free choice in which couples do not carry out the dictates of a contract but fulfil a promise. They donate each to the other freely and lovingly and in the process enrich each other as persons. Through their joy and pleasure they acknowledge the privilege of their mutual commitment and, with or without words, render thanks.

Intercourse is also an act of hope. Implicit in sexual desire is the hope that the husband will want the wife and the wife the husband. What is desired is a repetition of sexual intercourse, and, through the act, the recurrent union of persons. Thus this hope sustains the bond between husband and wife by constantly renewing their sexual intimacy.

In the third place, the sexual act brings reconciliation. The sexual intimacy of the couple can be bruised and sometimes radically broken by quarrels, because intimacy is very closely linked with acceptance by the partner. Apology and forgiveness may not totally overcome the hurt and pain of feeling temporarily out of touch with the other. More than words are needed for healing: an act of equivalent restoration is required, and that act is sexual intercourse, which restores sexual intimacy and mutual recognition and acceptance through making love.

The fourth function of sexual intercourse is to confirm sexual identity. At the heart of sexual intimacy is the encounter of two persons with differentiated sexual characteristics. The sexual act powerfully recognises these differences socially, emotionally and physically. The husband can make his wife feel truly a woman, the wife can make her husband feel truly a man.

The gift of life

Last, the sexual act brings confirmation of personhood. This is the pinnacle of its meaning. Each partner integrates body, mind and heart into a personality that is the self. Each self seeks constant recognition, acceptance and appreciation, and that is precisely what the sexual act confers. It is a recurrent expression of mutual love through the confirmation of personhood.

One of the fears about sexual intercourse which is found in the Christian tradition is that the powerful physical and emotional experience which occurs at the peak of sexual intercourse, and which we call orgasm, is a moment when reason and control are lost. This has been a cause of suspicion and anxiety in the attitude of the Church to intercourse. For a long time, this lack of moderation was identified with brute animal behaviour. That can indeed be an apt description of men and women who desire sexual contact without personal encounter. Sexual attraction detached from the personal does become lust. The supreme challenge which sex presents to the Christian faith is not how to protect its biological component, but how to harmonise instinct with personhood, in and through love.

When personal love exists, the orgasm is not the culmination of uncontrolled lust, but is the fusion of two persons who now become one. Their unity as persons who retain their individuality mirrors the unity and separateness of the persons of the Trinity. We should recognise orgasm as the psychomatic reality that brings together the physical and spiritual.

Sexual intercourse, then, is the act which gives life to the couple on each and every occasion – and, on a few occasions, creates new life. These latter occasions are so few and the biology which gives rise to them so determined that it embraces only a minute part of the physiological cycle of the month. By every criterion, that is to say from the design of the biological pattern and its psychological meaning, the act does not remotely require that reproduction should be an essential characteristic of each and every act of intercourse. The purpose of each and every act of intercourse is to enhance the life of the couple.

As we come to see this more clearly, however, young people ask why intercourse should be confined to marriage. Condemnation of sex outside marriage was based on the risk of children being born outside marriage, and also upon a feeling that sexual pleasure should not be enjoyed outside the marriage relationship, although no specific reason was given why sexual intercourse should belong to marriage in this way.

The essential evil of fornication and adultery lies in the transient nature of the exchange, which cannot possibly do justice to the whole person. Sexual intercourse has such a range of meaning and is so rich in its possibilities that it needs a personal encounter of a continuous and enduring nature to express that richness fully. In adultery, there is also injustice to the other spouse. While the teaching on contraception has no biblical basis, the condemnation of fornication and adultery is deeply rooted in both the Old and the New Testament, and safeguards values which are of the deepest significance to sexual intimacy.

No one reading this article should come to the conclusion that the age-long link between intercourse and children has been finally snapped. That cannot be right. Children are the fruit of the joint love of the couple and in turn cement that love, although at times this is done at the cost of the personal relationship. No parent would wish to deny this. But a hundred years of child psychology has taught us that the wellbeing of the child depends on the stability, friendship and love of the parents. Their welfare is the guarantee of the welfare of the child, and their happiness in turn encourages the happiness and mature growth of the children. Just as an act of love expressed through intercourse initiates life, so love expressed through intercourse sustains the sexual intimacy of the couple and is responsible for the growth and maintenance of life.

(4) The need for reform
Jack Dominian

The Tablet, 17 November 1984

I drew attention in my last article to the dangerous divide between the official teaching of the Church in *Humanae Vitae* and the belief and practice of so many of the faithful. Surely, this is a situation which should not be allowed to continue. Everyone suffers, but above all the Church. Too many people have come to the conclusion that, if the Church can get it wrong, then it can be wrong on other matters also. It is essential for the whole people of God to impress upon Rome that we cannot continue indefinitely along the present path.

The values which *Humanae Vitae* is defending must be understood and safeguarded. The document taken as a whole can be divided into two parts: one is concerned to defend the integrity of the sexual act, and the other to protect sexual morality. But such fundamental values can be affirmed without making the biological aspect of sexuality determinative, as the encyclical does. In this series, I have argued strongly that the essence of the sexual act is to be found in the life-giving, personal exchange between the couple.

The encyclical argues from the natural law. But its interpretation is based entirely on the male point of view. Hence depositing of semen in the vagina is considered to be the life-giving component of every act. But the woman's role is just as much part of the natural law – and she is fertile for only 24 hours in each cycle of her reproductive life. Her voice has never been heard, and that throws enormous doubt on the existing interpretation of natural law. If fertility is only possible for 24 hours in every 28 days, the argument from design should clearly conclude that fertility does not belong to every act. The biological deductions which the encyclical draws from natural law are extremely weak.

There is, however, another even more important value which the encyclical seeks to safeguard when it insists that the unitive and procreative elements of intercourse should not be separated by contraceptives: namely, the inter-personal integrity of the couple in the sexual act. There is no doubt that contraceptives do impair the total exchange of the couple.

Each form of contraception has its own disadvantage. *Coitus interruptus* severely dislocates the integrity of the act. The use of condoms also interrupts intercourse. Caps and diaphragms also impair the exchange though to a lesser degree. The contraceptive pill produces changes in the woman's body, as does sterilisation, and therefore reduces the full availability of the couple to each other.

However, the pill does not interfere with the act itself and provides maximum security, which is why it has proved so attractive.

Everyone can recognise that all forms of contraception do interfere with the integrity of the sexual act and limit the availability of the couple to each other. *Coitus interruptus* does the greatest violence to the sexual act and the pill the least. This is where an effective form of the safe period method of birth control would be most welcome. If it only involved abstention from intercourse for 24 hours each month, there would be an instant rush to adopt it. The advantages would be clear to everyone.

In a reformed encyclical, the central emphasis would be on the importance of the inter-personal integrity of the couple. An argument along those lines would be readily understood. Total sexual integrity does ideally necessitate the exclusion of contraceptives. But love comes first, and so the contraceptives which least damage sexual integrity should be tolerated until such time as science can move forward and succeed in regulating conception without, as at present, such long periods of abstinence being necessary.

It should be added, however, that the encyclical's arguments about the alleged dangers of contraceptives are extremely weak. The basic assumption is that contraceptives encourage people to give in to sexual temptation because they remove the risk of pregnancy. This argument is full of fallacies. Long before the effective contraceptives of today were discovered, history has seen periods when sexual morality was lax. The desire for sexual transgression is part of the disorganised nature of mankind, allied to sin, and it is naive to think that contraceptives are more than just one of the factors responsible for promiscuity. Moreover, the sexual revolution of the last 25 years is the result of a complex social and psychological process which cannot be explained primarily as the result of the arrival of widespread contraception.

Marital infidelity is an example. In 25 years of marriage counselling, I have frequently had to deal with cases of adultery. I can say, without fear of contradiction, that the reasons are overwhelmingly personal ones. It is not the use of contraceptives that leads to adultery; contraceptives are used when extra-marital relationships have been formed for other reasons. It is easy to assume that contraceptives play a part in marital breakdown when in fact far more complex causes are basically responsible.

Or take promiscuity among the young. This is another concern of the encyclical, unfortunately. However, young people do not use contraceptives with diligence that the encyclical assumes. If they did, abortion would disappear and so would much illegitimacy. It is vital not to make contraceptives carry the blame for the much more complicated reasons for the behaviour of young people. Otherwise we shall make ourselves blind to the real drives: desire for experiment, the tendency of the sexes to exploit each other, the search for self-identification through intercourse and so on.

Another fear expressed in the encyclical is that the reverence due to a woman from a man may be lessened when contraceptives are used. But women do not say that this has been their experience. Women are used and exploited in many other ways and the most common is when men do not express adequate affection in making love, disregarding feminine sensitivity. The fault is not that they use contraceptives, but that they are poor lovers.

Authority in question

In order to rationalise the ban on artificial methods of contraception, *Humanae Vitae* makes contraception bear a responsibility for immorality which cannot be sustained. The use of contraceptives is the symptom of much deeper changes in society: for example, emancipation of women, their desire for equality, the search for sexual fulfilment and so on. It is these on which we should be concentrating.

The Church has accused the world of having a contraceptive mentality. But there is a real danger that the Church has developed a contraceptive mentality of its own, namely a naive approach to sexual problems which attributes the main blame to contraceptives. It is important that the basis for morality should be positive and not negative. In Christian terms, it is love of neighbour, rather than fear of pregnancy, which should prevent misuse of sexuality. Fear and love are incompatible.

The truths in *Humanae Vitae* need to be preserved. The encyclical defends sexual integrity and sexual morality. But the basis of its argument has proved unacceptable to many, and in this series of articles I have tried to show why. Perhaps we need a council to treat the whole field of sexuality. In this area, the updating carried out by Vatican has not been effective, so that the Church remains behind the times. Yet the world is hungry to hear sound teaching on sexuality which is concerned with human nature. For their part, ordinary Catholics long for the voice of their Church to be heard instead of being ignored. At present this is not happening, and I have tried to show that the reason is not disloyalty or a desire to attack authority, but because the encyclical is not true to the experience of married people. The Church will not be successful in speaking to hearts and minds if that failure is not corrected.

20.

THE *HUMANAE VITAE* CRISIS

(1) Inside the Commission
John Marshall

The Tablet, 24 July 1993

Young people marrying today cannot comprehend the anguish which followed the publication of Pope Paul VI's encyclical *Humanae Vitae* 25 years ago; still less are they aware of the work of the papal commission which preceded it, and whose story has not been fully told.

The commission was set up by Pope John XXIII in response to the decision of the United Nations and the World Health Organisation to tackle the issue of population control. Hitherto, they had been deterred by an unholy alliance between the Communist countries, which argued that a Communist economy could sustain any amount of population growth, the developing countries, which saw in proposals for population control a Western plot to keep them down, and the Catholic countries, which objected on moral grounds. The unprecedented growth in population forced the international organisations to overcome this opposition and consider the question. The brief given to the commission by the Pope was to help the Holy See respond to this challenge.

The commission originally consisted of three priests – two sociologists and the Swiss Dominican Henri de Reidmatten as secretary-general – and three laymen – two medical doctors, of whom I was one, and an economist. Notably, there were no theologians. We met in Louvain. It was clear to us that though the wilder projections about global population growth could be discounted, there was a real dilemma, not only about space and food but about how poorer countries with rapid population increase could provide the necessary schools and health care. We further decided that correction of distortions in the world economy, were that possible, would not in itself provide a solution. We also concluded that natural family planning, the method of birth regulation acceptable to the Holy See, could not be made available to the extent necessary to meet the short-term need.

The commission toyed with the idea that the new oral contraceptive might prove to be the solution. It was not, it was argued, a contraceptive in the traditional sense of interposing a barrier between ovum and sperm; nor was it sterilisation in the traditional sense of causing mutilation. Flirtation with this idea was short-lived as more fundamental issues emerged but it served to show the confusion that existed over the teaching that contraception was intrinsically evil. The commission concluded that theological input was needed if the position of the Holy See was to be expounded properly and recommended.

Meanwhile, Pope John XXIII had died and it fell to Pope Paul VI to expand the commission to 18, adding theologians, demographers and others. The venue was moved to Rome and it was at the first meeting at Domus Mariae that someone, in response to questions put by the Belgian priest Canon de Locht, said, "But you are raising questions of fundamental theology", to which he responded, "I suppose I am". At this point it was found convenient to take a coffee break while discussions continued privately. On resumption of the formal session, it was agreed that fundamental issues about the nature of the marital relationship could not be avoided. There was considerable apprehension about the way things were going but the Pope was informed and responded by encouraging the commission to continue its work in an open and responsible fashion. Two factors contributed to this openness: the commission, because it originated in response to international diplomatic pressure, was the responsibility of the Secretary of State, not the Congregation for the Doctrine of the Faith; perhaps more important was the fact that the secretary-general had direct access to the Pope.

Of course, the commission had not suddenly stumbled upon a problem of which no one was aware. For some years theologians had been tentatively exploring the nature of the marital relationship, leading in some instances to censure by the Holy Office. Prelates, such as Archbishop Roberts SJ, had publicly stated that they could not understand the arguments against contraception. Cardinal Suenens, whilst making no pronouncement on the issue, had, through his sponsorship of a series of symposia at Louvain, encouraged open and scholarly discussion of the nature of sexuality, the marital relationship and related issues.

Confirmation of the work of the commission was accompanied by further expansion to some 64 members to include cardinals, bishops, priests and laity, men and women, both married and single, from all relevant scientific disciplines and the different countries and cultures of the world. It says much for the resources available in the Church that such a wide diversity of callings and expertise could be encompassed in such a relatively small number.

There was some apprehension that this expansion of numbers might change the nature and style of the discussion but this did not happen, in part because the members chosen were scholars and scientists accustomed to taking a dispassionate view. (Only one person, or at most two, took a polemical approach.) This calm and persistent search for truth was typified in a session chaired by Cardinal Heenan in which those for change were required to put the case against and vice versa. The experiment was not an unqualified success; nevertheless, it illustrated the tone of the discussion. There were no factions or lobbying. This atmosphere was helped by the fact that the majority of members lived together in the Spanish College to which the commission had moved. Most important was the introduction of the newly available, daily concelebrated Mass which created a real eucharistic community at work.

Discussion ranged widely over relevant demographic, sociological, medical and psychological evidence but the essential issue which had clearly emerged was not the nature of contraception but the nature of the marital relationship itself. The traditional view of a contract involving "acts apt for generation" was seen to be a totally inadequate description of marriage. Rather, marriage emerged as a relationship of love uniquely, though not solely, expressed through sexual intercourse which may or may not be reproductive. In reaching this conclusion great emphasis was placed on the evidence which had emerged from married couples themselves. Space restrains any account of all that flows from this basic standpoint but gradually, over the three years the commission was at work, an increasing number of members recognised that the intrinsic evil of contraception could not reasonably be demonstrated. Formal votes were taken which showed the great majority to be of this opinion, which was sustained above all by the well-argued reports.

In reaching this conclusion members were not unmindful of the implications for authority and the pastoral problem that would arise. How could they be, when each in different ways and at different times had undergone an agony of reappraisal? I myself had started out with the view that contraception was intrinsically evil, but in light of the evidence about the nature and purpose of marital intercourse, I was forced, like the vast majority of the others, to change my mind. In their deliberations members were helped by the relationships developed during the course of the commission's inquiry but such support would not be available to those outside. Accordingly, work was put into the production of some very fine chapters to be used to explain developments to the wider world, chapters which, alas, never received the extensive publication they deserved.

Openness prevailed among commission members until very near the end. At this stage there was some evidence that the small minority who were against change may have been seeking support outside the commission. Within the commission one member would now put an objection to change which would be carefully answered whereon, without response, he would move on to another objection; this was a different type of dialogue than had hitherto prevailed, But overall, harmony prevailed; the report was completed expressing both sides of the argument but quite clearly recommending change, and sent to the Pope. It is believed that the four who could not accept change sent the Pope a private communication.

There followed two years of silence. This did not indicate inactivity, for the Roman Curia was hard at work. A secret commission composed entirely of carefully chosen clerics was set up, and produced a report which even the Curia found too extreme. A second commission was then appointed, again entirely composed of clerics, which produced something less extreme but upholding the traditional line. As though a group of selected clerics would have greater insight into the nature of marriage than the papal commission with its wide range of relevant expertise! These endeavours cast a revealing light on how the Curia works. Finally, the encyclical, *Humanae Vitae,* appeared on 29 July, 1968.

The long delay between the conclusion of the commission's work and the publication of the encyclical was not without its effects. During this period Cardinal Heenan, in a private remark to me, said, "It does not matter now what the Pope says. It is too late. The people have made up their minds." *The Tablet,* with great courage, published in concert with the *National Catholic Reporter* of Kansas City a leaked (not by me) copy of the final report of the commission. This clearly helped many people wrestling with the question to reach a conclusion.

The Curia, like all bureaucracies, may have hoped that by delay some heat would have been taken out of the situation. In this they were wrong. The encyclical met with widespread dissent both within and without Catholic circles. The latter felt able to comment as the teaching was addressed to all men and women as being a part of the natural law. In Catholic circles the dissent was distinguished by the fact that it did not cause people to leave the Church as many would have done in former times. Rather, people formed a moral judgement that the teaching was wrong and that they could practise contraception and remain in full communion with the Church. A number of surveys have shown that this is precisely how many Catholics have reacted. None of this was achieved without great anguish for people and their pastors, anguish which for many of the older generation still persists. This could have been avoided had the Pope listened to his commission rather than to the Curia.

(2) Authentic teaching
David Knowles

The Tablet, 24 July 1993

I will begin by saying that I feel that some, at least, of all those who have written and spoken about the encyclical *Humanae Vitae* cannot have read and reread it with reverent care. For myself, its full power was only revealed after constant rereading.

It is, taken as a whole, a majestic and eloquent document, a careful exposition of a theme in which no consideration of importance is omitted. It is solemn and magisterial, yet intensely personal and compassionate. It is fully cognisant of modern conditions of life and modern ways of thought. It is perfectly clear and simple – would that all comments upon it had been so – but it assumes in the reader a recognition of his complete creaturely dependence upon God, as also a living faith in his vocation, aided by God-given powers, to be a child of God, and to rise to Christian fullness of life here, and to the fellowship of the divine nature hereafter. Unlike almost all his commentators, the Pope allows for both sin and divine grace as practical, "situational", factors in the human predicament.

His declaration, if I may try to summarise it, is this. Our body – as we know it here and now, however it may have evolved to what it is – is a wonderful and most delicate organism, each part with uses and functions and relations and effects that we know by living with them. Among these none is more wonderful than the organs for the transmission of life, and no merely natural and human condition is more marvellous than the combination of these physical powers with the most intimate and fulfilling experiences of marriage and parenthood. The physical process and the human love, which in the case of baptised and married Christians is also at least potentially spiritual, are in God's design indissolubly linked, and to put one of these (either the love or the physical process) out of action, or to prevent the possibility of the physical action having the consequence for which it exists throughout the animal creation, is to thwart the design of the Creator.

This connection of sexual love and sexual process can be and is known instinctively and intuitionally and is in no sense a creation of the Church or of the Pope. The proper use of the sexual organism is an intuitive realisation of moral truth, and it is a part of chastity in its widest sense as a human, and still more as a Christian, virtue. But it can be obscured, like many of the simplest truths, by original and personal sin, by the culpable loss of sensitivity, by contrary instruction, by misunderstanding, by sophisticated argument, or by mere human confusion. For this reason it can be and needs to be reasserted by the Church.

The Church has also the right and duty of reminding us that Christian marriage is not solely a natural union; that in the Creator's design for the human race the physical instincts and impulses are to be subordinated to the reason, and the reason to the light of faith and the Gospel teaching. It was for this, as a part of our Redemption, that the Son of God became man and died to repair in us what sin had broken and to make possible, nay joyful, a harmony of the whole man under the law, that is the freedom of the sons of God. It is therefore the teaching of the Church, not that of Paul VI apart from the Church, that "each and every marriage act must remain open to the transmission of life".

Natural law disputed

The Pope is well aware of the extrinsic arguments against this teaching, which have pullulated since the perfecting of the oral contraceptive. Particular attention has been given in the press to his appeal to natural law, as if this of itself invalidated both his argument and his teaching. The existence of natural law is denied, or alternatively it is said that the natural law is what is discovered by man's own reason and cannot be imposed on him.

It is true that many schools and climates of present-day thought reject the traditional conception of natural law. They also, in many different ways, reject much else that Christians hold and always have held, explicitly or implicitly, to be reasonable and right. As the Pope himself said in his recent declaration of the Catholic faith, a reflecting Christian must needs make basic assumptions which some systems of thought, both ancient and modern, have refused to accept. Thus we hold that the intellect which God has given us reaches reality, that which is, in the universe outside our minds, and that it can also ascertain that which is right in human conduct. But indeed the flight from natural law is far from universal, even at the present day. Moreover, many of those who expel it from their systems verbally make use of something very like it translated into their own technical language.

As for the suggestion that the natural law, in order to be recognised as law, must be something that each individual ascertains for himself, one can only say that the term law, even when used as here only by analogy, implies indeed that a general ability to recognise an obligation exists, but this does not imply a universal personal recognition, still less one that cannot be obscured, very widely and commonly, by the consequences of original sin and by personal sin, contrary teaching, contrary habit, insensitivity and the like. It is precisely for this reason, as the Pope says, that the teaching organs of the Church can reassert and interpret natural law.

I would earnestly beg any of my readers who are troubled by the references to natural law in the papal encyclical to read and ponder a familiar passage in St Matthew, chapter 19, verses 1-12. It is not a "proof-text" of *Humanae Vitae,* nor an exact parallel, but it shows Our Lord dealing with a cognate problem, familiar in our time also, the indissolubility of marriage, and the same elements are present: the primeval "natural" law of the Creator's design; the failure in its observance through human "hardness of heart"; the reassertion by Christ of the principle both natural and spiritual; the objections of the disciples to the consequent hardship; and the calm maintenance of the teaching with an invitation to chastity aided by grace.

Much has been written about the individual conscience both as regards contraception and the acceptance of the encyclical itself. The word conscience has a terrible ambiguity, which cannot be bypassed by a kind of bland assumption that we are all always acting with clear minds and pure motives. Those who have had dealings with the claims of conscientious objection to military service, and those who consider for a moment those two great champions of the individual conscience, King Henry VIII and St Thomas More, will have a different, a truer, and a more truly "situational" appreciation of man's condition.

We all agree that in the ultimate resort we must do good as we see it at the moment of action. Vatican II in a welcome (but not infallible?) pronouncement declared that in all matters of belief the sincere conscience of the individual must be respected, and that freedom is of the essence of moral action and *a fortiori* of a credal assent. But the Council was also very careful to define the conditions of an objectively good conscience.

As Christians we know that we must always act with what present light we may have, but we know also that there is for us, in every event of our lives, a course of action entirely in harmony with God's will for us as individuals ("Thy will be done on earth as it is in heaven"). This we may fail to see here and now through ignorance, carelessness, education, emotion, present or past moral failing. But Christians, and above all Catholics, know that they have in grave matters of belief and morals a wholly reliable yardstick, agreement with the teaching of the Church

("I believe whatsoever else the Church proposes to be believed"). To follow that is never to renounce true reason, though it may sometimes imply transcending the conclusion to which our own reasoning has apparently brought us.

Theologians who extend the realm of "free responsibility" to solemn pronouncements of the magisterium must weigh their words. Do they suggest that the attitude of the faithful to a dogmatic papal pronouncement should be a suspension of judgement and a critical examination of anything that seems to shock their presuppositions?

What shall we say of the degree of authority inherent in *Humanae Vitae?* It is agreed that it lacks the external ticket, so to say, of infallibility. But it cannot be agreed that it is, in the words of some commentators, only the private opinion or the personal view of Pope Paul VI. He is expressly teaching us as *Pope,* and the Second Vatican Council's constitution on the Church reaffirms what Catholics already believed, that "We owe the offering of the religious allegiance of mind and will in a unique way to the authentic teaching of the Roman pontiff, even when he is not speaking *ex cathedra* ... This should result in a sincere adherence to the judgements on faith and morals which he has delivered, complying with his obvious meaning and intention."

No candid reader can mistake the "obvious meaning and intention" of Paul VI in *Humanae Vitae.* But is it the "authentic teaching" of Paul VI alone that we are hearing? A superficial reader (the present writer was one such) may fail at first to notice how often the Pope puts forward what he says not as *his* teaching (it is noteworthy that in the doctrinal part of the text the first person is never used) but the teaching of the Church.

It is the teaching of the Church, not the natural law, to which we are asked to give our assent. Do we, simple Christians, know better than the Pope what the Church teaches?

Attempts have been made to draw parallels between previous declarations of popes that have either been reversed by the successors or passed into desuetude as social habits changed. One who has for the past ten years been engaged in reading and writing the history of the thousand medieval years of the Church's life would have no difficulty in adding to their number. Some of them are indeed "motes to trouble the mind's eye", and there were sore eyes enough before the decrees of Vatican I were passed. But I have not seen either in this paper or elsewhere a single example alleged that is within hailing distance of being a parallel to *Humanae Vitae.*

Here, then, is the matter as it stands. We have a grave moral problem affecting in one way or another almost every Catholic Christian (and many other Christians and men of goodwill). Nor does it affect our generation alone, for papal pronouncements do not die when the writer is no more with the Church militant. Two successive popes, one being the dearly loved Pope John, withdrew a consideration of the matter from the agenda of Vatican II. The present Pope engaged himself to give an answer more than four years ago, as to whether the Church could modify its teaching. The Pope has, as we have been told in sincere and moving words, read much, spoken much, thought much and, what is more, prayed and suffered much, and devout souls throughout the Church have prayed with him and offered the Holy Sacrifice for his intention. We know, he knew better, what a tremendous and agonising responsibility was his; indeed, greater responsibility can rarely if ever have confronted a pope; and he knew that he would be, like his Master, "a sign of contradiction". We are told that gradually he saw more and more clearly what he must say. He answered on the spiritual level, transcending all debates on natural law and reasserting, though in ampler terms, the constant teaching of the Church of which he is head. Is any Catholic believing in Christ's promise to Peter and in the guidance of the Holy Spirit prepared to assert that he answered not only inopportunely or unwisely, but faultily and wrongly?

We are in a tangle, and argument, good or bad, will not restore peace and unity to us. Silence and prayer and quiet thought alone can restore peace. And peace can only come through union, in faith and filial obedience and understanding, with the Vicar of Christ.

(3) Consulting the faithful
Bernhard Häring

The Tablet, 24 July 1993

Twenty-five years after Paul VI's encyclical *Humanae Vitae,* we should look on the controversy in the context of the collegial government of the Church. How did the process of consulting the faithful on this question affecting responsible parenthood and world population work in the past and what might be the prospects for the future?

An authoritarian ethics of obedience does not lead to the maturity which befits Christians called to be the "salt of the earth", especially as witnesses in a pluralistic culture. John Henry Newman could only reconcile himself with the dogmas of the First Vatican Council by setting them in a collegial perspective, including the need to consult the faithful in matters of faith and especially in matters of morals.

The Bishop of Rome in union with all the bishops can teach authentically in so far as they are witnesses of the faith of the people of God. This means systematically consulting the faithful, especially those who enjoy a particular experience and professional competence.

Almost all theologians agree today that methods of family planning are not a matter of revealed faith. There are four main sources for all theology and teaching in the Church and in its name: Scripture, tradition, experience and rational discourse – in other words, mutual sharing of experience and reflection. Since Scripture does not say anything relevant to contraception and tradition has various mainstream opinions relating to it as expressing responsible parenthood and fostering conjugal love and fidelity, a well grounded teaching must rely on human and Christian wisdom, experience and discernment.

In 1930 the Lambeth Conference collegially and after a process of consultation and discourse broke away from a long-standing Augustinian tradition which considered conjugal intercourse onesidedly as a procreative act. For St Augustine only the explicit intention to transmit human life could condone *(co-honestare)* conjugal intercourse. Although the original rigorism had been mitigated in the course of the centuries, even at times tolerating conjugal intercourse in circumstances when procreation was not possible, any contraceptive mentality or practice was severely branded as licence, grave sin and so on. The Lambeth Conference recommended the virtue and practice of continence as a noble way of family planning, yet also considered contraception as justified where necessary (abortion was ruled out).

Pius XI and the Holy Office reacted quickly and sharply. The resulting encyclical *Casti Connubii* was the work of two moral theologians of the Holy Office, Fr Arthur Vermeersch SJ and Franz-Xaver Mirth SJ, though Pius XI in person supplied an alleviating influence. Contraception was now condemned not only as a grave sin, but also as a crime, side by side with abortion.

Casti Connubii was not only a sharp reaction against the Lambeth Conference, but also a break with a long-standing tradition of pluralism within the Roman Catholic Church. Along with the broad stream of Augustinian rigorism went a tradition which emphasised the unitive dimension of conjugal intercourse and tended to tolerance regarding interrupted intercourse in situations where procreation was not desirable. Representatives of this tradition included saints like Gregory Nazianzen, John Chrysostom, and Dionysius who wrote that he never published anything on the subject of matrimony without consulting married people. The same is true of St Alphonsus Liguori who dared to take an explicit and strong stand against the kernel of Augustinian rigorism, teaching emphatically that as an expression of the conjugal covenant intercourse between spouses is good and legitimate in itself, without any actual intention to transmit human life being necessary, adding even: *"Et hoc est de fide"* (a matter of faith on the basis of Scripture). For almost five centuries most confessors followed the advice of St Alphonsus.

Casti Connubii, therefore, made a radical change in favour of just one tradition without any practice of collegiality or consultation of the faithful. After its publication all discussion or expression of dissent was severely repressed. An appearance of public assent was enforced.

From the moment that John XXIII announced the Second Vatican Council, dissent came to the fore. The Holy Office did all it could to stifle it and even to solemnicise *Casti Connubii* through the Council. But the resistance was strong. The commission charged to draft the pastoral constitution on the Church in the modern world, *Gaudium et Spes,* raised the question openly, and vigorous consultation began of bishops, theologians, and experts in the field. No wonder, then, that great Christian churchmen like Cardinals Suenens, Leger, Döpfner, and Patriarch Maximos Saigh became spokesmen for a profound change. They received an astonishing warmth of applause from the majority of the bishops present in general session in St Peter's.

Then, alarmed by the men of the Holy Office, Paul VI suddenly intervened to stop the discussion. Was that an anti-collegial act by the Pope? I do not think so. His intention was to foster a broader consultation of the faithful. Paul VI ordered the Council's subcommission on marriage to take the issue up jointly with the members of the special Papal Commission on Population, Family and Birth.

In these joint meetings there was a clear majority in favour of change. The outcome was a text, part of *Gaudium et Spes,* laying down important premises for such a development. This text received a clear majority vote – well over two-thirds of the bishops favoured it. When, pressed by the Holy Office, Paul VI intervened by proposing new formulations in line with *Casti Connubii,* there was a huge storm, a few days before the close of the Council. A compromise was reached, pointing to the intention of the Pope to decide the question after a more profound study by an enlarged commission, truly representative for a consultation of the faithful. I was filled with optimism, as were many others, that Cardinal Newman's insistence on the consultation of the faithful would now and in the future be part and parcel of the papal teaching ministry, and that a genuine collegiality would be applied to all vital problems.

What then happened is well known. The strong men of the Vatican tried after the publication of *Humanae Vitae* to engineer a show of enthusiastic assent from the side of the bishops, in repetition of the methods that had been used to rally opinion round *Casti Connubii.* But times had changed. Pius XII had emphasised that freely expressed public opinion was necessary for the health of the Church, and that is what now took shape. Experts, marriage counsellors, therapists, Christian family movements, numerous theologians devoted to pastoral ministry, raised their voices publicly in many encounters with their bishops.

In this way, although the process was somewhat disorderly, a consultation of the faithful took place. Numerous bishops' conferences released well-prepared collegial expressions allowing broadminded pastoral interpretations of *Humanae Vitae* and honouring the sincere convictions of the faithful as they searched for more light and acted according to their conscience.

It is a part of the greatness of Paul VI that he could live in peace with this kind of collegial response – it was more than a "reaction" – to his encyclical, grounded on the conscience of the faithful. He had opened the door and given the go-ahead when through his spokesman Mgr Lambruschini he had declared that the norm declared in his encyclical, "Every marriage act must remain open to the transmission of life", was neither an infallible declaration nor an irrevocable decision.

Look forward in hope

In any case *Humanae Vitae,* like the Council texts, sanctioned profound changes in comparison with *Casti Connubii.* A process of development and refinement had thus been set in motion by the church authorities, part of which were the collegial procedures and some ways of consulting the faithful that were adopted. It is well documented that John Paul I intended to proceed in this direction.

The Congregation for the Doctrine of the Faith (the former Holy Office), however, and other organs of the Vatican could not live in peace with this openness, with this understanding of the Church as a learning community. Doctrinal pressures against some theologians (including myself) and some bishops had already begun during the last years of the elderly Paul VI. In the last decade, we have seen strong forces in Rome trying to reverse everything and to reintroduce *Casti Connubii's* criminalisation of all artificial methods of family planning, to such an extent that it now seems that full consent to this rigorism is considered the main criterion of orthodoxy and a condition for the nomination of episcopal candidates. This is surely the exact contrary of what Cardinal Newman meant when he called for the faithful to be consulted, for by such procedures the bishops are cut off from the convictions of experts and of the majority of their people.

The present situation is causing the Pope increasing pain as he gradually comes to know the breadth of dissent not only among theologians but especially among the spouses concerned and marriage counsellors. Equally great is the pain of millions of spouses who despite total goodwill cannot internalise the Pope's teaching, arguments and emphases.

I dare to predict, nevertheless, that the present suffering on all sides will be fruitful for the future of the Church. Popes and bishops will ever better realise that the competence of their office cries out for them to take account of the conscience of all who are experts in their respective fields, and of the experience of all the faithful. The Church of the future will – after all these sufferings – be more and more a great ecumenical learning community where all the charisms and experiences of life and faith flow together. In this future Church, all will understand better and better the words of Jesus, "You have one teacher, and you are all learners". Faith in Christ will honour "his majesty", as Newman called the upright conscience, and the unwavering search for more light.

21.

TRUE MEANING OF MARRIAGE
John Marshall

***The Tablet,* 4 September 1993**

The rising tide of divorce – in Britain 40 per cent of marriages now end in this way – and the ever-increasing number of single parents – in Britain currently around 1.3 million – pose a threat to marriage and family probably without precedent. In this situation, there was never greater need for the voice of the Church to be heard, for the Christian view of marriage should inspire people. But the Catholic Church seems mainly to speak in the negative, and therefore is not being heard.

Marriage is a relationship between a man and a woman based on love. To love is to give; in Christian marriage each gives himself or herself to the other in a shared life together to the exclusion of all others and without term. How different this is from the view expressed by, "Well, if things don't work out we can always get a divorce".

The basis of this Christian view lies in Scripture. Christ spoke of two great commandments, the first to love God and the second to love our neighbour; no one has greater right to be called our neighbour than our husband or wife. St Paul specifically commanded husbands to love their wives (Eph. 5:25) and likened their relationship to that between Christ and his Church. The Church sees this relationship as a sign of grace – a sacrament.

Love between spouses is expressed in every aspect of the life they share but uniquely through sexual intercourse. Intercourse both expresses love and nurtures love. In particular, love between spouses may bring children, who are also loved and will, in turn, learn to love. The unitive and procreative aspects of the married relationship are but two sides of the same coin.

The unique role of intercourse in marriage requires that it be properly understood. The official teaching of the Church has portrayed intercourse as essentially a procreative act. This it is not. Married couples themselves experience intercourse as an act of union which above all expresses and fosters love in a way that nothing else can. It may or may not be procreative. Since the work of Ogino and Knaus in 1929 it has been known that, because of the relatively short life of ovum and sperm, on only a minority of days in a cycle can intercourse be fertile. This provides the basis for natural family planning of which the Catholic Church officially approves.

Thus the majority of acts of intercourse in the reproductive phase of life are non-productive and cannot be otherwise. And, once the reproductive phase of life is over, none of the acts of intercourse can be procreative. With increased life expectancy, the post-reproductive phase of life now equals, or even exceeds, the reproductive phase. So during the entire marriage the vast majority of acts of intercourse are non-procreative. It is in the context of the marriage as a whole, not in individual acts of intercourse, that union and procreation should be one.

It is here that official Catholic teaching runs into difficulty by insisting that every act of intercourse must remain open to the transmission of life. It allows couples, for good reason, to choose acts of intercourse which they know are not open to the transmission of life, but will not allow acts which are open to the transmission of life to be converted to acts which are not. We enter a circular type of argument. Why cannot procreative acts be made non-procreative? Because it interferes with the nature of the act. But we have already seen that most acts of intercourse are non-procreative. By what moral principle are men and women forbidden to make intercourse, for good reason, what nature at other times makes it? Because it shows "contraceptive intent". But are not couples who deliberately choose non-procreative acts showing "contraceptive intent"? No, because they are not interfering with the nature of the act of intercourse. So, we go round the circle again.

In addition, the official Church warns that contraception leads to infidelity and a lessening of regard for women – the contemporary decline in the standard of sexual behaviour being quoted in evidence. This reveals a misreading of the sociological data. Most teenagers entering upon intercourse do not use contraceptives at first. Likewise in an affair, contraceptives are often abandoned, especially at a time when the partners think – often wrongly – that they are "safe". It is not the availability of contraceptives but the demeaned and demeaning contemporary attitude to sex that leads them on. Sex is portrayed solely as a physical pleasure to be taken whenever and with whomever you wish. Condemning contraception will not change this. What is required is an inspiring teaching which shows intercourse as a unique expression of love between a man and a woman who have committed themselves to one another.

The ban on contraception has clearly not been accepted by the Catholic Church as a whole. Surveys have shown that the majority of Catholics now practise contraception in good conscience. The supremacy of conscience has always been taught by the Church. Conscience, of course, must be properly informed – which, the teaching authority seems to imply, means following the official line. But only the couples concerned know what their actual situation is. While listening carefully to the teaching, therefore, only they can apply it. This is not dissent; it is the proper exercise of moral responsibility.

How has Catholic teaching got itself into this difficulty? The problem started with the adoption of St Augustine's view of intercourse, tainted as it was by his experience of illicit unions prior to his conversion. Sexual pleasure had such attraction for him that he had great difficulty in giving it up and only succeeded in doing so by condemning it. He held that intercourse was only justified by the intention to procreate; intercourse for any other reason was sinful. Pope Gregory the Great went even further in stating that, even when there was intention to procreate, intercourse was likely to be sinful because of the associated pleasure. A fear of sexual pleasure has its effects on official teaching to this day.

This bad start might have been corrected but for two factors. Extraordinary though it may seem, women have had no input whatsoever into the development of the theology of marriage. Their experience and understanding of intercourse has remained a closed book in official church archives. The other factor is that the theology of marriage has been developed and expounded in the Latin Church by celibate priests who either had no experience of intercourse, or experience that was guilt-laden. In no area was there greater need to heed Newman's recommendation to consult the faithful in matters of doctrine, yet this was not done. The nature of intercourse is not a matter of revelation; special knowledge about it can be obtained rather from those who experience intercourse as an expression of love in marriage. Had the married faithful been consulted, the real nature of God's gift of intercourse and its associated pleasure would have been properly understood.

Paradoxically, one of the casualties of the condemnation of contraception has been natural family planning (NFP). Initially derided by family planning organisations as "Vatican roulette", patient research by those working in NFP gradually led to its acceptance by the scientific world to the point at which the International Planned Parenthood Federation, which was hitherto opposed, commissioned a booklet on NFP for use in the field. Increased use of the method has now been followed by a decline – in the United States, for example, it was the choice of 8 per cent of those practising birth control in 1982, but only of 4 per cent in 1988 – because NFP is seen as being officially promoted by the Catholic Church to bolster the condemnation of contraception, rather than as a valid method of family planning in its own right. Moreover, there is a suspicion that it is accepted by the Catholic Church because it entails abstinence from intercourse (back again to fear of sexual pleasure). Abstinence is not in itself of value; its value depends on how and why it is embraced. Abstinence which is followed by a binge, whether in sex or drink or food, is not of value. Likewise, abstinence which is associated with either solitary or mutual masturbation – which 20 per cent of NFP users resort to – does no good. On the other hand, abstinence which is mutually and freely accepted and is used to develop a greater appreciation of the joy of intercourse can greatly strengthen a marriage. NFP is, therefore, a valid method of family planning which can be as effective as barrier methods and is free from physiological side-effects. It does not, however, despite the claims of some of its over-enthusiastic promoters, meet the need of all couples all the time. There is a need for other methods.

Discussion about contraception has now continued for more than 25 years. Surely the time has come for us to stop wasting our energies in this way, so that we can turn them fully to the task of promoting an ideal of love and marriage which will help to heal the sickness in society. A truly Christian view of marriage could carry a message of hope to those, especially among the young, who are disillusioned by the contemporary scene to the point that they no longer formally marry.

22.

HOW NATURAL IS NFP?
Annabel Miller

The Tablet, **2 December 2000**

"RHYTHM AND BLUES" was one headline prompted by a recent article in the *British Medical Journal* which indicated that "natural" methods of family planning could not work because there are such wide variations in the time when a woman can become pregnant during the month. The article, by Wilcox et al., declared: "There are few days in the menstrual cycle during which some women are not potentially capable of becoming pregnant."

Practitioners of Natural Family Planning brushed this study aside, pointing out that it was concerned with the old-fashioned "calendar method" of predicting fertility which has long since been replaced with far more sophisticated methods based on temperature, the monitoring of mucus and urine tests. It is interesting that the Family Planning Association – usually the *bête noire* of the Catholic lobby – issued a statement on the *BMJ* article which took a similar view to that of the NFP practitioners.

Wherever one stands in the moral debate over contraception, it is indisputable that NFP is not what it used to be. Modern methods, if practised correctly, do appear to work. Success rates quoted by practitioners are in the high nineties in percentage terms; equivalent to condoms and almost as high as the Pill. Another change is that NFP is no longer a Catholic preserve. A survey carried out in 1998 by Fertility UK, the NFP service of the Catholic agency Marriage Care, found that only 12 per cent of their clients cited their Catholicism as their main reason for using NFP. Another 58 per cent who chose NFP, some of whom were Catholics, explained that they simply did not like other methods. Twenty-two per cent cited health reasons and eight per cent religious views which were not Catholic.

Another study carried out in the United Kingdom in the mid-1980s showed that 31 per cent of those using a modern method of NFP were also using barrier methods of contraception during the fertile times.

So what are the modern methods of NFP? There are a variety of schools of thought worldwide; in Britain the most popular are the sympto-thermal method, the Billings Method and a hormone monitoring kit called Persona, which only works with regular cycles between 23 and 35 days. The sympto-thermal method requires the woman to take her waking temperature and chart it, along with observing the changes in the healthy mucus which appears most days at the vaginal entrance. The Billings Method relies on the observance of mucus alone. Persona uses urine tests to monitor hormone changes. The idea is that couples restrict sexual intercourse to their infertile days – the number depends on which method is being used and the length of the menstrual cycle. According to the Billings Method, for example, 50 per cent of an average or short cycle is available for intercourse.

The subtle differences between the providers of these various methods could be observed at a recent study day held in London by Fertility UK. This NFP provider of the Catholic Marriage Care organisation, funded by the Department of Health, gives training in NFP to health professionals, many of whom are not Catholic. The idea that couples might use condoms on their fertile days was discussed at the study day, and many of the NFP teachers who attended the day were also prepared to give information to their clients about contraception.

But some other participants in the event, whose promotion of NFP was driven by their Catholic faith, looked on with some distaste as one speaker showed slides of demonstrating condoms in Romania. The Billings method is the one most identified with the Catholic Church, although religion is not brought into the teaching and it is made available to all – even to unmarried couples. Billings was not discussed in detail at the Marriage Care study day, which focused on the sympto-thermal method and on Persona. Persona has been heavily and expensively marketed (it is produced by the major diagnostics company Unipath) and has also been exhaustively tested. It is sold as a modern method of family planning for health-conscious young couples. German television advertisements for Persona show gorgeous young things in fashionable night-wear having a flirty time in the bedroom. A Dutch study showed "Persona Woman" to be in a steady relationship, highly educated, with an above-average income; someone who "wants a contraceptive method with no side effects".

The idea which links all these modern methods of NFP is that of using one's sexuality in harmony with nature. This is an idea which would appeal to anyone – particularly those who do not want to use drugs to stifle their menstrual cycles or mess around with bits of latex at their most romantic moments.

But what is it like to use NFP? An advertisement in *The Tablet* produced a number of individuals and couples who were happy to tell me about their experiences with NFP. The sample was, admittedly, skewed in that interviewees were mainly Catholic *Tablet* readers. But even they had very different experiences to report.

Jim, who is now in his 50s and has two children, swears by the sympto-thermal method. "Abstinence is part of the real world as well as pleasure", he told me. "The beauty of NFP is that both husband and wife have to practise joint responsibility for the family. There are no pills, no ointments, no bits of latex, no surgery. There is an enormous joy about the process. It is also so unbelievably sexy! Every session of making love is like total ecstasy after having had to wait for it." He went on to say that NFP had taught him and his wife to be "counter-cultural".

John, who works for a computer company in Canada and is in his 40s and has four children, is equally positive about NFP. He and his wife used it to space their children, and now continue to use it to avoid having any more. "Other methods of family planning take sex for granted", he told me. "This one makes it very special. It takes two people to do this, so it is something they fully share." He explained that NFP forces couples to use other ways to express their affection during the fertile times, such as giving each other a hug or going out for dinner. This gives a "real grounding" to the relationship, he said. When asked whether it was frustrating, he replied: "Studies show that people who can delay satisfaction in any area of their lives are more likely to be successful in whatever they do."

But, I asked him, what about those people who are not motivated enough to make NFP work, who find it hard to delay sexual satisfaction? Should the Catholic Church be forcing those people to use a method which does not suit their personalities? "What the Church is trying to do is say: 'Here are the guidelines'", Jim answered. "The Church challenges people with the ultimate. Jesus knows we can't be perfect because we are human, and that sometimes we fail but we should not give up trying to be better in our marriages." The Church offered "ideals", he said, and this could be seen as one of them.

But the distinction between ideal and reality can be little comfort to those who find it impossible to make NFP work. Susan, who is in her 40s, has three children. She and her husband used the sympto-thermal method early in their marriage. "At that point it would not have been the end of the world if I had fallen pregnant", she told me. "The crunch came after my third child, and I did not want to have any more. I was exhausted. The whole issue caused a crisis in our marriage."

She explained that with three children, the time which she and her husband had to themselves was very limited. The notion of planning to make love at the right time was unrealistic. "We could only do it on ten days of the month, and that was not always when we felt like it", she said. "And I never felt totally confident that I would not get pregnant. There was always anxiety in the back of my mind and that is not good for a relationship."

In the end, and after much painful heart-searching, she and her husband realised that they had been making the Church's teaching on contraception more important than the health of their marriage. So they decided to use a method of contraception. "Our life has changed for the better", she said. "I feel now that we are able to relax and enjoy each other."

Sandra is a devout Catholic who likes the idea of NFP and believes that it can enhance communication between the couple, and encourage partnership in managing fertility. But for her and her husband, a principled agnostic, attempting to use NFP in the early part of their marriage presented insurmountable difficulties. A serious illness first showed up on her honeymoon, and went on to disrupt her menstrual cycles which lasted anything from 30 to 90 days. She carried on using NFP with the help of an instructor. "My husband did not like waiting in the bedroom while I was talking to the instructor on the telephone", she told me. Her husband lost faith in NFP, particularly after they had an unplanned child. To have another child within a year would have posed a serious risk to Sandra's health, so they abstained from sex for a year. After a few years, they had another child.

Eventually, after much searching of her conscience, Sandra decided to use contraception. "What is the most important thing? Sticking to the rules and damaging a marriage or putting the relationship first?", she said. "What would Christ do?" She and her husband now use condoms during the fertile period. "I decided it was not right to burden him," she told me. "'He has done his best and it is just not fair; this has caused so much trouble." She acknowledges, however, that NFP is not solely to blame for this trouble; the fact that she is a Catholic and her husband is agnostic was bound to cause a problem somewhere. But Sandra feels easy in her conscience now. "My husband and I have done all we could do to live according to Catholic teaching. If, in the eyes of the Church, my husband and I are 'one flesh', his principled views have to be taken into account."

Does that teaching make theological sense? One man, a devoted Catholic who found that, some years ago, the old-fashioned method of NFP destroyed the physical side of his relationship so that he turned to contraception, told me: "Ethically, the difference between NFP and contraception is so small. Why are we bothering about it? This is actually a debate about church authority."

Whether a couple uses NFP or contraception, he points out, the intention is the same: to make love without producing a child. The Catholic Church's argument is that NFP is "open to life" whereas artificial methods are not. But this is where double-speak creeps in. Advocates of NFP say that it is as effective in preventing pregnancy as contraception. If so, how is it any more "open to life"? Either it works or it does not.

The evidence which is available indicates that if used correctly, modern methods of NFP do work. But to say that NFP "works" is to assume that the couple are highly motivated, organised enough to measure symptoms and keep charts every day, and that they find that limiting their love-making to certain times in the month does not damage their relationship by causing undue frustration.

But there are many couples who do not fit that mould. Church authorities would argue that they must practise more self-control. But others might reply that some couples don't fit that mould because their personalities are not suited to it. Because their relationship is especially physical and passionate. Because they have been created differently by God.

For some couples, NFP is a joy. Others describe it as a destructive burden. Should the latter group be told there is something wrong with them, and that they should try to change so as to conform happily with church teaching on birth control? Or should they just concentrate on continuing their joyful and fruitful relationships in their own way? More than 30 years after *Humanae Vitae,* the time is overdue for another look at that one.

Part III

Marriage and Family in the Modern World

INTRODUCTION

The 1980 Synod of Bishops that gathered at the Vatican in the fall of 1980 was widely anticipated as a potential watershed session. Episcopal conferences in many countries held preparatory consultative sessions with their diocesan communities, and consultation, as several synod delegates have observed, implies responsibility. In England and North America, for example, the Catholic faithful had made their thinking clear with respect to the church's teaching concerning the regulation of birth. When their delegates left for Rome, therefore, Catholics on the home front were left with high expectations. Change was in the air. G. Emmett Carter, the Archbishop of Toronto and a cultured advocate for change, wrote a series of articles for *The Catholic Register* in which he argued that it was time for a change, a change in the voice from Rome – it was time to speak in a language the people would understand and time to treat in a dignified manner an educated church, a church for whom a respectful response would consist of a reasoned explanation presented in everyday language rather than formulae from the past couched in philosophical abstractions. There should be no "ready-made solutions," no "laying down of the law"; it was time to abandon the old bromides that posited the supremacy of the virgin state, time for compassion and understanding; and it was time to recognize that "There is no use in simply telling a married couple in difficulty that they should love each other or without explanation that they must follow the teaching of the Church on artificial contraception under penalty of sin." Carter was to be disappointed. As were Worlock and Hume of England, from whom much had been expected. As were many of the faithful in Canada, the United States, England and Wales, and eastern Europe.

The Tablet published the summary paper from the 1980 synod in full. Pope John Paul II's *Familiaris consortio,* issued on November 22, 1981, is Rome's formal statement on the nature of the proceedings and the recommendations of the delegates. *Familiaris consortio* insists that the sacred assembly had formally confirmed the teachings of *Humanae vitae,* "particularly that love between husband and wife must be fully human, exclusive, and open to new life," to which John Paul added that it was the "fundamental task" of the married couple to serve life through the act of procreation. At the same time, he reminded the faithful that the most perfect state is the virginal one, and that the church has always taught its superiority over that of marriage: by "liberating the human heart in a unique way" virginity makes it "burn with greater love for God and all humanity." To be sure, *Familiaris consortio* has as much to say about the family as a community of love and about the equality of woman as it does about the "contraceptive mentality," the "consumer mentality" and the "anti-life mentality"; there is an effort to redefine the traditional anthropological hierarchy of husband and wife just as long as women are not forced to work outside the home or that their redefined role does not result in "a renunciation of their femininity or an imitation of the male roles." Just what that means is not entirely clear, except that John Paul does explain his vision of the respective roles of husband and wife when he notes that "a man is called upon to ensure the harmonious and united development of all the family," a task he will perform "under the heart of the mother." There is here an effort to read the signs of the times, but there is also a commitment to the constant tradition, an inculcated inner instinct about maleness and femaleness that runs contrary to what are clearly the best of intentions.

And yet there is obviously within the Roman Catholic church a new theology of family and sexuality struggling to be born. One of its most respected and most articulate spokesmen is Jack Dominian: psychiatrist, sexologist, family counsellor, and wholly dedicated Roman Catholic. In a talk that he gave at St. Jerome's University in Waterloo, Canada, in 1988, Dominian made clear his early puzzlement over the fact that a celibate clergy should be the prime movers in the conception of the church's thinking with respect to sexuality and marriage; he also learned at an early age that the theology he had learned and the reality of his professional practice were at odds with one another. As a result, Dominian became a serious student of matters relating to marriage and sexuality as well as to the related teachings of the church. Through two personal friends Dominian became a prolific and highly respected author on marital issues, writing books and developing a productive relationship with *The Tablet*. Dominian argues that the church's preoccupation with procreation is misdirected. Experience had taught him that the starting point is all wrong. While working for the Catholic Marriage Advisory Council in London, Dominian began his professional life with an uncritical eye to traditional Catholic teachings with respect to the primary and the secondary ends of marriage: procreation and mutual help/the remedying of concupiscence. But he quickly discovered that something was wrong with the theory and that the grace of the sacrament simply was not sufficient to prevent marriage breakdown. As a result, "Little by little, I formulated the view that the principal feature of marriage was relationship. The second conclusion was that the language of primary and secondary ends, the language of the church for nearly a thousand years, was mistaken and should go." Dominian's altered perspective is neatly encapsulated in the observation in his *Tablet* article, "The Use of Sex: Christian Marriage in a Changing World," where he states that "every sexual act gives life to the couple and on one or two occasions gives new life." Sex is about relationship: a relationship of love, of sealing that loving relationship and giving it new life.

Writing in *The Regis News* back in the fall of 1998, the president of Regis College, the Jesuits' internationally respected theological graduate school at the University of Toronto, observed that the majority of the students registered at Regis were lay and that 58 per cent of them were women. The situation is hardly peculiar to Regis College. Is it any wonder, therefore, that educated women have begun to ask educated questions, or that educated women should begin to argue that the theory of natural law on which much of the church's teaching rests was conceived by men about men? Educated women have begun to argue that what is natural for men is not necessarily natural for women. The observation and the argument raise compelling questions that strike at the root of the constant tradition. Writers like Lisa Sowle Cahill and Susan A. Ross have unlidded Pandora's box.

There is much we do not know – except perhaps that we all have a lot to learn.

23.

THE SYNOD ON THE FAMILY

Emmett Cardinal Carter

At the request of *The Catholic Register,* I have agreed to write a series of articles on matters of immediate importance for the Catholic community and, hopefully, for others as well. The prime reason for undertaking this admittedly delicate assignment is the pastoral care of the faithful people of the Archdiocese of Toronto, entrusted to my care. However, it also helps to discharge my responsibility as one of the four delegates elected to the International Synod which will be in session in Rome through the month of October. The Holy Father has commissioned the Synod to consider "the role of the Christian family in the modern world."

Hence it is fitting that the first article of this series be concerned with this topic. Its importance is matched only by its complexity, which means that what I offer is obviously and necessarily presented in the clear perception of its inadequacy. These will be meant to be subjects for consideration, not necessarily for solution.

My first preoccupation is to attempt to portray what I perceive as the mind-set of the Canadian delegation to the Synod on the Christian Family. This opinion is based on the series of meetings we have held jointly with the delegates from the United States at the University of Notre Dame, Indiana, where the host team assembled some of the leading thinkers of the day. This we have followed up by our own team meetings, bringing together married people who are experts in their own fields: sociologists, anthropologists and theologians to assist the Canadian delegates and alternates in their preparatory studies.

Our major concern is with our own "ecclesiology." I recognize that this is a "big" word and hardly understandable. It means the context of the approach we feel the Church should be making to this subject at the Synod and it is much more accurate than the catch-all expression of "theology."

We feel very strongly, without any discernible negative voice, that we must, at all cost, avoid trying to "lay down the law" to the real and already agonized Christian families, who are not abstractions, but tangible, vibrating human beings, caught up in the problems of human relations in all of their stark dimensions. I know that there is, and will be, in the Church a body of opinion that runs exactly contrary to this position. Some quite legitimately in view of the present disarray, will be hoping for a Synod which will propose to the world a series of formulae to solve the difficulties of sexual mores, of marriage and of the family, which are all pervasive and which even threaten to destroy the whole structure of our civilization.

I cannot deny that in my heart I yearn for that possibility. How wonderful it would be if, from on high, we could impose a series of dicta and of orientations which could lead our faithful people and all of the well-meaning families of the world out of the wilderness of confusion! Alas, we are convinced that, if such a time ever existed, it has now lapsed.

We see ourselves rather as pastors whose duty is to present to the believing people of our world the Gospel message of the Lord as it applies to marriage in all its ramifications. To the love and sexual expression of husband and wife, to the relationships of parents with children and children with parents. The response to that call of the Lord can never be triggered in compulsion because it is, itself, a call of love, and love can never be adequately met except by love.

Let no one read these words as an abdication of responsibility. I do not share the current popular view that the teaching Church is limited and confined to a sociological consensus, that anything which does not have popular assent cannot be proclaimed. To hold such a view is to deny the prophetic role entrusted by the Lord to His apostles and their successors. The "magisterium" or the teaching Church is founded in the "sensus fidelium," but this term must never be adduced to deny the right and duty of the bishops of the Church in union with the See of Peter to proclaim even unpopular views that may well run counter to the opinion even of a majority. The question is not one of democratic election or even of the findings of pollsters, but rather of the revelation of God as found in the teaching of Jesus.

All of this notwithstanding, we feel that we are here dealing with issues which are so personal, so intimate, so bound up with the personalities of married couples and the dynamics of families, that our best effort is to call forth from the believing hearts of our people their own convictions and their own adherence to the teaching of the Lord.

It is only in this type of context that we can understand why premarital sex is wrong – because it fails in the completeness of self-donation for a lifetime of giving as willed by God; why masturbation is not acceptable – because turned inward; why homosexual practice cannot share in the fruitful image of God's own life, and so on.

But we must not return to the sterile strictures of "don't," "it's forbidden," "it's bad," "it's a sin." It may be all of those things but people today demand to know "why." We will have to make a heroic attempt to tell them "why" in the most beautiful, most positive, most cogent presentation available to us.

SEPTEMBER 27, 1980

THE SYNOD STARTS

ROME – The fifth general Synod of Bishops opened with the celebration of Mass in the Sistine Chapel presided over by His Holiness Pope John Paul II. The concelebrants were the newly-appointed moderators who will chair the plenary assembly. They are: Cardinal Raul Francisco Primatesta of Cordoba, Argentina; Cardinal Bernardin Gantin, the president of the Pontifical Commission for Justice and Peace; and Cardinal Lawrence Trevor Picachy, the archbishop of Calcutta. The secretary general of the Synod office, Archbishop Tomko, also concelebrated.

The Pope's homily centred on the beautiful text of the Lord's Prayer at the Last Supper and His Holiness seemed to place great stress on the petition of Jesus that these men, His disciples, that the Father had given Him, would not be removed from the world but rather preserved from evil.

The working session began in the afternoon at 5 p.m. and we had the opportunity to hear the hour-long presentation of this meeting's coordinator, (relator) Joseph Cardinal Ratzinger, the well-known theologian who is now archbishop of Munich.

Although it is manifestly impossible to give even a summary of all the points he raised, the method of approach was parallel to that of the Holy Father, although he naturally addressed more concrete problems. He presented his stance by saying that the principal role of this Synod will be to offer a critical but prophetic word against those ideologies and abuses of our times which tend to alienate man from himself.

Secondly, in this context we must try to present the Gospel values in such a way that man will be able to break the shackles which hold him captive in modern society. In a word, we are hearing the same theme: We are not asking the Father to remove us from the world. This would be an abdication of our responsibility and a kind of false otherworldliness from which the Church has suffered at times.

Moreover, here we see the clear position of the Canadian delegation coming into focus. The Synod cannot afford to use the methods of the past. Our people will not accept ready-made solutions or absolutes. At the same time, without that prophetic word, however contrary to modern trends, the healing of the wounds of society can hardly be envisaged.

Our criticism, then, is a positive act which leads to real hope since it flows from the spirit of the Gospel which gives light and strength in man's search for the freedom of true life and for the love which characterizes the children of God.

The Canadian delegation strongly supports both of these ideas. We do not propose a watering-down of Christian principles or an ignoring of Gospel teaching. But we are convinced unanimously that we must bring people to see these values in their own lives and out of their own convictions. In our considerations, of how we must address ourselves to the vital questions of the family, we must take cognizance of the massive change in the attitudes of many people, not least of all of many theologians.

When most of us who now debate these issues were young, in our families, in our schools, in our whole social structure there were *a priori* principles which were the starting point of our perception of right and wrong and the unchallenged guide to our conduct whether or not we lived up to them. We must recognize that that is not the present situation particularly, although not exclusively, for the young. Our society is predominated by an almost totally existential approach to life and particularly to moral life, which includes marriage and the family relationship.

Television, radio, newspapers, journals of all kinds and the whole social structure speak with one voice and it is the voice of situationism, of materialism, of secular and temporal values. The Christian ideal is simply not known to most of our people, or when known is under constant challenge.

This, as stated, represents a historical reversal. Formerly, we adjusted our conduct and practice to the teaching of the Church. Today, social acceptability has become the norm. We have often heard it said that parents do not teach their children enough and tend to abdicate in favor of the school. There may be some truth in this, but I have heard it respectably maintained that many parents are attempting to teach more than ours did but with a notable lack of success.

Who, after all, is really teaching our children? It's not the secularized world. All of which leads us to the conviction that our only hope of success in our responsibility of leadership is to teach people through their lived experiences, which does not, however, preclude our fidelity to the Gospel message enshrined in traditional teachings and sharpened in focus by the second council of the Vatican, notably in *Gaudium et Spes*.

OCTOBER 11, 1980

THE FAMILY SYNOD CLOSES

By the time this article appears in print, the fifth general Synod of bishops will have passed into history and, God willing, our strike-infested country co-operating, I'll be home gratefully.

The confrontation that a few days ago seemed imminent has mercifully and almost miraculously disappeared. Obviously, this does not connote a form of sterile unanimity which would speak only of intellectual bankruptcy or some form of coercion. Neither of these unhappy states of mind is present or prevalent. Something more positive and more encouraging has appeared.

A few days ago, a minority of the Synod seemed anxious to close the door to progressive and open-minded approaches to many of the major controversial issues we were beefing. We decided on two concrete steps to express our findings. These were, first, a message to the families of the world, second, a set of propositions, which in more technical and precise language would summarize the contributions of the Synod members and present our conclusions. These propositions would be submitted to vote and would require a two-thirds majority to pass. They would then be presented to the Holy Father.

Well, contrary to what some of us had feared, the propositions are not satisfying those who, on one hand, seemed to desire a totally inflexible and immovable attitude on every question, or those, most of whom are not here, who seemed to hope that this Synod would attack the indissolubility of marriage, abolish the teaching of *Humanae Vitae* and endorse every permissive stance now prevalent in our decaying society. The practices, I repeat, are remarkably open to thoughtful, positive progress in the pedagogical role the Church must assume at this juncture.

Bishop Agnellus Andrew, reporting for the Pontifical Commission on communications, made this noteworthy statement. "The Church is about communications. The Church is for communications. The Church is itself communication, leading to communion between God and man. And between man and his brother."

And this is what I find encouraging about the propositions and, in general, about this Synod. Pope Paul VI in his great summation of the 1974 Synod *(Evangelii Nuntiandi)* wrote this: ". . . evangelization risks losing its power and disappearing altogether if one empties and adulterates its contents under the pretext of translating it: if, in other words, one sacrifices this reality and destroys the unity without which there is no universality, out of a wish to adopt a universal reality to a local situation." (No. 63)

But he also wrote in the same passage ". . . evangelization loses much of its force and effectiveness if it does not take into consideration the actual people to whom it is addressed, if it does not use their language, their signs and symbols, if it does not answer the questions they asked, and if it does not have an impact on their concrete lives."

If this applies in general terms of teaching Christian values, it must assuredly apply even more to the moral content of the Christian message. The Second Vatican Council in very precise language recognized a certain priority of individual conscience as did the Canadian bishops in their Winnipeg statements and in their longer presentation on Christian conscience some two years later. This need of pastoral judgment is inspired, guided, sustained and authenticated by the teaching Church and must still be exercised in concrete circumstances which are so varied they can hardly be categorized. Under these always changing circumstances new and adequate response must be forthcoming to meet the challenge and the need.

To try and sum up, I believe this Synod has achieved two things. We have clearly stated the need for new insights into the Gospel values underpinning marriage and the family. These new insights must not be handed down from above as if the bishops had, in some mysterious way, a private pipeline to the Holy Spirit. We have to discover them along with the married people and the families that must live them.

The second thing is that not only must we learn to communicate in the language of the times but we must recognize what one might call the agony of the times. It is no use telling a blind man that he should look where he is going. There is no use in simply telling a married couple in difficulty that they should love each other or without explanation that they must follow the teaching of the Church on artificial contraception under penalty of sin. We have to reach into the resources not only as God's loving design expects, but to the new technologies, a more personalist view of human love, not neglecting the need for self-giving, for sacrifice and so forth. We have to leave the ideal plane, the level of doctrinal principles without denying either, and enter into a more concrete order of moral understanding and compassion. Above all, we must show that we believe in good will and the age-old adage that "to him (or her) who does his best God never denies Grace."

NOVEMBER 8, 1980

24.

THE SYNOD OF BISHOPS ON THE FAMILY

Closing business

The Synod of Bishops on "The role of the Christian family in the modern world" came to an end on Saturday 25 October. The 43 propositions, which were drawn up under the aegis of the *relator* Cardinal Joseph Ratzinger, and of which the content so far remains secret, have been submitted to the Pope for his approval or possible rejection. Meanwhile the bishops' "Message to Christian families in the modern world" has been published, together with the Pope's final address to the Synod (see below). Before the closure of the proceedings, elections were made to the Council of the General Secretariat of the International Synod of Bishops, the standing committee of the Synod, the main task of which will be to prepare for its next meeting in 1983. The new membership of the council is as follows: Cardinal Paul Zoungrana, Archbishop of Ougadougou (146), Cardinal Maurice Otunga, Archbishop of Nairobi (107), Bishop Stephen Naidoo, auxiliary of Capetown (83), Cardinal Aloisio Lorscheider, Archbishop of Fortaleza (148), Archbishop Joseph Bernardin of Cincinnati (121), Cardinal Gerald Emmett Carter, Archbishop of Toronto (87), Cardinal Jaime Sin, Archbishop of Manila (144), Cardinal Joseph Cordeiro, Archbishop of Karachi (132), Archbishop Angelo Fernandes of Delhi (65), Archbishop Godfried Danneels of Malines-Brussels (124), Cardinal Joseph Ratzinger, Archbishop of Munich (121), Cardinal George Basil Hume, Archbishop of Westminster (110). The figures in brackets indicate the number of votes received.

Bishops' message to Christian families

I. Introduction

(1) We have come to the end of the Synod. For the past month we bishops from all over the world have met here in Rome in union with the Holy Father and under his leadership. Before returning to our own countries, we wish to address these few words to you. It is not our intention to give answers to all the complex questions raised in our day about marriage and the family. We only want to share with you the love, confidence, and hope which we feel. As your bishops and pastors, who are also your brothers in the faith, we have been united with you during these weeks: nor have we forgotten that we, too, grew up in families, with all their joys and sorrows. To you and to our own families we are deeply grateful.

II. The situation of families today

(2) In our discussions of family life today we have found joys and consolations, sorrows and difficulties. We must look first for the good things and seek to build on them and make them perfect, confident always that God is present everywhere in his creatures and that we can discern his will in the signs of our times. We are encouraged by the many good and positive things that we see. We rejoice that so many families, even in the face of great pressure to do otherwise, gladly fulfil the God-given mission entrusted to them. Their goodness and fidelity in responding to God's grace and shaping their lives by his teaching give us a great hope. The number of families who consciously want to live the life of the Gospel, giving witness to the fruits of the Spirit, continues to grow in all our lands.

(3) During this past month we have learned much about the many and varied cultural conditions in which Christian families live. The Church must accept and foster this rich diversity, while at the same time encouraging Christian families to give effective witness to God's plan within their own cultures. But all cultural elements must be evaluated in light of the Gospel, to insure that they are consistent with the divine plan for marriage and the family. This duty – of acceptance and evaluation – is part of the same task of discernment.

(4) A more serious problem than that of culture is the condition of those families who live in need in a world of such great wealth. In many parts of the globe, as well as within individual countries, poverty is increasing as a result of social, economic, and political structures which foster injustice, oppression, and dependence. Conditions in many places are such as to prevent many young men and women from exercising their right to marry and lead decent lives. In the more developed countries, on the other hand, one finds another kind of deprivation: a spiritual emptiness in the midst of abundance, a misery of mind and spirit which makes it difficult for people to understand God's will for human life and causes them to be anxious about the present and fearful of the future. Many find it difficult to enter into and live up to the permanent commitment of marriage. Their hands are full, but their wounded hearts are waiting for a Good Samaritan who will bind up their wounds, pouring on them the wine and oil of health and gladness.

(5) Often certain governments and some international organisations do violence to families. The integrity of the home is violated. Family rights in regard to religious liberty, responsible parenthood and education are not respected. Families regard themselves as wards and victims rather than as human beings responsible for their own affairs. Families are compelled – and this we oppose vehemently – to use such immoral means for the solution of social, economic, and demographic problems as contraception or, even worse, sterilisation, abortion, and euthanasia. The Synod therefore strongly urges a charter of family rights to safeguard these rights everywhere.

(6) Underlying many of the problems confronting families and indeed the world at large is the fact that many people seem to reject their fundamental

vocation to participate in God's life and love. They are obsessed with the desire to possess, the will for power, the quest for pleasure. Instead of looking upon their fellow human beings as brothers and sisters, members of the human family, they regard them as obstacles and adversaries. Where people lose their sense of God, the heavenly father, they also lose their sense of the human family. How can human beings see one another as brothers and sisters if they have lost their consciousness of having a common Father? The fatherhood of God is the only basis, the unity of the human family.

III. God's plan for marriage and the family

(7) God's eternal plan (cf. Eph I, 3ff.) is that all men and women should participate and share in the divine life and being (cf. Jn 1, 3; II Pt 1, 4). The Father summons people to realise this plan, in union with their fellow human beings, thus forming the People of God (cf. *Lumen Gentium*, 9).

(8) In a special way the family is called to carry out this divine plan. It is, as it were, the first cell of the Church, helping its members to become agents of the history of salvation and living signs of God's loving plan for the world.

God created us in his own image (cf. Gn 1, 26) and he gave us the mission to increase and multiply, to fill the earth and subdue it (cf. Gn 1, 28). To carry out this plan man and woman are joined in an intimate union of love for the service of life. God calls spouses to participate in his creative power by handing on the gift of life.

In the fullness of time, the Son of Man, born of woman (Gal 4, 4) enriched marriage with his saving grace, elevating it to the level of a sacrament and causing it to share in the covenant of his redemptive love, sealed with his blood. Christ's love and gift to the Church and those of the Church become the model of the mutual love and self-giving of man and woman (cf. Eph 5, 22-32). The sacramental grace of matrimony is a source of joy and strength to the spouses. As ministers of this sacrament, they truly act in the person of Christ himself and bring about their mutual sanctification. Spouses must be conscious of this grace and of the presence of the Holy Spirit. Each day, dear brothers and sisters, you must hear Christ saying to you: "If only you recognised God's gift" (cf. Jn 4, 10).

(9) This divine plan shows us why the Church believes and teaches that the covenant of love and self-giving between two people joined in sacramental marriage must be permanent and indissoluble. It is a covenant of love and life. The transmission of life is inseparable from the conjugal union. The conjugal act itself, as the encyclical *Humanae Vitae* (9 and 11) tells us, must be fully human, total, exclusive and open to new life.

(10) God's plan for marriage and the family can only be fully understood, accepted and lived by persons who have experienced conversion of heart, that radical turning of the self to God by which one puts off the "old" self and puts on the "new". All are called to conversion and sanctity. We must all come to the knowledge and love of the Lord and experience him in our lives, rejoicing in his love and mercy, his patience, compassion, and forgiveness, and loving one another

as he loves us. Husbands and wives, parents and children, are instruments and ministers of Christ's fidelity and love in their mutual relationships. It is this which makes Christian marriage and family life authentic signs of God's love for us and of Christ's love for the Church.

(11) But the pain of the cross, as well as the joy of the resurrection, is part of the life of one who seeks as a pilgrim to follow Christ. Only those who are fully open to the Paschal Mystery can accept the difficult but loving demands which Jesus Christ makes of us. If because of human weakness one does not live up to these demands, there is no reason for discouragement. "Let them not be discouraged, but rather have recourse with humble perseverance to the mercy of God" (*HV* 25).

IV. The family's response to God's plan

(12) Just as we are doing, you also are seeking to learn what your duties are in today's world. In looking at the world, we see facing you certain important tasks of education. You have the tasks of forming free persons with a keen moral sense and a discerning conscience, together with a perception of their duty to work for the betterment of the human condition and the sanctification of the world. Another task for the family is to form persons in love and also to practise love in all its relationships, so that it does not live closed in on itself but remains open to the community, moved by a sense of justice and concern for others as well as by a consciousness of its responsibility toward the whole of society. It is your duty to form persons in the faith – in knowledge and love of God and eagerness to do his will in all things. It is also your task to hand on sound human and Christian values and to form persons in such a way that they can integrate new values into their lives. The more Christian the family becomes, the more human it becomes.

(13) In fulfilling these tasks the family will be, as it were a "domestic church," a community of faith living in hope and love, serving God and the entire human family. Shared prayer and the liturgy are sources of grace for families. In fulfilling its tasks the family must nourish itself on God's word and participate in the life of the sacraments, especially reconciliation and the Eucharist. Traditional and contemporary devotions, particularly those associated with the Blessed Virgin, are rich sources of growth in piety and grace.

(14) Evangelisation and catechesis begin in the family. Formation in faith, chastity, and the other Christian virtues, as well as education in human sexuality, must start in the home. Yet the outlook of the Christian family should not be narrow and confined only to the parish; it should embrace the whole human family. Within the larger community it has a duty to give witness to Christian values. It should foster social justice and relief of the poor and oppressed. Family organisations should be encouraged to protect their rights by opposing unjust social structures and public and private policies which harm the family. Such organisations should also exercise a healthy influence on the communications media and build up social solidarity. Special praise is due to those family organisations whose purpose is to

help other married couples and families appreciate God's plan and live by it. This like-to-like ministry should be encouraged as part of comprehensive family ministry.

(15) Out of a sense of fidelity to the Gospel, the family should be prepared to welcome new life, to share its goods and resources with the poor, to be open and hospitable to others. Today the family is sometimes obliged to choose a way of life that goes contrary to modern culture in such matters as sexuality, individual autonomy, and material wealth. In the face of sin and failure, it gives witness to an authentically Christian spirit, sensitive in its life and in the lives of others there to the values of penance and forgiveness, reconciliation and hope. It gives evidence of the fruits of the Holy Spirit and the Beatitudes. It practices a simple style of life and pursues a truly evangelical apostolate toward others.

V. The Church and the family

(16) During the Synod we have grown in awareness of the Church's duty to encourage and support couples and families. We have deepened our commitment in this regard.

(17) Family ministry is of very special interest to the Church. By this we mean efforts made by the whole People of God through local communities, especially through the help of pastors and lay people devoted to pastoral work for families. They work with individuals, couples, and families to help them live out their conjugal vocation as fully as possible. This ministry includes preparation for marriage; help given to married couples at all stages of married life; catechetical and liturgical programmes directed to the family; help given to childless couples, single-parent families, the widowed, the separated and divorced, and, in particular, to families and couples labouring under burdens like poverty, emotional and psychological tensions, physical and mental handicaps, alcohol and drug abuse, and the problems associated with migration and other circumstances which strain family stability.

(18) The priest has a special place in family ministry. It is his duty to bring the nourishment and consolation of the word of God, the sacraments, and other spiritual aids to the family, encouraging it and in a human and patient way, strengthening it in charity so that families which are truly outstanding can be formed (cf. *Gaudium et Spes,* 52). One precious fruit of this ministry, along with others, ought to be the flourishing of priestly and religious vocations.

(19) In speaking of God's plan, the Church has many things to say to men and women about the essential equality and complementarity of the sexes, as well as about the different charisms and duties of spouses within marriage. Husband and wife are certainly different, but they are also equal. The difference should be respected but never used to justify the domination of one by the other. In collaboration with society, the Church must effectively affirm and defend the dignity and rights of women.

VI. Conclusion

(20) As we reach the end of our message, we wish to say to you, brothers and sisters, that we are fully aware of the frailty of our common human condition. In no way do we ignore the very difficult and trying situation of the many Christian couples who, although they sincerely want to observe the moral norms taught by the Church, find themselves unequal to the task because of weakness in the face of difficulties. All of us need to grow in appreciation of the importance of Christ's teachings and his grace and to live by them. Accompanied and assisted by the whole Church, those couples continue along the difficult way toward a more complete fidelity to the commands of the Lord. "The journey of married couples, like the whole journey of human life, meets with delays and difficult and burden-some times. But it must be clearly stated that anxiety or fear should never be found in the souls of people of goodwill. For is not the Gospel also good news for family life? For all the demands it makes, is it not a profoundly liberating message? The awareness that one has not achieved his full interior liberty and is still at the mercy of his tendencies and finds himself unable to obey the moral law in an area so basic causes deep distress. But this is the moment in which the Christian, rather than giving way to sterile and destructive panic, humbly opens up his soul before God as a sinner before the saving love of Christ" (Pope Paul VI, Address to the Equipes de Notre Dame, 4 May, 1970).

(21) Everything we have said about marriage and the family can be summed up in two words: love and life. As we come to the end of this Synod, we pray that you, our brothers and sisters, may grow in the love and life of God. In turn we humbly and gratefully beg your prayers that we may do the same. We make St Paul's words to the Colossians our final words to you: "Over all these virtues put on love, which binds the rest together and makes them perfect. Christ's peace must reign in your hearts, since as members of the one body you have been called to that peace. Dedicate yourselves to thankfulness" (Col 3, 14-15).

Pope's final address to the Synod

(1) We have just heard the apostle St Paul giving thanks to God for the Church at Corinth "that in every way it was enriched in Christ Jesus, with all speech and all knowledge" (cf. I Cor 1,5). We too feel impelled at this moment first and foremost to give thanks to the Father, the Son and the Holy Spirit, before we bring this Synod of Bishops to an end. We came together to celebrate it, whether as members or as assistants, in the mystery of that supreme unity which belongs to the most Holy Trinity. It is to the Holy Trinity therefore that we express our thanks that we have completed the Synod, which is an outstanding sign of vigour and of great importance for the life of the Church. For the Synod of Bishops – to use the words of the council, in accordance with whose wishes the Supreme Pontiff Paul VI instituted it – "acting for the whole Catholic episcopate, is a sign that all the bishops in

hierarchical communion share in the cares of the universal Church" (*Christus Dominus*, 5).

We give thanks together for these four weeks during which we have been working. This period of time, even before the issuing of the final statements (that is, the message and the propositions) has borne fruit in us, because truth and love seem to have matured in us by a gradual process as the days and weeks have passed.

It is right to mention this process, and briefly to describe how it became clear. It thus becomes plain how honestly and sincerely were manifested in it both liberty and a responsible sense of duty regarding the theme that we were discussing.

We wish today to give thanks first to him "who sees in secret" (Mt 6,4) and works as a "hidden God," because he has directed our thoughts, our hearts and our consciences and enabled us to press on with our work in fraternal peace and spiritual joy. Indeed, such was our joy that we hardly felt the burden of work or exhaustion. And yet, how tiring it in fact was! But you did not spare yourselves in the work.

(2) We must also express thanks among ourselves. First of all, this must be said: we must all attribute that process by which, in a way that gradually matured, we "did the truth in charity," to the urgent prayers which the whole Church as it were standing around as has been pouring out at this time. This prayer was for the Synod and for families: for the Synod, in that it was concerned with families, and for families, because of the tasks they have to perform in the Church and in the world of today. The Synod benefited from these prayers in a quite extraordinary way. Continual and abundant prayer was made to God, especially on 12 October, when couples, representing the families of the entire world, came together to St Peter's basilica to celebrate the sacred rites and to pray with us. If we must thank one another, we must also thank so many unknown benefactors who, throughout the world, helped us with their prayers and offered their suffering to God for this Synod.

(3) Now we come to the time for thanking one another by name, and in this we include everybody who has helped in the celebration of this Synod: there are the presidents, the secretary general, the relator general, the members themselves, the special secretary and his assistants, the auditores and auditrices, the people appointed to help the media, the departments of the Roman Curia and especially the Consilium for the Family, and others, from the ushers to the technical assistants, typists and so on.

We are all grateful that we have been able to complete this Synod. It was an outstanding manifestation of the collegial care for the Church of the bishops of the whole world. We are grateful that we have been able to see the family as it really is in the Church and in the world of today, considering the many different situations in which it finds itself; the traditions drawn from various cultures which influence it; the aspects of civilised life that shape and affect it; and other matters of this sort. We are grateful that we have been able again, with the obedience of faith, to look at

God's eternal plan for the family manifested in the mystery of creation, and strengthened with the blood of the Redeemer, the Spouse of the Church. And finally we are grateful that we have been able to define. according to the eternal design regarding life and love, the tasks of the family in the Church and world of today.

(4) The fruit which this Synod of 1980 brings forth here and now is contained in the propositions, accepted by the assembly, of which the first is entitled: "On knowing the will of God in the pilgrimage of the People of God. On the sense of faith." This rich treasury of propositions, 43 in number, we (sic) now receive as a singularly precious fruit of the works of the Synod. At the same time we express our joy that the assembly itself, publishing its message, has spoken to the whole Church. The General Secretariat, with the help of the organisations of the Apostolic See, will take care that this message is sent to all whom it concerns, and the episcopal conferences will help in this.

(5) The deliberations of this Synod of 1980 and the contents of the propositions certainly enable us to see the Christian and apostolic tasks of the family in the world of today, and in a special way (*quodammodo*) to draw them from the total teaching of the second Vatican Council. Thus we make effective progress along the road which must enable this Synod to put its doctrinal and pastoral plans into effect.

With regard to this, this year's Synod is closely connected with the previous synods and is a continuation of the synods celebrated in 1971 and especially in 1974 and 1977, which have helped to put the second Vatican Council into practical effect and must continue to do so. These synods help the Church in a fitting way to be as she must in the conditions of our age, and so to present herself.

(6) Within the work of this Synod must be considered of the greatest usefulness the careful examination of doctrinal and pastoral questions that especially needed such examination, and, in consequence, a sure and clear judgment of these questions.

In the wealth of interventions, relations and conclusions of this Synod, which greatly arouse our admiration there are two cardinal points – namely, fidelity to the plan of God for the family, and a pastoral way of acting which is full of merciful love and of the reverence that is owed to men, and embraces all of them, in what concerns their "being" and "living." In all this there are some parts which have especially occupied the minds of the Synod fathers, for they realised that they were expressing the expectations and hopes of many couples and families.

It is right to mention these questions among the work of the Synod, and to recognise the very useful examination that has carefully been made of them: that is, the doctrinal and pastoral examination of questions which, although they were not the only ones to be treated in the Synod's discussions, nonetheless had a special place there, in that they were discussed in an especially open and free way. This means that importance must be attached to the opinions that the Synod clearly and powerfully expressed on these questions, while still retaining that Christian view, according to which marriage and the family are regarded as a gift of divine love.

(7) So the Synod – when speaking of the pastoral care of those who after divorce have entered on a new union – rightly praised those couples who in spite of great difficulties witness in their life to the indissolubility of marriage. In their life the Synod recognises that good news of faithfulness to love which has its power and its foundation in Christ. Furthermore, the fathers of the Synod, again affirming the indissolubility of marriage and the Church's practice of not admitting to eucharistic communion those who have been divorced and – against her rule – again attempted marriage, urge pastors and the whole Christian community to help such brothers and sisters. They do not regard them as separated from the Church, since by virtue of their baptism they can and must share in the life of the Church by praying, hearing the word, being present at the community's celebration of the Eucharist, and promoting charity and justice. Although it must not be denied that such people can in suitable circumstances be admitted to the sacrament of penance and then to eucharistic communion, when with a sincere heart they open themselves to a way of life that is not in contradiction to the indissolubility of marriage – namely, when such a man and woman, who cannot fulfil the obligation of separation, take on the duty of living in total abstinence, that is, abstaining from acts that are proper only to married couples – and when there is no scandal.

Nonetheless, (tamen) the lack of sacramental reconciliation with God should not deter them from perseverance in prayer, in penance and in the exercise of charity, in order that they may eventually receive the grace of conversion and salvation. Meanwhile the Church, praying for them and strengthening them in faith and hope, must show herself a merciful mother towards them.

(8) The fathers of the Synod were close in mind and spirit to the great difficulties that many couples feel in their conscience about the moral laws concerning the transmission of life and the protection of human life. Knowing that every divine precept carries with it promise and grace, they openly confirmed the validity and the sure truth of the prophetic message, full of deep meaning for the conditions of today, which is contained in the encyclical *Humanae Vitae*. The Synod has encouraged theologians to join forces with the hierarchical magisterium so that the biblical basis and the "personalistic" reasons (as they are called) for this doctrine may be ever more clearly made known, so that the entire teaching of the Church may become accessible to all men of good will, and may be every day more clearly understood.

Thinking of those who have pastoral care of married couples and families, the synod fathers rejected any split or "dichotomy" between instruction (which is necessary for any progress in fulfilling the design of God) and doctrine (taught by the Church with all its consequences and which includes the command to live according to that doctrine). It is not a matter of keeping the law as a mere "ideal" to be obeyed in the future. It is a question of the command of Christ the Lord that difficulties should constantly be overcome. In fact, the "law of gradualness," as it is called, is not possible unless a person sincerely obeys the divine law and seeks those benefits that are protected and promoted by that law. For "the law of gradualness" (or gradual progress) cannot be the same as "gradualness of the law" as if there were various grades or forms of commandment for different men and circumstances in the divine law.

All couples are called to holiness in marriage according to the divine plan; and the dignity of this vocation becomes effective when a person is able so respond to the command of God with a serene mind, trusting in divine grace and his own will. So it is not enough for couples – if they are not both of the same religious persuasion – to accommodate themselves passively and easily to their circumstances, but they should strive with patience and good will to come to a common intention to be faithful to the duties of Christian marriage.

(9) The Synod fathers have acquired a deeper knowledge and awareness of the riches that are to be found in the cultural forms of different peoples and of the good things that every cultural form has to offer, the more fully the unsearchable mystery of Christ is understood. They have also recognised that – even within the confines of marriage and the home – there is a great field for theological and pastoral study, so that the adaptation of the gospel message to the character of each people may be better fostered and so that it may be learnt how the customs, special characteristics, the sense of life and the unique spirit of each human culture may be combined with the data of the divine revelation (Ad Gentes, 22).

This research – if carried on according to the principle of communion of the universal Church and with the encouragement of local bishops, who should be united among themselves and with the See of Peter "which presides over the whole assembly of charity" (LG 13) – will bring forth its fruits for families.

(10) The Synod spoke timely and persuasive words with reverence and gratitude about woman, about her dignity and vocation as a daughter of God, as wife and mother. Reproving whatever harms her human dignity, the Synod stressed the dignity of motherhood. It therefore rightly said that human society should be so constituted that women are not obliged to work outside the home at a job or profession, but that the family should be able to live properly even when the mother devotes herself entirely to the family.

(11) If we have mentioned these important questions and the replies that the Synod gave to them, we do not wish to value any less the other matters that the Synod dealt with, for, as has been shown in many interventions in these useful and fruitful weeks, these are questions worthy of being treated in the teaching and pastoral ministry of the Church with great reverence and love, full of mercy, towards men and women, our brothers and sisters, who fly to the Church for words of faith and hope. May pastors, taking their example from the Synod, address themselves to these problems, as they truly are in married and family life, with care and a firm will, that we may all "do the truth in charity."

Now we wish to add something as the fruit of the labours that we have been carrying out for more than four weeks: that is, that nobody can "do charity" except in the truth. This principle can be applied to the life of every family no less than to the life and work of pastors who truly mean to serve families.

So the principal fruit of this session of the Synod is that the tasks of the Christian family, of which charity is as it were the heart, should only be fulfilled according to the whole truth. All in the Church who wish to help in the fulfilment of these tasks – be they lay people, clerics, or religious of either sex – can only do this in the truth. For it is truth that sets free; it is truth that brings order: it is truth that opens the way to holiness and justice.

We have seen what the love of Christ is, what that charity is that is offered to all who make up a family in the Church and in the world: not only to husbands and wives, but also to boys and girls and young people, and also to widows and orphans, to grandparents, and to all who in any way share in family life. For all of these the Church of Christ wishes to be and wishes to remain both a witness and a gate to that fulness of life of which St Paul speaks to the Corinthians in the words that we heard at the beginning: for we have been made rich in all things in Christ Jesus with all speech and all knowledge (I Cor 1,5).

25.

SEXUALITY: FROM LAW AND BIOLOGY TO LOVE AND PERSON
Jack Dominian

My theme is sexuality considered first in terms of marriage and, secondly, sexual intercourse in the life of the Roman Catholic Church in the last fifty years. I have deliberately chosen marriage as my first theme because society and the world tend to confine sexuality to sexual intercourse. In doing this we impoverish and diminish sexuality. Physical attraction, social encounter, psychological complementarity, and physical union form a whole range of rich human experiences leading to the attachment of marriage of which sexual intercourse is only a part.

I have been thinking, writing, and praying about these two topics for nearly thirty years and I want to start off by offering an explanation regarding this preoccupation. From time to time I have been criticized on the grounds that I have been sucked in by the wave of secular interest in sex, which has emerged since the sixties, and that I might have done better if I had been concerned with more appropriate and traditional themes.

My answer is that my interest in the subjects of marriage and sexuality started before sex became a popular issue in the sixties. I have thought and felt for a long time that, whilst the church has always taken these subjects seriously, it has never done proper justice to them. The Roman Catholic Church throughout its history has been preoccupied with the single state dedicated to God, and from the church's very inception virginity has held a strong fascination. In *Familaris consortio* Pope John Paul II has this to say about virginity: "Virginity or celibacy, by liberating the human heart in a unique way, 'so as to make it burn with greater love for God and all humanity' bears witness that the kingdom of God and his justice is that pearl of great price which is preferred to every other value no matter how great, and hence must be sought as the only definitive value. It is for this reason that the church, throughout her history, has always defended the superiority of this charism, to that of marriage, by reason of the wholly singular link it has with the kingdom of God."

Innate in this statement is a situation of intrinsic tension in the life of the church. Whilst it is true that the church has recognised marriage as a sacrament and has given it due honour, the fact is that its spiritual life has been largely in the hands of celibates whose main concern is to develop the qualities of support for the single state and suppress in themselves the pull of sexuality. To this very day the life of

Roman Catholics is shaped through the sacraments and prayers organised by the clergy, for whom the inner life of marriage and sexuality is largely a closed book.

And yet 80% of Roman Catholics marry, and thus the overwhelming majority of the People of God will find God and the major elements of their spirituality *within* marriage. There is thus an inherent contradiction in the life of the church which struck me very early on in my life. I thought and felt that it was my duty and vocation as a Catholic to do all I could to reveal the wonderful mysteries of marriage and sexuality, and I have been pursuing this aim since 1959 when I started working in Britain for the Catholic Marriage Advisory Council.

To assist me in this task I have had the privilege of my own marriage, the love and devotion of a unique wife, and the experience of working with hundreds of marriages in distress. But the Lord works in mysterious ways. This interest of mine needed channels of communication, and here I found myself fortunate to have the unconditional support of two men who played a crucial role in the dissemination of my ideas. The first was John Todd, who was one of the partners of the publishing firm Darton, Longman & Todd, and was responsible for publishing all my books on this topic since 1967. The second was Tom Burns, the editor of the influential British weekly, *The Tablet,* who was also sympathetic to my views. *The Tablet* is read throughout the English-speaking world and in this way I have been fortunate to have been received in many parts of the world. This combination of the freedom and experience of marriage and sexuality from a lay person, coupled with these two channels of communication, has largely shaped my life for nearly the last thirty years. I have received much appreciation whilst others have been astonished at what I have written. I am frequently asked what is the attitude of bishops to my writings. The answer is that, with a single exception in 1976, no bishop has ever criticized my writings. The reason for this, I believe, is two-fold. The first is that my intention has never been to attack the church or the magisterium. I have a strong love and reverence for both. But in the matter of love and sexuality there have been – and still are – considerable limitations both in theory and in the practice of understanding these wonderful gifts of the creation. My respect for the church has never made me blind to its limitations. I have never been the sort of Catholic who believes in the adulation of authority. I am totally committed to the church as the Body of Christ, but I believe that the witness of the laity in its life is an urgent necessity and, despite current difficulties, will be all the richer for having this input. This article is an attempt to summarize the interaction between the teaching of the church on marriage and sexuality and my own thoughts on these subjects over nearly thirty years of work in the field.

My story begins in 1959 when I was training as a psychiatrist and, having always given some of my time voluntarily to the church, I found myself working for the Catholic Marriage Advisory Council in London, England. This is a national body concerned with counselling in marriage and sexuality. Week after week I saw marriages in difficulties, and I had to try to understand the theology of marriage, the reasons for marital breakdown. My preoccupation with marital pathology is a separate subject: in this article I am concerned with the theology. I began to read the available material and I soon realized that there was a fundamental problem as far as marriage was concerned.

All the textbooks described marriage in terms of the prevailing canon law of the day, with ideas that had existed since the Middle Ages. Essentially, this official teaching of the church, which had been present for nearly a thousand years, saw marriage as a contract. Without bothering you with too many details, let me say only that the church at the time taught that marriage was a sacrament. The sacrament took place when a contract was exchanged by the irrevocable mutual consent of the man and the woman to take each other as spouses, and the sacrament became indissoluble when this union was consummated by the first act of sexual intercourse. Thus, the principal mark of marriage as a sacrament was essentially legal and took place at the wedding. The canonical language, to be found in Canon 1013 of the 1917 Code, stated that the primary end of marriage was the procreation and upbringing of children and the secondary end that of mutual help and the remedying of concupiscence. Today, this is the language of history but we should not forget that it was the official terminology of the church since the Middle Ages and that it played an enormous part in the context of marriage. It is the language many of us grew up with and it was enormously influential at the time I started work within marriage.

The grace of the sacrament was intrinsically related to what took place at the wedding and, provided the canonical requirements were met, the couple continued to pray, participate in the sacraments, have children and remained faithful to each other, then – by definition – their marriage should have prospered.

Every week at the Marriage Council I saw couples who had met all these conditions and yet their marriages were in serious trouble; in fact, many were breaking down. Given my upbringing and the theology in which I was nurtured, the reality I met in practice contradicted the theological theory. The grace of the sacrament, as understood at the time, was apparently not sufficient to prevent marital breakdown. This was a crisis of faith which was beginning to occur in me about 1961.

Up to then I had never questioned such fundamental teaching. And yet what I was seeing week after week made me think afresh about the nature of marriage. This thinking and praying had to be done privately. It is hard for us today to appreciate the prevailing atmosphere in the Roman Catholic Church before the Second Vatican Council. Any doubts about such fundamental issues as the theology of marriage coming from anyone, but particularly a layman, were tantamount to heresy and in another historical period carried the risk of burning. In addition, I was a psychiatrist and the views of psychiatry some thirty years ago were not particularly welcomed in the church.

Nevertheless, I persisted with my thoughts and gradually came to two conclusions. The first was that, whilst the irrevocable consent of the partners to take each other as husband and wife was essential, the key feature of marriage was not this contract. I believed that the essence of marriage was its relational characteristics. Little by little, I formulated the view that the principal feature of marriage was relationship. The second conclusion was that the language of primary and secondary ends, the language of the church for nearly a thousand years, was mistaken and should go. I felt so sure about these conclusions that I observed in my first book, *Christian Marriage* (1962), long before the Second Vatican Council made its pronouncements, that "Christian marriage seen in this way is a God-given, lifelong community, created to ensure the most appropriate conditions for the promotion of life, the life of the children and that of the spouses. It is based on a series of relationships of love which in a chronological order are those of the spouses, the spouses and their children, and the children amongst themselves. It is upon the physical, psychological and social integrity of these relationships, participating in the sacramental life of grace, that the essence of marriage ultimately rests." Both my conclusions were approved by the teaching of Vatican II on marriage and the family. Few of us are privileged to see in our own lifetime such verification of major theological changes.

But before I come to the Second Vatican Council on marriage I want to share with you a bit of history in the life of the church which I consider vital.

This is the history of the internal struggle within the church between 1930 and the Second Vatican Council with regard to the theology of marriage. During the current debate on contraception, those who cannot accept the idea of change will attest repeatedly in articles and books that the church does not change in fundamentals. The issue, of course, is the question of what is fundamental but, as will be seen, much of the teaching on marriage was considered unalterable before the Second Vatican Council and yet the Council made radical changes.

The internal debate in the life of the church was focussed on the ends of marriage. In very simple terms, the prevailing notions were that the church saw procreation as the key of marriage, whereas others wanted to emphasize the mutual help of the couple. Pius XI, conscious of this debate, wrote in his famous encyclical *Casti connubii* (1930): "This mutual interior formation of husband and wife, this persevering endeavour to bring each other to the state of perfection, may – in a true sense – be called as the Roman Catechism calls it, the primary cause and reason for matrimony, so long as marriage is considered not in its stricter sense, as the institution destined for the procreation and education of children, but in the wider sense as a complete and intimate life-partnership and association."

Armed with this section of the encyclical, Professor H. Doms wrote his book on marriage in 1939, *The Meaning of Marriage,* with this question in mind. After quoting a number of theological opinions favouring his point of view, he wrote: "We may now go on to say that there is a meaning imminent not only in the biological act but also in marriage itself. But the meaning is not, as has often been thought, merely 'love.' It is rather that fulfilment of love in the community of life of two persons who make one person. ... The inner meaning of marriage includes the performance of the sexual act, although it has no conscious interest in procreation. ... The constitution of marriage, the union of two persons, does not then consist in their subservience to a purpose outside themselves, for which they marry. It consists in the constant vital ordination of husband and wife to each other until they become one. If this is so, there can be no longer sufficient reason, from this standpoint, for speaking of procreation as the primary purpose (in the sense in which St. Thomas used the phrase) and for dividing off the other purposes as secondary. ... Perhaps it would be best if in the future we gave up using such terms as 'primary' and 'secondary' in speaking of the purposes of marriage."

Such outright challenge to the teaching of the church could not pass unnoticed. In fact, the heavens opened and – not unlike the official situation on contraception nowadays – Pius XI, the Holy Office, and the judges of the Roman Rota in turn, all criticized the book severely. The Holy Office was short and to the point. It formulated the following question: "Can we admit the opinion of some recent writers, who either deny that the primary end of marriage is the generation and upbringing of children, or else teach that the secondary ends are not essentially subordinated to the primary end, but are in fact equally primary and independent? The answer given to this question is 'No.'" Thus, in one sentence, the book was dismissed and the author put in his place. But twenty years later what the Holy Office described as impossible came to pass in the documents of the Second Vatican Council. The Sacred Roman Rota also set aside the views of Doms in authoritarian language, arguing that the ideas were innovations which depart from the certain doctrine concerning marriage. Thus spoke authority, and, as is usual, it hoped that the matter would end there. But, of course, it did not. The truth has greater priority than any individual, authoritative statement.

The answer came in the extraordinary richness of the Second Vatican Council's Pastoral Constitution on the Church in the Modern World (*Gaudium et spes*). As against the emphasis on law, the Vatican Council calls marriage and the family a *community of love* and thereafter emphasizes the supreme importance of love in its life. This view is still poorly comprehended by the church as a whole and yet its contents are absolutely vital. We have moved truly now from law to love. Instead of a legal contract, emphasis is now placed on marriage in the biblical sense of covenant, and in terms of relationship. In the words of the Council: "It is rooted in the conjugal covenant of irrevocable personal consent. Hence, by that human act whereby spouses mutually bestow and accept each other, a relationship arises which by divine will and in the eyes of society too is a lasting one." This relationship is based on conjugal love and the Council goes on to say – "This love is eminently human since it is directed from one person to another through an affection of the will. It involves the good of the whole person. ... This love the Lord has judged worthy of special gifts, healing, perfecting and exalting gifts of grace and of charity." The emphasis on personal love is balanced by the concept of procreation. "By their very nature, the institution of matrimony itself and conjugal love are ordained for the procreation and education of children and find in them their ultimate union."

But the language of primary and secondary ends, despite its use over centuries, disappears overnight. The personal and procreative elements of marriage are placed on the same footing. Thus, all the main objectives of the critics, including my own, were realized at the Council.

Since the Second Vatican Council there have been two main statements on marriage. The first was issued in 1968, *Humanae vitae,* and the second was published in 1981, *Familiaris consortio,* the report by John Paul II after the synod held in Rome in 1980 on Marriage and the Family. My comments on *Humanae vitae* will be reserved for the second part of my article when I will consider sexuality. As far as *Familiaris consortio* is concerned, all one can say is that it has received very little attention in the church. It is rarely mentioned in writings on the topic. The reasons for its demise are not clear. One thing that can certainly be said on its behalf is that it follows very closely the Vatican Council and is very strong on love. "The family, which is founded and given life by love, is a community of persons. ... Its first task is to live with fidelity the reality of communion. ... The inner principle of that task, its permanent power and its final goal is love: without love the family is not a community of persons and in the same way without love the family cannot live, grow and perfect itself as a community of persons."

As far as my own contributions to the subject of marriage and the family since the Council are concerned, I will summarize here my three main considerations. The conclusion of the Vatican Council has coincided with a phenomenal rise of divorce in Western society. I have studied this increase in detail and have written three books about it. Suffice to say here that I consider marital breakdown one of the most serious moral issues of our age – infinitely greater than contraception, and I go around the world urging the church to respond to it by far more than moral condemnation. The reasons for this escalation of divorce are many and complex. But there are two widespread factors. The first is that as material standards have risen in the West, that is to say as work, housing, food, clothing, and shelter have become more secure, men and women are imperceptibly seeking fulfilment in the next layer of their being, which involves feelings, emotions, and sexuality. Secondly, there has been a massive rise in woman's emancipation and women are not only tolerating much less violence, alcoholism, and infidelity but they expect a great deal more in affection. Thus, there is a real rise in marital expectations which is likely to be a permanent feature of all societies attaining Western standards, and the church must respond by appreciating these factors and understanding how they are translated into marital conflict. With this in mind, I set up in 1971 the Marriage Research Centre at the Central Middlesex Hospital in London, with a specific commitment to the prevention of marital breakdown through research.

As a result of my understanding of marital breakdown I have come to appreciate that there are three key elements in the inner life of marriage and I have described these as sustaining, healing, and growth. Through sustaining, the couple needs both an outer material security and an inner world of love. We experience love, first, during our childhood and again in our second relationship of intimacy in marriage. Through sustaining, we experience afresh the loving components of intimacy, trust, giving and receiving, availability, conflict, forgiveness, and reconciliation. In the process of sustaining, we reveal our strength and our weaknesses, and through complementarity we are able to heal slowly, over a lifetime, the wounds in our personality with which we come to marriage. And, finally, beyond sustaining and healing we need to grow in marriage. We mature in marriage by developing our social skills, moving from intelligence to wisdom, and increasing our capacity to love. The frustration of this growth leads to marital conflict; fulfilment leads to the richest realization of our potential. I believe that sustaining, healing, and growth are the three key expressions of love in contemporary marriage.

My third and final contribution to this topic is a vision of marriage as the key sacrament for salvation. I believe that we are incorporated in Christ through baptism and that we celebrate the essence of the Incarnation in the eucharist; but, in fact, for married people the main gateway of their salvation is matrimony and I am passionately concerned to put this sacrament on the map. At the present moment, the Roman Catholic Church commends a spirituality which is based on the sacraments and a life of prayer that is largely celebrated and experienced in the building of the church. But for the overwhelming majority of Christians their main preoccupation is with their family and their work, and I believe that the main thrust of evangelization is to be found in discovering God in these two situations. I am preoccupied with the phenomenon in the West that many people are interested in the reality of God, have transcendental experiences, and yet continue to withdraw from the institutional churches. This is a huge topic to consider, but I believe that one explanation is to be found in the fact that the churches are increasingly failing to communicate the sense of God where people experience it. Marriage and the family is one such area, and the Roman Catholic Church has recognized the importance of both but has not translated this realization into action. The Second Vatican Council was aware of the importance of marriage for evangelization: "For from the wedlock of Christians there comes the family in which new citizens of human society are born. By the grace of the Holy Spirit received in baptism these are children of God, thus perpetuating the People of God through the centuries. The family is, so to speak, the domestic church." The idea of the "domestic church" is considered in broad theological terms in *Familiaris consortio*. But I want to examine it in different terms.

For me, the concept of the "domestic church" means that throughout their twenty-four hours per day, spouses and children meet God in each other through their moment-to-moment encounter with each other. From the moment the husband and wife wake up in the morning, right through the processes of washing, dressing, eating, arranging for children to go to school, caring for the house, preparing food, socializing, coming together to eat, going to bed, making love, I see all as a liturgy of the community of love in which the members of the family encounter God in and through each other. We are accustomed to see and experience every detail of the eucharist as participating in the integral encounter with Christ and through him with God the Father. I believe the same should apply to married life in which the ordinary becomes the extraordinary. Through their personal encounters spouses and their children encounter Christ in each other.

If my vision is correct, then the pastoral challenge to the church is immense. I believe we have a task of preparing young people for this sacrament and then recognizing that the wedding is not the conclusion of the church's involvement with marriage but the beginning of support for an unfolding relationship of love that lasts over its whole lifetime. We have to support marriage and celebrate it, and that means understanding it in depth, having a theology which penetrates its immense mystery, and developing a liturgy of celebration of its key moments.

All this cannot be done by the church as it is presently constructed. We cannot expect a celibate clergy to make marriage a pastoral reality for the spiritual life of the church's community. The spadework has to be done by the married and we have to work in close co-operation with the clergy. This development will take different shapes and forms in various parts of the world, but I consider it one of the most crucial issues for evangelization.

This brings me to the conclusion of the section on sexuality seen through marriage. The whole encounter of men and women is steeped in the mystery of sexuality which is revealed in marriage. In the Roman Catholic Church – indeed, in Christianity as a whole – the richness of this mystery of sexuality has yet to be explored. As far as the male is concerned, the Son of God, Jesus, led a celibate life but, as I have to remind people again and again, that does not mean he was asexual, hence his rich insights into sexuality. As far as the female is concerned, Mary is held in high esteem, and rightly so, as a virgin. It is inconceivable that the Son of God, who was the prototype of loving openness to God the Father, could have married, narrowing down his availability to one other person in marriage. He was the prototype of the fullness of the kingdom of God in which love will remain supreme and will not require marital exclusiveness to be realized. But marriage and sexuality are the principal means of experiencing love, which is the nature of God, and we must not forget that in the Hebrew Scriptures, sexuality as expressed in marriage was one of the key symbols of God's covenant with humankind. So, whilst we must undoubtedly appreciate virginity, Christianity has yet to explore further the mystery of sexuality.

Turning now to sexuality in terms of the social, emotional, and physical attraction leading to sexual intercourse: there is little doubt that this precious gift of God celebrated so fully in the Song of Songs and elsewhere has had a relatively poor reception in the Christian tradition. Against a background which exalted virginity, sexual intercourse was safeguarded from being considered evil, as Manichaeism, Gnosticism and subsequent heresies regarded it, but has nonetheless been treated with great caution by the church. Given that its pleasure-producing qualities were approached with great suspicion, its ultimate salvation was seen in its relationship to procreation. From the earliest centuries its greatest justification was its link with children; thus, a biological emphasis has existed from the beginning of Christianity to this very day.

The connection of sexual intercourse with love was extremely slow to develop and, although it had its disciples throughout the Christian tradition, its adherents were few. Love, as a main expression of sexual intercourse, never established itself in the life of the church, whereas its dangers were never far from the church's thoughts.

Returning to the last fifty years, we have seen how canonical language saw coitus as a remedy for concupiscence. In the fullness of theological thought, the concept of "remedy of concupiscence" is not a term of abuse. Concupiscence, in general, refers to the human disorder of uncontrolled passion and instincts to which fallen human nature is susceptible because of Original Sin. At its best, the idea behind the phrase is the concept that grace offers a healing strength which directs sexuality to a much more ordered, organized, and integrated channel of proper human expression. Thus, marriage translates promiscuity into exclusive faithful intercourse and pure instinctual gratification into procreative potential with pleasure, a proper reward for an authentic human activity. Alternatively the phrase "remedy of concupiscence" has overtones such that the sexual drive has elements which are sick and that sexual desire is suspect, that at its worst it is not much better than animal instinct and it needs tight control to overcome its dangers. There is little doubt that the canonical language before Vatican II was totally devoid of the link between intercourse and love: the accent was on its procreative potential, and that the atmosphere which prevailed in Roman Catholic schools and from the pulpits of the church throughout the world was about sex's dangers. That is the theology and the atmosphere in which the ordinary Roman Catholic of the time grew up.

There are those who wish to deny all this and paint a rosy picture. But those of us who grew up in the thirties, forties, and fifties – and even later generations – will not easily forget the negativity. I was a child of that generation and from the very moment I had any possibility of contributing to the subject, I felt obliged to do all I could to restore to this unique gift of the creator, the richness that it possesses. I was convinced from my earliest and most tentative thinking that the secret of understanding coitus was to appreciate its link with love and, therefore, with God.

Here, as elsewhere, in this area, the Second Vatican Council had some wonderful things to say about sexual intercourse. "This love [of the spouses] is uniquely expressed and perfected through the marital act. The actions within marriage by which the couple are united intimately and chastely are noble and worthy ones. Expressed in a manner which is truly human, these actions signify and promote that mutual self-giving by which spouses enrich each other with a joyful and a thoughtful will."

We have seen that the language of primary and secondary ends is dropped by the Council and that the personal and procreative elements of marriage are put on the same footing. Nevertheless, the Council asserts clearly that having and educating children is absolutely crucial, and the link between sexual intercourse and procreation is paramount. There cannot be any shadow of a doubt that the church is absolutely correct when it states – as it does at the Council: "Hence, while not making the other purposes of matrimony of less account, the true practice of conjugal love, and the whole meaning of the family life which results from it, has this aim: that the couple be ready with stout hearts to co-operate with the love of the Creator and the Saviour who, through them, will enlarge and enrich His own family day by day." Without this co-operation between the Creator and spouses, life will cease to exist. But having underlined this profound truth, I believe that the Roman Catholic Church – indeed Christianity as a whole – has yet to grasp the central truths about the meaning of sexual intercourse. I have developed my thoughts on the meaning of coitus in several papers and two books. The first of these appeared in 1977 and was called *Proposals for a New Sexual Ethic* and the second appeared in 1987 under the title *Sexual Integrity: The Answer to AIDS*. In these various writings I have proposed that, as far as sexual intercourse is concerned, our understanding of it will be immensely enhanced if we move from primarily linking it to the biology of procreation to a personal encounter of love. Inevitably, that has meant that I have to dissent from the teaching of the church on contraception and I have had to put forward what I consider to be more fundamental interpretations of the meaning of coitus.

The most fundamental issue to be faced is that throughout the world a combination of advances in medicine, coupled with birth regulation of the contraceptive or the infertile period variety, has severed the link between sexual intercourse and procreation. Conservative thinkers are liable to interpret this, particularly in the contraception debate, as an anti-life tendency. It is nothing of the sort. It is simply the result of the fact that within the means available the average family size can be created with a few acts of intercourse leaving the rest.... Leaving the rest for what? To me this is one of the most fundamental questions of our age and intimately linked with sexual morality. There are broadly two groups of answers. The first is offered by the church, which is that sexual intercourse has a unique loving element and a pronounced and important link with procreation demanding that every act of intercourse be open to life. The second is that of secular society, which has assumed that now that the procreative element can be controlled effectively the pleasure component is released and should be pursued in every possible set of circumstances before marriage and outside it. The world is locked in this polarity, and generally the secular response has had a field day during the last quarter of a century with the Roman Catholic Church persisting with its anti-contraceptive campaign as one of the main answers to this dilemma. I have little doubt that both responses are profoundly wrong and I deplore the attitude of the

Roman Catholic Church, for it has in its tradition the elements of the correct answer.

As the link between coitus and procreation recedes, we are being released from this blind alley to see the wider perspectives of the meaning of sexuality. The first and most obvious is that sexual attraction is a most powerful energy, a precious gift of the Creator, the main purpose of which is human attachment or bonding. Sexual attraction is singularly ordained to bring men and women together, to form an exclusive relationship in marriage and then through intercourse to maintain the bond for their own and that of their children's interest. The pleasure of sexual attraction and coitus is not an end in itself but serves human bonding. All theology which has compared the sexual drive with animal instinct directed towards procreation is fundamentally wrong. The sexual drive in human beings is markedly different, and is linked with a personal dimension whose proclivity is what we have come to understand as love.

So sexuality is not primarily to be used before marriage for its orgiastic qualities, but is to bring two people together: hence, the abiding importance of premarital continence. Having established this bond in marriage, what then? Sexual intercourse has now the central task of maintaining the relationship and a minute part in procreation (which it can achieve very effectively with a few acts). The relationship is maintained, not so much by the number of orgasms attained, but by the personal encounter of love which the orgasm facilitates. Every time a couple make love they have the possibility of realising the following experiences.

Firstly, intercourse verifies their personal significance to each other. Each act of intercourse is a reminder that they are the most important person in each other's life and that they recognize, want and appreciate each other by donating the whole of their person in total physical and emotional unity.

Secondly, coitus is one of the most powerful acts through which they reinforce each other's sexual identity, making the woman feel most fully feminine and the man masculine. Thirdly, every bond is threatened by dissensions. Quick reconciliation is the order of the day, but sometimes forgiveness doesn't work. The hurt is too severe. It is at these times that coitus can facilitate reconciliation as the joy it mobilises heals the wound. Fourthly, at the very heart of attachment is the desire for its continuity; coitus is a peak moment of confirming this unity of relationship. Sexual desire is a powerful hope for that continuity of a loving relationship and it anticipates that powerful yearning for continuity of being which we look for in the mystery of the Trinity. Finally, every time the couple make love there is a rich vein of thanksgiving which is rendered with or without words. For me, therefore, every act of intercourse is a moment of personal life-giving which, by reinforcing the relationship of marriage, is its most powerful meaning: on a few occasions it is actually life-giving in procreative terms, but its chief link with procreation is to promote the unity and stability of the parents who are essential for the development of the children.

If what I am saying about sexuality is remotely correct, it is such a rich and meaningful personal encounter that it needs a continuous, reliable, and predictable relationship to do justice to it, and that is precisely what marriage does. For me, marriage justifies the Judaeo-Christian stance against fornication and adultery. But it in no way justifies the position against contraception taken by the Roman Catholic Church. In fact, I consider the energy consumed in the Roman Catholic Church by the contraception controversy one of the saddest wastes of time when we consider the urgent need for work to be done in preserving marital stability against the ravages of divorce, and the urgency to find a new meaning for sexuality against the proliferation of the secular belief that the only thing worth counting in sex is the number of orgasms. The need for a profound, in-depth answer to both moral dilemmas has been heightened by the crisis of AIDS.

Let me now conclude with a quick summary. There is little doubt in my mind that the Second Vatican Council has been the most important Council in the life of the church on the topic of marriage, and has moved the church from a theology of law to where its roots properly belong – love. As far as sexuality is concerned, the initial steps in the appropriate direction have been taken, but the contraceptive argument has been a hiccough. But I think future historians will see the last twenty years as a vital step in negotiating this transition. I have no doubt that the essence of Christianity is to be found in an ever-deepening understanding of love and human sexuality. For this to happen everyone – but particularly the married – have to play their part and it is my sincere hope that my contributions, whatever their intrinsic worth, will act as a stimulant for men and women all over the world to come forth with their experiences and help the church perceive more clearly the richness of the gift that the Creator has given us.

26.

CHRISTIAN MARRIAGE IN A CHANGING WORLD

(1) Person to person
Jack Dominian

***The Tablet*, 4 February 1984**

In 1967 I wrote a number of articles in *The Tablet* with the title "The Church and the sexual revolution". They marked the beginning in these columns of a special and regular interest in the subjects of marriage and sexuality. The sexual revolution has continued, but is not the subject of this series of four articles. Instead, I am confining myself to the relation between marriage and sexuality. Many people are conscious that there have been changes in both areas since Vatican II but are not aware of how marked these are and – even more important – of how many questions they leave open.

When I joined the Catholic Marriage Advisory Council in 1959, the theology of marriage was still in the hands of canon lawyers and the language used was that of canon law. The Roman Rota summarised the position in 1944: "There are several ends of marriage, and one of these is primary and the others are secondary. As Canon 1013 states, the primary end is the procreation and upbringing of children, the secondary end is the mutual help and the remedying of concupiscence." The secondary ends were subordinated to the primary end of procreation.

This division into primary and secondary ends was challenged in 1939 by Professor Doms amongst others, and by myself in 1967 in the book *Christian Marriage*. The challenge of Professor Doms was taken very seriously but, although Pius XII tried to ensure that the procreative end was not disproportionately favoured, the overall answer from Rome was categorically negative. The division between primary and secondary ends was to stand unaltered until Vatican II.

The reason why I criticised this formulation was that, as it stood, it could be interpreted to imply that the Church favoured procreation at the expense of the personal side of marriage, while "the relief of concupiscence", without any mention of the word "love", was a concept that mutilated the richness of sexuality.

Anyone participating in the discussion in the thirties, forties and fifties would have assumed that the Church would never change its formulations. In fact it did so in the Vatican Council without any damage to its standing. So often Catholics in the conservative tradition make the point that, if the Church has spoken, the last word has been said and the integrity of the teaching office would be at stake if it altered. Millions of words have been spilt on the possibility of change, without realisation that, whilst the Church must remain faithful to Christ and the Gospel, our understanding of what that faithfulness means will continue to develop until the end of time. So many Catholics are persecuted for suggesting change when in fact change does come sooner or later.

The deliberations of Vatican II produced an extraordinary transformation. Almost overnight, the legal language that had existed for nearly 50 years, based on the medieval concept of ends, was removed. Instead of this legal language the whole of *Gaudium et Spes* is infiltrated with the concept of love. It is worthwhile recalling here the words of John Paul II in *Familiaris Consortio:* "Without love the family cannot live, grow and perfect itself as a community of persons." Love permeates the concept of marriage in Vatican II: so much so that the family is now defined as "a community of love" and the biblical language of covenant is used in this context. The covenant is the word used for the relationship between God and his people, which is saturated with love and fidelity, and these are the characteristics which adorn marriage.

Everyone will agree that here are ideas which elevate marriage to a wonderful level. But there are problems. In what way is this love to be expressed?

Facing reality

It will be remembered that in the period before Vatican II, the personal and sexual element were subordinated to the creation and education of children. Vatican II no longer draws this order of priorities and apparently pays equal attention to the relationship of the spouses and the procreation of children, However, if one looks carefully at the language, the predilection towards procreation remains.

I quote the relevant passages to illustrate the point. "This love [of the spouses] involves the good of the whole person [and] the Lord has judged it worthy of special gifts, healing, perfecting and exalting gifts of grace and of charity" and "such love pervades the whole of their lives" (*Gaudium et Spes,* 49). "Thus a man and a woman, who by the marriage covenant of conjugal love 'are no longer two, but one flesh' (Mt 19,6) render mutual help and service to each other through an intimate union of their persons and of their actions" (ibid, 48). All these remarks offer an ideal but rather a vague one and at first sight would not spell out to a couple what are the contents of their personal relationship or its significance. However, when we come to procreation there is a clarity and firmness which stands in contrast to the above statements. "Hence, while not making the other purposes of matrimony of less account, the true practice of conjugal love, and the whole meaning of the family life which results from it, have this aim: that the couple be ready with stout hearts to cooperate with the love of the Creator and Saviour, who through them will enlarge and enrich his own family day by day" (ibid, 50).

It is clear that, whilst Vatican II and subsequent documents have shifted towards the personal aspect of marriage, the concept of procreation still holds a tremendous attraction for the Church. Many will say at once that this is correct. Marriage is for children; what is the fuss about? The concern is threefold. First, 100 years of psychology have taught us that the welfare of children depends on the stability and happiness of the couple. Secondly, divorce is a reflection of the breakdown of personal relationships and then it is the children who suffer. Thirdly, for some couples there is an interval between marriage and the first child, and for most couples 20 or 30 years after the children have grown up.

All these factors suggest that the key to the life of the family is not the children, but the relationship of the couple. This is not to say that children are not important or precious, they certainly are. But it does mean that marriage is primarily about the life of the couple, from whose love everything else emanates. It is about time that the Church's preoccupation with procreation gave way to reality.

Reality certainly requires that life should continue but, if we believe that human life should reflect the image of God, then we need to concentrate on the relationship of the couple which reflects that image for the children. Such a redirection has also fundamental pastoral implications. One of these implications is that we need to spell out more clearly what the love of the couple implies.

In my writings I have tried to hint at how this love is recognised in the daily life of the couple. I have suggested that there are three characteristics which identify the nature of this love: sustaining, healing and growth. By sustaining I mean that the couple support each other materially and practically in the roles they adopt, but above all emotionally. In the intimacy of contemporary marriage, couples want to know about each other, to understand and be understood: sometimes without words, as they were understood by their parents, at other times after much communication.

When they reach such depths of understanding, couples touch those parts of themselves which are their wounds. When they feel safe, they disclose the wounds which they bring with them into marriage and also the new wounds which emerge throughout the marriage. They expect to receive healing from their partner. Healing may involve understanding, acknowledgment of deprivation, alteration of some fear or bad habit, or any basic change that promotes the physical, emotional and spiritual healing of the person. In fact, marriage encourages a great deal of healing which goes on unrecognised and is probably the most important source of healing in society.

Finally, there is growth. In the process of living together for 50 or more years, a couple change. What form does this change take? Physically the change is towards development and integration, with sexual fulfilment as one of the ultimate achievements. Intellectually, the inter-personal impact becomes one vital source by which intelligence is sharpened and transformed into wisdom. Eventually the couple will develop their capacity to show affection, control their emotions of anger and irritation, acquire tolerance, understanding, and a capacity to forgive and assist at times of difficulty. There is no doubt that emotional change is one of the keys to the happiness of marriage.

(2) The use of sex
Jack Dominian

The Tablet, 11 February 1984

Despite individual dissenters, Christians have traditionally taken a pessimistic and negative view of sexuality. Much of the conflict between the modern world and Christianity arises because Christianity has failed to assimilate the social and psychological effects of the sexual revolution – indeed, has misunderstood and fought them as evil. It is true that sex can he distorted and cheapened, but it can also be deepened, clarified and expanded. It is important, therefore, for Christianity to use discernment to differentiate when this is a precious gift of God and when it is trivialised by cheap distortions. What Christianity cannot do is remain aloof and persist in the tradition of 2,000 years which seeks to safeguard sex by linking it always to procreation.

As I stated in my previous article, Vatican II transformed the Church's previous attitude by placing the relationship of the couple and the procreation of children side by side. But there is no doubt that procreation is still regarded as the supreme characteristic of matrimony.

What does Vatican II pronounce about sex itself? What it says is truly beautiful, but it is limited and does not help a couple to understand deeply the meaning of their sexuality. "This love is uniquely expressed and perfected through the marital act. The actions within marriage by which the couple are united intimately and chastely are noble and worthy ones. Expressed in a manner which is truly human, these actions signify and promote that mutual self-giving by which spouses enrich each other with joyful and thankful will" (*Gaudium et Spes,* 49). But what do the couple in fact give to each other? The depths of the meaning of intercourse are not explored except in the procreative sense. And, indeed, the whole post-Vatican II history of the Church has been preoccupied with procreation and the means of birth regulation.

The fact that Paul VI removed the subject of birth regulation from consideration by the council, received the advice of a special commission but ultimately took his own decision in the document *Humanae vitae* is part of history. *Humanae vitae* reiterated the right to birth regulation but insisted that this must be confined to the normal physiological rhythms of fertility and infertility – the so-called "safe period".

The persistent unhappiness over *Humanae vitae* indicates that a deeper examination of sexuality is needed. Even couples who use only natural rhythms to regulate their fertility will find that, after they have had two or three children, they will intend the vast majority of their sexual acts to be deliberately non-procreative. In fact, after completing their family in their late twenties or early thirties, most couples will consciously plan that for the next 30 years or more their intercourse will be non-procreative.

This is where the Church – and indeed the whole of Christianity – have to face fundamental questions. What is the meaning of intercourse which is not for procreation? There is some tension in Christianity about this. Intercourse pursued for purely erotic purposes has traditionally been regarded by Christianity as very unacceptable. There are many passages in the official documents which refer to chastity, self-control, discipline. They all hint that purely erotic activity is dangerous and that control is indicated.

At the very heart of Catholic morality is the examination of what is truly and authentically human because such activity reflects the image of God in man. A couple who have intercourse are seeking to realise the highest pleasure from each other's body. This is the erotic component which has always been eyed with suspicion by Christianity. But this is not the whole story. The body becomes a source of communication. There is a body language which should be at the very heart of sexual love. Thus intercourse is a body language in which the erotic becomes the channel of communication for personal love.

Identity

What do the spouses say to each other?

First, the sexual experience is saturated with pleasure and joy and in the course of making love the couple are thanking each other. They may do this with or without words, but they are in total closeness in the process of mutual appreciation.

Secondly, the act, which, as already stated, is a source of immense pleasure, calls for repetition. This may be immediately, soon, the next day, the day after or as soon as possible. Implicit in this repetition is the hope of being wanted and responded to. This mutual trust is constantly reinforced. From childhood, we hope that we are loved; we build that hope through adulthood. The hope that God loves us permeates the whole of our spiritual life. In a truly incarnate faith, we move from the physical to the spiritual and vice versa and this is precisely what happens in sexual intercourse.

Thirdly, the couple will have conflicts and hurt each other. There will be mutual forgiveness, but some hurt will remain. In the depths of intercourse there will be found a powerful joy which will wipe away the hurt. So this is an act of forgiveness and reconciliation.

Fourthly, intercourse most economically confirms the sexual identity of each other. The man is able to make his wife feel most completely a woman and the wife able to make her husband feel most completely a man. Thus this is the recurrent way in which the couple confirm the divine image in each other as sexual beings.

Fifthly, from the very beginning of life we depend on the sense of our personhood being affirmed by those who love us. Every time a couple make love, they indicate to each other that they recognise, want and appreciate the other.

Intercourse is therefore a recurrent affirmation of each other and in a sense participates in the recurrent self-affirmation of the members of the Trinity.

All this can be summed up by saying that every sexual act gives life to the couple and on one or two occasions it gives new life.

We must, therefore, not be afraid of encouraging couples to exploit their erotic capacity, for through it they are addressing each other as persons and, indeed, finding the sense of God in the depths of their love. Chastity, discipline and control are indeed needed. Chastity should be seen as unselfish mutual attention to what pleases both, as opposed to unilateral pleasure-seeking. Discipline and control should be exercised where one person is ill, not inclined to have sex, or incapacitated. But Christianity must learn that, for married couples, chastity, control and discipline refer to quality and not to quantity. The more a couple can experience love through sex, the greater is their participation in the life of God who is love. It is about time that Christianity came to reconcile God and sex in love. If we can move in this direction, we can restore communication with a world that is waiting for such a lead from us.

When intercourse is described in these terms, the question arises whether it is legitimate before marriage or outside marriage. If it is so good and a couple find themselves in love, why not participate in intercourse? My position is unequivocal. I believe that both fornication and adultery are wrong. But my reasons are not simply the traditional ones.

Traditionally, fornication was regarded as a sin because sex should be used only for procreation, within marriage. I take the view that predominantly sex conveys love in such a unique and precious way that it needs an appropriate relationship to safeguard it, characterised by continuity, reliability and predictability. That relationship is marriage.

The same approach condemns adultery. Sex is a gift of such richness that the transient experience of adultery cannot do justice to it. In marriage, sexual intercourse becomes an expression of love which conveys fidelity, trust and mutuality, all of which are breached in adultery.

(3) The scourge of divorce
Jack Dominian

The Tablet, **18 February 1984**

I have no doubt that marital breakdown is by far the most important pastoral issue which faces the Church. I have, therefore, regretted the energy that the question of contraception has absorbed because I have remained convinced from the very beginning that the evil involved in divorce is enormous. This is not to say at all that those who divorce are evil people; rather, it is a reflection on the repercussions of widespread marital breakdown and the recognition that our Lord himself reminded us that indissolubility is of the very nature of the original creation. Something truly momentous is at stake. I am not making a special plea, merely attempting to put on paper the agony I have shared with thousands of men and women.

The seriousness of marital breakdown has in fact been increasingly noted, and in particular by the bishops at the last synod and by Pope John Paul II in *Familiaris Consortio.* So far, the wave of divorce has hit western societies, but I believe that it is only a matter of time before the Third World also will be afflicted.

The statistical evidence from Europe and the United States shows divorce increasing from about 1960 onwards. The rate has fluctuated but has remained persistently high, so that in the United States the figures suggest that one in two marriages is heading for dissolution.

The same phenomenon has been observed in England and Wales. The rise began in 1960 but took a sharp turn after 1971 when the new Divorce Act came into operation. Currently some 500,000 men, women and children are involved annually in divorce. One in three marriages is heading for dissolution and one in five of children under 16 is involved. These figures are horrendous, and there is no evidence of any marked reduction. As far as the Catholic population is concerned, one study has suggested that the numbers involved in divorce are proportionately the same as for the rest of the community.

Divorce is of its very nature a private affair and only those who experience it – or the immediate family – appreciate the vast devastation caused by it. But besides the private agony – the pain of the spouses, their ill-health, the distress to the children and possibly the long-term damage to their personalities – there is a public cost. It has been calculated by the Marriage Research Centre as £1 billion: the cost of taking children into care, of supplementary benefit, of legal proceedings, of national health service care, and of time lost to industry. Few people can really assess the impact of divorce, but something of its effect can be gauged when we see that cumulatively more people are involved than are unemployed, and when we reckon up how many suffer in their health, take drink and drugs, attempt suicide or kill themselves.

I have been amazed that all the churches have not made divorce the leading social evil of our day.

If we are to cope successfully with marital breakdown, we must understand the reasons for it. These are not local and isolated, but involve virtually the whole western society over a period which has clear and delineated beginnings in the early sixties. Sociologists and psychologists have tried to isolate these reasons.

Prevention

Some are due to major cultural shifts in society as a whole – the rise of material standards, women's emancipation and the demise of religion. As western society has gained enhanced material security – food, shelter and employment – so men and women have had time and energy to attend to their personal relationships. As material standards rose, so their expectations in marriage rose too. Couples now see marriage as a personal relationship and do not tolerate emptiness or cruelty. The growth of material standards coincided with the emancipation of women, both in terms of rights and of entry into work. Women have played a crucial role in marital breakdown as they have steadily refused to put up with the lack of love or the presence of cruelty. And finally, the demise of religion has made divorce possible for people who would not have dreamt of divorcing in the past.

I have stated that the increase in divorce will hit the developing countries in due course. The Christian churches must be on the alert for this. They are concerned with advancing the status of these countries and ensuring the rights of children, women and men, and so must not be surprised if the rise in standards results in marital breakdown, particularly as women have an increasing say in family life. The understanding and control of divorce in the West has implications for all countries.

Such are the causes on the wider stage. Within a particular society, sociologists have identified other factors which are specifically linked with marital breakdown. Those who marry under the age of 20 are especially liable to divorce: so are those who begin marriage because the woman is pregnant. Where youth and pre-marital pregnancy coincide, the couple are particularly at risk. There is also evidence that certain social classes are very prone to divorce: among them, workers like clerks and bus drivers, and labourers. Clearly this knowledge is useful in helping us to try to prevent divorce.

Pregnancy is no reason for marriage unless the couple can cope with it. On the other hand, abortion is not the answer either. We need to ensure that marriage does not overwhelm people, socially and materially.

We will further understand the reasons for divorce within particular societies if we understand the typical married life cycle of the couple. Basically, I divide this into three phases: the first five years, which often brings the couple up to 30; from 30 to 50; and lastly from 50 to the death of one spouse. Each phase has social, emotional, sexual, intellectual and spiritual aspects.

From marriage to the age of 30, the couple has to adjust socially, by setting up a home, defining their roles, taking work and earning money. They have to adjust emotionally, by developing the capacity to relate to each other, to communicate and to resolve conflict. Sexually, they must consummate the relationship and have sex lovingly. Intellectually and spiritually, they need to communicate rationally and share intellectual and spiritual values.

From 30 to 50, the main reason for conflict between them is that one partner may change in such a way as no longer to make sense to the other. The change may be in any one of the five dimensions I have outlined. Another major reason for conflict is that one partner may realise that he or she is no longer in love with the other.

Finally, from the age of 50 to death, a breakdown is liable to occur if the spouses find, after the children have grown up and left, that they themselves have nothing in common. In other words, they discover that they have lived entirely through their children, and have not formed a relationship through each other. Equally, this is the time when people are free to express changes which have occurred in their personality, which again is liable to cause conflict.

Such then are the reasons for divorce. We must exert every effort to prevent it. Little by little the Church has responded, for at the parish level the breakdown of family life is one of the most disturbing events and the sorrow of parish priests has been voiced repeatedly. The Catholic Marriage Advisory Council is probably the leading organisation for preparing couples for marriage, although we have a long way to go before we can cover all of them.

Even more fundamental is the care needed by couples after marriage. This is a new notion. Traditionally the wedding was seen as the climax of the Church's involvement with the couple and not until the baptism of the first child did the Church reappear. Now we are beginning to realise that the wedding is not the end but the beginning of marriage. As the marital relationship starts, the early years, particularly the first five, are crucial. The couple need to be supported, and every parish should have a structure for this purpose.

Many Catholics do not appreciate that in the Church there is a delicate balance between the firmness of Christian marriage and the just stipulation that a marriage should only be considered as such when it fulfils the criteria of Christian marriage. The marriage tribunals of the Church have come in for much criticism from Anglican and some Catholic sources, on the ground that they really give divorce under another name. Recently however, the Anglican Church has come to a greater appreciation of the value of such tribunals, as it struggles with its plans to remarry the divorced. The tribunals do not give annulments easily, but neither do they deny the freedom of individuals when no marriage exists. Meanwhile, the interaction between the practice of the tribunals and the reflection of theology advances the understanding of marriage. What is now needed to complete this understanding is a much greater contribution by the married whose sacrament it is.

A huge challenge

Not everyone is able to get an annulment, and so there are many divorced Catholics who have remarried. They need to remain within the life of the Church. Much attention has been given to the fact that they cannot receive communion, and the present sacramental ruling is most unsatisfactory. But Christ can be reached in many other ways, through the sacraments apart from the Eucharist, through the word and pastoral care. We must focus on ensuring that these men and women are not isolated, but remain our neighbours in Christ.

Divorce is an evil and should be fought. But we should not fight it negatively, by attacking the idea of it or those involved in it. Rather, we must recognise that generally speaking the divorced are seeking a greater expression of love in their lives. This is a goal which the Christian churches must accept; but they will aim to help couples achieve it by a much greater preparation for marriage, and continuing support after marriage, rather than by divorce. This is a huge challenge.

One way of meeting it is to create and maintain a centre for research. The Marriage Research Centre has been set up for exactly this purpose, and has deeply appreciated the help which it has received from the Church. Its task is to examine contemporary marriage and spread its findings to every corner of the Church and society in order to support the work of prevention. The Catholic Marriage Advisory Council also does research, but in a limited manner. Its main effort is to prepare, educate and counsel couples, and here it does invaluable work.

The overall challenge is overwhelming. Every diocese needs a priest to be a catalyst on the work of the Church in the field of marriage and the laity need to be involved extensively in supporting each other in their marriages. All this cannot succeed without repeated and concentrated direction from the hierarchy.

(4) Domestic sacrament
Jack Dominian

The Tablet, 25 February 1984

In the Judeo-Christian tradition, the sacredness of marriage is clear throughout the Old Testament from Genesis onwards. This is particularly expressed in the concept that marriage represents the covenant. In the New Testament, St Paul's letter to the Ephesians draws a parallel between the husband-wife relationship and the relationship between Christ and his Church. In the gospels our Lord reminds his audience of the indissolubility of marriage and performs one of his major miracles in the wedding feast of Cana. All this is evidence that marriage is steeped in the life of God.

St Augustine described the goods of marriage as children, fidelity and indissolubility. At a later stage the Church reached the conclusion that marriage was a sacrament. The goods of marriage now became the ends, and after the Council of Trent the language of marital theology was increasingly couched in these terms.

As we have seen, this legalistic approach came to an end in Vatican II, and was replaced by the idea of a "community of love" expressed in relationship and covenant. This is undoubtedly a tremendous step forward, reflecting accurately the nature of marriage as a personal relationship steeped in a loving encounter. Nevertheless, if we were to ask the ordinary married Catholic couple about their spiritual life, they would be very likely to say it was situated in their Sunday Mass, as though they met God in Church only. This is not the case. The married have their own sacrament – their married life, where they encounter Christ minute by minute. Nowhere in the relevant documents is this reality spelled out in detail. Reference is made to the family as being the "domestic church" but this idea needs considerable expansion.

At the very heart of marriage lies the fact that it is a sacrament, in which the couple encounter Christ through their unity, indissoluble commitment, and creativity. I would like to extend the notion of "the domestic church" by suggesting that in the course of this sacramental encounter with Christ the couple participate also in the other sacraments by the very nature of their married life.

If we take each sacrament in turn, we see that baptism, which is essentially the entry into relationship with Christ, is extended by the affirmation of the personal encounter of the couple. In so far as they relate to each other as spouses and meet Christ in each other, they also perpetuate their links with Christ and become reborn as children of God.

Similarly, the sacrament of penance is extended when a couple have arguments, fights, conflicts and then forgive each other and become reconciled. Confirmation is extended as the couple affirm their commitment to each other. Again, healing is something that takes place constantly within the couple, who in this way share in the divine healing.

I have left the Eucharist to the last. The Eucharist is the actualising of the redeeming reality of Jesus and the reception of his person in communion. It is the supreme sacrament. It is extended in the same way when spouses encounter Christ in each other and in their union incorporate Christ through each other. Through marriage, their own sacrament, they not only receive special graces of unity, indissolubility and procreativity but, in the course of these activities, they participate in the life of grace itself.

All the sacraments are essential links with Christ through relationship with him. If the life of the couple is an encounter with Christ, it participates in the characteristics of the other sacraments, though it cannot, of course, replace them.

Renewal

No doubt many will rush to attack this idea and yet it is precisely what happily married couples experience, and it is their experience that is of crucial importance. There is no doubt that their spiritual experience is much richer than has hitherto been realised. Justice has not been done to this. It is therefore not surprising that the married have seen themselves as in touch with God only when they attend church. The tragic result has been a split between home, work and church. I am convinced that the people of God must see the sacrament of marriage as vibrating with the presence of Christ in *their home*.

The sacrament of marriage has received very little attention over the centuries, and the time for highlighting it has now arrived. We must help people to see that their life together at home participates in the life of Christ through the sacrament of marriage and therefore has a meaning and dignity which is unique. If we are going to help people really to unfold the characteristics of their own sacrament – unity, permanency and the gift of life – then we must help them to see that their ordinary experiences are stamped with the extraordinary presence of Christ and that all this does not require any external approval because it is taking place in their home.

Some might misinterpret this as an attempt to put married people ahead of the clergy and the single who have dedicated their lives to God. Such an interpretation is always possible but it belongs to infantile power politics. The Christian community should not be concerned about who is first. It seems to me that our Lord made that clear a long time ago.

What really matters is that the laity should be helped by the clergy to realise their spiritual worth. The re-evangelisation of western society largely depends on the laity rediscovering God, and the sacrament of marriage is a cornerstone of this process.

The married are aware intuitively of their spiritual position, but not formally. They need their priests to help them appreciate in depth the significance of their sacrament. This will make demands on priests, who have been trained to act as ministers of the sacraments in church, and whose pastoral work is only beginning to integrate such ideas as I have described in this article. In addition to the present liturgical events we need a cycle of liturgy in which courtship, the early years, the middle years and the late years are celebrated annually. This would provide a meeting point between church and home.

For too long, however, the laity have sat back and expected their priests to illuminate their life and tell them what to do. The time has come when they must contribute to the understanding of their own sacrament. They need to support each other in their street, town, parish and arrange groups to share their experience and illuminate each other about the interaction between their life and Christ. There is no doubt that a spiritual upsurge of married life is crucial for the renewal of our society.

This renewal means that men, women and children have to look at their own home and to see how closely it approximates to the Gospel. They have to examine their relationship with each other and see how it compares with the love they promised each other. They have to ask themselves whether they truly appreciate what Christian marriage is and whether they have shaped their own life accordingly.

Support needed

Marriage is the sacrament of the vast majority of the laity. If they do not put it on the map and attend to it, they should not be surprised if they are ignored. I am often told that the emphasis I put on the married ignores the single and the widowed, that the parish is really for everyone, not just the married. My answer is that we are a long way from the point where the married are singled out for attention. Moreover, if we strengthen family life in a truly Christian sense, this will do something fundamental for the single and the lonely. We shall learn to open the doors to them and welcome them into family life. If married people are supported, then everyone else will gain – including priests and religious: in a truly Christian community married people should receive them and they should open their lives to the married.

The experience of marriage and married love is shared by Christians with the rest of society. It offers unique opportunities for ecumenical work and as a bridge of love through which we reach others who are not Christian. This is the one sacrament that penetrates deeply and widely in the life of the whole community. In the past we have tended to criticise others for marital behaviour of which we disapprove. Clearly we must uphold principles, but there is much we share – for example, the sustaining, healing and growth that occur in the family. In this way we can begin to talk. through love about God.

Marriage is of unique importance today. The Church would confirm its recognition of this if a bishop was appointed whose sole responsibility was for marriage matters. For it is within the "domestic church". which is marriage, that the majority of human beings are going to find themselves. love and God.

27.

MARRIAGE PREPARATION AND COHABITING COUPLES: INFORMATION REPORT

U.S. National Conference of Catholic Bishops, 1999

INTRODUCTION

Today almost half the couples who come for marriage preparation in the Catholic Church are in a cohabiting relationship.[1] Cohabitation, in a commonly understood sense, means living together in a sexual relationship without marriage. Living together in this way involves varying degrees of physical and emotional interaction. Such a relationship is a false sign. It contradicts the meaning of a sexual relationship in marriage as the total gift of oneself in fidelity, exclusivity and permanency.

Over the past 25 years cohabitation has become a major social phenomenon affecting the institution of marriage and family life.[2] It is also an extremely perplexing issue for priests, deacons and lay pastoral ministers who help couples prepare for marriage in the church.

In 1988 the National Conference of Catholic Bishops' Committee on Pastoral Practices published *Faithful to Each Other Forever: A Catholic Handbook of Pastoral Help for Marriage Preparation.* The intent of this volume was to be a resource for those involved in marriage-preparation work. It remains a very useful and comprehensive pastoral tool.

Faithful to Each Other Forever discussed (pp. 71-77) the question of cohabitation under two headings: (a) input on cohabitation from personal experiences and the behavioral sciences, and (b) pastoral approaches to cohabiting couples. In this latter section the handbook drew upon the written policies of a few dioceses to present a range of possible options for working with cohabiting couples who come seeking marriage in the church.

Now, nearly 12 years after the original work of *Faithful to Each Other Forever,* the cumulative pastoral experience of ministering to cohabiting couples has broadened and deepened. This is reflected, at least partially, in the increased number of dioceses that now include a treatment of the issue within their marriage-preparation policies.

In this present resource paper the NCCB Committee on Marriage and Family builds upon the foundation provided by *Faithful to Each Other Forever* when it first treated the question of cohabitation. The paper adopts the same two-part structure: empirical data and pastoral approaches. Its purpose is twofold:

1. To impart information that is current and relevant to all who participate in the church's ministry with engaged couples, including those in diocesan leadership who might be in the process of revising their marriage preparation policies.

2. To offer a descriptive overview of common pastoral approaches now being taken in U.S. dioceses to the various situations and issues connected with the phenomenon of cohabiting couples.

This paper is neither an official statement of the Committee on Marriage and Family nor of the National Conference of Catholic Bishops. It does not offer formal recommendations for action. It is intended as a resource paper, offering a compilation of resources and a reflection of the present "state of the question" regarding certain issues of cohabitation.

In this way, it wishes to help:

1. Bishops and diocesan staff who are reviewing and possibly revising their marriage-preparation policies.

2. Priests, deacons, pastoral ministers and lay volunteers who want to become more informed and effective in working with cohabiting couples who come to marriage-preparation programs.

3. Those who are responsible for in-service and continuing education of clergy and laity who carry out the church's ministry or marriage preparation.

As pointed out in *Faithful to Each Other Forever* (p. 71), the committee acknowledges a distinction between sexual activity outside of marriage and cohabitation. They are not identical matters. One can exist without the other. Couples may engage in sexual intercourse without living together other couples may share the same residence but not live in a sexual relationship. The focus of this paper, however, is on cohabitation understood as both having a sexual relationship and living together in the same residence. Moreover, in Part 2, the paper focuses even more narrowly on a segment of cohabiting couples, namely those who choose to move out of this type of relationship and into the life-long commitment of marriage. It is this group of engaged couples who pose certain unique pastoral challenges.

In both sections of the paper the committee has chosen a question-and-answer format in order to organize the material in a concise manner. The committee is very grateful to Sister Barbara Markey, ND, Ph.D., director of the Family Life Office in the Archdiocese of Omaha, for helping to compile and edit the first section. In order to develop the second section, committee staff collected marriage-preparation policies representing 129 dioceses from around the country. The pastoral approaches outlined in this section emerge from an analysis of these policies, from knowledge of current pastoral practice and from consultations with pastoral ministers. In particular, the committee thanks Dr. James Healy, Ph.D., director of the

Center for Family Ministry in the Diocese of Joliet, for his assistance with this part of the paper.

Finally, in the course of preparing this report, the Committee on Pastoral Practices and Bishop David E. Fellhauer, chairman of the Committee on Canonical Affairs, reviewed and recommended changes in the text. We are very grateful for their expert involvement.

PART I: EMPIRICAL INFORMATION ABOUT COHABITATION AND MARRIAGE

Those couples who are in a cohabiting relationship and who come to the church for marriage preparation represent only a percentage of the total cohabiting population. Nonetheless, to understand and respond to them one must appreciate some aspects of the broader phenomenon of cohabitation. This, in turn, is set within a context of widespread sexual activity outside of marriage. In this section we provide highlights of what social science has discovered about cohabitation in general and with specific reference to cohabiting couples who eventually marry.

1. How Widespread Is Cohabitation?

Cohabitation is a pervasive and growing phenomenon with a negative impact on the role of marriage as the foundation of family. The incidence of cohabitation is much greater than is indicated by the number of cohabiting couples presenting themselves for marriage. Slightly more than half of couples in first-time cohabitations ever marry; the overall percentage of those who marry is much lower when it includes those who cohabit more than once. Cohabitation as a permanent or temporary alternative to marriage is a major factor in the declining centrality of marriage in family structure. It is a phenomenon altering the face of family life in first-world countries.

• Eleven percent of couples in the United States cohabited in 1965–74; today, a little over half of all first marriages are preceded by cohabitation (Bumpass and Lu, 1998; Popenoe and Whitehead, 1999).

• Across all age groups there has been a 45 percent increase in cohabitation from 1970 to 1990. It is estimated that 60 percent to 80 percent of the couples coming to be married are cohabiting (U.S. Bureau of the Census, 1995; Bumpass, Cherlin and Sweet, 1991).

• Overall, fewer persons are choosing to be married today; the decision to cohabit as a permanent or temporary alternative to marriage is a primary reason (Bumpass, National Survey of Families and Households paper No. 66, 1995). The percent of couples being married in the United States declined 25 percent from 1975 to 1995. The Official Catholic Directory reported 406,908 couples married in the Catholic Church in 1974; in 1995, it reported a 25 percent decline to 305,385 couples.

• Only 53 percent of first cohabiting unions result in marriage. The percentage of couples marrying from second and third cohabitations is even lower (Bumpass and Lu, 1998; Bumpass, 1990; Wu, 1995; Wineberg and McCarthy, 1998). Ten percent to 30 percent of cohabitors intend never to marry (Bumpass and Sweet, 1995).

• All first-world countries are experiencing the phenomenon of cohabitation and the corrosive impact it has on marriage as the center of family (Bumpass, National Survey of Families and Households paper No. 66, 1995; Hall and Zhao, 1995; Thomasson, 1998; Haskey and Kiernan, 1989).

2. What Is the Profile of the Cohabiting Household?

The profile of the average cohabiting household is both expected and somewhat surprising. Persons with low levels of religious participation and those who have experienced disruption in their parents' marriages or a previous marriage of their own are likely candidates for cohabitation. Persons with lower levels of education and earning power cohabit more often and marry less often than those with higher education. The average cohabiting household stays together just over one year, and children are part of two-fifths of these households. Men are more often serial or repeat cohabitors, moving from woman to woman, while women tend to cohabit only one time.

• Forty percent of cohabiting households include children, either the children of the relationship or the children that one or both partners bring to the relationship (U.S. Bureau of Census, 1998, Wu, 1995; Schoen, 1992).

• Median duration of cohabitation is 1.3 years (Bumpass and Lu, 1998; Wu, 1995; Schoen and Davis, 1992). Previously married persons cohabit more often than never-married; two-thirds of those separated or divorced and under age 35 cohabit. They are more likely than never-married cohabiting couples to have children in the household, and they are much less likely than never-married to marry their current partner or someone else (Wineberg and McCarthy, 1998; Wu, 1995; Bumpass and Sweet, 1989).

• Those not completing high school are almost twice as likely to cohabit as those who complete college. Forty percent of college graduates, however, do cohabit at some time. Only 26 percent of women with college degrees cohabit, compared to 41 percent of women without a high school diploma. The higher the level of education, the more likely the cohabitor is to marry the partner (Qian, 1998; Bumpass and Lu, 1998; Thornton, Axinn, Teachman, 1995; Willis and Michael, 1994).

• Women are likely to cohabit only once, and that with the person they subsequently marry; men are more likely to cohabit with a series of partners (Bumpass and Sweet, 1989, Teachman and Polanko, 1990).

• Individuals, especially women, who experienced disruption in their parents' marriage are more likely to cohabit than those who had parents with stable marriages (Axinn and Thornton, 1992; Kiernan, 1992; Black and Sprenkle, 1991; Bumpass and Sweet, 1989).

• Persons with low levels of religious participation and who rate religion of low importance are more likely to cohabit and less likely to marry their partner than those who consider religion important and practice it. There is no difference in frequency of cohabitation by religious denomination; there is a significant difference in cohabitation frequency by level of religious participation (Krishnan, 1998; Lye and Waldron, 1997; Thornton, Axinn and Hill, 1992; Liejbroer, 1991; Sweet, 1989).

• In general, those in cohabiting households are more independent, more liberal in attitude and more risk oriented than noncohabitors (Clarkberg, Stolzenberg and Waite, 1995; Cunningham and Antill, 1994; Huffman, Chang, Rausch and Schaffer, 1994; DeMaris and MacDonald, 1993).

3. What Are the Reasons for Cohabitation?

The declining significance of marriage as the center of family is in large part a result of growing secularization and individualization in first-world cultures. Aversion to long-term commitments is one of the identifying characteristics of these trends and a major reason for cohabitation. Key milestones previously associated with marriage, such as sexual relationships, childbearing and establishing couple households, now occur without marriage. Individuals choose to cohabit under the influence of these cultural values but also for very individual reasons. Some are seeking to ensure a good future marriage and believe that a "trial marriage" will accomplish this; many are simply together because it seems more economically feasible or because it has become the social norm. In general, cohabitors are not a homogenous or monolithic group, however fully their general characteristics can be described. The reasons for choosing cohabitation are usually mixed: Cohabitation may be in equal parts an alternative to marriage and an attempt to prepare for marriage.

There are both broad cultural reasons and a range of individual reasons for cohabitation.

• The cultural reasons are descriptive of most first-world countries: changing values on family and decline in the importance of marriage (Bumpass, National Survey of Families and Households No. 66, 1995; Clarkberg, Stolzenberg and Waite, 1995; Parker, 1990).

• Declining confidence in religious and social institutions to provide guidance (Nicole and Baldwin, 1995; Thornton, Axinn and Hill, 1992).

• Delaying of marriage for economic or social reasons while sexual relationships begin earlier. Eighty-five percent of unmarried youth are sexually active by age 20. "Marriage no longer signifies the beginning of sexual relationship, the beginning of childbearing or the point at which couples establish joint households"

(Bumpass, No. 66, 1995). (Popenoe and Whitehead, 1999; Peplau, Hill and Rubin, 1993; Rindfuss and Van den Heuvel, 1990).

The individual reasons for cohabitation are varied:

• Fear of or disbelief in long-term commitment (Nicole and Baldwin, 1995; Bumpass, DeMaris and MacDonald, 1993).

• Desire to avoid divorce (Nicole and Baldwin, 1995; Thornton, 1991; Bumpass, 1990).

• Desire for economic security (Rindfuss and Van den Heuvel, 1990; Schoen and Owens, 1992).

• Stage of personal development, escape from home, "rite of passage" (Nicole and Baldwin, 1995).

• Desire for stability for raising of children (Wu, 1995; Bumpass, Sweet and Cherlin, 1991; Manning and Lichter, 1996).

• Pressure to conform to current mores that having cohabiting partner is measure of social success, personal desirability, adult transition (Rindfuss, Van Den Heuvel, 1990; Schoen and Owens, 1992).

• Desire to test the relationship (Nicole and Baldwin, 1995; Bumpass, Sweet and Cherlin, 1991; Bumpass, 1990).

• Rejection of the institution of marriage and desire for an alternative to marriage (Sweet and Bumpass, 1992; Rindfuss, Van den Heuvel, 1990).

4. What About Cohabitors and Marriage?

Overall, less than half of cohabiting couples ever marry. Those who do choose to marry are in some part counterculture to the growing view that it is certainly not necessary and perhaps not good to marry. Those who choose to marry instead of continuing to cohabit are the "good news" in a culture that is increasingly anti-marriage. Those cohabiting couples who move to marriage seem to be the "best risk" of a high-risk group: They have fewer risk factors than those cohabitors who choose not to marry. Even so, they still divorce at a rate 50 percent higher than couples who have never cohabited. They are a high-risk group for divorce, and their special risk factors need to be identified and addressed, especially at the time of marriage preparation, if the couples are to build solid marriages.

Only 50 percent to 60 percent of cohabitors marry the persons with whom they cohabit at a given time. Seventy-six percent report plans to marry their partner, but only about half do. The percentage of couples marrying after second and third cohabitation is even lower (Brown and Booth, 1996; Bumpass and Sweet, 1989).

• Up to 30 percent of cohabitors intend never to marry (Bumpass and Sweet, 1995).

• Twenty percent of cohabiting partners disagree about whether or not they intend to marry (Bumpass, Sweet and Cherlin, 1991).

• When cohabitors do marry, they are more at risk for subsequent divorce than those who did not cohabit before marriage. In the United States the risk of divorce is 50 percent higher for cohabitors than noncohabitors. In some Western European countries, it is estimated to be 80 percent higher (Bumpass and Sweet, 1995; Hall and Zhao, 1995; Bracher, Santow, Morgan and Trussell, 1993; DeMaris and Rao, 1992; Glenn, 1990).

• When previously married cohabitors marry, their subsequent divorce rate is higher than that of cohabiting couples who have not been previously married (Wineberg and McCarthy, 1998; Wu, 1995; Bumpass and Sweet, 1989).

• Those who cohabit more than once prior to marriage, serial or repeat cohabitors, have higher divorce rates when they do marry than those who cohabit only once (Brown and Booth, 1996; Stets,1993; Thomson and Colella, 1991).

• There is some indication that the divorce rate is higher for people who cohabit for a longer period of time, especially over three years. The data on this are mixed (Lillard, Brien and Waite, 1995; Thomson and Colella, 1991; Bennett, Blanc and Bloom, 1988).

• Cohabitors who marry break up in the earlier years of marriage. Cohabitors and noncohabitors have the same rate of marriage stability if the marriage remains intact over seven years (Bumpass, Sweet and Cherlin, 1991; Bennett, Blanc, and Bloom, 1988).

• Cohabitors who do choose to marry appear to be of lesser risk for later divorce than those cohabitors who choose not to marry would be. They appear to be the best risk of a high-risk group (Thomson and Colella, 1991).

5. What Are the Factors That Put Cohabitors Who Marry at Risk?

Individuals who choose to cohabit have certain attitudes, issues and patterns that lead them to make the decision to cohabit. These same attitudes, issues and patterns often become the predisposing factors to put them at high risk for divorce when they do choose to move from cohabitation to marriage. The cohabitation experience itself creates risk factors, bad habits, that can sabotage the subsequent marriage. These attitudes and patterns can be identified and brought to the couple preparing for marriage for examination, decision making, skill building, change. Without creating "self-fulfilling prophecies," those preparing cohabiting couples for marriage can help them identify and work with issues around commitment, fidelity, individualism, pressure, appropriate expectations.

Many studies explore why cohabitors are more at risk when they marry. The research suggests that there are two overlapping and reinforcing sources for risk:

• Predisposing attitudes and characteristics they take into the marriage.

• Experiences from the cohabitation itself that create problem patterns and behaviors.

Predisposing Attitudes and Characteristics

• Cohabitors as a group are less committed to the institution of marriage and more accepting of divorce. As problems and issues arise to challenge the marriage, they are more likely to seek divorce as the solution (Lillard, Brien and Waite, 1995; Bracher, Santow, Morgan and Trussell, 1993; Thomson and Colella, 1991; Bennett, Blanc, and Bloom, 1988).

• "Sexual exclusivity" is less an indicator of commitment for cohabitors than for noncohabitors. In this regard, cohabitation is more like dating than marriage. After marriage, a woman who cohabited before marriage is 3.3 times more likely to be sexually unfaithful than a woman who had not cohabited before marriage (Forste and Tanfer, 1996).

• Cohabitors identify themselves or the relationship as poor risk for long-term happiness more often than do noncohabitors. There is evidence that some cohabitors do have more problematic, lower-quality relationships with more individual and couple problems than noncohabitors. Often this is why they feel the need to test the relationship through cohabitation. There is the probability that some of these significant problems will carry over into the marriage relationship (Lillard, Brien, Waite, 1995; Thomson and Colella, 1991; Booth and Johnson, 1988).

• Cohabitors tend to hold individualism as a more important value than noncohabitors do. While married persons generally value interdependence and the exchange of resources, cohabitors tend to value independence and economic equality. These values do not necessarily change just because a cohabiting couple decides to move into marriage (Clarkberg, Stolzenberg and Waite, 1995; Waite and Joyner, 1992; Bumpass, Sweet and Cherlin, 1991).

• Cohabitors can allow themselves to marry because of pressure from family and others, and because of pressure to provide a stable home for children. While it is generally better for the children in a cohabiting household or a child to be born to a cohabiting couple to be raised in a stable marriage, this is not by itself sufficient reason for the marriage. While family and friends are often right to encourage marriage for a cohabiting couple, a marriage made under such pressure is problematic unless the couple chooses it for more substantial reasons (Barber and Axinn, 1998; Wu, 1995; Mahler, 1996; Manning and Smock 1995; Teachman and Polanko, 1990).

• Cohabitors are demonstrated to have inappropriately high expectations of marriage that can lead them to be disillusioned with the ordinary problems or challenges of marriage. Cohabitors generally report lower satisfaction with marriage after they marry than do noncohabitors. There is danger that they think they have "worked out everything" and that any further challenges are the fault of the institution of marriage (Brown, 1998; Nock, 1995; Booth and Johnson, 1988).

Experiences From the Cohabitation Itself

• The experience of cohabitation changes the attitudes about commitment and permanence, and makes couples more open to divorce (Axina and Barber, 1997;

Nock 1995; Schoen and Weinick 1993; Axinn and Thornton, 1992).

• Cohabitors have more conflict over money after they marry than noncohabitors do. Often they have set patterns of autonomy or competition about making and handling money during the time of cohabitation, and this carries over to the marriage. Many couples have one pattern of money handling in the cohabitation household and have not discussed clearly how one or the other individual expects this pattern to change after marriage (Singh and Lindsay, 1996; Ressler, Rand, Walters and Meliss, 1995; Waite, 1995).

• Domestic violence is a more common problem with cohabitors than with married persons, and this pattern will carry over to a subsequent marriage relationship. Cohabiting partners can have a lesser-felt need to protect the relationship while they are cohabiting because they do not see it as permanent. If this is the case, some will begin dysfunctional patterns of problem-solving. The existence of the partner's children in the relationship or stress over the permanency of the relationship are common causes of conflict and sometimes violence (Jackson, 1996; McLaughlin, Leonard and Senchak 1992; Stets and Straus, 1989).

• Cohabitors who marry are less effective at conflict resolution than those who did not cohabit. Either a fear of upsetting an uncommitted relationship or the lack of need to protect a temporary relationship can be factors that lead cohabiting couples into poor patterns of conflict resolution which they then carry into marriage (Booth and Johnson, 1988).

• Using sex as a controlling factor can be a negative pattern, which cohabiting couples can bring to their subsequent marriage. Reinforcement of negative family of origin patterns can also have occurred in the cohabiting relationship and be carried over to marriage. Both of these patterns are common issues that dating couples carry into marriage, but they can be exaggerated by the cohabitation experience (Waite and Joyner, 1996; Waite, 1995; Thornton and Axinn, 1993).

PART 2: PASTORAL ISSUES WITH COHABITING COUPLES IN MARRIAGE PREPARATION

Preparation for marriage begins long before the couple approaches the priest or pastoral minister. In his apostolic exhortation on the family *(Familiaris Consortio,* 81), Pope John Paul II strongly urges that young people be educated about chastity, fidelity and the meaning of marriage as a sacrament. Religious education, parish-based catechetical programs and chastity curricula in elementary schools are all part of this effort. The Catholic Chastity Curriculum Directory (NCCB/USCC, fall 1999), a directory of available materials that follow Catholic teaching, can be a helpful resource.

The high school years, in particular, can be a prime time for dealing with these issues when dating, and the desire to date, are foremost in the minds of adolescents. During this time they can be given the spiritual foundation that helps them to make informed, faith-filled and life-giving choices throughout their lives. With this foundation it can be hoped that couples will choose not to cohabit before marriage.

Nonetheless, we know that many couples do live together before they marry. Many pastoral ministers identify cohabitation as the most difficult issue they deal with in marriage preparation. They are faced with the dilemma of addressing a situation that is contrary to our moral principles while attempting to validate and sanctify the relationship of the couple through the sacrament of marriage (Archdiocese of Miami, "Marriage Preparation Guidelines," 1997; Diocese of Phoenix, *Marriage Preparation Policy Handbook,* 1998).

We offer the following pastoral suggestions to priests, deacons and pastoral ministers who prepare couples for marriage. They are intended to provide general guidance only, since each couple's pastoral needs and circumstances are unique. In developing these suggestions we join with many dioceses in turning to *Familiaris Consortio* for inspiration. "In *Familiaris Consortio* the Holy Father offers sound guidance," says the Miami Archdiocese's marriage-preparation policy, referring to the challenge posed by cohabiting couples.

In Section 81 of *Familiaris Consortio* Pope John Paul II points out that de facto free unions, i.e. those unions without any publicly recognized institutional bond, are an increasing concern. He recognizes that various factors can lead a couple into a free union. These include difficult economic, cultural or religious situations, extreme ignorance or poverty, and a certain psychological immaturity that makes couples afraid to enter into a permanent union.

The pope continues: "Each of these elements presents the church with arduous pastoral problems by reason of the serious consequences deriving from them, both religious and moral ... and also social consequences.... The pastors and the ecclesial community should take care to become acquainted with such situations and their actual causes, case by case. They should make tactful and respectful contact with the couples concerned, and enlighten them patiently, correct them charitably and show them the witness of Christian family life in such a way as to smooth the path for them to regularize their situation" *(Familiaris Consortio,* 81).

In the discussion below we attempt to take the Holy Father's advice and apply it to concrete questions that arise during marriage preparation with cohabiting couples. Our goal is to work through the challenges – "smooth the path" – so that cohabiting couples will be able to celebrate a sacramental marriage.

1. How to Begin Working With Cohabiting Couples Who Approach the Church for Marriage Preparation

Faithful to Each Other Forever notes that two extremes are to be avoided: (1) immediately confronting the couple and condemning their behavior, and (2) ignoring the cohabitation aspect of their relationship. In the decade following the document's publication, pastoral experience and diocesan policies have borne out the wisdom of this approach. The majority of policies and practices follow a middle way between the two extremes, one that integrates general correction with understanding and compassion.

The U.S. bishops' plan for young-adult ministry, "Sons and Daughters of the Light," points out that during marriage preparation the church connects with more young adults than at any other time outside Sunday Mass. "For some this may be their first step back into church life" ("Sons and Daughters of the Light," p. 30). Marriage preparation is an opportunity for evangelization and catechesis. The Gary Diocese points out that "this is a 'teachable moment,' and the parish priest must be cautious lest he alienate the couple from the church community. This calls for pastoral support in the couple's plans for the future rather than chastising them for the past" ("Guidelines for Marriage as a Sacrament," Diocese of Gary, 1996).

While couples need to be welcomed with the Gospel values of love, understanding and acceptance, they also need to be challenged by the Gospel message of commitment and faithfulness. *Faithful to Each Other Forever* points out that in the past pastoral ministers often overlooked the cohabitation, not pressing the couple too hard for fear of alienating them from the church. Because of the awkwardness of dealing with the situation, some chose to ignore the entire issue. Increasingly, however, pastoral ministers have abandoned this approach in favor of addressing the cohabitation gently but directly.

The church has consistently taught that human love "demands a total and definitive gift of persons to one another" that can only be made in marriage (*Catechism of the Catholic Church,* No. 2391). Since cohabitation violates the church's teaching about sexual love and marriage, church ministers must speak and teach about it. Doing so, as one diocese points out, "is an act of love for the couple in the process of spiritual growth" ("Pastoral Care of Sexually Active/ Cohabiting Couples Before Marriage," Diocese of Peoria, 1997).

How can pastoral ministers know if a couple is cohabiting? This can be a delicate situation. Very few diocesan policies offer suggestions for surfacing this issue during marriage preparation. Given the potentially harmful effects of cohabitation on marital stability, however, pastoral ministers are beginning to recognize a responsibility to raise the issue.

Certain tipoffs (e.g. giving the same address and/or telephone number) can alert the pastoral minister that the couple may be cohabiting. Some couples are quite open about their living arrangements. A pastoral minister who is sensitive but straightforward can encourage a similarly candid attitude on the part of the couple. Some pastoral ministers discuss cohabitation in general terms, noting the issues it raises and the potentially harmful effects on the marriage.

However it surfaces, cohabitation should be discussed early in the marriage preparation process. If it is not possible or advisable to discuss it immediately, it should be flagged as an issue to be addressed at a subsequent face-to-face meeting.

Some marriage preparation programs use the premarital inventory FOCCUS (Facilitating Open Couple Communication, Understanding and Study). FOCCUS now includes discussion questions for cohabiting couples, and the FOCCUS manual includes additional material on facilitating discussion with this group.

2. What Are Specific Objectives in Doing Marriage Preparation With Cohabiting Couples?

The general goal of marriage preparation with all couples is the same: to create a clear awareness of the essential characteristics of Christian marriage: unity, fidelity, indissolubility, fruitfulness; the priority of the sacramental grace that unites the couple to the love of Christ; and the willingness to carry out the mission proper to families in the educational, social and ecclesial areas (Pontifical Council for the Family, "Preparation for the Sacrament of Marriage," 45).

For cohabiting couples, a specific goal may be added: to encourage the couple to reflect on their situation and why they decided to cohabit, and to provide insights into possible consequences, factors that may present special challenges to them or put them at risk for later marital disruption. (See, for example, marriage preparation policies in the Dioceses of Rockford, 1992, Sioux Falls, 1988, and Peoria, 1997, among others).

To accomplish this second goal, the pastoral minister invites the couple to reflect on their experience of living together and its implications for sacramental marriage. The following questions (or appropriate variations), drawn from a newly developed section in FOCCUS, can be discussed:

1. Why did you originally choose to live together? How does the commitment you wish to make now differ from the commitment you made when you decided to cohabit?

2. How does your family and community feel about your living together? How do these feelings affect you?

3. What are your reasons for wanting to marry at this time? Is there any reluctance to marry? Is pressure from family or around children a major reason for marriage now?

4. What have you learned from your experience of living together? How do you expect your relationship to grow and change in the future? Does either of you expect marriage to be free from times of discontent? How well do you deal with conflict? Have you agreed on any changes in the way you will handle money after you are married?

5. Why do you want to marry in the Catholic Church at this time? Do you understand the concerns the church has had about your cohabiting situation?

6. What does marriage as a sacrament mean to you?

7. What do you think will be the largest barriers to a life-long marriage for you? How do you think you will be especially challenged by the vow of faithfulness?

After these discussions the pastoral minister may ask the couple how the information gained from the preparation process has raised their understanding of church teaching and cohabitation, and what response they will make in light of this knowledge. At this point the pastoral minister may ascertain the couple's readiness and ability to enter into a sacramental marriage.

3. What Distinctions Are Made Among Cohabiting Couples?

Some diocesan policies (e.g. Cleveland, 1988, Buffalo, 1992, Michigan dioceses' common policy) note the following differences among various types of cohabiting couples, based on the reasons given for the cohabitation. Each has distinct pastoral implications.

1. For couples who have seriously planned for marriage and who decided to live together for practical reasons such as finance or convenience, the pastoral minister can focus on their understanding of the meaning of sacrament and the commitment to permanence and stability in marriage.

2. For couples whose cohabitation seems more casual, and for whom no previous commitment seems to have been made, in addition to the treatment of commitment and sacrament, special attention is given to overall readiness for marriage and for permanent lifetime commitment.

3. For couples whose reasons for seeking marriage are more for the sake of appearance or to accommodate social or family needs, and little evidence is presented to indicate either spiritual or psychosocial maturity for marriage, a postponement of further marriage preparation, at least at this time, can be considered.

4. Should Cohabiting Couples Be Encouraged to Separate Prior to the Wedding?

Many diocesan marriage preparation policies suggest that pastoral ministers encourage cohabiting couples to separate. They recognize that this is a desirable goal to propose and to achieve – not because the church is so concerned with the fact of separate addresses but because it declares that conjugal love needs to be definitive; "it cannot be an arrangement 'until further notice'" (*Catechism of the Catholic Church,* No. 1646). Even if the couple chooses not to separate, they can be encouraged to live chastely before marriage. "They should see in this time of testing a discovery of mutual respect, an apprenticeship in fidelity and the hope of receiving one another from God" (*Catechism of the Catholic Church,* No. 2350).

The challenge to separate or, if continuing to live together, to live chastely, can be fruitfully posed at the end of a process in which the church's teaching on marriage and sexuality is carefully explained. This approach has been adopted by the bishops of Kansas, among others. They point out that during marriage preparation couples must make decisions. One of these concerns living together. Priests and pastoral ministers point out the many good reasons not to cohabit and invite couples to follow the teachings of the church. As the Kansas bishops stress:

"Ultimately, the engaged couple must make the decision to follow Christ and his church" ("A Better Way," 1998).

The Diocese of Peoria follows a similar approach. After suitable instruction, the priest must ask the couple to consider chaste and separate living and give the couple time to reflect on their decision ("Pastoral Care of Sexually Active/Cohabiting Couples Before Marriage, Appendix E).

Priests and pastoral ministers report that couples who separate often benefit from the experience. "Priests say that many couples return ... expressing amazement at new insights through living separately. The couple's experience has changed their hearts" (Sioux Falls). Separation can give the couple new perspectives on their relationship; it is also a tangible sign of the couple's free, loving decision to accept the church's vision of marriage and sexuality.

Some couples are not normally asked to separate, e.g. those with children. Ideally, before challenging a couple to separate, the minister knows their particular circumstances and why they decided to live together. A couple may have what seem to them good reasons (e.g. finances, safety) for living together. A change in living arrangements can pose practical problems. The Diocese of Sioux Falls, recognizing this situation, notes that "parishes may be challenged to help couples cope with such difficulties so that they can live apart" ("Preparing for Marriage in the Diocese of Sioux Falls").

5. If a Couple Is Cohabiting, Can Marriage Be Denied or Delayed?

1. Denial of marriage: Since cohabitation is not in itself a canonical impediment to marriage, the couple may not be refused marriage solely on the basis of cohabitation. Marriage preparation may continue even if the couple refuses to separate. Pastoral ministers can be assured that to assist couples in regularizing their situation is not to approve of cohabitation.

2. Delay or postponement of the marriage: Some diocesan policies note that in certain circumstances a postponement of the wedding might be in order. In these cases additional time might be needed to address the issues raised by cohabitation. For example a concern for the impact of cohabitation on the couple's freedom to marry could be a reason to delay the marriage until this issue is sufficiently explored as part of marriage preparation (Archdiocese of Detroit; Archdiocese of Miami).

A few dioceses point out that cohabitation may prolong the marriage preparation process because of the need to evaluate the couple's attitudes and understanding of the church's teachings on marriage and sexuality. One policy states: "If there is not sufficient awareness on the couple's part of the essential elements of Catholic teaching on the sanctity of marriage and sexual relations, and of the commitment, fidelity and permanence needed in marriage, then the marriage should be postponed until such awareness has developed" ("Preparing for Marriage," Diocese of Rapid City).

Since couples have a natural and canonical right to marriage, any delay beyond the normal waiting period for all couples is a serious matter. Care must be taken to ensure that delay is not used as a punishment for a couple's continued cohabitation. (See Bishop John D'Arcy's letter to priests of the Diocese of Fort Wayne-South Bend, *Origins,* Oct. 1, 1998.)

6. Should Cohabiting Couples Be Encouraged to Celebrate the Sacrament of Reconciliation Prior to Their Wedding?

With all couples, celebration of the sacrament of reconciliation is properly encouraged as part of marriage preparation for the Catholic party or parties. The catechism states, "It is therefore appropriate for the bride and groom to prepare themselves for the celebration of their marriage by receiving the sacrament of penance" (*Catechism of the Catholic Church,* No. 1622).

It should be noted that absolute moral rectitude is not demanded for sacraments to be celebrated. *Familiaris Consortio* offers this guidance: "The faith of the person asking the church for marriage can exist in different degrees, and it is the primary duty of pastors to bring about a rediscovery of this faith and to nourish it and bring it to maturity. But pastors must also understand the reasons that lead the church also to admit to the celebration of marriage those who are imperfectly disposed" (68). The document further points out that the baptized couple, by their right intention, have already accepted God's plan regarding marriage and, at least implicitly, consent to what the church intends to do when it celebrates marriage. It cautions: "As for wishing to lay down further criteria for admission to the ecclesial celebration of marriage, criteria that would concern the level of faith for those to be married, this would above all involve grave risks" (68).

7. Is It Possible for Cohabitation to Scandalize the Community?

Many diocesan marriage-preparation policies note the possibility of scandal. Scandal is a multifaceted reality. In society as a whole, cohabitation neither carries the stigma nor causes the scandal that it did just two generations ago. As the bishops of Kansas point out, "As society no longer adheres to traditional moral values and norms, scandal becomes less and less a concern to many people" ("A Better Way," p. 9). The burden of scandal falls not just on the cohabiting couple, but on our sexually permissive society.

The cohabiting couple is living contrary to the church's teaching on marriage and sexual love. By acting as if they are married when they are not, they risk scandalizing the believing community. It is also possible to cause scandal, however, through a lack of understanding and compassion for couples in irregular situations. Whether and how couples are welcomed can mean the difference between alienation from the church or renewed involvement.

Moreover, parents and pastoral ministers may have a different opinion of how scandal occurs. Parents who are deeply distressed by their children's cohabitation are relieved when the son or daughter approaches the church for marriage. They believe the scandal is easing. At this point, however, priests and pastoral ministers fear that the scandal is about to start. Both viewpoints have some merit and point to the need for understanding different perspectives on scandal.

8. Is a Simple Wedding Ceremony Most Appropriate for Cohabiting Couples?

A few diocesan policies suggest that a simple wedding ceremony is most appropriate for cohabiting couples. (Those policies that explain *simple* usually do so in terms of number of people in the wedding party.) This is the most common consequence of a failure to separate. One policy states that since the couple is choosing to appear as husband and wife to the community, then their wedding ceremony should reflect this choice and be small and simple. Others (e.g. Memphis) state that a large wedding raises the possibility of serious scandal.

The Code of Canon Law gives no special consideration for marriages of cohabiting couples. The general norm states that the pastor and the ecclesial community are to see that the couple has a "fruitful liturgical celebration of marriage clarifying that the spouses signify and share in the mystery of unity and of fruitful love that exists between Christ and the church" (Canon 1063.3).

The catechism states, "Since marriage establishes the couple in a public state of life in the church, it is fitting that its celebration be public, in the framework of a liturgical celebration, before the priest (or a witness authorized by the church), the witnesses and the assembly of the faithful" (No. 1663).

Some pastoral ministers are concerned that a simple celebration hinders the couple's ability to understand the communal dimension of the sacrament. They point out that cohabiting couples are the least likely to realize the involvement of the Christian community in their marriage. Having a wedding with only immediate family and witnesses simply underscores their impression that marriage is a private event. They need to appreciate the reciprocal commitment between the couple and the Christian community.

The Archdiocese of Omaha points out that even for cohabiting couples the celebration of marriage is an act of the church's public worship. It states: "The same liturgical principles and norms apply for a cohabiting couple as for any other couple. Marriage preparation for cohabiting couples should not begin with or be based upon a decision about the kind or size of the wedding ceremony that will be allowed."

CONCLUSION

Since widespread cohabitation is a fairly recent phenomenon, many pastoral ministers are still learning how to address the issue in marriage preparation. The Committee on Marriage and Family hopes that this paper provides helpful guidance, but it acknowledges that more can be done. One challenge is to provide additional formation for those who prepare couples for marriage so that they can more effectively handle the issues raised by cohabitation. Another challenge is learning how to discuss cohabitation in the various settings in which marriage preparation takes place.

Above all, when cohabiting couples approach the church for marriage we encourage pastoral ministers to recognize this as a teachable moment. Here is a unique opportunity to help couples understand the Catholic vision of marriage. Here, too, is an opportunity for evangelization. By supporting the couple's plans for the future rather than chastising them for the past, the pastoral minister can draw a couple more deeply into the church community and the practice of their faith. Treated with sensitivity and respect, couples can be helped to understand and live the vocation of Christian marriage.

---

[1] In 1995 a national study of Catholic-sponsored marriage preparation found that 43.6 percent of couples were living together at the time of their marriage preparation. The average length of cohabitation had been 15.6 months. See "Marriage Preparation in the Catholic Church Getting It Right," Creighton University Center for Marriage and Family, 1995, p. 43.

[2] In a report titled "The State of Our Unions: The Social Health of Marriage in America" (The National Marriage Project, Rutgers University, 1999) authors David Popenoe, Ph.D., and Barbara Dafoe Whitehead, Ph.D., identify the rise in unmarried cohabitation as partly responsible for the 43 percent decline, from 1960 to 1996, in the annual number of marriages per thousand unmarried women.

28.

WHAT HAPPENS WITHOUT THE NATURAL LAW
Mary Kenny

"Scandal of Single Gays' Baby Factory", splashed the *Mail on Sunday* last week. The report concerned a new service set up by the Regent's Park Clinic in London which facilitates lesbians and homosexuals in search of parenting. "Lesbians who want to become mothers are paying a clinic £190 to be introduced to homosexuals who will father their children," went the report. "The shocking new 'matching service' includes lessons in self-insemination and take-home, do-it-yourself kits for the prospective parents."

The service is already advertised on the Internet, and will appear in special gay and lesbian magazines.

Shocked? Horrified? I don't quite see how anyone can be. Indeed, it all seems to me to be the perfectly logical outcome of "the woman's right to choose" ideology which now has such widespread approval. If people have the right to terminate a pregnancy, then it follows that they feel they have the right to instigate one, by whatever means. If "personal choice", rather than conjugal love, is the criterion for conception and birth, then why shouldn't lesbians and homosexuals be accorded the same consumer choice as others?

Once you dispense with the natural law – which affirms that the transmission of human life is inextricably linked with sexual intercourse – then every single "choice" and deviation follows. It follows that the medical profession will sterilise healthy young women of 25, then expend enormous effort in assisting a 60-year-old woman achieve a pregnancy. It follows that sperm will be sold through commercial outlets, and women will shop for sperm donors much as they shop for Gucci shoes. It follows that human eggs will be traded according to need and purchased according to "choice". And it follows that homosexuals will come to believe they are discriminated against because their sexual practices are not productive of pregnancy. They will be angry and aggrieved; they will demand equality (and in the sphere of adoption are already getting it). In the fullness of time, perhaps National Health services will follow the Regent's Park Clinic and supply self-insemination kits for lesbians, from homosexuals. After all, there is a demand for it: the Regent's Park Clinic said it was responding to "a huge demand from gay people who want to become parents". There will be those who say if rich gay people can get this service privately, then it's "not fair" if poorer gay people cannot get it on the national health.

The Regent's Park Clinic, incidentally, has been carrying out private abortions for 25 years, and to my certain knowledge will perform them as late as British law allows. In a way, providing assisted conception is not only a logical extension to their services, but a smart business move. In one wing of the clinic they destroy pregnancies; in another, they create them. And there will be a fee remitted on both counts. Neat.

This is not to say, by the way, that homosexuals might not be good parents. Indeed, famous examples exist to prove the case. Harold Nicholson and Vita Sackville-West, the Bloomsbury writers, had a kindly and affectionate marriage although he was a homosexual and she a lesbian. Their sons loved them dearly and their grandchildren and great-grandchildren honour their memory to this day, as does anyone who visits Vita's splendid garden at Sissinghurst. Yet, to have their children, they did submit themselves, if you like, to a heterosexual union; and having done so, and subsequently discovered their inclinations, they maintained that union and were genuinely devoted. They were good parents and they were homosexual in orientation. So it certainly can be done: education, leisure, space and money also help, by the way. As does the fact that the parents stayed together and remained loving as a mother and a father.

Whether it is ideal to set out to give birth to, and bring up a child, in a lesbian union, with episodic, or perhaps no, contact with the father is another question. Nature intended us to be, wherever possible, raised by a man and a woman, and the natural law would not favour deliberately taking another course. People can survive odd or eccentric upbringings but whether it is selfish to create unusual circumstances for a child's birth is another matter.

Still, the gay couples in question are only following where "the right to choose" culture has pioneered. People can now have whatever they want. Study the full menu and select your choice. Everyone must have equal access to all desires and science and technology must serve these consumer wants. Not coincidentally, perhaps, the report about this new service appeared on the 21st birthday of the first test-tube baby, Louise Brown, the technique which enhanced, still further, the notion that there is no more natural law that laboratory intervention cannot alter.

29.

THE RATIFIED AND CONSUMMATED SACRAMENTAL MARRIAGE
John Paul II/Roman Rota

1. Every year the solemn opening of the tribunal of the Roman Rota's judicial activity offers me the welcome opportunity for a personal meeting with all of you who form the college of prelate auditors, the officials and the advocates of this tribunal. But it also gives me the occasion to tell you again of my esteem and to express my deep gratitude for the valuable work you perform with generosity and professional skill in the name and by mandate of the Apostolic See.

I greet you all with affection, extending a special welcome to the new dean, whom I thank for the respectful words he just addressed to me in his own name and that of the tribunal of the Roman Rota. At the same time, I wish to express my thanks and gratitude to Archbishop Mario Francesco Pompedda, recently appointed prefect of the Supreme Tribunal of the Apostolic Signature, for the long service he has rendered at your tribunal with generous dedication and with remarkable preparation and competence.

2. This morning, urged as it were by the dean's words, I would like to reflect with you on the supposed juridical effect of the current divorce mentality on a possible declaration of marital nullity and on the doctrine of the absolute indissolubility of ratified and consummated marriage as well as on the limit of the Roman pontiff's power over such marriages.

In the apostolic exhortation *Familiaris Consortio,* published Nov. 22, 1981, I highlighted the positive aspects of the new family reality such as a more lively awareness of personal freedom, greater attention to personal relationships within marriage and to the advancement of women's dignity as well as those negative aspects connected with the degradation of certain fundamental values and with the "mistaken theoretical and practical concept of the independence of the spouses in relation to each other," pointing out their impact on the "growing number of divorces" (No. 6).

At the root of these negative phenomena, I wrote, "there frequently lies a corruption of the idea and the experience of freedom, conceived not as a capacity for realizing the truth of God's plan for marriage and the family, but as an autonomous power of self-affirmation, often against others, for one's own selfish well-being" (No. 6). For this reason I stressed that the church's "fundamental duty" is "to reaffirm strongly, as the synod fathers did, the doctrine of the indissolubility of marriage" (No. 20), in order to dispel the shadow that seems to be cast over the value of the indissolubility of the conjugal bond by certain opinions stemming from theological and canonical research. I am referring to theories in favor of rejecting the absolute incompatibility of a ratified and consummated marriage (cf. Code of Canon Law, Canon 1061.1) with a new marriage by one of the spouses while the other is still alive.

3. In fidelity to Christ, the church must firmly stress "the good news of the definitive nature of that conjugal love that has in Christ its foundation and strength (cf. Eph. 5:25)" *(Familiaris Consortio,* 20) to those in our day who think that it is difficult or even impossible to be bound to one person for their whole life and to those who are unfortunately caught up in a culture that rejects the indissolubility of marriage and openly mocks the couple's commitment to fidelity.

In fact, "being rooted in the personal and total self-giving of the couple, and being required by the good of the children, the indissolubility of marriage finds its ultimate truth in the plan that God has manifested in his revelation: He wills and he communicates the indissolubility of marriage as a fruit, a sign and a requirement of the absolutely faithful love that God has for man and that the Lord Jesus has for the church" *(Familiaris Consortio,* 20).

The "good news of the definitive nature of conjugal love" is not a vague abstraction or a beautiful phrase reflecting the common desire of those who decide to marry. This message is rooted instead in the Christian newness that makes marriage a sacrament.

Christian spouses who have received "the gift of the sacrament" are called by the grace of God to bear witness "to the holy will of the Lord: 'What therefore God has joined together, let not man put asunder' (Mt. 19:6), that is, to the inestimable value of the indissolubility ... of marriage" *(Familiaris Consortio,* 20). For these reasons, the *Catechism of the Catholic Church* says, in fidelity to the words of Christ (Mk. 10:11-12) ... the church maintains that a new union cannot be recognized as valid, if the first marriage was" (No. 1650).

4. Certainly "the church, after an examination of the situation by the competent ecclesiastical tribunal, can declare the nullity of a marriage, i.e., that the marriage never existed," and in this case the parties "are free to marry, provided the natural obligations of a previous union are discharged" (Catechism, 1629). However, declarations of nullity for the reasons established by the canonical norms, especially for the lack or defects of marital consent (cf. Canons 1095-1107), cannot conflict with the principle of indissolubility.

No one can deny that the current mentality of the society in which we live has difficulty in accepting the indissolubility of the marital bond and the very concept of marriage as the *'foedus, quo vir et mulier inter se totius vitae consortium constituunt"* ["covenant, by which a man and a woman establish between themselves a partnership of the whole of life" (Canon 1055.1), whose essential properties are *"unitas et indissolubilitas, quae in matrimonio christiano ratione sacramenti peculiarem obtinent firmitatem* ["unity and indissolubility, which in

Christian marriage obtain a special firmness by reason of the sacrament"] (Canon 1056). But this real difficulty does not amount *sic et simpliciter* to a concrete rejection of Christian marriage or of its essential properties. Still less does it justify the presumption, as it is unfortunately formulated at times by some tribunals, that the predominant intention of the contracting parties in a secularized society pervaded by strong divorce currents is to desire a dissoluble marriage so much that the existence of true consent must instead be proven.

In order to affirm the exclusion of an essential property or the denial of an essential end of marriage, canonical tradition and rotal jurisprudence have always required that this exclusion or denial occur through a positive act of will that goes beyond a habitual, generic will, an interpretive wish, a mistaken opinion about the goodness of divorce in some cases or a simple intention not to respect the obligations one has really assumed.

5. In conformity with the doctrine constantly professed by the church, therefore, we must conclude that opinions opposed to the principle of indissolubility or attitudes contrary to it, but without the formal refusal to celebrate a sacramental marriage, do not exceed the limits of simple error concerning the indissolubility of marriage, which, according to canonical tradition and current legislation, does not vitiate marital consent (cf. Canon 1099).

Nevertheless, in virtue of the principle that nothing can replace marital consent (cf. Canon 1057), an error concerning indissolubility, by way of exception, can have an invalidating effect on consent if it positively determines the will of the contracting party to decide against the indissolubility of marriage (cf. Canon 1099).

This can only occur when the erroneous judgment about the indissolubility of the bond has a determining influence on the will's decision because it is prompted by an inner conviction deeply rooted in the contractor's mind and is decisively and stubbornly held by him.

6. Today's meeting with you members of the tribunal of the Roman Rota is an appropriate setting for also speaking to the whole church about the limits of the Roman pontiff's power over ratified and consummated marriage, which "cannot be dissolved by any human power or for any reason other than death" (Canon 1141; Code of Canon of the Eastern Churches, Canon 853). By its very nature this formulation of canon law is not only disciplinary or prudential, but corresponds to a doctrinal truth that the church has always held.

Nevertheless, there is an increasingly widespread idea that the Roman pontiff's power, being the vicarious exercise of Christ's divine power, is not one of those human powers referred to in the canons cited above, and thus it could be extended in some cases also to the dissolution of ratified and consummated marriages. In view of the doubts and anxieties this idea could cause, it is necessary to reaffirm that a ratified and consummated sacramental marriage can never be dissolved, not even by the power of the Roman pontiff. The opposite assertion would imply the thesis that there is no absolutely indissoluble marriage, which would be contrary to what the church has taught and still teaches about the indissolubility of the marital bond.

7. This doctrine that the Roman pontiff's power does not extend to ratified and consummated marriages has been taught many times by my predecessors (cf., for example, Pius IX, *Verbis Exprimere,* Aug. 15, 1859; *Insegnamenti Pontifici,* ed. Paoline, Rome 1957, Vol. 1, No. 103; Leo XIII, *Arcanum,* Feb. 10, 1880: *Acta Sanctae Sedis* 12 [1879-1880], 400; Pius XI, *Casti Connubii,* Dec. 31, 1930: *Acta Apostolicae Sedis* 22 [552]; Pius XII, address to newlyweds, April 22, 1942: *Discorsi e Radiomessaggi di S.S. Pio XII,* ed. Vaticana, Vol. 4, 47).

I would like to quote in particular a statement of Pius XII:

"A ratified and consummated marriage is by divine law indissoluble, since it cannot be dissolved by any human authority (Canon 1118); while other marriages, although intrinsically indissoluble, still do not have an absolute extrinsic indissolubility but under certain necessary conditions can (it is a question, as everyone knows, of relatively rare cases) be dissolved not only by virtue of the Pauline privilege, but also by the Roman pontiff in virtue of his ministerial power" (address to the Roman Rota, Oct. 3, 1941: AAS 33 [1941], pp. 424-425).

With these words Pius XII gave an explicit interpretation of Canon 1118, corresponding to the present Canon 1141 of the Code of Canon Law and to Canon 853 of the Code of Canons of the Eastern Churches, in the sense that the expression *human power* also includes the pope's ministerial or vicarious power, and he presented this doctrine as being peacefully held by all experts in the matter.

In this context it would also be appropriate to quote the *Catechism of the Catholic Church,* with the great doctrinal authority conferred on it by the involvement of the whole episcopate in its drafting and by my special approval. We read there:

"Thus the marriage bond has been established by God himself in such a way that a marriage concluded and consummated between baptized persons can never be dissolved. This bond, which results from the free human act of the spouses and their consummation of the marriage, is a reality, henceforth irrevocable, and gives rise to a covenant guaranteed by God's fidelity. The church does not have the power to contravene this disposition of divine wisdom" (No. 1640).

8. The Roman pontiff in fact has the *sacra potestas* to teach the truth of the Gospel, administer the sacraments and pastorally govern the church in the name and with the authority of Christ, but this power does not include per se any power over the divine law, natural or positive. Neither Scripture nor tradition recognizes any faculty of the Roman pontiff for dissolving a ratified and consummated marriage; on the contrary, the church's constant practice shows the certain knowledge of tradition that such a power does not exist. The forceful expressions of the Roman pontiff's are only the faithful echo and authentic interpretation of the church's permanent conviction.

It seems quite clear then that the nonextension of the Roman pontiff's power to ratified and consummated sacramental marriages is taught by the church's magisterium as a doctrine to be held definitively, even if it has not been solemnly declared by a defining act. This doctrine, in fact, has been explicitly proposed by the Roman pontiffs in categorical terms in a constant way and over a sufficiently long period of time. It was made their own and taught by all the bishops in communion with the See of Peter, with the knowledge that it must always be held and accepted by the faithful.

In this sense it was reaffirmed by the Catechism of the Catholic Church. Besides, it is a doctrine confirmed by the church's centuries-old practice, maintained with full fidelity and heroism, sometimes even in the face of severe pressures from the mighty of this world.

The attitude of the popes is highly significant; even at the time of a clearer affirmation of the Petrine primacy, they show a constant awareness that their magisterium is at the total service of the word of God (cf. *Dei Verbum,* 10), and in this spirit, they do not place themselves above the Lord's gift, but endeavor only to preserve and administer the good entrusted to the church.

9. Distinguished prelate auditors and officials, these are the reflections that I wished to share with you on so important and serious a matter. I entrust them to your minds and hearts in the certainty of your fidelity and adherence to the word of God, interpreted by the church's magisterium, and to canon law in its most authentic and complete interpretation.

I invoke upon your difficult ecclesial service the constant protection of Mary, *regina familiae.* While assuring you of my closeness, esteem and appreciation, I cordially give you a special apostolic blessing as a pledge of my constant affection.

30.

JUST THE FACTS, MAN: CATHOLICS STILL MARRY CATHOLICS

Andrew H. Greeley

For reasons that escape me, the conviction is widespread that younger Catholics are drifting away from the church. Thus an article about Catholics in their thirties in *Commonweal* [July 17, 1998] by a team of scholars associated with The Catholic University of America was headlined with the suggestion that their faith was "loosely held." More recently, Professor Scott Appleby of Notre Dame, in an address to a convocation of Chicago priests, opined that the church was faced with mass defection in his generation. Now Professor James D. Davidson of Purdue University has argued in the September 11, 1999 *Commonweal* that religious mixed marriages have increased because younger Catholics are "less attached to the church" than their predecessors.

I would have thought that the article by the Catholic University team really indicated that young people strongly identify with key elements of their heritage. Professor Appleby's apocalypse was not notably encumbered by data; in fact, available data indicate that the defection rate from Catholicism for non-Hispanics has not changed dramatically from the turn of the [20th] century (up only 11 percent). Professor Davidson's findings, however, do deserve more serious attention.

Davidson's essential finding – that more and more American Catholics are marrying outside the church – is a factoid. One ought to, therefore, search for an explanation. Professor Davidson hints at one in his discussion of mixed marriages: There is less pressure now on the partner who is not Catholic to convert to Catholicism – before, during, or after the marriage. Might the increase in exogamy (marrying outside one's faith) be nothing more than that? If, in other words, one allows for that change, might the exogamy rate across various generations or "birth cohorts" be constant? Might those Catholics who were raised Catholic be choosing Catholic-raised spouses at approximately the same rate as earlier in the [20th] century?

These questions can be answered by analyzing data from the National Opinion Research Center's *General Social Survey*. Annually, or more recently, biennially, since 1972, NORC has surveyed probability samples of the American population for the National Science Foundation (and other sponsors). Trained interviewers have talked face-to-face (not simply on the telephone, as Davidson seems to suggest) with more than 38,000 respondents of whom 9,408 iden-ified themselves as Catholic. Of these, 7,450 married Catholics, and 5,472 were currently married to a Catholic when interviewed. With a sample of the duration and size of the GSS, it is possible to compare birth cohorts from the beginning of the twentieth century with all birth cohorts throughout the century, and to measure changing patterns of behavior and attitudes. The GSS data, for example, included 520 Catholics born before 1910, interviewed in great part in the early years of the project. How does their exogamy rate compare with that of those born in the 1960s?

The first column of the accompanying table indicates the correctness of Professor Davidson's analysis. More than eight out of ten Catholics born before 1940 were currently married to other Catholics. Moreover, the rates for each cohort (using a technique called dummy variable multiple regression analysis) are significantly different from that of the 1940s' cohort. Those born before the 1940s had higher endogamy rates – that is, they married other Catholics – whereas those born in the 1950s and '60s had lower rates (though there is not a significant difference between those born in the '50s and those born in the '60s, which suggests that the decline may have bottomed out).

Catholic Endogamy Rate by Birth Cohorts

Birth Cohorts	Catholic with Catholic spouse	Raised Catholic with Spouse Raised Catholic
Before 1910	88 percent*	82 percent*
1910–19	84 percent*	73 percent
1920–29	85 percent*	68 percent
1930–39	81 percent*	70 percent
1940–49	76 percent	68 percent
1950–59	71 percent*	65 percent
1960–69	69 percent*	64 percent

* Difference from 1940–49 is statistically significant.

The question remains, however, as to whether the absence of pressure for conversion on partners who are not Catholic may account for the decline in endogamy. To answer this question one must look at the propensity of Catholics who were raised Catholic to choose as spouses others who were raised Catholic, a "pure" endogamy rate, as it were, in which there was no pressure for conversion. Fortunately, the GSS also asked questions about the religion in which both the respondent and the spouse were raised.

The second column in the table shows this "pure" endogamy rate – the propensity of Catholics who were raised Catholic to choose as spouses those who were also raised Catholic. Here the results are very different. The endogamous rate of those born before 1910 is significantly higher than the rates of those born after 1910, but, it should be noted, none of the other birth cohorts is significantly different from the 1940s' benchmark. Beginning with the cohort of the 1920s, two out of three Catholic respondents who were raised Catholic have chosen as spouses those who were also raised Catholic. Under a different statistical technique in which the religion in which the spouse was raised and age are taken into account, the correlation between year of birth and endogamy is reduced to statistical insignificance.

It would appear, therefore, that the increase in what the older *monsignori* used to call "those damn mixed marriages" is almost entirely the result of the relaxing of pressures for marital conversions. I doubt that Davidson or anyone else would want to go back to those pressures, even if it were possible – which it certainly is not.

I am prepared for priests to argue that the data do not apply to the situation in their parishes, or for laity to argue that there have been far more mixed marriages in their families. I can only respond, with respect, that they should collect their own national sample data to prove that their experiences are typical and that our data are flawed.

We cannot tell from the data how many of these Catholic/Catholic marriages were contracted in the presence of a priest. Moreover, I am skeptical about trying to manipulate *The Official Catholic Directory* to answer this question. Bad data tend to drive out good data, especially when it is relatively easy to ask a question about the subject in a survey.

Many young couples report that rectories these days greet them with hostility instead of enthusiasm when they come to apply for marriage, that registration in the parish has replaced baptism as a criterion of a right to the sacrament, that preparation for marriage has become an obstacle course instead of a celebration, and that priests or parish staffs frequently simply deny them the sacraments (for example, if they are living together), usually in direct violation of canon law. I know of some couples who simply go down the street to the local Lutheran church to contract marriage and then continue to attend Mass and receive Communion in the Catholic church. However, in the absence of data, I doubt that this strategy has become common. Most Catholic/Catholic marriages will occur in the Catholic church, despite what bitter taste in their mouths the bride and the groom might have after encountering parish staff. I agree with Davidson that more attention should be paid to young adults by the church (many parishes have no programs at all for them). I also believe that parishes should emphasize celebratory instead of rule-dominated preparation for marriage (many of which rules violate canon law).

Nonetheless, two-thirds of those Catholics who were raised Catholic and were born since 1940 (and, for the most part, came of marriage age after the Second Vatican Council) have chosen marriage partners who were also raised Catholic.

Moreover, despite all the social, economic, demographic, cultural, and religious changes in this century, the "pure" endogamy rate has not changed significantly since the 1910–19 cohort. I would suggest that these data lend support for a conclusion opposite from that of Davidson. Young people are still strongly attached to Catholicism, if in their own way. Despite all that we (bishops, priests, lay staff, lay intellectuals) have done to them, we have not been able to drive them away from Catholicism.

I realize that I am virtually the only one in the public arena of the church who holds this position. Nonetheless, the phenomenon which must be explained is not why they leave but why they stay, not why they marry those who were not raised Catholic, but why most of them marry those who, like themselves, were also raised Catholic. It is folly to try to make ecclesiastical policy without asking and attempting to answer these questions. There are several reasons which we might consider.

Religion in our society is still an important element in a person's social identity (even though the media and the academy often try to pretend that it is not or perhaps should not be). To choose a Catholic spouse protects and reinforces one's Catholic identity.

Religious affiliation is a form of what George Stigler and Gary Becker have called consumption capital: a collection of habits, customs, attitudes, and behaviors in which one has invested considerable time and energy and hence a capital that one is loath to lose or to compromise in an exogamous marriage.

Catholics like being Catholic. The Catholic stories which reflect the sacramentality and the community and are the core of the Catholic heritage are too good to give up; on the contrary, it is good to have a spouse who shares them.

Faith – which may well subsume the first three reasons.

To those who think these explanations are absurd, I can still say, again with infinite respect, derive your own explanations for the consistency of the "pure" exogamy rate.

In conclusion, I have always been astonished at the propensity of the clergy (from the pope on down) and the serious thinkers in Catholicism to believe the worst about the Catholic young people and indeed about all the Catholic laity. Granted, the young are Catholic on their own terms now. So, for weal or woe, is everyone else.

Priests seem to exult when they tell me that the latest "October count" (bad data drive out good data, just as bad money drives out good money) shows a decline in church attendance. See how bad the laity are, they seem to be saying. Not one has ever wondered what he might have done to cause the problem. Similarly, the European bishops assembled in synod in Rome this fall were busy blaming everyone and everything in sight (especially vague cultural forces) for the "crisis" in the European church without asking what mistakes they might have made.

No one seems interested in the enormous residual power which might be latent in the Catholic heritage, much less in the solid empirical evidence that this power is still strong, perhaps even indestructible.

Part IV

Contemporary Issues with Respect to Marriage and Sexuality

INTRODUCTION

The Catholic church's dogged insistence on an adherence to "the constant tradition" does, of course, create its own problems. Some of these problems result from the fact that the tradition is inherently selective and, equally important, that it is posited on a 2000-year period over which attitudes have changed but the inbred prejudices within the tradition have not, or have only changed marginally. Not only have attitudes changed, but our scientific knowledge with respect to human reproduction, human psychology, the social implications of outmoded stereotypes, and indeed to the social/physical world in which we live has expanded dramatically; in addition, our understanding of the Bible, enculturation, the prejudices that one brings to one's scholarship, and a whole range of other considerations have affected the way we approach our appreciation for the way our past influences our present.

With this in mind, a number of religious communities have issued formal apologies for their lack of sensitivity towards the cultures of indigenous peoples whom they have evangelized: the Jesuits in North America and the Oblates in Canada, for example. In addition, John Paul has issued a limited recognition of the church's errors in dealing with the Galileo affair and in the unwitting promotion of anti-Semitism; more to the present issue, the bishops of Quebec have formally recognized the role the Christian churches have played in promoting violence and discrimination against women by fostering a falsely-based hierarchical anthropological perception of what it means to be male and female, husband and wife. Recognizing that we do have a lot to learn, Eileen Flynn has suggested that the church would do well to be less doctrinaire in its attitudes towards homosexuals, lest it create a situation through lack of information that future developments may well prove to have been simply in error. Similarly, Shawn Zeller worries about the church's involvement with organizations which seem to assume that homosexual behaviour is learned rather than being innate. And Susan Ross has raised concerns about the church's traditionally male-centred approach to our understanding of human anthropology.

Clearly, to define the absolutely primary end of sexual activity to be procreation leaves one with no option in dealing with questions of homosexual behaviour. If the divine order actually requires that all sexual activity be directed towards a procreative end, then homosexual activity will by its very nature be "disordered," as the Congregation for the Doctrine of the Faith insists it is. If, however, as Jack Dominian and many other Roman Catholic professionals are now arguing, family units are primarily about relationships and sexuality is one means for reaffirming that relationship, then there is some new-found latitude to reflect more sensitively about the homosexual couple. It is not inconceivable that future generations will be apologizing to homosexual couples for the role the church has played in fostering violence against gays as a result of policies articulated with the best of intentions but posited on incomplete information.

In this light, the church's suppression of the work in which Sister Jeannine Gramick and Father Robert Nugent had been engaged in their New Ways Ministry for gays and lesbians in the Archdiocese of Washington, D.C., is a serious issue both for the church and for the gay community. The Congregation for the Doctrine of the Faith took final action against the two when Gramick and Nugent balked at providing a formal declaration of their acceptance of the church's teaching with respect to homosexual activity; the Congregation found that the teaching of Gramick and Nugent "regarding the intrinsic evil of homosexual acts and the objective disorder of the homosexual inclination are doctrinally unacceptable because they do not faithfully convey the clear and constant teaching of the Catholic church in this area." One might well wonder how, in light of the Congregation's conclusions, the church is to provide effective pastoral ministry to the gay community. Lisa Sowle Cahill and Father Robert Gahl Jr. provide opposing views on that question.

The homosexual issue is an important one both as an issue in itself and as a benchmark for the adequacy of the constant tradition. There are, however, other pressing issues that relate to sexuality and marriage in the modern world. The instance of cohabitation, for example, has risen to such a level that both the bishops of the United States and the Vatican's Pontifical Council for the Family have issued formal statements on the matter. In addition, instances of AIDS among members of the ordained ministry have often been handled awkwardly by the church; Jon Fuller provides a provocative insight into this question. And then, of course, there is the problem of a church preaching lofty doctrine with respect to marriage and sexuality while advocates of those positions are living in secret violation both of the vows they have taken and the principles they are articulating. There is a here a serious matter of institutional credibility in a society already chary of institutions.

When Rembert G. Weakland, the Archbishop of Milwaukee, published his very frank "Reflections for Rome" in an April 1998 issue of *America* magazine he provided findings whose import might well apply well beyond his diocese; indeed, Weakland's comments on sexual morality and the married life would seem to capture the present state of affairs for the church in much of the Western world and be a cause for concern about the receptivity of the church's message by the Church at large. The archbishop reports:

The largest group of Catholics in my archdiocese can be found in a kind of middle ground.... They seem to ignore much of the church's teaching on sexuality and just do not talk about it, especially about birth control. They use common sense, they say, in dealing with many of these problems, having long ago ceased believing that all acts of masturbation were mortal sins, having accepted gays as human beings to be respected and loved but having many doubts about so many aspects of gay lifestyle, being secretly sad that their children are living with partners before marriage but not wanting to break bonds with them....

Clearly, the church's voice is a crucial one crying out to be heard in a world awash in an individualistic ethic and mired in a grasping for gratification. But, as Cardinal G. Emmett Carter has pointed out, the old bromides will not do. If the church wants its teachings to be taken seriously it has to leave the old philosophical abstractions behind. It has to learn instead to converse with its people in language they can understand, speaking not from the universals of the cloister but from a demonstrated sensitivity to the actual human conditions in which real people – men and women – struggle with the practical concerns which constitute their everyday lives.

31.

A HERITAGE OF VIOLENCE?

A Pastoral Reflection on Conjugal Violence
Social Affairs Committee of the Assembly of Quebec Bishops, 1989
English Translation by Antoinette Kinlough

FOREWORD

The Church, as well as society in Quebec, is more and more aware today of the existence of conjugal violence, an intolerable problem, the gravity and extent of which have long escaped the scrutiny of public opinion. We owe it to the feminist movement and to certain individual women to have first drawn attention to this reality, which saps the dignity of so many people and undermines marital relationships.

The rise of public indignation at reports of violence inflicted on women is a sign of society's rejection of this type of violence. Wife battering is an outrageous form of behaviour but the implementation of assistance programmes creates some hope. The fact that the media as well as legal, social and community agencies are taking an interest in this problem shows that one segment of society is looking for new approaches and calling for a less violent world.[1]

Statistics do not reveal the whole extent of this reality. According to an inquiry conducted by Linda MacLeod, "every year, one out of ten Canadian women who are married or in a common-law relationship is battered."[2] The report "Une politique d'aide aux femmes violentées" published by the "ministère des Affaires sociales" states that, in Quebec in 1985, nearly 300,000 women over the age of 15 were victims of conjugal violence.[3] The experts consulted by the Rochon Commission suggested that one out of every seven women is a victim of violence.[4]

Members of the Christian community must break their silence; they must join forces with and complement the work of those associations and groups which are already involved in preventing and fighting this form of violence. This task is one of evangelization and humanization. To undertake it is to perform an essential task and to live up to the first commandment of Jesus: "Love one another as I have loved you." Christ's exhortation speaks not only to the universality of love but also to the manner in which we are to love. In every action of his life, Jesus taught us how to love: love must not be possessive; it must, instead, be respectful of the other's physical and psychological integrity, of the other's freedom and dignity.

Violence and injustice are unacceptable. To work at preventing them and at alleviating the sufferings caused by them is to actualize as well as to name our collective values and to manifest our compassion in the face of human suffering: Those who believe in Christ have no right to shirk the duty which is theirs to embody God's tender love and his concern for the oppressed."[5]

INTRODUCTION

In the month of March 1986, the Assembly of Quebec Bishops held a study session on the theme: "The women's movement and the Church." One of the twenty-eight recommendations to come out of this session stipulated the following:

"That a Commission composed of women and men of different socio-economic milieus and members of the Social Affairs Committee study every aspect of the problem of violence against women and prepare a declaration of the Assembly of Quebec Bishops on this subject."

The Social Affairs Committee was given the mandate to implement this recommendation. At its meeting of August 25, 1987, it formed a Task Force on violence against women, which it entrusted with the following mandate:

– to prepare a declaration of the Assembly of Quebec Bishops on violence against women, in which avenues of renewal would be presented in the light of the Gospel to counter existing prejudices;

– to prepare a pastoral letter for priests and pastoral workers dealing with appropriate attitudes towards the situation of women who are victims of violence.

Considering the magnitude of the task assigned to it, the Social Affairs Committee narrowed down its original mandate to focus strictly on the issue of conjugal violence. Without denying or forgetting other forms of violence, the Committee chose this course of action in order to develop a more significant reflection on a problem which is so widespread and which has such direct and obvious consequences for the cohesiveness of social and family life.

For pedagogical considerations, the Social Affairs Committee decided to present its findings, not in the form of a declaration of the Assembly of Quebec Bishops or of a pastoral letter, but rather in the form of two related documents:

– a consciousness-raising document;

– a pedagogical tool for priests and pastoral workers.

Tentative Definition

It is no simple matter to try and define what conjugal violence is, for this kind of violence takes on many forms. For the purposes of this document, we shall consider conjugal violence to be that in which the wife is the victim of verbal, physical or psychological abuse on the part of her husband or partner, and which takes place within the relationship of a couple.

A rather broad definition of conjugal violence was retained:

"A woman is a victim of violence in the conjugal home when she is battered (physical violence), threatened to be battered or subjected to violent scenes which give her reason to expect being battered (verbal violence), or else when she is humiliated by criticism, sarcastic remarks and insults which can eventually destroy her personality and self-confidence (psychological violence). The violence referred to in this context is perpetrated by the woman's husband or partner, whether the couple is married or living in a common-law situation, or whether this happens after the woman has left her husband or partner."[6]

It is a well-known fact that violence against women occurs mostly within couples and that this sort of violence takes on different forms, as we shall see later on.

Objectives of the Process

Through the publication of this document, it is the intent of the Social Affairs Committee of the Assembly of Quebec Bishops to become involved in the social struggle against conjugal violence. The Committee demonstrates its commitment by denouncing this social phenomenon and by striving to develop a greater sense of responsibility with respect to the whole problem.

This consciousness-raising document was written with the following objectives in mind:

– to help priests and pastoral workers to become more aware of the reality of conjugal violence, of all the factors involved in this problem and of the need to recognize this destructive force in our milieu;

– to initiate a process of psychological, social, anthropological, ethical and theological reflection in order to define more accurately the causes of conjugal violence;

– to single out a few leads which the Church might pursue in order to arrive at appropriate solutions.

To respond to the mandate stated above, the document is coupled with a pedagogical tool designed to:

– sensitize priests and pastoral workers to the phenomenon of conjugal violence;

– elicit on the part of these people a response which will lead them to question their own attitudes, behaviour and prejudices;

– enable them to look at conjugal violence from the standpoint of the Gospel and to develop a pastoral approach;

– encourage them to acquire new skills along the lines of a helping, communal approach to women who are victims and to men who are violent.

This tool intended for clergy and pastoral staff should help them to support those who speak out against conjugal violence, to facilitate the detection of violent situations and to encourage the creation of more adequate services to both victims and aggressors. For it is in the reality of every day life that a timely intervention can help a woman trapped in a violent situation to break out of her silence and seek the help she needs from existing resources in a spirit of autonomy and self-respect.

The Consciousness-Raising Document

The consciousness-raising document, which is the theoretical part, does not offer an exhaustive study of the phenomenon of conjugal violence. Instead, it gathers together the most significant research conducted in our milieu and a synthesis of the findings which are generally accepted regarding this phenomenon. The ecclesial and pastoral aspect will be dealt with in the light of history and Gospel principles in which are the foundation of any action to be taken by Christian communities.

To nourish their reflection and help them get a better grasp of every facet of this problem, the members of the Task Force called on the cooperation of many people.

They consulted with resource persons (see Annex 1) in order to identify more clearly the different aspects to be developed:

– bible and theology,

– sociology and anthropology,

– real life experiences of intervention in women's shelters,

– pastoral experiences of diocesan contact persons for the status of women.

Through their competence and the quality of their experiences, these resource persons provided new paths of reflection and compelled the Task Force to examine more thoroughly certain aspects of the question.

A summarized report of these consultations and the analysis of a considerable amount of literature on the subject supplied the basic materials for putting together the consciousness-raising document on conjugal violence.

The Pedagogical Tool

Besides presenting a consciousness-raising document on conjugal violence, the Task Force decided to develop a tool to help assimilate the theoretical document, based on the well-known educational method "see, judge, act."

This pedagogical tool is in the form of a workbook to be used during the sessions to initiate participants into a process of conscientization and learning. Without claiming to turn these people into specialists in dealing with problems of conjugal violence, it seems important to equip more adequately those engaged in pastoral work to enable them to understand the mechanisms of conjugal violence, question their own prejudices and attitudes towards this phenomenon and acquire certain intervention skills.[7]

Content of the Consciousness-Raising Document

Having defined the general outlook and described the process, we shall now introduce the three major chapters of this document. First, the *Basic Information* in which we describe the different types of violence, its escalation, its cycles and its consequences for the family.

A second chapter discusses the *Causes of Violence* seen as an individual and social problem recorded in the pages of history, born of the patriarchal system and reinforced by economic structures.

A third chapter offers *Pathways Towards Solutions* for all Church communities. Even if this document is primarily addressed to priests and pastoral workers, it is also intended to challenge any person who is actively involved in society and in the Church. Our hope is that it reaches all social groups concerned to encourage them to continue developing the necessary services; we also hope it reaches government agencies working to shape and articulate policies regarding this issue.

BASIC INFORMATION

For centuries a hidden wound and a taboo, violence against women is now talked about openly. The outcry and activity of the feminist movements have raised the awareness of vast segments of society.

Although the phenomenon of violence is acknowledged, its individual victims continue to remain invisible for fear of being labelled, for fear of the aggressor, for shame, confronted as they are by the forces of prejudice. Even though many of them do call on existing resources (when they can find any), a large number continue to suffer violent treatment in isolation and guilt.[8]

1. Who is the Woman Victimized by Violence?

In her study, Linda MacLeod describes the battered woman as:

"...one who has lost her dignity, her autonomy and her security, who feels like a prisoner without any protection, being directly assaulted, either continuously or repeatedly, by physical, psychological, economic, sexual or verbal violence."[9]

The battered woman is also:

– one who seeks help in times of crisis but finds herself faced with friends, relatives, professionals (doctors, police, social workers, priests and pastoral workers) who, by their words and attitudes, ask that she defend her credibility and justify such behaviour of hers which may (consciously or unconsciously) have provoked the violence, while they fail to perceive through "the language of pain"[10] her crying need for safety and the expression of her despair when she tolerates the violence which is destroying her;

– one who finds herself faced with professionals who back away from offering any help out of respect for her privacy and who, without any discernment, seek to preserve the family unit at the cost of condoning the violence as inevitable.

2. Types of Violence

There are four types of violence which women suffer at the hands of their partners:[11]

– psychological violence, which consists of degrading the other as a person, humiliating her through criticism or sarcastic remarks, or using crude behaviour;

– verbal violence, which consists of intimidating the other by threats of physical aggression or by insults;

– physical violence, which consists of physically assaulting the other by pushing or striking her, causing her wounds, burns, bruises, fractures, and even death;

– sexual violence, which consists of forcing the other to have sexual relations in a climate of fear or under threat of physical violence, by what amounts to conjugal rape.

When psychological, verbal, physical or sexual assaults are set off by trivial domestic quarrels or passing outbursts of anger, does this mean that these are disturbed people likely to perform irrational acts? No, such behaviour is that of normal men. The Rochon Commission notes that, with rare exceptions, wife abusers "are not characterized by any particular pathology."[12] Nor are the assaults caused by an argument that has taken a bad turn. These forms of behaviour, which can be serious and frequent, are the outcome of being carried away by the escalating cycle of violence. The blows are often serious. In one out of three cases, medical care is needed[13] and 20% of the homicides committed in Canada are perpetrated by spouses taking their grievances out on each other. In practically every one of these cases, what we have is a husband who has killed his wife.[14]

To these four types of violence, which are now widely recognized, we will add the social violence generated by patriarchy, structures and institutions:

– patriarchal, structural and institutional violence consists in perpetuating those stereotypes, prejudices and warped visions of reality which discredit women or subject them to male domination. Social violence also consists in the laws, policies, regulations and general organization of society which maintain women in a state of dependence and exploitation.

Recognizing violence and looking for effective ways to reverse its course requires an understanding of its progression, its cycle and the lived experience of all members of the family. These processes and their consequences for the people concerned will be described in the following section.

3. Escalation of Violence[15]

Ginette Larouche notes that it is only gradually that violence becomes part of the life of a couple. In most cases, it worsens with time. It may escalate rapidly or it may take months or even years before coming to a head. Too often, the victims deny it or accept it as a disagreeable element of their lives, until a new development occurs which makes the violence unbearable. The intervals between two onsets of violence, sometimes experienced as loving respites, can lead the persons involved to relax their vigilance and prevent them from recognizing the violence and taking action to control it.

The following diagram by Ginette Larouche enables us to visualize the escalation.[16]

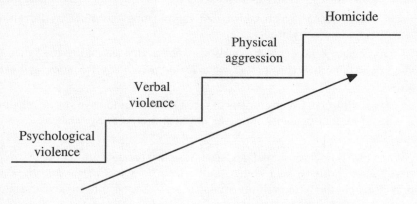

Violence generally begins with psychological attacks disparaging the person for what she is, for what she says and for what she does. Verbal abuse, insults and threats often precede physical aggression. The latter becomes more severe as time goes on.

When physical violence is part of the pattern of a couple's relationship, we can be sure that the other forms of violence exist. The study done by Hofeller (1982) shows that 44% of aggressors say they lose contact with what is going on at the moment of the physical assault and are not even aware of the blows they deliver.[17]

One can understand, therefore, that such a loss of self-control helps increase the cruelty of the treatment while providing the aggressor with a convenient excuse for appealing to his wife for clemency. The excuse of "a moment of madness" only serves to secure his control over her and to lift the burden of guilt from his shoulders. Moreover, what is quite revealing of the aggressor's "self-interest" is the fact that he never feels the urge to go to a therapist for help to prevent him from ever again experiencing such a loss of control. On the contrary, he continues to have relapses until his wife leaves him.[18]

4. Cycle of Violence

Walker describes three phases in the cycle of violence.[19]

4.1 Phase One: Tensions Build

– <u>starting from elements which trigger violence</u>: alcohol, stress, pregnancy, etc.;

– <u>starting from incidents or conflicts between the partners</u>;

– <u>starting from scenarios which are conditioned by the violence</u> experienced by the man in his original family and often reinforced by his own adult experiences;[20]

- <u>starting from a process of socialization</u> patterned after economic relations, social role models and sexual stereotypes ascribed to one sex or the other.

4.2 Phase Two: Explosion and Aggression

– <u>characterized by the man's loss of self-control,</u> a phase which may vary in length from a few minutes to twenty-four hours;

– <u>characterized by a reinforcement of the act of violence</u>; for the woman is in a state of panic and, to ward off the blows, she yields to her partner's demands or tries to remove the source of his irritation. "It is essential to consider the reinforcement stage in order to understand the repetitive and, at the same time, self-righteous nature of the abuse which women endure from their partners."[21]

– <u>characterized by varying reactions on the part of the women involved</u>. Some women react with anger and violence. In the great majority of cases, women are soon reduced to a position of self-defence. They lack the physical strength of the men. Since women have usually not been educated to use their strength, their reaction is generally to protect themselves and to seek shelter of some sort. Often left in a state of shock, many women try to reassure themselves by minimizing the damage, or by rationalizing or excusing their partners' behaviour, even going so far as to deny the violence of which they are the victims.

Later on, the wave of shock caused by the assault subsides, only to make way for the third phase.

4.3 Phase Three: Reconciliation and Remission[22]

– <u>characterized, for the majority of violent men, by feelings of guilt and remorse</u>, which may be expressed by apologies or affectionate behaviour, presents or other pleasing deeds. For example: he will suggest an outing, offer some flowers, give a child the bicycle he had been promising for a long time;

– <u>characterized by the reinforcement which it gives the victim in her intent to keep the couple together</u>. The hope associated with this period of the cycle leads the battered wife to forget or even deny the tension she has lived through. "He has changed, he is sorry and he will not do it again." Helped by his own defense mechanisms against his feelings of guilt, the aggressor uses his wife's denial and minimization of the event to resolve his inner discomfort. He will say, for instance: "Everything is fine; she still loves me; let's forget the past and start all over," or "I didn't really hurt her, she shouldn't have said or done such or such...", and when all is said and done, it is the victim who takes the blame for the act of violence. Since the aggressor has done nothing to get hold of himself and learn a better way to communicate, the cycle of violence starts again with a new buildup of tensions;

– <u>characterized by the decreasing length of the periods of remission</u>. They may extend over several days, several weeks or even months. However, the length of these periods gradually becomes shorter as the number of relapses into violent behaviour increases.

A good grasp of the three phases of the cycle of violence enables us to understand why it is so difficult to obtain any involvement from the victim outside the period of shock which occurs after the assault.

The Cycle of Violence[23]

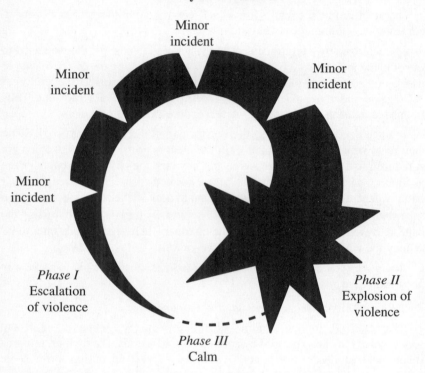

Women who have been victims of violence need time to understand this cycle. Before reaching out for help, most of them will have gone through the complete cycle many times.

It is usually within forty-eight hours after the assault that the victim first takes the initiative of asking for help. Help must be available immediately when requested, as soon as the victim indicates her intention to escape from the aggressor, for she is then in a most vulnerable position. Experience in emergency shelters shows that the very fact of asking for help puts the victim in danger.

Consequences of Violent Behaviour

Communication of a violent nature undermines the very foundation of human development, both that of the aggressor and that of their victims. Their need to be respected, considered and loved is overrun by feelings of failure and guilt and replaced by a state of ambivalence in which love and hate are closely intertwined and confused. Conjugal violence also has an impact on the children, who sometimes continue to suffer the physical and, above all, the psychological aftermath.

5.1 For the Woman

Upset emotionally and physically, she is often left to struggle with:

– physical wounds: According to Kérouac's study of battered wives, more than half of them had bruises; approximately one out of ten had suffered lacerations, and close to one third had serious wounds such as fractures, cuts and burns;[24]

– pervasive feelings of apprehension or intense fear at the thought of being attacked again. The Rochon Commission reports that "all the experts consulted emphasized the problems of stress, anxiety and depression experienced by these women. This observation is supported by the findings of a study of Montreal shelters;[25]

– loss of self-esteem. Some women, who see themselves as the barometers of the emotional stability of the couple, take more than their share of responsibility for the breakdown of the family. They say to themselves: "Somewhere along the line, I must have done something wrong;"

– withdrawal into passivity and paralysis leading her to a state of learned helplessness. This psychological condition brings the woman to believe that there is absolutely nothing she can change in the events which affect her; no matter what she says or does, she is convinced that the situation cannot be changed. Gradually, she gives up defending herself or trying to do anything about it and settles for the victim's role, adopting submissive, self-reproaching attitudes.[26] She will even look upon the violence as normal and adjust to it as a means of survival. The cost to her is very high, for living in such an environment leads to a sense of interior emptiness and to feelings of degradation and despair;

– pressures from people around her who do not believe her and who even blame her, advising her to use a different approach with her partner;

– the temptation to turn to alcohol or drugs, or escape by attempting suicide. As a result of serious bouts of depression, many need psychiatric treatment. Despite controversies over the figures, all studies show that the longer the violence lasted, the higher is the rate of these kinds of consequences;[27]

– the urge to retaliate with violence, to defend herself and her children. Living in an environment in which the threat of violence is always present, she too ends up using it as a means of control;

– the need to completely reconsider her future, for she is faced with failure in that which had been her fondest dream, namely, to have a happy family. Her whole life had revolved around this ideal.

5.2 For the Man

The violent man also pays the price for his own actions:

– he feels even more contemptible, frustrated, guilty and isolated, and has a very poor self- image. His problems have been part of his psychological makeup long before the violence erupted. Even if he denies all responsibility, he knows what he has done is wrong, but he is unable to express anger in any other way;[28]

– he associates self-affirmation with violent behaviour. Having lost touch with the whole gamut of his emotions, he knows no other way but anger to relieve his tensions and handle his conflicts. The more he resorts to violence, the more beset he is by the need to be loved and by feelings of fear and distress, and the more he seeks to control his wife. "Slowly, she becomes the one to manage his emotions, which he never was able to do; he transfers onto her the responsibility for his joys, his pleasures, his sorrows and his anger. She is made to take the blame for everything that happens to him;"[29]

– he cuts himself off, little by little, from the possibility of experiencing any real intimacy with his wife. When love is conditioned by fear it becomes servile, devoid of true relationship and unfit to gratify anyone;

– he slips into compulsive behaviour, for violent behaviour has physiological consequences for the one who indulges in it;

– he ends up having a criminal record if declared guilty by a court of law. There are men who jeopardize their professional future in this way;

– he loses his family in the case of separation, divorce or imprisonment.

5.3 For the Children

Children also are big losers in violent situations. Whether they are victims or witnesses, the pain and consequences which they suffer cannot be measured. Many studies show that:[30]

– they suffer from the atmosphere of tension which exists in their homes and are profoundly marked by having witnessed scenes of violence or by having themselves been the targets of ill-treatment on the part of their fathers or mothers;

– boys who grow up in families where there is violence have more adjustment and behaviour problems than others;[31]

– boys tend to use violence to handle their conflicts with their siblings or peers. Adolescents become violent either to defend their mothers, or to join in the abuse inflicted on them.[32] One may wonder why boys reproduce violent patterns of behaviour once they reach adulthood, while this happens less frequently in the case of girls. This may be seen as an indication that violent behaviour is not simply an hereditary mechanism, but that it also results from a differentiation in the process of socialization.

– boys who suffered physical abuse as children become violent when they reach adulthood in 61.7% of cases.[33] Helpless witnesses, they absorb these forms of behaviour and learn to see them as normal means of communication. Very likely, they will approve of them and reproduce them in their adult lives;

– 33% of battered wives were abused as children[34] and 35.1% of women who are victims of aggression witnessed violent behaviour in their original families.[35] These statistics confirm the theory that girls who were battered and who witnessed violence as children become adults with patterns of behaviour which are typical of victims.

CAUSES OF VIOLENCE

Before looking for solutions or attempting to prevent and counteract conjugal violence, we need to examine its causes and recognize in ourselves some of its features. To do this, we shall first go to the roots of conjugal violence, and then, look at some of the ways in which it is reflected in our speech and in our social and ecclesial structures. Next, we shall examine two analytical approaches which seem the most significant to us: one which looks at violence as an individual problem, and one which studies it as a social problem.

1. Violence, a Problem Deeply Imprinted in History

The Book of Genesis opens with these words:

"God created man in his image; in the divine image he created him; male and female he created them." (Gn 1,27)

"In creating the human race "male and female", God gives man and woman an equal personal dignity, endowing them with inalienable rights and responsibilities proper to the human person."[36]

Yet, how many civilizations over the course of history have taken it upon themselves to amend God's original plan! Even now, in our own world, conjugal violence is still a cause for great concern because it has roots which are deeply imbedded in history. Supported by a whole hierarchical system of social, political, economic and religious structures, it has endured throughout the centuries and in every civilization. The interplay between these structures has established and maintained male dominance. The problem of wife battering originates in the social and cultural belief that women are less important, that they are worth less than men and are not entitled to the same status and respect as men are.

1.1 In the Old Testament

The concept of the personal and social inequality of man and woman founded on the myth that Eve was formed out of Adam's rib (Gn 2) has, for centuries alas! been transmitted through a negative interpretation of the Creation narratives in the opening chapters of Genesis. The findings of contemporary exegesis have set the record straight, showing that, on the contrary, these texts present woman as equal to man, created with the same dignity and for the same destiny.[37] Male domination, which begins to appear in chapter three of the Book of Genesis, is a result of the sin committed by the couple, and not as part of God's original plan.

There are, however, numerous stories of the Old Testament which testify to the deplorable condition of women. Stripped of all autonomy, objects of lust, contempt and violence, women were frequently made to endure terror, loneliness, abandonment, mutilation and even death: such was the case of Hagar (Gn 21,9-11), of Tamar, sister of Absalom (2 Sam 13, 1-22), of the unnamed concubine of the Levite of Ephraim (Jg 19,1-30) and of the daughter of Jephthah (Jg 11,29-40).

Yet, the Book of Deuteronomy curses him "who slays his neighbour in secret." (Dt 27,24) But "Who is my neighbour?" This question resounds even in the New Testament (Lk 10,29) and still in our day when, not so long ago, "it was not a crime to beat one's wife." Obviously, women were not considered "neighbours" to men, a fact which reveals a whole concept of humanity. The Old Testament reflects an age which had not yet adjusted its mores to the emerging revelation of a God who rejected injustice and violence.

1.2 In the Hebrew World

"Even though the Law of Moses applied some restraint to the father's unlimited power, and the fourth commandment restored equality between mother and father,"[38] the Hebrew world considered the wife to be the exclusive property of her husband, no different, sometimes, from his material possessions. (See the verb "to belong" in Ex 20,17 and Dt 24,2.) A woman was treated as a perpetual "minor" under the guardianship of her father, her brother, her husband or her husband's brother. (Dt 25,5-6) There was no place for her except in domestic duties; she acquired social status solely through her sexual functions as wife and mother, and not through her personal worth or basic dignity as a human being. Denied access to any kind of learning, even of the Torah, women were not allowed to speak in public, not even to their husbands. Their testimony was not admissible in a court of law and they had no say whatsoever in political decision-making. In the Temple, women could not enter the court of the Israelites and even less the sanctuary where sacrifices were offered.

It was in this context that Jewish men would thank God every day, saying: "I give you thanks for not making me a pagan, a woman or an ignorant man."[39] It was in this social and cultural environment that Jesus carried out his ministry.[40]

1.3 In the New Testament

The New Testament certainly opens for women the way to freedom and dignity. Jesus brings grace "to renew all things." Through his work of liberation, Christ restores the original order according to which human beings are created in the image of God. Destined as they both are to be united with the Creator, men and women are equal in their calling to the dignity of the children of God. Jesus gave back to the wife her rightful honour and made her equal to her husband when he declared, for instance, that husbands may not repudiate their wives any more than wives may repudiate their husbands (Mk 10,11). He restored to health the woman who suffered with a hemorrhage (Mk 5,25-34) and fought against those laws on ritual impurity which weighed so heavily upon women; he disrupted the observance of the Sabbath to cure the bent woman (Lk 13,10-17), enabling her to stand up straight again; he defended the adulteress who was accused alone, while her partner went free (Jn 8,1-11). More importantly, he involved women in his work of liberation, among them Mary Magdalene and the women disciples who constantly walked with him along with the Twelve (Lk 8, 1-3; Mt 27,55-56; Mk 15,40-41).Witnesses to the Resurrection, they were sent to announce the Good News (Mt 28,10; Jn 20,17). "In a deeper sense, Jesus judges women by their faith, and not primarily by their ability to perform as wives, mothers and homemakers."[41]

Jesus singled out in a very special way in his teaching those who, like battered women, are vulnerable and disadvantaged: those without a voice, without power, without help, and not at models, roles and statutes, he looked at the totality of their existence and allowed them, women in particular, to go forward, to grow and to live.

1.4 In the Early Christian Communities

In the early Church, Saint Paul acknowledged the work of liberation which Jesus had initiated. To him we owe this key verse:

"There does not exist among you Jew or Greek, slave or free man, male or female. All are one in Christ Jesus." (Gal 2,28)

However, other verses of his letters, reflecting a rabbinical influence, and some of his instructions conditioned by his own and his communities' cultural backgrounds have been used in support of sexual stereotypes, which prevailed over the new spirit in Jesus Christ. In subsequent centuries, the significant part played by women in the establishment of the early churches, as evidenced in the accounts of the New Testament, was obscured.

1.5 In the Period of the Fathers of the Church

To the authority of Paul the Apostle was added that of the Fathers of the Church, heirs to the same sexual stereotypes. Likewise men of their time, they failed to see the contradiction between the Christian message of the equality of men and women and the deplorable inferiority of the social condition of women. They explained the latter as a natural deficiency and a consequence of the guilt of Eve, blaming women for all the tribulations of the human race since original sin, including the crucifixion of Jesus Christ. Such harsh judgments, supported by biblical texts quoted out of context or belonging to an earlier stage of Revelation or to one not yet fully understood, have influenced theology ever since.

Based on the patristic exegesis of the Pauline texts about women, Gratian wrote that the state of slavish subjection allotted to women is founded on this verse of the letter to the Ephesians: "Wives should submit to their husbands in every-thing." (Eph 5,24)[42]

In the Middle Ages, the Church as well as the State gave husbands the legal right to inflict corporal punishment. There were laws which specified in which cases of bad conduct women could be severely beaten with a whip or a stick, and in which cases a moderate chastisement was in order.[43] Some within the Church went so far as to demand that this be done with dignity!

1.6 From the Renaissance to Our Day

The Renaissance failed to improve the lot of women. Society still believed that, good or bad, women needed a good beating. Molière testified to this in the seventeenth century and his voice carries through to our own day.

According to Badinter, "patriarchy is not merely a system of sexual oppression. It is (first of all) the expression of a political system which finds support, in our societies, in a theology of some sort. Depending on whether the going theology was authoritative or tolerant, respectful or not of individuals, patriarchy has had different faces in the course of history, ranging from the worst to the merely tolerable. For example, in the seventeenth century, Catholic monarchies wielded power more harshly than the great Protestant countries."[44] Their keyword was submission!

Throughout the course of history, through revolutions and reforms, men have sought to build a new world founded on equality and liberty. Their plan, however, which was initially political, and then, economic and social, was only intended for their own benefit. They fought to gain rights from which women were excluded for a long time. In France, "while the ideal of the Revolution placed formal equality above natural differences, sex remained the ultimate criterion of distinction. Jews were emancipated by decree on September 27, 1791; Black slavery was abolished on February 4, 1794; but in spite of efforts on the part of a few individuals, the condition of women was not transformed. Natural human rights deriving from the very fact of their personhood were denied them."

Badinter goes on to ask: "What need did they have to vote, to be educated or protected like men in their places of work? Equality could not break through the barrier of sex..." The Convention (which followed the French Revolution) opposed women's right to vote, forbade them to form any kind of association and sent them back to their homes, alleging that "each of the sexes is called to a specific type of occupation..." For, while most men attempted to rid themselves of political patriarchy, they sought to maintain family patriarchy, as can be inferred from this seventeenth century warning repeated by conservatives and by the Church: "...by fighting for more freedom and equality, you attack the father's authority and undermine the foundation of the family..."

It took two more centuries before women began to bring their fathers and husbands to admit that they too are part of the human race, entitled to share in the same rights and duties as their partners." Indeed, the first law ever to forbid using force against one's wife dates back barely one century (1890). It was only in 1929 that women in Canada acquired the legal status of persons, and in 1940 in Quebec that they finally obtained the right to vote. On both sides of the Atlantic, the feminist movement had worked at this with determination.

The law, however, failed to eliminate conjugal violence. Both the Church and the State were reluctant to take effective action on this problem out of fear of violating in any way what they considered to be the sacred character of marriage and the privacy of the couples

The 1968 Federal Divorce Act stipulated that physical and mental cruelty were sufficient grounds for divorce. Later, the principle of spousal equality was introduced by the "Office de révision du Code civil;" and finally, the Charter of Rights and Freedoms condemned all discrimination based on sex. Some of the restrictions of the past seem laughable to us... and yet, in spite of laws and changing attitudes, the "macho" spirit is still alive and well!

2. Violence as an Individual Problem

The individual approach to violence emphasizes those factors which trigger violent behaviour, and those which exist because of attitudes transmitted from one family generation to another.

2.1 Provoked by Triggering Factors

Alcoholism, drug addiction, stress caused by unemployment, poverty or the expectation of a new child in the family can, indeed, perturb family life to the point of provoking various forms of conjugal violence. This individual approach analyzes the problem on the basis of pretexts – called triggering factors – which are not, in fact, the fundamental causes of conjugal violence.

Alcohol is related to a good number of cases of wife battering: 50% according to MacLeod. Nevertheless, the belief that alcohol generates abnormal behaviour too often provides the easy excuse to condone acts of violence. "In other words, a man does not beat his wife because he is drunk; he drinks in order to justify the fact that he beats his wife."[45] The potential for violence is already a problem for this individual, whether or not he has had a drink. Not all alcoholics are violent people.

Too often we tend to think that violence exists only among the disadvantaged, who are faced with such problems as unemployment, illiteracy, etc. Surveys conducted in recent years show clearly that there are battered women in every kind of environment.[46] They can be found in wealthy homes, in situations where both spouses work, in all races and nationalities, at all ages and regardless of whether or not a couple has children.

Some will stress provocation as the triggering factor. The victim then becomes the tormentor, who verbally and endlessly harasses the aggressor until he loses all control of himself and retaliates with blows. This approach blames the victim for the assault, giving the aggressor the excuse of self-defence. Such a view of conjugal violence limits the problem to a few individual cases, while statistics show that, in Canada, one couple out of ten lives in this sort of warped relationship.[47]

2.2 Linked with Fundamental Attitudes Transmitted by the Parents and the Social Environment

We recognize the vital influence of what we learn at an early age and of our first significant affective relationships. Depending on whether we live these experiences in an environment where control and force prevail, or in one that thrives on mutual respect and understanding, we develop differently as individuals, with different ways of relating to others. How many children learn to accept family violence as a fact of life and hence, to justify men's violent treatment of women? These children become adults burdened with unmet needs, ill-equipped to express their feelings and frustrations. They know no other means but violence to express their anguish. Thus another link is forged in an endless chain.

Statistics gathered from most studies confirm the following facts: 50% of wife batterers were battered as children, compared with approximately one third of their wives;[48] 52% of aggressors witnessed violent behaviour in their original families, compared with 31.5% of their wives.[49]

Too frequently, conjugal violence is minimized by being presented as a personal problem, an individual case of deviant behaviour. It has even been made the butt of jokes, trivializing its seriousness. This problem is too heavy with consequence to be made a laughing matter. It is much more than a personal dilemma or the result of an occasional crisis. It is a way of life perpetuated through our families, our beliefs, our traditions and our institutions. As we have seen earlier, it has causes which are rooted in our history.

3. Violence as a Social Problem

The second approach reveals the existence of social reinforcement based on sexual differentiation and on inadequate visions regarding love and the family. Social reinforcement also comes from the political, legal, social and ecclesial structures, which are closely connected with patriarchy and the economic system.

3.1 Generated by Patriarchy

Patriarchy is a social system which supports and authenticates the predominance of men, brings about a concentration of power and privilege in the hands of men and, consequently, leads to the control and subordination of women, generating social inequality between the sexes.

This disparity of power, privilege and prestige entrenches and perpetuates patriarchy in society. It gives men power, domination and advantage over women and explains much of the continuing violence.

3.1.1 Patriarchy Transmits Sexual Stereotypes

Consider, for example, the best known stereotypes which relate to the nature of man and woman:

• Human nature is male.

• Woman is by nature the companion of man; she exists only in relation to him.

• The natural qualities of man are strength, rationality, authority, initiative and emotional control.

• The natural qualities of woman are sensitivity, intuition, submission, passivity and compassion.

Thus do men learn and convince themselves of their superiority and women learn and convince themselves of their inferiority.

Their education has impressed upon them that there is nothing worse than for one sex to behave like the other; a man must suppress his emotions: a man "never cries." A woman who exhibits attitudes which are thought of as masculine is quickly branded "mannish." Some psychoanalysts have described intellectual women as "suffering from a masculinity complex!"

Acceptance of the masculine model associated with strength, domination and the censure of emotions encourages the use of violence to resolve marital conflicts.[50]

Acceptance of the feminine model linked with passivity and submission imposes upon women a feeling of inferiority and predisposes them to become victims.

The dual concepts of male and female, superior and inferior, soul and body, poisons at its very source, both for men and women, the human ability to relate to each other as equals.[51]

"By dint of thinking of the One and the Other in terms of contrary elements such as good and evil, strength and weakness, etc., we end up failing to perceive what they have in common."[52]

We must admit that the institutional Church has not been free from this lopsided vision. To the extent that it loses sight of the "essential quality"[53] of man and woman as human beings, and ' to the extent that it looks at women only in terms of their specific nature and role, it encourages women to have a false image of themselves...."[54]

Moreover, this vision tends to exalt as women's prerogatives qualities which all human beings should possess: intuition, sensitivity, patience, gentleness, compassion, understanding and love. Today, when members of the Church speak of Mary solely or mainly with reference to her traditional image as a submissive listener, are they not sanctioning the stereotypes and undermining the recognition of the human person as a whole? Is not the same true when they refer to a concept of nature which seems to ignore the advances of modern science?

3.1.2 Patriarchy Distributes Roles, Tasks and Functions in an Inequitable Fashion

To illustrate this point, consider a few of the most common prejudices:

• The man is the breadwinner.

• The woman must perform the family tasks in exchange for economic security.

In reality, this security soon becomes precarious, a source of dependence and, at times, poverty – situations, unfortunately, conducive to violence. When conflicts arise, the dependence and poverty of women, which result from their devalued and unesteemed roles in society, open the door to violence against this subordinate person.

• The man pursues his career plans.

• The woman frequently subjects her vocational development to the concerns of the family, either by leaving her job or by limiting her career or education plans.

Yet, if we look at reality, we learn that "four out of five women will, at some time or other, have to support themselves and their families."[55] Living in dependency, they are at the mercy of destiny; their future is far from assured.[56]

The economic dependence of women can hinder the egalitarian relationship between spouses: being oneself, affirming one's autonomy, deciding on one's own development require having the means to affirm oneself and, therefore, the means of refusing to invest in undesired endeavours. When all is said and done, those means always come down to economics.

– *Women were excluded for a long time from public and sacred areas, higher education and positions of responsibility.*

– *Women were absent, because they were rejected, from the spheres of economics, science and politics.*

For some years now, they have been wending their way into those areas, carefully and in small numbers, after going through a stringent selection process, having to fight prejudice and male interests. Moreover, for many of them, the price to pay includes being repeatedly scoffed at and heroically carrying a "double load."

The majority of women remain confined to the traditional roles of health care, education and service. Housework, done almost exclusively by women, is hardly given any recognition.

– Status is too often related to income and professional occupation.

– Until quite recently, housework was not considered by the courts as having direct economic value to family assets.

– The tax system considers the homemaker as a dependent of her partner.

– Domestic and volunteer work are considered trivial, providing little opportunity for skills development. Such are the obstacles a woman has to overcome the day she must reenter the labour market, in order to be given proper credit for her knowledge and experience as a homemaker.[57]

Labour structures, which are patriarchal, since they are oppressive and insensitive to the need for equality, make it difficult for families to organize their lives so that men can share more actively in the care the family and women take their place in the labour force. Neither government nor business have made the necessary changes for a swift transformation to occur.

This lack of interest was shown by the absence of labour from the forums on family policy in 1986.[58] Paternity leaves, flexible time schedules and the creation of childcare facilities are not yet a political priority.

In the ecclesial institution itself, is there not still a patriarchal mentality:

– when it continues to specify the function of women by insisting almost exclusively on their role as mothers and on their own distinct psychology;

– when it uses exclusive language;

– when Canon Law excludes women from certain functions and positions of responsibility, for example, lectors, acolytes (Can. 230, par. 1), from sacred ordination (Can. 1024), from giving homilies (Can. 767, par. 1), from positions such as judicial vicar and diocesan judge (Can. 1420, par. 2 and 1421, par. 1).[59]

Social and ecclesial structures and institutions, which exert an influence upon each other, need to be converted if they are to promote equality between men and women; thus, conditions conducive to peace and harmony instead of violence will be established.

3.1.3 Patriarchy Perpetuates a Narrow Vision of Love

There are other prejudices illustrating this vision:

– In our cultural and religious heritage, there are still traces of the concept of woman as sub-human because of her bonds with nature and the evil one and because of her complicity with disorder.

In such imaginary assumptions, women are hardly considered capable of friendly, fraternal relationships. When a man's partner is looked upon as unworthy of trust, there is little chance for cooperation and tenderness in their relationship.

In patriarchal cultures, men and women are more familiar with brute desire, fear and lust than with the kind of love akin to friendship which feeds on equality, trust and the possibility of identifying with the other.[60]

– Society still idealizes romantic love and passion: "to fall in love" is the popular term.

– Our culture prizes intense feelings and sudden outbursts; witness, for example, those television series in which passions generate violence.

Violence is frequently an integral part of love relationships, which can involve isolation, possessiveness and more or less brutal sexual games.

Are not romantic love, passion, exclusivity, withdrawal into a separate world with the loved one the brighter side of the jealousy and isolation which women encounter when they are assaulted?

3.1.4 Patriarchy Turns us Away from a Realistic Vision of the Family

Still more prejudices illustrate this vision:

– The age-old myth that man is the natural protector of woman.

Yet, we know from experience that all human beings need protection at some time or other in their lives, no matter what sex or age they are.

– As a result of the above statement, women are relegated to a passive role, doubtful of their ability to take on roles such as protectress, breadwinner and head of the family.

"In fact, they are denied these roles. It is, undoubtedly, this belief which has enabled society to maintain and nurture the insidious structural and financial dependence of women and to continue limiting their options."[61]

– The family is still too frequently viewed as an oasis of security and conviviality. This distorting prism makes it seem like a dream world of harmonious relationships.

What a difference between this ideal and what numerous families actually experience! "According to statistics, it is in marriage and common-law unions that women are the most at risk of suffering violent assaults."[62] There is nothing wrong with wanting to make the family a harbour of peace, a place of safety and tenderness, provided that this does not keep us from facing the way things really are.

Honesty demands the recognition of conflicts, of destructive and alienating elements present in certain conjugal relationships. It is only realistic to look squarely at some of the failures before couples begin to fall apart and before human beings destroy themselves and each other irremediably.

A certain discourse within the Church sacrifices persons for the sake of the conjugal bond when it seeks to maintain the conjugal union "for better or for worse", by exhorting women to forgive endlessly and often unconditionally, and forever to make peace in the name of a mystical ideal which is very difficult to attain. All the resource persons we consulted, who work with victims of violence, have made this observation.

In some cases, the conjugal bond no longer has any meaning. It is certainly no longer a sign of the covenant between Christ and His Church, upon which is founded the enduring character of marriage. In the name of the truth of the sacramental sign, many Catholics, both men and women, have asked us to give them an answer on the part of the institutional Church regarding this issue.

There is only one way to curb the dynamic of the cycle and the unavoidable escalation of violence: a radical break of this infernal circle in order to save the dignity of people whom God loves.

3.2 Reinforced by the Economic System

Capitalism in its purest form is akin to patriarchy, i.e. when it is not tempered by the acknowledgement of values higher than profit, such as solidarity, sharing, the quality of life and the protection of the rights of the weak. It might be called institutional patriarchy. It dominates, crushes, subjects human beings to its laws, imperatives and strength. It practices a form of violence which has become widely accepted in society.

3.2.1 The Economic System Perpetuates Power as the Basis of Relationships

Violence is also reinforced by the economic structures of society, which value power as the basis of relationships and the subjection of the weak. Indeed, our economic structures rest on:

– personal initiative at the expense of solidarity,

– unrestrained competition whereby the strongest, the shrewdest, the most efficient get the upper hand, regardless of the means they use and of the human and ecological price to be paid,

– exorbitant profits which make the rich even richer with no thought whatsoever about equitable distribution of wealth.

Do such economic structures not advocate a model of relationships which is oblivious of values such as just sharing, solidarity, self-actualization and the quality of life for all people?

The model of relationships and transactions learned and practiced in the economic world is quite naturally reproduced in marital and family relationships. The man who suffers frustrations at work comes home expecting to exercise, at last, in his family the kind of domination which prevails in the workplace. Economic structures themselves benefit from this transfer of the tensions they provoke. No wonder some workers, subjected to alienating circumstances, bring home a considerable amount of repressed anger. In such cases, it is their wives who literally substitute for them as victims of overbearing employers or foremen.

3.2.2 The Economic System Serves Its Own Interests by Exploiting Women

The same economic system also serves its own interests through the economic exploitation of women. "The overall gap between the salaries of men and those of women with a paid job is 40%."[63]

In spite of existing programmes for equal access to employment for women in Quebec, women are paid, for work of equal value, an average of 32.2% less than men.[64]

3.2.3 The Economic System Profits from Pornography

Using little or no discernment in its choice of means and solely intent on reaping huge profits, the economic system uses pornography as an important source of revenue. The annual sales of pornography are estimated at over 50 billion dollars worldwide.[65] While pornography is primarily a money-making industry, it encourages contempt for women. It is not surprising, therefore, that men who are violent or prone to violence find in pornography a space where they can feel justified and even reinforced in their behaviour."[66]

Pornography, especially the kind that seems the most harmless and is shown every day on television, in commercials, movies and fashion advertisements, eroticizes aggression, making it seem commonplace and associating it with the partner's sexual desire.[67]

3.2.4 The Economic System Commercializes Violence

Completely obsessed with gain, this economic system also uses the media and the sale of arms and war toys to commercialize violence, presenting criminal techniques and male aggressiveness as means of resolving problems.

In this way, it employs various means of communication to teach children as well as the general public that violence is a normal part of life.

Considering the amount of violence caused by the existing social order, the human and Christian community cannot remain silent. It is not enough to denounce the social order; what we must do is transform it.

3.3 Diagnostic Conclusion

We have tried to diagnose the phenomenon of conjugal violence. Looking beyond the triggering factors, we aimed at bringing to the fore the causes and origins of this evil.

We went back in time and discovered that a great many factors (anthropological, religious, psychological, sociological) have contributed to promoting and defending the negative vision men have of women. Those same factors fashioned the relationships between the sexes and the economic and social structures we know, which explain both the violence of the past and that which still occurs today.

In our view, the causes of conjugal violence are less immediate and deeper than the behavioural problems of individuals. They also originate in social, economic and political attitudes and structures. They are rooted in patriarchy and in its influence over our institutions.

Are we faced with a problem so complex and pervasive that we must give up on it?

We think not. It is our duty to lead the way towards solutions and point out pathways of hope.

III. PATHWAYS TOWARDS SOLUTIONS

"Then I saw a new heaven and a new earth..." (Ap 21,1)

Violence can be overcome. Under pressure from feminist movements, a transformation is already beginning to emerge. This renewal will be neither profound nor complete until:

– it begins with a conversion of the hearts and consciences of people;

– it comes out of a greater sensitivity to oneself, to others, to events and to the presence of the Spirit;

– it results from a greater realization that certain realities are accepted because they are overly familiar and that persisting prejudices make one incapable of recognizing the truth;

– it brings about a transformation of patriarchal, social and economic structures.

"...to change behaviour patterns is what Jesus tried to do in his life. The very first words he spoke in public, according to Saint Mark, were to call everyone to conversion and penance. (Mk 1,15) He pointed to bonds other than biological between human beings to bring to light their fundamental capacity – that of women as well as men – to do the will of God and thus become "his brother, sister and mother." (Mk 3,31-35) He continuously rejected domination as a rule of conduct for his disciples: Anyone among you who aspires to greatness must serve the rest." (Mk 10,42-45) It was by such teachings that Jesus laid the foundation of a Christian doctrine regarding the human person..."[68]

The Gospel gives the Church the boldness and ethical principles which should motivate her to combat violence. Today, she must be an agent of change by becoming aware, first, of her own violence, and then, of that which surrounds her. She will thus be able to detect the violence hidden in customs, language, gestures, attitudes, manipulations and structures. She will have the courage to denounce it openly before both the secular and the Christian community. Remaining silent would be a form of complicity.

1. Positive Achievements

In the last few years, several projects have been initiated in an attempt to respond to the needs of battered women, and public opinion has been sensitized through a number of campaigns.

It is important to recognize the individual and collective achievements of women who have established shelters and hospitality houses and to acknowledge the involvement of female religious communities who have supplied both human and financial resources to assist battered women.

It is also important to mention a more rigorous application of the law as well as training programmes for professional staff in social service centers, particularly the CLSC's and, more recently, a few services for violent men.

In June 1985, the "ministère de la Santé et des Services sociaux" (Quebec) made public the "Politique d'aide aux femmes violentées," which acknowledges the essential role of emergency shelters in providing refuge for battered women and which increases financial subsidies to these shelters by setting objective norms. This policy also capitalizes on public awareness and on the concerted efforts of all those involved in this work.

In March 1986, the "ministère de la Justice et du Solliciteur général" (Quebec) made public the "Politique d'intervention en matière de violence conjugale." This policy "restates the fact that 'to beat one's wife is a crime' and rules that police officers, judges and procurators must apply the Criminal Code in cases of conjugal violence. The police are bound to respond to calls; in cases of serious offence, they may proceed without warrant to the arrest of the violent spouse. The judicial system must provide the victim with appropriate information and support; it now has the capacity to provide treatment instead of imprisonment for the aggressor."[69]

In June 1988, the Minister of Health and Welfare Canada and the Minister responsible for the Status of Women announced that six federal ministries would spend a total supplement of 40 million dollars in the next four years for the struggle against family violence. Moreover, the Federal Government plans to cooperate closely with the provinces and territories to find effective solutions to the problems of family violence.[70]

2. Limitations of Current Initiatives

These improvements, policies and structures do not, however, automatically transform mentalities. These initiatives have some limitations, because hardly any solutions are proposed to deal with the problem as a whole. "We put out fires everywhere", say counsellors and directors of emergency shelters, who are forced to turn away one out of every two women for lack of space.

The number of cases of legal prosecution multiplied five times in 1988.[71] Criminalization plays an important preventive role:

– It makes concrete and credible the statement that violence is intolerable and that the refusal to live in fear of violence is a right;[72]

– It enables victims to protect themselves temporarily from violence;

– It allows aggressors to face the natural consequences of the criminal act which they committed and to assume responsibility for the seriousness of their actions and for the resulting social reprobation.

However, criminalization as a deterrent has its limits:

– It can trap victims in painful dilemmas. Few women agree to have their partners imprisoned, regardless of the complaints filed against them. Instead, in 91% of cases, they express a wish for their partners to get professional help;[73]

– If society's response is merely one of repression, it will likely engender a childish attitude in the aggressor.

As matters now stand, women and children are the ones to leave home for their own safety after an assault. It is important, therefore, to provide other forms of protection and to strengthen the network of emergency shelters or battered women. The present financial situation of shelters is quite precarious since they are subsidized for 50% of their real operational needs.[74]

"S.O.S. Violence conjugale" responded to an average of 920 requests per month from January to August 1989. Nearly 44% of the 7354 calls recorded during those eight months of the hotline's operation were from victims of conjugal violence.

Moreover, 213 male aggressors took the initiative of calling, some in an attempt to track down their female partners, others to tell off the receptionist, and still others, a small minority (17.8%), to seek help;[75] which shows the urgency of developing aid programmes for aggressors.

In order to transform the violent behaviour of individuals, it is necessary to work on both the individual and social aspects of the problem. Violence is not only an individual problem; it is also a social, hence, collective phenomenon. Therefore, there is a need to find collective solutions and to consider ways and means of sensitizing, informing and educating society as a whole.

3. Proposals for Action

All of Quebec society and the whole community of the Church, especially pastors and pastoral workers, should be mobilized if we are to combat conjugal violence effectively. Whatever the form of their commitment, they may follow a process involving reflection, a compassionate response, conscientization, education and social transformation.

3.1 The Path of Reflection

To avoid deviation and remain effective, any action aimed at resolving a problem and correcting a practice must be based on reflection. Reflection provides a deeper foundation for action, strengthens its principles and motives and clarifies its purpose. Through reflection, we analyze the circumstances of time and place in which action is to be performed. This means that reflection needs to be updated periodically. This is why the Church seeks to renew her theology in light of the signs of the times.

To comply with this necessity, the Church in Quebec along with her theologians and the whole Christian people, prompted by the Spirit, should:

3.1.1 Make available the human and financial resources for task forces of men and women who, aided by recent developments in theology, exegesis and Christian anthropology, would help to update the prevailing perception of women and their role, marriage and the family, as well as the ethical discourse on these subjects.[76]

3.1.2 Recognize, by word and community action, that men and women are equal partners with the same dignity.

There is a need to question the rules, cultural traditions and institutional policies which keep women in a state of inequality. Already, the lives of many couples have changed: they relate to each other as equals on a daily basis; they agree to premarital contracts, stress equal access to resources, equal input in decision-making and mutual consultation before making changes that affect each other. Women's claims to equality (in terms of training, hiring, wages and career advancement), some of which have been taken up even by the government, are gradually changing the face of society and of certain business firms. More flexible time schedules, giving both men and women greater freedom to look after children, now appear possible. As well, some dioceses appoint women to important positions.

3.1.3 Listen receptively to the theological reflection offered by women when they name God, speak of Mary and read the Bible.[77]

Until a few decades ago, theology was the work of men alone. Today, more and more women are educated in religious as well as secular sciences. They should be allowed without discrimination to contribute to the progress and advancement of the different sacred disciplines. Their scientific discourse should not be distrusted because they are women.

3.1.4 Demystify and support the feminist movement, so that the Christian community may be more accepting of the humanistic and evangelical values which it defends.

Today, the Church does not frown upon economic, scientific and artistic movements, even if some of their proponents support questionable positions; why should the feminist movement be frowned upon when it can be credited with raising public awareness and denouncing unjust and unacceptable situations?

3.2 The Path of Compassion

Pastors and pastoral workers who meet or receive people living with a problem of conjugal violence must neither deny nor minimize the problem, nor should they attempt to resolve it by exhorting these people to be more patient, more tolerant, more, forgiving, or to practice greater self-control in the future.

Victims must be assisted and aggressors made aware of their responsibility. How can this be done without making an error and without taking the place of trained, experienced professionals whose work it is to provide such services? The role of priests and pastoral workers is to:

3.2.1 Receive warmly those coming to confide their problem.

Let them express their pain without showing boredom or being excessively upset; never ridicule them or make them feel guilty; avoid proposing band-aid solutions, and never pass judgment. State that violence is unacceptable and intolerable.

3.2.2 Direct women who have been assaulted to the proper resources.

It is essential to know the addresses and phone numbers of organizations and emergency shelters in your area in order to provide quick assistance and thus, demonstrate true willingness to support the victim. Give special support to those women whose access to service is made even more difficult by their ethnic origin, their culture or the place where they live.

3.2.3 Direct aggressors to appropriate programmes.[78]

The unhappiness, sorrow and disarray felt by the violent man, now a subject of social reprobation and legal penalties, can lead him to true liberation. Nothing is completely lost for someone who has enough hope to take part in a process of rehabilitation.

3.2.4 Support the community in its commitment against violence so that everyone – neighbours, friends and relatives – may give victims their help and support.

A little encouragement, a gesture or a few words of appreciation are sometimes all that is needed to trigger active charity on the part of those in a position to help.

3.3 The Path of Conscientization

As a credible social institution in Quebec, the Church should exert her influence to increase public awareness of the problem of conjugal violence seen as a global reality.

In order to accomplish this, the Church should:

3.3.1 Raise public awareness of conjugal violence and denounce it by stating clearly that it is unacceptable.

This could involve publicity campaigns, texts for parish bulletins, the publication of pedagogical tools, so that everyone in the community can say: "Peace is our concern."

3.3.2 Call for collaboration by all levels of organizations involved with this problem, as well as those which should be more concerned with it.

A problem which, in its causes and effects, prevention and repression touches the worlds of labour (management and unions), education, health, social and legal services and the Churches, cannot be dealt with unless there is cooperation. Regional advisory groups are already in place. They should provide orientation and follow-up to meet needs while recognizing and respecting the different fields of competence and intervention.

3.4 The Path of Education

The Church has always played an important part in the human and Christian formation of both adults and young people. Pastors and pastoral workers, who are dedicated to education through preaching, services of preparation for marriage and life, pastoral services in schools and adult faith education, must contribute as educators in the struggle against violence.

In order to perform this task effectively, they should:

3.4.1 Inform young people preparing for life as a couple and those already involved in such a relationship of the causes and consequences of violence and of the autonomy and respect which are essential in a couple.

3.4.2 Pursue, together with professionals in the field of human relations, a process of reflection on conflict resolution and stress management.

Conflict and anger inevitably occur in a relationship, but violence can be avoided.

Simply advocating tolerance and adjustment, as is too frequently done, creates groundless hopes for change and urges couples to give precedence to family unity over the physical and psychological security of persons.

Ruptures too have evangelical value: they are a part of living.

The stresses and clashes of life can be overcome creatively without resorting to violence. No human being has the right to victimize another.

Communication and cooperation between man and woman must be the rule of life both in the family and in society.

3.4.3 Recognize women, not only in their role as wives and mothers, but as human persons with vast potential as well as limitations, who are entitled to their autonomy and to respect for their dignity.

Before being a mother, a woman is a person with her own identity. Motherhood, however noble, is not what defines womanhood. While many women find fulfillment in physical or spiritual motherhood, others also find it elsewhere.

3.4.4 Encourage those who reflect on the status of men and promote a new concept of manhood.

Is it not possible for men, who are perceived as competitive, power-oriented, domineering and, at times, violent, to be also seen as partners eager to cooperate and capable of tenderness?

The abuse of power and control is not an essential component of manhood or of the affirmation of one's masculinity.

3.4.5 Redefine and re-emphasize paternity as a man's equal responsibility for life and for the child.

This responsibility goes far beyond the role of a provider. The father must take on his share of those daily tasks which are generally thought of as "maternal" by a society accustomed to seeing them performed almost solely by women.

Unfortunately, the term "father" is itself misleading because it all too often means only the kind of authority that bullies, punishes and dominates. The father is also someone who wishes to see his child grow, who calls him or her forth to freedom, who supports, rewards and loves with no strings attached.[79]

3.4.6 Rediscover man and woman free of the stereotypes and models which predetermine what is to be expected of their sex.

Today, men and women are gradually learning to reconcile love of the other with love of oneself, and to harmonize the desire for freedom with the desire for close relationship. Maturity involves recognizing the autonomy of both oneself and the loved one.

Pedagogical materials that transmit sexual stereotypes, used in the Church, especially in marriage preparation programmes, must be revised.

3.4.7 Include in the training of future priests sensitization to the causes of conjugal violence, and training for appropriate pastoral intervention.

3.5 Path of Social Transformation

Priests and pastoral workers, as members of the Christian community and along with this community, must encourage political and economic authorities (management as well as labour) towards action aimed at correcting the current form of capitalism.

This system exemplifies the use of brute force in economic relations, the abuse of power and money and insensitivity to the rights and needs of weaker members of society.

The role of Christian communities must be to:

3.5.1 Denounce to public authorities oppressive situations which could cause rebellion: unemployment, homelessness and all kinds of exploitation.

3.5.2 Mobilize and coordinate efforts to demand fair and equitable social policies for disadvantaged members of society.

3.5.3 Raise social consciousness by using symbolic actions, on appropriate occasions, in support of the poorest of the poor.

Some religious communities, parishes and Catholic action groups are already playing this prophetic role. Could not even more Christian communities take up this cause? The "new heavens and the new earth" of Saint Peter (2 P 3,13) will come to be through the combined efforts of all.

The problem of conjugal violence is not merely an individual problem; it is also a comprehensive social problem.

CONCLUSION

Whatever our situation may be and from whatever standpoint we may observe this issue, the liberation of women is unquestionably a sign of our times. If we use the word "liberation", it is because women have, in fact, been bound and oppressed. This liberation has neither occurred everywhere, nor been completed where begun. It is, therefore, a Christian issue consistent with the fundamental option of Jesus Christ.

The liberation of women is a challenge and a responsibility for men as well as women, the hierarchy as well as the whole people of God, the clergy as well as the laity. Everyone working together must actualize in this world the values proposed by the Gospel. Such is the Mission we are asked to fulfill.

BIBLIOGRAPHY

Association canadienne des travailleurs sociaux. Symposium sur la violence, Ottawa, Juin 17-18, 1981, 77 pages.

BADINTER, Elisabeth. *L'un est l'autre, Des relations entre hommes et femmes,* Paris, Editions Odile Jacob, 1986, 362 pages.

BILODEAU, Angèle. *La violence conjugale, Recherche d'aide des femmes,* Quebec, Les Publications Quebec, 1987, 1A7 pages.

CARRIER, Micheline and MICHAUD, Monique. *La violence faite aux femmes en milieu conjugal: Le produit d'une société sexiste,* Ottawa, Secrétariat d'Etat, Programme de promotion de la femme, 1982, 108 pages.

Church Council on Justice and Corrections, Canadian Council on Social Development. *Family Violence in a Patriarchal Culture, A Challenge to Our Way of Living,* Ottawa, 1989, 142 pages.

Code of Canon Law, A Text and Commentary (The), Canon Law Society of America, Paulist Press, New York, 1985, 1152 pages.

Comité de la consultation sur la politique familiale. *Le soutien collectif reclamé pour les familles québécoises,* Première partie, 114 pages, and *Le soutien collectif recommandé pour les parents québécois,* Deuxième partie, Rapports du Comité de la consultation sur la politique familiale, Gouvernement du Québec, 1986, 152 pages.

Comité ministériel permanent du développement social. *Pour les familles québécoises,* Document de consultation sur la politique familiale, Governement du Québec, 1984, 114 pages.

Commission d'enquête sur les services de santé et les services sociaux. *Programme de consultation d'experts, Dossier "Femmes",* Quebec, 1987, 222 pages.

Concilium, Revue internationale de théologie, Paris, Editions Beauchesne, nos. 111, 154 and 188.

Conseil canadien de développement social. *Vis-à-vis,* Bulletin national sur la violence familiale, numéro spécial sur la violence familiale et les organisations spirituelles, Ottawa, vol.4, no. 4, 1986.

Conseil du statut de la femme. *Pour les Québecoises: égalité et indépendance,* Gouvernement du Québec, 1978, 335 pages.

Corporation des travailleurs sociaux professionnels. *Intervention,* numéro spécial sur la violence conjugale, Montreal, no. 75, October 1986.

DANKWORT, Jürgen. "Une conception alternative de la violence conjugale: vers une intervention efficace auprès des hommes lents", *Service social,* Ecole de service social de l'Université Laval, vol. 37, nos. 1 and 2, 1988, p. 86-119.

DAVID, Hélène. *Femmes et emplois: le défi de l'égalité,* Montreal, Institut de recherche appliqué sur le travail, Presses de l'Université du Québec, 1987, 477 pages.

DEMERS, Dominique. "Le mariage, un passeport pour la violence", *Châtelaine,* September 1988, p. 63-73.

DE VAUX, Roland. *Les institutions de l'Ancien Testament,* vol. 1, Paris, Cerf, 1958.

DOBASH, R.E. and DOBASH, R. *Violence Against Wives, A Case Against the Patriarchy,* New York, Free Press, 1979.

DUMAIS, Monique. *Les femmes dans la Bible, expériences et interpellations,* Socabi et Editions Paulines, 1985, 96 pages.

DUMAIS, Monique, ROY, Marie-Andrée. *Souffles de femmes, Lectures féministes de la religion,* Montreal, Editions Paulines, 1989, 239 pages.

FORTUNE, Marie M. *Keeping the Faith, Questions and Answers for the Abused Women,* New York, Harper and Row, 1987, 94 pages.

FOX, Bonnie J. "Conceptualizing Patriarchy", *Revue canadienne de sociologie et d'anthropologie,* vol. 5, no. 2, 1988, p.163-181.

FRENCH, Marilyn. *La fascination du pouvoir,* [Engl. Ed.: *Beyond Power,* Summit Book, New York, 1985.] Paris, Editions Acropole, 1986.

HANMER, Jalna. "Violence et le contrôle social des femmes," *Questions féministes,* Paris, Editions Tierce, November 1977, p. 69-89.

John-Paul II. Apostolic Letter *"Mulieris Dignitatem" on the Dignity and Vocation of Women,* Canadian Conference of Catholic Bishops, 1988, 119 pages.

John Paul II. Apostolic Exhortation *"Familiaris Consortio" on the Role of the Christian Family in the Modern World,* Canadian Conference of Catholic Bishops, 1981, 175 pages.

JEREMIAS, Joachim. *Jérusalem au temps de Jésus,* Paris, Cerf, 1967, 525 pages.

LAROUCHE, Ginette. *Guide d'intervention auprès des femmes violentées,* Montreal, Corporation des travailleurs sociaux du Québec, 1985, 93 pages.

LAROUCHE, Ginette. *Agir contre la violence,* Montreal, Editions La pleine lune, 1987, 554 pages.

MACLEOD, Linda. *La femme battue au Canada: un cercle vicieux,* [Engl. Ed.: *Wife Battering in Canada: The Vicious Circle*] Ottawa, Canadian Advisory Council on the Status of Women, 1980, 72 pages.

MACLEOD, Linda. *Pour de vraies amours.... prévenir la violence conjugale,* [Engl. Ed.: *Battered But Not Beaten... Preventing Wife Battering in Canada*] Ottawa, Canadian Advisory Council on the Status of Women, 1987, 191 pages.

Ministère de la Justice. *Rapport, Colloques régionaux sur la violence envers les femmes et les enfants et dans la pornographie,* Gouvernement du Québec, 1980, 83 pages.

Ministère de la Justice, Ministère du Solliciteur général. *Politique d'intervention en matière de violence conjugale,* Gouvernement du Québec, 1985, 36 pages.

Ministère des Affaires sociales. *Une politique d'aide aux femmes violentées,* Gouvernement du Québec, 1985, 59 pages.

MOLTMANN, Elizabeth and Jurgen. *Dieu Homme et Femme,* Montreal, Fides, 1984, 149 pages.

MORRIS, Roberta. *Ending Violence in Families, A Training Program for Pastoral Care Workers,* Toronto, The United Church of Canada, 1988, 78 pages.

NOEL, Lise. *L'intolérance, Une problématique générale,* Boréal, 1989, 308 pages.

Ordre des infirmières et des infirmiers du Québec. *Ecouter le langage des maux... La violence conjugale, intervention infirmière auprès des femmes,* Montréal, 1987, 32 pages.

PAQUETTE, Louise. *La situation socio-économique des femmes, faits et chiffres,* Secrétariat à la condition féminine, Les Publications du Québec, 1989, 168 pages.

PELLAUER, Mary D., CHESTER, Barbara, BOYAJIAN, Jane A. *Sexual Assault and Abuse, A Handbook for Clergy and Religious Professionals,* New York, Harper and Row, 1987, 278 pages.

PHILIPPE, Robert. "Pro-Gam, un service pour hommes violents", *Nursing Québec,* vol. 5, no. 5, Juillet-Août 1985, p. 39-41.

PROULX, Monique. *Cinq millions de femmes, Une étude de la femme canadienne au foyer,* [Engl. Pd.: *Five Million Women, A Study of Canadian Housewives*] Ottawa, Canadian Advisory Council on the Status of Women, 1978, 98 pages.

Regroupement provincial des maisons d'hébergement et de transition pour femmes victimes de violence. *La sexualité blessée: Etude sur la violence sexuelle en milieu conjugal,* Montreal, 1987, 87 pages.

Revue Notre Dame. "Les femmes battues", Québec, no. 1, Janvier 1987.

Revue Notre Dame. "La pornographie", Québec, no. 9, Octobre 1988.

RONDEAU, Gilles, GAUVIN, M. et DANKWORT, Jürgen. *Les programmes québécois d'aide aux conjoints violents,* Rapport préliminaire sur sept organismes subventionnés, Université de Montréal, Ecole de service social, 1988, 87 pages.

SCHUSSLER FIORENZA, Elisabeth. *En mémoire d'elle, Essai de reconstruction des origines chrétiennes selon la théologie féministe,* [Engl. Ed.: *In Memory of Her, An Essay Reconstructing the Origins of Christianity according to Feminist Theology*] Paris, Les Editions du Cerf, 1986, 482 pages.

Secrétariat à la condition féminine. *Vers l'égalité, Orientations triennales en matière de condition féminine 1987–1990,* Gouvernement du Québec, 1987, 44 pages.

SINCLAIR, Deborah. *Pour comprendre le problème des femmes battues: guide de formation pour les conseillers et les intervenants,* [Engl. Ed.: *Understanding Wife Assault, A Training Manual for Counsellors and Advocates*] Toronto,

Ontario Ministry of Community and Social Services, Family Violence Programme, 1985, 204 pages.

STARK, Evan et al. *Les sévices exercés sur les femmes et l'établissement médical,* [Engl. Ed.: *Wife Abuse in the Medical Setting, An Introduction for Health Personnel*] Ottawa, National Clearing House on Family Violence, Health and Welfare Canada, 1980, 78 pages.

THERRIEN, Rita, COULOMBE-JOLY, Louise. *Rapport de l'AFEAS sur la situation des femmes au foyer,* Montreal, Boréal Express, 1984, 214 pages.

Vie ouvrière, Dossier violence conjugale, no. 206, Décembre 1987.

---

[1] Linda MacLeod, *Pour de vraies amours... Prévenir la violence conjugale.* [Engl. Ed.: *Battered But Not Beaten: Preventing Wife Battering in Canada*], Ottawa, Canadian Advisory Council on the Status of Women, 1987, p. 8.

[2] Linda MacLeod, *La femme battue au Canada: un cercle vicieux,* [Engl. Ed.: *Wife Battering in Canada: The Vicious Circle*], Ottawa, Canadian Advisory Council on the Status of Women, 1980 p. 23.

[3] Ministére des Affaires sociales, *Une politique d'aide aux femmes violentées,* Gouvernement du Québec, 1985, p. 10.

[4] Commission d'enquête sur les services de santé et les services sociaux, Programme de consultation d'experts, Dossier "Femmes", Gouvernement du Québec, 1987, p. 132.

[5] Robert Lebel, "Le panneau de l'armoire, Billet de l'évêque de Valleyfield, mars 1982," text no. 48, *La justice sociale comme Bonne Nouvelle, Messages sociaux, économiques et politiques des évêques du Québec, 1972–1983.* Recherche et présentation par Gérard Rochais, Centre Justice et Foi, Montréal, Les Editions Bellarmin, 1984, p. 291.

[6] Sandra Shee, *Des victimes de violence conjugale: les femmes battues au Québec,* Ecole de criminologie, Université de Montréal, 1980, p. 14, quoted by Angèle Bilodeau, *La violence conjugale, recherche d'aide des femmes.* Québec, Les Publications du Québec, 1987, p. 54.

[7] See in Annex 3 the Formation Programme proposed for these sessions. Participants only will receive the pedagogical tools during the sessions. (Translator's Note: These tools will he available in French only.)

[8] Commission d'enquête sur les services de santé et les services sociaux, op. cit., p. 145.

[9] Linda MacLeod, op. cit., 1987, p. 17.

[10] Phrase used in the *"Guide d'intervention infirmiére auprés des femmes", Ecouter le langage des maux...,* Ordre des infirmiéres at des infirmiers du Québec, 1987.

[11] These types of wife abuse are outlined by Ginette Larouche, *Guide d'intervention auprés des femmes violentées,* Montréal, Corporation des travailleurs sociaux du Québec, 1985, p. 13.

[12] Commission d'enquête sur les services de santé et les services sociaux, op. cit., p. 140.

[13] Linda MacLeod, op. cit., 1980, p. 10.

[14] Canadian Advisory Council on the Status of Women, 1982, quoted in *Une politique d'aide aux femmes violentées,* Ministére des Affaires sociales, Gouvernement du Quéhec, 1985, p. 10.

[15] This section is largely inspired by Ginette Larouche, op. cit., p. 13-14.

[16] Ibid., p. 14.

[17] Ibid., p. 14.

[18] Regarding this question, see the article by Jürgen Dankwort "Une conception alternative de la violence conjugale: vers une intervention efficace auprés des hommes violents", *Service social,* Ecole de service social de l'Université Laval, vol. 37, nos. 1 and 2, 1988, p.86-119.

[19] L.E. Walker, "Battered Women and Learned Helplessness," in *Victimology: An International Journal,* 1977–1978, vol. 2, nos. 3-4, p. 525-534, quoted by Ginette Larouche, op. cit., p. 14-16 and by the Commission d'enquête sur les services de santé et les services sociaux, op. cit., p. 137-140. This section is larpely inspired by these texts and by that of l'Ordre des infirmiéres et des infirmiers du Québec, op. cit., p. 9.

[20] Dale Trimble, "Faire face à sa responsabilité: l'homme qui bat sa femme" [Engl. Ed.: Confronting Responsibility: Men who Batter their Wives], *Mutual Aid Groups and The Life Cycle,* revised by Alex Gitterman, University of Columbia and Lawrence Shulman, University of Boston, Itasca, Illinois, F.E. Peacock Publishers, Inc., 1986, p. 10.

[21] Ibid., p. 11-12.

[22] In the texts referred to in footnote 19, this phase is called the "Honeymoon" phase.

[23] Graphic illustration reproduced with the kind permission of l'Ordre des infirmiéres et des infirmiers du Québec, op. cit., p. 10. Adapted from Walker's model.

[24] S. Kérouac, M.E. Taggart and J. Lescop, *Portrait de la santé de femmes violentées et de leurs enfants,* Faculté des sciences infirmières, Université de Montréal, 1986, p. 39, quoted by the Commission d'enquête sur les services de santé et les services sociaux, op. cit., p. 142-143.

[25] Commssion d'enquête sur les services de santé et les services sociaux, op. cit., p. 143. See S. Kérouac et al., op. cit., p. 19 and p. 70-75.

[26] This theory of learned helplessness, developed in a laboratory by Seligman to explain the docile behaviour of animals subjected to excessive stress, is taken up by Walker to explain, by extrapolation, why assaulted women seem indifferent to their own plight as victims. This theory is cited by Evan Stark et al., *Les sévices exercés sur les femmes et l'établissement médical,* [Engl. Ed.: *Wife Abuse and the Medical Setting: An Introduction for Health Personnel*] Ottawa, National Clearing House on Family Violence, Health and Welfare Canada, 1980, p. 4, and described by Ginette Larouche, op. cit., p. 17-18.

[27] Evan Stark et al., op. cit., p. 46.

[28] Linda MacLeod, op. cit., 1987, p. 37.

[29] Robert Philippe, "Pro-Gam, un service pour hommes violents," *Nursing Québec,* vol. 5, no. 5, Juillet–Août 1985, p. 40.

[30] Several studies, among which those of L. MacLeod (1980), M. Roy (1982), S. Kérouac et al. (1986), are quoted by the Commission d'enquête sur les services de santé et les services sociaux, op. cit., p. 141-142.

[31] Linda MacLeod, op. cit., p. 35-37.

[32] Ginette Larouche, op. cit., p. 84.

[33] S. Kérouac et al., op. cit., p. 39, quoted by the Commission d'enquête sur les services de santé et les services sociaux, op. cit., p. 142.

[34] M. Roy, *The Abusive Partner: An Analysis of Domestic Battering,* Van Nostrand Reinhold, New York, 1982, quoted by the Commission d'enquête sur les services de santé at les services sociaux, op. cit., p. 142.

[35] S. Kérouac at al., op. cit., p. 39.

[36] John Paul II, *The Role of the Christian Family in the Modern World, Apostolic Exhortation "Familiaris Consortio,"* Canadian Conference of Catholic Bishops, 1981, p. 43.

[37] In his "biblical meditation" *Mulieris Dignitatem,* Pope John Paul II uses the new interpretation in relation to this point and, at the very start of his argumentation, he forcefully affirms, on the basis of these biblical texts, the essential equality of man and woman.

[38] Elisabeth Badinter, *L'un est l'autre, Des relations entre honnes et femmes,* Editions Odile Jacob, 1986, p. 116.

[39] Elisabeth Fiorenza, "Le rôle des femmes dans le mouvement chrétien primitif," *Concilium* 111, 1976, p. 17 and Monique Dumais, *Les femmes dans la Bible, expériences et interpellations,* Socabi and Editions Paulines, 1985, p. 22.

[40] These statements are also supported by the works of the following authors: Roland De Vaux, *Les institutions de l'Ancien Testament,* Vol. 1, Paris, Cerf, 1958 and Joachim Jérémias, *Jérusalem au temps de Jésus,* Paris, Cerf, 1967, Annex: 'La situation sociale de la femme," p. 471-492.

[41] Marie de Mérode-de-Croy, "Rôle de la femme dans l'Ancien Testament," *Concilium* 154, 1980, p. 90.

[42] Ida Raming, "De la liberté de l'Evangile à l'Eglise masculine pétrifiée," *Concilium* 154, 1980, p. 19.

[43] R.E. Dobash and R. Dobash, *Violence Against Wives: A Case Against the Patriarchy,* New York, Free Press, 1979, p. 137.

[44] This historical section is largely inspired by Elisabeth Badinter, op. cit., p. 191-205.

[45] Linda MacLeod, op. cit., 1987, p. 23-24.

[46] Ibid.

[47] Linda MacLeod, op. cit., 1980, p. 23.

[48] Ibid., p. 15.

[49] Commission d'enquête sur les services de santé et les services sociaux, op. cit., p. 142.

[50] Ginette Larouche, Agir contre la violence, Editions La pleine lune, 1987, p. 50-52.

[51] Elizabeth Carroll, "La domination masculine peut-elle être renversée?" *Concilium* 154, 1980, p. 60.

[52] E. Badinter, op. cit., p. 160.

[53] Phrase used by Pope John Paul II, *Apostolic Letter "Mulieris Dignitatem" on the Dignity and Vocation of Women,* Canadian Conference of Catholic Bishops, 1988, p. 62.

[54] Elizabeth Carroll, op. cit., p. 60.

[55] Secrétariat à la condition feminine, *Vers l'égalité, Orientations triennales en matière de condition féminine 1987–1990,* Gouvernement du Ouébec, p. 30.

[56] Rita Therrien, Louise Coulombe-Joly, Rapport de l'AFEAS sur la situation des femmes au foyer, Boréal Express, 1984, p. 147.

[57] On this subject, see the study by Monique Proulx, *Cinq millions de femmes, Une étude de la femme canadienne au foyer,* [Engl. Ed.: *Five Million Women, A Study of the Canadian Housewife*] Ottawa, Canadian Advisory Council on the Status of Women, 1978.

[58] *Rapport du comité de la consultation sur la politique familiale, Première partie, Le soutien collectif réclamé pour les familles québécoises,* Gouvernement du Québec, 1986, p. 56.

[59] *The Code of Canon Law, A Text and Commentary,* Canon Law Society of America, Paulist Press, 1985, p. 167, 553, 723, 954, 955.

[60] On this subject, see E. Badinter, op. cit., chap. II "La logioue des contraires ou la guerre des sexes," p. 149-189.

[61] Association canadienne des travailleurs sociaux, *Symposium sur la violence entre les conjoints,* Ottawa, 1981, p. 59.

[62] Jalna Hanmer, "Violence et contrôle social des femmes," *Questions féministes,* Paris, Editions Tierce, novembre 1977, p. 82.

[63] Hélène David, *Femmes et emplois, le défi de l'égalité,* Montréal, Institut de recherche appliquée sur le travail, Presses de l'Université du Québec, 1987, p. 59.

[64] Statistics Canada, Salaire annual salon le sexe 1987, quoted in *La Presse,* Samedi, 4 mars 1989, p. 85.

[65] *Revue Notre-Dame,* "La pornographie est fondée sur le mépris de la femme," an interview with Monica Matte and Ginette Drouin-Busque, no. 9, Octobre 1988, p. 17.

[66] Regroupement provincial des maisons d'hébergement et de transition pour femmes victimes de violence, *La sexualité blessée: Etude sur la violence sexuelle en milieu conjugal,* Montréal. 1987, p. 74.

[67] Linda MacLeod, op. cit., 1987, p. 43.

[68] Elizabeth Carroll, op. cit., p. 63.

[69] Martine D'Amours and Marie-Luce Garceau, "Réseau public vs. réseau communautaire L'Ogre at le Petit Poucet" *Vie ouvrière,* no. 206, December 1987, p. 17.

[70] Government of Canada, *Nouvelles initiatives fédérales de lutte contre la violence familiale,* [Engl.Ed.: *Federal Government Announces New Family Violence Initiatives,*] News Release, June 7, 1988.

[71] André Noël, "S.O.S. Violence conjugale a servi 400 femmes par mois depuis sa création," Montréal, *La Presse,* Mercredi, 25 mai 1988, p. A4.

[72] Ibid.

[73] Colin Meredith and Ellie Conway, *The Study for the Planning of Victim Assistance Services on P.E.1.: Summary Report for the P.E.I. Committee on Victim Assistance, Programmes Management,* a report for specialists, no. 1984-34, Ottawa, Solicitor General of Canada, 1984, p. 25, quoted by Linda Macleod, op. cit., 1987, o. 101.

[74] According to the calculations of Ruth Rosa, professor of Economics at the Université du Québec à Montréal, in *Etude économique, Budget d'opération d'une maison de 15 places et moins,* a study which was part of a joint project of the UQAM and Relais-Femmes, 1986.

[75] Statistics made available by "S.O.S. Violence conjugale" on the use of the hotline between January and August 1989.

[76] The anthropological roots of human beings are described in the works of Kari Elisabeth Böresen, as found in her article "Fondements anthropologiques de la relation entre l'homme at la femme dans la théologie classique" *Concilium* 111, 1976, p. 27-39.

[77] On this subject, see Monique Dumais, Marie-Andrée Roy, *Souffles de femmes, Lectures féministes de la religion,* Editions Paulines, 1989 and *Concilium* 111, 1976.

[78] Even if existing programmes for violent men sometimes give rise to contradictory conclusions, they are the only sources of help we presently have. New resources need to be created. On this subject, see Jürgen Dankwort, op. cit., and Gilles Rondeau, M. Gauvin and J. Dankwort, *Les programmes québécois d'aide aux conjoints violents,* Rapport préliminaire sur sept organismes subventionnés, Université de Montréal, Ecole de service social, 1988.

[79] The "no losers" approach in Thomas Gordon's *Parents efficaces* is interesting in this regard, Collection Actualisation, Le Jour Editeur, 1976.

32.

A SOCIETY WITHOUT SHAME
Clifford Longley

***The Tablet*, September 11, 1999**

The indications are that Britain's Churches have pulled off a spectacular coup against the forces of secular political correctness at the heart of government. David Blunkett, the Education status Secretary, has rewritten the official recommendations for the national curriculum to put back the stress on marriage and stable family life that was omitted from the first draft that reached his desk. That omission produced an outspoken protest from those representing Anglican and Catholic schools, which he has heeded. He will now incur the displeasure of those who regard the decline of marriage as natural, inevitable and desirable, the gradual abandonment of the religion-based social conventions of another age.

It is not difficult to work out that the Prime Minister knew about all this when he gave an interview to the *Observer* last weekend. He called for a new moral crusade to build a better future — a call that would have been embarrassing had the Government then gone on to ignore the Churches' complaints about the lack of moral content in the school curriculum. In the event, all the increasingly irrelevant Opposition was left to grumble about was the absence of tax incentives for marriage — incentives that they had spent most of their own 18 years in power dismantling.

But marriage was not the only focus of the Government's new interest in promoting a more conservative morality. It has also committed itself to turning back the tide of teenage pregnancy. The press has been rightly appalled by the phenomenon of a 12-year-old girl made pregnant by a 14-year-old boy, who, far from contrite, proceeded to blame the sex education he had received in school. This was a reversal of the usual argument that sex education was the best antidote to teenage pregnancy; it suggests that there was some weight after all to the complaint that sex education can actually encourage earlier experimentation. The Government's own investigation into teenage pregnancy, a field in which Britain leads Europe and most of the rest of the world, had earlier this year produced a mixed bag of proposals that did include more sex education, but with the proviso that it had to be the right sort. But did that include the promotion of marriage? His advisers said it didn't. Mr Blunkett has decided that it does.

Knowledge of the nuts and bolts of sex is obviously not by itself the key to a chaste society. If it merely dismantles social and psychological constraints, it can have the opposite effect. Boys prefer sex without condoms, we are told, as a knowledgeable, street-wise, thing to do. Girls with little else happening in their lives don't always get pregnant by accident, but because they know motherhood brings status and, indeed, a baby to love. The urge for instant gratification is overwhelmingly a characteristic of adolescence; and there is a whole world of commerce out there making a lot of money by spreading the knowledge of how to achieve it.

Those who promoted sex education have always talked about blowing away the cobwebs of ignorance that made sex a taboo subject for earlier generations, leading, they would always have added, to "immense misery". But wittingly or not, that joined them to another agenda which saw all taboo, shame and stigma as damaging, rather than as psychological barriers discouraging harm to ourselves and others.

If we wanted to name it, we could call it emotional libertarianism: the view that the free and spontaneous expression of whatever we feel is the only mentally healthy approach to life. The equation of stigma and taboo with neurosis goes back to Freud at least, and it became part of what women's liberation was about in America in the 1960s. And to an extent, they had their reasons. Stigma, shame and guilt had certainly been used to keep women in their place. But the attempt to run a society without shame and guilt of any sort is looking increasingly dangerous, not just in the area of sex but also of drugs and other forms of petty crime. A society without shame is ultimately a society without standards.

These are not things the Government can do much about, except by trying not to make them worse. The real channels of influence are between parents and children (the foundations of which are either laid long before adolescence or not at all), and among an adolescent's own peer group. It is the latter we have never really tried to work through in Britain, though there have been some interesting ideas on the Continent and in America. The power of peer-group pressure among adults is well illustrated by the changed public attitude to racism, to smoking and to drunk-driving. The harnessing of peer pressure against early teenage sex is the only factor likely to make a real difference to that. It isn't brilliant or wicked or cool; it is dumb. But whether that attitude can be spread by sex education, by adults talking at adolescents in a formal classroom setting, is very doubtful. It will take something much more ingenious than that. I wonder what Catholic sixth-formers would suggest as a way of mobilising opinion.

33.

THE PASTORAL CARE OF HOMOSEXUAL PERSONS
Doctrinal Congregation's Letter to Bishops (1986)

1. The issue of homosexuality and the moral evaluation of homosexual acts have increasingly become a matter of public debate, even in Catholic circles. Since this debate often advances arguments and makes assertions inconsistent with the teaching of the Catholic Church, it is quite rightly a cause for concern to all engaged in the pastoral ministry, and this congregation has judged it to be of sufficiently grave and widespread importance to address to the bishops of the Catholic Church this letter on the pastoral care of homosexual persons.

2. Naturally, an exhaustive treatment of this complex issue cannot be attempted here, but we will focus our reflection within the distinctive context of the Catholic moral perspective. It is a perspective which finds support in the more secure findings of the natural sciences, which have their own legitimate and proper methodology and field of inquiry.

However, the Catholic moral viewpoint is founded on human reason illumined by faith and is consciously motivated by the desire to do the will of God, our Father. The church is thus in a position to learn from scientific discovery but also to transcend the horizons of science and to be confident that her more global vision does greater justice to the rich reality of the human person in his spiritual and physical dimensions created by God and heir, by grace, to eternal life.

It is within this context, then, that it can be clearly seen that the phenomenon of homosexuality, complex as it is and with its many consequences for society and ecclesial life, is a proper focus for the church's pastoral care. It thus requires of her ministers attentive study, active concern and honest, theologically well-balanced counsel.

3. Explicit treatment of the problem was given in this congregation's "Declaration on Certain Questions Concerning Sexual Ethics" of Dec. 29, 1975. That document stressed the duty of trying to understand the homosexual condition and noted that culpability for homosexual acts should only be judged with prudence. At the same time the congregation took note of the distinction commonly drawn between the homosexual condition or tendency and individual homosexual actions. These were described as deprived of their essential and indispensable finality, as being "intrinsically disordered" and able in no case to be approved of (cf. No. 8).

In the discussion which followed the publication of the declaration, however, an overly benign interpretation was given to the homosexual condition itself, some going so far as to call it neutral or even good. Although the particular inclination of the homosexual person is not a sin, it is a more or less strong tendency ordered toward an intrinsic moral evil and thus the inclination itself must be seen as an objective disorder.

Therefore special concern and pastoral attention should be directed toward those who have this condition, lest they be led to believe that the living out of this orientation in homosexual activity is a morally acceptable option. It is not.

4. An essential dimension of authentic pastoral care is the identification of causes of confusion regarding the church's teaching. One is a new exegesis of Sacred Scripture which claims variously that Scripture has nothing to say on the subject of homosexuality or that it somehow tacitly approves of it or that all of its moral injunctions are so culture-bound that they are no longer applicable to contemporary life. These views are gravely erroneous and call for particular attention here.

5. It is quite true that the biblical literature owes to the different epochs in which it was written a good deal of its varied patterns of thought and expression (*Dei Verbum*, 12). The church today addresses the Gospel to a world which differs in many ways from ancient days. But the world in which the New Testament was written was already quite diverse from the situation in which the Sacred Scriptures of the Hebrew people had been written or compiled, for example.

What should be noticed is that in the presence of such remarkable diversity there is nevertheless a clear consistency within the Scriptures themselves on the moral issue of homosexual behavior. The church's doctrine regarding this issue is thus based not on isolated phrases for facile theological argument, but on the solid foundation of a constant biblical testimony. The community of faith today, in unbroken continuity with the Jewish and Christian communities within which the ancient Scriptures were written, continues to be nourished by those same Scriptures and by the Spirit of truth whose word they are. It is likewise essential to recognize that the Scriptures are not properly understood when they are interpreted in a way which contradicts the church's living tradition. To be correct, the interpretation of Scripture must be in substantial accord with that tradition.

"It is likewise essential to recognize that the Scriptures are not properly understood when they are interpreted in a way which contradicts the church's living tradition."

Vatican Council II in *Dei Verbum,* No. 10, put it this way: "It is clear, therefore, that in the supremely wise arrangement of God, sacred tradition, Sacred Scripture and the magisterium of the church are so connected and associated that one of them cannot stand without the others. Working together, each in its own way under the action of the one Holy Spirit, they all contribute effectively to the salvation of souls." In that spirit we wish to outline briefly the biblical teaching here.

6. Providing a basic plan for understanding this entire discussion of homosexuality is the theology of creation we find in Genesis. God, by his infinite wisdom and love, brings into existence all of reality as a reflection of his goodness. He fashions mankind, male and female, in his own image and likeness. Human beings, therefore, are nothing less than the work of God himself and in the complementarity of the sexes they are called to reflect the inner unity of the Creator. They do this in a striking way in their cooperation with him in the transmission of life by a mutual donation of the self to the other.

In Genesis 3, we find that this truth about persons being an image of God has been obscured by original sin. There inevitably follows a loss of awareness of the covenantal character of the union these persons had with God and with each other. The human body retains its "spousal significance," but this is now clouded by sin. Thus, in Genesis 19:1-11, the deterioration due to sin continues in the story of the men of Sodom. There can be no doubt of the moral judgment made there against homosexual relations. In Leviticus 18:22 and 20:13, in the course of describing the conditions necessary for belonging to the chosen people, the author excludes from the people of God those who behave in a homosexual fashion.

Against the background of this exposition of theocratic law, an eschatological perspective is developed by St. Paul when, in 1 Corinthians 6:9, he proposes the same doctrine and lists those who behave in a homosexual fashion among those who shall not enter the kingdom of God.

In Romans 1:18-32, still building on the moral traditions of his forebears but in the new context of the confrontation between Christianity and the pagan society of his day, Paul uses homosexual behavior as an example of the blindness which has overcome humankind. Instead of the original harmony between Creator and creatures, the acute distortion of idolatry has led to all kinds of moral excess. Paul is at a loss to find a clearer example of this disharmony than homosexual relations. Finally, 1 Timothy 1, in full continuity with the biblical position, singles out those who spread wrong doctrine and in Verse 10 explicitly names as sinners those who engage in homosexual acts.

7. The church, obedient to the Lord who founded her and gave to her the sacramental life, celebrates the divine plan of the loving and life-giving union of men and women in the sacrament of marriage. It is only in the marital relationship that the use of the sexual faculty can be morally good. A person engaging in homosexual behavior therefore acts immorally.

To choose someone of the same sex for one's sexual activity is to annul the rich symbolism and meaning, not to mention the goals, of the Creator's sexual design. Homosexual activity is not a complementary union able to transmit life; and so it thwarts the call to a life of that form of self-giving which the Gospel says is the essence of Christian living. This does not mean that homosexual persons are not often generous and giving of themselves; but when they engage in homosexual activity they confirm within themselves a disordered sexual inclination which is essentially self-indulgent.

As in every moral disorder, homosexual activity prevents one's own fulfillment and happiness by acting contrary to the creative wisdom of God. The church, in rejecting erroneous opinions regarding homosexuality, does not limit but rather defends personal freedom and dignity realistically and authentically understood.

8. Thus, the church's teaching today is in organic continuity with the scriptural perspective and with her own constant tradition. Though today's world is in many ways quite new, the Christian community senses the profound and lasting bonds which join us to those generations who have gone before us, "marked with the sign of faith."

Nevertheless, increasing numbers of people today, even within the church, are bringing enormous pressure to bear on the church to accept the homosexual condition as though it were not disordered and to condone homosexual activity. Those within the church who argue in this fashion often have close ties with those with similar views outside it. These latter groups are guided by a vision opposed to the truth about the mystery of Christ. They reflect, even if not entirely consciously, a materialistic ideology which denies the transcendent nature of the human person as well as the supernatural vocation of every individual.

The church's ministers must ensure that homosexual persons in their care will not be misled by this point of view, so profoundly opposed to the teaching of the church. But the risk is great, and there are many who seek to create confusion regarding the church's position and then to use that confusion to their own advantage.

9. The movement within the church, which takes the form of pressure groups of various names and sizes, attempts to give the impression that it represents all homosexual persons who are Catholics. As a matter of fact, its membership is by and large restricted to those who either ignore the teaching of the church or seek somehow to undermine it. It brings together under the aegis of Catholicism homosexual persons who have no intention of abandoning their homosexual behavior. One tactic used is to protest that any and all criticism of or reservations about homosexual people, their activity and lifestyle are simply diverse forms of unjust discrimination.

There is an effort in some countries to manipulate the church by gaining the often well-intentioned support of her pastors with a view to changing civil statutes and laws. This is done in order to conform to these pressure groups' concept that homosexuality is at least a completely harmless, if not an entirely good, thing. Even when the practice of homosexuality may seriously threaten the lives and well-being of a large number of people, its advocates remain undeterred and refuse to consider the magnitude of the risks involved.

The church can never be so callous. It is true that her clear position cannot be revised by pressure from civil legislation or the trend of the moment. But she is really concerned about the many who are not represented by the pro-homosexual movement and about those who may have been tempted to believe its deceitful propaganda. She is also aware that the view that homosexual activity is equivalent to or as acceptable as the sexual expression of conjugal love has a direct impact on society's understanding of the nature and rights of the family and puts them in jeopardy.

10. It is deplorable that homosexual persons have been and are the object of violent malice in speech or in action. Such treatment deserves condemnation from the church's pastors wherever it occurs. It reveals a kind of disregard for others which endangers the most fundamental principles of a healthy society. The intrinsic dignity of each person must always be respected in word, in action and in law.

But the proper reaction to crimes committed against homosexual persons should not be to claim that the homosexual condition is not disordered. When such a claim is made and when homosexual activity is consequently condoned or when civil legislation is introduced to protect behavior to which no one has any conceivable right, neither the church nor society at large should be surprised when other distorted notions and practices gain ground, and irrational and violent reactions increase.

11. It has been argued that the homosexual orientation in certain cases is not the result of deliberate choice; and so the homosexual person would then have no choice but to behave in a homosexual fashion. Lacking freedom, such a person, even if engaged in homosexual activity, would not be culpable.

Here, the church's wise moral tradition is necessary since it warns against generalizations in judging individual cases. In fact, circumstances may exist or may have existed in the past which would reduce or remove the culpability of the individual in a given instance; or other circumstances may increase it. What is at all costs to be avoided is the unfounded and demeaning assumption that the sexual behavior of homosexual persons is always and totally compulsive and therefore inculpable. What is essential is that the fundamental liberty which characterizes the human person and gives him his dignity be recognized as belonging to the homosexual person as well. As in every conversion from evil, the abandonment of homosexual activity will require a profound collaboration of the individual with God's liberating grace.

12. What, then, are homosexual persons to do who seek to follow the Lord? Fundamentally, they are called to enact the will of God in their life by joining whatever sufferings and difficulties they experience in virtue of their condition to the sacrifice of the Lord's cross. That cross, for the believer, is a fruitful sacrifice since from that death come life and redemption. While any call to carry the cross or to understand a Christian's suffering in this way will predictably be met with bitter

ridicule by some, it should be remembered that this is the way to eternal life for *all* who follow Christ.

It is, in effect, none other than the teaching of Paul the apostle to the Galatians when he says that the Spirit produces in the lives of the faithful "love, joy, peace, patience, kindness, goodness, trustfulness, gentleness and self-control" *(5:22)* and further (Verse 24), "You cannot belong to Christ unless you crucify all self-indulgent passions and desires."

It is easily misunderstood, however, if it is merely seen as a pointless effort at self-denial. The cross *is* a denial of self, but in service to the will of God himself, who makes life come from death and empowers those who trust in him to practice virtue in place of vice.

To celebrate the paschal mystery it is necessary to let that mystery become imprinted in the fabric of daily life. To refuse to sacrifice one's own will in obedience to the will of the Lord is effectively to prevent salvation. Just as the cross was central to the expression of God's redemptive love for us in Jesus, so the conformity of the self-denial of homosexual men and women with the sacrifice of the Lord will constitute for them a source of self-giving which will save them from a way of life which constantly threatens to destroy them.

Christians who are homosexual are called, as all of us are, to a chaste life. As they dedicate their lives to understanding the nature of God's personal call to them, they will be able to celebrate the sacrament of penance more faithfully and receive the Lord's grace so freely offered there in order to convert their lives more fully to his way.

13. We recognize, of course, that in great measure the clear and successful communication of the church's teaching to all the faithful and to society at large depends on the correct instruction and fidelity of her pastoral ministers. The bishops have the particularly grave responsibility to see to it that their assistants in the ministry, above all the priests, are rightly informed and personally disposed to bring the teaching of the church in its integrity to everyone.

The characteristic concern and good will exhibited by many clergy and religious in their pastoral care for homosexual persons is admirable and, we hope, will not diminish. Such devoted ministers should have the confidence that they are faithfully following the will of the Lord by encouraging the homosexual person to lead a chaste life and by affirming that person's God-given dignity and worth.

14. With this in mind, this congregation wishes to ask the bishops to be especially cautious of any programs which may seek to pressure the church to change her teaching, even while claiming not to do so. A careful examination of their public statements and the activities they promote reveals a studied ambiguity by which they attempt to mislead the pastors and the faithful. For example, they may present the teaching of the magisterium, but only as if it were an optional source for the formation of one's conscience. Its specific authority is not recognized. Some of these groups will use the word "Catholic" to describe either the

organization or its intended members, yet they do not defend and promote the teaching of the magisterium; indeed, they even openly attack it. While their members may claim a desire to conform their lives to the teaching of Jesus, in fact they abandon the teaching of his church. This contradictory action should not have the support of the bishops in any way.

15. We encourage the bishops, then, to provide pastoral care in full accord with the teaching of the church for homosexual persons of their dioceses. No authentic pastoral program will include organizations in which homosexual persons associate with each other without clearly stating that homosexual activity is immoral. A truly pastoral approach will appreciate the need for homosexual persons to avoid the near occasions of sin.

We would heartily encourage programs where these dangers are avoided. But we wish to make it clear that departure from the church's teaching or silence about it, in an effort to provide pastoral care, is neither caring nor pastoral. Only what is true can ultimately be pastoral. The neglect of the church's position prevents homosexual men and women from receiving the care they need and deserve.

An authentic pastoral program will assist homosexual persons at all levels of the spiritual life: through the sacraments, and in particular through the frequent and sincere use of the sacrament of reconciliation, through prayer, witness, counsel and individual care. In such a way, the entire Christian community can come to recognize its own call to assist its brothers and sisters, without deluding them or isolating them.

16. From this multifaceted approach there are numerous advantages to be gained, not the least of which is the realization that a homosexual person, as every human being, deeply needs to be nourished at many different levels simultaneously.

The human person, made in the image and likeness of God, can hardly be adequately described by a reductionist reference to his or her sexual orientation. Everyone living on the face of the earth has personal problems and difficulties, but challenges to growth, strengths, talents and gifts as well. Today the church provides a badly needed context for the care of the human person when she refuses to consider the person as a "heterosexual" or a "homosexual" and insists that every person has a fundamental identity: the creature of God and, by grace, his child and heir to eternal life.

17. In bringing this entire matter to the bishops' attention, this congregation wishes to support their efforts to assure that the teaching of the Lord and his church on this important question be communicated fully to the faithful.

In light of the points made above, they should decide for their own dioceses the extent to which an intervention on their part is indicated. In addition, should they consider it helpful, further coordinated action at the level of their national bishops' conference may be envisioned.

In a particular way we would ask the bishops to support, with the means at their disposal, the development of appropriate forms of pastoral care for homosexual persons. These would include the assistance of the psychological, sociological and medical sciences, in full accord with the teaching of the church.

They are encouraged to call on the assistance of all Catholic theologians who, by teaching what the church teaches and by deepening their reflections on the true meaning of human sexuality and Christian marriage with the virtues it engenders, will make an important contribution in this particular area of pastoral care.

The bishops are asked to exercise special care in the selection of pastoral ministers so that by their own high degree of spiritual and personal maturity and by their fidelity to the magisterium, they may be of real service to homosexual persons, promoting their health and well-being in the fullest sense. Such ministers will reject theological opinions which dissent from the teaching of the church and which therefore cannot be used as guidelines for pastoral care.

We encourage the bishops to promote appropriate catechetical programs based on the truth about human sexuality in its relationship to the family as taught by the church. Such programs should provide a good context within which to deal with the question of homosexuality.

This catechesis would also assist those families of homosexual persons to deal with this problem which affects them so deeply.

All support should be withdrawn from any organizations which seek to undermine the teaching of the church, which are ambiguous about it or which neglect it entirely. Such support or even the semblance of such support can be gravely misinterpreted. Special attention should be given to the practice of scheduling religious services and to the use of church buildings by these groups, including the facilities of Catholic schools and colleges. To some, such permission to use church property may seem only just and charitable; but in reality it is contradictory to the purpose for which these institutions were founded, it is misleading and often scandalous.

In assessing proposed legislation, the bishops should keep as their uppermost concern the responsibility to defend and promote family life.

18. The Lord Jesus promised, "You shall know the truth and the truth shall set you free" (Jn. 8:32). Scripture bids us speak the truth in love (cf. Eph 4:15). The God who is at once truth and love calls the church to minister to every man, woman and child with the pastoral solicitude of our compassionate Lord. It is in this spirit that we have addressed this letter to the bishops of the church, with the hope that it will be of some help as they care for those whose suffering can only be intensified by error and lightened by truth.

During an audience granted to the undersigned prefect, His Holiness Pope John Paul II approved this letter, adopted in an ordinary session of the Congregation for the Doctrine of the Faith, and ordered it to be published.

Given at Rome, Oct. 1, 1986.
Cardinal Joseph Ratzinger, prefect
Archbishop Alberto Bovone, secretary

34.

FROM AN INTERVIEW WITH THOMAS GUMBLETON, AUXILIARY BISHOP, ARCHDIOCESE OF DETROIT

Interviewed by Michael W. Higgins and Douglas R. Letson for Grail: An Ecumenical Journal (September 1998)

Grail – I said earlier that there were two things you were known for. One is for your association with Pax Christi. The other is, of course, for your sensitivity to the whole gay issue in Roman Catholicism. Do you see the church as being able to provide some openness or are bishops obligated to maintain some canonical rigidity on the front and then work out some quiet pastoral solution behind the scenes?

Thomas Gumbleton – It is certainly true that bishops generally are conservers. It's their role to make sure you keep continuity with the tradition and keep the tradition. So they tend to hold back to maintain that tradition. But at the same time, part of our tradition is that it evolves. So if we're genuinely conservative we have to be open to the evolution of teaching. And this is clearly true in moral teaching. We have evolved tremendously in our whole understanding of sexuality, morality, and human sexual relationships.

This is maybe not as coherent as I would like it. I talk about it a lot these days. This is one of the things I point out to people because it's such a frustration to the homosexual community, that we have finally recognized there is such a thing as orientation but we keep on condemning action or activity. You can go back to Pope Gregory the Great when he sent Augustine to England. He sent him with a letter in which it says something about not allowing people to come into the church after they have had marital relations because they can't do that without experiencing pleasure and, of course, that's a sin. That was our teaching and it was constant through a thousand years or more. Almost never could married people engage in sexual intercourse without committing at least a venial sin. Most of the time it was going to be a lot worse than that, because with passion you lose control and so you're not human any longer.

That has changed. You read what John Paul writes about marriage and it's so idealistic and mystical almost, but it's clearly accepting the human body, sex, and the pleasure that goes with it as all part of marriage. It's all part of deepening intimacy. Well, that evolution has happened. My point is that I can't predict what's going to happen but I say two things to the homosexual community. One is that even in the human sciences, we don't know enough about sexuality right now and how people integrate their sexuality into their personhood in the healthiest way possible. And I say every one of us has to struggle to do that, whether we're heterosexual in a marriage relationship or whether we're a celibate like I am. I have to integrate my sexuality with how I continue to grow as a human person. I can't repress everything or be self-destructive. I have to have friends, I have to have intimacy, and yet I'm committed to a celibate life. I have to struggle to do that. Well, homosexual people also have to figure out how sexuality integrates into life in the healthiest way possible, because ultimately what is morally right and morally good is what leads us to become the full human person God intends us to be. There aren't predesigned rules out there, nor do you have to jump through hoops that make you good. What God has intended is that we become the full person that we have the capacity to become. Part of that is our human relationships that nourish or nurture us as a person. If they're destructive, well then there is something wrong with them. They can't be wrong just on a human scale but, rather, morally wrong too. Because if you deliberately choose to be self-destructive, however much freedom there is in your choice, that is a moral flaw or defect.

And so I point out that through evolution we haven't come to the point of having a definitive understanding of everything that has to do with sexuality. The church is still learning and we have to continue to learn. Part of this learning needs to be from the experience of homosexual people. That's never previously been part of the content that the moral theologians put in the textbooks. They never drew out of the homosexual experience to say what is nurturing, what is life-giving, and what makes them free to be fully human. So we need their experience.

But then the other key thing is primacy of conscience. That's a very traditional part of Catholic teaching. The ultimate arbiter of what is right or wrong for you is the well-informed conscience. You have to consult scripture, the tradition, your own prayer life, take consultation with other people and try to discover what is right for you. Then when you have made your choice in conscience you follow that.

The latest pastoral that we put out called *Always Our Children* had half a page in there on the primacy of conscience. First, we clearly set forth the teaching. Again we're conserving so we're not going to jump way out in front. Then there was this section on primacy of conscience which would have been helpful to the homosexual community. The pastoral said this is what the church is saying and, yet, in my life I have to follow my conscience. But then we pulled that. It's not in the final text. But I give it out. I share that with people. Or I've been to some colleges or universities where they have student groups that are trying to become accepted or in some cases they are accepted on campus. But their frustration is that the church tells them, "It's okay to be who I am, but then you tell me I can't act on who I am. That is frustrating and it's stifling to me."

So I talk about the evolution of the teaching and how no one knows how it's going to evolve and I also talk about primacy of conscience. At least this gives an opening for people. They feel less alienated from the official church even though they're not being affirmed and told it's okay to act on who they are. But within the primacy of their own conscience they can act on who they are.

Grail – Just to follow that up – it seems to me that a good bit of our background has been Thomistic and syllogistic and cerebral and there has been a real effort to provide sensitive reaction to sexual questions generally. But the responses from Rome and even the response on gays that the bishops in the United States put out six or seven months ago, have got a rational tone to them. How you take that rational tone and explain to people who are trying to live decent lives and have them be convinced by it, is just beyond me.

TG – I don't think you can do it on that intellectual level. I really do think it has to be on an interpersonal level. To me one of the main things that would help the bishops would be to listen to the experience of the homosexual community and to take that into consideration when they're trying to write something to respond to their pain, their hurt, and their sense of alienation. But they didn't do that. The committee didn't do that. They did it all from an abstract intellectual background and then came forward with this letter. Now it's a major step in the right direction but it's only a step.

I must say for the most part in the States the homosexual community accepted the letter and they were very appreciative of the fact that we got that far at least. It is a lot further than what came out of the Congregation for the Doctrine of the Faith about intrinsic disorder and that sort of thing. The second one practically justified violence by saying that it's your own fault and if you're acting out in this way and somebody kills you, well, then, you asked for it. They didn't quite say that but there is that sort of tone.

So this is a step in the right direction, especially as it says that there is no reason why a homosexual person can't be fully active in their parish. They should be able to be teachers in schools, they should be able to be eucharistic ministers and be recognized as a gay or a lesbian person and still be fully active. Well, that's a big step forward but the text itself is kind of cold.

When the bishops did try to write a pastoral letter drawing on the experience of people, it was the Women's Pastoral. The first draft of that was really good because they had listened to the pain, the anguish, the anger and yet the love for the church that so many women had. That was reflected in the first draft. But it got slammed by the conference when it was presented. Then we went to two other drafts and each one got worse by moving in the direction you're talking about. Each one became more analytical, abstract and theoretical to the point where it became clear to give it up. So the thing was voted down and we don't have one.

Grail – Just one final question. The whole debate about [former U.S. President] Clinton these days is interesting from several points of view, but one of them is that it has become almost Thomistic in its argumentation. The fact that the man may well be engaged in an adulterous relationship seems to bother no one any longer. It's more a question of what constitutes intercourse. That's almost Thomistic and one wonders what is happening to the moral fibre of the United

States and what the role of the church is in a country when adultery seems to be completely acceptable.

TG – Well, the role of the church is to try to maintain a higher moral standard, to teach it, and to try to live it. But I don't think it is a healthy thing for us in the States to have everything about the private life of public people put out into the open. No one is a saint. If everything every bishop did was on the front page of the newspaper every day it would be pretty disastrous for the church.

I really do think we have gone too far in making private life public for public figures. It almost forces a lot of deception which further causes deterioration in the moral atmosphere so that people try to lie and hide.

35.

NOTIFICATION REGARDING SISTER GRAMICK
AND FATHER NUGENT

Doctrinal Congregation/Homosexuality (1999)

Positions advanced by Salvatorian Father Robert Nugent and School Sister of Notre Dame Jeannine Gramick "regarding the intrinsic evil of homosexual acts and the objective disorder of the homosexual inclination are doctrinally unacceptable," says a notification by the Vatican Congregation for the Doctrine of the faith made public at the Vatican July 13.

Sister Jeannine Gramick, SSND, and Father Robert Nugent, SDS, have been engaged in pastoral activities directed toward homosexual persons for more than 20 years. In 1977 they founded the organization New Ways Ministry within the territory of the Archdiocese of Washington in order to promote "justice and reconciliation between lesbian and gay Catholics and the wider Catholic community."[1] They are the authors of the book *Building Bridges: Gay and Lesbian Reality and the Catholic Church* (Mystic, Conn.: Twenty-Third Publications, 1992) and editors of the volume *Voices of Hope: A Collection of Positive Catholic Writings on Gay and Lesbian Issues* (New York: Center for Homophobia Education, 1995).

From the beginning, in presenting the church's teaching on homosexuality, Father Nugent and Sister Gramick have continually called central elements of that teaching into question. For this reason, in 1984 Cardinal James Hickey, the archbishop of Washington, following the failure of a number of attempts at clarification, informed them that they could no longer undertake their activities in that archdiocese. At the same time, the Congregation for Institutes of Consecrated Life and for Societies of Apostolic Life ordered them to separate themselves totally and completely from New Ways Ministry, adding that they were not to exercise any apostolate without faithfully presenting the church's teaching regarding the intrinsic evil of homosexual acts.

Despite this action by the Holy See, Father Nugent and Sister Gramick continued their involvement in activities organized by New Ways Ministry, though removing themselves from leadership positions. They also continued to maintain and promote ambiguous positions on homosexuality and explicitly criticized documents of the church's magisterium on this issue. Because of their statements and activities, the Congregation for the Doctrine of the Faith and the Congregation for Institutes of Consecrated Life and for Societies of Apostolic Life received numerous complaints and urgent requests for clarification from bishops and others in the

United States of America. It was clear that the activities of Sister Gramick and Father Nugent were causing difficulties in not a few dioceses and that they were continuing to present the teaching of the church as one possible option among others and as open to fundamental change.

In 1988 the Holy See established a commission under the presidency of Cardinal Adam Maida to study and evaluate their public statements and activities, and to determine whether these were faithful to Catholic teaching on homosexuality.

After the publication of *Building Bridges,* the investigation of the commission focused primarily on this book, which summarized their activities and thinking. In 1994 the commission issued its findings, which were communicated to the two authors. When their responses to these findings were received, the commission formulated its final recommendations and forwarded them to the Congregation for Institutes of Consecrated Life and for Societies of Apostolic Life. While not overlooking the presence of some positive aspects in the apostolate of Father Nugent and Sister Gramick, the commission found serious deficiencies in their writings and pastoral activities, which were incompatible with the fullness of Christian morality. The commission, therefore, recommended disciplinary measures, including the publication of some form of notification, in order to counteract and repair the harmful confusion caused by the errors and ambiguities in their publications and activities.

As the problems presented by the two authors were primarily of a doctrinal nature, in 1995 the Congregation for Institutes of Consecrated Life and for Societies of Apostolic Life transferred the entire case to the competence of the Congregation for the Doctrine of the Faith. At this point, with the hope that Father Nugent and Sister Gramick would be willing to express their assent to Catholic teaching on homosexuality and to correct the errors in their writings, the congregation undertook another attempt at resolution by inviting them to respond unequivocally to certain questions regarding their position on the morality of homosexual acts and on the homosexual inclination.

Their responses, dated Feb. 22, 1996, were not sufficiently clear to dispel the serious ambiguities of their position. In these, Sister Gramick and Father Nugent demonstrated a clear conceptual understanding of the church's teaching on homosexuality, but refrained from professing any adherence to that teaching. Furthermore, the publication in 1995 of their book *Voices of Hope: A Collection of Positive Catholic Writings on Gay and Lesbian Issues* had made it clear that there was no change in their opposition to fundamental elements of the church's teaching.

Given the fact that certain of the statements of Father Nugent and Sister Gramick were clearly incompatible with the teaching of the church and that the wide dissemination of these errors through their publications and pastoral activities was becoming an increasing source of concern for bishops in the United States of America, the congregation decided that the case should be resolved according to the procedure outlined in its "Regulations for Doctrinal Examination" (Chapter 4).[2]

In the ordinary session of Oct. 8, 1997, the cardinals and bishops who make up the congregation judged that the statements of Father Nugent and Sister Gramick, which had been identified through the above-mentioned procedure of the "Regulations for Doctrinal Examination," were in fact erroneous and dangerous. After the Holy Father had approved the formal *contestatio* of the authors, the above-mentioned erroneous statements were presented to them through their respective superiors general. Each was asked to respond to the *contestatio* personally and independently from the other, to allow them the greatest freedom in expressing their individual positions.

In February 1998, the two superiors general forwarded the responses to the congregation. In the ordinary sessions of May 6 and May 20, 1998, the members of the congregation carefully evaluated the responses after having received the opinions of members of the episcopate of the United States and of experts in the field of moral theology. The members of the congregation were unanimous in their decision that the responses of the two, while containing certain positive elements, were unacceptable. In each case, Father Nugent and Sister Gramick had sought to justify the publication of their books, and neither had expressed personal adherence to the church's teaching on homosexuality in sufficiently unequivocal terms. Thus, it was decided that they should be asked to formulate a public declaration, which would be submitted to the judgment of the congregation. In this declaration they were asked to express their interior assent to the teaching of the Catholic Church on homosexuality and to acknowledge that the two above-mentioned books contained errors.

The two declarations which arrived in August 1998 were examined by the congregation in the ordinary session of Oct. 21, 1998. Once again, they were not sufficient to resolve the problems associated with their writings and pastoral activities. Sister Gramick, while expressing her love for the church, simply refused to express any assent whatsoever to the teaching of the church on homosexuality. Father Nugent was more responsive, but not unequivocal in his statement of interior assent to the teaching of the church.

It was decided by the members of the congregation, therefore, that Father Nugent should be given yet another opportunity to express unequivocal assent. For this reason the congregation formulated a declaration of assent and, with its letter of Dec. 15, 1998, forwarded it to Father Nugent, through his superior general, for his acceptance. His response, dated Jan. 25, 1999, showed that this attempt had not met with success. Father Nugent would not sign the declaration he had received and responded by formulating an alternative text which modified the congregation's declaration on certain important points. In particular, he would not state that homosexual acts are intrinsically disordered, and he added a section which calls into question the definitive and unchangeable nature of Catholic doctrine in this area.

Given the failure of the repeated attempts of the church's legitimate authorities to resolve the problems presented by the writings and pastoral activities of the two authors, the Congregation for the Doctrine of the Faith is obliged to declare for the good of the Catholic faithful that the positions advanced by Sister Jeannine Gramick and Father Robert Nugent regarding the intrinsic evil of homosexual acts and the objective disorder of the homosexual inclination are doctrinally unacceptable because they do not faithfully convey the clear and constant teaching of the Catholic Church in this area.[3]

Father Nugent and Sister Gramick have often stated that they seek, in keeping with the church's teaching, to treat homosexual persons "with respect, compassion and sensitivity."[4] However, the promotion of errors and ambiguities is not consistent with a Christian attitude of true respect and compassion: Persons who are struggling with homosexuality, no less than any others, have the right to receive the authentic teaching of the church from those who minister to them.

The ambiguities and errors of the approach of Father Nugent and Sister Gramick have caused confusion among the Catholic people and have harmed the community of the church. For these reasons, Sister Jeannine Gramick, SSND, and Father Robert Nugent, SDS, are permanently prohibited from any pastoral work involving homosexual persons and are ineligible, for an undetermined period, for any office in their respective religious institutes.

The sovereign Pontiff John Paul II, at the audience of May 14, 1999, granted to the under-signed secretary, approved the present notification, adopted in the ordinary session of this congregation and ordered its publication.

Rome, from the offices of Congregation for the Doctrine of the Faith, May 31, 1999.

Cardinal Joseph Ratzinger, Prefect
Archbishop Tarcisio Bertone, SDB, Secretary

---

[1] *Voices of Hope: A Collection of Positive Catholic Writings on Gay and Lesbian Issues* (New York: Center for Homophobia Education, 1995) ix.

[2] Cf. Congregation for the Doctrine of the Faith, "Regulations for Doctrinal Examination," Art. 23-27: *Acta Apostolicae Sedis* 89 (1997), 834.

[3] Cf. Gn. 19:1-11; Lv. 18:22; 20:13; 1 Cor. 6:9; Rom. 1:18-32; 1 Tm. 1:10; Catechism of the Catholic Church, 2357-2359, 2396; Congregation for the Doctrine of the Faith, "Declaration on Certain Questions Concerning Sexual Ethics," 8: AAS 68 (1976), 84-85; "Letter to Bishops on the Pastoral Care of Homosexual Persons," AAS 79 (1987), 543-554.

[4] *Catechism of the Catholic Church,* 2358.

36.

SILENCING OF NUGENT, GRAMICK, SETS A NOVEL STANDARD OF ORTHODOXY

Lisa Sowle Cahill

***America*, August 14, 1999**

It is well known that Catholicism, along with traditional Christianity and most other religions, sees homosexual relationships as a sin. It is less well known that, since at least 1975, the year of the publication of the Vatican's *Declaration on Certain Questions Concerning Sexual Ethics,* the Catholic Church has made it clear that it is not a sin to be a homosexual (i.e., to have a homosexual "orientation"). The sin is in engaging voluntarily in homosexual acts. Even this latter teaching is moderated by the traditional Catholic premises that one's responsibility for sin is diminished to the degree that one acts "involuntarily" out of compulsion, impulse or passion; or if one's conscience is in error, even though one has made a sincere effort to properly inform it through respectful attention to religious authorities. While sexual acts between persons of the same sex have been deemed objectively immoral and termed "intrinsically disordered" or "intrinsically evil," homosexual persons are certainly not condemned simply on the basis of their sexual orientation.

Catholic sexual teaching of generations past dealt mightily in negatives and threats, and portrayed all sexual sins as "mortal." The documents of Vatican II, Paul VI's *Humanae Vitae,* and writings of John Paul II, however, place the emphasis more on positive models of sexuality (as a form of "mutual self-gift"), urge pastoral understanding for human failure and offer support to all who struggle with sexual identity or toward truly moral sexual behavior. According to the *Catechism of the Catholic Church* (1992), homosexual persons "must be accepted with respect, compassion and sensitivity" (No. 2358). This command is quoted in a 1997 pastoral message from the Committee on Marriage and Family of the United States Conference of Catholic Bishops, *Always Our Children.* Addressed to the families of gays and lesbians, as well as to the church's pastoral ministers, this message emphasizes that, while the church summons all Christians "to a higher standard of loving," it also offers "its homosexual sisters and brothers understanding and pastoral care."

Admittedly, it will always be a difficult challenge for any religious or moral community to affirm high standards while still accepting and encouraging those who have not yet fully lived up to them, or who may even be in violation. This is certainly a challenge for Catholic ministry to gays and lesbians, as well as to divorced and remarried Catholics, couples living together while preparing for marriage, clergy whose sexual attractions and relationships threaten their commitment to celibacy, teen-agers pressured toward sexual experimentation and women exploited by the sex industry.

Pastoral care must always be personal and contextual; it requires prudence and sometimes involves risk. The pastoral minister, as well as the author of pastoral theology, must discern what will constitute a life-giving and grace-filled message capable of converting hearers to the fullness of life in Christ in an atmosphere of forgiveness and reconciliation. No such message can arise unless it truly engages the experiences and needs of its intended audience. Learning and listening must go both ways, as is admirably clear in *Always Our Children.*

To say the least, pastoral ministry to those who have been hurt and excluded, or even been the victims of hatred and violence because of distorted Christian or Catholic teachings, should not always begin with or stress sin and judgment. The healing word of God's love must be preached, even at the risk of misunderstanding. Often the focus must lie, as in *Always Our Children,* on love, mercy and grace. That message ends by addressing homosexual persons in the following way: 'Though at times you may feel discouraged, hurt, or angry, do not walk away from your families, from the Christian community, from all those who love you. In you God's love is revealed. You are always our children."

The Charge

In a "notification" released by the Vatican on July 14 of this year two members of Catholic religious congregations, Robert Nugent, S.D.S., and Jeannine Gramick, S.S.N.D., who have worked together in ministry to gay and lesbian Catholics and their families since the early 1970's, were barred from further such pastoral work and prohibited from holding office in their religious orders. The central charge against them is a failure, in their ministry to gays and in writing, to clearly condemn homosexual activity.

Although Gramick has made no public comment (as of my writing), Nugent issued a statement that his ministry had been motivated by the "respect, compassion and sensitivity" to homosexual persons that has been mandated by the *Catechism of the Catholic Church.* Moreover, he said, he accepted and adhered to the Catholic doctrine on sexuality contained in prior Vatican documents and the catechism, and, in fact, had never even been accused of public dissent from any teaching of the church about homosexuality, but only of "ambiguity" in his level of support for condemnations.

Even after repeated investigations over the course of two decades by the Archdiocese of Washington, the Vatican Congregation for Institutes of Consecrated Life and the Congregation for the Doctrine of the Faith, as well as lengthy written exchanges with the two accused, the Vatican has apparently been unable to identify any specific point in the writings or pastoral teaching of Nugent and

Gramick in which they reject church teaching on homosexuality. In other words, absent any evidence of direct, public dissent from church teaching, or even from authoritative, noninfallible teaching, the Vatican is silencing Gramick and Nugent for not having adequately clarified points they in fact chose not to address out of pastoral concerns. The Congregation for the Doctrine of the Faith is thus reduced to bolstering its strong measures with vague references to "errors and ambiguities," and charging that the two accused have not emphasized sufficiently "the intrinsic evil of homosexual acts."

Even without denying the moral analysis of such acts as wrong in principle, it is certainly possible to take issue with the Vatican condemnation, which, finding no actual departure from Catholic teaching by Gramick and Nugent, revolves instead around a judgment about how they should present that teaching in ministry to gays. While *Voices of Hope,* a book edited by Nugent and Gramick, contains "positive" Catholic views of homosexuality that may collide with magisterial analyses, the volume also includes examples of official teaching itself. Gramick and Nugent's own book, *Building Bridges,* presents debates in the church about homosexuality, and presents in a positive light authors who affirm gay experience, but does not actually endorse any "dissenting" position. Moreover, New Ways Ministry, which they founded, has also published and circulated *Homosexuality and the Magisterium* (edited by John Gallagher), a collection of documents from the Vatican and the U.S. bishops, which presents the magisterium's arguments against homosexuality, as well as statements advancing compassion and reconciliation. In New Ways Ministry workshops, according to Nugent, a "handout" is distributed that presents five points of church teaching, of which the latter three are least familiar, and thus typically attract more attention. These five are: the objective disorder of homosexual acts, the intrinsic evil of homosexual acts and the civil rights of, pastoral care for and human dignity of homosexual persons.

In 1998 Jeannine Gramick and Robert Nugent were each asked by the Congregation for the Doctrine of the Faith to compose declarations of faith and adherence to church teaching. These were submitted to the C.D.F. and found wanting. Gramick expressed her love for the church but refused to give assent to any church teachings on homosexuality. Nugent's statement was found to be "not unequivocal." Therefore a declaration of assent was formulated for him by the congregation, which he agreed to sign only in revised form. The revisions concerned two points in particular that caused this statement also to be rejected by the C.D.F. First, Nugent rejected the phrases "objectively evil" and "intrinsically evil" as applied to homosexual acts and substituted the phrases "objectively speaking, morally wrong" and "objectively immoral." The rationale he offered was that the stipulated designations can cause "serious pastoral harm or confusion among people whom I have attempted to reconcile with the church." Second, Nugent added a paragraph referring to "difficulties in determining whether a particular teaching has in fact been taught infallibly by a nondefining act of the ordinary and universal magisterium," although he still affirmed "the authoritative and binding nature of such teaching." Finally Nugent did include above his signature the statement, "I adhere with religious submission of will and intellect to the teaching that the homosexual inclination, though not in itself a sin, constitutes a tendency toward behavior that is objectively immoral and therefore must be considered objectively disordered."

Objectively/Subjectively Immoral?

In its rejecting response, the Vatican replied that the terminology "objectively immoral" could be interpreted to imply that homosexual behavior could be subjectively moral, or that homosexual acts are not intrinsically wrong, but can become objectively wrong through the presence of certain circumstantial factors, an argument used by so-called "proportionalists." It added that allusions to the possible noninfallibility of authoritative teaching could only be meant to suggest that that teaching might in the future change.

Although the Vatican's extrapolations are not, in my opinion, completely without foundation, a fact that must be kept in sight is that Nugent, though he has signed a statement agreeing that homosexual acts are immoral, is being condemned on the basis of suspicions about his tone, motives, implications and possible association with others whose ethical methodology has fallen under a cloud. And on the point of the subjective morality of homosexuality, the author of the C.D.F. response himself contradicts Catholic moral teaching by denying that an objectively immoral act could be subjectively moral for the sincere but erroneous conscience. As the catechism has it, "If... the ignorance is invincible, or the moral subject is not responsible for his erroneous judgment, the evil committed by the person cannot be imputed to him" (No. 1793). From Nugent the Vatican wants not only conformity of doctrine and practice, but a soul-selling "internal assent" to descriptions of homosexuals that Nugent believes are not only wrong but destructive. Again the catechism: "A human being must always obey the certain judgment of his conscience. If he were deliberately to act against it, he would condemn himself" (No. 1790). Finally, if there were no "difficulties" in determining infallible and irreversible moral teaching, controversies over Catholic sexual morality would never erupt in the first place.

It is of some interest that, on the day the Vatican notification was released, Bishop Joseph A. Fiorenza of Galveston-Houston, president of the National Conference of Catholic Bishops, made a public statement that the silencing of Nugent and Gramick should not be read as a condemnation of ministry to gay people, and that the bishops in fact are committed to ministry to gays as "brothers and sisters in the Lord." This move seems to represent a perception within U.S. episcopal leadership that words of understanding toward gays are in this culture and at this time an important corrective to generations of painful rejection, including very recent examples of violence and homicide perpetrated against gays in our society. Perhaps Fiorenza discerns that the clear and present danger of "confusing the faithful" in North America lies on the side of strong statements against gays and their sympathizers, made publicly by high church representatives, not on the side of advocates of the other part of Catholic moral teaching about homosexuals, namely, that they are sisters and brothers in the community of Christ.

Homosexuality and the Magisterium, published by New Ways Ministry, ends by quoting the more balanced voice of Cardinal Joseph Bernardin: "I firmly deplore acts of violence, degradation, discrimination, or diminishment of any human person – including anyone with a homosexual orientation.... At the same time, as a bishop in the Catholic Church, I am equally bound to teach that homosexual activity and patterns of life which promote it are immoral."

So it would not be true to say that Gramick, Nugent or New Ways Ministry (in which they have now been forbidden to participate) conceals either part of the official Catholic message about homosexuality. Instead, their choice of a positive emphasis should be seen as a prudential judgment about an effective Catholic presence in the gay and lesbian community. Along the same lines, Archbishop Raymond Hunthausen of Seattle, in an interview in the same book, responds to criticism that he allowed Dignity – a Catholic-oriented gay support group that does overtly encourage gay people to form committed unions – to celebrate a Mass in the archdiocesan cathedral. "I decided that this was a risk that ought to be taken in order to deal with this delicate and highly charged issue in a Christian manner."

New Maximalist Criterion of Conformity

While one might argue that the fullness of Catholic teaching includes points pastorally downplayed by Nugent and Gramick (the intrinsic evil and immorality of homosexual acts), Vatican policy on conformity and dissent has certainly taken a novel turn by focusing on this fact. Now the bottom line of orthodoxy is full disclosure of church teaching on an issue, rather than the avoidance of any claims that contradict it. In other words, a minimalist standard of non-contradiction has been replaced by a maximalist standard that requires not only theologians but pastors to present a range of specified points of Catholic teaching around a given issue, and to do so in precisely the language prescribed by Vatican authorities. Now people are being silenced *not* for contradicting any doctrine, and not even for contradicting any "noninfallible teaching," but for staying within church teaching while not equally emphasizing or including other points.

Will this maximalist criterion be applied equally to moral theologians writing in other areas, such as just war theory or economics? Must every defender of just war make an equally clear statement that violence violates Christian identity, or the defender of democratic capitalism a clear statement that Western market societies and economic "globalization" violate the rights of the poor? Will those who fail to do so be silenced? The anti-Christian nature of war and the "preferential option for the poor" have been given much more attention by Pope John Paul II than the intrinsic evil of homosexual acts. Moreover, the Vatican's demand that Nugent take a submissive posture goes far beyond the conformity of his formal, public positions in theology or in ministry and reaches to the renunciation of his own conscientiously held values, a renunciation to be expressed in formulae imposed by Vatican investigators.

One is left to wonder if this type of response can reasonably be expected of someone subject to a Vatican investigation without annihilating his or her personal dignity and integrity and betraying the Christian values of charity and reconciliation in the process. One wonders indeed whether the outcome of this transaction was decided at its beginnings in Washington and Rome, making the long, draining inquiries and negotiations with Nugent and Gramick mere ancillary procedural accompaniments to the predestined condemnation of what had been (wrongly) determined in advance to be "dissenting" sexual theology.

The new, expanded criterion of crime and punishment enacted through this case is ominous in a time in which bishops, theologians and Catholic universities are debating the meaning and implementation of *Ex Corde Ecclesiae,* a Vatican document requiring that theologians obtain a "mandate" to teach from the local bishop. The Vatican argues to concerned U.S. academics that the purpose of expanded episcopal control over theology is merely to guard against egregious error while respecting and even fostering a spirit of community and mutual dialogue between bishops and theologians. But the C.D.F.'s action against Gramick and Nugent may be a more accurate harbinger of the goals of some of those who insist on firmer control over Catholic theologians and pastoral ministers. Those few who desire such control do not represent the U.S. bishops as a whole. But the condemnation of Robert Nugent and Jeannine Gramick suggests that demands by a minority can have ecclesial and juridical consequences that are not only unjust, but endanger the very credibility of the church as a pastoral leader and inspiring voice on matters of sexual virtue.

37.

MINISTRY TO HOMOSEXUALS MUST USE AUTHENTIC CHURCH TEACHING

Gerald D. Coleman

***America*, August 14, 1999**

The Congregation for the Doctrine of the Faith's public notification on July 14 that Sister Jeannine Gramick and Father Robert Nugent "are permanently prohibited from any pastoral work involving homosexual persons" and are ineligible "for an undetermined period, for any office in their respective religious institutes" was accompanied by a written explanation from Cardinal Joseph Ratzinger to Bishop Joseph A. Fiorenza, president of the National Conference of Catholic Bishops. The Cardinal stated that "The Bishops of the United States are to understand it in the following manner: The two religious are certainly prohibited from any involvement with workshops, retreats, liturgical celebrations and any other pastoral initiative for homosexual persons or their parents...." And, "Concerning the publications of books, the canonical norm presently in force, binding all religious... must be observed. Finally with regard to Father Nugent, he may continue to preach and administer the sacraments, but not for gatherings of homosexual persons."

Sorrow that this decision would be "particularly hurtful" to gay and lesbian Catholics was expressed by Francis DeBernardo, executive director of New Ways Ministry, the group founded by Gramick and Nugent in 1977. The San Francisco Examiner headline over the story read, "Vatican Nixes Catholic Gay Ministry." The Washington Post labeled the decision "a kind of public shaming," telling parishes across the nation that Gramick and Nugent "are anathema to the church." The July issue of the St. Anthony Messenger Press series Catholic Update calls homosexuality one of the "hot-button" or "red-flag" issues in the church and society today. With this in mind, and in light of the congregation's decision, what might be said about this whole matter?

Ministry to Homosexuals

The story of New Ways Ministry begins in 1971 with Sister Gramick, a School Sister of Notre Dame. This was the year she recalls meeting a young gay Catholic in Philadelphia named Dominic Bash who asked her, "What is the Catholic church doing for my gay brothers and sisters?" The question challenged her to study the topic of homosexuality and eventually led her to meetings with a group of Catholic and Anglican gay men.

After a newspaper account of her associations, she received more than a dozen responses, one from Father Nugent, a member of the Society of the Divine Savior (Salvatorians), in Philadelphia. He was at that time in transition from parish work and suggested to Gramick that he might help her out in her new work and interest. Thus began their ministry to gay and lesbian Catholics, a work initiated with the hope of building a bridge between homosexual Catholics and Catholic moral teaching. Their 1992 book, *Building Bridges: Gay and Lesbian Reality and the Catholic Church* describes the results of their work.

The notification from the congregation mentions the presence of some positive aspects in their writings and pastoral activities," so it seems critical in analyzing this whole matter that the pastoral sensitivities of Gramick and Nugent not be thoughtlessly disregarded, or that they themselves be summarily condemned. Certainly the church should continue its important ministry to gay and lesbian Catholics. The Vatican and the U.S. bishops have promised that the church's ministers will not be lacking in compassion and understanding when caring for gay and lesbian people *(Catechism of the Catholic Church,* No. *2358; Human Sexuality,* No. *55-56; Declaration on Sexual Ethics,* No. 8; and *To Live in Christ Jesus,* No. *52).* Reports drawing the conclusion that this notification "nixes," or ends Catholic gay and lesbian ministry are simply wrong and irresponsible.

The Notification

It is important to make five points in relation to the congregation's statement.

First, the congregation has not come to this judgment quickly or rashly. It carefully studied the questions and entered into a long conversation with Gramick and Nugent for nearly 15 years and reached its decision, with papal approval, only after continued efforts to reach mutual understanding and agreement.

Second, Gramick and Nugent separated themselves from leadership roles in New Ways Ministry in 1984 at the direction of their respective religious orders, although they did continue some work with this group.

Third, the congregation directed Gramick and Nugent to "faithfully present the Church's teaching regarding the intrinsic evil of homosexual acts," and they were not to "present the teaching of the church as one possible option among others and as open to fundamental change."

Fourth, the 1988 commission chaired by Cardinal Adam Maida of Detroit found "errors" in the authors' book, *Building Bridges.* The commission attempted a "resolution" by asking Gramick and Nugent to "respond unequivocally to certain questions regarding their position on the morality of homosexual acts and on the homosexual inclination."

The two major questions were whether a homosexual orientation is in any sense a defect, and are there any moral limitations on homosexual activity that do not apply to heterosexual activity? In replying to these questions, Gramick and Nugent were asked to acknowledge errors in *Building Bridges* and their 1995 book,

Voices of Hope: A Collection of Positive Catholic Writings on Gay and Lesbian Issues, and to "express their interior assent to the teaching of the Catholic Church on homosexuality."

The notification concludes that Gramick and Nugent did in fact promote errors and ambiguities in view of the church's teaching on homosexuality. It states that such pedagogy is "not consistent with a Christian attitude of true respect and compassion: Persons who are struggling with homosexuality no less than any others have the right to receive the authentic teaching of the church from those who minister to them."

Fifth and finally, the notification points out that it attempted to resolve this case by using the procedures outlined in the Congregation for the Doctrine of the Faith's Regulations for Doctrinal Examination (Origins 27 [1997], 221-24). These regulations point out that the congregation "renders a service to the truth by protecting the right of the people of God to receive the Gospel message in its purity and entirety" (Art. 1). It further indicates that this responsibility belongs fundamentally to "all pastors of the church," but that it is necessary that the Holy See intervene when "the influence of a publication exceeds the boundaries of an individual episcopal conference or when the danger to the faith is particularly grave" (Art. 2). While the regulations provide for this moral and pastoral responsibility on the part of bishops and the Holy See, they likewise acknowledge and respect the rightful place for dialogue and clarification by those whose "writings and opinions" have appeared to be "contrary to correct faith or dangerous" (Art. 1).

What Are the Errors?

Since the 1988 commission focused primarily on *Building Bridges,* I will attempt to list here briefly some major points of teaching that appear in this work that either create ambiguity about the church's teaching on homosexuality or explicitly call the teaching into question.

It should be noted that the authors sometimes present theological opinions that are clearly at odds with church teaching without making efforts to critique or correct these views. The impression is left that the authors endorse and support these theological opinions.

Furthermore, this list is not meant to be exhaustive, nor is it intended to aggravate an already difficult pastoral situation. It is meant to help clarify why the congregation came to its conclusions.

The following contentions are presented in *Building Bridges:*

First, various forms of sexual intercourse, for example, homosexual acts, might be morally acceptable since these acts are not necessarily "unnatural" (p. 44). In specific cases the "general objective norm about the morality of homogenital acts" can be "qualified" or "even suspended" (p. 151). It is wrong for the church to "punish lesbian and gay persons" when they are simply being "true to their natures" (p. 187). Second, the homosexual orientation itself is "morally neutral" and can be compared to being "left-handed" (p. 60). The congregation's teaching, in its 1986 *Letter to the Bishops of the Catholic Church on the Pastoral Care of Homosexual Persons,* that the homosexual orientation is an "objective disorder" does not reflect the real experience of homosexual persons and needs to be rejected in order to assist gay and lesbian people to know that they are not "abnormal, sick, sinful, or criminal" (p. 189).

Third, if a homosexual relationship is stable and faithful, this fact can possibly justify homosexual acts within such a relationship (p. 61-63). Fourth, the congregation's *Letter to the Bishops* betrays "little pastoral concern" (p. 72) and sets back for at least 20 years "outreach to lesbian and gay Catholics" (p. 72, 119).

Fifth, the strong need for "relatedness and connection" in celibates necessitates "rejecting [the] traditional approach to celibacy and intimacy in favor of an alternative interpretation" (p. 132).

Conclusions

In view of the complex issues in this case, it seems most important to reassert first the positive affirmations of the church's teaching on homosexuality, as articulated in the *Letter to the Bishops:*

- "The particular inclination of the homosexual person is not a sin" (No. 3).

- "Homosexual persons are often generous and giving of themselves" (No. 3).

- "It is deplorable that homosexual persons have been and are the object of violent malice in speech or in action. Such treatment deserves condemnation from the church's pastors wherever it occurs... [and] the intrinsic dignity of each person must always be respected in word, in action and in law" (No. 10).

- "What is essential is that the fundamental liberty that characterizes the human person and gives him dignity be recognized as belonging to the homosexual person as well" (No. 11).

- "The characteristic concerns and good will exhibited by many clergy and religious in their pastoral care for homosexual persons is admirable and, we hope, will not diminish" (No. 13).

- "A homosexual person, as every human being, deeply needs to be nourished at many different levels simultaneously.... The human person, made in the image and likeness of God, can hardly be adequately described by a reductionist reference to his or her sexual orientation.... Today the church provides a badly needed context for the care of the human person when [it] refuses to consider the person as a 'heterosexual' or a 'homosexual' and insists that every person has a fundamental identity: the creature of God and, by grace, His child and heir to eternal life" (No. 16).

Second, it is important to consider the responsibilities that Catholic ministries to homosexual persons have to respect the dignity of all homosexual persons by:

• Ministering to them in such a fashion that the church's authentic teaching about homosexuality and homosexual activity is unambiguously presented. They have a right to receive the church's teaching in its clarity and entirety;

• Clearly and adequately teaching what the church means when it names the homosexual orientation as an objective disorder. This teaching has been explained in "Toward an Understanding of the Letter on the Pastoral Care of Homosexual Persons," by Archbishop Quinn (AM., 2/7/87), and in an article I co-authored with the Rev. Stephen Rossetti, "Psychology and the Church's Teaching on Homosexuality" (AM., 11/1/97);

• Condemning all violence and malice against them;

• Supporting those who clearly uphold the church's teaching on homosexuality and homosexual activity, and who work with local bishops in fostering a viable outreach and ministry to homosexual people;

• Positively presenting the church's teaching on friendship and chastity, as well as the critical place in every Catholic's life of the sacraments of reconciliation and the Eucharist.

The *Letter to the Bishops* gives good and helpful advice that might serve as a guiding endnote: "Departure from the church's teaching or silence about it, in an effort to provide pastoral care, is neither caring nor pastoral. Only what is true can ultimately be pastoral. The neglect of the church's position prevents homosexual men and women from receiving the care they need and deserve" (No. 15).

38.

A RESPONSE

**Two persons whose ministry to gays and lesbians
has come under scrutiny respond to a critic.**

Jeannine Gramick and Robert Nugent

***America*, October 9, 1999**

Our painful and protracted dealings with the Vatican were analyzed with care and sensitivity by Lisa Sowle Cahill ("Silencing of Nugent, Gramick Sets a Novel Standard of Orthodoxy") and Gerald Coleman ("Ministry to Homosexuals Must Use Authentic Church Teaching") in the Aug. 14 issue of *America.* We are pleased by the discussion that has ensued in the Catholic community.

We would like to clarify the record concerning the alleged errors catalogued in Father Coleman's article. Coleman lists eight contentions, grouped in five points, from our book, *Building Bridges: Gay and Lesbian Reality and the Catholic Church,* to illustrate why the Congregation for the Doctrine of the Faith concluded that we create ambiguity or call the church's teaching on homosexuality into question. We would like to comment on each of Coleman's contentions, which are italicized below:

1. Homosexual acts might be morally acceptable since these acts are not necessarily "unnatural" (p. 44).

The chapter, "What is Natural?" examines various definitions of the word *natural* found in such disciplines as history, anthropology, psychology, biology, theology and philosophy. Each discipline has its own notions of what *natural* means. The chapter is not concerned about "morally acceptable" acts, only about understanding the meanings of the word *natural.*

Coleman replicates the mistake of the Maida commission. According to Scholastic philosophy and theology, *natural* and *morally acceptable* are not equivalent. Some sexual acts are natural, but not morally acceptable. A sexual act is natural if it is open to procreation. Thus, adultery and fornication and even rape would be considered natural sexual acts, though certainly not morally acceptable.

2. In specific cases the "general objective norm about the morality of homogenital acts" can be "qualified" or "even suspended" (p. 151).

In the original text, this quotation is preceded by "McCormick believes that," a clear indication that we are presenting the view of Richard A. McCormick, SJ., not necessarily our own.

3. It is wrong for the church to "punish lesbian and gay persons" when they are simply being "true to their natures" (p. 187).

Coleman, like many people, seems to interpret the "punishment" to be the magisterium's condemnatory judgment on homosexual activity. Why, we ask, do people constantly place genital meanings or sexual interpretations on any statement having to do with lesbian and gay people?

As pastoral ministers, we often see lesbian and gay people being punished for being true to their nature—i.e., for simply being homosexual in orientation. For example, many are denied the opportunity to serve as eucharistic ministers in their parishes. Some church leaders describe their civil rights as a "threat to the family." Many experience job terminations in church institutions when a homosexual orientation is discovered. It is wrong to impose these, as well as similar punishments, on lesbian and gay people.

4. The homosexual orientation itself is morally neutral" and can be compared to being "left-handed" (p. 60).

We are at a loss to understand why Coleman believes that this is an example of error.

The 1986 letter from the C.D.F. states that "the particular inclination of the homosexual person is not a sin" (No. 3). Cardinal James Hickey's 1984 pastoral letter on homosexuality states, "a homosexual orientation is not morally wrong in and of itself."

Left-handedness is also morally neutral. Both are non-chosen characteristics of minority populations and, in that sense, can be appropriately compared.

5. The congregation's teaching, in its 1986 "Letter to the Bishops of the Catholic Church on the Pastoral Care of Homosexual Persons," that the homosexual orientation is an objective disorder" does not reflect the real experience of homosexual persons and needs to be rejected in order to assist gay and lesbian people to know that they are not "abnormal, sick, sinful, or criminal" (p. 189).

Coleman's selection of these quotes from two adjacent but transposed sentences posits a causal connection that we did not make. The original text is as follows:

"A positive and affirming lesbian/gay theology or spirituality rejects the notion that a homosexual orientation is abnormal, sick, sinful or criminal. The 1986 letter from the Vatican's Congregation for the Doctrine of the Faith, which contended that a homosexual orientation was 'objectively disordered' obviously did not begin from the experience of being lesbian or gay" (p. 189).

As in point No. 2 above, we are reporting the assertions of authors writing about lesbian/gay theology today. On page 189 in our book, there are numerous references to these authors, who rely on their own experience, confirmed by the judgments of contemporary psychological and psychiatric associations that a homosexual orientation is not "abnormal or sick."

In regard to "sinful or criminal," the magisterium itself rejects the notion that a homosexual orientation is sinful; furthermore, the Government does not consider it a criminal offense to *be* lesbian or gay.

6. If a homosexual relationship is stable and faithful, this fact can possibly justify homosexual acts within such a relationship (p. 61-63).

Once again Coleman quotes us citing contemporary theologians, but does not acknowledge that we also state, "the present pastoral ministry of the Church requires gay and lesbian people to live in chaste celibacy with the help of the sacraments, spiritual direction, and works of charity" (p. 61).

If Coleman assumes that the mere presentation of any views means that we endorse or support them, why would he not conclude that we also endorse the magisterial teaching because we present it as well?

In presenting contemporary theological views, we write:

A growing number of reputable theologians allow, on the pastoral level, for the formation of stable, faithful homosexual relationships. These relationships would embody some of the traditional values associated with heterosexual marriages such as fidelity, monogamy, and permanence. Referring to such relationships, the Catholic bishops of England and Wales stated that while the moral norms were clear, when we help people apply their consciences to such situations as stable relationships, the clear-cut application of such moral norms may be complicated (p. 6l).

To say that the application of moral norms "may be complicated" is not equivalent to "justify(ing) homosexual acts."

In a later chapter, we refer again to this question and quote the bishops of England and Wales directly:

The pastor may distinguish between irresponsible, indiscriminate sexual activity and the permanent association between two homosexual persons, who feel incapable of enduring a solitary life devoid of sexual expression *(An Introduction to the Pastoral Care of Homosexual People,* 1979).

We conclude the quote by noting that "They refused, however, to compare this situation analogously with the marriage relationship as objectively good" (p. 144).

7. The congregation's "Letter to the Bishops" betrays "little pastoral concern" (p. 72) and sets back for at least 20 years "outreach to lesbian and gay Catholics" (p. 72, 119).

In 1986, a great number of responsible Catholic leaders and thinkers criticized the letter and noted that the already fragile rapport between the church hierarchy and gay and lesbian Catholics was further harmed. This has been amply documented in the book we co-edited, *The Vatican and Homosexuality* (1988).

For example, The (London) *Tablet* (11/8/86) characterized the document as "violently hostile" to Catholic groups ministering to lesbian and gay people and noted that "not a word of appreciation is offered." *America* (11/22/86) editorialized that the "letter explicitly aims at pastoral care for homosexuals, but it is doubtful they will feel especially cared for. Despite the stated intention of the letter's title, it makes a series of decidedly unpastoral missteps." After an interview with Cardinal Basil Hume about church pronouncements on homosexuality, Msgr. James Lisante reported, "Cardinal Hume said he felt compelled to challenge Cardinal Joseph Ratzinger about the teachings. He did this because they lacked a true pastoral compassion. They did not, he suggested, reflect the faith of the always empathetic Jesus" (The Long Island Catholic, 8/26/92).

Therefore, Coleman's contention of "error" should more properly be called an assessment of the reception by the faithful of the 1986 letter.

8. *The strong need for "relatedness and connection" in celibates necessitates "rejecting [the] traditional approach to celibacy and intimacy in favor of an alternative interpretation" (p 132).*

Again, Coleman does not state that we are reporting, not endorsing, a lived reality among some women religious. In our book we state:

Lesbian religious, particularly those in the middle years, are rejecting this traditional approach to celibacy and intimacy in favor of an alternative interpretation. They believe that celibacy, to be authentically human, must maximize opportunities for developing close, intimate relationships. This conception of celibacy springs from women's strong inclinations for relatedness and connection (p. 132).

In conclusion, we have not been accused of opposing church teaching. As Coleman and the C.D.F. pointed out, we presented others' opinions without critiquing them. We did this for the following reason.

We are pastoral ministers, not professional theologians. It was not our purpose to analyze alternative theological views or to present our own opinions. What we intended to do, and believe we have done, was to present clearly and comprehensively the magisterial position, as well as the views of lesbian and gay Catholics we have heard in our pastoral ministry of almost 30 years.

We believe this is necessary in order to foster an open discussion among the magisterium, theologians, and lesbian and gay Catholics involving sound reasoning, without short-circuiting the discourse by appeals to authority. Through genuine dialogue we hope that some common ground will emerge.

Finally, as rightly noted in Professor Cahill's article, our endeavor has been to present the *full* range of church teaching, giving primary attention to the less known elements of that teaching, which the church community sorely needs to hear. The well-known teachings about homosexual acts and orientation, while not ignored or impugned in our presentations receive less emphasis for reasons we, and others, judge as pastorally sound and prudent. With all due respect, Coleman's defense of the C.D.F.'s decision has not persuaded us otherwise.

39.

TOWARD EFFECTIVE PASTORAL CARE OF HOMOSEXUAL PERSONS
Father Robert Gahl Jr.

"Because they contradict the plan of the Creator, homosexual acts are intrinsically disordered. Anyone who freely consents to homosexual activity is personally guilty of grave sin," said Father Robert Gahl Jr., a professor of ethics in Rome at the Pontifical University of the Holy Cross, the international university of Opus Dei. An article by Gahl was published in L'Osservatore Romano, the Vatican newspaper, the day after the newspaper published the Congregation for the Doctrine of the Faith's notification barring Salvatorian Father Robert Nugent and School Sister of Notre Dame Jeannine Gramick from pastoral work involving homosexual persons.

1. Human Love and Sexuality

"It is not good that the man should be alone" (Gn 2:1 8). With these words, the Book of Genesis introduces the creation of Eve, the first woman. The inspired creation story explains the origin of the difference between man and woman by indicating that human beings, made in the image and likeness of God (cf. Gn. 1:26), are called to loving communion. In addition, according to the Genesis account, the complementarity between man and woman, a reflection of "the inner unity of the Creator," is directed toward this communion.[1]

Ever since the creation of our first parents, sexual intercourse was always meant to be a beautiful expression of human love for the sake of bearing fruit within a family and for unifying husband and wife. The church therefore "celebrates the divine plan of the loving and life-giving union of men and women in the sacrament of marriage."[2] Consequently, in accord with natural law, the church teaches that any use of the sexual faculty outside of conjugal intercourse is sinful and thus can only lead to frustration and remorseful separation from the divine Creator.

2. Homosexuality: Definition and Evaluation

When Adam and Eve misused their freedom by disobeying God, they committed the original sin which wounded human nature. The effects of original sin are experienced by each one of us. Sin obscures man's likeness to God, clouds our perception of the spousal meaning of the human body and makes difficult the permanent, self-giving love between husband and wife.[3] Because of original sin, human nature is wounded in the natural powers proper to it and inclined to sin.[4]

Homosexuality is one of the many manifestations of the disorder in human inclinations introduced by original sin. Homosexuality is the condition of those "who experience an exclusive or predominant sexual attraction toward persons of the same sex."[5] Like any other disorder brought about by the wounds in human nature, the experience of homosexual inclinations is a summons to spiritual battle.[6]

The church distinguishes between inclinations and the active following through on those inclinations. The church therefore also distinguishes between persons who experience homosexual temptations and homosexual activity. Men and women who experience sexual inclinations directed predominantly toward members of the same sex are considered homosexual persons. Voluntary sexual activity, or any form of sensual contact for the sake of sexual gratification, between persons of the same sex is considered homosexual activity. While original sin is the remote cause of homosexuality, the proximate cause seems to be a combination of various phenomena not totally understood by science.

Because they contradict the plan of the Creator, homosexual acts are intrinsically disordered. Anyone who freely consents to homosexual activity is personally guilty of grave sin.[7] Homosexual activity nullifies the rich symbolism, meaning and purpose within the Creator's design. In its intrinsic sterility, homosexual activity thwarts the call to a life of loving self-gift expressed by the complementary conjugal union between man and woman.[8] Homosexual activity lacks the essential finality indispensable for the moral goodness of sexual acts. Sacred Scripture condemns homosexual activity as a serious depravity and even "as the sad consequence of rejecting God"[9] (cf. Rom. 1:24-27).

The church helps homosexual persons to struggle courageously against disordered inclinations and to conform themselves to the splendor of truth found in Jesus Christ (cf. Jn. 14:6). By "rejecting erroneous opinions regarding homosexuality," the church "defends personal freedom and dignity."[10] Social harmony depends in part on the proper living out of the mutual support and complementarity between the two sexes, which is why the church cannot support civil legislation protecting "behavior to which no one has any conceivable right."[11]

While denouncing homosexual activity, the church also defends homosexual persons from those forms of discrimination which are unjust[12] and seeks to help them find joy and peace in living the virtue of chastity. Those who suffer from homosexual inclinations are not necessarily responsible for their condition. No one ought to judge such persons as inferior. The church's long experience proves that with the help of the grace of Jesus Christ, frequent reception of the sacraments of reconciliation and holy communion, ascetical struggle and – in some cases – medical treatment, they can avoid sin and make progress on the path toward holiness.

All must struggle to do what is right, and it is only with God's grace and great effort that men and women succeed in achieving their own inner integrity. The church recognizes the equal dignity of all persons and offers a maternal welcome to those who experience homosexual inclinations. Likewise, the church absolutely condemns all malice in speech or action toward homosexual people and teaches that such behavior endangers the most fundamental principles of a healthy society. Consequently, the church teaches that human law should promote respect for the intrinsic dignity of each person.[13]

3. Guidelines for Ministry to Homosexual Persons

Through her apostolic action, the church opens her arms to all men and women. "The church is the place where humanity must rediscover its unity and salvation."[14] "All salvation comes from Christ the head through the church, which is his body."[15] With creative initiative motivated by charity and without any fear, the Christian faithful express God's fatherly love for all by seeking them out and meeting their desire for salvation. Believing that the salvific perfection of human freedom may be found only in the truth of Jesus Christ, the church must always courageously proclaim Christian morality, even when facing opposition or, in extreme cases, persecution and martyrdom.[16]

Therefore, any Catholic ministry or apostolate to homosexual persons should fulfill the following conditions.

1) Respect for the equal dignity of homosexual persons requires recognizing that sinful actions such as homosexual acts are beneath human dignity. The church's ministers therefore must ensure that no homosexual persons in their care are misled by the widespread erroneous view that homosexual activity is an inevitable consequence of the homosexual condition.[17]

2) To be effective, authentic and faithful, all pastoral care of homosexual persons must convey the serious sinfulness of homosexual behavior. Without driving away anyone of good will, ministry to homosexual faithful must communicate, as soon as possible, the demanding yet attractive requirements of moral truth. Since some people may feel rejected by the church, pastoral care of homosexual persons is most effective by helping them to recognize that the church accepts them as persons while also helping them to understand the church's teaching.

3) With their effort to live according to the Gospel, homosexual persons gain peace and mastery of their disordered tendencies. They are encouraged to learn that with the love of Christ, "they can and should gradually and resolutely approach Christian perfection."[18] All pastoral outreach to homosexual persons should therefore privilege personal ascetical struggle, generous acceptance of God's will, recognition of being a child of God and the joining of their sufferings and difficulties to the sacrifice of the Lord's cross.[19]

With compassionate understanding, the church's ministry should encourage homosexual faithful to hope in the power of the Lord's resurrection, with the confidence that the Holy Spirit will produce in them "love, joy, peace, patience, kindness, goodness, trustfulness, gentleness and self-control" (Gal. *5:22*). As St. Paul admonished the Galatians: "Those who belong to Christ have crucified their flesh with its passions and desires" (Gal *5:24*). Homosexual persons, therefore, should make use of the proven means for growing in the virtue of chastity, including frequent reception of the sacraments of penance and holy communion.

4) The authenticity of the church's public proclamation of the Gospel must be guaranteed by assuring that all involved in ministry to homosexual persons, especially clergy and religious, be personally convinced of the church's teaching and ready to profess the church's teaching as their own. The public accountability of ministers of the church requires that they believe and profess the teachings of the church. Attracting new members to the church requires firm personal conviction and dedication. An effective apostolate to homosexual persons, even to those who may feel ostracized from the church, requires readiness to communicate the church's moral teaching with personal adherence. Reluctance to express the whole of Christian morality only hinders the pastoral care of homosexual persons and thereby does them a serious injustice.

5) All public ministry to homosexual persons should be done in very close unity with and under the guidance of the local bishop in order to guarantee that the ministry will always reflect the fullness of Catholic teaching.

6) Ministry toward homosexual people should courageously speak against the claim that the condemnation of homosexual activity is a kind of unjust discrimination of homosexual persons or a violation of their rights.[20] Those who accept the homosexual condition as though it were not disordered and condone homosexual activity "are guided by a vision opposed to the truth about the human person, which is fully disclosed in the mystery of Christ."[21] Even without recognizing it, their approval of homosexuality reflects "a materialistic ideology which denies the transcendent nature of the human person as well as the supernatural vocation of every individual."[22]

7) To avoid misunderstandings or confusion, ministry to homosexual persons must always be entirely independent from any group which favors a "gay lifestyle" or claims that the homosexual condition is equivalent or somehow superior to the chastity lived in marriage or celibacy. Church ministries to homosexual people should not associate with organizations that promote changes in civil legislation which would jeopardize the juridical recognition of marriage and family by giving equivalent status to homosexual unions.[23]

The church is conscious of the responsibility to preserve the priceless gift of revelation and to defend it against every harmful influence. Pastoral programs, when undertaken in conformity with the truth of revelation, contribute to the human and spiritual benefit of homosexual persons and to the integrity of society. It must never be forgotten that "departure from the church's teaching or silence about it in an effort to provide pastoral care is neither caring nor pastoral. Only what is true can ultimately be pastoral. The neglect of the church's position prevents homosexual men and women from receiving the care they need and deserve."[24]

---

[1] Congregation for the Doctrine of the Faith, Letter to Bishops on the Pastoral Care of Homosexual Persons (Oct. 1, 1986), 6.

[2] Ibid., 7.

[3] Cf. ibid., 6.

[4] Cf. Catechism of the Catholic Church, 405.

[5] Ibid., 2357.

[6] Cf. ibid., 405.

[7] Cf. ibid., 2396.

[8] Cf. "Pastoral Care of Homosexuals," 7.

[9] Congregation for the Doctrine of the Faith, Declaration on Certain Questions Concerning Sexual Ethics (Dec. 29, 1975), 8.

[10] "Pastoral Care of Homosexuals," 7.

[11] Ibid., 10.

[12] Cf. Catechism, 2358. However, "there are areas in which it is not unjust discrimination to take sexual orientation into account, for example, in the placement of children for adoption or foster care, in employment of teachers or athletic coaches, and in military recruitment" (Congregation for the Doctrine of the Faith, "Observations on Legislative Proposals Concerning Discrimination Against Homosexual Persons," in L'Osservatore Romano, July 24, 1992, 11).

[13] Cf. "Pastoral Care of Homosexuals," 10.

[14] Catechism, 845.

[15] Ibid., 846.

[16] Cf. John Paul II, Veritatis Splendor (Aug. 6, 1993), 91.

[17] Cf. "Certain Questions on Sexual Ethics," 8.

[18] Catechism, 2359.

[19] "Pastoral Care of Homosexuals," 12.

[20] Cf. ibid., 9.

[21] Ibid., 8.

[22] Ibid.

[23] Cf. ibid.

[24] Ibid., 15.

40.

SEXUALITY & HOMOSEXUALITY
The church's Gordian knot
Sidney Callahan

Commonweal, **September 10, 1999**

Resolved: However provoked, no Christian will use the word "homophobia" or "patriarchy" in heated debate over sex. The current test case is the Vatican's "notification" to Jeannine Gramick, S.S.N.D., and Robert Nugent, S.D.S., that they are permanently barred from further pastoral work with homosexual persons. Their joint ministry of writing, teaching, and building bridges to gay Catholics has been judged to be insufficiently condemnatory of the intrinsic evil of homosexual acts.

Gramick and Nugent are found guilty of ambiguity for overemphasizing the church's positive teachings on homosexuality, that is, that the homosexual condition is not in itself sinful, that homosexuals must be accorded full civil rights, and that homosexuals possess human dignity as children of God and must be pastorally cared for. But, Rome declares, it is erroneous to mislead gays by neglecting the teaching that homosexuality is an objective disorder that predisposes a person to intrinsically evil acts. Homosexuals have a right and a need "to receive the gospel message in its purity and entirety."

This latest condemnation by the Congregation for the Doctrine of the Faith (CDF) sets off a firecracker-like string of questions. Was the CDF's appraisal of the work of Gramick and Nugent fair? The investigation and negotiations dragged on for two decades and concluded when the CDF requested written statements of internal assent to the church's teaching on homosexuality. Gramick refused and Nugent's nuanced statement of assent was rejected as unacceptable. Was this request for internal assent, which goes beyond the requirement of obedient conformity to church teaching, a chilling effort to coerce conscience? Almost certainly, since as Thomas More (1478–1535) explained to his inquisitors, silence implies consent. No person should legally or morally be punished for his or her private thoughts, only for an action that breaks the law.

Of course, as More's friends and enemies knew, in his heart of hearts More did not approve of King Henry VIII's divorce and elevation to the headship of the English church. And I would bet my bottom dollar that in their heart of hearts Nugent and Gramick do not give internal assent to the whole of the church's current teachings on homosexuality. (I can't.) Despite their careful obedience, they are being punished for a private dissent of conscience. Who knows, they may even have had a procedurally adequate hearing, but the larger questions remain: First, do

Catholics have the right in good conscience to dissent from teaching that is authoritatively taught but not infallibly defined? And second, is the CDF's current teaching on homosexuality God's pure and entire gospel truth?

Clearly the answer to the first question is yes and hardly needs to be reargued with references to the hierarchy of truths and the sacredness of conscience. The cutting edge in the present fight is the challenge presented by question number two to the validity of the Vatican's teaching. I am not alone in finding the CDF's current teaching on sexuality and homosexuality to be rationally unconvincing, morally unsound, and theologically inadequate – but not, note well, because of its homophobia or display of patriarchy.

No, the church's teaching on homosexuality, sexuality, and gender is a tightly wrapped package that many intelligent, charitable, and holy men and women believe to be true. Why? First, because they think sexuality is ordered to biological procreation, and this ordering cannot be dispensed with to serve any other human good, such as unity or love. Second, taking biological procreation as the critical standard, men and women are believed to be differentiated in gender and to possess different and complementary vocations in the family and in the church. From the first two premises comes the third. Homosexuality is a fundamental defect because it is not ordered to biological procreation, and same-sex unions cannot be complementary in gender. Homosexual acts are intrinsically evil because they are not procreative and do not take place within marriage. Obviously, these teachings about sex and human nature can be seen as interdependent. If you say that gender differences are not essentially complementary or determinative of vocations, you end up ordaining women and weakening the arguments against same-sex unions. A concession that not every sexual act need be open to procreation as long as it is expressing love in a committed heterosexual marriage leads to the approval of contraception and opens the way to nonprocreative homosexual unions. To accept homosexuality as solely a sexual variation and not a fundamental defect will weaken the assertion that in nature all sexuality must be ordered to procreation. If loving, committed same-sex unions can be moral, what happens to the gender complementarity that sustains the ban on ordaining women? And so it goes, circling round like the blind ox driving the gristmill.

Two final ironies: Homosexuals are told that they must abide by the same sexual morality as heterosexuals. Well and good. A universal principle of equal moral responsibility for all validates the human being's freedom to direct sexual behavior in accord with moral standards. But heterosexual individuals can freely enter into marriage with a beloved partner and express their love sexually, whether or not procreation is possible. Homosexuals are told that since the only sexual intimacy morally permitted is in marriage, and marriage is impossible for them, they have to be permanently chaste. The homosexual orientation is viewed by the church as involuntary and not sinful, nor is it seen as a defining characteristic of the whole person; but if it is defined as a defect, it forces persons to endure lifelong deprivations that heterosexuals do not face.

In explanations of the church's position, it's often admitted that suffering is being imposed upon homosexuals, a suffering that is justified as morally necessary to follow God's will and to preserve the goods of traditional marriage. But some defenders of the faith go on to claim that since gay persons can pursue friendships, extended family bonds, and charity, what's the problem? This argument denies the reality that experiencing erotic love and sexual joy in committed unions of mutual self-giving is uniquely human and a gift from God.

These current ambiguities, conflicts, and lack of reception of the church's teaching on sexuality signal a crisis in the development of doctrine. More moral, theological, and scientific argument is needed to correct the rigid overvaluation of procreation and gender differences, and the undervaluation of erotic joy. While it may be small comfort to Christians like Jeannine Gramick and Robert Nugent who are being punished for doing good, a new uniquely personal understanding of sexuality is emerging. Of course, pecking this particular ugly duckling out of its hard shell isn't going to be easy; but when the chicken yard is left behind, the swan is going to fly.

41.

RESPONDING TO THE 'GAY AGENDA'
Three reasons why dialogue might be an appropriate response
Eileen P. Flynn

America, **September 30, 2000**

How should the Catholic Church in the United States respond to what some have labeled the "gay agenda"? One way would be simply to restate what has been declared repeatedly. This approach, however, may not meet the challenge.

The so-called gay agenda has been in the making roughly since 1969, when the patrons of Stonewall, a gay nightclub in Greenwich Village, fought back against a police raid. The closet door was opened, the battle was joined by others, and momentum continues to build. As recently as last April 30, a crowd estimated by its organizers to number 800,000 gathered in Washington, D.C., to protest hate crimes and discrimination against gays and lesbians. Supporters have lobbied for protection of civil rights and partnership recognition as well as adoption and parental rights. Dennis and Judy Shepard, parents of Matthew Shepard, whose horrific murder revealed the depth of homophobic malice that can be harbored in the soul, attended the April rally. In solidarity with the marchers, Mr. and Mrs. Shepard provided a reminder of the serious and critical demands for which gays and lesbians argue.

This agenda faults many institutions in society for fostering homophobic attitudes that lead to misconduct against gays – and the Catholic Church ranks high on the list. The Catholic Church, an entity identified with a hierarchically structured leadership and uncompromising religious and moral doctrines, is often depicted by gays and lesbians as against them and their agenda because of its positions. These positions include an evaluation of the homosexual orientation as objectively disordered and condemnation of all homosexual genital or homoerotic acts as immoral. Furthermore, church opposition to the legalization of gay partnerships has angered gays who have mobilized to secure recognition of same-sex relationships.

Catholic leaders have repeatedly rebutted criticism of the church as an institution that fosters homophobia. Many in the hierarchy do not accept generalizations that portray the church as intolerant and have repeatedly sought to set the record straight. In so doing, Catholic spokespersons often reiterate familiar distinctions: The church accepts gays and lesbians; it welcomes them and provides appropriate ministry to them and their families. Church leaders do not blame gays for being homosexual; the church teaches that the etiology of sexual orientation is complex and defies facile explanation. Being homosexual is not morally wrong; what is morally wrong is to choose to act on a homosexual orientation by engaging in sexual acts. Homosexual acts are always wrong because these acts are contrary to natural law and scriptural teaching.

This said – and consistently restated – many church leaders insist that the Catholic Church and its teaching supports respect for homosexual persons and opposes discrimination, humiliating remarks including jokes and slurs, and the denial of legitimate civil rights.

The rationale that undergirds Catholic opposition to homosexual acts stems from the way the church understands the meaning and purpose of sex: God created humans as male and female and designed their genital complementarity for pro-creation. The church teaches that God intends sex to occur only within the context of heterosexual marriage. It maintains that it is important for society to support the institution of marriage in order to validate the lifelong commitment marriage requires, as well as parental responsibilities for the well-being of their children. This fundamental premise presupposes that the family is the basic unit of society and that the well-being of society cannot be maintained unless the nuclear family is preserved.

The "gay agenda," in radical opposition to Catholic teaching, does not hold that sexual acts between consenting adults are immoral or that alternative lifestyles – including same-sex couples and biological or adoptive parenthood by homosexual persons or couples – are ethically problematic.

Rejecting the tactics of some gay advocacy groups that seek to rewrite long-held moral and cultural standards, many Catholic leaders adamantly hold the line. But is this attitude of absolute certitude justified, or are there reasons why dialogue might be an appropriate response to the "gay agenda"? Those familiar with the formulation of Catholic moral teaching as well as the climate in the church for the past 20 years might advocate dialogue. There are three reasons.

First, a technical issue needs to be resolved before one can proclaim the rational adequacy of Catholic teaching that all homosexual acts are immoral. The issue entails deciding whether it is reasonable to include acts described *solely by their objects* in the same category as acts classified as evil based on analysis of acts *in their entirety,* i.e., taking into account object, intention, circumstances and foreseeable consequences. Currently, official church teaching places homosexual genital acts in the same category as lying, stealing and murder.

There is a problem with putting homosexual acts into the same category as lying and murder. Lying can be defined as speaking falsely without a justifying intention in circumstances that do not require false speech, with awareness of negative consequences. Similarly, murder is taking the life of an innocent person for an evil reason, not required by circumstances or consequences. Thus, speaking falsely and killing *become* evil acts based on intention, circumstances and consequences. Moral conclusions about specific instances of speaking falsely or taking life are not made until these relevant aspects are considered. In contrast, the homosexual act of a person with a homosexual orientation is condemned by church teaching without regard for why the act is engaged in, the circumstances of the persons involved or the consequences for them as individuals as well as for the broader society.

Evaluating actions based on the *object* of the act (that which is done) rather than in a broader context that includes intention, circumstances and consequences has been criticized by some moral theologians as a biologistic and unreliable rendering of natural law thinking. Biologism can be described as an "oughtness" ascribed to the biological structure of the heterosexual act of intercourse. Here, a moral law is perceived in the way the act is configured, and human sexual acts that do not conform to this structure are said to be immoral. Morality is thus identified with physical or biological processes rather than with human decisions about how to exercise sexuality in loving and responsible ways.

Since natural law morality is first and foremost rational, a theoretical criticism is made that church teaching is not on firm ground when it crafts its response to homosexual acts in a biologistic vein that fails to take into account the intentions, circumstances and consequences – all of which are inherent aspects of human actions. This criticism, reaching as it does to the core of official Catholic teaching, calls for serious and sustained dialogue by able theoreticians from across the Catholic ideological spectrum. That the magisterium does not recognize this need and that Catholic moral theologians, for the most part, have stopped discussing it, does not mean that it does not exist. On the contrary, the uneasy silence indicates the present climate in the church, in which questions go unaddressed for fear of reprisals.

Second, the current situation calls for humble tentativeness rather than pulpit-thumping certitude. Scientific and genetic knowledge are ever-expanding, and scientists still do not know the root causes of homosexuality. Until more is understood about the degrees and varieties of same-sex orientation, it makes sense to be tentative.

As far as empirical data from gays and lesbians are concerned, church leaders need to listen in order to learn about sexual and spiritual experiences of gay and lesbian Catholics. Requesting that gays and lesbians speak openly and freely would be helpful for church leaders, as it would enable them to learn how gays and lesbians experience their sexuality. In its pastoral practice the church maintains both its relevance and sensitivity. Neither of these attributes can be claimed by leaders who are not open to dialogue with those who receive church teaching.

Third, the church should manifest reverence for God and Scripture. In its teaching on homosexual acts, however, the church may actually be showing disrespect. How so?

According to the doctrine of creation, God created all that is and blessed humans with the gift of sexuality. But, according to some surveys, as many as 10 percent of humans experience their sexuality as an attraction for same-sex partners. Because God is not capricious, it is difficult to imagine why God would have created humans with a sexual orientation destined to be a source of frustration and embarrassment. Might it not be that the search by the pilgrim church to discover in what truly moral human sexual conduct consists has not yet been completed? Might this not also leave open the door to a possible revision in respect to its teaching on homosexual acts?

As far as Scripture is concerned, the church ironically finds itself in the company of fundamentalist evangelical Christians in citing biblical verses as proof texts that homosexual acts are evil and contrary to God's will. In light of the fact that the Catholic Church supports scientific study of Scripture, credibility for its teachings on homosexuality demands a similar openness to Scripture scholarship to determine what moral guidance can be gleaned from Bible verses that seem at first glance to be germane to the contemporary debate. Uncritical literalism cannot provide justification for Catholic teaching. Fully nuanced exegesis, as complex and time-consuming as this process is, is required. Anything less should be rejected out of hand.

A New York Times story about the April 2000 gay rights rally in Washington recounts: "There were tiny clusters of protesters. As the march began, a man with a bullhorn shouted, 'Sick! Sick! Sick!' The marchers chanted back, 'Shame! Shame! Shame!' Another protester yelled: 'You're despicable before God. You know nothing about families.' And a marcher shouted back, 'Jesus loves me.'"

Jesus loves us, each and every one. There is no question about that. But we would love one another more fully if we could determine how to move beyond attacks and counterattacks, suspicions and threats. This is not a task for Catholic leaders alone, but there is no underestimating the significance of the role they play in establishing fundamental insights about who gay and lesbian people are and what standards they should observe in their sexual conduct. If this is an open question, it goes without saying that truth, justice and charity require that it be faced.

42.

STATEMENT ON PROPOSITION 22, SAME-SEX MARRIAGE INITIATIVE
Cardinal Mahony (2000)

Proposition 22, the "limit on marriage" initiative, will appear on the March 7, 2000 ballot. Earlier this year the Califoria Catholic Conference voted to support the measure's definition of marriage as "a union between a woman and man."

The limited language of Proposition 22 makes the initiative seem rather straightforward. In reality, the issue is highly complex because of the emotional and political dynamics that surround the measure and the limitations and inadequacy of the initiative process in our state to set sound public policy.

The Califoria Catholic Conference has endorsed this initiative to assure that God's plan for marriage and family life described so fully in both the Old Testament and New Testament, as well as in other religious beliefs, remains the bedrock upon which marriage is respected within our society. In addition, the church has found no legitimate justification to redefine and extend the marriage contract to include same-sex unions.

At the same time, there still remains the question of whether homosexual partners and other domiciled relationships can have legal access to certain prerogatives and benefits that accrue to couples within the marriage contract. These issues, however, should not be resolved by extending the definition of marriage to same-sex unions. Prudent public policy needs to be explored through appropriate legislative bodies to address some of these concerns.

Unfortunately, some will use this initiative to advance attitudes that foster ill will against homosexual persons, their parents and their families. Those who use this measure to degrade others act in a manner that is wholly inconsistent with Catholic Church teaching that affirms the inherent dignity of every human person, including women and men with a homosexual orientation.

I call upon our Catholic community and all people of good will to join me in deploring and denouncing the degradation of dignity and respect toward any of our brothers and sisters.

As the 2000 election season nears, individual Catholics and Catholic parishes face a profound challenge in discerning appropriate responses to Proposition 22. I call upon all Catholics to make clear our focus and position on this initiative:

– First, we must promote the traditional understanding of marriage as contained so clearly in God's revelation and defined in the initiative as "a union between a man and a woman." We must also take this opportunity to strengthen and expand our parish ministries that support married couples and their families.

– Second, we must oppose those persons and organizations that will use this measure to promote hatred against homosexual persons, and

– Third, we must reaffirm the pastoral directives for ministry and outreach with homosexual persons articulated in church teaching. In our own Archdiocese of Los Angeles, this has been embodied through our well-established ministerial commitmnent to homosexual persons and their families through our Pastoral Ministry With Lesbian and Gay Catholics.

In addressing this issue, pastors and parish leaders should discern and employ educational activities that address all three of these challenges. Proposition 22 should not be a disguised opportunity to demean a segment of our population.

I am saddened that some people have interpreted the Catholic Church's support for Proposition 22 as a lessening of our commitment to serve the gay and lesbian communiity with any less interest or zeal. Nothing could be farther from the truth.

In the Archdiocese of Los Angeles, I continue to support our ministry with gay and lesbian Catholics and their families in order to bring their gifts, talents and experiences to enrich the local church. We will continue to extend our welcome and our ministry to gay and lesbian Catholics throughout the archdiocese, a ministry that will continue to remain a priority for our church.

I invite all of us, Catholics and all people of good will, to reflect more thoughtfully and calmly on the church's position on this initiative in light of the three essential components I have outlined above. May we continue to cherish each person as a son or daughter created in God's image and likeness, and work together to build up a community of justice, compassion and care for all.

43.

DIGNITY'S CHALLENGE
Can homosexuals feel at home in Catholicism?
Shawn Zeller

Commonweal, July 14, 2000

On any given Sunday in Washington, D.C., a group of Catholic exiles gathers. Because they have openly disavowed the church's teachings on homosexuality, they are not allowed to convene for Mass on church property. So the members of Dignity gather apart, at Saint Margaret's Episcopal Church in Washington's gay-friendly Dupont Circle neighborhood. Some come in pairs. Some are alone. Most, by far, are men, and most are white. Most, but not all, are gay. Some are friends or relatives of homosexuals.

The parishioners list numerous reasons for their attendance. Some view Dignity as a social gathering place, where like-minded homosexuals can meet. Others view it as purely spiritual. It's a place where gay Catholics can reconcile their faith and their sexuality, they say. And many see Dignity, at least partly, as a political organization. Their goal is to persuade Vatican authorities to change the church's official teachings on homosexuality and to work with local, state, and federal governments on gay-rights issues.

To many Americans, the idea of a religious homosexual is an oxymoron. God and gays don't mix, they say. That perception has led many gay people to abandon religion, according to former Dignity president Robert Miailovich. But, he explains, Dignity members have held onto their Catholic identity. "We're Catholics because we say we're Catholics and we're not going to let anybody define us out. We define ourselves in," says Miailovich, sixty-one, a Dignity member for twenty-two years and a retired federal government employee.

Still, as Dignity enters its fourth decade as an alternative ministry for gay Catholics, the group's commitment to Catholicism is facing renewed strains. On matters of politics and sexuality, the group finds itself more at odds than ever before with mainstream Catholicism. At the same time, Dignity has struggled to bring in a new generation of gay Catholics. Its congregations are graying, and becoming more male-dominated. Lesbians, upset with the church for what they see as sexist as well as heterosexist policies, have abandoned the group in droves and joined more lesbian-friendly denominations or ceased to worship altogether.

Founded in 1969 by gay Catholics in Los Angeles, Dignity was an officially recognized church group until 1986. To that point, Dignity had never openly questioned church teaching. But in 1986, the Vatican issued a "Letter to the Bishops of the Catholic Church on the Pastoral Care of Homosexual Persons" and ordered dioceses to withdraw all support from groups like Dignity. The next year, Dignity countered with its own statement challenging the church's position. It argued that gay people can practice their sexuality in accordance with Christ's teachings. Dignity was then barred from church facilities in most dioceses. The church continues to hold that homosexuals do not choose their condition, but argues nonetheless that homosexual sex is sinful and that gays and lesbians should seek to lead chaste lives.

At its seventy-five chapters around the country, Dignity counts thousands of members unwilling to accept the church's view. Many chapters have opened lines of communication with diocesan officials in an effort to find common ground but, in many ways, the rifts have only grown deeper. Dignity has issued statements assailing the church's failure to ordain women and to approve the use of birth control. Some of its members have vocally criticized the church's opposition to abortion and the canonical regulation on priestly celibacy, although the organization takes no official position on either issue. And many Dignity chapters have rewritten sections of the Mass to eliminate what members view as sexist rhetoric. Dignity members were outraged a year ago when the Vatican ordered Father Robert Nugent and Sister Jeannine Gramick to cease their ministry to gay Catholics because it allegedly strayed too far from Catholic doctrine. Nugent and Gramick were the founders of the Maryland-based New Ways Ministry. (It continues to minister to gay Catholics.) "For many gay Catholics, unfortunately, that was the last straw," Miailovich says.

For those who've remained, "There's definitely an aspect of trying to find a new self-identity," says Father Christian Mendenhall, a fifty-year-old gay priest who left the active ministry in 1990. Mendenhall is now an assistant professor of drama at American University in Washington, D.C., but he still says Mass for Dignity's Washington chapter.

A Washington service earlier this year underscored just how far Dignity has moved from mainstream Catholicism. Parishioners were urged to refer to God in the terms with which they were most comfortable, a reference to the view that calling God "He" and "Father" is sexist. Likewise, at the offering of petitions, parishioners responded with "God hear our prayer" because, says Miailovich, the more traditional "Lord" is a "male imperial term." Mendenhall also skipped recitation of the Nicene Creed because many Dignity parishioners deem its terminology sexist.

The sermon's content and presentation also differed from those of the traditional Catholic parish. Mendenhall told parishioners to love themselves, homosexuality and all. We should "love the fullness of things about who we are, and that God already loves."

Overall, the Mass felt something like a group therapy session. Before the kiss of peace, Mendenhall encouraged the gathered to "hug the work of art that is sitting next to you." And before the celebration of the Eucharist, he walked the room offering the sacrament of the anointing of the sick. Several parishioners took him up on it, and he made the sign of the cross on the forehead of each while other parishioners laid their hands on the anointee.

"I think we try to cure or heal people who have had a lot of garbage laid on them in their lives," explains Miailovich. "We don't deny that sin exists, but our people have had that message in spades. What they need is the message that God is 'Yes,' that God is there for them."

With the gay-rights agenda gaining currency in many states, Dignity has also expressed increasing anger with the church's active opposition to gay-rights initiatives. Dignity members in Vermont, for example, weighed in with the state legislature as it considered how to implement a December 1999 state supreme court decision that required Vermont to provide equal benefits and rights to gay couples as to married heterosexuals. Vermont state lawmakers passed legislation last spring establishing a system of "civil unions" for gay couples, and the state's Democratic governor, Howard Dean, signed the bill in late April. Vermont Bishop Kenneth Angell publicly opposed the measure.

Meanwhile, San Francisco's Dignity chapter helped publicize the nearly $300,000 that California bishops donated to promote Proposition 22, a ballot initiative that banned California from recognizing same-sex marriages. In December 1999, Dignity members had marched from San Francisco's predominantly gay Castro neighborhood to Saint Mary of the Assumption Cathedral and handed out leaflets protesting against the church's spending and its alliance with the Mormon church, which also backed the initiative. Despite such efforts, California voters approved the gay marriage ban on March 7 of this year by a vote of 69 to 31 percent.

"We really have felt that it's very important to be a presence and an authentic Catholic voice on issues that affect our community," explains Dignity's current executive director, Marianne Duddy, thirty-nine, of Boston. Duddy, who works part-time as a consultant to nonprofit organizations, thinks it is important for Catholic gays to show that church membership is divided on issues like gay marriage.

In that regard, the group has taken steps to form alliances with other liberal Catholics. In February, Dignity members participated in a panel discussion on homosexuality and Catholicism at a meeting of Call to Action, an Illinois-based progressive Catholic group. Dignity is also a member of the Virginia-based Women's Ordination Conference.

Duddy stresses, however, that not all of Dignity's interactions with the church hierarchy have been combative. She points to several meetings with Boston's Cardinal Bernard Law, where she and other Dignity members encouraged him to take a stand against antigay violence and in favor of legislation that would label such violence a hate crime. They also sought financial assistance from the cardinal for the group's charitable work with the homeless and with AIDS patients, and they urged him to implement fully "Always Our Children," the letter issued by the National Conference of Catholic Bishops in 1997. It stresses that parents of homosexuals should treat their children with compassion. Though the cardinal made no promises, Duddy says the meetings were cordial and productive. New York City's Dignity chapter, meanwhile, was successful last year in persuading Cardinal John O'Connor to remain neutral on a state hate-crimes bill, which the late cardinal had opposed in previous years. The bill recently passed in both houses of the state legislature, and is set to be signed into law by George Pataki, New York's Republican (and Catholic) governor.

A few bishops have taken stands supportive of Dignity. The Archdioceses of Baltimore and Detroit both continue to permit Dignity to hold Mass at Catholic churches. Detroit Auxiliary Bishop Thomas Gumbleton spoke at Dignity's last national convention on August 6, 1999, in Denver. "Dignity members feel very much marginalized by the bishops," he says. "I think it's important for the church to reach out to them and keep them connected. They are sincere in their commitment to the church."

Frank DeBernardo, the executive director of the New Ways Ministry, also urges reconciliation with Dignity. "I think the dialogue should continue. They are the largest gay and lesbian Catholic organization in the country, and the church needs to listen to what these people are saying."

But many in the church, like Father Jim Lloyd of New York City, stress that Dignity "leads people down the wrong path because it encourages the rationalization that if it feels good, it must be okay." Lloyd works for the controversial Courage program, an officially recognized church organization that helps homosexuals lead chaste and, if they want, heterosexual lives. The New York City-based group has chapters across the country, but is banned from some dioceses, which feel it treads too closely to the reparative therapy endorsed by some evangelical Protestants. The Archdiocese of Los Angeles, for one, bans Courage, according to Father Peter Liuzzi, who heads the diocese's lesbian and gay outreach program. Liuzzi says Courage's policy of working to help gay men "grow into heterosexuality" is risky since those men may marry, only to then find that they still harbor homosexual desires. "In my view," he says, "the cost of marriage is too dear."

Other dioceses have sought to win over Dignity members by setting up gay and lesbian outreach programs. The National Association of Catholic Diocesan Lesbian and Gay Ministries counts fifty-five dioceses that now have outreach programs. That's up from just thirteen six years ago, when the association was founded, according to its president, John Good. He says the programs seek to help gay Catholics come to terms with church teaching and to make them feel welcome in the church. Good admires Dignity's efforts to work for change in the church but says, "I don't think the way they've gone about their advocacy is the best way to influence change. I think the fact that we work within the formal church structure, we are able to accomplish more because we sit at the table." Good said outreach groups have won greater funding for AIDS ministries, and have persuaded priests to speak out against antigay violence. California members have also weighed in on the church's support for Proposition 22, particularly its alignment with the Mormons. The Mormon church goes beyond the Catholic church in condemning homosexuality itself as sinful.

Still, the arrival of these church-outreach groups has outraged Dignity members in many dioceses. In Chicago, for example, the introduction of an outreach program a decade ago decimated the local Dignity chapter. Half of its membership bolted for the outreach program, recalls Martin Grochala, a member of Dignity/Chicago. Although much of the anger has blown over now, Grochala says that there was a lot of animosity. "There were friendships destroyed and a lot of hard feelings."

Dignity has also struggled to find its place in the larger gay-rights movement. Many gay activists are openly skeptical of religious homosexuals. "There's a segment in the movement that's fairly antireligious," acknowledges Thomas Fleury of Dignity/Vermont. "They hear that I'm a practicing Catholic and they roll their eyes and shrug their shoulders and can't imagine that anyone would want to worship as a Roman Catholic." Last year, a controversy arose among planners of the gay pride 2000 Millennium March on Washington this April 30, over whether to stress faith as one of several march themes. Some even condemned the use of the term "Millennium," calling it a purely Christian marker of time. Fleury says the antireligious attitude is typical among gay activists since so many organized religions consider homosexuality sinful.

Several Dignity members told me they often volunteer time with their local gay-rights organizations. Many members of Washington, D.C.-based PELAG – Parents, Families, and Friends of Lesbians and Gays – attend Dignity services throughout the country. Dignity's national chapter has joined the National Religious Leadership Roundtable, an arm of the National Gay and Lesbian Task Force (NGLTF), a major Washington-based gay-rights group. The roundtable seeks to help gay religious organizations share strategy for working within their own denominations, and also seeks to mobilize religious gays on political causes. "We want to amplify the voice of the pro-gay religious movement," explains Urvashi Vaid, the executive director of the NGLTF Policy Institute. "We want to have different voices speaking out for gay rights."

Dignity's aggressive advocacy and alignment with other gay-rights organizations further lessens the chance of reconciliation with the church, according to skeptics. Still, Dignity leaders insist that they cannot compromise on principle. "When we talk about wanting to dialogue and trying to reach some understanding with the church, it's not on bended knee asking for favors," insists Miailovich. "It has to be equal to equal."

But that's impossible, according to Father John Harvey, the founder of Courage. Dignity's position can never overrule or compromise church teaching "based solidly on Scripture and natural law," he says. If there is to be dialogue, he adds, it must begin with the premise that the "church's position is correct and is not going to change." Whether or not dialogue will end with that is the unanswered question.

44.

GAY CATHOLICS LOOK TO THEIR FAITH

The church's teachings on homosexual sex pose a tough challenge
Anne Bacani

The Catholic Register, **week of June 19, 2000**

TORONTO – Amateur sketches of nude bodies in cheap imitation gold frames are nailed against hollow walls inside the cramped cafe on Charles Street West. The air is cloying with the smell of nicotine from cigarette-smoking patrons. David (not his real name), a 35-year-old office clerk who epitomizes the word thin – thin physique, nose, eyeglasses and blond hair – is comfortably ensconced in a scarred, wooden pew-like chair. He stirs two cream cups into his first of three mugs of Canadian blend coffee.

"My story is nothing special," he says, looking at me warily. "It's not at all interesting. I wasn't sexually abused as a child and I have a good relationship with my dad."

David, who hasn't disclosed his same-sex preferences to his devout Roman Catholic parents, dismisses his testimony as boring. He says he doesn't fall in a tidy niche that gay activists and Christian ex-gay ministries have created for the homosexual. Ex-gay ministries say being gay is a learned behaviour that can be reversed by coming to terms with childhood events and dynamics which may have affected a person's understanding of his/her masculinity and femininity.

David's Wednesday nights for the last five years have been spent at Courage – a spiritual support group for men and women who strive to live chaste lives in accordance with the Catholic Church's teaching on homosexuality. The late Cardinal Terence Cook of New York and Fr. John Harvey of the Oblates of St. Francis de Sales founded Courage about 20 years ago. Courage is the only national, Vatican-approved Catholic ministry to homosexuals.

Forty years-ago, Harvey ministered to priests and religious struggling with sexual identity and chastity. In his work, he discovered the value of support groups and the power they had in helping people confront their tendencies and habits. He realized support groups gave individuals living with same-sex attraction a chance to connect with others and offered them a clearer perspective on their struggles:

"Courage doesn't require anyone coming to its meetings to commit to diminishing their same-sex attraction or changing it to a more heterosexual focus," says Christina Nair, secretary for New York's Courage chapter. "Courage's focus is on the person's personal relationship to Christ."

There is a reason why people come to Courage, says Oblate Father Vaughan Quinn, facilitator of Toronto's Courage. It is a place of support, prayer and friendship for men and women with homosexual tendencies who want to live chastely in a world that devalues chastity.

"People come to Courage because they're sick and tired of being sick and tired of their life situation. Of not being the person who they want to be," says Quinn. "Courage is about how to set people free. To strive for personal integrity, overcome debilitating compulsive behaviour and to follow Christ's teachings that homosexual acts are intrinsically evil."

Bob, another group member, says Courage is a source of love and renewal. People opposed to chastity have a misperception of it being "a life of loneliness and darkness," he says. In fact, Bob says he enjoys his single state in life because he has more time for community outreach, going out with friends and meeting new people.

"I don't sit alone Friday or Saturday nights wishing I had a boyfriend sitting next to me," Bob says. "It's a challenge to see single life as a vocation. You have to learn how to use your time and money wisely for moral good."

Bob is adamant in pointing out Courage is not at war with anyone. He explains Courage is not here to engage in a "we're right and you're wrong" battle with any existing groups in opposition to the Catholic Church's teaching on homosexuality. The church stands on the periphery of the debate raging over sexual reorientation between militant gays and ex-gay Christian ministries.

For David, elementary school was a hellish ride punctuated by name-calling, such as gay and fag, by older girls. He was teased by his peers for preferring the girls' game of jump rope. Amidst the cruel taunts of schoolyard bullies, David's parents reaffirmed him as a man. His mom would say, "You are a very masculine boy, David," and his dad taught him self-defence and football.

David has always been attracted to both sexes; he went to his high school prom with a girl he liked. But same-sex attraction, he explains, overrides his attraction towards the opposite sex. He sexually fantasized about older men and male movie stars but never acted on his impulses, he says. As well, he never identified himself as gay because he didn't feel the word captured who he was.

"I take my faith very seriously. The church's teaching on homosexuality is rooted in Scripture, tradition and the biblical understanding of sexuality in general," he says.

Gay activists argue that same-sex attraction is biological and eschew the possibility it may be environmentally caused. Rob Goetze, the London, Ont., director of a Christian ex-gay support and counselling group called New Direction for Life Ministries Canada, advocates reparative therapy. He offers some explanations for homosexuality. Victims of sexual, physical or emotional abuse lose their sense of self. Other events that can increase the likelihood of being gay, he says, include peer rejection and labelling, sexual misinformation and birth trauma. In addition, boys with absent fathers and girls with absent mothers feel rejected and their psychological needs for love and affirmation as boys and girls are not met. Thus they seek masculine and feminine fulfilment through same-sex relationships.

The American Psychological Association labelled reparative or "conversion" therapy as potentially harmful in 1997. The therapy raises the hackles of gay activists.

"Ex-gay ministries encourage people to feel negative about the homo- or bisexual inclinations of themselves and others," says Christine Donald, a spokesperson for the Coalition for Lesbian and Gay Rights in Ontario. She contends you can certainly encourage homosexuals and lesbians to deny aspects of their inclination and not act on their feelings, but that doesn't mean they have ceased to become gay. They have only ceased to act on their desires, says Donald. Ex-gay ministries, she says, also perpetuate homophobia. Homophobia is the irrational fear and hatred of homosexuality.

If you ask Jay, he'll tell you something different.

"New Direction for Life Ministries is not a smokescreen for homophobia," says Jay, 25-year-old special education teacher from southwestern Ontario. He joined New Direction for Life at 16.

"They don't teach you techniques of suppression. Healing comes with talking and dealing with past issues – social issues and nurture versus nature issues – that caused you to be gay. I don't think I'm suppressing who I am. My homosexual orientation was a consequence of living in a broken world."

Growing up in a broken family was difficult, he says. His parents divorced when he was two and his biweekly visits to his father's house were insufficient in building a relationship with his dad who gave little positive feedback to his only child.

Being called "Tinker Bell, Cindy, sissy and fag" all throughout grade school aggravated his gender confusion, Jay adds. He was ostracized by the boys at school for spending more time with girls who were kinder to him.

As his Protestant faith grew and the communication lines between him and his dad opened, Jay says he was stirred to change his unsatisfying homosexual lifestyle which consisted of quick, anonymous sexual encounters with men in mall washrooms.

"I remember going through puberty and scratching my head thinking, 'Lord if you made me this way then why is homosexuality condemned in the Bible?' I realized my homosexuality wasn't a consequence of God making me this way. It was because of different factors in my life," he says. "But God has provided a way out for me, too."

Jason Van Tassel, a 26-year-old information technology student, is frank about what he thinks of ex-gay ministries and other groups advocating chastity as an option.

"I'm sure 100 per cent of homosexuality is biological. If it wasn't otherwise, who in their right mind, in this day and age, would choose to be discriminated against," Van Tassel argues. "As long as I can remember, I've always felt different. In Grade 6, when we played spin the bottle I'd always want to get Harry."

The possibility of living a straight life or practising celibacy is impossible for Van Tassel, who says he is happy with his homosexual lifestyle of nearly 10 years. Similarly Luis Rodriguez, a good-looking Colombian Catholic, says if someone offered him a pill that would remove his "gayness," he wouldn't take it. Why? Because he is content about who and what he is even though he says he often grows weary of the superficiality that runs rampant among people in the homosexual community.

"There's times when I say, 'I don't want to be gay' because I see how superficial the gay community is. I see everyone is miserable because of excessive use of drugs which has escalated in the last five years."

The Catholic teaching about chastity is really about love: love of God, of self and of others, says David. He finishes his last mug of coffee, foots the bill and we get up to leave. As he pushes his chair back, he confides his self esteem has increased ever since he started attending the meetings. In those meetings, he says, they voice out the difficulties of living a life aligned with their faith. They talk about developing healthy, male friendships and respecting other men by seeing them for who they are instead of mere sex objects.

45.

PRIESTS WITH AIDS

Jon Fuller

America, **March 18, 2000**

During the last three days of January, after an 18-month exploration of the topic, The Kansas City Star published a series of articles on cases of AIDS among Catholic priests. Propelled by the assertion that "priests are dying of AIDS at a rate at least four times that of the general U.S. population" the story was picked up by news outlets across the country and around the world. In response to criticism of the authors' methods for comparing death rates in the general population and those of priests, The Star subsequently modified its story. The amended version indicated that the rate was about double the death rate of the adult male population, although this detail was apparently not included in the original, nationally circulated story.

First, what about the numbers? In my experience with religious orders of men, it is not uncommon to observe H.I.V. rates of 0.25 percent to 1 percent, comparable to the United Nations AIDS Program's estimate of 0.5 percent for the rate of H.I.V. infection among adults in the United States. So yes, The Star's numbers are plausible. But even though the proportion of priests and religious who are homosexual appears to be higher than in the general population (with variation probably occurring by geographic region and in different historical periods), the data for priests do not compare with highly sexually active gay populations, in which rates as high as 50 percent have been documented.

But beyond concern about accuracy of the numbers, my initial reaction was to ask: "Why is this story getting so much attention now?" Is it that people are surprised priests have developed AIDS, or that some are homosexual? The data are certainly not new. The fact that priests have been stricken with H.I.V.–AIDS has been noted in local and national newspapers and magazines, in The National Catholic Reporter and Origins, in books written by priests living with AIDS and in AIDS quilts made for the Names Project. Many have been quite open about their diagnoses while remaining actively engaged in ministry.

Nevertheless, these articles have brought the issue to a markedly wider audience and provide the opportunity to highlight a series of related developments. These include my impression that the number of new infections among clergy and religious has actually trended downward over time, that the church's response to infected clergy has become more enlightened and compassionate and, most important, that there has been a significant evolution in how sexuality and psychosexual development are understood and incorporated into formation programs.

My association with this topic has involved caring for priests and religious living with H.I.V.-AIDS since the 1980's. But it has also included efforts (with the National Catholic AIDS Network and the National Federation of Priests Councils) to inform superiors, vocation directors and bishops who have struggled to deal with cases of infected individuals and who have also sought to understand how to diminish the risk that other members could also become H.I.V.-infected.

Central to many workshops on AIDS for religious and diocesan leaders have been panels of priests and religious living with H.I.V. infection. During the first such conference (organized by Damien Ministries in 1988), participating priests felt so stigmatized and fearful of negative repercussions that they wore paper bags over their heads as they shared their experiences.

Over the years panelists have spoken of never being able to talk about their sexuality, and of living in fear that they would be rejected or ostracized if their homosexuality were discovered. They have reported internal or external pressure to appear or to "pass" as heterosexual, and have felt inhibited from discussing the challenges of being faithful to their vows as they have moved through different stages of adulthood. They have spoken of living in fear that they might have acquired H.I.V., of how difficult it was to come to terms with the reality of their infection once diagnosed and of how denial and shame sometimes delayed their seeking medical attention. They have spoken of being afraid and ashamed to disclose their infected status to superiors and peers, and of worrying that they might cause scandal. They have feared that they might be withdrawn from ministry and relocated geographically, or that they might be dismissed and cut off from personal and financial support. They have described their desires to remain active in ministry and to be open about their H.I.V. status with the communities they serve. And they have shared the difficulties of living with complicated medical regimens, amid how they have approached – sometimes with fear – their own process of dying.

These workshops and conferences have addressed caring for infected members, as well as the ethical, clinical and juridical complexities in developing policies on the testing of candidates for H.I.V. infection. But they have also drawn attention to what conference participants frequently pointed out were fundamental issues underlying the stories they had heard: how human sexuality has been inadequately considered and incorporated into formation programs.

If there is a silver lining to the tragedy of priests and religious dying of AIDS, it is in the vastly increased attention given to the area of psychosexual development in the training of clergy and religious. For example, not 20 years ago I was chastised by a major superior for being involved with efforts to promote dialogue between heterosexual and homosexual members of a religious order. I was told that such conversations were inappropriate because "we have put sexuality behind us and we don't need to deal with those questions." This attitude has unfortunately led to an atmosphere in which sexual issues were simply not talked about, and where shame and stigmatization prevented an open discussion of the challenges that all vowed religious and priests face as they grow into mature expression of their vows.

Experience has taught that authentic psychosexual development simply cannot occur when sexuality in general, and sexual orientation in particular, are treated as subterranean topics. Whether or not it is permissible to speak about one's sexuality and orientation in seminaries or religious life, sooner or later individuals will come to terms with who they are, whether at age 25, 35 or 65.

It is true that one should never presume that H.I.V. infections among clergy and religious are the result of sexual activity in violation of the vows; cases have occurred from transfused blood, from administration of clotting factors and from H.I.V. infections acquired before entering the seminary or religious order. However, in my estimation, many instances of AIDS among religious and priests in the United States are at least partly related to a history of inattention to psychosexual development in formation programs and to the strongly negative attitude of the church toward homosexuality. This has made it difficult, if not impossible, for many gay persons to feel confident and healthy about who they are, and even to accept the fact that they are homosexual. As J.A. Loftus, S.J., former director of the Southdown treatment center in Canada has described, some gay persons are so homophobic and afraid of being stigmatized that they are unable to acknowledge themselves as gay even though they may be engaging in frankly homosexual behavior (*Clergy and Religious Exposed to AIDS, Emmanuel Convalescent Foundation,* 1989). In addition to making it impossible for them to hear preventive messages directed toward the gay community, this is evidence of a pathological disconnection between self-identity and evident sexual orientation.

In many circumstances in which vowed religious have become infected with H.I.V., this has been the result of finally dealing with sexual feelings that have erupted after years or decades of being submerged. Where there has been silence on these issues, instead of a proactive, systematic treatment of integrating sexuality with celibacy, an adolescent-like exploration of relationships may occur. If one's orientation has been treated as unacceptable and one has never learned to develop authentic and appropriate intimate friendships, this exploration may include furtive sexual contacts that can place individuals at high risk for acquiring H.I.V. infection.

Partly as a result of the church's experience with H.I.V.-infected clergy and religious, I believe that a sea change is occurring in this area (albeit more often in religious orders than in the training of diocesan clergy). We are recognizing the absolute necessity of dealing openly, realistically and respectfully with the fact that orders and dioceses are made up of human beings who share the same spectrum of sexual orientations as the population at large. Religious orders in particular have recognized that, if they are to form individuals who can minister effectively in contemporary society, their members cannot be "asexual" but must be possessed of a consolidated understanding of their sexuality. They must be able consciously to attend to the challenges of living celibacy that will continue to evolve as they advance through the stages of adult development.

As superiors have learned to care for infected clergy and religious, they have also learned to listen attentively to the lived experience of gay priests and religious. This has led to a more widespread acknowledgment that diocesan presbyterates and religious communities include gay members, and to the realization that the strength of such an organization and the union of its members depend upon mutual trust, understanding and respect. It has revealed that the central issue is not one's sexual orientation, but that one be fully integrated, authentic, faithful to the vows and capable of working and living with persons of other sexual orientations as one exercises the priestly ministry or lives the order's charism. It has spawned formation programs that develop individuals with interior freedom, integrity, self-knowledge and self-confidence because they believe that along with their vocations, their sexual orientations, whether heterosexual or homosexual, are also gifts from God.

It gives me hope to observe developments in religious formation over the last 20 years, but the process of moving forward in our understanding of human sexuality through reflection on experience needs also to occur in the church at large. Even a cursory review of comments that readers have posted on The Star's Web site indicates a wide spectrum of perspectives and feelings on this topic, ranging from relief that the issue is finally being aired, to rage at the very concept of homosexual priests, to compassionate awareness that clergy are so human that they, too, can make mistakes.

In every instance I know in which a priest has revealed his H.I.V.-AIDS status to the parish or school he serves, the response has not been judgment or ostracism but an outpouring of concern and support. Parish members providing 24-hour care to their priest as he approaches death is a revelation of the loving energy of reconciliation radiating from the heart of the church, an energy that I hope can empower our continued efforts to engage in dialogue on the complexity and mystery of God's gifts of sexuality and human dignity.

46.

CATHOLICS IN SHOCK

Michael Higgins

The Tablet, 22 September 1990

The sight was both pathetic and noble. There on the most important public affairs programme of the Canadian Broadcasting Corporation – *The Journal* – was Alphonsus Penney, Archbishop of St John's, Newfoundland, publicly acknowledging his pastoral failure over the vexatious issue of clerical paedophilia and the lamentable and wholly inadequate response of the institutional Church to the complaints of the victims. It was an indictment complete and entire; it was an act of repentance on the part of a culpable but honourable prelate quite simply overtaken by the enormity of it all. Earlier on that fateful day, 18 July 1990, he had proffered his resignation as archbishop.

At the press conference convened on his own authority, Penney remarked: "I apologise and express my sincere regrets for failing the victims and their families in their moment of acute pain and desolation. I also express to the people of God in our local Church my regrets for the deficiency in my leadership, ministry and management. I take full responsibility and candidly acknowledge that 'it is I the shepherd', indeed the chief shepherd, who has failed. Upon becoming aware of the significantly negative evaluation of my leadership, ministry and management, I immediately wrote our Holy Father, Pope John Paul II, and submitted my resignation as Archbishop of St John's."

The "negative evaluation" of his pastorship to which he alluded was expressed in particular in the report on child sexual abuse by members of the clergy of Newfoundland drawn up by the archdiocesan commission of inquiry, widely known as the Winter Commission after its chairman, Gordon Winter, a former Lieutenant Governor, who is an Anglican. Ironically, Penney himself established the commission and set its mandate. Although it was clearly intended to respond to the mounting criticism of the archbishop's performance, and was a constructive effort to assure the Catholic community of Newfoundland of the chief shepherd's determination not to play down the gravity of the issue, Penney could not have anticipated the harsh verdict that his leadership would be accorded. The two-volume report's 55 conclusions and recommendations are hard-hitting.

Since 1988 the Church in Newfoundland has been under severe public scrutiny. The series of sex scandals involving altar boys and orphans has shaken the Catholic community in the province to its very roots. In the major newspapers of the nation, principally in the *Globe & Mail* and the *Toronto Star,* as well as in such national newsmagazines as *L'Actualité* and *Maclean's,* detailed coverage has been provided on a regular basis. Weekly, or even daily, instalments about the behaviour of the Newfoundland clergy have provoked rage, indignation or titillation.

It began with the trial of Fr James Hickey, one of the most popular priests in all of the Maritimes. It was Hickey who figured prominently as a master planner during the papal visit to Canada in 1984, and it was Hickey who could be relied upon to employ his native charm to stunning effect with the media. This same Hickey was found guilty of a score of sexual assaults upon altar boys spanning several years, and was sentenced to five years in prison, to be served at the Dorchester penitentiary in New Brunswick. He has been repeatedly denied early parole.

During the Hickey trial other allegations concerning priests and ex-priests surfaced, fanning the flames of outrage, embarrassment and confusion. Penney elected silence as his legal and moral strategy. He was counselled so. It may have proven to be legally wise, although that is doubtful, but morally his leadership suffered irreparable damage, to an extent of which he only became truly apprised upon receiving the Winter Commission's report. After the shock and incredulity with which the initial disclosures were met by an anxious laity, Penney found himself increasingly targeted by angry Catholics for his "policy" of inaction, a form of pastoral solicitude they could easily do without. There were calls for his resignation. He declined to visit the parishes whose resident priests stood accused or were facing charges – frequently dispatching the articulate and affable Fr Kevin Molloy in his stead – and chose to avoid the media completely.

As a consequence, Penney's credibility and that of many of his clergy plummeted in the public eye. The clerical authority was replaced by a highly credible moral authority invested in several women religious and in an increasingly vocal laity, composed of many activist mothers and aggrieved parents. In a manner consonant with the method of liberation theology, these unofficial spokeswomen have provided a cogent dissection of the pathology of patriarchy and a painful analysis of the dangers of a rampant clericalism.

As if these disclosures were not enough, the headlines were soon taken over by allegations of sexual and physical abuse made against several Christian Brothers by past residents of Mount Cashel Orphanage. These charges, and the accusations of a cover-up perpetrated by a Church-State alliance of feudal proportions, resulted in the establishment of the Hughes Commission and the closure of Mount Cashel.

Religious controversy and religious shenanigans are not new to Catholics in Canada's youngest province. But the shame and seediness associated with paedophilia and pederasty have eroded, irreversibly, the exaggerated esteem the clergy commanded, particularly in the out-ports. Things will never be the same again.

Not a few of the priests and scores of the religious sisters will be comforted by that knowledge at least. Clericalism is dying in Newfoundland – a region more devoutly and fiercely Catholic than almost anywhere else in Canada, including the pockets of Acadian and Celtic Catholicism found on the East Coast or the Latin immigrant communities of Toronto and Montreal.

The nasty drama unfolding in the province prompted the distinguished writer and editor of *Saturday Night* magazine, the Anglican John Fraser, to observe in the January/February 1990 issue: "From the Church in Canada recently we have been learning more than we ever wanted to know about the dark side of trust. This has to be corrected in a forthright, public manner, no matter how painful the process is. And it will be painful because reforms in the public sector are caught up with all those thorny 'family matters' that have to be struggled with urgently and alone."

And now the reforms are with us; the thorny "family matters" struggled with in stark relief against the backdrop of the Winter Commission and an archbishop's impending resignation. Many of the commission's recommendations are predictable, but many others are blunt assessments of inadequate and morally, if not criminally, culpable actions on the part of the church leadership. The archdiocesan administration is urged to accept its full share of guilt and responsibility, indulging in no waffling or evasionary tactics, recognising the vulnerability of the victims and seeking in every public way to provide compensation and healing. But what is especially surprising is the commission's strong insistence that broader initiatives be undertaken by the Canadian Conference of Catholic Bishops to develop a "national programme of research and study which might contribute to the development of the Church's theology of sexuality". In addition, the commission boldly recommends that Penney and his episcopal brothers across Canada address "fully, directly, honestly and without reservation questions relating to the problematic link between celibacy and the ministerial priesthood."

Moment missed

The first major occasion for the bishops to respond to this recommendation came with their plenary assembly, held in August just a few weeks after the release of the Winter Commission's report. They set aside a part of their time to address, yet again, the problem of sex abuse, but hesitated to do more. They had their own committee to examine the issue with all its ramifications, and had demonstrated their willingness to establish diocesan procedures to cope with complaints and the need to guarantee due process of law. There were other urgent items, they reasoned, that required attention, and the sex scandals had sapped the energy of an already over-extended and demoralised clergy. But the bishops missed an ideal moment. As they mulled over their drafts of the interventions for the Synod in Rome this October – refining, clarifying and tightening – they managed to compose a series of presentations empty of any real substance.

The history of Canadian synodal interventions is an heroic one; they have raised questions other episcopal conferences have either not contemplated or have not dared to express in public. It was the 1971 intervention of Cardinal Flahiff, for instance, that first took up the issue of women and ministry, to which the CCCB returned with tenacity and creativity at the Synods in 1980, 1983, 1985 and 1987.

Pope John Paul has made it clear that he does not want a discussion of clerical celibacy at the 1990 Synod on the training of priests, and an intervention specifically focused on celibacy could be seen as rank insubordination. However, given the problems facing the ministerial priesthood in Canada – an increasing number of priestless parishes, particularly in the prairie provinces; a high burn-out rate among active clergy; flourishing rehabilitative services for clergy: an average clerical age hovering around 60; starkly inadequate seminary enrolments and so on – that it is hard to justify the exclusion of the subject from the interventions. Temerity, not timidity, is what Canadian Catholics want from their bishops at this time.

The drafts do not inspire confidence considering that three of the five delegates – Archbishop Aloysius Ambrozic of Toronto, Auxiliary Bishop Frederick Henry of London, and Bishop Henri Goudreault of Labrador-Schefferville – are former seminary professors or rectors, would not be unreasonable to expect interventions of an immediate and pointed nature. Such had been the tradition of the past. This time, however, prudence has displaced candour. The drafts fail to examine alternatives to seminary education or new models of priestly ministry. Given the highly charged atmosphere in Canada over the sex-abuse scandal, and the continued failure of recruitment programmes to attract a significant number of high-quality candidates for the priesthood, what could possibly have motivated the bishops to choose so tame and tepid an approach as can be found in these synod drafts?

The continuing events in Newfoundland, with trials, judicial inquiries and committee reports, can easily obscure the need for a more accurate historical and ecclesial evaluation of what is, in effect, a national crisis. The accountability of the hierarchy, the training of church personnel, fair financial compensation for victims of clerical crime, sexual and emotional rehabilitation and the subsequent reincorporation into the service of the Church of those who have undergone restorative therapy – all these are questions that need to be faced with earnest immediacy by the Church in Canada, and not just by the beleaguered Catholics of St John's.

The formation of a Coalition of Concerned Canadian Catholics, and the increasing boldness with which various lay Catholics are demanding accountability from those who exercise church office, are signs of the times. Though Canadian Catholics are not restive or rebellious by nature – after all, Canada retains historical and political links with the British Crown – the sex-abuse scandals in Newfoundland have brought to a head their many worries about whether those who govern the Church have the capacity to effect deep and authentic structural change.

The first step, at least, has been taken, with the report of the Winter Commission showing the way to turn tragedy into the beginning of wisdom. As the editorial in the 10 August issue of the *National Catholic Reporter* of Kansas City commented: "It is a commendable piece of work, revealing that what is really required in the face of scandal and seemingly endless mire is the will to act as a pastoral Church."

Was it naive to think that step two could have been the Canadian voice at the Synod?

47.

FOCUS ON SEXUAL ABUSE
Michael Higgins

***The Tablet,* 13 February 1993**

In my previous article in *The Tablet* on the sex scandals that had shaken the Canadian Catholic Church (22 September 1990) I wrote of the Newfoundland revelations that led eventually to the resignation of Archbishop Penney and the abuses at a Christian Brothers orphanage called Mount Cashel. That was a sordid business that in great measure prompted the Canadian Conference of Catholic Bishops to set up in October 1989 an ad hoc committee on child sexual abuse. It has had its hands full.

The committee published its report, "From Pain to Hope," in June last year, and earlier a collection of materials for discussion called "Breach of Trust, Breach of Faith". They are both significant and estimable efforts showing an honesty and determination even the Church's critics must admire. But it is not the end of the crisis for, as the committee wrote, "In the eyes of a good number of our fellow citizens, the Church has lost a great deal of credibility over the past few years due to these scandals and the suspicion that there were attempts to conceal these intolerable acts".

The committee was chaired by Archbishop Roger Ebacher of Gatineau-Hull, and composed of two other archbishops, a lay social worker, a woman social development officer, the national president of the councils of priests, and a Sister of Charity who is a paediatrician. It had four specialist assistants.

"From Pain to Hope" contains 50 recommendations, many of them bold, all of them urgent. The report is neither timid nor delicate in acknowledging the abuse that has flourished without accountability. It even looks at the priesthood in Canada in order to detect signs of institutional pathology that go beyond the simple recording of sexual disorder and occasional aberration.

The committee notes that "relatively recently in our history, Catholic priests in Canada could, on account of their ministry and their status as priests, exercise considerable authority over the day-to-day lives of their communities". This "excessive power", it declares, "unchecked by any kind of social control, placed certain individuals beyond the reach of legitimate questioning and made it possible to prevent detection. The fact that priests were placed on a pedestal was actually a kind of trap. This contributed to their becoming more and more isolated from the people they served and not developing healthy relationships built on simple friendship —something essential to a balanced humanity."

It is recommended that in the spirit of humility "more energy be put into correcting wrongs than into safeguarding appearances; into humble care of the wounded than into attempts to justify, into effective forms of education and careful research into ways of improving services for children, the poor and the most vulnerable in our society."

These are the words of an institution that is contrite, wounded, moving "from pain to hope".

The first five recommendations are addressed to all the Catholics of Canada and vigorously encourage the citizenry to become informed about all the aspects – juridical, psychological and social – concerning child sex abuse and the demands of healing.

The report then addresses the Catholic bishops of Canada (recommendations 6 to 23), mostly on legal and procedural matters, including the process to be invoked should consideration be given to the possible return to active ministry of a priest who, having been convicted of child sexual abuse and having served his sentence or having received a suspended sentence, asks to resume his ministry. These recommendations have come under some heavy criticism. There are many parishes in the country that are smarting from ill-advised shuffles in the past when abusive priests were simply reassigned to a different parish or transferred to a different diocese without the new congregation or bishop being made fully aware of the priest's record. The report, however, makes clear that the priest who is to be reintegrated "should be prepared to meet with the members of the parish council or with a group of parishioners to ask for their support, understanding and prayer".

The hard investigative work in exposing these abuses was done, particularly in the early days, by the secular media. John Redekop, a political science professor and columnist for the Evangelical and Reformed newspaper *Christian Week,* has rightly pointed out that the defensive posture adopted by the fundamentalist media in the United States over the televangelist sex scandals (Jimmy Swaggart and Jim Bakker) was matched in Canada with an alarming timidity in the religious over the Roman Catholic clerical sexes. In fact when *Catholic New Times* of Toronto republished a news item from a Calgary newspaper concerning allegations against a British Columbia bishop of sexual assault, the editors were inundated with complaints, cancellations, and more than a mite of outrage. The rumours, however, were translated into formal charges and the bishop resigned, admitting to consensual sex with at least two women.

Perhaps an awareness of the consequences of damage control is behind the committee's clear call for openness: "...our suggestions and recommendations are clearly oriented toward the search for truth: the truthfulness of statements made to the media; personal truthfulness and honesty in the preparation of candidates for the priesthood; insistence on the truth throughout the therapy of the abusers; truthfulness with those few parishes asked to accept a priest who is being reintegrated into the ministry".

This is meant to exorcise the demon of secrecy, the fear of causing scandal. Yet, as Andrew Britz, the blunt-speaking Benedictine editor of *The Prairie Messenger,* has noted: "The report calls on Catholics to 'break the silence' about child sexual abuse, but is itself silent about the magnitude of the problem. When reporters asked for figures on the number of cases involving child sexual abuse by priests and religious, the committee was unable to as much as hazard a guess. Yet an Ottawa newspaper was later able to come up with a list of 70 priests and members of religious orders who have been charged with sexual offences in recent years." The committee needs to understand that modified openness is not openness at all.

Another set of recommendations (24 to 33) is addressed to those who are responsible for priestly formation. In an accompanying preliminary note the authors remark that these recommendations are not "intended to replace the orientation document of the Holy See in 1980". It was discreet to say so, but in so doing the committee reveals the considerable difficulty it faces when addressing national issues in a universal institution. The recommendations argue for the formation of seminarians "within a context of integral human development" and rely rather heavily on the insights and methods of the social sciences. They do not jettison the philosophical and theological curricula so dear to the heart of Rome but they do support such things as human formation counsellors, and they make a point of emphasising "how necessary it is that women be among those who collaborate in the formation of candidates for the priesthood. The involvement of women is considered essential at all stages and in every aspect of the formation (including teaching, counselling and pastoral work)".

The presence of Dr Jeannine Guindon as one of the four principal advisers to the committee is instructive. She is the professional psychotherapist who was invited by Pope John Paul II to attend the 1990 Synod on priestly formation as a lay auditor. Her presence might well have emboldened the committee to press some of these matters of priestly training that Rome continues to be suspicious of, like the enhanced presence of women in priestly formation.

It may be that the psycho-affective emphases proposed by Dr Guindon's work group can be accommodated without any serious substantive changes to the seminary structure, but I do not myself see how it is possible.

The presence of women in all aspects of priestly formation at the two major English-speaking seminaries, St Augustine's in Toronto and St Peter's in London, Ontario, is lamentably restricted. Women do not function as spiritual directors (a Roman requirement) and they are noticeably absent in the administrative structure and as instructors in the "hard" disciplines, like systematics. The Atlantic School of Theology and St Paul's in Ottawa fare much better, but their broader and more ecumenical design is less favoured by an increasingly more cautious English-Canadian episcopate.

To those responsible for priests in a diocese the committee proposes various ways of diminishing clerical isolation and loneliness and of enhancing opportunities for mutual support. The last seven recommendations of the report are addressed to the bishops' conference, encouraging it in its role as facilitator and urging the composition and implementation of a code of professional ethics for clergy and pastoral agents.

The bishops of Canada have the daunting task of implementing the recommendations made by their ad hoc committee, and Catholic Canada will be watching closely. Although the report does not employ a hard ecclesiological critique of the inadequacies of church structure and formation, it does admit to the presence of such serious problems as "the failure to fully implement ecclesial communion proposed by the Second Vatican Council", and the committee's working papers include several passages from the hard-hitting report into the Newfoundland scandals (the Winter commission). This on the ravages of patriarchy: "Paternalism and sexism are very much in evidence, the commission was told, among both young and old priests in the archdiocese. Many who spoke and presented briefs to the commission described an alarming lack of awareness and insensitivity in the use of patriarchal language and imagery in worship, and in preaching and teaching throughout the archdiocese . . . Many have argued that patriarchal thinking is one of the contributing factors to the sexual abuse of children." This brave inclusion is, however, provided with an italicised note indicating that "the quotations pertaining to each factor are discussion starters only. Debate and further study of these complex matters are needed and encouraged". I would have thought that to be self-evident. Some senior hierarchical sensibilities — in English Canada most notably — are easily ruffled by references to sexism and patriarchy, hence the sop.

But the report of the bishops' ad hoc committee and its discussion materials are on the whole significant, sound, and sane. They are in the best Canadian episcopal tradition of forthright and probing analyses. But now to the implementation.

It should be noted that the purview of the committee was limited to the issue of child sexual abuse. Crimes of sexual assault, allegations of sexual impropriety and harassment regarding those aged 18 and older of either sex, and the highly vexatious issue of abuse in the Indian residential schools (which is being addressed by a separate process established by the bishops' conference) fall outside its mandate. The sexual abuse incidents in the St John's and St Joseph's training schools run by the Christian Brothers in Ontario did fall within the mandate, and the committee's work was applauded by David McCann, the founder of Helpline (a support group for survivors of physical and sexual abuse) and a major force in bringing to public awareness the appalling legacy of abuse.

The Roman Catholic Church is not the only one facing major challenges to its institutional integrity on matters of sexual injustice. Revelations about the Mennonite community in the prairie provinces, the highly publicised trials of two Anglican choirmasters in Toronto and Kingston respectively, and a recent report on sexual abuse by the clergy of the United Church of Canada demonstrate only too clearly that the Catholic Church is not alone in its painful exercise in self-scrutiny.

In fact, with institutional resolve, the Roman Catholic Church can lead the way to a more just and equitable society and proclaim its message of the reign of God with renewed vigour and recovered credibility. Much good has come out of these two documents. A sense of urgency and honesty now characterises the treatment of these matters by the official Church.

48.

FIFTY RECOMMENDATIONS:
THE CHURCH AND CHILD SEXUAL ABUSE

Canadian Bishops' Committee (1992)

Fifty recommendations to the Catholic Church in Canada for responding to the problem of the sexual abuse of children are offered in a report titled "From Pain to Hope" by the Canadian bishops" Ad Hoc Committee on Child Sexual Abuse. The report was released June 11.

SUMMARY

Where Does the Church Stand?

At the beginning of the sixth part of our report, we expressed the firm conviction that the concerted effort of many people will be needed to stem the tide of sexual abuse against children. To conclude this section, let us state where the Catholic Church should stand in the context of this plan for action.

– On the side of openness and truth: We would like to see our church guided by a spirit of openness and truth when responding to allegations of child sexual abuse by a priest or a religious. We want our church to cooperate fully with child-protection agencies and the judiciary, not claiming preferential treatment for one of its ministers when suspected or formally accused in such cases.

– On the side of extensive cooperation by Catholics: In our minds, our church would be socially irresponsible if it participated in the fight against child sexual abuse only when one of its ministers is implicated. We know that such cases represent only a small proportion of the total number of cases in our country.

We would like to see our church, inspired equally by belief in the cause itself and by a sense of responsibility, actively encourage all Catholics to cooperate fully with Health and Welfare Canada in its efforts to curb family violence and, in particular, child sexual abuse. Our church should call its members to unite with those who condemn such forms of aggression.

– On the side of transforming persons and institutions: We would like to see our church face, with clarity and courage, the decisions that must be taken in light of the failure that child abuse represents for society and the church itself. Indeed, it is simply intolerable that a society should degenerate to the extent of closing its eyes to the injustices which are destroying the foundations on which children build their identity.

These decisions will call for change in the attitudes of those who are whole-heartedly to defend children and other vulnerable people in society. They also call for change in institutions themselves, both those in civil society and those within the church.

Child sexual abuse flourishes in a society that is based on competition and power and which is undermined by sexual exploitation and violence against women. Contemporary society has shown itself quick to reject traditional values, to be unable to offer new ones and to be unfair to women and children. The challenge to transform society becomes enormous when we begin to realize the terrible social cost when child abuse is tolerated.

Another contributing factor to child sexual abuse is a church that too readily shelters its ministers from having to account for their conduct; that is often tempted to settle moral problems behind a veil of secrecy, which only encourages their growth; that has not yet fully developed a process of internal reform in which the values of familial communion would predominate. Challenges for personal conversion and institutional change are far from lacking. We would like to see our church take firm steps which would leave no doubt as to its genuine desire to eradicate the phenomenon of child sexual abuse.

Such is our understanding of the findings which flow from our mandate. We will let our readers study the recommendations we have made and decide for themselves whether or not we have been true to it.

RECOMMENDATIONS

Preliminary Observations

1) Most of the following recommendations concern the sexual abuse of children by priests. Those for whom these recommendations are intended will easily make the adaptations needed for cases that have some similarities but remain different – for example, sexual abuse by deacons or male religious; abuse committed by lay personnel of the Catholic Church; or the sexual abuse of adults.

2) The recommendations made to church authorities call for the maximum reconciliation of the following three principles:

– Justice toward all who are implicated.

– Diligence.

– Respect for civil authorities and their proper jurisdiction in these matters.

3) The following recommendations try to reconcile two attitudes essential for an adequate church response: compassion and responsibility.

Compassion toward the victims of abuse will be demonstrated by showing that the church does care and will do everything possible to respond to the situation. The same compassion should also affect the response of the church to those who are accused. The church must manifest the compassion of Christ.

Responsibility calls for getting to the truth of a difficult situation while firmly maintaining the principle that a person is innocent until proven guilty. It also calls for a search for appropriate remedies, various forms of response and, eventually, reconciliation through the actions of an authorized representative of the church.

Both compassion and responsibility are facets of the church's love. How the church responds will be a determining factor in eliciting positive cooperation on the part of all those involved in this painful situation.

4) A certain number of guiding principles underlie the recommendations we are making and indicate the spirit in which we have labored. These guiding principles include:

– Giving priority to the protection of children and vulnerable adults.

– Taking allegations of sexual misconduct seriously, independently of esteem for and the reputation of the accused.

– Presuming an accused person's innocence until proven otherwise.

This presumption of innocence should not, however, disregard a healthy need for prudence. Necessary measures must be taken in order to avoid all risk of future abuse.

– Respecting both the civil and canonical legislation which is applicable in these cases, while avoiding any undue interference.

– Respecting the rights of all persons implicated in allegations of sexual misconduct and in the proceedings following an allegation.

– Carefully avoiding any word or gesture that risks dissuading someone from carrying out his or her duty of reporting a case of child sexual abuse.

5) Despite the technical, clinical or juridical character of many of the recommendations made in this report, those to whom these are addressed are invited to implement them thoughtfully and humanely. To do otherwise would risk injustice.

A. Recommendations to the Catholics of Canada

We recommend that our Catholic brothers and sisters of Canada:

1. Move beyond the fear and shame they experience when confronted with cases of child sexual abuse perpetrated by adults (even when these are priests or religious whom they esteem and admire), and so become free to search out the truth about this socially tragic issue. By so doing, Catholics will be able to break silence and become actively involved in addressing and eradicating this social affliction of which we are becoming more and more aware.

We suggest that Catholics who have become aware about questions concerning the prevention of sexual abuse take the initiative in promoting a frank dialogue within the Christian community.

2. Become involved, in a spirit of generosity, determination and hope, in the whole process of healing the sometimes serious and long-lasting aftereffects that mark those who have been victims of child sexual abuse and those near to them, who are also often profoundly affected.

Such involvement is rooted in a strong trust in divine grace. It will demand that many people acquire new skills and abilities.

3. Support those who, with great difficulty, struggle to allow a painful truth to be heard despite the conspiracy of silence which develops so readily as a way of self-protection against the fear of scandal.

The committee suggests that Catholics take advantage of the mechanisms put in place by the institutional church for responding fairly and openly to all instances of child sexual abuse alleged to have been committed by priests or religious. The committee also invites Catholics not to trivialize or minimize the seriousness of child sexual abuse by priests or religious.

4. Become informed about the requirements of provincial and territorial reporting laws on child sexual abuse (see Recommendation 6 and Appendix 2), and become involved in information, education and prevention programs on child sexual abuse.

5. Support, sustain and encourage in their mission and daily lives the thousands of Canadian priests who, living their ministerial vocation in dignity and honesty, are unjustly smeared by the misconduct of a small minority of their colleagues.

Finding the adequate means by which Catholic individuals and communities can actualize this recommendation is closely linked with the need for new models of parish community life, as we have suggested in Part 6. There is need for considerable creativity in this regard.

B. Recommendations to the Canadian Catholic Bishops

We recommend that the Catholic bishops of Canada:

6. Appoint in their respective dioceses a priest, hereinafter called the bishop's delegate, for issues regarding sexual abuse or allegations of misconduct or sexual abuse (Canon 1717.1). Any allegation of sexual abuse by a priest should be referred to this delegate (or to the deputy delegate), whether such allegations are doubtful or appear to be founded on fact.

A bishop's deputy delegate should also be appointed at the same time as the delegate, who would have the same duties and functions as the bishop's delegate in the latter's absence or incapacity.

The bishop's delegate and the deputy delegate should participate in a special training session before taking on the delicate responsibilities entrusted to them.

Social workers and specialists in police investigation should be involved in their training.

It is recommended that the delegate or the deputy delegate not be the judicial vicar of the diocese; if a process of canonical adjudication is later initiated, the person who carried out the preliminary inquiry cannot act as judge in the judicial process (Canon 1717.3).

The delegate should be empowered and directed by the bishop to act immediately (i.e., within 24 hours or as soon thereafter as possible), with a view to determining in a discreet and pastoral manner whether there are reasonable and probable grounds to believe there was child sexual abuse by a priest. If such is the case, the delegate must ensure that any applicable child protection laws for reporting are complied with immediately (see Appendix 2: diocesan protocol). The priest under inquiry should be placed on administrative leave with pay, according to Recommendation 41.

7. Establish, in their respective dioceses (or group of dioceses), an advisory committee of at least five persons to whom, under the authority of the bishop's delegate, is referred any issue of sexual abuse or any allegation of sexual abuse.

The membership of the advisory committee, without being too large should be as diversified as possible; in addition to the delegate (as chairperson) and the deputy delegate, it should include a canonist (who must not be the judicial vicar), a civil lawyer, a professional person experienced in the treatment of those who have suffered sexual abuse or a professional specialized in the treatment of persons who suffer from sexual integration disorders. The advisory committee's members should include men and women, parents and professionals or others with experience well suited to deal with emotionally-charged issues.

Experience shows that rather than increase the size of the advisory committee, it is preferable for it to invite specialists as required (for example, in criminal law, education or communications).

8. Mandate the advisory committee to prepare and maintain a current basic protocol regarding situations of sexual abuse; after being prepared and updated, the protocol should of course be approved by the diocesan bishop in order to be implemented.

Integral to this protocol should be a decision-making process which is prompt, reasonable and fair to all those involved. The protocol should also ensure that appropriate action is taken when facts are established or suspicions are linked to circumstantial evidence, according to the civil and ecclesiastical laws involved. [Appendix 2 lists elements necessary to prepare an adequate diocesan protocol.]

There are those who favor a common protocol for a civil province; others maintain that because of regional differences it is better to choose from a variety of protocols. In any case, dioceses can inform one another of their experiences in this regard.

9. Communicate to priests and the religious personnel concerned the duly approved text of the diocesan protocol.

Priests and religious personnel thus become aware of both their responsibility to oppose any possible instance of child sexual abuse and also their obligation to report every allegation of sexual misconduct (even if the alleged abuser is a colleague).

10. Provide a sympathetic and attentive hearing within the church to each victim of sexual abuse committed by a priest or a religious.

Victims often need to express their sufferings and conflicting feelings. Sometimes it is better that the victims have the opportunity of addressing someone chosen from the staff of the church, since they had been betrayed by one of its ministers.

11. Form a committee for the victims, distinct from the advisory committee (see Recommendation 7) but of an equally multidisciplinary composition, which will provide individualized support to each minor who is the alleged victim of sexual abuse by a priest until the competent civil authorities have concluded whether the allegations are valid. This support does not imply, at this stage, any admission regarding the guilt of the accused.

This support will include, if necessary, arrangements for treatment and counseling as well as any other form of assistance considered necessary by the victim or his/her representative and judged pertinent. Such support must not however entail meetings with the child, unless proper authorization is obtained from police or judicial authorities, in order to avoid unwarranted interference.

12. Provide victims, after sentence has been pronounced against a priest for sexual abuse, the services of qualified resource persons who can provide the pastoral support wanted, counseling and, if necessary, therapy. The diocese of course may refer to existing outside facilities.

It is the committee for the victims (see Recommendation 11) that is involved in this process.

13. Designate, if this has not already been done, one competent person who will be responsible for dealing with the media and who will answer all questions concerning sexual abuse or allegations of abuse in the diocese; this person should not be the bishop's delegate (see Recommendation 6).

Designating one mandated spokesperson allows for better mutual understanding and collaboration with the media and helps avoid a variety of statements, which could give the impression of divergent or contradictory declarations (see Appendix 7).

There will be openness and trust in relations with the media when based on the following principles:

– Acknowledging the right of the public to know what information of general nature is available.

– Protecting the right of the accused to a fair trial.

– Safeguarding the right of the victims to maximum privacy.

– Safeguarding the right of the state to initiate legal proceedings.

The spokesperson should especially be diligent in providing information to the parish community whose priest is under suspicion.

14. Decide, when there are allegations of child sexual abuse by a priest, on the advisability and timing for introducing a preliminary canonical inquiry. Canonical proceedings should not be pursued at the same time as the secular proceedings (criminal and civil). The decision should be made by the bishop and his judicial vicar in consultation with the bishop's delegate (see Recommendation 6).

The precise canonical details about the canonical preliminary inquiry are found in Appendix 3 of the present document. Information on both the administrative procedure and the canonical trial is found in Appendix 4. As a point of fact, few dioceses conduct a canonical penal process in such cases.

For the sake of clarity, in this report we group everything together that concerns the preliminary canonical investigation (Appendix 3) and the administrative proceedings and the canonical penal process (Appendix 4), in case they might be lost in the series of different recommendations addressed to the bishops.

15. Ensure, whether or not additional canonical procedures are undertaken, that the canonical norms are carefully observed by the diocesan authorities.

Because religious authorities are subject to ecclesiastical legislation, they therefore must be able to document their defense if charges are brought against instances within the jurisdiction of the Holy See.

The juridical formulations used in the foregoing should not be construed as neglecting the fact that the bishop (or the religious superior) is the primary pastoral care giver for the accused at a very difficult moment in life. This pastoral care should be characterized by understanding of and respect for the person accused and by a non-judgmental attitude.

16. Provide, to the extent possible, depending on prevailing laws, the maximum confidentiality for all written documents related to allegations of sexual abuse by a priest. The documents should be recorded as having been prepared for the benefit and assistance of the diocesan counsel.

This rule of confidentiality should also be applied, as much as possible and with due respect for the existing canonical or civil laws and regulations, for the benefit of the victims and their parents.

Legal experts might remark on the many precautions taken in the wording of this recommendation: "to the extent possible," "depending on prevailing laws," "the maximum confidentiality"; "as much as possible and with due respect for the existing canonical or civil laws and regulations." The authors of this recommendation are very aware of the difficulties concerning privileged confidentiality: Each case is special (the reader is referred to Appendix 6).

17. Identify in each diocese experts from many disciplines involved in the serious study of issues connected with sexual abuse in order to approach the whole problem from a multidisciplinary perspective (in its legal, psychological, sociological, spiritual, moral and pedagogical dimensions). This will make it easier to propose a form of therapy which takes into account the varied aspects of this complex problem.

There is one prerequisite before a priest implicated in child sexual abuse can begin specialized treatment: He must have begun to reexamine his own emotional, spiritual and sexual life. He should be capable of recognizing that this admission of his own limitations and failings is a sine qua non and that it is vital for him to cooperate with competent people in the field of psychiatry, counseling and spirituality who are ready to help him. It is of paramount importance that he seek to overcome denial and resistance to truth if he wishes to be as free as completely possible for the rest of his life.

It would be useful to consult a recent document from the Family Violence Prevention Division (Health and Welfare Canada), which has been produced by the Canadian Child Welfare Association: "National Inventory of Treatment Programs for Child Sexual Abuse Offenders" (April 1989), 125 pages.

For the therapy required for priests implicated in child sexual abuse, the specialists can help locate an appropriate clinic, that is, with personnel specifically trained in the treatment of sexual abuse; having access to a variety of up-to-date tools for diagnosis; and offering different forms of treatment adapted to specific individual needs. The contract between the diocese and the clinic should specify that professional information acquired during the course of treatment can be shared with the diocesan authorities.

For the therapy required by victims and their families, see Recommendations 11 and 12.

18. Verify with insurance companies the particular clauses of a contract required, so that the diocese can fulfill its obligations in regards to maximum pastoral support to all persons concerned as well as appropriate services for counseling and therapy.

In the same context, the diocese or religious institute could establish a contingency fund, where applicable, in view of covering legal, medical and psychotherapeutic expenses. These contingent measures should consider taking into account possible revelations of cases dating back several decades.

The priest who has been convicted should be asked to contribute as much as possible, even if it be only in a symbolic way, toward paying the expenses incurred because of his conduct.

19. Manifest particular pastoral care for the sufferings of the parish community when one of its priests is accused or convicted of child sexual abuse and encourage the parish congregation to participate in the recovery process by offering assistance and understanding to those affected.

Among those affected by the accusation or sentencing of a priest for child sexual abuse, we must not forget his brother priests, whether in the same parish or neighboring parishes. They feel through association the negative impressions circulating on the priestly ministry.

20. Decide, in consultation with the treatment center, about the possible return to active ministry of a priest who, having been convicted of child sexual abuse and having served his sentence or having received a suspended sentence, asks to resume his ministry. Such a decision must give the protection of children first priority and, correspondingly, evaluate the potential risk constituted by the priest's eventual return to the ministry. Appendix 9 outlines the services available from treatment centers in such cases.

The bishop should neither promote re-entry of priests at all costs nor refuse re-entry of priests under any circumstances. The bishop or the religious superior should make the decision in consultation with the treatment center. The following points should be kept in mind:

– A complete and reliable diagnosis and prognosis has to be available.

– The priest would have to accept or at least recognize the problem exists.

– There would need to be adequate probation time between the period of incarceration and eventual acceptance for re-entry.

– The priest would have to agree to maintain a relatively low profile in the community.

– An effective system of monitoring has to be available.

– Other mechanisms such as support groups and after-care programs need to be available in the diocese which can and will provide continuing support and guidance to the priest.

– An assurance that any ministerial assignment would avoid bringing the priest into contact with potential victims (e.g., individuals or groups with characteristics similar to the previous victims or persons who had previously been victims of sexual abuse).

– In each individual case, the relationship between the occurrence of the offense and the existence of a personal crisis or risk factors would have to be assessed. (It should be emphasized that not all sex offenders have the same motivations or behavior patterns.)

Prudential judgments are necessarily difficult, since risks can occur outside the identifiable ministerial context.

21. Obtain the informed opinion of the diocesan presbyterium about reintegrating a priest into the ministry after his period of incarceration and give this advice full consideration.

The ways for consulting the diocesan presbyterium will be set by each diocese. In most cases, the dioceses will establish representative groups, that is, the members of the priests' council, of a special committee (see Recommendation 22) or of the advisory committee to the clergy office, etc.

22. Institute in each diocese, if required, a re-entry committee to assist the bishop in his decisions regarding reintegration. Members of this committee should be recruited from among those who already know the facts and from people in neighboring parishes or the actual parish where the priest would be accepted for reintegration into pastoral ministry. This committee would be under the responsibility of the bishop's delegate or the priest responsible for diocesan clergy, who should evaluate all the factors discussed in Recommendation 20 and meet with the priest who is seeking to return to active ministry.

The personal intervention of the diocesan bishop is recommended in such circumstances. The priest who would be reintegrated should be prepared to meet with the members of the parish council or with a group of parishioners to ask for their support, understanding and prayer.

23. Offer to priests who have completed a prison sentence for child sexual abuse and who cannot meet all the established conditions for re-entry into pastoral ministry, one of the following options:

– To remain as priests under a formal prohibition of exercising any pastoral ministry whatsoever; in this situation, they should be independently capable of earning their living for their own sake and for the good of the church.

– To retire, if they have reached the age to do so and if they are financially able to provide for their own needs.

– To ask for their laicization voluntarily.

– To accept canonical penal proceedings, which could result in their being removed from the clerical state.

C. Recommendations to Those Responsible for Priestly Formation

Preliminary Note

Those responsible for priestly formation receive a mandate from the diocesan bishop to prepare the future priests of a particular diocese. These persons cooperate at different levels (for example, archdiocesan, interdiocesan, civil province or larger pastoral region) in order to develop common policies which then are submitted for the approval of the bishops concerned. However, it is the diocesan bishop who commits to those responsible the specific task of forming his priests.

Those responsible for priestly formation will readily recognize in this report the main emphases of a particular movement in psychoeducation. This movement has inspired the whole dynamic behind a formation plan we consider especially appropriate to the contemporary world and church. Even though we believe this movement has already proven itself in many formation and therapeutic settings in Canada, we do not claim that it represents the only valid approach. We invite those responsible for priestly formation to make the necessary adjustments in order to achieve, perhaps through different means, the same basic objectives as envisaged by this particular movement.

The following recommendations do not pretend to be a replacement or substitute for a complete program for the formation of future priests in its full philosophical, theological and spiritual dimensions. Nor are these recommendations intended to replace the orientation document approved by the Holy See in 1980, to which we will subsequently return. Their purpose is rather to indicate some of the conditions needed for the psychoaffective development of the candidate to the priesthood in order to foster the interiorization of his vocation, the strengthening of his commitment and the integration of his vocation as a priest and his pastoral work.

We recommend that those responsible for priestly formation:

24. Advocate, in the groups which journey with priesthood candidates in order to discern their vocation, that the candidates be accompanied by a spiritual guide who can also serve as mentor (for example, an adviser who is a wise and experienced counselor and whose life work is proven and inspiring).

This accompaniment, even for candidates journeying without such groups, helps the candidate to come to know Jesus Christ better and develop a significant relationship with him. In the case of an aspiring candidate who has recently undergone a conversion experience, vocation discernment over several years is advised.

25. Propose and enforce criteria for a candidate's admission to the priesthood based on his personal fundamental strengths as these relate to the stages of the candidate's human growth. Special attention should be paid to the harmony or disharmony which exists between the candidate's chronological age and his lifestyle.

A candidate who applies to a formation center in his 20s is still attempting to integrate Gospel values into his decision making. A candidate in his 30s has already met the earlier challenges of his professional life and his community commitments. He must become more autonomous in his choices and deepen his sense of pastoral commitment. Last, a candidate in his 40s has already arrived at midlife and should be capable of renouncing external expectations, accepting solitude as part of a more intense interior life, and understanding that celibacy has a spiritual significance and also provides greater availability in terms of priestly ministry.

26. Implement a selection process for candidates which focuses more on the candidate's personal fundamental strengths, rather than on factors of vulnerability, without however disregarding the latter. In the same spirit, it is recommended that there be an initial meeting with the candidate and those responsible for his formation even before there is psychological testing.

Most bishops ask that those responsible for formation be assisted in the formation process by experts on the team of an accredited center so as to obtain a detailed assessment of each candidate. The results of the psychological tests, recorded in a report given to the candidate and, with his permission, forwarded to the rector of the seminary, are an important and indispensable part of his admission file.

27. "Personalize" the whole process of the candidate's formation, paying special attention to each candidate's personal strengths, history, age, the progress of his achievements and his development toward maturity.

The objective is life as a priest, with achievements to be realized and challenges taken on during the course of the journey (see Appendix 5).

28. Pay particular attention to the candidate's progress in the following areas: his assumption of commitments; his becoming truly responsible for his own personal development; concern for others; his lifestyle and the attainment of a certain financial independence; the adequate satisfaction of his basic needs and the presence of a healthy balance in life; his emotional stability.

It would be helpful to refer to a document prepared through a joint effort of representatives from seven English-language seminaries in Canada and members of the Canadian Conference of Catholic Bishops' Secretariat. Its final version was approved Sept. 28, 1978, by all the bishops of the English-speaking sector of the CCCB. The document was submitted by the conference to the Congregation for Catholic Education as a revision of the 1971 *ratio fundamentalis* for English Canada and later published under the title "The Program of Priestly Formation," Ottawa, CCCB, 1981, 35 pages.

Those responsible for priestly formation should also be attentive to the following factors: the candidate's functional or dysfunctional relationship with the members of his family, particularly with the authority figures (father and mother); his emotional development in relationships with women and men as well as the special case of an only child, etc. This is intended to help the candidate acquire the self-knowledge necessary for progressing in his interpersonal and community life.

It would be advantageous for those involved in the formation process to know the seminarian's family background in order to better understand the origins of certain dysfunctional relationships between a candidate and his family. This would help a candidate overcome specific obstacles to his personal growth (for example, an alcoholic parent, a difficult relationship with a brother or sister, a parent's overauthoritarian attitude, the trauma of abuse at an early age).

29. Examine with the candidate his own insight into himself and identify the strengths and weaknesses of his key life experiences.

A human formation counselor, as distinct from the spiritual director, should be appointed who will guide each candidate in his integral human formation. Some seminaries prefer a formation process involving small groups of seminarians, but with the same objective of the candidates obtaining better insight into themselves. This group work could, as needed, be complemented with an individualized approach.

The human formation counselor, with special training in the basic principles of human development, should be clearly and unambiguously concerned with the external (observable) behavior of the candidate, which includes the manifestations of his psychosexual identity. This form of accompaniment should help the candidate acquire and develop a greater self-awareness and to take a more conscious possession of his integrated self. He will be required to do this throughout his life in order to live his commitment to celibacy. This personal accompaniment should be recognized, by common agreement, as being in the external forum, thus leaving the human formation counselor free to participate in the evaluation of the candidate and of his call to the diaconate and priesthood.

Human formation counselors should be chosen from among men and women who are well established in their faith and convinced of the essential reality of the ministry of priests, and should have the necessary training to do this important task. It would be hoped that those involved in such formation would be able to acquire and integrate into their own respective areas of responsibility a vision of integral human formation and of the role of the human formation counselor.

30. Advocate the formation of priesthood candidates within the context of integral human development. This implies in particular:

– A clear view of the theological identity of the priest, and a global (holistic) view of the human person which integrates all the dimensions of human identity.

– The practice of supervised reflection on their human experiences so that candidates might have a deeper understanding of themselves and the capacity to make choices that are clear, free and consistent with their vocation.

– The development of altruistic and impartial relationships with others, in a spirit of collaboration with lay people (men and especially women).

For a fuller explanation of what integral human development involves, see Appendix 5.

The concept of integral human development must be understood as a process in which the seminarian can gradually grow in human maturity in an atmosphere of trust and accountability with the help and accompaniment of the human formation counselor (or a formation group) as well as with the collaboration of other resource persons, in particular the spiritual director. Growth in maturity reveals itself through increased self-awareness and the deliberate integration of the various facets of personal identity. It is linked to the age of the candidate, his background and his understanding of life as well as to the quality of his relationships with others. Such growth is realized through a process of self-revelation of the seminarian's life experience (with particular attention to his accomplishments). Its objective is to actualize the candidate's strengths from the approach and perspective of human growth and development.

31. Foster agreement and collaboration among the various resource people who have special responsibilities in the formation of candidates (including the

academic, spiritual, human, pastoral, artistic, missionary and community dimensions).

It is important to emphasize how necessary it is that women be among those who collaborate in the formation of candidates for the priesthood. The involvement of women is considered essential at all stages and in every aspect of the formation (including teaching, counseling and pastoral work).

Moreover, it will be noted that the collaboration recommended goes beyond a team of "directors" or those responsible. Collaboration should result in an experience of community life in which there is a true life-sharing among all the members of the community, both those responsible for giving the formation and the candidates, in an atmosphere of confidence and clarity about the goals and criteria of the formation process.

32. Foresee, within the formation process of seminarians, the presentation of up-to-date statistics on the present-day phenomenon of family violence; noting especially the frequency of child sexual abuse and paying special attention to child sexual abuse by priests (i.e., its incidence, the psychological profile of offenders, the risk factors, pastoral care of victims, etc.).

Such a formation program should reflect clearly and unequivocally the position of the church in this regard:

a) Child sexual abuse has been committed by priests in the past and could happen again in the future.

b) Child sexual abuse is tolerated neither by the church nor by society.

c) In the course of their ministry, priests can become aware of situations of child sexual abuse and should know how to respond properly in such circumstances. In particular, they should know the requirements of provincial legislation for reporting (see Recommendation 8 and Appendix 2).

d) In times of personal crisis, certain priests may feel overwhelmed by the urge to act out their sexual fantasies. Church authorities must be able to listen to their problems before abuse actually occurs and provide a pastoral and clinical response. Once a sexual offense has been committed against a minor, the canonical and secular laws must be allowed to follow their course without hindrance, since the life of a child could be seriously affected (see Appendix 6, which compares the concurring requirements of confidentiality and reporting).

33. Ensure that those responsible for the formation of seminarians provide the diocesan bishop and/or the clergy office with a profile of each deacon to be ordained priest, which would be helpful in determining what first assignments are appropriate for the priest.

This profile should be prepared in an open manner and in collaboration with the different resource people on the formation team and with the candidate himself. It would show the candidate's various accomplishments with respect to the aims and objectives of the formation process. In some dioceses, the profile is prepared in progressive and gradual stages and given to the bishop at the time of ordination.

D. Recommendations to Those Responsible for Priests in a Diocese

Preliminary Note

The carrying out of the recommendations concerning the life and ministry of priests ultimately comes under the diocesan bishop. However, at least in dioceses with several hundred priests, the bishop will usually entrust the immediate and direct pastoral responsibility to the Clergy Office (responsible for both religious and diocesan priests).

We recommend that those responsible for priests:

34. Appoint, in consultation with the diocesan bishop, an experienced priest to be available to newly ordained priests as their mentor and to assist them in the transition from seminary life to the many forms of pastoral experience in the local church community.

This priest could be the pastor with whom the newly ordained is called to serve or preferably a priest in a neighboring parish.

35. Put in place, when opportune, a plan of action (including time for meeting, resource persons, etc.) for sustaining the spiritual direction which the newly ordained priests began during the years in seminary.

This form of support is crucial to maintaining and furthering a sustained life of daily prayer, the development of which can be observed. The new priest obviously remains responsible for his own spiritual growth.

36.   Invite newly ordained priests to set personal and ministerial goals for the period of their initial assignments; these goals should be reviewed periodically, especially when the priest takes on new pastoral assignments.

Attention should be paid in these evaluations to the various facets of a priest's personal identity: the use of his physical energies, productiveness in his work, awareness of his responsibilities and talents, his psychosexual integration, receptiveness to others, the meaning he gives to his life, etc.

37. Prepare policies regarding the need for periodic updating, renewal and specialized training. This will foster a lifelong, ongoing formation of all the priests of the diocese.

This implies that the means and resources which the priest can call on to enhance his personal and professional development be well publicized.

38. Provide priests with regular opportunities for updating their pastoral knowledge through seminars. These seminars should periodically address the issue of child sexual abuse, from three angles:

– New scientific knowledge.

– Church policy as well as civil and criminal laws.

– Issues concerning moral theology, professional ethics and the theology of sexuality.

39. Pay particular attention to priests who are experiencing a major personal or pastoral crisis, offering them counseling if requested or judged necessary. In such circumstances, immediate consideration must be given to evaluating whether it is preferable to allow the priest to continue his ministry or to invite him to take on another type of work which would be more suited to this temporary situation.

40. Make sure that an accused priest is informed about the availability and possibility of supportive treatment or counseling during the judicial process and is encouraged, according to the advice of his counselor, to use these services (see Recommendation 17).

41. Place a priest accused of child sexual abuse on administrative leave with pay from the time there are reasonable and probable grounds to believe that child sexual abuse occurred until completion of the investigative or judicial process. This leave does not imply either the guilt or the innocence of the person under investigation.

When a priest has been financially assisted by his diocese in order to choose and retain legal counsel, it is suggested that suitable arrangements be made, when possible, for the priest to reimburse the diocese for its financial out-lay should he be found guilty.

42. Ensure that the bishop's delegate, the diocesan vicar general or the bishop himself (or the religious superior, if such is the case) continue caring for the incarcerated priest, visiting him periodically, offering him the moral support needed, and never forgetting that he is a fellow human being and a child of God in need of compassion.

The incarcerated priest should be treated as a priest with his rights as long as he has not been canonically removed from the clerical state. Fellow priests and laypersons should also be encouraged to visit him in prison.

43. Clearly inform the parish council or representative parishioners in an open and responsible manner before appointing a priest who has been reintegrated into the pastoral ministry and ensure that the receiving parish community will support the initiative of this appointment.

This sharing of information is not without problems, given the additional pressure it puts on the candidate for reentry. Nonetheless, experience tends to indicate that those few who are involved in the situation will be fully supportive.

E. Recommendations to the CCCB

We recommend that the CCCB:

44. Prepare and implement a code of professional ethics for clergy and pastoral agents.

45. Continue to cooperate with the Canadian Religious Conference, according to the situation as it evolves, in working toward healing as initiated with the native peoples following revelations concerning the former Indian residential schools (this is in reference to the meeting in Saskatoon, March 1991).

46. Support and foster the present involvement of the diocesan churches of Canada in their efforts to emphasize baptismal priesthood and promote an ecclesial communion in which the ministerial priesthood serves the priesthood of all the faithful.

Throughout the country we see a progressive transformation in the way certain diocesan structures function, e.g., greater accent on the partnership of women and men; clearer expressions of the ministries of priests and pastoral agents; diocesan synods, etc.

We recognize that there is a direct connection between a certain model of church life and the deviations we deplore in the behavior of some of the church's ministers. We do not claim this relationship is one of cause and effect but suggest, based on certain studies, particularly the Winter Commission, that a model of church life in which priests live their ministry as if it were an undebatable power provides a more favorable environment for committing and continuing acts of child sexual abuse (see Winter Commission, Vol. 1, pp. 137-138). However, rather than belatedly putting hypothetical blame on outdated social structures that still exist, we ask the CCCB to support and promote all that is being done to implement the true spirit of the Second Vatican Council. Indeed, it is through fidelity to their own vocation of renewal and conversion that our diocesan churches will indirectly become less vulnerable to possible deviations by some of their ministers.

47. Explore ways of participating in a telephone service designed to provide assistance to troubled youth. Dioceses or groups of dioceses could consider a similar project at the local or regional level.

48. Collect suggestions and recommendations submitted by local groups throughout Canada, using the discussion materials prepared by our ad hoc committee, and provide the best follow-up possible.

49. Have the competent authorities undertake an updated outline of the *ratio fundamentalis* for the formation of future priests (see Recommendation 28).

This updating could take advantage of three recent studies: the synod document on this subject, the evaluations from the apostolic visitations of the Canadian seminaries and findings of the work group that was commissioned by the ad hoc committee.

50. Call for immediate and continuing research in the social sciences regarding the complex reality of human sexuality (both heterosexual and homosexual orientations), the sexuality of celibates and the issues linked to the deviant expression of sexuality.

According to some researchers, it is urgent to establish a scientific basis on which clear guidelines can be made for the treatment of sexually dysfunctional priests.

Conclusion

The two years of study we undertook in response to the request of the Canadian Conference of Catholic Bishops have taught us a great deal about the insidious character of sexual abuse. Within the limits of our studies, our discussions and the reports of our work groups, we have been able to come to a better understanding of the extent of the devastation caused by this abuse. The devastation touches the whole community to one degree or another: the families and friends of the victims; those in their immediate community (school, neighborhood, parish, Scout troop, sports club, activities center, etc.); and the groups linked to the abusers (teaching staff, medical institutions, clergy, psychologists and psychiatrists, therapists, etc.). In varying degrees, these persons or agencies were obliged to live in an atmosphere of mistrust, suspicion, insidious accusations and at times contempt.

But abuse also causes profound damage. We became aware of the traumas that still resound within adults who lived through repeated abusive experiences in the past. Many or most have had to go through a long process before being able to recover, as adults, some belief in their own personal worth. Groups and institutions felt stigmatized when it was revealed that some of their members had been implicated in incidents or allegations of abuse. Our church, people and clergy, has been deeply affected by the devastation. These profound effects on others, as well as on the actual victims, illustrate how the consequences of evil are transmitted and how difficult it is to control their damaging spread even when the abusers are not numerous.

Rather than let ourselves be discouraged by these devastating effects, we chose to rely upon another kind of infectiousness. Goodness is also able to spread among people! We remembered the words and actions of Jesus and how some were scandalized by the contacts he maintained with publicans and sinners. This reminded us that the effects of the good news can also be contagious.

We began our work firmly rooted in the hope that life and resurrection will triumph over the seeds of death, provided we remain true to the message of the one who told us he is the resurrection and the life, and who showed us the paths that lead to him: truth, humility, conversion and forgiveness. The path of truth becomes immediately evident. All our considerations convinced us that child sexual abuse occurs and will continue in a climate of deception, hypocrisy and lies. This is why our suggestions and recommendations are clearly oriented toward the search for truth: the truthfulness of statements made to the media. Personal truthfulness and honesty in the preparation of candidates for the priesthood. Insistence on the truth throughout the therapy of the abusers. Truthfulness with those few parishes asked to accept a priest who is being reintegrated into the ministry.

The path of humility is no less important. Even if only a tiny fraction of Canada's 11,000 priests in active ministry have been implicated in cases of abuse, the church must humbly admit that some of its ministers are in flagrant contradiction to the message they have been commissioned to preach. In this spirit of humility, we suggest that more energy be put into correcting wrongs than into safeguarding appearances; into humble care of the wounded than into attempts to justify; into effective forms of education and careful research into ways of improving services for children, the poor and the most vulnerable in our society.

The path of conversion is also most necessary. Priest abusers are not numerous, but they are a painful indication that something is lacking within the church. It is in this spirit that we have drafted a number of recommendations calling for: particular attention to all the measures of prevention possible in the formation of future priests; multiple ways to assure better pastoral and spiritual care for newly ordained priests; new insistence on communities and of fraternal support; and the progressive transformation of how our parish communities and their pastors live the insights of the Second Vatican Council.

Forgiveness is certainly not the easiest path the Lord has indicated to us. In cases of sexual abuse it can, at times, become confused with other paths erroneously called "the road to pardon." We must never forget, for example, that sacramental forgiveness can be used as a kind of security or a form of "cheap grace," to use Dietrich Bonhoeffer's expression. Nor should we demand premature forgiveness on the part of victims, particularly as a means of more or less silencing the demands of justice or concealing an unhealed wound. In this report we have tried to indicate what truly leads to forgiveness and how to avoid becoming sidetracked.

Knowing well that we have not said the final word in response to these difficult questions, with humility we ask our readers: "Are we right in believing that we, as church, can pass from pain to hope?"

49.

"THE PSYCHOSEXUAL MATURITY OF CANDIDATES FOR THE PRIESTHOOD"

Intervention to the 1990 Episcopal Synod
"On the Formation of Priests in the Circumstances of the Present Day"

Bishop Frederick B. Henry

Preamble

Recent cases of sexual abuse by some priests in Canada have caused deep soul-searching on the part of the Canadian Church. After much discussion, it was felt that the best way to address this concern *at the Synod* was to focus on an effective formative program of psychosexual development in the seminary. It is recognized, of course, that this is only a part of the solution to a complex and lamentable problem, but it is that part which addresses itself most specifically to the theme of this Synod and, it is hoped, will be effective in uncovering some of the problems at their root.

This intervention refers primarily to the *Instrumentum Laboris*, chapter III, Sections iv and v, which deal with "chastity" (paragraph 35) and "human formation" (paragraphs 37-38). It is given on behalf of the Canadian Conference of Catholic Bishops.

Introduction

The charism of celibacy, which the Church looks for in candidates for the order of presbyter, is often depicted only in negative terms by society and even in the church. This situation requires the evolution of a positive exposition of the rich potential for human relationships inherent in this grace of the Spirit. For celibacy freely accepted and nurtured is both a sign of God's love and the proof of the Father's tenderness. As such, it points to the value of those sound human relationships which characterize the mature human person, whether married or celibate. The priest's celibacy ought not to reflect a fear of, but rather should symbolize a capacity and love for, deep human relationships. Celibacy demands a high degree of psychosexual maturity.

Psychosexual development is a critically important area of human growth, whether a person enters the priesthood or religious life, marries or remains single. When we speak of the psychosexual maturity of seminarians and priests we are really addressing the issue of the integration of a man's total personhood; his self-image, interpersonal skills, the way he copes with responsibility and authority, how he rélates with women and other men, how he comes to terms with his own sexuality and psychosexual organization, etc.

An Integrated Formation Program

To help assure the desired psychosexual maturity of future priests, the following program, adapted to local conditions, is recommended for the four stages of a priest's formation:

1) Prior to Seminary Admission

Each candidate should be interviewed by persons experienced in formation ministry and pastoral life, and be evaluated psychologically by a competent professional to determine: stability of character, absence of serious pathology, behavioural evidence of a positive attitude toward himself and his own sexuality, current pattern of personality traits, absence of extreme mannerisms which would impede leadership, and an expressed intention to live a chaste-celibate lifestyle.

Since the spiritual struggle to maintain the integrity of one's celibate calling is challenge enough, it is unlikely that individuals struggling with basic developmental problems will have the capacity or the energy for ministry. Grace builds on and permeates, but rarely substitutes for, nature. Candidates whose, sexual understanding is so confused or damaged that they could harm God's people and undermine the task of evangelizing society should be denied entry to the seminary.

When assessment indicates a candidate's need for psychological counselling, therapy should be completed before acceptance into the seminary. Given the prevalence of unmarried sexual activity in society, a reasonably lengthy cessation from frequent sexual intimacies should be sought as an indicator that an individual will be able to undertake a chaste-celibate commitment.

Candidates, whatever their sexual tendencies, need to give evidence of a positive integration of their sexuality that will allow them to live a chaste-celibate lifestyle. What needs to be examined in all cases is whether such persons have successfully completed the developmental task of relational trust, whether they have latent or manifest difficulty with male authority and whether there are indicators of hostility toward women.

2) The Period of Seminary Residence

The candidate should be expected to manifest a capacity for both private and communal prayer and engage well in the process of spiritual direction which enables this.

The seminarian should be expected to handle the stress and anxiety of studies and seminary life without choosing negative or addictive behaviour patterns such as overeating or a dependency on alcohol or drugs. Individuals unable to maintain a healthy lifestyle, including adequate exercise and good nutrition, within ordinary seminary routine, should receive counselling in these matters. Continued failure ought to be interpreted as a predictor of collapse under the stresses of ministry.

Seminarians engaged in genital behaviour should be put on leave. During this time, the individual should be requested to continue regular spiritual direction and, if deemed necessary, therapy as well.

The seminary program should be set up in such a way as to facilitate the mastering of the tasks of adult development. One of the essential skills which must be learned is that of intimacy, the ability to relate personally in a non-possessive, caring manner to others in the various encounters of adult life – in cooperative work, healthy competition, friendship and love relationships. A closed male environment will not adequately facilitate this task.

In addition, seminaries must provide a forum for seminarians to uncover the false symbols of manhood provided by our society. With other men they must be able to relate compassionately, unimpeded by homophobia. With women they must be able to be peer, friend, leader or follower without their behaviour being determined by sexual stereotypes or sexual expectations. They must be given the opportunity to articulate their own experience of what it means to be male and above all must focus on the manhood of Jesus Christ as their exemplar.

Given the negative influences on many individuals reared in our contemporary society due to alcohol and drug dependency, family breakdown and violence, sexual permissiveness, child abuse, etc., we must expect that a certain amount of energy will be required to help some seminarians and priests deal with their psychological and affective woundedness. It is essential that the seminary program promote an environment of trust so that candidates can openly admit difficulties and be helped in resolving them.

3) The Early Years of Priesthood

It has become routine to consider stress as a feature of contemporary life. The question is not whether priests and bishops will experience stress but rather how they will choose to respond to it. The experience of health professionals indicates that many members of the clergy have chosen ways of managing their stress which inflict severe psychological damage over time, such as compulsive work-routines, the abuse of alcohol, denial of personal needs, repression of anger, the neglect of a structured daily life, etc. The sexual permissiveness and consumerism of modern society exacerbates the tendency of some to either use sexual behaviour or the accumulation of material goods as a means of managing anxiety.

The difficult transition from seminary to active priestly life, anticipated somewhat through the seminary's pastoral internship program, can be facilitated by offering the newly-ordained the assistance of a priest-mentor outside his own pastoral setting and diocesan support groups based on common values or life commitments.

Consideration should also be given to regular gatherings of priests in the first five years following ordination for purposes of review, renewal and mutual support. The place and leadership of such conventions should be non-threatening and the explicit purpose be to identify and improve the ways each priest is persevering in an adequate prayer-life, managing his time in ministry, maintaining personal health habits, living within his financial constraints and meeting his needs for friendship and support. Providing sound spiritual direction for the newly ordained priest, which can build on what began in the seminary and take account of the new realities of full-time ministry, should be considered a priority of the diocese.

4) Lifelong Formation

Each priest must continue to develop the psychosexual maturity requisite for celibate ministry and Christian asceticism. Such a goal is part of a lifelong process and challenge. There are no easy or absolute methods for identifying psychosexual dysfunctions, but consultation with professionals current with contemporary science developments ought to be encouraged.

Some basic expectations or requirements, and systems of evaluation and accountability, and support mechanisms designed to address the real needs of priests must be seen as a normal part of diocesan priestly life. The responsibilities of bishops and others charged with dealing with Church personnel demand that they facilitate and challenge priests to the continuing tasks of personal and spiritual development for their own good and the well-being of God's people.

50.

DID CANADIAN BISHOPS CAVE IN AT SYNOD?
Newfoundland sex abuse scandal is swept under carpet in Rome
Rose Simone

Kitchener-Waterloo Record, **November 17, 1990**

The performance of Canada's Roman Catholic bishops at the synod on the formation of priests in Rome last month is being graded a "D," for "disappointing."

Douglas Letson, president of St. Jerome's College in Waterloo, and Michael Higgins, assistant academic dean, have closely followed past synods, so they went to Rome knowing "not much happens at synods." But this synod was particularly disappointing because Canadian bishop delegates were unusually reluctant to speak out, Letson and Higgins said.

"In the past, there were (Canadian) bishops willing to go on the public record to express their dissatisfaction and their hopes. There would be at least one bishop who was prepared to go the extra mile and take a risk, but there was no one like that this time," Higgins said.

"This time, there was a tremendous timidity among the bishops. There was a remarkable homogeneity in style."

The synod acts as an advisory body to the Pope and brought together about 200 bishops from around the world. Canada sent four elected bishop delegates, plus a Ukrainian Catholic representative.

Letson and Higgins were at the 1985 extraordinary synod in Rome which was called to review the documents of the second Vatican Council, and also closely followed and wrote about the 1987 special synod on the laity.

At those synods, Canadian bishops developed a reputation for boldly representing the feelings of Canadian Catholics. "They didn't do that this time," Letson said.

In both an early memo and a press release from the office of the Canadian Conference of Catholic Bishops, there were indications the findings of the church-ordered Winter commission inquiry into the sex abuse scandals in Newfoundland would be part of the presentations at the synod.

"But something happened in the final analysis," Letson said. He thinks a decision to "cool it," was made during the plenary meeting of bishops in Ottawa prior to the synod.

"At the plenary in Ottawa, in the in-camera sessions – that's where it seems things were sifted out. That's when the memo disappears and after that, there is no mention of the Winter report."

Letson and Higgins' disappointment is shared by lay people who are members of the Coalition of Concerned Canadian Catholics, a group lobbying for reform in the Roman Catholic church.

On the heels of the inquiry hearings into the sexual abuse of children by some priests in Newfoundland, they were hoping Canadian bishops would display strong leadership.

"Canadian bishops have had a good track record in raising controversial issues, but this time, they seem to have completely caved in to Vatican pressure," Joanna Manning of Toronto, a founding member of the Coalition of Concerned Canadian Catholics, said in a telephone interview.

"Our bishops did not seem to be speaking from the Canadian context. They didn't seem to be presenting the findings of the Winter commission report," she said.

"We were hoping major questions about priests coming from the community and being accountable to the community would be addressed." But from the written summaries of the presentations made at the synod, there was no indication this took place.

"It was as if they were rearranging the chairs on the deck of the Titanic," Manning said.

Higgins said one of the major faults of synods is that speeches are made behind closed doors and there is almost complete secrecy about what is being said.

"Very little is done to facilitate access to information. There are press briefings and conferences, but they are depressingly managed affairs," said Higgins, who is writing about the synod for *Grail* magazine.

"In the first week, the bishop delegates give short talks called interventions. Then they break into discussion groups. We don't get the complete transcripts of these discussions. What we get are extremely succinct, bland summaries that are produced by the secretaries for each session," Higgins said.

Auxiliary Bishop Frederick Bernard Henry of London, Ont. made a presentation at the synod about the need to provide training and counselling to men who are seeking to become priests.

Later, in a public statement by Henry, the Canadian scene was mentioned, but the problem of sexual abuse was not part of the intervention in the hall of the synod.

There was no public mention by the Canadian delegates of the criticism that has been levelled in Canada of celibacy and the hierarchical, patriarchal structures of the church – linked by some people as indirect factors contributing to the sexual abuse having gone on to the extent that it did and for as long as it did.

A Caribbean delegate, Bishop Lawrence Burke of Nassau-Antille, did openly question the church's priestly celibacy requirement, but on the whole, it wasn't discussed because the synod moderator had declared the subject closed.

"Celibacy was celebrated as the jewel in the crown on various occasions by various bishops, but there was no formally mandated or allowed discussion on the discipline of celibacy in the Latin rite," Higgins said.

"The Pope didn't want it discussed, and in a very real way, the Pope sets the agenda."

One of the difficulties for Canadian delegates at an international synod is that Canada represents a tiny fraction of the world's Roman Catholics. Only about 11 million of the world's 950 million Roman Catholics are in Canada.

But Higgins said that is not a good excuse for Canadian delegates not speaking out. "The vitality of the local church should be what is considered important and not the size of the church numerically."

In Third World countries, Roman Catholicism is booming and is in a "spring-time of vocations," with plenty of people seeking to get into the priesthood. "But that doesn't take into account the historical developments and the relatively recent arrival of Christianity in Africa," Higgins said.

In Canada, about 15 per cent of parishes don't have priests and many other parishes have priests nearing retirement age. The priest shortage is now mainly affecting parishes in isolated areas of the country, but eventually, the problem will reach the Hamilton diocese, Letson and Higgins said.

"The debate among theologians now is simple: does the church exist for the priesthood or does the priesthood exist for the church?" Higgins said.

"In the Roman Catholic church you must have a priest presiding over the Eucharist. How many millions of Roman Catholics will go without Sunday Eucharist in order to maintain a law that can be changed by a pope in a moment?"

John MacRae, another member of the concerned Catholics group, predicts that eventually people will stop supporting the church financially. "That's always difficult, because there are so many things that are worthy of support, but maybe that will be the only thing left. I think that unless we see some leadership from the bishops, this will be really traumatic for the church."

What Canadian Catholics want is "an honest dialogue," MacRae said. "It is the arrogance of the leadership that is most insulting – the fact they don't even feel any obligation to talk about it." MacRae said his one hope is that Canadian bishops did talk about the problems "unofficially," behind the closed doors of the synod. "But I would have liked to have seen that take place on some official level, and quite clearly, it didn't."

Letson and Higgins said trying to "shore up" the priesthood by sweeping problems under the carpet will hurt the church even more. "That is what you might expect from politicians – that no matter how bad things get, the Prime Minister and cabinet members will put on a unified face," Higgins said.

"But this standard should not exist in the church, where there should be a level of honesty and full disclosure. The church is a healing community, and there cannot be healing unless the full truth comes out. If there is a fear of the press and a fear of lay Catholics somehow being scandalized by such openness, then they have it all wrong. They are being scandalized by the perceived suppression of information."

The Canadian Coalition of Concerned Catholics is trying to "build a consensus of lay people in Canada who will keep mounting pressure for change, and make sure the Winter report is not quietly allowed to die," Manning said.

Higgins said it is up to the lay people to continue the fight.

Some people have romantic notions of what the church should be, Higgins added. "The church is a community like any other community – it struggles; it fights; it is torn apart; it is flawed. Roman Catholics have to be brought to the awareness that if it matters so much to them, then they should want to be part of the church in a full way, and not leave because of politics."

51.

EXTRAVAGANT AFFECTIONS
Women's Sexuality and Theological Anthropology
Susan A. Ross

It is one of the marvels of a Catholic education that the impulse of a few words can bring whole narratives to light with an immediacy and a clarity that are utterly absorbing. "The poor you have always with you... And until that moment, climbing the stairs in a rage to my ugly room, it was a passage I had not understood. . . But now I understood. What Christ was saying, what he meant, was that the pleasures of that hair, that ointment, must be taken. Because the accidents of death would deprive us soon enough. We must not deprive ourselves, our loved ones, of the luxury of our extravagant affections...

Final Payments

It is difficult to be on equally good terms with God and your body.

An Interrupted Life

When it comes to sexuality, Christians have inherited a very mixed tradition. On the one hand, God has come to dwell with humanity, having a first home – as do we all – in a woman's womb, thereby gracing our entire existence. Within Catholicism, marriage bears sacramental status, an acknowledgment of the holiness of physical union. On the other hand, Etty Hillesum's observation is also painfully true. Our sexuality, we are told, is that dimension of our nature that we share with nonrational animals: it is powerful, sometimes dangerous, and always potentially sinful. How often has Paul's remark, "Better to marry than to burn," been used to suggest that human sexuality is a necessary but unfortunate part of human being?

For women, this heritage is doubly mixed. In art and literature as well as theology, women have been portrayed as the very embodiment of sexuality and, consequently, of sin. As the fourteenth-century authors of the *Malleus Maleficarum* put it, "All witchcraft comes from carnal lust, which in women is insatiable."[1] Thomas Aquinas states that women lack "eminence of degree," the result of a lessened capacity for reason and grounds for denial of ordination.[2] For women, reflection on sexuality is at once both a reflection on our being as it has been socially and theologically constituted and a redefinition of sexuality on our own terms, only newly learned.

In this chapter, I will attempt to sketch out possibilities for a Christian theology of sexuality from a feminist perspective. Certain assumptions should be made clear from the beginning. First, the incarnational, sacramental dimension of the Christian tradition has the potential, as yet far from developed, for a theology that holds the body and sexuality of women as sacred. Isabel, the heroine of *Final Payments,* came to this realization almost too late. She finally saw that Jesus did not scorn earthly pleasures but urged that we delight in them while we can. Second, women and men both come to understand our sexuality within cultural and religious frameworks that privilege the experiences of men. As feminist theologian Carol Christ put it, "In a very real sense, women have not experienced their own experience."[3] Women, therefore, must develop a new language for understanding sexuality that values it on its own terms, a language that places women as subjects of our sexuality, not simply as the objects of others' desires.[4]

Finally, there can be no adequate feminist theology of sexuality without an intrinsic ethical concern for the integrity and safety of women. That is, I write within a cultural context that is often hostile and dangerous for women. It is a context that commodifies and exploits women's sexuality and teaches most women that their bodies are inadequate. An adequate feminist theology of sexuality will both counter and condemn these currents while at the same time offer a more adequate vision of the beauty and delights of human sexuality for all people, women and men alike. In other words, an adequate feminist theology of sexuality is also a social ethics that values embodiment.

It is an axiom of feminism that we begin with our experience. But this is more easily said than done. Human experience is not an undivided unity, and it is interwoven within the multiple cultural frameworks that shape it. Especially in the last fifteen years, feminist theory has been challenged to be more attentive to the diversity of the experiences of women from many racial, class-based, and ethnic contexts.[5] Making any generalization about "women's experience" is fraught with the dangers of exclusion and oversimplification. Nevertheless, I will venture some generalizations, since I am convinced that the embodied experiences that women have had across cultures and time have some common characteristics and have also been the objects of some common perceptions that have helped to shape our present.[6] These generalizations always need, however, to be tested against the experiences of diverse women. Certain emphases will be more true for some groups of women than others.

In her informative and lucid article "Sexuality and the Family," theologian Christine B. Gudorf writes, "More than boys, girls are taught that their bodies are not their *selves,* but rather a commodity."[7] In contemporary American culture, where women's bodies are used to sell consumer products, it is difficult for women to attain a sense of subjectivity – of "ownership," if you will – in relation to their sexuality.[8] This is especially true for poor women, whose ownership of self, much less of possessions, cannot be taken for granted. In addition, as Lisa Sowle Cahill writes, our culture faces "a new dualism about sex."[9] The "sexual body" has become separated from morality, with the result that "our sexual lives [do] not really 'count' in defining whether we are good persons."[10] Cahill notes the universal sympathy extended to "Magic" Johnson upon his announcement that he had contracted HIV. The fact that he had had hundreds of sexual contacts did not detract from the concern expressed by the public and the press, and Cahill wonders what the reception would have been had a woman contracted HIV through similar circumstances.

The difficulty for women in gaining a sense of our own sexuality is further complicated by the Christian tradition's suspicion of female sexuality, as well as female subjectivity. In the Hebrew scriptures, the importance of women resided largely (but not entirely) in their potential for childbearing. A woman who had many children, especially many sons, was greatly blessed. The barren woman was a reproach, both to herself and to her husband. The woman whose sexuality was not under the control of her father or her husband was outside the realm of normative conduct: an adulteress or a prostitute. Rape was treated as a violation of the property of a man, and a woman who was not a virgin at marriage was liable to death by stoning (this was not true for men).[11]

While the Jewish tradition has always looked upon sexuality as a God-given gift of human life and has largely avoided the dualism of soul vs. body that has plagued Christianity through its Greek inheritance, sexuality in Judaism is nevertheless a powerful and potentially dangerous arena. Menstruation, childbirth, nocturnal emissions all require that the person be purified before public worship. Such ritual purity prescriptions affected women far more than men. And while some contemporary Jewish feminists such as the Orthodox Blu Greenberg argue for a retrieval and appreciation of practices such as *niddah,* the laws pertaining to menstruating women, it remains clear that the ability of women to define sexuality was at best highly circumscribed.[12]

In the New Testament, Jesus' attitude toward women is not, at least as the Gospels tell the story, determined by their sexuality. Contemporary feminists draw on Jesus' apparently egalitarian approach to women and their participation in his ministry.[13] But the early eschatological framework, in which neither sexuality nor the patriarchal family was of paramount concern, gave way to an attitude more in line with the culture, in which the roles of women were again subordinated to fathers and husbands. In addition, the dualism of soul and body in the Greek tradition profoundly influenced Christian thinking on the body and sexuality, and women in particular came under fire from some Christian thinkers – Tertullian being one of the most often mentioned – for responsibility in leading men to sin.[14]

But any consideration of sexuality in the Christian tradition must ultimately deal with the heritage of Augustine of Hippo (354-430). Augustine's reflections on Christian belief in the light of his own experience led him to interpret the nature of original sin as *concupiscence:* the inordinate drive to gratify one's own desires. Although found in all of human life, concupiscence was especially evident in human sexuality. Sexual expression could be redeemed only through its exercise in marriage, and then only for procreation. Indeed, Augustine argued that in paradise, procreation would have been untainted by desire and entirely rational.[15]

Augustine's writings on sexuality and marriage, because they have been profoundly influential in the Roman Catholic tradition, have led feminists to question the extent to which his understanding of *human nature* is, in effect, an understanding of *masculine nature.* That is to say, despite his own experience of partnership and parenthood with his unnamed companion, Augustine's interpretation of sexual desire and sinfulness seems to be so rooted in his own lived and embodied experience that its applicability to women's lives is not as clear as it is to men's.[16] For Augustine, one's sexuality is always linked with desire – and ultimately, desire for the self – and therefore must be subordinated to a higher good than pleasure: procreation. But women's experience, not only of sexual intercourse but also of the process of procreation, is very different from men's. Women can engage in intercourse without desire, although this is certainly not the optimal experience, and the process of procreation engages women's lives to a far greater extent than it does for men.[17] While I would not want to suggest that women's experience of sexuality could not be and is not also one of concupiscence, nevertheless Augustine's understanding of sin and sexuality reflects his own (necessarily male) experience and perspective and fails to account for the different perspective women's experience of sexuality would bring to its interpretation.

Thomas Aquinas's understanding of sexuality, derived as it is from an Aristotelian (i.e., a non-Platonic and empirical) framework, is somewhat more positive than Augustine's. While Augustine had thought that paradisiacal procreation would have been entirely rational (and thus very unlike our present physical experience), Aquinas argued that the pleasure that our first parents experienced in paradise was far greater than our own pleasures, since ours are muted by sin.[18] For Aquinas, rationality *enhances,* rather than diminishes, pleasure; therefore, pleasure in paradise would not have been overcome by concupiscence, as it is now. Nevertheless, sexuality belongs to our lower nature where rationality pertains to our higher. And since men are more rational than women, naturally women are closer both to lower human nature and to sexuality. In fact, God's ultimate purpose in creating women was to assist men in procreation.[19]

The Protestant Reformers rejected the Roman Catholic valuation of celibacy as higher than marriage; indeed, they saw marriage as a *vocation* for both men and women. Martin Luther argued that it was against nature to be celibate; only a very few are able to live such a life.[20] Yet Luther, like Augustine and Aquinas before him, saw women's participation in sexuality as pertaining mainly to reproduction. For him as well, sex was impossible without sin. Later, the development of the "cult of domesticity" in the nineteenth century further removed women in dominant classes from subjectivity in regard to sexuality: white, middle- and upper-class women were the repositories of innocence and purity, especially with regard to sex, where lower-class women and women of color (as well as men) were seen to embody sexuality.[21]

This all-too-brief survey of Christian thought on women's sexuality reveals two related strands: women are either so immersed in bodily existence that they are unable to rise above it; *or* women are innocent of carnal desire and engage in sexual acts only to quell the lusts of their husbands.[22] In neither case are women the *subjects* of their sexuality.

While it is possible to argue – indeed, I would say it is necessary to do so – that treatments of sexuality throughout the Christian tradition are more diverse than they are generally acknowledged to be, they are still overwhelmingly from the perspectives of men and overwhelmingly negative towards, as well as ignorant of, women's sexuality. Women's sexuality is rarely a subject spoken of or written about *by women*. Rather, women are described as the objects of male sexual desire. When women are spoken of as having such desires, they are usually prostitutes, slaves, or witches. Criteria for sexual sins, and even for sexual pleasure, have been consistently drawn from male experience. This is true both in the secular literature and the religious traditions. Consider, for example, Sigmund Freud's conviction that in mature women, orgasm is normatively experienced in intercourse, not through clitoral stimulation.[23] Or consider Paul VI's encyclical *Humanae Vitae,* which condemns the use of "artificial" contraceptives in part because... "it is feared that the man, growing used to the employment of anti-conceptive practices, may finally lose respect for the woman..."[24] Only in more recent years, especially with the advent of the women's movement in the 1960s and 1970s, have women begun to explore the nature of female sexuality from our own perspective. What does it mean, then, to understand sexuality from a perspective that is both feminist and Christian?

FEMINIST PERSPECTIVES ON SEXUALITY

In 1973, a group of women who called themselves the Boston Women's Health Book Collective published a book called *Our Bodies, Ourselves.*[25] That volume, now in its third edition, provided basic information on women's physical and emotional lives, including doing vaginal self-examinations, learning how to masturbate and achieve orgasm, and getting a safe abortion. The emphasis throughout the book is that women need to "take charge" of their whole lives, especially including sexuality. Against the background of a medical establishment dominated by men, women have sought to redefine sexual pleasure, pregnancy and childbirth, and reproductive control from the perspective of women's own lived experience. Gudorf terms this "bodyright."[26]

Given contemporary American culture's emphasis on individualism, it is hardly surprising that control emerges from *Our Bodies, Ourselves* and other feminist books on sexuality as key for women's sexual self-determination. "The right to control our bodies" is the linchpin of the movement for women's reproductive rights, especially abortion. But not only in sexuality is control of such importance. Consider the emphasis in contemporary culture on the importance of being thin and the horror of obesity. Those who are overweight, our cultural "wisdom" holds, lack self-control, and eating disorders such as anorexia nervosa and bulimia are characterized by the person's having "total control" over how much she eats.[27]

But a larger context for considering the issue of "control" is raised by Delores Williams, who writes poignantly about the lack of control experienced by the biblical figure Hagar.[28] As the surrogate for another woman, Hagar was subject to rape, forced labor and forced pregnancy. Williams draws parallels between the situation of African-American women in this country who have continued to serve in surrogate roles for privileged white women with that of Hagar. "Control" is thus an essential dimension of a feminist understanding of sexuality, although it requires careful analysis. I will return to the issue of control later.

The rethinking of the term *erotic* has been a key theme in recent feminist writing, especially that of the late poet and activist Audre Lorde. Lorde defines the erotic as "the assertion of the lifeforce of women."[29] The erotic is that creative energy which comes from deep within our being, which we have been taught to fear, but which fuels joy, relationships, and mutuality.[30] The fear and loss of the erotic have resulted in its denigration into pornography. Many feminists have noted the need to articulate women's capacity for the erotic in language that affirms its joys as well as its pains.[31]

French feminism has also been concerned about the erotic. While a complex movement, French feminism is characterized by a concern to see women's experience, and in particular, sexuality, from a woman-centered perspective.[32] In general, French feminists have emphasized the quality of *jouissance* in women's sexuality, a term meaning enjoyment and delight that contrasts with male sexuality's emphasis on phallic power. While much of the language is more suggestive than formally descriptive, it is helpful in pointing out the limits of our dominant (French feminists would say phallocentric) language for female sexuality.[33]

Another source is in the growing area of feminist ethics. While her work has been controversial, Carol Gilligan and her colleagues have nevertheless raised many crucial questions in relation to women's sexuality.[34] Gilligan argues that the women she interviewed (e.g., in her abortion decision study) tended to be very concerned about relational issues in making moral decisions. While their concerns for issues of principle (e.g., rights, justice) were not absent, these more abstract issues were often interpreted in the context of relationships. What this suggests is that many women most often see their sexuality in the context of their whole lives and their relationships, with women as well as men.[35] Thus, an "act-centered" focus on sexual ethics – characteristic, as I would argue, of male sexuality and, not surprisingly, central to the Roman Catholic tradition in sexual ethics – can fail to do justice to women's experiences when it looks at sexuality in terms of particular sexual acts (intercourse, masturbation, etc.) and not in the context of the relationships in which these acts take place. Within relationships of mutuality, sexuality serves as an avenue for enhanced touch, tenderness, intimacy. Sexuality is thus far more than intercourse; it is that way of communicating and sharing one's entire existence, both body and spirit. This broadened conception of sexuality is much indebted to the work of lesbian and gay writers, some of whom have argued that homosexual relationships have greater potential for mutuality than heterosexual ones.[36]

That sexuality can never be entirely separated from reproduction is also important to note. While not all women are mothers, all mothers are women. The consequences of heterosexual activity fall more heavily on women. A man's participation in insemination may take only a few minutes, but pregnancy is not only for a far longer period of time, it also has long-ranging physical consequences. My point is not to identify sexuality with procreation, as the Roman Catholic magisterial tradition does, but to note that they cannot be completely separated.

In connection with reproduction, sexuality is inevitably connected with the physical world. Feminist perspectives on sexuality have noted how the treatment of women and the treatment of the earth have shared many unfortunate characteristics: women and the earth are means to greater ends (children, mineral resources), lack (full) rationality, are passionate and unpredictable, and need to be tamed or cultivated. Sherry Ortner's classic controversial article, "Is Female to Male as Nature is to Culture?" put this connection concisely.[37] A more adequate theology of sexuality will also have ramifications for the way in which human beings relate to the physical world.[38]

Finally, feminist perspectives on sexuality emphasize the role that women's bodies have played in consumer society. Women's bodies are used to seduce potential consumers into desire for more objects. Pornography portrays women in demeaning ways, and its status as protected "free speech" continues to provoke heated debate among feminists and First Amendment rights advocates.[39] Not least among these concerns, women are at risk of rape and domestic violence from both strangers and, more often, their own (overwhelmingly male) partners.[40] A woman is not free to enjoy her embodiment in public (on a beach or a street) without the assumption being made that she is "asking for it" – "it" being a sexual encounter. Women's physical safety is most at risk in the home, where partners abuse women (and their children) both physically and emotionally. The incidence of child sexual abuse is probably much more frequent than has been recorded.[41] Feminist perspectives on sexuality condemn such treatments of women as bodies to be used or abused and argue that our culture's understanding of women (and children) needs major transformation.

All of these issues – autonomy and control, the erotic joy and *jouissance* of female sexuality the relational context the connection with reproduction and the physical world, the rejection of pornography and violence – are crucial elements for an adequate understanding of women's sexuality. But while they are necessary, they are not sufficient for a theology that is also rooted in a critical interpretation of the Christian tradition. I turn now to such an interpretation, arguing that there are elements within the Christian tradition which could support an adequate feminist theology of sexuality. In connection with the more secular feminist perspectives outlined above, this theology is at times critical of the Christian tradition, and at times of the culture as well. There are also, inevitably, points of tension between secular and Christian feminism.

A FEMINIST *THEOLOGY* OF SEXUALITY

Christian feminist theology is possible because it is based in the conviction that the message of Jesus is one that brings salvation to all: women and men, poor and rich. In the words of Elizabeth Johnson,

> By Christian feminist theology, I mean a reflection on God and all things in the light of God that stands consciously in the company of all the world's women, explicitly prizing their genuine humanity while uncovering and criticizing its persistent violation in sexism, itself an omnipresent paradigm of unjust relationships. In terms of Christian doctrine, this perspective claims the fullness of the religious heritage for women precisely as human, in their own right and independent from personal identification with men.[42]

My own perspective draws on what I consider to be two essential (although not exhaustive) dimensions of the Christian tradition: the incarnation and the Christian community. Put in more traditional theological language, the first includes the christological affirmation that God has come among humanity in fully human form, that all creation is graced, that God is mysteriously present in all things. The second has to do with the way we live with others, as modeled by Jesus: that all are God's children, especially the least among us; that we are called to love and to live in justice, mutuality, and peace. In both of these dimensions, the radical potential for affirming the full humanity and the contributions of women as well as men has gone unfulfilled, with grave consequences for understanding human sexuality as well as all of human life.

In the history of Christian theology of the incarnation, it is unfortunate that the virginity of Mary and Jesus' virginal conception have been given the kind of emphasis they have. Mary's obedience and receptivity to God's message and her purity both before and after the birth of Jesus have suggested that women's role is to be the vessel of the will of God: "Let it be done unto me according to your word." What has not been remembered is Mary's active participation in the incarnation: the discomfort of pregnancy, the pain of labor, the energy and intelligence required in raising a child. Who could better say in relation to Jesus, "This is my body; this is my blood?"[43] The fact that virginity is less a statement about the body than about the power of God is largely ignored in the tradition.

If anything, the incarnation is about "beauty of body," to use Robert Penn Warren's felicitous phrase.[44] God has come to dwell among us, in our flesh and blood, in our desires and joys. All that is created, including our sexuality, is good and is to be delighted in. But Christians have tended to see the body, and certainly sexuality, as obstacles to be overcome on the way to eternal life. To be sexual in the service of future generations is permissible, but intercourse for mutual pleasure and joy, masturbation, homosexual love are inherently evil because they are not oriented to procreation.

The folly of this view becomes evident when we look at the perspective of women's physical experiences. While the potential for future life is present in every man's ejaculation, a woman ovulates but once a (usually monthly) cycle. The Roman Catholic teaching that permits "natural" forms of birth control neither takes into account the hormonal fluctuations that affect women's sexual desires nor that women's ovulatory cycles fluctuate widely, making reliable "natural" contraception extremely difficult. Or take the issue of masturbation – almost always discussed in terms of male experience. Unlike the penis, the clitoris has one function only: exquisite female sexual pleasure. It is not at all connected with procreation. To say that learning about and delighting in one's body through self-stimulation is inherently sinful suggests that physical pleasure for its own sake is evil. Is this the message of the incarnation? Episcopal feminist theologian Carter Heyward suggests that to think one must justify sexual pleasure is to misunderstand profoundly the erotic power of God. "We do not need to justify pleasure. Let us rather have to justify pain..."[45]

The second of the characteristics basic to the Christian tradition is that we are called to live in community – a community of justice. It is necessary to emphasize our communal nature and calling to put the sexual body in its proper context. Human beings do not live in isolation: we require human contact to survive, let alone thrive. And is it here that the renewed emphasis on the beauty and joy of our sexuality, found in flawed ways in the "sexual revolution" of the late twentieth century, needs to be balanced by our communal calling.

One of the most helpful contributions of feminist ethics has been its reminder that we do not emerge from the womb as full-blown "rational men." This is something that women are likely to remember better than men, since it is largely women who raise both women and men.[46] Human relationships are to some extent voluntary, as the mainstream ethical tradition holds, but our first relationships are not. We learn how to be in relationship from parents and siblings. This relational context is where we must locate the delight and joy – and also the frustration and pain – of our sexuality. In a Christian context, this relational nexus has further implications. It means that we are called to live in relationships of justice and mutuality and to have special care for the least among us – poor women and children. Christians are called to spread the good word of God's "extravagant affections" to all and through all. God's power comes alive in the dynamic of mutual relation.

A feminist Christian theology of sexuality is thus critical of elements both within the Christian tradition and within secular, including feminist, culture. In relation to Christianity, this theology critiques the male- and act-centered focus on sexuality that often fails to consider the relational context. This theology would thus judge sexual expression in heterosexual relationships both inside and outside of marriage and homosexual relationships in terms of the commitment and fidelity of the partners. This entails the very concrete dimensions of these relationships and their potential for future life. By the same token, this theology would look with concern upon secular culture's (and frequently also the feminist) emphasis upon rights, autonomy, and control because of the communal context in which all human beings live.

Let me make this more explicit in terms of particular issues in sexual ethics: abortion and reproductive technology. Abortion is surely one of the most neuralgic issues in both public and parochial debate. The Roman Catholic church's position is that all direct abortion is evil. But the church's position focuses on the particular act itself, outside of the context in which painful moral decisions must be made. Unlike the question of whether or not it is just to go to war (which always involves killing), where a pluralism of moral discourse has been the norm in the Christian tradition,[47] there is no pluralism in regard to abortion, and in fact little discussion at all of the contexts in which unplanned pregnancies take place. The church's position simply does not consider women's own experiences as a valid source of moral decision making.[48] Indeed, one wonders whether the church trusts women's capacity to make moral decisions. Not coincidentally, war is an issue that is almost always decided by men.

But this is not to suggest that secular feminism has all of the answers, either. The focus on "my body, my choice" emphasized so strongly by prochoice feminists is surely a necessary correction of long-standing laws and practices that regard women's bodies as male property. But is it really only "my" body? and only "my" choice? Are our bodies our own singular possessions, to be guarded as carefully as our homes, cars, computers? For Christian feminists, the fact that we are part of a moral community of mutual responsibility means that, to some extent, our bodies and choices are also the community's bodies and choices. But this mutual "ownership" cannot be maintained unless there is an intrinsic sense of the sacrality of all bodies and the integrity of each person's relationship to her own body. Sadly, we are far from this point. This does not mean, in my view, that some abortion decisions cannot be morally justified. But it is unfortunate that the emphasis on autonomy and control so characteristic of contemporary American culture, and so unquestioned by at least some feminist moral theorists, has become so central to the issue of reproductive "choice."[49] The language of mutuality and responsibility to the other, so central in much feminist discussion of ethics, seems to disappear in this discussion. A fully adequate sexual morality, from a feminist Christian perspective, must be accountable to person and community.

The feminist literature on women and sexuality rightly celebrates its positive and graced dimensions; to speak of women's sin and sexuality risks losing this needed emphasis. But it is important to recognize the ambiguity of sexuality for women as well as men. While Augustine's focus on uncontrollable desire may not be as historically or psychologically relevant for women as well as men, *dishonesty* might be an appropriate category for women's "sexual sin." In part because women have lacked or been afraid to use a voice, women have failed to communicate sexual needs and desires, have given "double messages," have "faked" sexual responses. Much of this dishonesty may result from being in a context where honest communication is difficult. But women's sexual dishonesty is not always the result of victimization or lack of voice. Feminist theologians need to exercise careful discernment of the potential for grace and for sin in all human action. While sexuality may have unjustly borne the brunt of sin, a feminist analysis ought not to exempt it from all potential for sin.

In relation to the issue of "the right to choose," Lisa Sowle Cahill has been critical of the use of reproductive technologies that suggest that all of us have the "right" to have a child.[50] Along similar lines, the moral issue of reproductive technology ought not to revolve solely around the right of partners to make their own decisions, as the 1987 Vatican statement warns.[51] Other questions, such as who pays and, in some cases, who bears and rears the child need to be answered in the light of the Christian tradition's focus on mutuality and community.[52]

A feminist Christian theology recognizes that women are fully human moral agents and therefore are responsible for their moral decision making.[53] But what is an agent? Who is a person? In her book *Moral Boundaries,* Joan C. Tronto discusses "changing assumptions about humans" and notes that "humans are not fully autonomous, but always must be understood in a condition of interdependence."[54] That is, human autonomy is never absolute. The autonomy we have, Tronto reminds us, is something that is achieved only through a long period of dependence (largely upon women).[55] Moral decision making is done within this context of autonomy-interdependence, and in the Roman Catholic tradition, women's autonomy is rarely considered seriously.[56] It is worth pondering that when Milwaukee Archbishop Rembert Weakland sought simply to listen to the voices of women on the subject of abortion, he suffered attacks from both right-wing Catholics and the Vatican.[57]

In both secular consumer culture and church culture, the bodies of women have been problematic. Rarely if ever is a woman's body simply her body. Whether intended or not, a woman's body – especially a naked one – symbolizes sexuality. Consider the furor over Edwina Sandys' sculpture "Christa," which portrayed a naked crucified woman. While some argued that it was "theologically indefensible," others (including some feminists) argued that women's bodies are inevitably sex objects and that this sculpture perpetuated that perception.[58] Within the ecclesial context, women's embodiment has rendered women unfit for ordination and, in some cases, even for communion.[59] Women's bodies are considered "property," and the woman who ignores this does so at her own peril.

The violence that has been and continues to be perpetuated against women and children is tied to this understanding of women's (and children's) bodies as property. Secular culture supports this view by looking at all bodies as forms of property – both as abstracted from the moral life, as Cahill points out, and as instruments to be used determined by one's "personal choice." Church culture supports this view by overly identifying women with the bodily and by understanding men as "protectors," if not "owners," of women, as well as by its suspicion of sexual pleasure. As long as women are seen to comprise a different "psycho-symbolic" ontology than men,[60] women will be treated as less than fully human.

There is a connection between the refusal or failure to see women as fully human, as fully moral subjects, and violence toward women. As long as women cannot be seen by others as "the body of Christ," the message is that women are lesser than men and deserve to be treated as lesser than men. Christian social ethics, therefore, needs to be far more attentive than ever to the ways in which we care for an embodied community. The Roman Catholic natural law tradition, which has maintained a close tie between ethics and the body, has in my view failed to recognize that this tie takes place in a social context that does not view the body neutrally. This tie can only be maintained, at a far higher cost to women than men, within a theology that sees nature and the body "objectively" but is in fact a position defined from a male perspective. The Roman Catholic emphasis on objectivity is defective in that it has failed to take into account all of the data from human experience by systematically excluding the voices (and bodies) of women.

Sexuality is the avenue to deep and powerful feelings, to great joy. It can also be a deadly weapon. My intent in this chapter has been to suggest how feminist perspectives on sexuality can enhance joy, mutuality, and responsibility in human life. There is, of course, much more to be said on many issues. Further discussion is needed of the grace-filled dimensions of intentional procreation in a context of mutual love, of the capacity for sin in sexuality, of the need for changes in social policy. But in our present situation, aided by the critical perspectives of feminism as well as by the Catholic incarnational/sacramental reverence for the physical world, we can learn to cherish and delight in our extravagant affections, lavishing the love of God on ourselves and our communities.

Epigraphs: Mary Gordon, *Final Payments* (New York: Random House, 1978), pp. 288-89; Etty Hillesum, *An Interrupted Life. The Diaries of Etty Hillesum 1941-43* (New York: Washington Square Press, 1981), p. 34.

I am grateful to William P. George and Cristina L. Traina for their careful and critical reading of earlier drafts of this essay and for their many helpful suggestions.

1   Quoted in Elizabeth Clark and Herbert Richardson, eds., *Women and Religion: A Feminist Sourcebook of Christian Thought* (New York: Harper and Row, 1977); see also Mary Daly, *Gyn/Ecology: The Metaethics of Radical Feminism,* (Boston: Beacon Press, 1977).

2   Thomas Aquinas, *Summa Theologiae,* III (Supp.), Q. 39, a. 1

3   Carol Christ, "Spiritual Quest and Women's Experience," *Womanspirit Rising: A Feminist Reader in Religion* (San Francisco: Harper and Row, 1979), p. 228.

4   I am deliberately using the loaded language of "subjectivity" in this essay, well aware of the postmodern perils to which I open myself. In my view, it is essential, especially in dealing with sexuality, to argue for women's agency and selfhood.

[5] See Elizabeth V. Spelman, *Inessential Woman: Problems of Exclusion in Feminist Thought* (Boston: Beacon Press, 1988); and Cherrie Moraga and Gloria Anzaldua, eds., *This Bridge Called My Back: Writings by Radical Women of Color* (New York: Kitchen Table, 1983).

[6] See Jane Roland Martin, "Methodological Essentialism, False Difference, and Other Dangerous Traps," *Signs* 19 (Spring 1994): 630-57.

[7] Christine E. Gudorf, "Sexuality and the Family," *Second Opinion* 10 (March 1989): 32.

[8] For two feminist philosophical observations on this point, see Susan Bordo, *Unbearable Weight: Feminism, Western Culture, and the Body* (Berkeley: University of California Press, 1993); and Iris Marion Young, *Throwing Like a Girl and Other Essays in Feminist Philosophy and Social Theory* (Bloomington, IN: Indiana University Press, 1990), especially "Women Recovering Our Clothes."

[9] Lisa Sowle Cahill, *Women and Sexuality* (1992 Madaleva Lecture in Spirituality) (New York: Paulist Press, 1992), p. 3.

[10] Ibid.

[11] On rape and property: Deut. 22:28-29; on virginity at marriage, Deut. 22:20-21.

[12] See Blu Greenberg, *On Women and Judaism: A View from Tradition* (Philadelphia: Jewish Publication Society of America, 1981).

[13] See Leonard Swidler, "Jesus Was a Feminist," *Catholic World* (January 1971): 177-83, for one of the earliest articles. Swidler's position has been criticized for the implicit anti-Judaism suggested in the essay. Amid the vast literature on women and the New Testament, see Elisabeth Schüssler Fiorenza, *In Memory of Her: A Feminist Theological Reconstruction of Christian Origins* (New York: Crossroad, 1983).

[14] See Tertullian, "On the Dress of Women," I, 1, 2, quoted in Elizabeth Clark, ed., *Women in the Early Church* (Wilmington, DE: Michael Glazier, 1983), p. 39.

[15] Augustine, *City of God,* Book XIV, Ch. 26.

[16] See, for example, John Mahoney, *The Making of Moral Theology: A Study of the Roman Catholic Tradition* (Oxford: Clarendon Paperbacks, 1987), p. 66: "Lacking, of course, from Augustine's introspective make-up was any positive appreciation of women, and he seems to have considered them as little more than sex objects." See also Felisa Elizondo, "Violence Against Women: Strategies of Resistance and Sources of Healing in Christianity," in Elisabeth Schüssler Fiorenza and Mary Shawn Copeland, eds., *Violence Against Women, Concilium* 1994/1 (London and Maryknoll, NY: SCM Press and Orbis Books, 1994), p. 101, where she discusses Augustine's admiration of his mother's unquestioning acceptance of his father's infidelity.

[17] See Sidney Callahan, "Abortion and the Feminist Agenda: A Case for Pro-Life Feminism," in Patricia Beattie Jung and Thomas A. Shannon, eds., *Abortion and Catholicism: The American Debate* (New York: Crossroad, 1988), pp. 128-40, for a discussion of women's experience of sexuality as well as a discussion of abortion.

[18] Thomas Aquinas, *Summa Theologiae,* I, q. 98, a. 2, repl. obj. 3.

[19] Ibid., q. 92, a. 1.

[20] Martin Luther, "The Estate of Marriage," and "Lectures on Genesis," quoted in Clark and Richardson, pp. 131-48.

[21] See Nancy F. Cott, *The Bonds of Womanhood: "Women's Sphere" in New England, 1780–1835* (New Haven, CT: Yale University Press, 1977).

[22] For a study of literature that sees women in both of these characterizations, see my "The Bride of Christ and the Body Politic: Body and Gender in Pre-Vatican II Marriage Theology," *Journal of Religion* 71 (July 1991): 345-61.

[23] See Sigmund Freud, "Some Psychical Consequences of the Anatomical Distinction Between the Two Sexes," in *Standard Edition,* Vol. XIX, pp.248-258; also "Female Sexuality," ibid., Vol. XXI, pp. 225-43, trans. James Strachey (London: Hogarth Press, 1961).

[24] *Humanae vitae,* par. 17. I agree with Pope Paul VI that it is entirely possible that the use of contraceptives *may* contribute to a loss of respect for women, but so do many other things. What Pope Paul VI does not consider is the effect on a *woman's* sexuality if she does not have to worry about a pregnancy. A fear of pregnancy is seen by Pope John Paul II as "selfish, irrational, and unnatural" (John Paul II, *Love and Responsibility,* trans. H. T. Willetts [New York: Farrar, Straus, and Giroux, 1981, p. 280). I am indebted to Cristina Traina for pointing this out. See her "Oh, Susanna: John Paul II's Theology of the Body Confronts the Catholic Moral Theological Tradition," Midwest AAR Meeting, April 10, 1994.

[25] Boston Women's Health Book Collective, *Our Bodies, Ourselves* (New York: Simon and Schuster, 1973).

[26] Christine E. Gudorf, "Embodying Morality," *Conscience* XIV/4 (Winter 1993/94)' pp. 16-21: "every person has a right to control her or his own body," (16).

[27] See Bordo, *Unbearable Weight* (n. 8 above), for extensive discussion of this.

[28] Delores S. Williams, *Sisters in the Wilderness: The Challenge of Womanist God-Talk* (Maryknoll, NY: Orbis Books, 1993), esp. pp. 60ff.

[29] Audre Lorde, "The Uses of the Erotic: The Erotic as Power," in *Sister Outsider: Essays and Speeches* (Trumansburg, NY: Crossing Press, 1984), pp. 53-59.

[30] See also Carter Heyward, *Touching Our Strength: The Erotic as Power and the Love of God* (San Francisco: HarperCollins, 1989) and Rita Nakashima Brock, *Journeys by Heart: A Christology of Erotic Power* (New York: Crossroad, 1989).

[31] One such attempt is Mary D. Pellauer, "The Moral Significance of Female Orgasm: Toward Sexual Ethics That Celebrates Women's Sexuality," *Journal of Feminist Studies in Religion* 9, Nos. 1-2 (Spring-Fall 1993), pp. 161-82.

[32] See Arleen Dallery, "The Politics of Writing (the) Body: *Écriture Féminine,"* in Alison M. Jaggar and Susan R. Bordo, eds., *Gender/Body/Knowledge: Feminist Reconstructions of Being and Knowing* (New Brunswick, NJ: Rutgers University Press, 1989), pp. 52-67.

[33] During the time I wrote this chapter, I saw a film (*Sirens*) that seemed to express what Irigaray and others mean by the *jouissance* that characterizes women's sexuality.

[34] Carol Gilligan, *In a Different Voice: Psychological Theory and Women's Development* (Cambridge, MA: Harvard University Press, 1982).

[35] Mary E. Hunt, *Fierce Tenderness: A Feminist Theology of Friendship* (New York: Crossroad, 1991).

[36] See Carter Heyward, "Sexuality, Love, and Justice," in Judith Plaskow and Carol P. Christ, eds., *Weaving the Visions: New Patterns in Feminist Spirituality* (San Francisco: Harper and Row, 1989), pp. 293-301.

[37] Sherry Ortner, "Is Female to Male as Nature Is to Culture?," in Michelle Zimbalist Rosaldo and Louise Lamphere, eds., *Woman, Culture and Society* (Stanford: Stanford University Press, 1974), pp. 67-87.

[38] See Carol J. Adams, ed., *Ecofeminism and the Sacred* (New York: Crossroad, 1993).

[39] Most recently, see Catharine MacKinnon, *Only Words* (Cambridge, MA: Harvard University Press, 1993).

[40] For a thorough (and chilling) summation of this situation, see Elisabeth Schüssler Fiorenza, "Introduction," Schüssler Fiorenza and Copeland, pp. vii-xxiv.

[41] See Joanne Carlson Brown and Carol R. Bohn, eds., *Christianity, Patriarchy, and Abuse: A Feminist Critique* (New York: Pilgrim Press, 1989).

[42] Elizabeth A. Johnson, *She Who Is: The Mystery of God in Feminist Theological Discourse* (New York: Crossroad, 1992), p. 8.

[43] Frances Croake Frank, unpublished poem.

[44] Robert Penn Warren, "Auto-da-Fe," *The New Yorker* (December 31, 1979), p.28.

[45] Heyward, p. 47

[46] Both Virginia Held, *Feminist Morality: Transforming Culture, Society and Politics* (Chicago: University of Chicago Press, 1993) and Joan Tronto, *Moral Boundaries: A Political Argument for an Ethics of Care* (New York: Routledge, 1993) make this point central to their arguments. Sara Ruddick, *Maternal Thinking: Toward a Politics of Peace* (Boston: Beacon, 1989), was one of the first to make this a central point.

[47] I am indebted to William George for his reflections on this point. See his "War and Other Issues" lecture given at St. Joseph College, Renssalaer, IN, March 1994.

[48] See Christine E. Gudorf, "To Make a Seamless Garment, Use a Single Piece of Cloth: The Abortion Debate," in Beverly W. Harrison and Robert L. Stivers, eds., *The Public Vocation of Christian Ethics* (New York: The Pilgrim Press, 1986), pp. 271-86.

[49] See Sidney Callahan, "Abortion," n. 17 above.

[50] See Cahill, pp. 76-79.

[51] Congregation for the Doctrine of the Faith, *Instruction on Respect for Human Life in Its Origin and on the Dignity of Procreation: Replies to Certain Questions of the Day,* Feb. 22, 1987.

[52] See Delores Williams, *Sisters,* pp. 60ff.

[53] Beverly Wildung Harrison, *Our Right to Choose: Toward a New Ethic of Abortion* (Boston: Beacon, 1983).

[54] Tronto, *Moral Boundaries,* p. 162.

[55] Ibid., p. 163.

[56] It is worthwhile considering the enormous amount of literature in Roman Catholic moral theology that dealt with questions such as ectopic pregnancies, etc., that failed ever to mention the mother's own voice.

[57] An honorary degree was to have been bestowed upon Weakland, but under pressure from the Vatican, this was withdrawn.

[58] See *The New York Times,* April 28, 1984,1:27; also see Susan B. Thistlethwaite, *Sex, Race and God: Christian Feminism in Black and White* (New York: Crossroad, 1989), p. 93. Thistlethwaite comments here that her original reaction to the sculpture was negative, but that she later revised her view.

[59] In some Orthodox churches, my students tell me that menstruating women are not to receive the Eucharist.

[60] See Rosemary Radford Ruether, "Women's Difference and Equal Rights in the Church," in *The Special Nature of Women?, Concilium* 1991/6, ed. Anne Carr and Elisabeth Schüssler Fiorenza (London and Philadelphia: SCM Press and Trinity Press, 1991), p. 13.

SOURCES

I. Historical Background

1. Aristotle. From *Politics* and *On the Generation of Animals*

2. Thomas Aquinas. From *Summa theologica*

3. *The Bible.* Genesis 1, 2, and 3, and Song of Songs – The Scripture quotations contained herein aer from the New Revised Standard Version of the Bible, copyrighted, 1989, Division of Christian Education of the National Council of the Churches of Christ in the United States of America, and are used by permission. All rights reserved.

4. St. Augustine. *City of God* XIV, 26 and *The Good of Marriage*

5. Bede. From *The Ecclesiastical History of the English Nation*

6. Selections of Early medieval penitentials: a) From McNeill and Gamer *Medieval Handbook of Penances* and b) a modern translation of a section from the Old English Pseudo-Ecgbert penitential

7. Geoffrey Chaucer. From "The Parson's Tale": "Here followeth the Second Part of Penitence," "Lust" (14th century)

8. Three body and soul poems: a) Old English (11th century); Andrew Marvell (17th century); c) Gerard Manley Hopkins (19th century)

9. Joan Chittister, o.s.b. "Divinely Ordained?" reprinted with permission from *Sojourners* (800) 714-7474, www.sojo.net

10. Douglas R. Letson. "This Fair Defect of Nature: An Introduction to the Literary Image of Women." From *SIECCAN Journal,* 2(1), 18-24. Reprinted with permission of the Sex Information and Education Council of Canada (SIECCAN).

11. Douglas R. Letson. "The Soul Incarcerate." From *SIECCAN Journal*, 3(3), 14-18. Reprinted with permission of the Sex Information and Education Council of Canada (SIECCAN).

II. *Humanae vitae:* The Document and Its Context

12. Leo XIII. *Arcanum* [On Christian Marriage]

13. Pope Pius XI. *Casti connubii* [On Christian Marriage]
14. Michael W. Higgins and Douglas R. Letson. *"Humanae Vitae* and the Struggle over Personal Conscience." From *His Father's Business: The Biography of His Eminence G. Emmett Cardinal Carter.* Reprinted with permission.

15. The Report of the Papal Commission of the Regulation of Birth, April 1967. Originally appeared in *National Catholic Reporter,* Kansas City, MO. www.natcath.org

16. Pope Paul VI. *Humanae vitae [Of Human Life]*

17. The Canadian Bishops. Statement on *Humanae vitae.* Reprinted with permission.

18. The Canadian Bishops. Statement on the Formation of Conscience, December 1, 1973. Reprinted with permission.

19. Jack Dominian. A four-part series of articles on *Humanae Vitae,* "The argument goes on," "The flaw in the tradition," "Beyond biology," "The need for reform," *The Tablet,* 1984. Reprinted by special arrangement with Jack Dominian and *The Tablet.*

20. John Marshall, David Knowles, Bernard Haring. A three-part series on "The *Humanae Vitae* crisis": "Inside the Commission," "Authentic teaching," "Consulting the faithful." The Tablet, July 24, 1993. Reprinted with permission.

21. John Marshall. "True meaning of marriage," *The Tablet,* September 14, 1993. Reprinted with permission.

22. Annabel Miller, "How Natural is NFP?" *The Tablet,* December 2, 2000. Reprinted with permission.

III. Marriage and Family in the Modern World

23. G. Emmett Cardinal Carter. On the 1980 Synod of Bishops on Marriage and Family (A Shepherd Speaks*):* "The Synod Starts," "Synod divisions," "The Family Synod closes." Reprinted from *The Catholic Register* with permission.

24. Synod of Bishops (1980). The summary paper from the 1980 Episcopal Synod on Marriage and Family.

25. Jack Dominian. "Sexuality: From Law and Biology to Love and Person," *Grail: An Ecumenical Journal,* September 1988. Reprinted with permission.
26. Jack Dominian. A four-part series: "Christian marriage in a changing world: Person to person," "The use of sex," "The scourge of divorce," "Domestic sacrament," *The Tablet,* 1984. Reprinted by special arrangement with Jack Dominian and *The Tablet.*

27. Marriage Preparation and Cohabiting Couples: Information Report" © 1999 United States Catholic Conference, Inc., Washington, DC. Reprinted with permission. All rights reserved.

28. Mary Kenny. "What happens with the natural law," *The Catholic Herald,* July

30, 1999. Reprinted with permission.

29. John Paul II. "The Ratified and Consummated Sacramental Marriage."

30. Andrew M. Greeley. "Just the Facts, Man: Catholics Still Marry Catholics," *Commonweal,* December 17, 1999. © 1999 Commonweal Foundation, reprinted with permission. For Subscriptions, call toll-free: 1-888-495-6755.

IV. Contemporary Issues with Respect to Marriage and Sexuality

31. Social Affairs Committee of the Assembly of Quebec Bishops. *A Heritage of Violence? A Pastoral Reflection on Conjugal Violence* (Apology for the church's responsibility in the abuse of women), 1989. Reprinted with permission.

32. Clifford Longley. "A Society Without Shame," *The Tablet,* September 11, 1999. Reprinted with permission.

33. Congregation for the Doctrine of the Faith. "The Pastoral Care of Homosexual Persons."

34. Michael W. Higgins and Douglas R. Letson. From an interview with Thomas Gumbleton, Auxiliary Bishop, Archdiocese of Detroit, in *Grail: An Ecumenical Journal,* September 1998. Reprinted with permission.

35. Congregation for the Doctrine of the Faith. "Notification Regarding Sister Gramick and Father Nugent."

36. Lisa Sowle Cahill. "Silencing of Nugent, Gramick Sets A Novel Standard of Orthodoxy," *America.* This article was originally published in *America* (August 14, 1999) and is reprinted with the permission of America Press, Inc. Copyright 1999. All rights reserved. www.americapress.org.

37. Gerald D. Coleman. "Ministry to Homosexuals Must Use Authentic Church Teaching." This article was originally published in *America* (August 14, 1999) and is reprinted with the permission of America Press, Inc. Copyright 1999. All rights reserved. www.americapress.org.

38. Jeannine Gramick and Robert Nugent. "A Response: Two Persons Whose Ministry to Gays and Lesbians Has Come Under Scrutiny Respond to a Critic," This article was originally published in *America* (October 9, 1999) and is reprinted with the permission of America Press, Inc. Copyright 1999. All rights reserved. www.americapress.org.

39. Robert Gahl, Jr. "Toward Effective Pastoral Care of Homosexual Persons."

40. Sidney Callahan. "Sexuality and Homosexuality: The Church's Gordian Knot," *Commonweal,* September 10, 1999

41. Eileen Flynn, "Responding to the 'Gay Agenda.'" This article was originally published in *America* (September 30, 2000) and is reprinted with the permission of America Press, Inc. Copyright 2000. All rights reserved. www.americapress.org.

42. Cardinal Roger Mahony. "Statement on Proposition 22: Same-Sex Marriage Initiative," *Origins,* January 6, 2000

43. Shawn Zeller, "Dignity's Challenge: Can Homosexuals Feel at Home in Catholicism?" *Commonweal,* July 14, 2000. © Commonweal Foundation, reprinted with permission. For Subscriptions, call toll-free: 1-888-495-6755.

44. Bacani, Anne. "Gay Catholics Look to Their Faith." *The Catholic Register,* June 19, 2000. Reprinted with permission.

45. Jon Fuller, "Priests with AIDS." This article was originally published in *America* (March 18, 2000) and is reprinted with the permission of America Press, Inc. Copyright 2000. All rights reserved. www.americapress.org.

46. Michael Higgins, "Catholics in Shock," *The Tablet,* September 22, 1990. Reprinted with permission.

47. Michael Higgins, "Focus on Sexual Abuse," *The Tablet,* February 13, 1993. Reprinted with permission.

48. "Fifty Recommendations: The Church and Child Sexual Abuse," from *From Pain to Hope.* Copyright © Concacan Inc., 1992. All rights reserved. Used by permission of the Canadian Conference of Catholic Bishops.

49. Bishop Fred Henry. "The Psychosexual Maturity of Candidates for the Priesthood." Intervention at the 1990 Episcopal Synod on The Formation of Priests in Present Day Circumstances. Reprinted with permission.

50. Rose Simone, "Did Canadian Bishops Cave in at the Synod?: Newfoundland Sex Abuse Scandal is Swept Under the Carpet in Rome," *The Record,* November 17, 1990.

51. Susan A. Ross, "Extravagant Affections: Women's Sexuality and Theological Anthropology" in *In the Embrace of God: Feminist Approaches to Theological Anthropology,* Ann O'Hara Graff, ed. Reprinted by permission of the author.

AGMV Marquis

MEMBER OF SCABRINI MEDIA

Quebec, Canada
2001